Dependent-Arising and Emptiness

Dependent-Arising and Emptiness

A Tibetan Buddhist Interpretation of Mādhyamika Philosophy Emphasizing the Compatibility of Emptiness and Conventional Phenomena

Elizabeth Napper

Wisdom Publications · Boston

Wisdom Publications
199 Elm Street
Somerville, MA 02144 USA
www.wisdompubs.org

First published in 1989

Library of Congress Control Number: 2003101482

07 06
5 4 3 2

ISBN 0-86171-364-8

Cover image courtesy of Shelley and Donald Rubin; www.himalayanart.org

Cover design by Gopa & Ted2. Set in Plantin Medium 11/13

Wisdom Publications' books are printed on acid-free paper and meet the guidelines for permanence and durability of the Committee on Production Guidelines for Book Longevity of the Council on Library Resources.

Printed in Canada.

Contents

Preface to Second Edition VII
Acknowledgements IX
Technical Notes XI

PART ONE: ANALYSIS
Introduction 3
1 An Overview of the *Great Exposition* 17
2 Interpretation of Scripture 30
3 Dzong-ka-ba's Argument 39
4 Dzong-ka-ba and Modern Interpreters I: Not Negating Enough 67
5 Dzong-ka-ba and Modern Interpreters II: Negating Too Much 101
6 Dzong-ka-ba and Modern Interpreters III: Other Issues of Difference 123
7 Summation: Emptiness and Ethic 143

PART TWO: TRANSLATION OF DZONG-KA-BA'S *GREAT EXPOSITION*
Introduction 153
1 The Interpretable and the Definitive 158
2 Reliable Sources 164
3 The Stages of Entry Into Suchness 168
4 Misidentifying the Object of Negation 176
5 The Uncommon Feature of Mādhyamika 181
6 Dependent-Arising and Emptiness 188
7 Mādhyamika Response 198

PART THREE: TRANSLATION OF THE *FOUR INTERWOVEN ANNOTATIONS*
Translator's Introduction 219
Introduction 229
1 The Interpretable and the Definitive 247
2 Reliable Sources 268
3 The Stages of Entry Into Suchness 284
4 Misidentifying the Object of Negation 311
5 The Uncommon Feature of Mādhyamika 322
6 Dependent-Arising and Emptiness 339
7 Mādhyamika Response 361

APPENDICES
1 The Division of Mādhyamikas into Reason-Established Illusionists and Proponents of Thorough Non-Abiding 403
2 Alex Wayman's Translation Considered 441
3 Jan-yang-shay-ba's Outline 474
4 Emendations to the Delhi Edition of the *Four Interwoven Annotations* 499

GLOSSARY
1 English-Tibetan-Sanskrit 527
2 Tibetan-Sanskrit-English 550
3 Sanskrit-Tibetan-English 574

Bibliography 595
Notes 641
Index 825

Preface to Second Edition

Since the original publication of *Dependent-Arising and Emptiness* in 1989, I have become deeply involved in an effort to improve the standard and status of nuns in the Tibetan Buddhist tradition. My work focuses on nuns within the Tibetan exile community in India and those from the border areas of Ladakh, Zanskar, Spiti, and Kinnaur. Our main focus is on making available to nuns of the Tibetan Buddhist tradition the full range of education that has long been available only to monks. Since 1992, I have been living in Dharamsala, India, helping to create the Dolma Ling Nunnery and Institute of Higher Studies, along with a program to support Buddhist nuns under an organization called the Tibetan Nuns Project. It currently supports more than five hundred nuns representing all orders of the Tibetan Buddhist tradition.

Over the years, I have heard from a number of students of Mādhyamika philosophy and of the Tibetan Buddhist tradition that my book has been helpful, and I am delighted that it will continue to be in print.

Publisher's Acknowledgement

The Publisher gratefully acknowledges the kind generosity of the Hershey Family Foundation in sponsoring the publication of this book.

Acknowledgements

I would like to acknowledge the support of a Fulbright-Hays Doctoral Dissertation Research Fellowship that enabled me to spend nine months, from November 1981 through July 1982, studying in India, and of the Woodrow Wilson Foundation which, through a Charlotte W. Newcombe Doctoral Dissertation Fellowship, enabled me to spend the 1983–84 academic year engaged in fulltime writing. Regarding the Fulbright award, I would like to express special appreciation for the assistance I received from Mr. John Paul of the Department of Education and from the Director, Mrs. Sharada Nayak, and staff of USEFI in New Delhi. Also, I would like to thank my faculty advisor in India, Dr. K.K. Mittal of Delhi University. While in India I received invaluable assistance from Mr. E. Gene Smith of the Library of Congress, who helped me to secure an alternate edition of one of the texts of my translation and provided generous bibliographical assistance.

In addition, I would like to thank the many Tibetans who worked with me during my months in India – Ge-shay Palden Drakpa of Tibet House in New Delhi; Ge-shay Gönchok Tsering of Gan-den Shar-dzay in Mundgod, South India; Ken-sur Denba Dendzin and Ge-shay Jamyang Kendzay of Go-mang College of Dre-bung Monastery in Mundgod; Ken-bo Losang Nyima and Ge-shay Wangdrak of Nam-gyal Monastery in Dharmsala, North India – as well as those I worked with on this project at the University of Virginia – Gyu-may Ken-sur Jampel Shenphen and Lo-ling Ken-sur Yeshe Thupten.

Throughout the course of this lengthy project I have relied on the patience and generosity of Richard B. Martin, South Asia Bibliographer at the University of Virginia, and am tremendously grateful to him for his unfailing helpfulness. The work of many of us at the University of Virginia has been greatly enriched through his dedication to developing, cataloging, and making accessible such an exceptional collection of Tibetan and Buddhist materials.

I would like to express my deep appreciation to His Holiness the Dalai Lama, who, during an audience in Dharmsala, India, provided stimulating answers to my many questions, demonstrating a unique ability to speak directly to the heart of my qualms, and whose support for and encouragement of the translation project I have undertaken provides constant inspiration. In a similar vein I must express my profound gratitude and indebtedness to the Venerable Geshe Wangyal, teacher of unparalleled kindness, who set me on the path that has included this present work.

I thank my husband, Jeffrey Hopkins, who has worked closely with me throughout every step of this project, checking all of my translations against the Tibetan and offering copious and penetrating editorial suggestions, without whose support and encouragement this task would never have been brought to completion.

I would like to thank Professor Paul Groner who, with good humor and helpful suggestions, assumed the task of being my thesis director, and to thank the other members of my dissertation committee, Professors Julian Hartt, Karen Lang, and Jan Willis, all of whom offered many helpful and stimulating suggestions. Also, I am grateful to Professor Ashok Aklujkar of the University of British Columbia for his assistance in comparing my translations from Tibetan with the Sanskrit.

Finally, I would like to thank all those who, at various stages of this project, provided much needed help in many forms, such as proofreading, indexing, and moral support: Jules Levinson, Karen Saginor, Bill Magee, Ilia Durovic, Lark Hammond, Leah Zahler, John Powers, Cindy Swiatlowski, and Charlene Makley.

Technical Note

Throughout the text my practice is to phoneticize Tibetan and Sanskrit names when they occur in the body of the text and to cite them, within parentheses, in transliteration at their first occurrence.

With regard to Tibetan, the system of transliteration followed, with minor modification in that no letters are capitalized, is that devised by Turrell Wylie (see "A Standard System of Tibetan Transcription", *Harvard Journal of Asiatic Studies*, Vol.22, 1959, pp.261–7); this system has the great virtue of not requiring any diacritical marks and is easily used on standard typewriters and word processors.

The pronunciation system used is the "essay phonetic" system developed by Jeffrey Hopkins (see the technical note in *Meditation on Emptiness*, London: Wisdom Publications, 1983, pp.19–21). This follows Lhasa pronunciation, but is an "essay" phonetic system in that it is a simplified, easy to pronounce, system that does not attempt to mirror all minor variations. Hopkins' system takes account of the tonal element in Tibetan: a macron (¯) over a consonant indicates that the sound is high in tone. These high tone markers are indicated in a list of the Tibetan words used within this work that shows how the high tone markers should be affixed (see pp.x–xiii).

In the following chart of the transliteration and phonetic systems, the Wylie transliteration is given first followed by its equivalent in Hopkins' phoneticization.

ka	ḡa	kha	ka	ga	ga	nga	nga or n̄ga
ca	j̄a	cha	cha	ja	ja	nya	nya or n̄ya
ta	d̄a	tha	ta	da	da	na	na or n̄a
pa	b̄a	pha	pa	ba	ba	ma	ma or m̄a
tsa	d̄za	tsha	tsa	dza	dza	wa	wa
zha	sha	za	sa	'a	a	ya	ya
ra	ra	la	la	sha	s̄ha	sa	s̄a
ha	ha	a	a				

It should be noted that in Hopkins' phonetic system, the nasals (see far right hand column) are low in tone when they are not affected by a superscribed or prefixed letter (as in the word *nga*, "I") and high in tone when there is a prefix or superscription (as in the pronunciation of the word *n̄ga* [spelled *lnga*], "five").

A subjoined *la* is pronunced *l̄a*, except for *zla* which is pronounced *da*.

dbang is phoneticized as *w̄ang* and *dbyangs* as *ȳang*.

The letters *ga* and *ba* are phoneticized as *k* and *p* in suffix position.

Following is a list of all Tibetan names appearing in the text in "essay phonetics" followed by transliteration:

A-ḡya-yong-dzin	a kya yongs 'dzin
A-ku-ching S̄hay-rab-gya-tso	a khu ching shes rab rgya mtsho
Ba-s̄o Chö-ḡyi-gyel-tsen	ba so chos kyi rgyal mtshan
Ba-s̄o Hla-w̄ang-chö-ḡyi-gyel-tsen	ba so lha dbang chos kyi rgyal mtshan
B̄a-tsap Nyi-ma-drak	pa tshab nyi ma grags
Bo-dong Chok-lay-n̄am-gyel	bo dong phyogs las rnam rgyal
B̄o-d̄o-wa	po to ba
Cha-b̄a Chö-ḡyi-s̄eng-ge	cha pa chos kyi seng ge
Char-har Ge-s̄hay	char har dge bshes
D̄a-nak-nor-sang	rta nag nor bzang

D̄ak-d̄en-pun-tsok-l̄ing	rtag brtan phun tshogs gling
D̄ak-lung-drak-b̄a	stag lung brag pa
D̄ak-tsang	stag tshang
Dar-ma-drak	dar ma grags
D̄en-dar-hla-ram-b̄a	bstan dar lha ram pa
Dra-d̄i Ge-s̄hay	bra sti dge bshes
D̄ra-s̄hi-kyil	bkra shis 'khyil
D̄ra-s̄hi-hlun-b̄o	bkra shis lhun po
Dre-b̄ung	'bras spungs
Dro	'bro
D̄zong-ka-b̄a	tsong kha pa
Ḡa-dam-b̄a	bka' gdams pa
Ḡa-gyu-b̄a	bka' rgyud pa
Ḡa-wa-b̄el-t̄sek	ska ba dpal brtsegs
Gan-den	dga' ldan
Gang-gya-m̄ar-b̄a Jang-chup-drak	gangs rgya dmar pa byang chub grags
Ge-luk-b̄a	dge lugs pa
Ge-s̄hay	dge bshes
Ge-s̄hay Tsul-trim-n̄am-gyel	dge bshes tshul khrims rnam rgyal
Gen-dun-gyel-tsen	dge 'dun rgyal mtshan
Go-mang	sgo mang
Ḡön-chok-jik-may-w̄ang-b̄o	dkon mchog 'jigs med dbang po
Ḡun-kyen-rong-d̄ön	kun mkhyen rong ston
Gung-ru-chö-jung	gung ru chos 'byung
Gung-tang	gung thang
Gyel-tsap	rgyal tshab
Gyu-m̄ay	rgyud smad
Hla-s̄a	lha sa
Jam-b̄a Rin-b̄o-chay	byams pa rin po che
Jam-ȳang Ḡön-chok-chö-pel	'jam dbyangs dkon mchog chos 'phel
Jam-ȳang-shay-b̄a	'jam dbyangs bzhad pa
Jang-chup-l̄a-ma	byang chub bla ma
Jang-d̄zay	byang rtse

Jang-d̄zön	byang brtson
J̄ang-ḡya	lcang kya
Kay-drup	mkhas grub
Kay-drup Nor-sang-gya-tso	mkhas grub nor bzang rgya mtsho
Ku	khu
L̄a-ma Jang-chup	bla ma byang chub
Lay-chen-ḡun-gyal-wa	las chen kun rgyal ba
L̄o-den-s̄hay-rap	blo ldan shes rab
L̄o-drö-gya-tso	blo gros rgya mtsho
L̄o-sang-dor-jay	blo bzang rdo rje
L̄o-sang-ḡön-chok	blo bzang kun mchog
L̄o-s̄el-l̄ing	blo gsal gling
L̄ong-döl L̄a-ma	klong rdol bla ma
M̄a-ja Jang-chup-d̄zön-drü	rma bya byang chub brtson 'grus
M̄a-ja Jang-chup-ye-s̄hay	rma bya byang chub ye shes
Mi-ḡyö-dor-jay	mi bskyod rdo rje
N̄am-gyel	rnam rgyal
Nga-w̄ang-b̄el-den	ngag dbang dpal ldan
Nga-w̄ang-l̄o-sang-gya-tso	ngag dbang blo bzang rgya mtsho
Nga-w̄ang-rap-d̄en	ngag dbang rab brtan
N̄gok Lo-t̄sā-wa	rngog lo tsā ba
N̄ying-ma-b̄a	rnying ma pa
Pa-bong-ka	pha bong kha
Paṇ-chen Rin-b̄o-chay	paṇ chen rin po che
Paṇ-chen S̄hākya-chok-den	paṇ chen shā kya mchog ldan
Pur-bu-j̄ok	phur bu lcog
Ra	ra
Rong-d̄ön-s̄hākya-gyel-tsen	rong ston shākya rgyal mtshan
Rong-d̄ön-s̄hay-ja-ḡun-sik	rong ston shes bya kun gzigs
S̄a-ḡya-b̄a	sa skya pa
S̄a-ḡya Paṇḍita	sa skya paṇḍita
S̄am-yay	bsam yas
S̄ang-gyay-gya-tso	sangs rgyas rgya mtsho

S̄e-ra	se rwa
S̄e-ra Jay	se ra byes
Sha-m̄ar-d̄en-dzin	zhwa dmar bstan 'dzin
S̄har-d̄zay	shar rtse
Shön-nu-chok	gzhon nu mchog
Tang-s̄ak-b̄a	thang sag pa
Tri-rel-wa-j̄en	khri ral ba can
Tsay-chok-l̄ing	tshe mchog gling
Tu-ḡen L̄o-sang-chö-ḡyi-nyi-ma	thu'u bkwan blo bzang chos kyi nyi ma
Yar-l̄ung-chö-dzay L̄o-sang-d̄en-dzin	yar klung chos mdzad blo bzang bstan 'dzin
Ye-s̄hay-day	ye shes sde
Ye-s̄hay-gyel-tsen	ye shes rgyal mtshan
Yong-dzin	yongs 'dzin

This system of essay phonetics does not apply to the names of contemporary Tibetans and Mongolians who have developed their own forms of spelling their names for use in the West.

Regarding the transliteration of Sanskrit, standard transliteration is used for Sanksrit cited in parentheses. For names occurring in the body of the text, *ch* is used for *c*, *sh* for *ś*, and *ṣh* for *ṣ* to facilitate pronunciation.

The chapter breaks and titles in the translation of both Dzong-ka-ba's *Great Exposition* and the *Four Interwoven Annotations* are my own, added to facilitate understanding. All titles of texts cited are translated into English; at the first occurrence the Tibetan and Sanskrit (if it was originally a Sanskrit work) titles of the texts are provided, citing the Tibetan first, since this is the main language of translation. Many texts are cited in the Tibetan tradition by one or two short titles as well as occasionally a full elaborate title, and sometimes the author's name is mentioned, sometimes not. To avoid confusion in the translation, a text is always cited in the same way, giving both the author of the text and translation of a standard medium length title for the text, regardless of how it is cited in the Tibetan. At the first occurrence, reference to the full long form of the title as well as transliteration of the author's name and his dates, if available, is provided. Also, throughout the translation I supply the full form of outline headings even if in Tibetan only the number of the heading is indicated with the referent of that number to be understood from an earlier citation.

In translating quotations of passages for which Sanskrit survives, my translation follows the Tibetan. However, I have consulted the Sanskrit whenever it is available and note any significant variations between the Sanskrit and the Tibetan.

In the translation of the *Four Interwoven Annotations* I have inserted some explanation – both my own and that of contemporary Tibetan scholars – into the body of the text, deeply indented so that it is clearly set off from the rest of the text.

Part One
Analysis

Introduction

Dependent-arising and emptiness are two crucial concepts within Buddhism. Difficult to understand and subject to a variety of interpretations, an understanding of them and of their compatibility can serve as a key revealing the essence of the Buddha's teachings.

In very brief form, dependent-arising, labelled by the present Dalai Lama "Buddha's slogan", indicates the interrelatedness of all things in the universe. Things arise dependent on causes and conditions, they gain their identities in relation to other things. Nothing stands alone, autonomous and isolated, but instead exists only in a web of interconnectedness. Like near and far, all things are relative, dependent on their causes, on their parts, or on their relationship to something else. Things are always in flux, always changing; there are no independent autonomous entities.

Emptiness expresses this same idea from another viewpoint. All things are empty. Empty of what? Of being independent autonomous entities, of having some "own thing", some intrinsic nature that comes from their own side without depending on external causes and conditions or on a subjective factor of those who observe them. As solid, substantial, and graspable as things – persons, tables, chairs, or anything – may seem, when sought among the parts that make them up, there is nothing that can be pointed to as that thing itself. The non-finding of something when it is sought analytically is its emptiness. If things existed in the palpable, independent way we imagine them to, they would have to be such that they could be found when sought – but they cannot. In fact, when sought analytically in this way in meditation, they disappear altogether. When searching among the parts or collection of the parts of a table for the table or among the mind and body for the person and not coming up with the object sought, at some point the conventional phenomenon drops away and one is left with only the absence of what was sought, with a mere vacuity that is emptiness.

This fact of meditative experience might lead to the conclusion that emptiness and the conventional world are incompatible, that emptiness cancels ordinary phenomena, which would exist only so long as one has not realized emptiness and would cease to do so once emptiness is realized. Perhaps all that we see around us is only an illusion, a fabrication of our lack of understanding of the true nature of reality, which is only emptiness. But what is one to do then with dependent-arising? How does such a nihilistic emptiness fit with the Buddha's carefully formulated teachings such as the doctrine of karma – responsibility for the effects of all one's actions – and with the instructions on proper ethics and the precise delineations of the many varieties of phenomena? Why bother if all this is false, only illusion?

These are questions with which Buddhists have struggled over the more than two thousand years since the time of the Buddha, and numerous different schools and sects have arisen based on different ways of resolving these and other questions. The dilemma concerning the relationship of dependent-arising and emptiness is a particular issue for the Middle Way, or Mādhyamika (*dbu ma pa*), school. Founded by the great Indian scholar and yogi Nāgārjuna in the early centuries of our era, Mādhyamika has consistently been a focus of doctrinal controversy. Other philosophical schools do not take as uncompromising a stance regarding emptiness and the utter unfindability of objects, and, as a result, Mādhyamika has been accused by other schools, both Buddhist and non-Buddhist, of having gone too far and fallen into nihilism. Even within Mādhyamika, varying strands of interpretation have arisen as later commentators worked out their own solutions to the accusations of conflict between emptiness and conventional phenomena.

The Mādhyamika tradition developed in India over several centuries and was transmitted to Tibet along with the rest of the Buddhist teachings by the 9th century C.E. Buddhism underwent a period of repression in Tibet during the late ninth century and was essentially reintroduced to Tibet during the eleventh and twelfth centuries. The early centuries of Buddhism's flourishing in Tibet were intellectually lively as Tibetans newly studied and absorbed the Buddhist teachings, and during this period a number of different sects developed based on different traditions of textual study and interpretation, including varying assessments of the Mādhyamika teachings.

A number of individuals stand out during this period of development, brilliant thinkers whose interpretations gained them large followings and whose influence has continued up to the present as their followers have sustained and refined their views. One such figure is the great scholar and yogi Dzong-ka-ba (*tsong kha pa*) who lived from 1357 to 1419.[1] Widely acclaimed for his scholarly and meditative achievements during his lifetime, his followers evolved into the Ge-luk-ba order of Tibetan Buddhism, an order that has dominated Tibetan religious and political life from the mid-seventeenth century to the present.

The tradition of study during Dzong-ka-ba's lifetime was, for many, peripatetic, as students travelled from monastery to monastery taking instruction in various topics from many different teachers, seeking out those renowned as having special expertise in a particular text or lineage of teaching. Dzong-ka-ba participated in this tradition and received teachings from numerous teachers, including members of all the main orders that flourished at the time. Mādhyamika was widely accepted in Tibet as the highest of all the Buddha's philosophical sūtra teachings, and the focus of Dzong-ka-ba's study, as described in his writings, was his effort to gain a correct insight into Mādhyamika. Years of intense study culminated in 1398 in a vision during which he experienced a transformative realization of the meaning of the Mādhyamika teachings.[2] This experience radically changed his perception of the world as well as his understanding of the import of Buddha's teachings, causing him to disagree with many of the Mādhyamika interpretations prevalent at his time, which he felt had moved too far in the direction of nihilism, delineating an emptiness that was antithetical to valid maintenance of the conventional world.

Dzong-ka-ba undertook to formulate his own Mādhyamika interpretation which focused, in contrast, on the importance of valuing conventionalities within a sweeping negation of any inherent existence, setting forth a presentation that emphasized the compatibility of emptiness and dependent-arising.[3] He wrote five major works on Mādhyamika philosophy, of which the first, and the focus of this work, was his *Great Exposition of the Stages of the Path* (*lam rim chen mo*), written in 1402 when he was 45 years old.[4] It includes, as its final section, a presentation of special insight (*lhag mthong, vipaśyanā*) that is his earliest detailed exposition of Mādhyamika philosophy.

Dzong-ka-ba also wrote brief and middle length expositions of the stages of the path. The brief exposition, entitled the *Concise Meaning of the Stages of the Path* (*lam rim bsdus don*),[5] is a poem, giving in very condensed – forty-eight stanzas – and easily memorizable form a synopsis of the entire path to enlightenment; it contains no detailed treatment of special insight. The *Medium Exposition of the Stages of the Path* (*lam rim 'bring*),[6] written in 1415 when he was fifty-eight, is considerably shorter than the *Great Exposition* – 188 folios in the Peking edition as opposed to 444 folios – in large part because it omits the copious citation and discussion of Indian sources that characterizes the *Great Exposition*. It includes a section on special insight that is an interesting corollary to that in the *Great Exposition* since it is built on the same outline and contains many topical sentences identical to those in the *Great Exposition*, but on the whole was written as a complement to it rather than a summary, going into detail on topics not covered in the longer work and entirely omitting large sections that are the heart of the *Great Exposition*.

Between the composition of the *Great Exposition* and the *Medium Exposition*, Dzong-ka-ba wrote in quick succession two other works focused primarily on Mādhyamika – the *Essence of the Good Explanations* (*legs bshad snying po*)[7] and the *Ocean of Reasoning, Great Commentary on (Nāgārjuna's) "Treatise on the Middle Way"* (*rigs pa'i rgya mtsho rtsa shes ṭik chen*).[8] Finally, at age 61, one year before his death, he wrote his final work on Mādhyamika, the *Illumination of the Thought* (*dgongs pa rab gsal*) a commentary on Chandrakīrti's *Supplement to (Nāgārjuna's) "Treatise on the Middle Way"*.[9]

Each of these works is an independent and cohesive whole, yet they very much complement each other in that topics treated only briefly in one are analyzed in detail in another. For the most part, also, one does not supersede the others although there are a few points about which Dzong-ka-ba himself says that something in one text will explain a point in another. Also, there are a few places where the texts contradict each other, and the Ge-luk tradition has chosen to follow one rather than the other, usually preferring the later writings as representative of Dzong-ka-ba's more developed thought.[10]

These five works – the special insight sections of the *Great* and *Medium Expositions of the Stages of the Path*, the *Essence of the Good Explanations*, *Ocean of Reasoning*, and *Illumination of the Thought* – are the main sources for Dzong-ka-ba's views on Mādhyamika in that they focus on this system as their primary subject matter, delineating Mādhyamika positions in contrast to other systems. Still, the Mādhyamika view, and from among the two Mādhyamika subdivisions, Svātantrika-Mādhyamika and Prāsaṅgika-Mādhyamika, that of Prāsaṅgika-Mādhyamika, pervades Dzong-ka-ba's writings. His collected writings (*gsung 'bum*) are comprised of eighteen Tibetan volumes and contain over two hundred separate works covering a vast array of topics within both the sūtra and tantra systems; throughout, the view that Dzong-ka-ba himself adheres to, even if he is not specifically writing about it, is Prāsaṅgika-Mādhyamika. In his writings on tantra, he asserts explicitly that even within the highest tantric system, Highest Yoga Tantra (*rnal 'byor bla med kyi rgyud, anuttarayogatantra*), the emptiness described is not higher to or different from that set forth in the Prāsaṅgika-Mādhyamika system.[11]

In this volume, I consider the Mādhyamika interpretation found in the special insight section of Dzong-ka-ba's *Great Exposition of the Stages of the Path*, focusing specifically on Dzong-ka-ba's delineation of what is and is not negated in the view of selflessness and his resolution of the seeming conflict between a view of emptiness and the existence of conventional phenomena, including ethical actions. Mādhyamika philosophy is difficult to understand, especially because the works of the founder of that system, Nāgārjuna, are exceedingly terse and subject to a variety of interpretations. Thus, there has always been debate among those who claim to uphold the Mādhyamika systems as to exactly what that system is. Although in the *Great Exposition of the Stages of the Path*, Dzong-ka-ba newly set forth his understanding in contradistinction to interpretations prevalent in Tibet at that time, most of which from his viewpoint went too far and fell into nihilism, his argument also serves to counter the positions of the non-Prāsaṅgika Buddhist schools that, from a Mādhyamika viewpoint, do not negate enough and thus uphold an extreme of reification. Dzong-ka-ba makes very clear the "middle way" that he upholds.

As will be discussed in chapters four through six, many Western writers have concluded that Mādhyamika is a system at best agnostic and at worst nihilistic; that the purpose of the Mādhyamika dialectic is merely to demonstrate the inadequacy of language; that they reject all conceptuality whatsoever rather than just a misperception of the nature of reality; that Mādhyamikas merely refute others' systems and have no position, thesis, or view, of their own; that the Mādhyamika view is not the result of philosophical reasoning; and so forth.[12] Dzong-ka-ba sought to refute similar understandings of Mādhyamika, widespread during his lifetime, and thus his text addresses directly the qualms of many contemporary interpreters and serves as an excellent springboard from which to examine Mādhyamika philosophy.

In developing his Mādhyamika interpretation, Dzong-ka-ba relies heavily on four Indian commentators on the writings of Nāgārjuna – Āryadeva, Buddhapālita, Chandrakīrti, and Bhāvaviveka – the chief of these being Chandrakīrti. In a verse work, the *Essence of the Good Explanations, Praise of Munīndra* (also known as the *Praise of Dependent-Arising [rten 'brel bstod pa]*), written shortly before the *Great Exposition of the Stages of the Path*, Dzong-ka-ba describes his experience in discovering the commentaries of Chandrakīrti:[13]

> Although this good system [Mādhyamika]
> Is so wonderful,
> People who are unskilled in it
> Vie among themselves like tangling vines.
>
> Having seen this, I myself
> Followed after the skillful
> With manifold effort,
> Seeking again and again the intent of your teaching.
>
> At that time I studied many canons
> From my own sect and from the sects of others;
> My mind was tormented
> Again and again by a web of doubt.
>
> You predicted that the commentator
> On the system of the peerless vehicle
> That abandons the extremes of existence and non-existence
> Would be Nāgārjuna, whose commentaries are a lotus garden.
>
> Increscent sphere of undefiled knowledge,
> Traversing unimpeded across the sky of scriptures,
> Dispelling the darkness of heart of extreme views,
> Eclipsing the stars of wrong speech –

All is illumined by the rosary of moonbeams
Of good explantion of the Eminent Moon
[Chandrakīrti].
When by the kindness of the Lama I beheld this,
My weariness was relieved.

Dzong-ka-ba compares Nāgārjuna's explanation of the Mādhyamika system to a type of lotus that in Indian literary convention blooms only in moonlight; the moonlight opening the flower of Nāgārjuna's explanation is the good explanation of Chandrakīrti – "Eminent Moon" or "Moon-fame" – *candra* being the Sanskrit word for "moon" and *kīrti* meaning "fame" or "renown". Thus it was upon studying the commentaries of Chandrakīrti that Dzong-ka-ba settled his doubts and arrived at an understanding of the Mādhyamika system.[14]

Dzong-ka-ba's reliance on Chandrakīrti is a primary factor for understanding why his interpretation might differ from Mādhyamika interpretations prevalent in China and Japan. Nāgārjuna flourished during the first to second centuries A.D.;[15] Āryadeva was his direct disciple and thus is roughly contemporaneous with him. Buddhapālita, Bhāvaviveka, and Chandrakīrti lived considerably later, the former two in the sixth century and Chandrakīrti in the seventh.[16] Whereas major works of Nāgārjuna and Āryadeva were translated into Chinese, those of the three later commentators were not.[17] Hence Dzong-ka-ba was relying for his understanding of Mādhyamika on later texts than was the Chinese tradition.

A similar difference of sources applies to much of Western scholarship concerning Mādhyamika, which has relied heavily on extant Sanskrit materials. Among Mādhyamika texts, several of Nāgārjuna's works have survived in Sanskrit, fragments of one of Āryadeva's works, one of Bhāvaviveka's works, and one of Chandrakīrti's works along with fragments of another.[18] This hardly provides a basis for a complete picture of the Indian commentarial tradition. Dzong-ka-ba, in contrast, had access to Tibetan translations of Mādhyamika texts by Indian authors from Nāgārjuna to Atisha (eleventh century) which fill eighteen volumes of the Tibetan canon. Included are the major works attributed to Nāgārjuna, Āryadeva, Buddhapālita, Bhāvaviveka, and Chandrakīrti. In addition, Dzong-ka-ba was dealing with the material as a living tradition, actively studied and debated by the scholars of his time. Furthermore, the fact that it has remained a living tradition among the Tibetans right up to the present greatly increases access to Dzong-ka-ba's thought, as there are numerous written commentaries on his work in addition to well-versed contemporary scholars who can be consulted concerning difficult points.

The *Great Exposition of the Stages of the Path* is particularly useful for a study of Mādhyamika in that Dzong-ka-ba, because he was newly setting forth his interpretation, supports his positions with copious citation of Indian sources. Further, he presents a number of passages that are used by his oppon ents to support what he considers to be incorrect interpretations and then explains why he considers them to be incorrect, along with offering his own interpretation. Thus it is possible to judge whether Dzong-ka-ba's interpretation is in fact supported by Indian sources or is merely his own fabrication.

THE DEPENDENT-ARISING OF THIS STUDY

My initial study of the *Great Exposition of the Stages of the Path* was begun with Professor Jeffrey Hopkins. Over a period from May, 1979 to September, 1981, we read through slightly more than the first half of the special insight portion of the *Four Interwoven Annotations to (Dzong-ka-ba's) "Great Exposition of the Stages of the Path"* (*lam rim mchan bzhi sbrags ma*), a commentary on Dzong-ka-ba's *Great Exposition* that is itself a composite of four commentaries.[19] During this time I prepared a draft translation.

I also studied the first two-thirds of the portion of the *Four Interwoven Annotations* translated here with Gyu-may Ken-sur Jampel Shenphen, since appointed head of the Ge-luk-ba order, while he was in residence at the University of Virginia from June, 1980 to June, 1981. His extremely careful attention to the interplay of the different annotations helped me to become fluent in distinguishing between them and to develop a sense of the varying contributions of each annotator. In Dharmsala, India, during the summer of 1982, I read through the portion of the annotations translated here with the senior ge-shay of Nam-gyal Monastery, Ge-shay Wangdrak, and on my return to the US in the fall of 1982, read through the remainder of the portion of the text concerned with identifying the object of negation with Lo-ling Ken-sur Yeshe Thupten. While in India I also raised questions on the *Four Interwoven Annotations* with a number of Tibetan scholars, in particular Ge-shay Gönchok Tsering of the Shar-dzay College of Ganden Monastic University and Ken-sur Denba Dendzin of the Go-mang College of Dre-bung Monastic University.

In addition, while in India I read through the entire portion of Dzong-ka-ba's "Great Exposition of Special Insight" concerned with identifying the object of negation (slightly more than the first third of the text), separate from the *Four Interwoven Annotations*, with Ge-shay Palden Drakpa, resident scholar at Tibet House in New Delhi. I found him a brilliant scholar whose penetrating analysis went right to the heart of the many difficult issues raised by Dzong-ka-ba.

Other texts consulted as part of this study include four additional commentaries on the *Great Exposition of Special Insight*:

1 Sha-mar-den-dzin's *Difficult Points of (Dzong-ka-ba's) "Great Exposition of Special Insight"*,[20] a detailed analysis of key issues in Dzong-ka-ba's text that is highly recommended by the present Dalai Lama, which I studied with Professor Hopkins in India in 1982;

2 Lo-sang-dor-jay's *Decisive Analysis of Special Insight*,[21] a text that is less a commentary on Dzong-ka-ba's work than a summary of key points within it, supplemented with material from Dzong-ka-ba's other writings on Mādhyamika so as to provide a condensed picture of the major topics studied with regard to Mādhyamika philosophy, all phrased in the syllo-

gistic or consequential debate format, which I studied in Dharmsala with the then abbot of Nam-gyal Monastery, Losang Nyima;

3 A-gya-yong-dzin's *A Brief Explanation of Terminology Occurring in (Dzong-ka-ba's) "Great Exposition of the Stages of the Path"*,[22] a commentary first shown to me by Ge-shay Palden Drakpa of Tibet House, which is very helpful in explaining unusual terminology and providing background information on many points as well as historical information on the composition of the *Great Exposition* and the *Four Interwoven Annotations*;

4 Pa-bong-ka's *About the Four Interwoven Annotations on (Dzong-ka-ba's) "Great Exposition of the Stages of the Path to Enlightenment", Set Forth In Very Brief Form to Purify Forgetfulness and Nourish the Memory*,[23] miscellaneous notes set down by Pa-bong-ka to supplement the *Four Interwoven Annotations*.

I also read through the sections in Dzong-ka-ba's other major works on Mādhyamika that are appropriate to this study with Ge-shay Gönchok Tsering in Mundgod, South India. With Lo-ling Ken-sur Yeshe Thupten in Virginia, I read in Dzong-ka-ba's *Great Exposition of the Stages of the Path* other sections not translated in this volume but helpful for a deeper understanding of the topic: Dzong-ka-ba's introduction to the topics of calm abiding and special insight as well as the final sixty pages of the text, mainly concerned with how to cultivate the view of emptiness in meditation.

ON READING THIS WORK

Throughout my chapters, when I speak of Mādhyamika philosophy, I am speaking from the viewpoint of Dzong-ka-ba's interpretation of Mādhyamika — which is based, as described above, on Nāgārjuna, Āryadeva, Chandrakīrti, Buddhapālita, and Bhāvaviveka — and of that of Ge-luk-ba scholars who follow Dzong-ka-ba's interpretation.

Although I occasionally use the term "the Ge-luk-ba tradition" or "the Ge-luk-ba position", my use of it requires explanation. Dzong-ka-ba is considered the founder of the Ge-luk order, not in the sense that he himself announced such self-consciously, but that over time a school of his followers developed which eventually came to be called Ge-luk-ba. It is hard to define what makes someone a Ge-luk-ba, for certainly there is no doctrinal catechism that can be pointed to, and the ge-shay (*dge bshes*) training encourages individual analysis and interpretation of difficult philosphical points, not blind adherence to dogma. The main qualification perhaps would be that such a person relies *primarily* on the lineage of teachings and textual interpretation descended from Dzong-ka-ba, which in terms of spiritual practice would mean being based upon the "stages of the path" (*lam rim*) teachings that Dzong-ka-ba laid out in such detail in the *Great Exposition of the Stages of the Path*. The qualification "primarily" allows that one could rely on those teachings and not consider oneself a Ge-luk-ba, or that one could consider oneself a Ge-luk-ba and still rely on lineages of teaching descended from teachers of other Tibetan orders, and so forth.

I try to limit the term "*the* Ge-luk-ba position" to a philosophical assertion found in the textbook literature of all three of the great Ge-luk-ba monastic universities, Gan-den (*dga' ldan*), Dre-bung (*'bras spungs*) and Se-ra (*se rwa*). More frequently I use the indefinite article, "*a* Ge-luk-ba position" to indicate a position that is widely asserted within the tradition of scholars who are followers of Dzong-ka-ba, though not necessarily by members of all three monastic universities. Also, although the focus of this work is Dzong-ka-ba's interpretation of Mādhyamika, at times I bring in material from the commentarial tradition based on Dzong-ka-ba's writings that deals with issues not specifically addressed by him; I consider those "Ge-luk-ba" interpretations rather than specifically Dzong-ka-ba's. It is not that they contradict Dzong-ka-ba but that he did not necessarily say such.

My use of the term "Ge-luk-ba" is not intended to be

exclusive. If I say that something is a Ge-luk position, this does not mean that it is necessarily *not* a Nying-ma (*rnying ma*), Ga-gyu (*bka' rgyud*), or Sa-gya (*sa skya*) position. Since Dzong-ka-ba studied with teachers of all the great Tibetan orders, and especially those of the Sa-gya order, much of what he asserts is shared with those orders and not unique to Ge-luk. In some areas there are also significant differences from those schools, but delineation of these areas of similiarity and difference, though a fruitful field for further study, is not the focus of this work. Thus, identification of a position as "Ge-luk-ba" indicates that it is widely asserted within the tradition following Dzong-ka-ba but not necessarily asserted outside of that tradition.

The first three chapters of Part One are intended to supply the background material and explanation needed in order to understand and appreciate more fully Dzong-ka-ba's presentation. Chapters four though six consider some of the central issues in Mādhyamika philosophy around which Dzong-ka-ba's interpretation revolves, comparing his Mādhyamika interpretation with interpretations current in Western scholarship.

Part Two contains a translation of approximately one sixth of the special insight section of Dzong-ka-ba's *Great Exposition of the Stages of the Path*, his introduction to the topic of special insight and to the refutation of those who go too far in their estimation of what the Mādhyamikas negate, focusing on the compatibility of emptiness and conventional phenomena as the uncommon feature of the Mādhyamika system.[24] Part Three is a translation of the corresponding section of the commentary on Dzong-ka-ba's work, the *Four Interwoven Annotations to (Dzong-ka-ba's) "Great Exposition of the Stages of the Path"*.

The most fruitful way to read the translations is to read simultaneously the respective chapters of Dzong-ka-ba's text and the annotations on it. Once understood, Dzong-ka-ba's presentation is pellucid and his writing brilliant in its simplicity. However, approached initially, and particularly if one is unfamiliar with the topics he is discussing, it is possible to miss much of what he is saying, for he assumes an educated audience and does not supply a great deal of background material, referents, and so forth. The *Four Interwoven Annotations* are, therefore, invaluable in filling this gap. Having read them, it is then possible to reread Dzong-ka-ba alone with fuller appreciation.

1 *An Overview of the Great Exposition*

Dzong-ka-ba introduces his presentation of special insight with a few pages aimed at establishing that in order to gain release from cyclic existence, the endless cycle of birth and rebirth, mere meditative stabilization is not sufficient. Also needed is the special insight realizing emptiness. This starting point must be understood within its context in the *Great Exposition of the Stages of the Path* – in terms of what has come before it in the text, how special insight fits into the Buddhist path as a whole, and, within that, the level of the path on which Dzong-ka-ba's discussion focuses. To understand how Dzong-ka-ba approaches the Buddhist tradition, it is also important to be familiar with presuppositions and principles underlying his approach. These topics are addressed in this chapter.

SUMMARY OF THE GREAT EXPOSITION

The *Great Exposition* is a presentation of the entire path to enlightenment, laid out in the stages of practice of one individual, from the very beginning of religious practice through to the attainment of Buddhahood. It is based on Atisha's (982–1054) *Lamp for the Path to Enlightenment* (*byang chub lam sgron, bodhipathapradīpa*)[25] and the Ga-dam-ba (*bka' gdams pa*) tradition descended from Atisha, but Dzong-ka-ba has extensively extended and systematized the presentation. In terms of sheer size, Atisha's text is three folios in length whereas Dzong-ka-ba's is five hundred and twenty-three.

The text is structured around the mind-trainings (*blo sbyong*) of beings of the three capacities. A being of small capacity is one who has turned to religious practice, but is focused mainly on attaining a good rebirth in the future. In the section of the *Great Exposition* setting forth the practices shared with trainees of this capacity, Dzong-ka-ba presents teachings on developing mindfulness of the definiteness of death and the uncertainty of the time of death; on the sufferings of the three bad transmigrations – as hell-beings, hungry ghosts, or animals; on the importance, purpose, and benefits of going for refuge to the Three Jewels of Buddha, Doctrine, and Spiritual Community; on the relationship of actions committed and the effects they induce; on the different types of actions and their effects; and on the ways to purify negative actions done in the past.

A being of middling capacity is one who, rather than seeking merely a good rebirth in the future, has developed a perception of all of cyclic existence as pervaded by suffering, and has developed an attitude of renunciation – a determination to become liberated from cyclic existence altogether. In the section of the *Great Exposition* presenting the mind-trainings shared with beings of middling capacity, Dzong-ka-ba discusses the four noble truths, focusing particularly on the first two, true sufferings and true sources of suffering, describing the twelve links of dependent-arising and the sufferings of the six transmigrations; he identifies the afflictions and sets forth the path to liberation.

A being of great capacity does not stop merely with the intention to remove himself or herself from cyclic existence, but, understanding that as much as its suffering is unbearable for oneself so much so is it for all others as well, generates the altruistic intention to become a Buddha realistically able to work effectively to free beings from suffering. In the part of the *Great Exposition* describing the mind-training of a being of great capacity, Dzong-ka-ba sets forth the generation of the altruistic aspiration to enlightenment and the deeds in which a Bodhisattva is to train, including an extensive discussion of the six perfections – giving, ethics, patience, effort, concentration, and wisdom.

The final part of the *Great Exposition* is a more detailed and technical explanation of how to train in the last two perfections, now discussed in terms of calm abiding (*zhi gnas, śamatha*) and special insight (*lhag mthong, vipaśyanā*). For, taken loosely, all concentrative states (from a mere one-pointedness, or focusing, of the mind on a virtuous object on up through the concentrations [*bsam gtan, dhyāna*] and formless absorptions [*gzugs med kyi snyoms 'jug, ārupyasamāpatti*]) can be included within the class of calm abiding, and all wisdom (that is, all virtuous wisdoms differentiating individually either conventional or ultimate objects) can be included within the class of special insight.[26]

CALM ABIDING AND SPECIAL INSIGHT

As described by the Ge-luk-ba tradition, the etymology of the term calm abiding (*zhi gnas, śamatha*) is that it is an abiding (*gnas, sthā*) of the mind upon an internal object of observation having calmed (*zhi, śama*) its running to external objects.[27] Defined more technically, calm abiding is a meditative stabilization accompanied by a joy of mental and physical pliancy in which the mind abides naturally – without effort – for as long as one wishes, without fluctuation, on whichever virtuous object it has been placed.[28] This level of concentration is the degree of mental stabilization that must be present in order to progress to all the higher levels of the Buddhist path. Although not the most concentrated state that can be attained – the concentrations and formless absorptions are more highly concentrated states[29] – it is called the "not unable" (*mi lcogs med, anāgamya*) because it can serve as the mental basis for all of the path consciousnesses that are the antidotes to the afflictions that bind persons in cyclic existence.[30]

Calm abiding refers merely to the mind's being concentrated, drawn within so that it stays focused on whatever object it has been placed. That object can be any number of things – the visualized body of a Buddha, impermanence, the four noble truths, or whatever. Emptiness could be the object with respect to which calm abiding is achieved, but need not be, and because it is a more difficult object than many for achieving calm abiding, probably would not be the object initially.

Special insight is etymologized as sight (*mthong, paśya*) exceeding (*lhag, vi*), in that it is a special seeing.[31] It is an analytical wisdom defined as a wisdom of thorough discrimination of phenomena conjoined with special pliancy induced by the power of analysis.[32] In general, it need not be observing emptiness, but its main meaning within the Bodhisattva's training in the perfection of wisdom is as a wisdom consciousness realizing emptiness.

It is an analytical consciousness, but one based upon stabilization of mind – according to the sūtra system presentation, special insight can only be achieved after and upon a basis of calm abiding. Ordinarily, analysis harms the stability of mind, and great stability of mind harms analysis. The causal process utilized in the development of special insight is that having attained calm abiding, one repeatedly alternates stabilizing and analytical meditation, training in the harmonization of the two types of meditation until finally analytical meditation itself induces stability and that then induces special mental and physical pliancy. This is the point at which special insight can be said to have been attained, and the attainment of special insight is necessarily an attainment of a union of calm abiding and special insight.

In terms of progress on the Buddhist path, the attainment of such a union of calm abiding and special insight marks a rather advanced level of development. There are five paths which must be traversed by a practitioner intent upon the highest goal – those of accumulation, preparation, seeing, meditation, and no more learning. Discussed in terms of a Geluk-ba presentation of the Mahāyāna path, the path of accumulation (*tshogs lam, saṃbhāramārga*) is attained at the point at which one develops the Bodhisattva motivation, generating an altruistic aspiration to attain enlightenment for the sake of all sentient beings, this attitude arising spontaneously both in and out of meditation.[33]

On this path one accumulates the collections of merit and wisdom, the latter being primarily cultivation of the realization of selflessness. The path of preparation (*sbyor lam, prayogamārga*) is attained at the point at which one generates a union of calm abiding and special insight realizing emptiness, and the path of seeing (*mthong lam, darśanamārga*) is attained at the point at which one brings that realization to a level of direct perception, in which emptiness is realized directly rather than conceptually. During the path of meditation (*sgom lam, bhāvanāmārga*), which is divided into ten Bodhisattva grounds (*sa, bhūmi*), one is making that realization progressively more and more powerful, using it to eradicate ever more subtle levels of the innate conception of inherent existence. Finally, with the attainment of the path of no more learning (*mi slob lam, aśaikṣamārga*), one has attained Buddhahood, an omniscient state in which all good qualities have been perfected, all bad qualities eradicated forever, and one is fully effective in terms of being able to help other sentient beings.

According to the sūtra Mahāyāna system as studied in Geluk-ba monasteries, it takes three periods of countless aeons to progress over the five paths – one period of countless aeons for the paths of accumulation and preparation, one to go from the path of seeing through the seventh Bodhisattva ground, and a final period of countless aeons to progress over the last three Bodhisattva grounds and attain the path of no more learning.[34] Thus at the point when a union of calm abiding and special insight realizing emptiness is initially attained, one has already developed the Bodhisattva aspiration in fully qualified form and is well into the first period of countless aeons of practice of the Bodhisattva deeds. Further, the union of calm abiding and special insight is not merely a milepost marking the attainment of the path of preparation, but is an integral part of all the further levels of the path, being the concentrative basis for the progressively more penetrating realizations of emptiness that demarcate subsequent progress on the path. Even a Buddha's omniscient consciousness realizing all phenomena simultaneously is a union of calm abiding and special insight. Thus it can be said without exaggeration that calm abiding and special insight are at the heart of the Buddhist path.

Dzong-ka-ba begins his exposition of calm abiding and special insight with a general discussion of their benefits, the way in which all meditative stabilizations can be included within them, their natures, why it is necessary to cultivate both, and the definiteness of the order in which they are achieved – first calm abiding and then special insight.[35] He then discusses each in detail, devoting approximately fifty Tibetan folios to his explanation of calm abiding and one hundred and sixty to that of special insight.

THE CONTEXT OF DZONG-KA-BA'S DISCUSSION

The presentation of special insight is initiated with a brief indication that it is essential for gaining liberation from cyclic existence. Meditative stabilization alone is not sufficient. To support this point, Dzong-ka-ba relies chiefly upon citations from Kamalashīla's *Stages of Meditation* (*sgom rim*, *bhāvanā-krama*) and sūtra. In approaching the topic in this way, Dzong-ka-ba is alluding to the famous Sam-yay (*bsam yas*) debate that took place in the late eighth century between Kamalashīla and a Chinese monk identified as Hva-shang Mahāyāna. The outcome of the debate definitively settled that the Buddhist tradition in Tibet would take its impetus primarily from India rather than China.[36]

According to Tibetan traditions, Hva-shang was propounding as meditation on emptiness the mere withdrawal of the mind from everything. Dzong-ka-ba, for example, says of Hva-shang, "That one, holding all conceptuality (*rtog pa*, *vikalpa*) whatsoever as an apprehension of signs, abandons the wisdom of individual analysis and asserts as meditation on the profound meaning not taking anything at all to mind."[37] Such a premise is founded on the view that all conceptuality whatsoever is bad and to be gotten rid of, and is often expressed through the metaphor that just as black clouds obstruct the sky, so also do white clouds.

In refuting Hva-shang, Kamalashīla – martialling extensive scriptural support as well as using reasoning – is considered by Tibetan traditions to have successfully upheld the position that some conceptuality – e.g., that used in the analytical processes that are steps to penetrating the nature of reality – is not only acceptable but indispensible.

For Dzong-ka-ba the issue is settled, and rather than reworking the arguments in great detail, he merely summarizes the basic conclusion, relying primarily on Kamalashīla. From this beginning, Dzong-ka-ba then addresses the question of how special insight realizing emptiness is to be achieved. Special insight is an advanced level of realization of emptiness; the foundation from which it must be developed is the view (*lta ba*, *dṛṣṭi*) realizing emptiness. Thus Dzong-ka-ba immediately takes a position contrary to what many interpreters believe of Mādhyamika. For Dzong-ka-ba, Mādhyamika, far from being a systemless system intent only on refuting the views of others and positing none of its own, is a positive system built upon and directed towards the generation of a view – that realizing emptiness.[38] Emptiness, though a negative phenomenon – a non-affirming negative (*med dgag*, *prasajya-pratiṣedha*) that is the mere absence of the object of negation, inherent existence (*rang bzhin*, *svabhāva*) – does exist, is an object of knowledge (*shes bya*, *jñeya*), and as such, can be realized.[39]

The view realizing emptiness is generated through a careful process of reasoning and analysis, and most of the "Great Exposition of Special Insight" is focused on how to develop that view; of its one hundred fifty-eight folios, one hundred twenty-seven are concerned with the generation of the view, included within the topical heading, "Fulfilling the Prerequisites for Special Insight". The first step in that process is to identify the object of negation – what it is that phenomena are empty of. As part of that identification, Dzong-ka-ba refutes at length interpretations he felt negated too much. (The first part of this section, Dzong-ka-ba's general consideration of over-negation, is translated here.)

The *view* of emptiness is something that can be gained even prior to entry into the five paths in that, technically speaking, one is said to have gained the view at the point at which one initially generates an inferential cognition of emptiness.[40] Most of Dzong-ka-ba's discussion is thus carried on at a level considerably less lofty than actual special insight but very appropriate to the practical needs of his audience.

HOW DZONG-KA-BA APPROACHES THE TRADITION

To realize emptiness, one needs to rely on definitive scriptures – those in which the final mode of subsistence of phenomena is definite just as it is in the passage, not requiring any interpretation. However, Buddha taught for forty-five years, during which time he set forth a bewildering array of doctrines, many of them seemingly contradictory. Thus, Dzong-ka-ba next addresses the question of interpretation. How is one to know which scriptures to follow in seeking to understand emptiness? Through adhering to two basic principles: rely on reasoning, but also rely on a skilled guide. The emphasis on reasoning has its source in Buddha himself, for sūtra says:[41]

> Monks and scholars
> Should accept my words not out of respect
> But upon having carefully analyzed them,
> Like the way in which gold is scorched, cut, and rubbed.

Dzong-ka-ba and his Ge-luk-ba followers particularly took this teaching to heart. In their system, reasoning is essential in differentiating which scriptures are definitive and which require interpretation, for the sūtras themselves give contradictory indications. The teaching in a sūtra such as the *One Hundred Thousand Stanza Perfection of Wisdom* (*shes rab kyi pha rol tu phyin pa stong phrag brgya pa*, *śatasāhasrikāprajñāpāramitā*) that all phenomena are empty of true establishment is said to be definitive by one sūtra, the *Teachings of Akṣhayamati* (*blo gros mi zad pas bstan pa*, *akṣayamatinirdeśa*), and to require interpretation by another, the *Sūtra Unravelling the Thought* (*mdo sde dgongs 'grel*, *saṃdhinirmocana*). Thus, in the end, the differentiation must be made by reasoning.

However, this is not to say that every student of the teachings of emptiness is to begin anew, approaching the texts alone and relying only on his or her wits. Dzong-ka-ba indicates that one needs to rely on a teacher skilled in the texts teaching emptiness, and that further one must rely on one of the great Indian commentators. Otherwise, he says, "you are like a blind person without a guide going in a direction of fright".[42] He expresses this cautionary advice because emptiness, particularly as presented by the Mādhyamika system, is not a topic to be studied lightly. There is great danger of students' misunderstanding it – as evidenced by the centuries of controversy over how it is to be interpreted – with a consequent danger of generating strong wrong views that, in Buddhist religious terms, can bring great harm to a student in the future. Chandrakīrti's *[Auto]commentary on the "Supplement to (Nāgārjuna's) 'Treatise on the Middle Way'"* (*dbu ma la 'jug pa'i bshad pa*, *madhyamakāvatārabhāṣya*) says:[43]

> Further, [Nāgārjuna's] *Treatise*, which has the fruit of teaching the real dependent-arising just as it is, is to be taught only to those who through prior cultivation have established seeds [for the realization] of emptiness in their continuums. [It should] not [be taught] to others, for, even if they have heard about emptiness, since [such people] have thoughts wrongly oriented with respect to emptiness, it is disastrous. It is thus: Some people, through lack of

> skill, abandon emptiness and thereby go to a bad transmigration [upon rebirth]. Others, erroneously apprehending the meaning of emptiness, think that [these phenomena] do not exist. The wrong view deprecating all things, having been generated, increases. Therefore, a teacher should explain the view of emptiness to listeners upon having ascertained the particulars of [their] inclinations.

Thus, given the dangers of deprecation of the teachings or of a fall into nihilism, it is important if one is to study emptiness that it be done with the assistance of reliable commentaries. The scriptures themselves are vast and various, and, in isolation, without commentary, difficult to penetrate. Buddha is renowned to have prophesied two great commentators on his teachings – Asaṅga, founder of the Chittamātra school of tenets, and Nāgārjuna, founder of Mādhyamika – and Dzong-ka-ba says that one should rely upon their treatises.

THE THEME OF COHERENCE

The reference to relying on either the Chittamatra or the Mādhyamika commentators, in spite of Dzong-ka-ba's personal adherence to Mādhyamika as the highest of teachings, illustrates another of the principles underlying Dzong-ka-ba's presentation, that of the coherence and validity of all Buddha's teachings. Dzong-ka-ba extolls Atisha's *Lamp for the Path* and its teaching of the practices of the three types of beings, on which the *Great Exposition* is based, as particularly facilitating understanding that Buddha's teachings are a coherent whole. In the opening pages of the *Great Exposition*, he says that these instructions for practice are to be praised by way of their possessing four greatnesses:[44]

1 the greatness of realizing all of the teachings as without contradiction

2 the greatness that all of the scriptures dawn as instructions for practice

3 the greatness that the thought of the Conqueror [Buddha] is easily found

4 the greatness that one is prevented from the great wrongdoing [of abandoning the doctrine through accepting some teachings and rejecting others, saying that some are good and some are bad].

These emphasize what is for Dzong-ka-ba a central theme. Applying standards of reasoning and consistency, Dzong-ka-ba analyzed the vast corpus of Buddhist literature and derived an ordered system that attempts to uphold the validity of all the Buddha's diverse teachings within reconciling seeming contradictions between them. As he says with regard to the first of the four greatnesses:[45]

> Therefore, all of the scriptures are included as a branch of the Mahāyāna path for achieving Buddhahood, for, there is no saying of the Subduer which does not extinguish some fault or generate some good quality, and, of all those, there is none that is not accomplished by a Mahāyānist.

All the teachings are to be brought into the practice of a single individual, combining practical application with knowledge of the great texts based upon having come to know how they are to be interpreted.

Thus, the purpose of differentiating between which of Buddha's teachings are definitive and which interpretable is not to rule out some teachings, but to know how the teachings should be taken, to bring order to a variety of teachings that certainly on the surface appear to be contradictory.

The variety of practices, tenets, and levels is said to take account of the differences between individual practitioners and in fact is pointed to by the Buddhist traditions as yet another sign of Buddha's genius. He was not a quack with only one medicine to prescribe for all, but through his great skill in means taught many different doctrines to his many followers in accordance with their varying capacities. Fearing, because of the difficulty of understanding emptiness, that he would not be understood properly or that people would turn away from the teachings altogether, Buddha sometimes taught presentations of emptiness less subtle than his final teaching and, as such, more easily grasped by his less skillful trainees.

Within Dzong-ka-ba's system there is a clear ranking of the philosophical tenet systems – Vaibhāṣhika, Sautrāntika, Chittamātra, and Mādhyamika – in order of increasing subtlety, with preference for the highest. Also, the levels of practice set forth in the *Great Exposition* – practices of beings of small, middling, and great capacity – are a ranked order with preference for the Bodhisattva practices of a being of great capacity. However, even though Dzong-ka-ba states that in general Mādhyamika is the highest system and the Bodhisattva training the highest level of practice, this does not mean that everyone should seek this level immediately. For some, Mādhyamika is at present too subtle and the Bodhisattva training too difficult, and thus for them these are not the best. Rather than trying to follow them but failing, one should practice at a level appropriate to one's capacity.

Even for those capable of the higher levels, the higher levels are built upon the lower, and in fact require the lower as prerequisites; one must work one's way up, it not being suitable to just leap in at the top, nor to utterly reject the lower and accept only the higher. Thus, the levels of training described for beings of small capacity are described as those *shared* with beings of small capacity – shared in that beings of middling and great capacity must practice them as well.

Similarly, when seeking to understand Mādhyamika, one cannot study only it but must also have an understanding of the lower tenet systems, and, in fact, Mādhyamika asserts much of what is taught in the texts of the lower systems. It is not that Mādhyamika is just different from the lower systems, but that it builds upon them, accepting much of what is taught there, although refining and adding to it. Dzong-ka-ba himself on many occasions cites texts by non-Prāsaṅgika and even non-Mādhyamika authors. To give just two examples, much of his presentation of calm abiding is based on

Chittamātrin works by Asaṅga, for it was Asaṅga who developed the topic in most detail. (In addition, Asaṅga is the main source for the lineage of the teachings on the development of compassion, and these teachings are never overridden by any considered higher.) Also Dzong-ka-ba frequently cites Kamalashīla – a Svātantrika-Mādhyamika – on points to do with meditation and even for general comments about the view of emptiness. This does not mean that Dzong-ka-ba was a Chittamātrin or a Svātantrika or that he shifted his viewpoint within his writings with the result that the calm abiding section of the *Great Exposition* is Chittamātrin whereas the special insight section is Prāsaṅgika. It merely indicates that he accepted as valid and made use of non-Prāsaṅgika teachings that do not contradict Prāsaṅgika tenets.

Thus, in Dzong-ka-ba's statement that in seeking to understand Buddha's scriptures, one should rely on valid commentators who are openers of the chariot-ways — Asaṅga or Nāgārjuna – he is indicating the validity of both Mahāyāna traditions and emphasizing that one should follow a commentator whose interpretations are appropriate to oneself. However, he then goes on to specify that here, in this context of seeking the view realizing emptiness, one should rely on the texts of Nāgārjuna, and among the many commentators on Nāgārjuna's thought, those to be relied on are chiefly Buddhapālita and Chandrakīrti, and to a lesser degree and with some correction, Bhāvaviveka.

Thus, at the beginning of his presentation of special insight Dzong-ka-ba devotes a few pages to the need for special insight (see the introduction of the translation), a few to how one is to identify which scriptures are definitive and which require interpretation (see the next chapter and chapter one of the translation), and a few more to describing and categorizing the development of the commentarial tradition following Nāgārjuna (chapter two of the translation).

2 *Interpretation of Scripture*

For Dzong-ka-ba, the determination of which scriptures should be relied upon in seeking to realize emptiness is based on a differentiation of scriptures into those of definitive, or final, meaning (*nges don, nītārtha*) and those of interpretable meaning (*drang don, neyārtha*). One should rely on scriptures of definitive meaning, not on those requiring interpretation. This principle has its source in sūtra, it being one of the four reliances set forth by Buddha in the *Sūtra on the Four Reliances* (*rton pa bzhi'i mdo, catuḥpratisaraṇasūtra*):[46]

> Rely on the doctrine and not on the person.
> Rely on the meaning and not on the words.
> Rely on sūtras of definitive meaning and not on those of interpretable meaning.
> Rely on exalted wisdom [directly perceiving reality] and not on [ordinary] consciousness.

However, in order to rely on scriptures of definitive meaning, one must first determine which those are. How the various Buddhist schools make this determination is a major key to the differences between them and as such serves as the primary subject matter of one of Dzong-ka-ba's five major works setting forth his interpretation of the Mādhyamika view, the *Essence of the Good Explanations, Treatise Discriminating the Interpretable and the Definitive*.[47]

Within the Mahāyāna tenet systems, Chittamātra uses literal acceptability as the criterion for whether scriptures are definitive or require interpretation: a definitive scripture is one which can be accepted literally.[48] Thus, for example, scriptures teaching about impermanence or about the four noble truths, because they are literal, are of definitive meaning; scriptures such as the one that says, "Father and mother are to be killed," – which does not in the least mean what it would seem superficially to indicate, but rather means that existence (*srid pa*, *bhava*) and attachment (*sred pa*, *tṛṣṇa*), the tenth and eighth links of the twelve-fold chain of dependent-arising, are to be eradicated – are non-literal and hence of interpretable meaning.[49]

In the Mādhyamika school as presented by the Ge-luk tradition, the criterion shifts, based on the *Teachings of Akṣhayamati Sūtra* (*blo gros mi zad pas bstan pa'i mdo*, *akṣayamatinirdeśa*) and supported also by the *King of Meditative Stabilizations Sūtra* (*ting nge 'dzin rgyal po*, *samādhirāja*), and the differentiation between scriptures of definitive and interpretable meaning is made by way of the subject discussed. Those teaching emptiness as their subject matter are of definitive meaning and those teaching other topics require interpretation. The basis for the distinction thus rests on the ontological status of the subjects discussed: emptinesses, or ultimate truths, are definitive objects (*nges don*, *nītārtha*), and the taking of a definitive *object* as its subject matter will cause a sūtra to be considered a sūtra of definitive *meaning* (*nges don gyi mdo*, *nītārthasūtra*). (However it should be noted that the sūtra itself is ontologically an interpretable *object* in that it is a conventional phenomenon made up of letters, words, and sentences).[50]

All phenomena except emptinesses, that is, all conventional truths, are interpretable *objects* (*drang don*, *neyārtha*), and taking them as the subject of discussion will cause a sūtra to be one of interpretable *meaning* (*drang don gyi mdo*, *neyārthasūtra*).

This progression is based on a shift in meaning of the Sanskrit word *artha* which is mirrored by its Tibetan translation *don*. *Artha* can mean "object" or it can mean "meaning" or "purpose", and the same is true of *don*. There not being a comparable word in English, when translating these terms it is necessary to shift words depending on the context, translating it as "object" when it refers to emptinesses or conventional truths as definitive and interpretable *objects*, respectively, and translating it as "meaning" when it refers to the scriptures which are posited as of definitive or interpretable *meaning* by way of taking those definitive or interpretable objects as their subject of discussion.

Another point to be briefly noted is the meaning of the term *neyārtha*; *neya* and its Tibetan translation *drang* literally mean "to be led" or "drawn out", and, thus, scriptures of interpretable meaning (*neya-artha*, *drang ba'i don*) are scriptures of which the meaning must be led – to something other than what is explicitly taught on the literal level, namely to the final status of those things taught, their emptiness. As Dzong-ka-ba points out in his *Essence of the Good Explanations*[51] one should not mistake the term as meaning "scriptures that lead" but rather understand it as "scriptures that must be led". Although indeed trainees are led by scriptures of interpretable meaning, they are also led by those of definitive meaning, and thus this is not the significance of the term. What is under discussion is whether or not the scriptures themselves need to be led, or interpreted, in some way so as to get at the final mode of being of the objects discussed in them.

The Chittamātra system's use of literalness as the criterion for determining definitiveness or interpretability is not abandoned by the Mādhyamika differentiation but rather supplemented by it. As Kamalashīla's *Illumination of the Middle Way* (*dbu ma snang ba*, *madhyamakāloka*), a Svātantrika text relevant, according to Dzong-ka-ba, to both Svātantrika and Prāsaṅgika Mādhyamika, says:[52]

> What is [a sūtra] of definitive meaning? That of which there is valid cognition and which makes an explanation in terms of the ultimate.

That a sūtra has valid cognition means that there is a consciousness certifying it as correct – in other words, what is said in that sūtra can be accepted literally. Thus, the

Mādhyamikas agree with the Chittamātra system that non-literal scriptures, such as the one saying that father and mother are to be killed, require interpretation. However, in order to be of definitive meaning in the Mādhyamika system, a sūtra must also make an explanation in terms of emptiness, that is, it must teach about emptiness. Thus, many sūtras that the other tenet systems consider to be definitive are, for the Mādhyamikas, sūtras that require interpretation – for example, sūtras teaching about impermanence, or those teaching about the cause and effect of actions such as that giving leads to having good resources in the future, and so forth.

Svātantrika and Prāsaṅgika agree on this general presentation. However, in terms of specific interpretations and applications, they differ. For the Prāsaṅgikas, whatever is a sūtra mainly and explicitly teaching emptiness is necessarily a sūtra of definitive meaning, whereas for the Svātantrikas, there are both interpretable and definitive sūtras among those which mainly and explicitly teach emptiness.[53] An example of a sūtra on which they differ is the *Heart of Wisdom*, or *Heart Sūtra* (*shes rab snying po*, *prajñāhṛdaya*). The *Heart Sūtra* says in part:[54]

> . . . The great being, the Bodhisattva Avalokiteshvara, replied to the venerable Shāriputra: "Shāriputra, those sons and daughters of [noble] lineage who wish to train in the deeds of the profound perfection of wisdom should view the following: They should thoroughly view these five aggregates as empty of inherent existence. Forms are empty; emptiness is form. Apart from form, there is no emptiness; apart from emptiness, there is no form. Similarly also feelings, discriminations, compositional factors, and consciousnesses are empty.
>
> Shāriputra, in this way all phenomena are empty; they are without characteristics, without production, without cessation, without defilements, without separation from defilements, without decrease, and without increase. Shāriputra, since this is so, in

> emptiness, there are no forms, no feelings, no discriminations, no compositional factors, no consciousnesses; no eyes, no ears, no noses, no tongues, no bodies, no minds; no visual forms, no sounds, no odors, no tastes, no objects of touch, no [mental] phenomena....

Both Svātantrika and Prāsaṅgika agree that this is a sūtra mainly and explicitly teaching emptiness. However, for the Svātantrikas it is a sūtra requiring interpretation because while it says at the beginning that the five aggregates are empty of inherent existence, it does not add the qualification "ultimately" which they feel is required for an accurate statement of Buddha's thought. The Prāsaṅgikas find no need for the qualification "ultimate" since in their system, "inherent" and "ultimate" are qualifiers of equal strength and thus it is sufficient that Buddha said "inherent".

In the *Great Exposition* Dzong-ka-ba considers the qualm that if a sūtra of definitive meaning is necessarily literal, then does this not mean that the statements in the *Heart Sūtra*, "Forms do not exist," "Production does not exist," and so forth, must be taken literally. Dzong-ka-ba answers this qualm in two ways. The first demonstrates his consistent commitment to common sense – if production did not exist, then no produced things would exist, including even the sūtra saying that production does not exist. There would hence be no sūtras of definitive or of interpretable meaning, and such is clearly unacceptable.

Throughout his Mādhyamika interpretation, Dzong-ka-ba is unwilling to settle for a head-splitting paradox – it is unacceptable that a sūtra teach that which would deny its very existence. This commitment to common sense is demonstrated again and again, as for example in his treatment of the famous tetralemma which says that forms 1) do not exist, 2) do not not exist, 3) do not both exist and not exist, and 4) do not neither exist nor not exist. This will be discussed further in the next chapter, but, in brief, Dzong-ka-ba says that it is very clear the non-non-existence of the second branch of the tetralemma equals existence. Since existence is denied by the first and yet would seem to be affirmed by the second if they are taken just at face value, again some qualification is needed to understand Buddha's thought. The words must make sense. In this case, the qualification he finds needed is to say that the existence denied by the first branch is inherent existence and the non-existence denied by the second is an utter non-existence which would not even allow for conventional, nominal existence.

Dzong-ka-ba's resolution of the difficulty with the passage in the *Heart Sūtra* is to make the point that a qualification that is affixed in one part of a text must be considered to be carried over to all the other points at which it is not specifically affixed. Thus, because the *Heart Sūtra* at the beginning says, "The five aggregates are empty of inherent existence," the qualification "inherent existence" is implicitly present at the other points where it just says "Forms do not exist," and so forth; those passages mean that forms and so forth do not inherently exist and such passages are thus considered to be literal and definitive.

Carefully demarcated terminology has been developed by Ge-luk-ba scholars to deal with such situations; Sha-mar-den-dzin sets forth the following fine distinctions.[55] First, a differentiation must be made between the literal reading (*sgras zin*) of a passage – what the actual words are – and whether or not a passage is literal (*sgra ji bzhin pa*). Thus, even though the *Heart Sūtra* says in the literal reading that forms do not exist, which Prāsaṅgika does not accept, the passage can be said to be literal in that its actual subject of discussion (*brjod bya*) as well as explicit teaching (*dngos bstan*) is that forms and so forth do not *inherently* exist; this is what the sūtra teaches. It is thus possible to say that the literal reading of that passage is not literal – i.e., the passage out of context – but that the passage is nonetheless literal, since it is to be understood in context with an implicit (*don gyis*) affixing of a needed qualification. Further, even though the qualification "inherently" is not explicitly affixed (*dngos su sbyar ba*), nonetheless that passage explicitly teaches (*dngos su bstan pa*) that forms and so forth do not inherently exist.

Svātantrika requires the explicit affixing, somewhere in a particular sūtra, of any needed qualification in order for that sūtra to be considered literal and, hence, if it also teaches emptiness, definitive. Prāsaṅgika, in contrast, is quite generous in its willingness to carry over a qualification mentioned in one place in a sūtra to other sūtras of similar type. For instance, they say that the qualification "ultimately" which is affixed to the object of negation in the *One Hundred Thousand Stanza Perfection of Wisdom Sūtra* must be affixed similarly to all sūtras of the same class, including those in which a qualification of the object of negation is not clear. Hence, all of the Perfection of Wisdom Sūtras are to be posited as scriptures of definitive meaning teaching suchness.[56]

Such an understanding of the implicit carryover of qualifications is crucial to Dzong-ka-ba's Mādhyamika interpretation, for he applies it not only to the words of Buddha, but also to the great Mādhyamika commentators such as Nāgārjuna, Āryadeva, and Chandrakīrti. Although Nāgārjuna on many occasions makes the statement that such and such *does not exist*, since on a few occasions he qualifies his negation to say *does not inherently exist* and also on some occasions affirms conventional existence, the qualification is to be understood as implicit throughout.

Of the twenty-seven chapters of Nāgārjuna's *Treatise on the Middle Way*, twenty-five mainly refute inherent existence and thus mainly proceed in a negative vein. The twenty-sixth teaches the stages of the arising and cessation of the twelve links of dependent-arising, and the twenty-fourth sets forth the way in which all conventional presentations – of arising, cessation, cyclic existence and nirvāṇa – are feasible within an emptiness of inherent existence.[57] Dzong-ka-ba emphasizes that it is important to carry this teaching of the compatibility of dependent-arising and emptiness over to those chapters teaching by way of negation, so that one understands that what is being negated is an inherent existence of phenomena, not phenomena themselves.

Chandrakīrti makes more use of qualification than does Nāgārjuna and spells out in more detail just what is and is not being negated by the Mādhyamika reasonings. However, he also does not always qualify his statements of negation, and on those occasions qualification must be understood to be implicit.

One might wonder why, if the qualification is needed in order to correctly understand the meaning, it is not always stated. Two possible explanations suggest themselves. One is that the audience of the Perfection of Wisdom Sūtras and of Nāgārjuna and Chandrakīrti was not one tending towards the nihilism of overnegation, but rather one strongly adhering to what in the Mādhyamika system is an extreme of reification – imputing to phenomena a solidity, a palpability, that they in fact lack. In that it is said that prior to realization of emptiness, it is almost impossible to distinguish between existence and inherent existence, such strong statements as "Forms do not exist," "Production does not exist," are an effective pedagogical tool. The listener is forced to question his or her own strong adherence to the existence of those forms and so forth and is pushed closer to an understanding of their lack of inherent existence.

However, Dzong-ka-ba's audience was quite different. The Mādhyamika interpretation prevalent in Tibet at his time was one that he considered nihilistic, most who claimed to be Mādhyamikas asserting, according to Dzong-ka-ba's description, that in fact all phenomena were negated by the Mādhyamika reasoning and hence did not exist. Thus, for Dzong-ka-ba it was important to emphasize the affixing of a qualification in the negation of phenomena and, delimiting carefully the extent of the Mādhyamika negation, to stress the maintenance of conventional existence.

The other factor is simply ease of expression. Not only is it more dramatic and forceful to say simply, "Forms do not exist," but also if the qualification, "inherently" or "ultimately" or "truly" or whatever is repeated on each and every occasion where it is to be understood, it makes for a cumbersome and turgid writing style. Even Dzong-ka-ba, for all of his care in spelling out the limits of negation and emphasis on the need for qualification of the object of negation, does not spell out that qualification on each and every occasion where it is to be understood. To do so would be excessive.

To conclude, the purpose of this Buddhist hermeneutic – this "science of interpretation of sacred doctrine"[58] – is not to rule out any of Buddha's teachings but rather to understand how to take them. Dzong-ka-ba emphasizes very strongly that not only are the doctrines non-contradictory, but they must all be practiced and internalized by a person seeking Buddhahood. Through applying a system of interpretation, one is to arrive at an understanding of the scriptures such that one understands them in terms of their place within the entire path and then can begin to practice them according to the level of one's capacity.

3 *Dzong-ka-ba's Argument*

After settling what scriptures are to be relied on and identifying the commentarial tradition he is following (chapters one and two of the translation), Dzong-ka-ba then begins the transition to the actual topic of emptiness. He does this by locating the effort of realization of emptiness within the context of the religious path as a whole (chapter three of the translation): one seeks release from cyclic existence and the attainment of the state of Buddhahood. Ignorance – the misconception of "self" where there is none – is the root cause binding beings in cyclic existence, and thus those seeking release must meditate on selflessness. For this, one must identify that "self" whose non-existence, or the emptiness of which, is to be known. Through this approach, Dzong-ka-ba arrives at the major topic of the "Great Exposition of Special Insight": identifying the object of negation – determining the boundaries of what is refuted, or negated, by the Mādhyamika reasonings.

It is essential to identify the object of negation correctly. If one negates too little – and from the Mādhyamika perspective, this is the error of all the other Buddhist tenet systems – one will fall to an extreme of "permanence", or reification, conceiving something to exist that in fact does not, and hence one cannot attain liberation from cyclic existence. If, on the other hand, one negates too much, denying the existence of what actually does exist, then one has gone to an extreme of annihilation and falls into nihilism. Not only will one not attain liberation, but, losing belief in karmic consequences, one will engage in actions leading to unfortunate rebirths. A fall into nihilism is what the other Buddhist tenet systems accuse the Mādhyamikas of, and Dzong-ka-ba felt that many Tibetans who claimed to be Mādhyamikas had, in fact, fallen into this error. Thus he devotes one quarter of the "Great Exposition of Special Insight" to a refutation of those who negate too much. He sets forth their position – that all phenomena are negated by the Mādhyamika reasonings – along with the reasons and scriptural citations used to support such a view (see chapter four of the translation) and then carefully explains why he finds such an interpretation erroneous (chapters five through eleven; this volume stops with chapter seven).

In the course of his refutation Dzong-ka-ba elaborates his own Mādhyamika interpretation. He takes dependent-arising as the key to understanding Mādhyamika; in his verse work describing his own struggle to understand the meaning of emptiness, entitled *Praise of Dependent-Arising*,[59] Dzong-ka-ba lyrically extolls dependent-arising as the means through which one can realize that things do not have inherent existence, that is, are empty, and yet, by the very fact of their being dependent-arisings, can also understand that they are not utterly non-existent. Thus, in the "Great Exposition of Special Insight", Dzong-ka-ba begins his refutation of those who believe that the Mādhyamika reasonings utterly negate phenomena with a discussion of the compatibility of dependent-arising and emptiness. He cites numerous passages by Nāgārjuna, founder of the Mādhyamika system, in which Nāgārjuna speaks of the intimate connection between dependent-arising and emptiness of praises Buddha for his teaching of these two.

The compatibility of dependent-arising and emptiness is, in fact, a compatibility of the two truths, conventional truths and ultimate truths – the dependent-arisings of things such as sprouts, tables, persons, and so forth being conventional truths and their emptinesses of inherent existence being ultimate truths. Dzong-ka-ba emphasizes that the ability to posit these two as compatible such that the understanding of the one acts as an aid to understanding the other is the uncommon feature of Mādhyamika. He makes the key to proper understanding of Mādhyamika proper understanding of the compatibility of dependent-arising and emptiness, of conventional truths and ultimate truths.

In doing so, Dzong-ka-ba sets up a situation in which he uses the arguments found in the works of Nāgārjuna, Buddhapālita, and Chandrakīrti against opposing interpretations to support his refutation of the Tibetan interpretations prevalent at his time – even though the views being argued against by the great Indian scholars were very different from those of the Tibetans Dzong-ka-ba was seeking to refute. To explain this, a little background is necessary.

THE HISTORICAL PROGRESSION

Buddha lived from the sixth to the fifth centuries B.C.E.;[60] according to the Mahāyāna tradition, although Buddha taught all of the sūtras, both Hīnayāna and Mahāyāna, during his lifetime, forty years after his passing away the Mahāyāna sūtras had disappeared from view, and thus for several centuries after the Buddha, the form of Buddhism practiced by the vast majority of his disciples was Hīnayāna, or Low Vehicle. Four hundred years after Buddha's death (around 80 B.C.E. in Western dates), according with prophecies found in such scriptures as the *Descent Into Laṅkā Sūtra* (*lang kar gzhegs pa'i mdo, laṅkāvatārasūtra*) and the *Mañjushrī Root Tantra* (*'jam dpal rtsa rgyud, mañjuśrīmūlatantra*), Nāgārjuna was born and, reintroducing the Mahāyāna sūtras to India, formulated the Mādhyamika school of Buddhist philosophy.

All Buddhists assert a doctrine of selflessness.[61] It is one of the four seals certifying that a doctrine is Buddhist:

> All produced things are impermanent;
> All contaminated things are miserable;
> All phenomena are selfless;
> Nirvāṇa is peace.

However, concerning the third seal, the measure of selflessness – the identification of the self that is negated – differs greatly from one Buddhist school to another. In the Hīnayāna systems, selflessness refers to a selflessness of persons: persons lack being a particular sort of entity, or self, and Hīnayānists identify two forms of this personal selflessness, coarse and subtle. The coarse is the person's lack of being a permanent, unitary, and independent entity; the more subtle is a person's lack of being a self-sufficient entity.[62] These types of selflessness apply only to persons.

Nāgārjuna, based on the Perfection of Wisdom Sūtras, formulated the Middle Way, or Mādhyamika, system which advocates a far more radical doctrine of selflessness, one that applies equally to both persons and phenomena. The self that both persons and phenomena lack is ultimate, or inherent, existence. Because he was countering the strong adherence to inherent existence of the Hīnayāna schools, Nāgārjuna's texts are phrased, as are the Perfection of Wisdom Sūtras that are the basis for his interpretation, in strongly negative terms, emphasizing the non-existence of that to which persons habitually assent without question. Nāgārjuna wrote mainly in verse; his works are terse, pithy, and often appear to be enigmatic and even paradoxical.

Nine hundred years after Buddha's death according to traditional Tibetan chronology (this would be approximately 420 C.E.; most Western scholarship places him in the fourth century C.E.) Asaṅga was born. He formulated the Mind-Only, or Chittamātra, school which sought to mitigate somewhat the uncompromising and radical Mādhyamika negation.[63] Relying on the *Sūtra Unravelling the Thought* (*mdo sde dgongs 'grel, saṃdhinirmocana*), Chittamātra differentiates three turnings of the wheel of Buddha's teaching.

In that differentiation,[64] the first turning of the wheel represents the Hīnayāna scriptures; even though the selflessness of persons is taught there, the selflessness of phenomena is not. Rather, it is taught that the aggregates and so forth, the bases of designation of the person, exist by way of their own character as bases of conception by the thought consciousnesses apprehending them – from the Chittamātra viewpoint, an over-reification. In the middle turning of the wheel of doctrine, the Perfection of Wisdom Sūtras, it is said that all phenomena equally do not exist by way of their own character, or, are without entityness. Although Mādhyamika accepts this as Buddha's definitive teaching, for Chittamātra, this, if taken literally, would be an over-negation, and requires a qualification that they find explicitly stated in the sūtras of the third turning of the wheel of doctrine.

There, phenomena are divided into the three natures: imputations, other-powered phenomena, and thoroughly established phenomena, and it is explained that when Buddha said in the Perfection of Wisdom Sūtras that all phenomena are without entityness, what he was thinking was that imputations lack the entityness of own-character, other-powered phenomena lack the entityness of self-production, and thoroughly established phenomena are the ultimate, non-entityness. Thus, for Chittamātra, only imputations are not truly existent; other-powered and thoroughly established phenomena are truly and ultimately established. Chittamātra blunts considerably the force of the Mādhyamika dialectic.

Subsequent to the establishment of the Chittamātra system, Bhāvaviveka, who in a Tibetan chronology was born around 950 years after the death of Buddha (thus, approximately 470 C.E.), and is placed by many Western scholars in the sixth century, refuted Chittamātra and established the Svātantrika-Mādhyamika system. Bhāvaviveka reaffirmed the Mādhyamika system, but according to Dzong-ka-ba, his interpretation of the object of negation was not as radical as it might have been. As Dzong-ka-ba interprets his writings, although Bhāvaviveka refuted any sort of ultimate existence either ultimately or conventionally, he did accept that conventionally phenomena exist inherently, or by way of their own character.

Slightly after Bhāvaviveka, and in contradistinction to his

interpretation, Chandrakīrti developed the Prāsaṅgika-Mādhyamika system. According to a Tibetan chronology, Chandrakīrti lived for 300 years, from approximately 975 years until 1275 years after the death of Buddha (approximately 495–795 C.E.). Although his dates are controversial among Western scholars, most place him in the seventh century. He was following Buddhapālita, who had preceded Bhāvaviveka by a little and whom Bhāvaviveka had refuted, but it was Chandrakīrti who really elucidated the Prāsaṅgika system. According to Dzong-ka-ba, Chandrakīrti's interpretation of the object of negation in Mādhyamika goes farther than does Bhāvaviveka's, refuting any sort of ultimate or inherent existence, even conventionally.

THE OBJECT OF NEGATION IN THE FOUR TENET SYSTEMS

The above is a general historical picture pertaining to the identification of the object of negation. The course of study focusing on the different Buddhist schools and interpretations that is followed in the Ge-luk-ba monasteries takes this historical progression into account but is primarily concerned with philosophical content in a synchronic fashion. Comparing assertions on certain key points, they include all of the different Buddhist schools within four tenet systems (*grub mtha'*, *siddhānta*) ranked in an order of preference that is essentially based on the subtlety of their identification of the object of negation. The four with their subdivisions, ranked from bottom to top, are:[65]

- Mādhyamika
  - Prāsaṅgika
  - Svātantrika
    - Yogāchāra-Svātantrika
    - Sautrāntika-Svātantrika
- Chittamātra
  - Following Reasoning
  - Following Scripture
- Sautrāntika
  - Following Reasoning
  - Following Scripture
- Vaibhāṣhika
  - eighteen schools

In terms of what they negate in their view of selflessness, Vaibhāṣhika and Sautrāntika are Hīnayāna schools and, as discussed above, negate only a self of persons.

All Mahāyāna schools, in contrast, negate both a self of persons and of phenomena. The Chittamātra identification of the selflessness of the person is the same as that in the Hīnayāna schools – the coarse selflessness is the person's lack of being a permanent, unitary, independent entity, and the subtle selflessness is the person's lack of being a self-sufficient entity. However, Chittamātra also negates a self of phenomena, the selflessness of phenomena being considered more subtle and difficult to realize than the selflessness of persons. Chittamātra makes a twofold identification of the selflessness of phenomena: phenomena lack being a different substantial entity from the consciousness perceiving them; they also lack being established by way of their own character as bases for the designation of verbal conventions. In other words, in Chittamātra, phenomena do have some mode of existence by way of their own character, but do not exist by way of their own character as bases of names.[66]

Svātantrika's assertions with regard to the selflessness of persons are also shared with the lower tenet systems, asserting the same coarse and subtle forms. However, the Svātantrikas posit as the selflessness of phenomena the "lack of their existing by way of their own uncommon mode of subsistence without being merely posited through the force of appearing to a non-defective consciousness". This goes farther than does the Chittamātra refutation, but not as far as that of Prāsaṅgika, for Svātantrika is willing to accept that phenomena do have a common mode of subsistence even if it is posited through the force of appearing to non-defective consciousnesses.

Both Chittamātra and Svātantrika assert that merely to get out of cyclic existence, realization of the selflessness of the person is sufficient, but that for one seeking to attain Buddhahood in order to be of benefit to all sentient beings, it is necessary to realize the selflessness of phenomena, a realization that they posit as more subtle than that of the selflessness of the person.

Prāsaṅgika also asserts both a selflessness of persons and of phenomena, but differs from the lower tenet systems on what it identifies as those and on whether there is a difference of subtlety between the two realizations. What the lower tenet systems identify as the subtle selflessness of the person – the person's lack of being a self-sufficient entity – is, for Prāsaṅgika, only a coarse selflessness. The subtle selflessness of the person is the person's lack of inherent existence, and this same lack of inherent existence applied to phenomena other than persons is the selflessness of phenomena. The lack of inherent existence is the same in both cases, the only difference being the bases in terms of which it is understood; consequently, realization of the selflessness of persons and realization of the selflessness of phenomena are equally subtle.

Prāsaṅgika asserts that phenomena are merely posited by names and thought – phenomena have utterly no mode of subsistence which comes from their own side, that is to say, no existence in their own right. Also, unlike Svātantrika, which asserts that the mode of subsistence of phenomena comes from their appearing to non-defective consciousnesses, Prāsaṅgika asserts that there are no non-defective sense consciousnesses, for the error of inherent existence extends to the level of the sense consciousnesses. Even our sense data are mistaken; phenomena appear to the sense consciousnesses to exist inherently whereas they do not in fact exist that way. Further, Prāsaṅgika differs from the other Mahāyāna schools in asserting that even merely to get out of cyclic existence, it is necessary to realize the selflessness of phenomena. Thus, not just those seeking to attain Buddhahood, but even Hīnayānists must realize the selflessness of phenomena.

There are a number of synonyms used by Prāsaṅgika to describe the object of negation, or self – the non-existence of which must be realized in order to make progress at actually eradicating the afflictions. How much farther than the other tenet systems Prāsaṅgika goes in its refutation can perhaps be understood by comparing its list of synonyms with the assertions of the other Mahāyāna schools. In Prāsaṅgika, all of the following are non-existent, or phrased differently, all phenomena – everything that exists – lack all of these attributes:[67]

1 ultimate establishment (*don dam par grub pa*, *paramārtha-siddhi*)
2 inherent establishment (*rang bzhin gyis grub pa*, *svabhāva-siddhi*)
3 true establishment (*bden par grub pa*, *satya-siddhi*)
4 establishment by way of [the object's] own character (*rang gi mtshan nyid kyis grub pa*, *svalakṣaṇa-siddhi*)
5 establishment as [their own] reality (*yang dag par grub pa*, *samyak-siddhi*)
6 establishment as their own suchness (*de kho na nyid du grub pa*, *tattva-siddhi*)
7 establishment by way of their own entities (*rang gi ngo bo nyid kyis grub pa*, *svabhāvatā* or *svarūpa-siddhi*)
8 substantial establishment (*rdzas grub*, *dravya-siddhi*)
9 establishment from [the object's] own side (*rang ngos nas grub pa*, *svarūpa-siddhi*).

None of the other systems considers the above to be a list of synonyms but rather considers some members of it to be non-existent and others necessary qualifications of anything that exists. For example, the Svātantrika system rejects the following:[68]

ultimate establishment
true establishment
establishment as [its own] reality
establishment as [its own] suchness.

However, they accept conventionally:

inherent establishment
establishment by way of [the object's] own character
existence by way of its own entity
substantial existence
establishment from [the object's] own side.

In Chittamātra, the distinction is made that inherent existence and establishment from the object's own side, but none of the rest, are true of imputations. In other words, existent imputations – permanent phenomena – are *not* ultimately established, truly established, established by way of their own character, established as [their own] suchness, or established [as their own] reality. However, the entire list is true of other-powered phenomena – consciousnesses, tables, chairs, and so forth – as well as of thoroughly established phenomena – emptinesses.

This distinction of terminology comes down to the question, "What is found when you analyze an object?" What makes Prāsaṅgika more radical than any of the other tenet systems is that it says that nothing is found.[69] Take, for example, the person. Although all schools assert a selflessness of the person and say that the person is imputed in dependence upon the aggregates, nonetheless, all schools except Prāsaṅgika say there is something that can be pointed to as the person, something that serves as the basis for karmic continuity from one lifetime to another.

For the Saṃmitīya schools, a subdivision of Vaibhāṣhika, what is posited as the person is the collection of the aggregates; for the Kashmiri Vaibhāṣhikas and the Sautrāntikas Following Scripture, it is the continuum of consciousness; for the Chittamātrins Following Scripture, it is the mind-basis-of-all (*kun gzhi rnam shes*, *ālayavijñāna*), and for the Sautrāntikas Following Reasoning, Chittamātrins Following Reasoning, and Svātantrikas it is the mental consciousness. Based on their accepting some sort of establishment from an object's own side, all assert that if something were not found when sought, the person could not be posited and one would have the fault of nihilism.

Prāsaṅgika disagrees with this, positing as the person the mere I which is the object of an awareness thinking "I" in dependence upon the collection of the aggregates. That I exists conventionally and is the basis for karmic continuity, but it is merely imputed by thought and cannot be found at all when sought analytically. One must be satisfied with merely the verbal designations, "*I* saw this," "*I* remember this," and so forth. The I does not in the least exist from its own side, in its own right, inherently, truly, and so forth.

Further, Prāsaṅgika says that such is the case not only with respect to the I, but is also true of everything else – the mental and physical aggregates that are the basis of designation of the I, as well as tables, sprouts, and even emptiness. They say that when reasoning seeks to find any object, it is not found. Nonetheless, they maintain that despite this utter unfindableness, phenomena nonetheless exist conventionally and are able to perform functions. The challenge for Prāsaṅgika is to explain how they can maintain the conventional status of objects within their radical negation. This, essentially, is the purpose to which Dzong-ka-ba devotes the portion of the "Great Exposition of Special Insight" entitled "Identifying the object of negation by reasoning".

WHO IS BEING REFUTED

Nāgārjuna, in setting forth the Mādhyamika assertions, was, although he also refuted non-Buddhist schools, mainly refuting Hīnayānists, referred to as Proponents of True Existence (*dngos por smra ba, vastusatpadārthavādin*,[70] see just below for a discussion of the translation of this term), and as part of his refutation, he had to defend the feasibility of conventional phenomena within his negation of inherent existence. Those of his writings mainly teaching about emptiness through reasoning are referred to as the Six Collections of Reasonings. They are the *Treatise on the Middle Way*, (*dbu ma'i bstan bcos, madhyamakaśāstra*), the *Finely Woven* (*zhib mo rnam 'thag, vaidalyasūtra*), the *Seventy Stanzas on Emptiness* (*stong nyid bdun cu ba, śūnyatāsaptati*), the *Refutation of Objections* (*rtsod bzlog, vigrahavyāvartanī*), the *Sixty Stanzas of Reasoning* (*rigs pa drug cu pa, yuktiṣaṣṭikā*), and the *Precious Garland* (*rin chen phreng ba, ratnāvalī*).[71] Of those, the *Treatise on the Middle Way*, Nāgārjuna's most famous and longest work, mainly refutes the thesis of inherent existence; two others, the *Seventy Stanzas on Emptiness* and the *Refutation of Objections*, are considered to be spin-offs from the *Treatise on the Middle Way* and are devoted to teaching, respectively, the way in which activities in general are feasible even though there is no inherent existence and the way in which the activities of refutation and proof in particular are feasible within the absence of inherent existence.[72]

Chandrakīrti, in developing the Prāsaṅgika-Mādhyamika position, was arguing against both Hīnayānists and Chittamātrins; his opponents are also referred to as Proponents of True Existence, because even though the Chittamātra view is more subtle than that of Hīnayānists, Chittamātrins still propound that some phenomena – other-powered and thoroughly established phenomena – are truly existent. The Tibetan term *dngos smra ba* (Sanskrit *vastusatpadārthavādin*) is translated as "Proponents of True Existence" to make clear who are included when it is used to describe those the Mādhyamikas are arguing against. In general, the term *dngos po/vastu* has many different meanings, and further, *vastu* is not the only Sanskrit word that was translated into Tibetan by *dngos po*; often it was used as the translation for the Sanskrit *bhāva*. Usually, *dngos po* means "thing", or "entity", sometimes referring just to impermanent phenomena and sometimes referring to any phenomenon, permanent or impermanent; in many contexts it is best translated as "thing". It also can mean inherent existence, an over-reified nature or entity, which is, in Prāsaṅgika, the object of negation.

Here in the term *dngos smra ba* (Proponents of *dngos po*) it is being used to describe those propounding something not asserted by the Mādhyamikas. For the lower tenet systems, if something exists it must be truly existent in the Mādhyamika sense. The Mādhyamikas do not accept this concomitance, and thus although they do assert "things" in the general sense of the word, both functioning things and entities in general – thus making it unacceptable to translate the term as Proponents of *Things* – they do not assert truly established or ultimately established things. As discussed above, a refutation of truly established things both ultimately and conventionally is asserted by both Svātantrika-Mādhyamikas and Prāsaṅgika-Mādhyamikas although the two schools diverge with respect to whether inherent existence, establishment by way of object's own character, and establishment of phenomena by way of their own entities is to be refuted conventionally. Thus *dngos smra ba* is translated here as Proponents of *True Existence* (rather than, for example, Proponents of Inherent Existence) in order to include within its sphere only those whose views are refuted by both Mādhyamika schools – Svātantrika and Prāsaṅgika – namely, Chittamātra and below.[73]

Chandrakīrti was also involved in defending Mādhyamika from charges of nihilism, and sought to explain in various of his writings how the Mādhyamikas, in propounding an absence of inherent existence, are not propounding an absence of any capacity to perform functions. The writings of Chandrakīrti relied on by this Tibetan tradition are his *Clear Words* (*tshig gsal*, *prasannapadā*), which is a commentary on Nāgārjuna's *Treatise on the Middle Way*; his *Commentary on* (*Nāgārjuna's*) *"Sixty Stanzas of Reasoning"* (*rigs pa drug cu pa'i 'grel pa*, *yuktiṣaṣṭikāvṛtti*), his *Commentary on* (*Āryadeva's*) *"Four Hundred"* (*bzhi brgya pa'i 'grel pa*, *catuḥśatakaṭīkā*), and his *Supplement to* (*Nāgārjuna's*) *"Treatise on the Middle Way"* (*dbu ma la 'jug pa*, *madhyamakāvatāra*) along with its *[Auto] commentary* (*dbu ma la 'jug pa'i rang 'grel*, *madhyamakāvatāra-bhāṣya*).[74]

Dzong-ka-ba's situation was a bit different. He was not arguing against those who felt that within the Mādhyamika assertions on emptiness, conventional presentations would not be feasible and hence rejected Mādhyamika, but rather against those who, as he describes them, found conventional presentations to be negated by the Mādhyamika emptiness and, accepting this, called themselves Mādhyamikas and propounded a system in which there is no valid establishment of conventional phenomena and activities. This is verbalized in different ways, some saying that conventional phenomena are posited only by ignorance, others saying that the Mādhyamikas have no system of their own for the presentations of conventionalities but merely rely on the systems of others, and still others saying that conventionalities exist conventionally but that this does not function as existing, etc.

Given that Dzong-ka-ba does not cite his opponents by name, it is difficult to know exactly whom he is refuting and what their specific assertions are, or to distinguish within his refutations which are of positions held by specific historical opponents and which are merely hypothetical objections raised by Dzong-ka-ba himself so that he could more fully explore an issue. Later commentarial literature does identify some of those whose views disagree with those of Dzong-ka-ba: A-gya-yong-dzin names as those who negate too much the great translator Lo-den-shay-rap (*rngog lo tsā ba blo ldan shes rab*, 1059–1109) and his spiritual sons as well as the followers of Tang-sak-ba (*thang sag pa/zhang thang sag pa ye shes 'byung gnas*) and so forth, including among those named as followers of one or the other, Cha-ba Chö-gyi-seng-ge (*cha/phya pa chos kyi seng ge*, 1109–1169), Gun-kyen-rong-dön (*kun mkhyen rong ston*, 1367–1449), and Bo-dong Chok-lay-nam-gyel (*bo dong phyogs las rnam rgyal*, 1306–1386[?]).[75]

All of these figures are indeed likely referents of Dzong-ka-ba's refutation – persons whose views were influential at his time, with whom he would have been familiar, and with whom he would likely have disagreed.

Lo-sang-gön-chok (*blo bzang dkon mchog*) in his *Word Commentary on the Root Text of (Jam-yang-shay-ba's) "Tenets"*, gives a brief identification of some of those whom Jam-yang-shay-ba, a rather partisan late seventeenth and eighteenth century follower of Dzong-ka-ba, refers to as holding unacceptable Mādhyamika interpretations. The issues of disagreement remain the same although some of the figures named differ, reflecting the intellectual climate of a later time. He says that the Chinese abbot Hva-shang (*hwa shang*) and his Tibetan followers propounded that all conventionalities do not exist at all, like the horns of a rabbit; that Paṇ-chen

Shākya-chok-den (*paṇ chen shākya mchog ldan*, 1428–1507) asserted that conventionalities are not established by valid cognition; that Tang-sak-ba asserted that all phenomena do not exist conventionally and some of his followers qualified this by saying that the two truths exist conventionally but that this does not function as existing; that Jang-dzön (*byang brtson*, that is, *rma bya byang chub brtson 'grus*, d.1186[?]) and Gang-gya-mar (*gangs rgya dmar*, early twelfth century) asserted that Mādhyamikas did not have their own position or system; that "a certain scholar" asserted that establishment by valid cognition did not exist and that both the name and meaning of valid cognition (*pramāṇa*) were incorrect – and that all of the above claimed to be Mādhyamikas.[76]

From Dzong-ka-ba's viewpoint, all who propound such views within claiming to be Mādhyamikas have gone too far, negating too much, and in fact are susceptible to charges of nihilism. They have not correctly understood Nāgārjuna and Chandrakīrti, and Dzong-ka-ba bases his refutation of his fellow Tibetans on those Indian authors' refutations of Proponents of True Existence. He singles out as the uncommon feature of Mādhyamika the compatibility of dependent-arisings and an emptiness of inherent existence, which Nāgārjuna and Chandrakīrti emphasized in defending their views from charges by Proponents of True Existence that the Mādhyamika view was nihilistic. Dzong-ka-ba reasons that Proponents of True Existence and those Tibetans whom he feels negate too much could be considered to be similar in that both deny the compatibility of dependent-arisings and emptiness, although they draw different conclusions from that incompatibility. Proponents of True Existence see conventional phenomena and the Mādhyamika emptiness as incompatible and hence reject the Mādhyamika emptiness in order to preserve conventionalities; the Tibetans Dzong-ka-ba is refuting see the two as incompatible but choose the Mādhyamika view as they understand it at the expense of conventionalities.

Dzong-ka-ba, in hinging the argument, as he has, around

the compatibility of dependent-arisings and emptiness, is then able to use the arguments of Nāgārjuna and Chandrakīrti against Proponents of True Existence in support of his refutation of the over-negators. However, he still has to prove that he has understood those authors correctly and to show how one can interpret Mādhyamika in such a way that conventional existence is preserved. This is the task of the "Great Exposition". Dzong-ka-ba gathers together into one massive argument all the different reasons why misinterpreters would think the Mādhyamika reasonings negate all phenomena and then argues against those reasons one by one. His presentation of their arguments and subsequent refutation of them can be summarized as follows.

DZONG-KA-BA'S ARGUMENT

So-called "Mādhyamikas" who negate too much say that in the Mādhyamika system all phenomena are refuted by the reasoning settling emptiness, that is, by reasoning analyzing reality. Their reasons in support of such a view, in condensed form, are:[77]

1 because phenomena cannot withstand analysis by the reasoning of ultimate analysis;
2 because valid cognition certifying conventional phenomena does not exist;
3 because Buddha refuted all four alternatives – existence, non-existence, both, and neither – and there are no phenomena not included within those four;
4 because the production of things can be limited to the four – from self, other, both, and causelessly – and all four of those are refuted.

To refute this thesis and the reasons in support of it, Dzong-ka-ba has to make some fine distinctions. Let us consider the reasons one at a time.

Ultimate Analysis

With respect to the first reason, namely that, because phenomena cannot withstand analysis by the reasoning of ultimate analysis, all phenomena are refuted by reasoning, Dzong-ka-ba accepts that phenomena cannot withstand analysis by such reasoning. He agrees that if something could withstand analysis by reasoning, or ultimate analysis, then it would be truly, or ultimately, established. However, this does not for him entail that phenomena are therefore refuted by that reasoning. He maintains this position by making a distinction between (1) not being able to bear analysis by a consciousness and (2) being refuted by a consciousness, and (1) not being found by a consciousness and (2) being found to be non-existent by a consciousness.[78] He bases these distinctions on an understanding of the differing spheres of authority of different types of consciousnesses.

For example, the sphere of authority of visual consciousnesses is visible forms; the sphere of authority of ear consciousnesses is sounds. Eye consciousnesses do not "find" or realize sounds, but this does not mean that sounds are refuted by eye consciousnesses or found to be non-existent by them, the reason being that eye consciousnesses have no authority with respect to sounds. They do have authority with respect to visible forms, and if an eye consciousness looks for a form where it should be if it were present and does not find it, it can then be said that the existence of the form where sought has been refuted by that eye consciousness and that the form has been found to be non-existent at that place by the eye consciousness.

Similarly the reasonings of ultimate analysis have no authority with respect to merely conventionally existent phenomena. The sphere of authority of ultimate analysis is any sort of ultimate existence; ultimate analysis is seeking to find concrete or inherent existence, and if it did find that, then it would have to be said that there was such concrete or inherent existence. Because reasoned analysis does not find any such thing, it is said that ultimate, or inherent, or true existence is refuted by that consciousness and that it is found to be non-existent. Conventional phenomena cannot withstand analysis by reasoning and are not found by that reasoning, but they are neither refuted by that ultimate reasoning nor found to be non-existent by it, for they are outside its sphere of authority.

Phenomena cannot withstand analysis by reasoning in the sense that when reasoning seeks to find any sort of pointable, graspable existence, it is not found; what is found in its stead is emptiness, the mere absence of that inherent existence which was sought. However, the fact that emptiness is found by the reasoning of ultimate analysis does not mean that emptiness can bear analysis by reasoning. Emptiness was found by a consciousness seeking inherent existence; were that analysis to be applied to emptiness itself, emptiness would not be found but rather the emptiness of emptiness. Thus, being found by the reasoning of ultimate analysis and being able to withstand analysis by that reasoning are also not the same, for emptiness is found by the reasoning of ultimate analysis but is not able to withstand analysis by that reasoning. Nothing is able to bear analysis by reasoning; only emptiness is found by the reasoning of ultimate analysis. (Reasoning, here, refers to reasoning into whether an object inherently exists or not, such as by whether a thing is produced from self, other, both, or neither or whether an object is inherently one with or different from its bases of designation. It does not refer to conventional reasoning such as that used to understand impermanence and so forth.)

Conventional Valid Cognizers

The consciousnesses within whose sphere of authority conventional phenomena fall are conventional valid cognizers, and this brings us to the second argument advanced by those who negate too much, namely that all phenomena are refuted by the Mādhyamika reasonings settling emptiness because a valid cognizer that certifies conventional phenomena does not exist.

The reason for this aspect of the argument stems from the close tie in Buddhism between ontology and epistemology. As found in Ge-luk-ba textbooks for debate (their *bsdus grwa* literature), there are a number of synonyms for the broadest category of what exists:[79] existent, object of knowledge, established base, phenomenon, object of comprehension, object, object of comprehension of an omniscient consciousness, and hidden phenomenon. These terms represent the broadest ontological category – whatever exists is an object of knowledge, an established base, a phenomenon, and so forth. When one examines the definitions of these terms, one sees that, essentially, in order for something to exist it must be knowable, and it must be knowable in a valid way. Following is the same list of terms with their definitions:

existent:	that which is observed by a valid cognizer
object of knowledge:	that which is suitable as an object of an awareness
established base:	that which is established by a valid cognizer
phenomenon:	that which bears its own entity
object of comprehension:	object realized by a valid cognizer
object:	object known by an awareness
object of comprehension of an omniscient consciousness:	object realized by an omniscient consciousness
hidden phenomenon:	object realized in a hidden manner by the thought consciousness apprehending it

All except one of these terms is defined by way of its being known; something must be knowable if it exists. And, the way in which objects must be known if they are to exist is by a valid cognizer – a consciousness incontrovertible in its knowledge. Even emptiness, if it exists, must be knowable and must be certified by a consciousness.

Objects are certified by valid cognizers appropriate to them; ultimate objects, such as emptiness, are certified by ultimate valid cognizers – non-conceptual exalted wisdom consciousnesses realizing emptiness, and conventional ones by conventional valid cognizers – for instance, forms by eye consciousnesses, sounds by ear consciousnesses, and so forth. Thus, in Dzong-ka-ba's system, if one is to posit that conventional phenomena exist, one must be able to show that they are certified by some sort of valid cognizer. It is not sufficient, for instance, to say that they are merely posited by ignorance – a non-valid consciousness – for in that case their status of existing would be compromised.

The claim made by those who refute too much is that in fact conventional phenomena do not exist because a valid cognizer which certifies them does not exist. They give two reasons in support of this position, the first being that the supreme of valid cognizers, an exalted wisdom consciousness directly perceiving emptiness, does not establish, or certify, conventional phenomena such as forms, production, cessation, and so forth. For, according to them, that wisdom consciousness sees forms and so forth as non-existent. Their second reason is that such objects are not established by conventional valid cognizers because conventional valid cognizers do not exist; they cite in support of this view a passage from sūtra:[80]

> The eye, ear, and nose [consciousnesses] are not valid cognizers.
> The tongue, body, and mental [consciousnesses] are also not valid cognizers.

In countering these arguments, Dzong-ka-ba has no quarrel with the position that forms, production, and so forth are not seen, and consequently not certified, by an ultimate consciousness. For him, there is no reason why they should be: ultimate consciousnesses certify only ultimate objects – emptinesses. However, as discussed above, he does not accept the further conclusion that an exalted wisdom consciousness directly perceiving emptiness, or reality, sees conventional phenomena as non-existent.

Within this system, it is a psychological reality, undoubtedly stunning in its impact for a practitioner, that at the time of directly perceiving emptiness nothing else appears. One is apprehending only the ultimate, and the conventional world has utterly disappeared. However, this psychological reality – the non-appearance of conventional phenomena at the time of direct realization of emptiness – should not be mistaken for ontological fact; the mere non-perception of something does not mean it does not exist. The inability to directly perceive the two truths – ultimate truths and conventional truths – simultaneously is, in the Ge-luk-ba description, a perceptual problem caused by very subtle obstructions to omniscience. It is overcome by the eradication of those obstructions that takes place over the eighth, ninth, and tenth Bodhisattva grounds of the path of meditation, at the end of which, as a Buddha, one is able to perceive directly all conventional phenomena and their emptinesses simultaneously.

Dzong-ka-ba does not accept the second reason set forth by those who negate too much – that conventional valid cognizers do not exist. He explains that what the sūtra passage cited in support of this position is actually saying is that eye consciousnesses, ear consciousnesses, and so forth are not valid cognizers with respect to reality, the ultimate. For, if they were, then ordinary beings who have such ordinary consciousnesses would be perceiving reality already, in which case there would be no need to make the effort to develop an exalted wisdom consciousness capable of perceiving reality. He cites in convincing support of his interpretation numerous passages from Chandrakīrti, including Chandrakīrti's *Commentary on (Nāgārjuna's) "Sixty Stanzas of Reasoning"*, which says:[81]

> It is established that those [eye consciousnesses and so forth] which view those [forms and so forth] do not see reality. Therefore, the Supramundane Victor said, "Eye, ear, and nose [consciousnesses] are not valid cognizers. . . ."

However, having defended the existence of conventional valid cognizers, actually (1) to explain how these conventional consciousnesses can be valid cognizers in spite of the fact that, in the Prāsaṅgika system, all sense consciousnesses are mistaken in that phenomena appear to them to inherently exist whereas they do not so exist and (2) to explain in what way conventional consciousnesses certify conventional phenomena is not easy. Dzong-ka-ba addresses these questions in some detail, but that section of his text falls outside the scope of this volume and will be included in the next volume of this series.

The Tetralemma

The third of the reasons advanced by those who negate too much to support their claim that the Mādhyamika reasonings negate all phenomena is that Buddha refuted all four alternatives – existence, non-existence, both, and neither – and there are no phenomena not included within those four. Dzong-ka-ba accepts that Buddha made such statements, as did Nāgārjuna in his *Treatise on the Middle Way*, but he refuses to accept them at face value.

Demonstrating his commitment to common sense, Dzong-ka-ba points to the simple grammatical rule concerning double negatives. Thus he says that if one asserts that something does not exist (the first alternative), one has asserted that it is non-existent (the second alternative); if one then asserts that something is not non-existent (the second alternative), since one has perforce asserted that it is existent (which is denied by the first alternative), one has contradicted oneself. Also, if one asserts that something is not both existent and non-existent (the third alternative), and then goes on to say that it is *not* not both existent and non-existent (the fourth alternative), since "not not both" equals "both", again one has contradicted oneself. Thus, when they are interpreted literally, one cannot logically maintain a position that something is none of the four alternatives. Dzong-ka-ba is scathing in his indictment of those who try to maintain a literal interpretation of the four, taking them as simple negations:[82]

> When . . . you [try to] prevent falling to the extremes of existence or non-existence through putting hope in just propounding, "We do not propound [such and such] as non-existent (*med pa*); we say it is not existent (*yod pa ma yin pa*). We do not propound [such and such] as existent (*yod pa*); we say it is not non-existent (*med pa ma yin pa*)," you are propounding only a collection of contradictions and do not set forth even slightly the meaning of the middle way.

Dzong-ka-ba is firmly committed to the "law of the excluded middle" which T.R.V. Murti believes Mādhyamika rejects.[83] Dzong-ka-ba asserts a definite enumeration of the possibilities to be considered. That number can vary from situation to situation; often the situation is a dichotomy in which the possiblilities are limited to two and something must be one or the other. This is the case with inherent existence; whatever exists must either be inherently existent or not inherently existent. There are no other choices. In other situations as in the refutation of production from the four extremes, the possibilities are limited to four – production from self, other, both, or neither. The four are the only possibilities for *inherently existent* production, and when all four are rejected, this means that an inherent existence of production has been refuted and the absence of inherent existence affirmed. Some Mādhyamika interpretations reject this, feeling that it is possible to just eliminate – not this, not that – without there being any positive inclusion. They see this as a psychological process of transcending conceptuality, a means of forcing the mind to a different plane. In Ge-luk-ba also conceptuality is eventually transcended, but not by means of ceasing verbal conventions; rather, conceptuality is used to develop a level of insight which upon repeated meditative familiarization can be brought to the point of direct non-conceptual, non-imagistic perception.

Were one not to accept a definite enumeration in which the possibilities were limited, then analysis could never lead to certainty. One would only be left with doubt, waiting for new systems to come along and be refuted. This is not Dzong-ka-ba's position, and he offers his own interpretation of the four positions of the tetralemma, focusing on the first two (see chapter seven of the translation).[84] He makes a careful differentiation between existence, inherent existence, no inherent existence, and utter non-existence, and says that when the first of the four alternatives, existence, is denied, what is meant is that there is no *inherent* existence. When the second of the four alternatives, non-existence, is denied, what is denied is *utter* non-existence. Thus, when it is said that phenomena are neither existent nor non-existent, what is meant is that they are neither inherently existent nor utterly non-existent. Phenomena do exist – conventionally – but they do not exist inherently.

Dzong-ka-ba finds support for his interpretation in the writings of Chandrakīrti. For example, Chandrakīrti's *Clear Words* says:[85]

> We are not Nihilists.... We do not propound, "Actions, agents, effects, and so forth do not exist." What do we propound? "These do not inherently exist."

Also Chandrakīrti's *Commentary on (Āryadeva's) "Four Hundred"* says:[86]

> ... for our analysis is intent upon seeking out inherent existence. We [Mādhyamikas] refute that things are established by way of their own entities; we do not refute that eyes and so forth are products and are dependently arisen fruitions of actions. Therefore, those exist, whereby eyes and so forth which are explained as mere fruitions *just* exist.

Dzong-ka-ba's basic point is that the four alternatives of the tetralemma require some qualification so that they are not internally contradictory.

Refutation of Production

The final reason that Dzong-ka-ba describes those who negate too much as offering in support of their position that all phenomena are negated by the Mādhyamika reasonings focuses on whether production exists or not. Those who negate too much say that production does not exist because the production of things can be limited to the four – from self, other, both, and causelessly – and all four of those are refuted. In support of their view they have two seemingly potent quotes. Chandrakīrti says in his *Supplement to (Nāgārjuna's) "Treatise on the Middle Way"*:[87]

> By that reasoning through which [it is seen] on the occasion of analyzing suchness
> That production from self and other are not reasonable,
> [It is seen] that [production] is not reasonable even conventionally.
> If so, through what [reasoning] would your production be [established]?

Chandrakīrti seems to be saying that the reasoning that refutes production ultimately refutes it even conventionally and that, therefore, there is no way to establish conventional production. Also, there is a sūtra passage which says, "Whatever is produced from conditions is not produced."[88]

Dzong-ka-ba's response is that the production that is limited to the four possibilities of production from self, other, both, or neither – and that referred to by both of the above passages – is inherently existent production, not "mere" production. For all Buddhist schools except Prāsaṅgika, if production is to exist, it must be something that can be found when sought, and hence must be locatable within the four possibilities. Prāsaṅgika disagrees with this, saying that any production that could be found, ultimately or even conventionally, among the four possibilities would necessarily be inherently existent production. It, in contrast, asserts *mere* production, without investigation or analysis; the fact that such production cannot be found upon analysis does not damage its existence, since there was never any claim that it could be found under such analysis.

Thus, according to Dzong-ka-ba, Chandrakīrti is indicating in the above passage that the production of things *inherently* is refuted because the reasoning refuting production from any of the four possibilities, or four extremes, is refuting production from those four even conventionally. This is said also to be the meaning of the sūtra passage, "Whatever is produced from conditions is not produced," for the next line of that sūtra is, "It does not have an inherent nature of production."

Any sort of inherent production is refuted, both ultimately and conventionally, by means of the refutation of the possibilities of production from self, other, both, or causelessly. Mere production is not refuted.

CONCLUDING REMARKS

This brief summary of Dzong-ka-ba's refutation of Mādhyamika interpretations that he says take negation too far and deny the validity of conventional presentations provides an overview of Dzong-ka-ba's line of reasoning. Included within this volume is translation of Dzong-ka-ba's condensed exposition of the fallacious arguments of those who negate too much (chapter four of the translation), his delineation of the compatibility of dependent-arising and emptiness as the uncommon feature of Mādhyamika (chapters five and six of the translation), and his presentation of how a Mādhyamika responds to those who do not see or accept this compatibility (chapter seven of the translation).

In the remainder of his refutation of those who negate too much, Dzong-ka-ba considers in detail the meaning and functions of reasoned analysis, the meaning of valid establishment, how conventional existence is upheld, the way in which mere production is not refuted, and the way the four positions of the tetralemma require qualification.

He then moves on to a refutation of those Mādhyamika interpretations that negate too little. Dzong-ka-ba's refutation of those who negate too much, because of the way it is framed around the compatibility of dependent-arising and emptiness and relies on Nāgārjuna's and Chandrakīrti's refutations of the Proponents of True Existence, has already expressed a general refutation of non-Mādhyamikas who from the Mādhyamika viewpoint do not negate enough and fall into an extreme of reification, or eternalism. In the portion of his text labelled "a refutation of those who negate too little", Dzong-ka-ba considers a specific Mādhyamika interpretation that he says negates too little, namely, that based on what Dzong-ka-ba considers a misunderstanding of the fifteenth chapter of Nāgārjuna's *Treatise on the Middle Way*, the investigation of nature (*rang bzhin*, *svabhāva*), which says that the object of negation by ultimate analysis is merely the nature (*svabhāva*) possessing the three attributes of (1) its entity not being produced by causes and conditions; (2) its not depending on another positor; and (3) its status not changing to something else.

After refuting this view, Dzong-ka-ba presents at some length his own identification of the object of negation and then concludes the section on the object of negation with a brief explanation of when Prāsaṅgika does or does not use a qualifying term such as "ultimately" in its negations; this includes spelling out the difference between the Svātantrika and Prāsaṅgika schools in this respect.

The discussion of the object of negation along with the introductory material leading into it occupies 43% of the "Great Exposition of Special Insight". The next 18% of the text is devoted to a discussion of the difference between the Svātantrika and Prāsaṅgika schools based on whether they say the view realizing emptiness is generated through use of autonomous syllogisms (*rang rgyud kyi sbyor ba*, *svatantra-prayoga*) or whether only consequences (*thal ba*, *prasaṅga*) can be used. It includes a detailed discussion of whether there is or is not a commonly appearing subject to both parties in a debate. Along with a similar discussion in Dzong-ka-ba's

Essence of the Good Explanations, it is the basis of the Ge-luk-ba differentiation between the philosophical views of the Svātantrika and Prāsaṅgika schools.[89]

The final 39% of the "Great Exposition" is devoted to a description of the reasonings used in generating realization of emptiness and some concluding material. Dzong-ka-ba describes the sevenfold reasoning set forth by Chandrakīrti for realizing the selflessness of the person and explains how this realization is to be transferred to all other phenomena as well. He discusses the illusion-like mode of appearance of conventional phenomena that remains after emptiness has been realized, briefly states the different types of special insight, and describes how it is to be cultivated in meditation, including refutation of several, from his viewpoint, mistaken opinions on this point. Dzong-ka-ba concludes the *Great Exposition of the Stages of the Path* with a summary of the entire path to be followed by one wishing to train in the Bodhisattva practices and with an exhortation to enter into the tantric vehicle as it offers the quickest way to the attainment of Buddhahood.

4 *Dzong-ka-ba and Modern Interpreters I: Not Negating Enough*

Dzong-ka-ba says at many points throughout the *Great Exposition of the Stages of the Path* that it is extremely difficult to gain correct understanding of the middle way free from all extremes and that correct understanding of it is so rare as to be almost nonexistent. The disparity of opinions among modern interpreters as to just what Mādhyamika, the Middle Way school, is and what it purports to do, given their diversity, which is such that they cannot possibly *all* be correct, amply proves that Dzong-ka-ba's statements in this regard are not culture bound, applicable only to Tibetans. Listing just some of the labels that have been applied to Mādhyamika, D. Seyfort Ruegg says:[90]

> Over the past half-century the doctrine of the Madhyamaka school, and in particular that of Nāgārjuna, has been variously described as nihilism, monism, irrationalism, misology, agnosticism, scepticism, criticism, dialectic, mysticism, acosmism, absolutism, relativism, nominalism, and linguistic analysis with therapeutic value.

The first label given to Mādhyamika when it initially came to the attention of Western scholars in the mid-nineteenth century (and that given to it by rival non-Buddhist schools in India, as well as by other Buddhist schools) was of nihilism. The French scholar Eugène Burnouf called it a "nihilistic scholasticism", and this label stuck until the early twentieth century when its validity was finally questioned and ultimately rejected by such eminent scholars, active during the 1920s and 1930s, as Theodor Stcherbatsky, Stanislaw Schayer, Louis de la Vallée Poussin, and Poul Tuxen.[91] At this time the theory that Mādhyamika was monism was advanced by Stcherbatsky and, although he himself later retreated from that position, a tendency to view Mādhyamika as some sort of absolutism began and continues to the present.[92] However, the general trend among contemporary interpreters is to view Mādhyamika as a middle way between nihilism and absolutism, although opinions vary widely as to what this implies, leading to a continued imputing of "isms".

The majority of scholars writing about Mādhyamika base their interpretations on the writings of Nāgārjuna; many consider Nāgārjuna's writings in isolation, and, among those, some rely on only a portion of his works, many for example, utilizing only his *Treatise on the Middle Way* and *Refutation of Objections* (the two of his works on Mādhyamika reasoning wholly extant in Sanskrit). Others include the commentaries of Chandrakīrti, most basing their opinions on Chandrakīrti's *Clear Words* in addition to Nāgārjuna's *Treatise*. A relatively few work also with the commentaries of Buddhapālita and Bhāvaviveka. There has also been some excellent work done from Chinese sources, such as É. Lamotte's five volumes of translation of the *Ta chih tu lung*, Richard Robinson's *Early Mādhyamika in India and China*, and so forth. Until very recently, it has been the rare scholar who considered the native Tibetan tradition, in part because so few work in Tibetan, but even more, I suspect, because of the view that later developments of a religious or philosophical movement rarely remain true to the ideas of their founder. However, the various traditions in Tibet developed an extensive body of commentarial literature that can be of great assistance in seeking to understand Mādhyamika. Seyfort Ruegg sets forth an astute summation of the Tibetan contribution to the Mādhyamika tradition:[93]

(1) the textual exegesis of passages from the scrip-

tures (Sūtra) and, more especially, the canonical commentaries and treatises (Śāstra) found respectively in the bKa' 'gyur and bsTan 'gyur;

(2) the composition of commentaries and independent treatises showing wide learning, intellectual acumen and powers of synthesis in which (a) difficult individual points of doctrine are examined with care and penentration and (b) the overall purport of Sūtras and Śāstras is explicated in a systematic synchronic frame by means of a comprehensive hermeneutical method;

(3) the treatment of philosophical praxis deriving from Madhyamaka theory, including in particular guides to meditation and the theoretical and practical realization of reality (for example in the *lTa khrid* and *dMar khrid* literature); and

(4) the sustained attempt to situate the Madhyamaka in the overall frame of Buddhist thought, including not only the Bye brag tu smra ba (Vaibhāṣika), mDo sde pa (Sautrāntika) and Sems tsam pa (Cittamātra or Vijñanavada) schools but also the rDo rje theg pa (Vajrayāna) (in the *Grub mtha'* literature).

Of particular assistance is the development in Tibetan of very precise technical terminology that makes it possible to extract from the more loosely worded Indian texts greater specificity of meaning than might otherwise be gained. There are clearly Tibetan contributions to the development of Mādhyamika, and yet all Tibetan orders and scholars believe themselves to be true to their Indian antecedents, to such an extent that the present Dalai Lama says as the concluding sentence of his *Opening the Eye of New Awareness (blo gsar mig 'byed)*:[94]

> Tibetan lamas took these [doctrines that were translated into Tibetan] as the basis and root and thereupon listened to them, thought about them, and

> meditated upon them; among the main points they did not fabricate a single doctrine that does not accord with those [Indian traditions]. For example, any Tibetan Buddhist who has even the slightest need to remove a qualm about a point of doctrine or who needs a source will do so on the basis of sources in the statements of the Buddha or an Indian scholar-adept.

This is a strong statement that indicates clearly an intention to remain true to original teachings. Certainly Dzong-ka-ba believed that he was adhering correctly to the thought of the Mādhyamika founders and, particularly in the *Great Exposition of the Stages of the Path* where he was newly setting forth his Mādhyamika interpretation, is careful to document his every point with copious citation of Indian sources. Of course, in the main Dzong-ka-ba is a primary source, a great Mādhyamika writer. However, in another way, for the purposes of this analysis, he can also be viewed as a secondary source, someone describing the writings of the great Indian Mādhyamikas in a fashion comparable to that of contemporary academics. Viewed in this light, it is of interest to compare his opinions on Mādhyamika with those of modern scholars to see to what extent they agree or disagree. There is agreement on many points, but there are also many points of substantial disagreement; a detailed examination of some of those should help to illuminate central Mādhyamika teachings and perhaps to point out areas where further research is needed.

NĀGĀRJUNA AS A RELIGIOUS FIGURE

There is increasing recognition among Western scholars that Nāgārjuna must be seen as a religious figure working from and within a coherent religious tradition. This view has recently been stated succinctly by Christian Lindtner in the introductory remarks to his edited edition and partial translation of those works he considers to be authentically by Nāgārjuna:[95]

> Nevertheless, in my view, an attentive perusal of Nāgārjuna's authentic writings will show that his extraordinary genius succeeded in blending a great mass of inherited moral, religious and philosophical ideas into a harmonious whole.... Nāgārjuna arrived at this position from a desire to achieve a consistent exegetical result of his study of the Buddha's doctrine recorded in the scriptures. In the eyes of Nāgārjuna the Buddha was not merely a forerunner but the very founder of the Madhyamaka system.

Along with this understanding goes a perception of Nāgārjuna's purpose as primarily soteriological – that is, as directed towards a goal of liberation. One of the first to articulate clearly this view was Frederick Streng, who did so with eloquence in his *Emptiness: A Study in Religious Meaning*.[96] Such perspectives are part of a growing recognition that Nāgārjuna's very analytical works, stunning in the negative power of their refutations, cannot be viewed in isolation but must be seen within a context that includes also his more positive works such as the *Precious Garland* and his many "praises".[97] Although there is scholarly controversy over which of the many texts attributed to Nāgārjuna are authentically his, there is a core of works generally accepted to be in fact by Nāgārjuna, and all these must certainly be included in any assessment of Nāgārjuna's overall purpose and view.[98]

That the works of Nāgārjuna are to be viewed as part of a coherent religious tradition is definitely the position of Dzong-ka-ba and his followers. Nāgārjuna's teachings, far from being seen as merely destructive or negative, are taken as the key to development of the wisdom that, when combined with the practices of method, makes possible attainment of the perfect enlightenment of Buddhahood. Mādhyamika is not to be isolated from other facets of Buddhist doctrine or viewed only in reference to other philosophical systems, but is to be taken as the center of an integrated set of religious practices. Nāgārjuna is seen as part of a continuous tradition stemming from

Shākyamuni Buddha, albeit a particularly great figure, who articulated a correct philosophical understanding of Buddha's teaching, delineating the middle way between extremes of permanence and annihilation.

Because Nāgārjuna is not viewed as a solitary figure, but rather as the disseminator of a philosophical system interpreted in a valid fashion by many who came after him and to be combined with teachings and practices from many other aspects of Buddha's teachings, Dzong-ka-ba brings to his interpretation of Mādhyamika and even of Nāgārjuna a great deal of systematic understanding which is not explicit in Nāgārjuna but which, from Dzong-ka-ba's viewpoint, is either suggested or implicit given the coherence of the tradition. This fact notwithstanding, he does very much concern himself in his interpretation with ferreting out a correct understanding of Nāgārjuna's actual words, and thus he and modern Western interpreters are working with a comparable body of material. Many of Dzong-ka-ba's differences with Western scholars come from varying understandings of a number of "classic" passages that do, on the surface, lend themselves to interpretations of nihilism, scepticism, paradox, and so forth. Dzong-ka-ba is himself quite aware of the difficulties of these passages and devotes considerable analysis to working out interpretations of those passages that preserve the integrity of the system as a whole. Many that Westerners see as paradoxical he feels can be understood in a straightforward manner when taken in context. Concerning the lack of paradox, he is not without Western support; a similar position is held by Richard Robinson and Seyfort Ruegg.[99]

In what is a significant difference from a good many modern interpreters, it can fairly be said that Dzong-ka-ba approaches the material with a bias: he wants the system to work. He is not a neutral observer, but someone within the tradition. He is a Mādhyamika, not someone writing about Mādhyamika. In spite of some current opinion to the contrary,[100] this does not necessarily negate his validity; the Mādhyamika tradition was formed by just such individuals –

Nāgārjuna, Āryadeva, Buddhapālita, Bhāvaviveka, and Chandrakīrti – sharply analytical thinkers willing to rework and reject previously accepted dogma, but not necessarily carrying this to rejection of the Buddhist tradition as a whole. Dzong-ka-ba is sympathetic in his approach; however, he is not uncritical.

IDENTIFYING THE OBJECT OF NEGATION

Many Western interpretations of Mādhyamika are based on what, from Dzong-ka-ba's viewpoint, would be considered incorrect understandings of the Mādhyamika "middle way" and fall to one extreme or the other; he would say that this is in large part due to a failure to identify correctly the object of negation. Either too much or too little is negated. Thus, Mādhyamika interpretations that differ from Dzong-ka-ba's will be discussed here using the organizational headings of the "Great Exposition of Special Insight" – overly broad identifications of the object of negation and too limited identifications of it. The specific content of modern interpretations is in numerous instances directly addressed by Dzong-ka-ba, in some cases within the rubric of negating too much or too little, in some as topics that flow out of the main line of his argument. In other instances, modern interpretations differ markedly from what Dzong-ka-ba actually discusses, but his arguments against negating too much and too little are nonetheless interesting to consider, since his reasons are framed in such a way as to have broad applicability.

On the side of negating too little fall those contemporary interpreters who say that the Mādhyamika analyses are directed at other systems, or at language, or at reasoning, and on the side of negating too much come positions such as that Mādhyamika is a critique of conceptuality, that it refutes all conventional phenomena, and that Mādhyamikas have no views or system or theses of their own. These positions will now be considered individually.

MĀDHYAMIKA IS MERELY A REFUTATION OF OTHER SYSTEMS

A major proponent of the view that Mādhyamika merely seeks to discredit other philosophical systems was Richard H. Robinson, who called Nāgārjuna a sophist and, comparing his analyses to a shell game at a county fair, described the Mādhyamika "trick" as:[101]

> (a) reading into the opponent's views a few terms which one defines for him in a self-contradictory way, and (b) insisting on a small set of axioms which are at variance with common sense and not accepted in their entirety by any known philosophy.

This is stated even more strongly by Thomas McEvilley in an article comparing Mādhyamika to Scepticism, in which he says, "Skeptics, like Mādhyamikas, taught no positive doctrines but devoted themselves to undermining the doctrines of other schools without exception,"[102] and essentially is also set forth by Douglas Daye, who after differentiating four orders of description in Nāgārjuna's *Treatise on the Middle Way* says that the second, "rival metaphysical and epistemological theories which utilize such generic terms as Abhidharmic *dharmas*, prakṛti, etc.," are the "objects of the polemics" in the *Treatise* and that the *svabhāva* being refuted by Nāgārjuna is a general word for those generic terms.[103]

MĀDHYAMIKA IS AN ATTACK ON REASONING

The view that reasoning is the object of negation is advanced by Theodor Stcherbatsky and, implicitly, Richard Robinson, among others. For instance, Stcherbatsky says that Nāgārjuna's aim was "to undermine logical methods altogether and to demonstrate the hopeless contradictions of the principles upon which logic is built".[104] Robinson, in spite of saying, "There is no evidence that Nāgārjuna 'uses logic to destroy logic',"[105] nonetheless suggests that Nāgārjuna did intend to show an *inadequacy* of reason, the problem simply being that he did not succeed. In a passage that continues directly from his statement of the "Mādhyamika trick", cited above, he says:[106]

> It needs no insistence to emphasize that the application of such a critique does not demonstrate the inadequacy of reason and experience to provide intelligible answers to the usual philosophical questions.

MĀDHYAMIKA IS A CRITIQUE OF LANGUAGE

Currently far more prevalent than views that Mādhyamika is merely an attack on other systems or on reasoning is the idea that it is a critique of language. Fritz Staal says that Nāgārjuna's view is that there are "realms of reality where ordinary language is not applicable".[107] Edward Conze asserts that the Mādhyamikas wish to "remove all adherence to words, which always detract or abstract from reality instead of disclosing it".[108] Ives Waldo, limiting the sphere of Nāgārjuna's refutation to *statements*, says, "Nāgārjuna does not establish that all existence statements are incoherent, but only all statements involving the concept of *svabhāva* (a thing that conditions its own arising in significant experience)."[109] Douglas Daye is among those who have developed this interpretation with particular sophistication, and he sees Mādhyamika as primarily concerned with "metalanguage" – language about language. The Mādhyamikas' criticism of other schools is primarily a criticism of their use of language, of their "category mistakes". He says:[110]

> The Mādhyamikas attempted to show that the categories of description, the words used to describe the world in ordinary and philosophical language, of other schools was mistaken because it involved this

> fatal mistake of reification and the collapsing of levels of abstraction in the description of the way the world "really is"; thus they make a category mistake.

And, broadening the sphere of the Mādhyamika attack beyond only the language usage of other systems, he says, in describing the doctrine of the two truths:[111]

> ... one must progress to different levels of understanding ... until one reaches a point in the process of articulation and metacriticism where one is able to realize that there is a *reflexive* metacriticism directed at our medium through which we speak and learn – language.

Mark Siderits makes an argument that Nāgārjuna's analyses, rather than "seeking to show that the ultimate nature of reality cannot be adequately characterized, ... are meant to demonstrate that the phrase 'the ultimate nature of reality' is a non-denoting expression," and concludes:[112]

> Thus the Madhyamaka position would appear to be that it is not sufficient to attach to one's theory of knowledge the proviso that it is formulated entirely at the level of conventional truth; if one's theory purports to be more than a provisional description of conventional epistemic practices, if there is about it any pretense at systematicity, rigor, and theoretical elegance, it will inevitably come up against the fact that no metaphysical theory can be fully adequate to the nature of the world.

Shohei Ichimura, while concluding that Nāgārjuna's critique does leave room for the use of language on a conventional level, nonetheless sees it as mainly concerned with words:[113]

> Nāgārjuna's critique does not repudiate the practicality of convention (language and logic), but it leads to the twofold conclusion: (1) words have no real objective reference, and (2) they create only illusory subjective cognition.

And finally, Richard Robinson sees the concern of Mādhyamika as *abstractions*, not things, saying, "The concept of designation (*prajñapti*) provides a way of handling abstracts without concretizing them, or assigning ontological value to them."[114]

DZONG-KA-BA'S POSITION

1 THE PURPOSE OF THE "TREATISE"

A response to these three interpretations of what Nāgārjuna was refuting must be built around an assessment of Nāgārjuna's purpose in his analytical works such as the *Treatise on the Middle Way*. Many who hold views such as those cited above assess Nāgārjuna's effectiveness and conclude either that he did not succeed in his purpose or that his purpose was not terribly profound. Richard Jones sums up a generally perceptive article by saying:[115]

> Showing that the reality lies not in the conceptual understanding or that there is a linguistic basis to the idea of identity does not entail that what is labeled by our concepts is "unreal" in any normal sense of the term.... All of this shows I think that Nāgārjuna succeeds at best within a very limited scope. As Robinson also concludes, his procedure is a variation on the old shell game. Serious doubts thus arise about whether he can accomplish his religious intention by his method of stilling our conceptual preoccupation (and thereby ending suffering), once these problems are pointed out.

And Douglas Daye, finding Mādhyamika realization of emptiness to be merely a "therapeutic ploy by which one may realize the differences between languages and things (including the thing called 'self')," states as its result:[116]

> Thus Mādhyamika tends to generate epistemic nimbleness, linguistic respect, a new sense of human wonder, and an alert suspicion of the conventional

> view of the world which we have projected through our linguistically and culturally colored glasses.

If this were all that the Mādhyamika analyses achieved, Dzong-ka-ba would be the first to agree that their effectiveness was limited. However, he does not see such limited results primarily because he does not accept the above assessments of what Mādhyamika seeks to refute.

For Dzong-ka-ba, Nāgārjuna's *Treatise on the Middle Way*, far from being an "intellectual riddle", as described by Richard Robinson,[117] is a religious text with profound transformative purpose. He says, "All the reasoned analyses set forth in the *Treatise on the Middle Way* are only so that sentient beings might attain liberation,"[118] and finds support for this view in the writings of Buddhapālita and Chandrakīrti:[119]

> Buddhapālita says, "What is the purpose in teaching dependent-arising? The master [Nāgārjuna] whose very nature is compassion saw that sentient beings are beset by various sufferings and assumed the task of teaching the reality of things just as it is so that they might be liberated. Therefore, he began teaching dependent-arising." Also, Chandrakīrti's *Supplement to (Nāgārjuna's) "Treatise on the Middle Way"* (VI.118ab) says, "The analyses in the *Treatise* were not done for the sake of attachment to debate; such was taught for the sake of liberation."

Liberation is the goal – not merely the "removal of the 'linguistically colored sunglasses' with which we see the world",[120] but complete emergence from cyclic existence and all of its attendant suffering.

2 IDENTIFYING IGNORANCE

Since the purpose of Nāgārjuna's *Treatise* is not merely to refute other systems, but to teach a technique for the attainment of liberation, the *Treatise* must, from Dzong-ka-ba's viewpoint, be refuting something of sufficient potency to obstruct liberation. Although the wrong ideas of other systems fall within the scope of the refutation, they are not what bind beings in cyclic existence, and thus are not the main object of negation by the path. What are primarily to be refuted are a practitioner's own innate wrong ideas, specifically, the ignorance that is considered to be the root, or basic cause, of cyclic existence. Although Dzong-ka-ba would disagree with T.R.V. Murti's identification of "dogmatism", he would, if one substitutes "ignorance" for "dogmatism", accept Murti's assessment of a Mādhyamika's purpose:[121]

> The Mādhyamika is exorcising the devil of dogmatism from his own soul. The outward form of refutation is employed by him so that he can the better dissociate himself from the inherent dogmatic tendency of the human mind. The Mādhyamika dialectic is actuated by the spiritual motive of purifying the mind and freeing it of the cobwebs and clogs of dogmatism.

Ignorance (*ma rig pa, avidyā*), which literally means "non-knowing" is, for Dzong-ka-ba not just lack of knowledge in general, but the opposite of knowledge – and not just any knowledge, but knowledge of reality.[122] It is a specific misconception: the conception of inherent existence where there is no inherent existence. The way to overcome ignorance is to refute – that is, to recognize as non-existent – its object.

Thus, what Nāgārjuna's *Treatise* refutes is the object adhered to by ignorance, and, in his Mādhyamika system, that object is inherent existence. Inherent existence is the meaning of the *svabhāva* that Nāgārjuna denies, and its refutation is not a casual or easy thing that one must merely notice, as Christian Lindtner implies when he says:[123]

> By pointing out that nothing within the domain of experience can be conceived in and by itself independently of something else, Nāgārjuna merely

> intends to call attention to the fact that nothing has *svabhāva* (or, of course, *parabhāva* etc., cf. MK XV, 3).

Rather, the conception that things inherently exist, the adherence to *svabhāva*, is an ingrained, innate, misconception that operates within everyone within cyclic existence – educated, uneducated, human, animal, etc. It can be overcome only through extensive and prolonged effort and meditation. Hence Nāgārjuna's twenty-seven chapters of "limitless forms of reasoning", attacking the object of this conception again and again from many different approaches. For, it must utterly be overcome in order to achieve the religious goal of liberation from cyclic existence.

3 DZONG-KA-BA'S SOURCES

Dzong-ka-ba went through several steps to reach this position, and he attempts to support each one with the writings of the Indian Mādhyamika masters. That Nāgārjuna's basic intention is soteriological can be understood not just from the passages by Buddhapālita and Chandrakīrti cited above, but also in Nāgārjuna's own writings. For instance, in the final verse of his *Sixty Stanzas of Reasoning*, cited by Dzong-ka-ba in the *Great Exposition* (see below, p.181), he dedicates the merit from composing the text for the sake of all beings attaining Buddhahood. This is so much the message of Nāgārjuna's *Precious Garland* that it is almost too obvious to be said, this perhaps being the reason why Dzong-ka-ba did not cite it on this point. However, there are a wealth of passages available, beginning with opening stanzas (2–4):[124]

> O King, I will explain practices solely
> Virtuous to generate in you the doctrine,
> For the practices will be established
> In a vessel of the excellent doctrine.
>
> In one who first practises high status
> Definite goodness arises later,

For having attained high status one comes
Gradually to definite goodness.

High status is thought of as happiness,
Definite goodness as liberation,
The quintessence of their means
Are briefly faith and wisdom.

Following this, Nāgārjuna goes on to explain both virtuous practices leading to good rebirths within cyclic existence and teachings on selflessness, the realization of which leads to liberation from cyclic existence.

There are two ways to approach the topic of what prevents beings' liberation: objectively, by way of the object misconceived, or subjectively, by way of the misconceiving consciousness. Both are objects of negation. The objective – inherent existence – is the object of negation by reasoning; reasoning refutes inherent existence in the sense that through reasoning the absence of inherent existence is demonstrated, or made known, and one comes to disbelieve in inherent existence. The subjective object of negation – the ignorance misconceiving inherent existence – is the object of negation by the path; a path consciousness – a wisdom consciousness realizing emptiness – acts as a direct antidote to the ignorance misconceiving the opposite of emptiness and eradicates it such that it will not reoccur. For Dzong-ka-ba, the former object of negation is primary, for it is by way of refuting it that the latter is overcome. He explains:[125]

> This [former] object of negation must be one that does not exist among objects of knowledge because if it did exist, it could not be refuted. Nonetheless [that is, even though it does not exist], because superimpositions which apprehend it to exist are generated, it must be refuted. That refutation is not like destroying a pot with a hammer, but is a case of generating an ascertaining consciousness that recognizes the non-existent to be non-existent. When one generates ascertainment of it as non-existent, the

> mistaken consciousness apprehending it as existent will be overcome.

In the *Great Exposition*, the main focus in considering the object of negation is on the object of negation by reasoning, inherent existence, and Dzong-ka-ba's comments on ignorance, the misconceiving *consciousness*, come only near the end of the lengthy section on the object of negation, after the refutation of those who negate too much or too little, when setting forth his own identification of the object of negation.[126] To show the nature and pervasiveness of ignorance he cites numerous passages from Nāgārjuna, Āryadeva, and Chandrakīrti. For instance, Nāgārjuna's *Seventy Stanzas on Emptiness* says:[127]

> The Teacher said that that which conceives
> Things produced from causes
> And conditions as real is ignorance.
> From it, the twelve links arise.
> Knowing well that things are empty because of seeing
> The real, one is not obscured.
> That is the cessation of ignorance,
> Whereby the twelve branches cease.

Āryadeva's *Four Hundred* (VI.10) says:[128]

> Just as the physical sense power [pervades] the body,
> Delusion abides in all.
> Therefore, through destroying delusion
> All afflictions will also be destroyed.

Ignorance – or delusion (*gti mug*, *moha*), these being equivalent terms – is thus the root cause of all other afflictions, and its eradication is the key to their eradication.

In a very clear statement of just what that ignorance is, Chandrakīrti's *[Auto]commentary on the "Supplement to (Nāgārjuna's) 'Treatise on the Middle Way'"* says:[129]

> Ignorance superimposes an existence of things by way of their own entities that they do not have. It has a nature of obstructing perception of the nature [of things]. It is a concealer (*kun rdzob, saṃvṛti*).

Ignorance is a superimposition of existence by way its own entity (*rang gi ngo bo, svarūpa*), and "existence by way its own entity" is a synonym of inherent existence.

That inherent existence is what is being refuted is stated explicitly by Nāgārjuna and his Indian commentators on numerous occasions. Dzong-ka-ba cites a strikingly clear statement by Nāgārjuna in his *[Auto] commentary on the "Refutation of Objections"*:[130]

> . . . because beings are obscured with respect to the lack of inherent existence – the lack of a real entity – of all things which are like beings [emanated by] a magician, [the statements that things lack inherent existence] cause understanding that there is no inherent existence in those things which childish common beings, due to the obscuration of ignorance, superimpose as having inherent existence.

Also, Chandrakīrti says, identifying the object of the Mādhyamika analyses, ". . . our analysis is intent upon seeking out inherent existence. We [Mādhyamikas] are here refuting that things are established by way of their own entities."[131]

4 DIFFERENTIATING BETWEEN INHERENT EXISTENCE AND EXISTENCE

Based on the above identification of ignorance and the inherent existence that is its object, Dzong-ka-ba takes as one of the keys to his Mādhyamika interpretation a differentiation between four things: existence (*yod pa, bhāva*) and inherent existence (*rang bzhin gyis yod pa, svabhāva*), and no inherent existence (*rang bzhin gyis med pa, niḥsvabhāva*) and nonexistence (*med pa, abhāva*). Specifically, Dzong-ka-ba explains that it must be understood that when Nāgārjuna rejects existence, what he is actually refuting is inherent existence: things do not inherently exist. When he rejects non-existence, what he is actually refuting is utter non-existence: things are *not* utterly non-existent; they do not inherently exist, but do exist.

Another way to phrase this is that Dzong-ka-ba treats the terms "existence" (*yod pa*, *bhāva* or *asti*) and "non-existence" (*med pa*, *abhāva* or *nāsti*) which are used with great frequency in Nāgārjuna's *Treatise* as technical terms very specific in meaning. This is a view some Western interpreters have taken as well; Richard Jones says, for example:[132]

> "It is extremely important to note that even "is" (*asti*) and "is not" (*nāsti*) are technical terms for him, . . . "Is" refers only to what exists through own-nature – only to what would be real for Nāgārjuna. "Is not" is the notion of annihilationism (*uccheda*), the destruction of the real. "Is not" does *not* designate what does not exist by own-nature."

Such an understanding leaves one in a far better position to deal rationally with Nāgārjuna's writings than does a view such as that of Mervyn Sprung who feels that Nāgārjuna and Chandrakīrti "repudiate the ontological implications of the verb 'to be'," [133] this leading him to the not surprising conclusion that Mādhyamika is engaged in an "emasculation" of natural language,[134] which raises for Sprung the severe problematic: "how to carry on with meaningful talk about the central concerns of a philosophy which believes it can show that the idea of existence, of isness, of being, is empty? Language, without the force of the verb 'to be', would seem to be mere fantasy."[135]

Dzong-ka-ba seeks to maintain a coherent system in which the validity of language is upheld, and he sees Nāgārjuna's negations, including his apparent denial of valid use of the verbs of existence, as reflecting instead a psychological reality.

Prior to realization of emptiness, beings cannot differentiate between existence and inherent existence. Thus, an attack on inherent existence will be experienced as an attack on existence. Given the force of beings' adherence to inherent existence – this being the root cause that binds them in cyclic existence – Nāgārjuna's strongly worded negations, in which it seems that existence itself is under attack, are a very effective technique. However, it is important to distinguish between psychological reality and ontological fact; even though ordinary beings cannot, in experience, differentiate existence and inherent existence, nonetheless those two are different. Subsequent to realization of emptiness, that is, after the lack of inherent existence has been realized, existence – conventional existence – remains. Thus, Nāgārjuna is not negating all existence, but merely inherent existence. Further, to counter the nihilism that Dzong-ka-ba perceived among most of his Tibetan contemporaries who called themselves Mādhyamikas, he found it important to emphasize the verbal distinction between existence and inherent existence, even if it could not yet be verified in experience.

In that, for Dzong-ka-ba, inherent existence (*svabhāva*) is experientially coextensive with one's sense of existence (since everything *appears* to inherently exist) and that misconception with regard to it is considered to be what binds all beings in cyclic existence, it is clear that merely other systems, language, or reasoning could not be what is intended as the meaning of the *svabhāva* that Nāgārjuna refutes. For Dzong-ka-ba, those things posited by other systems with which Mādhyamika disagrees are not innate misconceptions, but merely artificial ones – learned through mistaken tenet systems and occurring only in those who have studied such tenets. Adherence to *svabhāva*, in contrast, is not just something learned, nor merely an "assumption" as B.K. Matilal describes it,[136] but is an innate, ingrained misconception, so potent that it even distorts the way things appear to us. Things *appear* to be inherently existent, although upon analysis they are found to be utterly devoid of inherent existence.

5 OTHER SYSTEMS ALONE ARE NOT WHAT IS REFUTED

According to Dzong-ka-ba, the assertions of other systems are not pervasive enough to be the root of cyclic existence nor, therefore, to be the primary referent of Nāgārjuna's refutations. Adherence to such ideas is to be eradicated – it is not that other tenet systems are not refuted, they are – but eradication of this is not the prime purpose and will occur naturally when the object of innate ignorance is refuted. Dzong-ka-ba says:[137]

> All those things posited through the force of tenets – the many different superimpositions by the Proponents of True Existence of our own [Buddhist] and other [i.e., non-Buddhist] schools, having taken as their basis just this referent object of the mode of apprehension of the ignorance explained earlier – will all be overcome when one eradicates the object of the mode of apprehension of ignorance, like a tree that is cut from the root. Therefore, those having wisdom should know that the referent object of innate ignorance is the basic object of negation and should not be intent on refuting merely those imputations imputed by only some proponents of tenets. This is (1) because refuting the object of negation in this way is not done upon being bereft of activity [that is, not having anything else to do], but rather, having seen that sentient beings are bound in cyclic existence by that wrong conceptual consciousness which has the object of negation as its object, one eradicates its object, and that which binds all sentient beings in cyclic existence is innate ignorance, and (2) because artificial ignorance, since it exists only in those who propound tenets, is not feasible to be the root of cyclic existence. It is very important to gain particular ascertainment with respect to this.

Thus, for Dzong-ka-ba, *merely* other systems are not what primarily is being refuted. However, other systems are refuted, for as Dzong-ka-ba explains Nāgārjuna, other systems' tenets concerning basic reality are *based upon* an assertion of inherent existence, whether those systems articulate their positions in such terms or not. This is because for those systems, if something exists, it must inherently exist. How is this? All Buddhist schools except Prāsaṅgika say that if something exists, there must be something that can be pointed to as it; Prāsaṅgika denies this and takes just such as indicative of inherent existence. If something were analytically findable, it would inherently exist. Thus, from the Prāsaṅgika viewpoint, other systems have asserted inherent existence with their very measure of existence, whether they say so or not.

The idea that other systems are based upon assertions of inherent existence, articulated as such or not, is the justification for Nāgārjuna's style of refutation. As Dzong-ka-ba interprets Nāgārjuna, Nāgārjuna is not, as Robinson accuses him, arbitrarily reading into his opponent's views a few terms defined in a self-contradictory way; rather, Nāgārjuna is drawing out the necessary implications of inherent existence. Robinson describes Nāgārjuna's mode of procedure:[138]

> Nāgārjuna has a standard mechanism for refutation, the pattern of which may be abstracted as follows: You say that C relates A and B. A and B must be either completely identical or completely different. If they are completely identical, C cannot obtain, because it is transitive and requires two terms. If they are completely different C cannot obtain, because two things that are completely different can have no common ground and so cannot be related. Therefore it is false that C obtains between A and B.

As Robinson then says, this formula arouses immediate suspicion since, among other reasons, it can be applied so readily to almost any hypothesis and also seems to contradict common sense. In a way, this is just the point. As interpreted by the Ge-luk-ba tradition, inherent existence, although conceived and assented to by all who have not engaged in active techniques to realize its non-existence, does contradict common sense – in this case, rational inquiry – and we should be suspicious. For becoming suspicious, applying analysis, and discovering an inability to withstand analysis is how the misconception of inherent existence is overcome.

The logical premise is not that we now conceive things to be either identical or completely different. Rather, we conceive things to be inherently existent, but in a non-analytical fashion, not considering its implications. Inherent existence is a solidity beyond what is there, an independence, an existence in its own right. It *requires* an ability to withstand analysis such as Nāgārjuna applies. Within such a mode of existence, the only possible relations between things are absolute oneness or total difference. This is a logical outflow of inherent existence, not something we necessarily conceive, and is the key to refuting the conception of inherent existence. For, if it can be shown that these relationships do not obtain, then the inherent existence of those things has been refuted and, through that, the conception of inherent existence can be overcome. Also, through refuting inherent existence, those systems based on an assertion of inherent existence are refuted.

As Robinson points out, "the validity of Nāgārjuna's refutations hinges upon whether his opponents really upheld the existence of a *svabhāva* or *svabhāva* as he defines the term," since he agrees with Nāgārjuna that "those who uphold the existence of a *svabhāva* are clearly self-contradictory."[139] A proof of such is not addressed by Nāgārjuna himself. Dzong-ka-ba considers it with regard to the non-Prāsaṅgika Buddhist schools' assertions concerning the person, saying that it is known that each asserts an inherently existent person because none is satisfied with the mere designation of the verbal convention "person", but must analyze to find something within the bases of designation of the person that can be pointed to as that person.[140] Thus, the tradition of commentary that stems from Dzong-ka-ba has developed the criterion discussed in the previous chapter of whether a system does or does not posit something that is analytically findable as indicative of whether inherent existence (*svabhāva*) is asserted or not. Presumably any system free from such an assertion would not be included within the sphere of Nāgārjuna's refutations.

6 LOGIC IS NOT REFUTED

Dzong-ka-ba does not explicitly address whether either logic or language is the intended referent of the Mādhyamika negations. However, much of his argument against Mādhyamika as being merely a refutation of other systems also applies here. Others' systems or mere logic or language are too limited to be what is intended by *svabhāva*, for all beings – not just humans or, among humans, not just those who use language or logic – are bound in cyclic existence due to the misconception of inherent existence.

Not only would a refutation of logical methods and principles not be sufficient to reverse innate misconceptions, but also Dzong-ka-ba does not see Nāgārjuna as *attacking* reasoning but rather as *using* reasoning, within acceptance of its basic principles, to refute inherent existence. This has been discussed briefly in the previous chapter (pp.60–1) and will be discussed further below (pp.123–6). In brief, Dzong-kaba sees no intrinsic flaw in reasoning. Instead he finds it a reliable vehicle for arriving at the truth. It is his primary resource in his Mādhyamika interpretation, and he finds it to be Nāgārjuna's as well.

7 MERELY LANGUAGE IS NOT BEING REFUTED

Language is not precisely the same issue in Buddhist philosophy that it is in Western philosophy. As Mervyn Sprung points out, the Indian Mādhyamikas – Nāgārjuna, Āryadeva, Chandrakīrti, and others – did not develop an explicit philosophy of language, and, in fact, there is no one Sanskrit word with a range of meaning comparable to "language".[141] Nor is there one Tibetan word. Further, the separation between objects and ideas so pronounced in the West from the time of Hume, with the consequent focus on language as totally divorced from the empirical world, never occurred in a comparable fashion within Buddhism.

There is, however, within Buddhism consideration of many of the topics that fall within Western analyses of language, and thus what must be determined for the purposes of this discussion are 1) whether specific understandings about the nature and function of language can be considered uncommon Mādhyamika understandings that set Mādhyamika apart from the other Buddhist schools and 2) whether interpretations of Mādhyamika based upon Western linguistic analyses accurately represent the Mādhyamika system.

Given that Dzong-ka-ba did not himself explicitly address the question of language as such, nor did the Indian Mādhyamikas who are his sources, the following discussion consists primarily of my own ideas and opinions, applying principles from Dzong-ka-ba's lines of argument and drawing supporting material from the post-Dzong-ka-ba Ge-luk-ba commentarial tradition.

Shared Understandings

My thesis with regard to the first point mentioned above is that many of what are often labelled "Mādhyamika" understandings are in fact not unique to Mādhyamika but are realized by lower Buddhist tenet systems as well, often being positions primarily worked out by epistemologists of the Dignāga-Dharmakīrti schools of logic.[142] They may be accepted by the Mādhyamikas as well, for Dzong-ka-ba, with his emphasis on the unity and coherence of the Buddhist teachings, sees no conflict in the tenets of one system being accepted by another so long as the tenets of the lower system do not conflict with those of the higher. However, being shared, they cannot be what sets Mādhyamika apart.

For example, if it is being said that Mādhyamika teaches that words cannot describe and thought cannot know impermanent objects exactly as they are, this is asserted even by the Sautrāntika tenet system. Nga-wang-bel-den (*ngag dbang dpal ldan*, b.1797), describing the two truths in the Sautrāntika system, explains, based on a passage from Dharmakīrti's *Commentary on (Dignāga's) "Compendium of Valid Cognition"* (*tshad ma rnam 'grel, pramāṇavārttika*), that specifically characterized, that is, impermanent, phenomena are those whose entity cannot appear fully to a mind merely from an expressional term.[143] In other words, direct perception knows its objects with a richness, vividness, and specificity that words cannot express and of which thought is incapable.

Also, that names do not inhere in objects but are designated arbitrarily is a concept realized and articulated in the Ge-luk-ba literature commenting on the Sautrāntika system.[144] That phenomena do not naturally exist as bases for the affixing of names is identified as the subtle object of negation in the Chittamātra system.[145] Thus neither of these can serve as uncommon Mādhyamika understandings.

Similarly, the idea that emptiness cannot be described exactly as it is and that direct realization of it is a non-verbal experience with profound transformative effect for the practitioner is not unique to Mādhyamika, but rather, with variations in the identification of emptiness, is a basic aspect of the path structure of all four tenet systems.[146] In both Chittamātra and Mādhyamika, ultimate truth (*don dam bden pa, paramārtha-satya*) is described as inexpressible and inconceivable, and Dzong-ka-ba takes such statements as indicating that at the time of directly realizing emptiness, all dualistic appearance as well as all conceptuality have disappeared,[147] not as showing that there are realms where language simply does not apply.

Linguistic Analysis

The question of whether or not linguistic analyses accurately represent Mādhyamika requires careful consideration. Such interpretations, frequently based upon comparison with the writings of Ludwig Wittgenstein, are currently a very popular way of looking at Mādhyamika, so much so that David Loy in a recent article in *Philosophy East and West* identifies it as one of two major streams of significant Western interpretations of Mādhyamika.[148] There is much in such comparisons that fits closely with Dzong-ka-ba's views. For example, Robert Thurman says:[149]

> The Wittgensteinian and Centrist non-egocentrist critical analyses intend to force him [the opponent] to look deeper into things and processes by examining his account of them . . .

If one then concludes, as Chris Gudmunsen asserts, that such analyses show that "There *are no* essences for the words to represent,"[150] this is, if one understands by "essences" some sort of intrinsic objective nature, very close to what Dzong-ka-ba says of Mādhyamika.

However, there are a number of ways in which the linguistic interpretation easily gives rise to ideas with which Dzong-ka-ba would disagree; there is also a danger of being led to read into Mādhyamika ideas not necessarily there and to distort the emphasis of those that are.[151] Thus, although there is much in Chris Gudmunsen's book, *Wittgenstein and Buddhism*, which I find helpful, and although Gudmunsen has clearly shown that there are many points of similarity between Mādhyamika and Wittgenstein, I would like to consider a few specific passages in order to highlight the fine line between what does and does not accord with Dzong-ka-ba's Mādhyamika interpretation.

Gudmunsen contrasts what he sees as the two primary approaches to Mādhyamika – one Kantian, or psychological, and the other Wittgensteinian, or linguistic – and says:[152]

> A Kantian approach to emptiness leads to just such an 'absolute ground.' A Wittgensteinian approach shows that the freedom which emptiness gives is

> freedom from assumptions about objects – assumptions based on a certain view of language. To know that X is empty is to know something about the way we can use and misuse language about X. But of course freedom is not simply a linguistic fact. The fact that I know that X is empty is a fact of psychology rather than of language. The human importance of understanding emptiness lies in that psychological fact and in its psychological implications, even though the fact that everything is empty is a linguistic rather than a psychological fact.

Insofar as a Wittgensteinian approach leads to an avoidance of seeing emptiness as an "absolute ground", Dzong-ka-ba would heartily agree with it. (See below, pp.129–31, for a discussion of Dzong-ka-ba's rejection of emptiness as an absolute.) He would also agree that the importance of understanding emptiness is primarily psychological – the effect it has on the mind of the person who understands it.

However, Gudmunsen in describing the positive effects of a Wittgensteinian approach suggests, based on Wittgenstein, that also in Mādhyamika because language is intimately bound up with our erroneous conceptions about objects, our "view of language" is the cause of them. This Dzong-ka-ba would not accept because, as mentioned earlier, of finding it too limited: If "view of language" means a particular philosophical theory about language, then only those holding that theory would be bound in cyclic existence; even if language in general is meant, then only those who use language – i.e., *not* babies and *not* most animals even if one were to concede language use to some of the more advanced species – would be caught within the snare of cyclic existence, and this contradicts basic Buddhist cosmology. For Dzong-ka-ba, the Prāsaṅgika-Mādhyamika view is that even the sense consciousnesses are mistaken, perceiving an inherent existence that is not in fact there.[153] Thus, the error involved in the misconception of inherent existence is pre-linguistic.

Finally, with regard to the above passage, I am uncomfortable with calling the emptiness of all phenomena merely a "linguistic fact". The trend within modern Mādhyamika interpretations to see it as such stems in large part from Richard Robinson's statement, which Gudmunsen cites in this context:[154]

> ... emptiness is not a term in the primary system referring to the world, but a term in the descriptive system (meta-system) referring to the primary system. Thus it has no status as an entity, nor as the property of an existent or an inexistent.

Emptiness is described thus in order to avoid the fault of reification, of elevating emptiness to the status of an absolute over and beyond the phenomena that are empty. However, relegating emptiness to the status of a second order term may take too much away from it,[155] and Dzong-ka-ba's interpretation seeks more of a middle ground.

The vocabulary of Dzong-ka-ba and the tradition following him leads me more toward calling the emptiness of all phenomena an "ontological" or "existential" fact, having to do with "being" more than language, for emptiness is described as the "mode of abiding" (*gnas lugs*), the "final nature" (*rang bzhin mthar thug*), and so forth of phenomena.[156] This does not mean that for Dzong-ka-ba emptiness is what Gudmunsen would describe as a Kantian absolute, and when I use the term "ontology" I do not mean to suggest an underlying absolute essence that is beyond all manifestations, a noumenon beyond phenomena. Dzong-ka-ba emphatically refutes such; emptiness no more inherently exists than do the phenomena it qualifies; emptiness too is empty. Emptiness is not seen as a unitary Absolute, but rather as multiple. There are as many emptinesses as there are phenomena. Each and every phenomenon has its own emptiness, and the emptiness of one is not the emptiness of another.[157] In such an interpretation, emptiness is very much a part of the primary system.

I am not suggesting that a linguistic interpretation is completely contradictory with Dzong-ka-ba's, and certainly Dzong-ka-ba would not dispute that language is intimately connected with the process of error, for language reinforces our innate tendency towards reification. However, David Loy, in describing what Nāgārjuna is seeking to overcome through his analysis of motion in the second chapter of the *Treatise on the Middle Way*, makes a statement that comes closer to what Dzong-ka-ba would be likely to say, speaking of:[158]

> ... our ingrained tendency (perhaps due to, and certainly enshrined in, the subject-predicate structure of language) to distinguish our experience into self-existing entities and their activities.

In Loy's statement, primary emphasis is focused not on the structure of language but on the self-existing entities and activities we imagine and whether or not those are logically feasible. This emphasis accords more with that of Dzong-ka-ba. Words, or language, point one to things – be they material or not, and, as interpreted in the Ge-luk-ba tradition, it is those things and their status that are of primary concern, not just the words themselves or ideas about the relationships between words and objects.

For instance, as is made very clear by the instructions in Ge-luk meditation manuals, the "self" that is being refuted in the refutation of a self of persons (in the eighteenth chapter of Nāgārjuna's *Treatise*) is not just an abstract concept, but a person's most palpable and deep-rooted sense of self. The pressent Dalai Lama said in a public lecture in 1972 that the sense of the self being refuted is one held so strongly that one feels, "If this does not exist, what does!"[159]

What the Mādhyamika analyses then reveal is the unreasonableness of this deep-rooted sense. Objects, activities, and so forth are not as substantial or as "other" as we imagine them, for analysis reveals that there is nothing substantial there to be grasped. Thus one is led to the understanding that objects are inextricably bound up with ideas; their actual status is that, rather than existing inherently, existing in their own right, or existing from their own sides, they are mere imputations, imputed by names and thought. They are functional, but not analytically graspable. All that exist are mere designations, and thus the concept of *prajñapti*, or designation, is not just, as Robinson says, a way of handling abstractions, (cited above, p.77) but is descriptive of even the most concrete.

Related to the question of emphasis, Gudmunsen, speaking of what remains to be done after deciding that all phenomena, or *dharmas*, are empty, lays out two tasks, one of which is, "We can try to understand how *words* function if they no longer derive their meaning from objects to which they refer."[160] Gudmunsen for his discussion of this focuses on the Mādhyamika doctrine of the two truths, specifically on conventional truths (*kun rdzob bden pa*, *saṃvṛti satya*) which he says means language and verbal thought.[161] As such, he has limited the scope of conventional truths far more than does Dzong-ka-ba and the tradition following him, for whom conventional truths are everything that exists except emptiness. Language and thought are included, but they are not primary or even much discussed. In this, Dzong-ka-ba finds support in both sūtra and the Indian Mādhyamika tradition. Chandrakīrti, for example, speaks of conventional truths objectively in his *Supplement to* (*Nāgārjuna's*) *"Treatise on the Middle Way"* (VI.28):[162]

> The Subduer said that because delusion
> Obscures the nature, it is the concealer (*saṃvṛti*);
> Those fabrications which it perceives
> As true are truths for a concealer (*saṃvṛti-satya*).
> Things that are fabrications [exist] conventionally.

And Chandrakīrti says in his autocommentary on that verse:

> In that way, truths-for-a-concealer are posited through the force of the afflictive ignorance which is

> included within the [twelve] links [of a dependent-arising] of cyclic existence. For Hearers, Solitary Realizers, and Bodhisattvas who have abandoned afflictive ignorance and who see conditioned phenomena as like the existence of reflections and so forth, [these] have a nature of fabrication and are not truths because they do not exaggerate [phenomena] as truly existent. To children these are deceptive, but to the others they are just conventionalities due to being dependent-arisings like a magician's illusions and so forth.

Thus, the emphasis within the Ge-luk-ba tradition is not on the linguistic elements of conventional truths but rather on their status as objects. Within their commentarial tradition, discussion of how words function is found in works dealing with the Dharmakīrti-Dignāga logicians and epistemologists, for whom it is an important and explicit topic unlike Mādhyamika where it is not explicitly addressed.

A potential danger with Mādhyamika interpretations that focus primarily on language is that they may lead to a devaluing of language. If one finds through comparing Wittgenstein and Nāgārjuna, for instance, as does Robert Thurman that in both there is a "reaffirmation of language, free of any supposed absolute substratum, as a practical, conventional process, an ordinary activity of human beings,"[163] then this is very much in line with Dzong-ka-ba's interpretation of Mādhyamika with its great emphasis on the valid establishment of conventional phenomena. However, should one, seeking a parallel with what Thurman describes as "the mature Wittgenstein's refusal to pretend to a system"[164] conclude, as many have (see above p.76), that any rigor or complexity of metaphysical theory is necessarily unsuitable, that terms cannot be defined, and so forth, this clearly is not Dzong-ka-ba's view as his own finely worked systematization demonstrates.

Again, from Dzong-ka-ba's viewpoint, systematization is

made possible by a valid establishment of conventionalities, conventional truths. Free from any overlay of inherent existence, conventional truths can be used, terms can be defined, systems can be formed. In fact, in accordance with Nāgārjuna's statement in the *Treatise on the Middle Way* (XXIV.10) that ultimate truths can be taught only by way of conventional truths, it is important to do so. Thus, unlike Edward Conze's opinion (cited above, p.121) that words only detract from reality, for Dzong-ka-ba, if used carefully, within awareness of their limitations and problems, they can and do *disclose* reality in the sense that they lead to the understandings that make possible a non-dualistic cognition of reality, the emptiness of inherent existence of each and every phenomenon in all world-systems.

A final issue of emphasis to consider is that of overall purpose. Mādhyamika is a religious system and Nāgārjuna's purpose is, as discussed previously, clearly soteriological, directed towards liberation. The system does not see itself as offering merely a "therapeutic ploy" or merely seeking to show that there is a "linguistic basis to the idea of identity", in contrast to the views of some who approach it through the avenue of linguistic analysis. Both Gudmunsen and Thurman address this question in their comparisons of Mādhyamika with Wittgenstein, each offering evidence that Wittgenstein too had a broader and more liberative intent.[165] Gudmunsen makes the case that when Wittgenstein says, "Philosophy is a battle against the bewitchment of our intelligence by means of language", he is not speaking of something that is a problem just for philosophers, but of something that affects us all. He finds Wittgenstein offering liberation in the statement, "What is your aim in philosophy? – To shew the fly the way out of the fly-bottle."[166]

Gudmunsen, having thus shown that statements of liberative intent can be found in the writings of Wittgenstein, makes the further point that although almost no one disputes that Nāgārjuna's intentions were liberative since this is "what Buddhism as a whole is all about," nonetheless, in Nāgārjuna's own writings, "there are almost no *other* clues to his being a 'religious writer'.[167] Gudmunsen's statement is only partially true since if one considers Nāgārjuna's "Praises" and his *Precious Garland* there is abundant evidence of his religious purpose; even within his *Treatise on the Middle Way*, the twenty-fourth chapter speaks specifically of the feasibility within emptiness, and in fact because of emptiness, of the religious framework of the four noble truths, the Three Jewels, the path structure indicative of religious progress, and so forth. In any case, the point I would like to make is that *even if* one were to accept Gudmunsen's statement, so that one has placed Nāgārjuna and Wittgenstein in a situation of relative parity as far as explicit statements demonstrative of religious intent, this omits the whole question of context. Nāgārjuna is within a religious tradition which thus reinforces that aspect of his work; Wittgenstein is within a philosophical one in which liberative intentions are an aberration. These differences cannot be ignored as one searches for similarities between the two systems.

It is not that comparison is not helpful or that linguistic analysis is inappropriate, but one must be careful not to be led by some areas of similarity to assume others that may not exist.

As Dzong-ka-ba frames the categories of negating too little and too much, the views that Mādhyamika is an attack on reasoning or on language fall into both. They negate too little in the sense that they do not go deeply enough to describe a basic misconception capable of binding each and every sentient being in cyclic existence. As such, they can be answered using Dzong-ka-ba's argument that mere refutations of learned as opposed to innate misconceptions are not sufficient to reverse the process of cyclic existence.

However, a negation of reasoning or of the language on which it is based also negates too much. As Dzong-ka-ba uses the category, negating too much is not a matter of negating correctly what should be negated but then negating something extra as well. Rather, something that should not be negated at all is denied, the very fact of such overnegation serving to show the lack of understanding of what should be negated. Dzong-ka-ba identifies the uncommon feature of Mādhyamika as the feasibility of conventional functionings within an utter absence of inherent existence. A blanket rejection of both reasoning and language goes too far, denying such feasibility and hence missing the unique Mādhyamika feature. Further, a denial of the validity of these two would remove our most potent tools for eradicating innate misconception. This is the context in which Dzong-ka-ba vigorously defends the use of reasoning, which will be discussed in detail below (see pp.123–6).

5 *Dzong-ka-ba and Modern Interpreters II: Negating Too Much*

Far more prevalent than Mādhyamika interpretations that, from Dzong-ka-ba's viewpoint, negate too little are those that negate too much. These would include the views that Mādhyamika is an attack on all conceptuality, or on all conventional phenomena, as well as the opinions of those who, while not necessarily claiming that Mādhyamika refutes all conventionalities, say that Mādhyamikas have no view or system or theses of their own and merely rely on others for the presentations of conventionalities. These positions are very much intertwined, but in the interests of clarity will be discussed in isolation as much as possible.

CONCEPTUALITY IS THE OBJECT OF NEGATION

That conceptuality is what Mādhyamika seeks to negate is a position advanced by, among others, T.R.V. Murti and Christian Lindtner, both of whom equate ignorance (*avidyā*) with conceptuality (*kalpanā*) as well as with views (*dṛṣṭi*) – as Murti says, "Kalpanā, (vikalpa) is avidyā *par excellence.*[168] (The idea that Mādhyamika is intent on a refutation of all views (*dṛṣṭi*) will be discussed in detail below, pp.111–16; here I will focus just on the question of conceptuality, since Dzong-ka-ba treats these as two separate issues.) It is also set forth by Peter Fenner, who, in a very complex articulation of how the Mādhyamika analyses lead to a stilling of conceptuality, argues that those analyses are intended to show a logical paradox inherent in thought.[169]

The idea that conceptuality is equivalent to ignorance and as such is what is to be removed, or negated, undoubtedly stems not only from passages in the writings of Nāgārjuna and Chandrakīrti that seem to suggest such, but also from the facts that (1) direct realization of emptiness is described as a non-dualistic cognition, totally free from conceptuality, and (2) a Buddha, a fully realized being, is said to be completely without conceptuality. Both of these points are widely accepted within the various Buddhist traditions, and Dzong-ka-ba has no disagreement with either. What he does disagree with, and he is not alone in this, it having been a primary topic of the Sam-yay debate mentioned in chapter one, is to draw the conclusion from this that all thought is bad and simply to be stopped and that the cessation of thought marks the attainment of liberation. Such is what Dzong-ka-ba describes as the position of the Chinese monk Hva-shang Mahāyāna, whom he sees as having been defeated by Kamalashīla in the debate at Sam-yay, and it can be found in modern manifestations as well. Ben-Ami Scharfstein writes:[170]

> ... since all these thoughts [analyzing self] like the world itself, are so troublesome, it is best to stop thinking. Plurality will then cease (and unity) and we (though not exactly) will remain (in a non-temporal sense) in a state of bliss.

Scharfstein has set forth exactly the view to which Dzong-ka-ba strenuously objects. For Dzong-ka-ba, non-conceptuality certainly does not constitute liberation. Were this so, then it would absurdly follow that non-conceptual states – fainting, deep sleep, and so forth – would be liberation. Further, the mere ceasing of conceptuality is also not sufficient for realization of emptiness; rather, emptiness must initially be realized through analysis, which entails conceptuality. Dzong-ka-ba supports this view with citations from Kamalashīla and from sūtra – the *King of Meditative Stabilizations Sūtra* (*ting nge 'dzin rgyal po, samādhirāja*) and the *Scriptural Collection of*

Bodhisattvas (*byang chub sems dpa'i sde snod*, *bodhisattva-piṭaka*). He opens the "Great Exposition of Special Insight" with this issue (see the Introduction of the translation), and he returns to it again near the end of his presentation when he discusses how to meditate on special insight, a topic he commences with a refutation of mistaken assertions.[171]

There are two basic aspects to the discussion of why thought, or specifically, analysis, is needed. The first is concerned with how the process of eradicating ignorance is conceived – not as a mere stopping of thought, but as the active realization of the opposite of what ignorance misconceives. Ignorance is not just mere absence of knowledge, but a specific misconception, and it must be removed by realization of its opposite. In this vein, Dzong-ka-ba says that one cannot get rid of the misconception of inherent existence merely by stopping conceptuality any more than one can get rid of the idea that there is a demon in a darkened cave merely by trying to not think about it. Just as one must hold up a lamp and see that there is no demon there, so the illumination of wisdom is necessary to clear away the darkness of ignorance.[172]

Although Dzong-ka-ba's main Mādhyamika source explicitly addressing, and refuting, the idea that progress can be made through a mere ceasing of conceptuality is a late Indian Mādhyamika, Kamalashīla (c.740–795), who in later exegesis is recognized, not as a Prāsaṅgika, but as a Svātantrika, the sense of an active removal of wrong conceptions by way of "seeing" reality rather than through a mere ceasing of conceptuality is also found in the writings of the early Mādhyamikas, as in the following passage from Āryadeva's *Four Hundred* (XIV.25):[173]

> The seed of cyclic existence is a consciousness;
> Objects are its sphere of activity.
> When one sees selflessness in objects,
> The seeds of cyclic existence are stopped.

Since a mere stopping of thought will not, in Dzong-ka-ba's system, lead to a realization of emptiness, one is led to the second aspect of the discussion: that at present thought is our only way to gain access to emptiness. One of the ways of dividing phenomena is into the manifest (*mngon gyur*, *abhimukhī*) and the hidden (*lkog gyur*, *parokṣa*). The manifest are those things presently accessible to direct perception, such as external forms, sounds, tastes, and so forth. The hidden are those things that must be initially realized conceptually, in dependence upon a process of reasoning. The division of phenomena into the manifest and the hidden is an all inclusive one; whatever exists must be one or the other, and emptiness falls within the latter. (See below, pp.126–33, for a discussion of the inclusion of emptiness among phenomena.) Emptiness is clearly not a manifest phenomenon; if it were, everyone would be perceiving it now, and obviously they are not. Rather, it is a hidden phenomenon, one which ordinary non-conceptual consciousnesses cannot reach. As such, conceptuality, reasoning, is our only avenue of initial approach to it.

It is undeniable that there are passages in Nāgārjuna, Chandrakīrti, and so forth – even in sūtras of the Buddha – that seem to reject all conceptuality. Dzong-ka-ba's response to these passages is that, just as the refutations of existence must be understood with qualification, as meaning "*inherent* existence", so also the refutations of conceptuality must be understood with qualification. Conceptions *of inherent existence* are being refuted, not all conceptions. Only one type of conceptuality – a very specific misconception – is being refuted, not the whole class. He finds support for this in Chandrakīrti who, commenting on a passage of Āryadeva's *Four Hundred* (XVI.23cd), "Conceptuality sees [and] one is bound; it is to be stopped here," glosses conceptuality as "that which superimposes a meaning of inherent existence which is not correct".[174]

In this way Dzong-ka-ba saves conceptuality from total denial, preserving the viability of scripture and reasoning as aids for spiritual progress and maintaining a valid distinction between good thoughts and bad thoughts – virtues and non-virtues. He would not quarrel with valuing non-conceptuality over conceptuality in terms of realizing a particular object, for his Mādhyamika interpretation does not override the Sautrāntika tenet system description of the way in which, whether the object is mundane or supramundane, direct perception exceeds conceptuality in richness and vividness.[175] However, this does not mean that non-conceptuality is *per se* better, for some objects such as emptiness could never be known without prior conceptual realization. One must understand the uses and limitations of both conceptual and non-conceptual cognition and make use of conceptuality to reach the higher non-conceptual states.

That the goal of Buddhahood is a non-conceptual state does not, for Dzong-ka-ba, imply any unsuitability in using conceptuality to reach that goal, a position he supports by citing the *Kāshyapa Chapter Sūtra ('od srung gi le'u'i mdo, kāśyapaparivarta)*:[176]

> Kāshyapa, it is like this: For example, fire arises from the rubbing together of two branches by the wind, and once arisen, the two branches are burned up. Similarly, Kāshyapa, if you have the correct analytical intellect, a Superior's faculty of wisdom is generated. Through its generation, the correct analytical intellect is consumed.

At higher levels of the path, conceptuality – the correct analytical intellect – is consumed by the fire of wisdom. Nonetheless, it is the fuel that makes the arising of wisdom possible. Prior to reaching the highest level, it is necessary to distinguish between different types of conceptuality and to make use of correct conceptuality in the struggle to remove the incorrect.

CONVENTIONALITIES ARE NEGATED BY THE MĀDHYAMIKA ANALYSES

That the intention of the Mādhyamika analyses is not a refutation of all conventionalities is the focus of the portion of

Dzong-ka-ba's "Great Exposition of Special Insight" translated in this volume and has already been discussed extensively in chapter three. Thus, it will be treated only briefly here, primarily drawing in material from portions of the *Great Exposition* not included in this translation. Much of the problem comes again from what, from the viewpoint of this tradition, is a mixing of psychological reality and ontological fact: At the time of direct cognition of emptiness, all conventional phenomena – everything except emptiness – disappear. Does this mean that those conventionalities do not exist? For Dzong-ka-ba the answer is no, and he takes his cue from Nāgārjuna and Chandrakīrti.[177]

Both Nāgārjuna and Chandrakīrti deny on numerous occasions that they propound nihilism, and the reason they give to prove they are not nihilists is their acceptance of conventional existence. For instance, Nāgārjuna says in the *Precious Garland*:[178]

> Having thus seen that effects arise
> From causes, one asserts what appears
> In the conventions of the world
> And does not accept nihilism.

Chandrakīrti, in the course of a long explanation in his *Clear Words* of how Mādhyamikas differ from Nihilists, concludes:[179]

> Because Mādhyamikas assert [actions and their effects and former and future lifetimes] as existing conventionally and these [Nihilists] do not assert them at all, they are just not similar.

Exactly what it means for things to exist conventionally is less explicit. The *locus classicus* for the fact that Buddhism is not denying all worldly conventions whatsoever is Buddha's statement, "What the world accepts, I too accept; what the world does not accept, I too do not accept," which is cited by both Buddhapālita and Chandrakīrti in their commentaries on Nāgārjuna's *Treatise on the Middle Way*, the *Buddhapālita*

Commentary on (Nāgārjuna's) "Treatise on the Middle Way" and the *Clear Words*, respectively, and is suggested by the above verse from the *Precious Garland*.[180]

Dzong-ka-ba, with his affinity for the epistemology and logic of Dignāga and Dharmakīrti, develops a complex systematization in which the measure of conventional existence is establishment by valid cognition (*tshad ma*, *pramāṇa*).[181] In this he goes far beyond what can be found explicitly in the writings of the Indian Mādhyamikas as well as beyond what many non-Ge-luk-ba Tibetan Mādhyamikas would accept;[182] however, from his viewpoint he is in accord with the intentions of his Indian antecedents, and he supports his argument with numerous citations from Chandrakīrti.

The essence of Dzong-ka-ba's argument is as follows.[183] The measure of something's existing conventionally is threefold: (1) it is renowned to a conventional consciousness; (2) it is not damaged by conventional valid cognition; (3) it is not damaged by ultimate valid cognition, that is, by reasoning analyzing whether or not it exists inherently. The first of these is essentially the first part of Buddha's statement – "what the world accepts, I accept". Dzong-ka-ba takes "worldly renown" as meaning a conventional consciousness. He describes this as a non-analytical consciousness in the sense that it "operates within the context of how things appear, or are renowned to it" rather than being engaged in analysis of the final status of what appears. This does not however mean that it is totally non-analytical or that what is intended is only what is renowned to illiterate persons or even to educated persons who have not studied tenets. All that is ruled out is that it be a consciousness analyzing the final mode of being; thus, those aspects of Buddhist doctrine that are clearly not within the sphere of renown to uneducated untrained persons such as path structure, the cause and effect of karma and so forth can be included within worldly renown.

The second of Dzong-ka-ba's threefold list reflects the second part of Buddha's statement, "What the world does not accept, I also do not accept." If something is damaged by conventional valid cognition, then it does not exist even conventionally. For example, if one mistakenly conceives a rope to be a snake or a mirage to be water, a subsequent worldly consciousness, a conventional valid cognition, can determine that there is no snake or no water, and thus, in those situations, the snake and water do not exist even conventionally. (The third part of Dzong-ka-ba's threefold list is not germane to this particular discussion although it is very important; it is the means of refuting the inherent existence asserted by other systems which Mādhyamika refutes. Since it cannot withstand analysis by the Mādhyamika reasonings, it does not exist even conventionally.)

Dzong-ka-ba is aware of the fact that even though he has tied the measure of conventional phenomena's existence to their not being harmed by conventional valid cognition, there is a question as to whether Chandrakīrti accepts valid cognition at all, and he addresses directly the more difficult passages in Chandrakīrti's writings concerning this subject.[184] He concludes that what Chandrakīrti is refuting is the specific assertion of logicians such as Dignāga that sense consciousnesses are valid with respect to the self-character (*rang mtshan, svalakṣana*) of objects.[185] Dzong-ka-ba argues that Chandrakīrti's thought is that the sense consciousnesses are not valid cognizers with respect to the self-character of the objects that appear to them because they are deceived in terms of the appearance of self-character: objects are empty of self-character, i.e., are empty of being established by way of their own character, yet appear to have such.

He says that if Chandrakīrti were utterly refuting the existence of valid cognizers among worldly consciousness, he would not have made such statements as, "An undeceived consciousness is viewed as a valid cognizer in the world," or "It is posited that the world realizes objects by way of the four valid cognizers," following which Chandrakīrti makes a presentation of valid cognizers that are direct, inferential, scriptural, and by example.[186] Dzong-ka-ba concludes that Chandrakīrti accepts valid cognizers as long as they are understood to be only conventionally and not inherently existent; he cites Chandrakīrti's *Clear Words*:[187]

> Those are established through mutual dependence. When valid cognizers exist, then there are objects which are objects of comprehension; when objects which are objects of comprehension exist, then there are valid cognizers. However, the two, valid cognizers and objects of comprehension, are not established by way of [their own] entities.

Thus, Dzong-ka-ba maintains for conventional phenomena a status of being validly established as mere conventionalities. A distinction is maintained between what exist conventionally – things such as tables and chairs – and what do not exist at all – for instance, the falling hairs seen by a person with cataracts – based on the reliability of the conventional consciousness perceiving them. Dzong-ka-ba cites Chandrakīrti's *Supplement to (Nāgārjuna's) "Treatise on the Middle Way"* (VI.24–5):[188]

> Also, perceivers of falsities [that is, worldly consciousnesses] are asserted as of two types, those with clear sense faculties and those with defective sense faculties. Consciousnesses of those having defective sense faculties are asserted to be wrong in relation to those having good sense faculties. Those objects realized by the world that are apprehended by way of the six unimpaired sense faculties are true in terms of just the world. The rest are posited as unreal in terms of just the world.

Thus, it is possible to maintain a difference within the conventional realm between truth and falsehood, right and wrong. However, conventional phenomena, even though validly established, are not nearly as substantial as we, with our misconception of inherent existence, conceive them to be. They are illusory in that they appear one way and exist another; nonetheless they do exist. This distinction is emphasized by the examples used to describe them. Dzong-ka-ba cites Chandrakīrti's *Commentary on (Āryadeva's) "Four Hundred"*:[189]

> Should someone assert that it is being taught that compounded phenomena are without production since production in all forms has been refuted by this analysis, then that [production of products and so forth] would not be like a magician's illusions. Rather, it would be comprehensible through [examples] such as the child of a barren woman, and so forth. Fearing that in that case it would [absurdly] follow that dependent-arisings would not exist, we do not make comparison with those [examples, such as the child of a barren woman and so forth] but rather with such things as a magician's illusions and so forth which are not contradictory with those [dependent-arisings].

Such an understanding of conventional phenomena as like illusions but nonetheless validly established allows for a valid presentation of the Buddhist teachings of the four noble truths, the cause and effect of karma, the path to enlightenment, and so forth.

Dzong-ka-ba's emphasis in his Mādhyamika interpretation on the valid establishment of conventionalities, even though he supports it with passages from the writings of the Indian Mādhyamikas, clearly represents a shift of emphasis from the writings of the Mādhyamika founders. For example, one of the arguments Dzong-ka-ba uses to show that Nāgārjuna did not refute conventionalities is the fact that of the twenty-seven chapters of his *Treatise on the Middle Way*, twenty-five refute inherent existence, the twenty-sixth teaches the arising and ceasing of the twelve links of dependent-arising, and the twenty-fourth shows how all activities, functionings, and Buddhist teachings such as the four noble truths and so forth, are feasible with the absence of inherent existence.[190] Dzong-ka-ba's point is that this twenty-fourth chapter emphasizing the feasibility of conventionalities must be carried over to all the others and taken as implicit throughout, even in passages that appear to be refuting everything whatsoever. What Dzong-ka-ba has done is to shift a chapter that was one out of twenty-seven to a position of prominence: The feasibility of conventionalities within an absence of inherent existence is now the focus around which everything else must take shape.

This might be considered a distortion of the *Treatise's* original intent. However, it might also be said to reflect a change in intellectual or religious climate. Nāgārjuna was writing to counter those convinced of the reality of the things around them, who, from his viewpoint, adhered to a solidity beyond what was there. Thus the strong negative tone. Dzong-ka-ba was writing to counter those convinced of just the opposite, that the things around them had no reality at all. Thus the need for a shift in tone to restore some status to things.

MĀDHYAMIKAS HAVE NO VIEW

Two positions taken by almost all Western writers on Mādhyamika are (1) that Mādhyamika has no view (*lta ba*, *dṛṣṭi*) or, as a slight variation, is an attack on all views, and (2) that Mādhyamika has no system, or theses (*dam bca'*, *pratijñā*), or, in alternate phrasing, is an attack on all systems and theses. These two positions tend to be blended together in the Western literature. For example, Chris Gudmunsen says:[191]

> In fact, the special quality of the Mādhyamika is generally taken to be that they criticize all possible philosophical views and theories without setting up anything in their place. Even the rejection of all views is not to be held on to as the 'correct' thing to do.

Thus, these two issues are difficult to separate for discussion, particularly when authors do not cite Sanskrit or Tibetan, for translation equivalents for the two tend to overlap – "theory" in particular being used for both "view" and "system". However, because the two positions come from two very different sets of passages in the Mādhyamika source literature, they will be discussed as much as possible as two separate issues, beginning first with the idea that Mādhyamikas have no view.

There are potent quotes in support of this position. For instance, Nāgārjuna's *Treatise on the Middle Way* (XIII.8) says, "The Conquerors said that emptiness eradicates all views; those who view emptiness were said to be incurable," and Nāgārjuna concludes the *Treatise* (XXVII.30) with an homage to Gautama Buddha for having "taught the excellent doctrine for the abandonment of all views".[192]

Based on such passages, numerous scholars have concluded that Mādhyamika is against all views. Douglas Daye says, "The Mādhyamikas deny *both* that other views are free from legitimate contradiction and that they possess a position (*dṛṣṭi*) to defend.[193] B.K. Matilal, taking his lead from T.R.V. Murti, denies that Mādhyamika is refuting *wrong* views and says that it is rather a criticism of having views at all:[194]

> The doctrine of *śūnyatā* 'emptiness' is, in fact, the critique of all views, all philosophical systems. But it is my contention that this doctrine may be dangerously misinterpreted not only by its opponents but also by its so-called proponents to the effect that it actually DISPROVES all views, all philosophy. If anything, this doctrine simply shows that it is neither proper nor is it logically (or, dialectically) justifiable to regard any particular metaphysical system as absolutely valid.

This leads Matilal, along with others such as Étienne Lamotte, to conclude that Mādhyamika is a form of agnosticism; Matilal says:[195]

> It needs to be emphasized, even at the risk of repetition, that the doctrine of emptiness does not actually consist in the rejection of the phenomenal world, but

> in the maintainance of a non-committal attitude toward the phenomena and in the nonacceptance of any theory of the phenomenal world as finally valid.

Numerous writers have questioned this blanket rejection of views, or at least refusal to uphold any view, since it seems not to be born out by Nāgārjuna's very act of writing the *Treatise on the Middle Way*. Richard Jones says:[196]

> To introduce the peculiarities of how Nāgārjuna goes about his task, consider his claim to expound no views (*dṛṣṭi*) – one who holds voidness, the remedy of all views, as a view is incurable (13.8). Of course by any commonsensical definition of "view," he has many, starting with the first verse of the *Kārikās*.

As L. Stafford Betty says, "Saying 'no' is saying something – and believing something. It is to hold a view about something."[197] Alex Wayman points out that Nāgārjuna does indeed adhere to views, for example, the view of dependent-arising, which would be counted as a right view (*yang dag pa'i lta ba*, *samyag-dṛṣṭi*).[198]

These latter opinions are very much in line with Dzong-ka-ba's approach to the question. Clearly Mādhyamikas do have views in spite of talk of refuting all views, and, furthermore, in some passages the term is used in a positive way. The *Heart Sūtra* says, "[A Bodhisattva] should thoroughly and correctly *view* (*paś*) these five aggregates as empty of inherent existence," and Chandrakīrti's *Supplement to (Nāgārjuna's) "Treatise on the Middle Way"* (VI.165cd) says, "Therefore, through the view of the emptiness of I and mine, a yogi will be released." Even more explicit is Chandrakīrti's *Commentary on (Āryadeva's) "Four Hundred"*:[199]

> The thorough extinguishment of attachment is the cause of attaining nirvāṇa, and, except for the view of the lack of inherent existence, there is no other doctrine which is a cause of thoroughly extinguishing such attachment.

Maintaining the viability of correct views is one of the reasons Dzong-ka-ba gives for rejecting Mādhyamika interpretations that would refute all conceptuality as well as the conventionalities realized by it, for, "in that case, since it would have to be that there was no correct view leading to the state of nirvāṇa, all the activities of hearing, thinking, and so forth with respect to the Mādhyamika texts would be senseless."[200]

Thus, from his viewpoint those passages that seem to be a blanket refutation of views must be understood in context and qualified in some way. Seyfort Ruegg, in discussing the Mādhyamika rejection of views, finds a difference in the Sanskrit terminology used; he distinguishes *śūnyatādarśana* (perhaps literally "seeing" emptiness) which is used in a positive way and in which Ruegg would translate *darśana* as "philosophical theory" from *śūnyatādṛṣṭi* (literally "viewing" emptiness) which is used negatively and in which Ruegg would translate *dṛṣṭi* as "speculative view" or "dogmatic opinion", thus limiting the meaning of the combined term to "a speculative view that hypostatizes emptiness."[201] One Tibetan term, *lta ba*, serves as the translation equivalent for both Sanskrit words, *darśana* and *dṛṣṭi*, both derivatives of the verb *dṛś* (Tib. *lta*), to see, and thus in the Tibetan literature this distinction is not possible. The lack of such a distinction would seem to be an important key to Dzong-ka-ba's more positive attitude towards the term "view" in general.

In any case, Dzong-ka-ba's interpretation of the passages in question accords with Ruegg's assessment and with the distinction in Sanskrit terminology (in cases where the Sanskrit exists to check against the Tibetan). For instance, the passage from Nāgārjuna's *Treatise*, "The Conquerors said that emptiness eradicates all views; those who view emptiness were said to be incurable," is interpreted by Dzong-ka-ba as meaning that emptiness was taught to remove all views of inherent existence and that those who view emptiness itself as inherently existent are incurable.[202]

In other situations where the term "view" is used negatively, but not specifically in the context of "viewing emptiness", Dzong-ka-ba interprets it as carrying an implicit qualification, "bad" or "wrong". There are examples, such as a passage from Āryadeva's *Four Hundred* (VIII.7cd), "The Tathāgatas said that one does not pass from sorrow through [such] wrong views,"[203] where the term "view" is used explicitly with the qualification "wrong". Similarly, Chandrakīrti's *Supplement to (Nāgārjuna's) "Treatise on the Middle Way"* (VI.115) says, "Therefore, this reasoning of dependent-arising cuts through all nets of bad views."[204] For Dzong-ka-ba, this then makes it suitable to carry those qualifications over to other places where they are not explicit, and thus, from Dzong-ka-ba's viewpoint, such a qualification can also be understood as intended by Nāgārjuna's concluding verse in the *Treatise* when he spoke of the abandonment of all views.

For Dzong-ka-ba and his followers, Mādhyamika, far from being either scepticism or agnosticism aimed at either refuting all views or, at least, refraining from any views, is a positive system directed towards the development of a particular view – the view of the middle way, the view of emptiness. Unlike Murti's opinion, "The Mādhyamika develops his characteristic 'middle position', which is really no position, by a trenchant criticism of the various systems and points of view, especially the Abhidharma position,"[205] for them, the view of the middle way is a positive meditative realization. It is developed after lengthy engagement in reasonings, such as those found in Nāgārjuna's *Treatise*, that are directed primarily not at other tenet systems but at the practitioner's own innate misconceptions. In the opening remarks of the "Great Exposition of Special Insight," Dzong-ka-ba calls the view of emptiness an "indispensible prerequisite" for special insight (see below, p.158) and descriptions of its development can be found in the meditation manuals of the Ge-luk tradition.[206]

From within the threefold division of wisdoms arisen from hearing, thinking, and meditating, the view of emptiness is a conviction, gained by means of the wisdoms of hearing and thinking, that "self", or "inherent existence" cannot be found.

It is not merely a verbal statement of such, but a decisive ascertainment based upon repeated seaching with the various types of analysis. The Fifth Dalai Lama says:[207]

> When the "I," which previous to now seemed to be perceivable by the eye and graspable by the hand as a true existent, is not found and is just vacuous, this is said to be the initial finding of the Mādhyamika view.

He continues:

> This initial generation of the Mādhyamika view is not actual special insight; however, like a moon on the second day of the month it is a small finding of the view. At that time, if you have no predispositions for emptiness from a former life, it appears that a thing which was in the hand has suddenly been lost. If you have predispositions, it appears that a lost jewel which was in the hand has suddenly been found.

The attainment of this view is a significant milestone in spiritual development.

MĀDHYAMIKAS HAVE NO THESES

The idea that Mādhyamikas have no theses has even more support among Western writers than does the idea that they have no views, and a list of those who express it in one form or another would include the majority of contemporary scholars – among others, Frederick Streng, B.K. Matilal, Mervyn Sprung, Karl Potter, Jacques May, T.R.V. Murti, Guy Bugault, Fritz Staal, Peter Fenner, G.C. Nayak, Shotaro Iida, Hans Schumann, and Herbert Guenther.[208] In any brief summary of Mādhyamika, it is sure to be stated as one of the dominant aspects of the system. This is not surprising, since it also finds wide support in Buddhist literature itself; it is the position, for instance, of the late Indian Mādhyamika Jayānanda (fl. second half of the eleventh century) and is almost universal in the Tibetan Mādhyamika interpretations that Dzong-ka-ba was refuting in the *Great Exposition*.

In fact, Dzong-ka-ba himself is said to have held this for a time as he was struggling to gain understanding of Mādhyamika. However, he came to see this as faulty, upon being corrected by Mañjushrī himself his biography reports,[209] and Dzong-ka-ba devotes a lengthy section of the *Great Exposition* to this topic.[210] Since it will serve as the focus of a later volume of translation of that text, I will only summarize parts of that discussion here.[211]

The source quotes – by Nāgārjuna, Āryadeva, and Chandrakīrti – in support of the view that Mādhyamikas have no theses or system of their own are numerous and Dzong-ka-ba himself lays them all out in the *Great Exposition*.[212] The most famous is the verse from Nāgārjuna's *Refutation of Objections* (verse 29):[213]

> If I had any thesis,
> Then I would have that fault.
> Because I have no thesis,
> I am only faultless.

In another instance of considering Mādhyamika paradoxical if taken literally, Fritz Staal says, "Unless this statement itself is not a proposition, we have a paradox here. But if Nāgārjuna got caught in paradoxes and contradiction, he is not worse off than most philosophers."[214] However, Seyfort Ruegg, defending Nāgārjuna from Staal's attribution of paradox, says:[215]

> But this sentence is not a *pratijñā* in Nāgārjuna's sense; for in his usage *pratijñā* denotes an assertion and more specifically a thesis (e.g. of an inference or syllogism) which seeks to establish something. What Nāgārjuna is saying here, then, is surely not that he is not uttering a meaningful sentence (something that would be not merely paradoxical but quite

> absurd), but rather that he is not propounding a proposition claiming probative force concerning the (positive or even negative) own being (*svabhāva*) of any thing. Whatever other logical problems may arise in connexion with Nāgārjuna's procedure in this respect, there would appear to be no paradox here at all.

Ruegg defends Nāgārjuna from Staal's charge of paradox by saying that one must understand the specific import of his statement, making a distinction between merely making meaningful statements about things and a technical meaning of the term "thesis". Dzong-ka-ba's defense of Nāgārjuna is similar. He says that clearly Nāgārjuna could not be saying that Mādhyamikas do not have any position, or any system, for then no one could claim to be a Mādhyamika or to establish points through citing passages from the writings of Nāgārjuna, Chandrakīrti, and so forth. Even if one, trying to be free from assertions, says that all presentations are only from others' point of view, this too is illogical, for even saying that much is an assertion, and thus one is not free from assertions.[216] Further, there are many cases in the writings of both Nāgārjuna and Chandrakīrti of the positive term "assert".[217] Two examples from Nāgārjuna can be found in chapter five of the translation: his *Sixty Stanzas of Reasoning* says:[218]

> Those who assert dependently
> [Arisen] things as not real but
> Not unreal, like a moon in water,
> Are not captivated by [such wrong] views.

And his *Praise of the Supramundane [Buddha]* (*'jig rten las 'das par bstod pa, lotātītastava*, 22) says:

> You [Buddha] asserted that whatever arises
> Dependently is empty;
> That there are no self-powered things
> Is your unequalled lion's roar.

Thus, Dzong-ka-ba does not accept that Nāgārjuna, Āryadeva, and Chandrakīrti intend a blanket denial of all assertions or positions. He also points out that when Chandrakīrti defends the Mādhyamikas from charges of nihilism, he does not say, "We are not nihilists because we make no assertions at all," but rather says, "We are not nihilists because we assert dependent-arising."[219]

Dzong-ka-ba also does not accept that Mādhyamikas reject all "theses" (*dam bca'*, *pratijñā*) when thesis is used as a technical logical term indicating one of the components of a syllogism (*sbyor ba*, *prayoga*), and he cites as an example Chandrakīrti's referring in the *[Auto]commentary on the "Supplement to (Nāgārjuna's) 'Treatise on the Middle Way'"* to the four "theses" – that a thing does not arise from itself, other, both, or neither.[220] Hence, Dzong-ka-ba has to explain the context of statements seeming to suggest a denial of having any theses and show how the scope of the negation is limited. Here, we will consider just the passage from the *Refutation of Objections:*

> If I had any thesis,
> Then I would have that fault.
> Because I have no thesis,
> I am only faultless.

Ruegg, with his statement that in this passage from the *Refutation of Objections* Nāgārjuna "is not propounding a proposition claiming probative force concerning the (positive or even negative) own being (*svabhāva*) of any thing," perhaps goes farther than does Dzong-ka-ba. For Dzong-ka-ba, this is a discussion *not* of having or not having theses in general, but of having or not having a *thesis of inherent existence*, as can be understood from the context of the statement within the argument in the *Refutation of Objections*.[221] A Mādhyamika has just said, "Phenomena do not exist inherently," and the opponent has answered, "In that case, if the words of your thesis inherently exist, then this contradicts your statement that all phenomena do not inherently exist. If they do not inherently exist, they cannot refute inherent existence." Such is an expression of the basic position of the Proponents of True Existence, that whatever exists must inherently exist and that whatever does not inherently exist, since for them it would not exist at all, is incapable of performing a function such as refutation. The meaning of Nāgārjuna's response is that if he asserted that the words of such a thesis existed inherently, he would have the fault of contradicting his thesis of no inherent existence; however, since he does not assert such, he does not have that fault.

The way in which Ruegg goes farther than does Dzong-ka-ba is in saying that Nāgārjuna is not making a statement concerning the positive *or negative* own-being (*svabhāva*) of any thing. According to Dzong-ka-ba, Nāgārjuna *is* making a statement concerning negative own-being. He is refuting inherent existence (*svabhāva*) and hence establishing the negative of it – the absence of inherent existence. For Dzong-ka-ba, inherent existence and no inherent existence, that is, the absence of inherent existence, are a dichotomy.[222] Something must be one or the other, and asserting a phenomenon that is neither of those two is "senseless babble". Thus Nāgārjuna, by refuting inherent existence, is establishing the absence of inherent existence, and Dzong-ka-ba cites in support of his view a passage from Nāgārjuna's *Refutation of Objections* (26cd):[223]

> If no inherent existence were overturned,
> Inherent existence would be thoroughly established.

Therefore, some of the statements which appear to reject all theses are to be understood as intending a rejection of all theses of inherent existence. Others, particularly those by Chandrakīrti which are found in chapter one of the *Clear Words* in the course of Chandrakīrti's refutation of Bhāvaviveka, have to do with the context of a particular debate and revolve around the question of how a particular opponent is being refuted. Chandrakīrti takes the position that opponents must be refuted on their own terms and thus the thesis that is implied by an absurd consequence need not be one asserted by oneself, but merely that which is forced on opponents by their own other assertions.[224] Thus T.R.V. Murti's statement:[225]

> He [the Mādhyamika] is a prāsangika – having no tenet of his own and not caring to frame a syllogism of his own. He [the Mādhyamika] has no reasons and examples which he believes to be true. Every endeavour of the Mādhyamika is, therefore, exhausted in reducing the opponent's position to absurdity on principles and consequences which the opponent himself would accept.

is from Dzong-ka-ba's viewpoint a case of confusing how Mādhyamikas argue with particular opponents with what Mādhyamikas themselves assert.

Syllogisms are not rejected *per se*, only autonomous syllogisms (*rang rgyud kyi sbyor ba*, *svatantra-prayoga*). In fact, syllogisms can be found throughout the writings of the Indian Mādhyamikas, even in those of Nāgārjuna, and thus Dzong-ka-ba and his Ge-luk-ba followers would have no quarrel with Shohei Ichimura who, however, treats this as a new and potentially controversial discovery;[226] they have long asserted it.

David Eckel, seeing a historical progression, takes the interesting position that Nāgārjuna proceeds only in response to claims made by his opponents, and "refuses to be drawn by their arguments into making positive assertions." He then sees Bhāvaviveka as making a significant step when he says in the *Blaze of Reasoning* (*rtog ge 'bar ba*, *tarkajvālā*, ch.3) "Our position is 'emptiness of intrinsic nature' and since this is the nature of things, we are not guilty of vitaṇḍā [just attacking without setting forth any counter position]." Eckel concludes:[227]

> Bhāvaviveka manages to deal with the objection but only at serious cost to the integrity of Nāgārjuna's method. He is now willing to admit something

> Nāgārjuna fought hard to resist: he accepts "emptiness of intrinsic nature" as a positive philosophical assertion.

Dzong-ka-ba does not see it this way. He does feel that Bhāvaviveka has made an admission that damages the integrity of Nāgārjuna's system: Bhāvaviveka's acceptance conventionally of establishment by way of an object's own character. But that is a different issue. (Dzong-ka-ba makes the case that Bhāvaviveka has done this, it being by no means obvious in Bhāvaviveka's writings, in great detail in a later section of the "Great Exposition" and in the *Essence of the Good Explanations*.) Dzong-ka-ba does not see Nāgārjuna as rejecting all theses and does see him as the first and foremost explicator of a positive doctrine set forth by the Buddha. Thus, he would not find any harm in Bhāvaviveka's statement, "Our position is 'emptiness of intrinsic nature'," and would not accept Eckel's distinction as valid, perhaps citing Nāgārjuna's rather similar statement in his *Praise of the Element of Qualities* (*chos kyi dbyings su bstod pa, dharmadhātustotra*), "The doctrine supremely purifying the mind is the absence of inherent existence."[228]

This concludes the consideration of points where Western interpretations of Mādhyamika differ significantly from that of Dzong-ka-ba insofar as those differences center around what the Mādhyamika reasonings refute. However, there are several further points requiring discussion as again they vary significantly from opinions widespread in the Western literature and reveal important aspects of Dzong-ka-ba's Mādhyamika interpretation. These, to be considered in the next chapter, are the role of reasoning in the attainment of the Mādhyamika goal and the ontological status of emptiness, the latter question leading to the related topics of Mādhyamika path structure and the ultimate goal.

6 *Dzong-ka-ba and Modern Interpreters III: Other Issues of Difference*

THE ROLE OF REASONING

Peter Fenner, in a recent article, "A Study of the Relationship Between Analysis (*vicāra*) and Insight (*prajñā*) Based on the *Madhyamakāvatāra*", begins with an assessment of Western opinions on this topic and concludes:[229]

> The problem at issue is essentially one of the *strength* of the relationship between analysis and insight, for it is difficult not to infer – given the prominent and extensive utilization of analysis in Mādhyamika texts *and* their placement of this in a genuine religious tradition – that analysis must have *some* bearing on at least some aspects of the Mādhyamikas' quest for spiritual liberation.

Thus Fenner sees the differing views of modern scholars as to the role of reasoning as reflecting an imputation of varying degrees of strength to that role, and he sees a chronological progression from weaker to stronger with Kenneth Inada as the weakest along with J.W. de Jong who also allows only a weak connection, and then progressively increasing degrees of strength in the views of T.R.V. Murti, Frederick Streng, Mervyn Sprung, Ashok Gangadean, and finally himself as advocating the strongest relationship of all. Although I accept Fenner's basic point about there appearing to be a chronological progression towards accepting a stronger relationship between reasoning and realization of emptiness, Fenner sees more imputation of strength to that relationship than do I; I see a gradual lessening of negativity, but not much statement of positive relationship.[230]

Fenner's thesis, which he believes to be Chandrakīrti's view, is that "analysis is meant to be a direct and efficient cause for producing the insight into emptiness, ... analysis induces the very realizations which are understood to free yogins from the bonds of *saṃsāra*".[231] This thesis is very much Dzong-ka-ba's viewpoint, although whether he would accept all that Fenner says is less clear, since Fenner's argument seems to be predicated on the fact that since thought is eventually transcended, thought is the object of negation, and this, as discussed above (see pp. 101–5), is not Dzong-ka-ba's view.[232]

Most of those who do not describe a strong relationship between reasoning and realization of emptiness do not dispute that the reasonings set forth by Nāgārjuna are soteriological in intent and have, in a religious sense, positive results. What seems to be in question is the mechanics of the process, specifically whether reasoning can lead *directly*, or *causally*, to wisdom (*jñāna*), knowledge of the highest reality, and the basis of such qualms seems to be twofold: one is the perception of analysis and meditation as two distinct and even incompatible activities; the other is the idea that emptiness, or reality, or, as some refer to it, the Absolute, is in no way whatsoever contactable by discursive thought.

Neither of these is Dzong-ka-ba's view. For him, reasoning and meditation are compatible: meditation is divided into two types, analytical and stabilizing, and reasoning can be included within analytical meditation. Not all analysis is meditation, and Dzong-ka-ba is aware of and warns against analysis being mere discursiveness, engaged in only out of love for argument. Nonetheless, a major component of meditation is analytical, and the analyses used are those such as are set forth in Nāgārjuna's *Treatise*.[233] As discussed in chapter one, the highest meditative states are unions of stabilization and analysis – of calm abiding and special insight – and thus it is not the case that the state of wisdom realizing emptiness is totally dissimilar from the analysis that has led to it. Also, although the supreme realization of emptiness is non-conceptual and non-dualistic in nature, prior to the attainment of such a level, emptiness can and, in fact, must be realized in a dualistic fashion by a conceptual consciousness.

Dzong-ka-ba's views on these points are undoubtedly heavily influenced by Kamalashīla's three *Stages of Meditation* and, even more, by the epistemological treatises of Dignāga and Dharmakīrti, and, in fact, in this instance he does not have explicit statements from Nāgārjuna or Chandrakīrti to cite in his support. Kamalashīla's arguments against the Chinese monk Hva-shang Mahāyāna provide the Indian Mādhyamika sources for the general framework of the need for both stabilizing and analytical meditation and the central role of reasoning in the attainment of wisdom. For instance, Kamalashīla says in the second of his *Stages of Meditation*:[234]

> The conceptuality of one who does not cultivate individual analysis on the entityness of things with wisdom, but cultivates only just an abandonment of mental application will never be reversed. Also, such a person will never realize non-entityness due to not having the illumination of wisdom. For, the Supramundane Victor himself said that when the fire of knowing the real just as it is arises from correct individual analysis, like the fire of sticks rubbed together, the wood of conceptuality is burned.

However, most of the specifics of how conceptual and non-conceptual realization relate to each other, and of how conceptual realization is developed to a level of non-conceptual understanding come from the epistemological tradition. The justification for the application of this general framework to the question of realization of emptiness is supplied by Bhāvaviveka's explanation of different etymologies for the term "ultimate truth" (*don dam bden pa, paramārthasatya*) and from elaborations on Bhāvaviveka's meaning by Kamalashīla and Shāntarakṣhita.[235]

The starting point for Dzong-ka-ba's integration of these is that "analysis", or "reasoning", is not, for him, an amorphous concept but refers to reasoning consciousnesses.[236] As such, it can be included within the systematization for dealing with minds, or consciousness. Not primarily for others, not merely, as Frederick Streng seems to indicate, "practical means for influencing other people who may be forced, by their own canons of validity, to analyze the co-dependent nature of their bases for knowledge,"[237] reasoning is to enhance the practitioner's own mental development. It is used within a formal process of logic to develop an inferential consciousness (*rjes dpag, anumāna*). Inference is necessarily conceptual, but can with repeated meditative familiarization be brought to a level of non-conceptual direct perception (*mngon sum, pratyakṣa*).[238] This is yogic direct perception (*rnal 'byor mngon sum, yogi-pratyakṣa*), one of the four types of direct perception described by Dignāga and Dharmakīrti,[239] and when directed towards emptiness is a non-dualistic cognition in which subject and object are fused like water poured in water. The content of the two types of realization – conceptual and non-conceptual – is the same, for their object, emptiness, is the same; also both can be called "reasoning consciousnesses". These facts allow for the continuity between the two even though they are very different in terms of manner of cognition and in potency as antidotes to the misconception of inherent existence, direct perception being tremendously more powerful.

THE STATUS OF EMPTINESS

What makes it possible for Dzong-ka-ba to include realization of emptiness within this schematization of the role of reasoning is the fact that for him emptiness exists. Far from being neither existent nor non-existent, or indeterminate, or merely a linguistic convention, emptiness is an existent (*yod pa*, *bhāva*), an object of knowledge (*shes bya*, *jñeya*), an object (*yul*, *viṣaya*), a phenomenon (*chos*, *dharma*), for all of these terms are synonymous in the Ge-luk epistemological schema. This position is controversial not only in terms of Western scholarship on Mādhyamika (contradicting the opinions of Étienne Lamotte, Jacques May, Edward Conze, Frederick Streng, Richard Robinson, Douglas Daye, G.C. Nayak, Mervyn Sprung, and Fernando Tola and Carmen Dragonetti among others)[240] but was, and is, also disputed by other Tibetan traditions.[241]

Dzong-ka-ba's case that emptiness exists is based on his equating a number of terms – emptiness (*stong pa nyid*, *śūnyatā*), ultimate truth (*don dam bden pa*, *paramārthasatya*), [final] nature (*rang bzhin*, *svabhāva*), reality (*chos nyid*, *dharmatā*), and suchness (*de nyid* or *de kho na nyid*, *tattva*). Unlike J.W. de Jong, who sees these as merely metaphors,[242] for Dzong-ka-ba these are equivalents; whatever is the one is the other, and he finds it legitimate to apply a discussion of such things as existence and so forth carried out in terms of one to another. Hence, in the *Great Exposition*, he uses Nāgārjuna's discussion in chapter fifteen of the *Treatise on the Middle Way* of the inherent, or final, nature (*rang bzhin*, *svabhāva*) and Chandrakīrti's discussion of the same topic in his *[Auto]commentary on the "Supplement to (Nāgārjuna's) 'Treatise on the Middle Way'"* as the locus for his proof that ultimate truth, that is, emptiness, exists.[243]

As Dzong-ka-ba sees it, Nāgārjuna indicates in chapter fifteen, the Analysis of *Svabhāva* (*rang bzhin*), two distinct meanings of the term *svabhāva*: one is *inherent existence*, the object of negation, which does not exist in the least; the other is emptiness, the *final nature* of each and every phenomenon.[244] Final nature is what Dzong-ka-ba, following Chandrakīrti, sees as intended by the last two lines of the second stanza of chapter fifteen:[245]

> It is not reasonable that an [inherent, or final] nature (*svabhāva*)
> Arise from causes and conditions.
> If it did arise from causes and conditions
> That [inherent, or final] nature would be something made.
>
> How could it be suitable
> For an [inherent, or final] nature to be "made"?
> An [inherent, or final] nature is non-fabricated
> And does not depend on another. (XV.1–2)

Numerous modern interpreters, not distinguishing in this way two separate meanings for *svabhāva*, see such passages as paradoxical,[246] whereas for Dzong-ka-ba, again, paradox and even misunderstanding are avoided by a careful delineation of terminology.

Having identified the referent of the *svabhāva* in the last two lines of the above stanzas as the final nature of phenomena, Dzong-ka-ba finds in Chandrakīrti's *[Auto]commentary on the "Supplement to (Nāgārjuna's) 'Treatise on the Middle Way'"* a definite statement that this final nature exists. Chandrakīrti says:[247]

> Does a nature, as asserted by the master [Nāgārjuna], that is qualified in such a way [as described in XV.2cd, which Chandrakīrti has just cited] exist? The "reality" (*chos nyid, dharmatā*) extensively set forth by the Supramundane Victor – "Whether the Tathāgatas appear or not, the reality of phenomena just abides" – exists. Also, what is this "reality"? It is the nature (*rang bzhin, svabhāva*) of these eyes and so forth. And, what is the nature of these? It is their non-fabricatedness, that which does not depend on another, their entity which is realized by knowledge free from the dimness of ignorance. Does it exist or not? If it did not exist, for what purpose would Bodhisattvas cultivate the path of the perfections?

> Why would Bodhisattvas initiate hundreds of difficulties for the sake of realizing reality?

After citing the above passage to show that emptiness exists, Dzong-ka-ba immediately makes explicit that he is *not* saying that it inherently exists and cites in support of this a passage from Chandrakīrti's *Clear Words*:[248]

> That which is the non-fabricated fundamental entity [abiding] ineluctably in fire even over the three times, that which is not the later arising of something which did not arise before, that which does not depend on causes and conditions like the heat of water or here and there or long and short, is called the "[final] nature". Does such a self-entity (*rang gi ngo bo*, *svarūpa*) of fire exist? By way of its own entity it does not exist and also does not not exist. Though it is so, in order to dispell the fear of listeners it is said upon imputation, "It exists conventionally."

Dzong-ka-ba concludes, "Thus [Chandrakīrti] refutes that the nature [of things] is established by way of its own entity and says that it exists conventionally."[249] For Dzong-ka-ba, emptiness is not an absolute. He grants it the status of an existent, but does not reify it to anything more than that. Although emptiness is the final nature of all phenomena, it no more inherently exists than does any other phenomenon. Thus, he would disagree with statements such as T.R.V. Murti's saying, "Tattva or the Real is something in itself, self-evident and self-existent," or Mervyn Sprung's contention, ". . . what is real . . . is precisely what the everyday world lacks . . . the real (*tattva*) which is *paramārtha-satya* (Ultimate Truth) can be said to be *svabhāva*, i.e., real in its own right," or B.K. Matilal's belief that "[The Mādhyamika] denies that the ultimate truth can be relative or that existence can be dependent on anything else."[250]

Dzong-ka-ba explains that the "non-fabricated" and "not depending on another" which are qualities of the final nature that is emptiness mean, respectively, not newly produced in the sense of something that did not exist before newly arising and not depending on causes and conditions.[251] Thus, for him, emptiness is not absolute, not real in itself, not self-existent, not independent in the sense of being non-relative. This he takes to be the meaning of Nāgārjuna's statement (XIII.7):[252]

> If there were anything not empty,
> Then something empty would also exist.
> If there is not anything not empty,
> How could the empty exist?

In other words, if things other than emptiness inherently existed, then emptiness would inherently exist as well; in that those things do not inherently exist, how could emptiness do so?

Emptiness is the final nature of phenomena, is, one might say, the substratum underlying phenomena, but it is not ontologically distinct from them in the sense of having a different status of existence. All – emptinesses and the phenomena qualified by emptiness – are equally without inherent existence.

Similar to Venkata Ramanan's statement, ". . . the relativity of the relative is not its ultimate nature; to cling to *śūnyatā* or relativity as itself absolute is the most serious of errors,"[253] Dzong-ka-ba calls the view that suchness, or emptiness, truly exists "an awful view of permanence",[254] and feels that such error is the referent of Nāgārjuna's verse (which follows immediately after the one cited just above), "The Conquerors said that emptiness eradicates all views; those who view emptiness were said to be incurable." If emptiness, the antidote to the misconception of inherent existence, is adhered to as inherently existent, then there is no hope. Dzong-ka-ba cites Buddhapālita's commentary on Nāgārjuna's *Treatise*:[255]

> Others cannot overcome the conceptions of those who conceive that emptiness is an [inherently existent] thing. For example, if you tell someone, "I have nothing," and that person then says, "Give me that nothing," how could you cause that person to enter into conceiving that you have nothing?

Just as the *bhāva* (*dngos po*) that Nāgārjuna refutes with respect to things other than emptiness must be understood to mean *svabhāva* (*rang bzhin*), inherent existence, and not mere existence, so must it also be understood with regard to emptiness. The fault is not in viewing emptiness, but in viewing it as an *inherently existent* thing.

In the context of his refutation of those who negate too much and refute the existence of conventional phenomena, Dzong-ka-ba cites a verse from Nāgārjuna's *Treatise on the Middle Way* (XXIV.14):[256]

> For whom emptiness is suitable,
> All is suitable;
> For whom emptiness is not suitable,
> All is not suitable.

He explains at that point that "suitable" (*rung ba*, *yujyate*) means "exists", and he demonstrates extensively in the *Great Exposition* how and why conventional phenomena "exist". Just as much as "suitable" applied to conventionalities means exists, so much so does it in terms of emptiness. The existence of emptiness makes possible the existence of everything else, for it is because phenomena are empty of inherent existence that they can be produced, developed, can function, and so forth. Furthermore, religious practice and the religious goal are possible and purposeful only if emptiness exists. Dzong-ka-ba quotes a sūtra that was cited by Chandrakīrti in the *[Auto]commentary on the "Supplement to (Nāgārjuna's) 'Treatise on the Middle Way'"*:[257]

> Child of good lineage, if the ultimate did not exist, behavior for purity would be senseless, and the

> arising of Tathāgatas would be senseless. Because the ultimate exists, Bodhisattvas are said to be skilled with respect to the ultimate.

He concludes that this sūtra proves that the ultimate truth exists because:[258]

> 1 if the ultimate truth did not exist, performing practice for the sake of the purity of the final nirvāṇa would be senseless
> 2 since realization of the ultimate by trainees would not occur, Buddha's coming to the world in order that trainees might realize the ultimate would be senseless
> 3 the great Conqueror Children would not be skilled in ultimate truths.

Emptiness as an object is distinct from the subject realizing it, and thus, unlike for many such as T.R.V. Murti, who says that the Mādhyamika "is convinced of a higher faculty, Intuition (*prajñā*) with which the Real (*tattva*) is identical,"[259] emptiness and wisdom (*shes rab*, *prajñā*) are different. Dzong-ka-ba acknowledges that a distinction of subject and object is not experienced at the time of direct realization of emptiness since this is a non-dualistic cognition in which the two are fused like water in water and must be posited as different from the viewpoint of some other conventional consciousness.[260] However, he maintains that they are nonetheless distinct, and by distinguishing ontological fact from psychological reality, Dzong-ka-ba is able to maintain a usage of terminology that unravels many difficult passages.[261]

His main source for this differentiation is Bhāvaviveka's explanation in his *Blaze of Reasoning* (*rtog ge 'bar ba*, *tarkajvālā*) of three different meanings of "ultimate" (*don dam*, *paramārtha*). (Whereas some Western interpreters see Bhāvaviveka as having made a significant departure from Nāgārjuna in laying out his different etymologies,[262] Dzong-ka-ba does not; this is one aspect of Bhāvaviveka's commentary that he accepts without criticism.) *Paramārtha* can mean "highest object" – emptiness – or "object of the highest" – object of the highest consciousness, that realizing emptiness. In both these cases the term refers to the object, emptiness. In Bhāvaviveka's third meaning, it indicates that which is concordant with the ultimate; this refers to the consciousness realizing emptiness, and, at another point in the *Blaze of Reasoning*, Bhāvaviveka specifies that not only can the term ultimate refer to a consciousness, but it can be used for both non-conceptual realization of emptiness and for conceptual understandings.[263]

Thus, it is made explicit at this point in the Mādhyamika commentarial tradition that the object, emptiness, and the subject, the wisdom realizing emptiness, are distinct and that emptiness can be an object of a mind – not merely of non-conceptual wisdom, but even of conceptual understanding. Dzong-ka-ba does not comment on this latter point as being a significant departure from Nāgārjuna's thought, perhaps because he sees it as a natural outflow from Nāgārjuna's emphasis on reasoning: if reasoning, a conceptual process, is the technique used to attain a non-conceptual realization of emptiness, it is only logical that there would be conceptual realizations of emptiness prior to attaining the level of non-conceptuality. Of course, conceptual realization of emptiness is a far lesser attainment than non-conceptual realization, and this is emphasized by those statements in the literature that would seem to exclude conceptual realization altogether. Nonetheless, for Dzong-ka-ba, it is an integral part of the process.

PATH STRUCTURE

A final point that warrants discussion is the tendency among many modern interpreters to equate "ultimate truth" with "ultimate state" and, as a consequence, for there to be no way to incorporate into the Mādhyamika system the path structure descriptive of progress towards the attainment of Buddhahood. T.R.V. Murti equates realization of emptiness with

Buddhahood – he says, "Prajñā is Nirvāṇa – the state of freedom. It is also the attainment of Buddhahood,"[264] and he sets forth an interpretation that reawakens the sudden versus gradual enlightenment controversy:[265]

> The Mādhyamika conception of Philosophy as Prajñāpāramitā (non-dual, contentless intuition) precludes progress and surprise. Progress implies that the goal is reached successively by a series of steps in an order, and that it could be measured in quantitative terms. Prajñā is knowledge of the entire reality once for all, and it does not depend on contingent factors as a special faculty, favourable circumstances or previous information. A progressive realisation of the absolute is thus incompatible.... The concept of progress is applicable to science, not to philosophy. It is however, possible to conceive of the progressive falling away of the hindrances that obstruct our vision of the real. But there is neither order nor addition in the content of our knowledge of the real.

Karl Potter cites this passage of Murti's and says:[266]

> In this passage Murti seems to waver to a certain extent. He says that *prajñā* is not reached by steps, but adds that it is possible to see it as a progressive series providing we do not draw the wrong inferences from that way of looking at the matter. This wavering is symptomatic of the issues which divide Nāgārjuna's Mādhyamika descendants. It would seem that what we may call the "pure" Mādhyamika position holds the no-progress interpretation, but there *are* attempts to construe the gaining of insight, *śūnya*, *nirvāṇa*, freedom – for these are the same, according to Nāgārjuna – as a progressive approximation, too.

Potter seems to be taking the position that Nāgārjuna's system was one of "sudden enlightenment" and that the writings of subsequent Mādhyamika commentators who describe a more gradual development have fallen from Nāgārjuna's initial purity.

This is *not* Dzong-ka-ba's understanding. Dzong-ka-ba never addresses the sudden vs. gradual controversy as such. Even though the preponderance of modern scholarship considers the famous Sam-yay debate (also called the Council of Lhasa and the Council of Tibet by numerous scholars) to have been primarily a debate about just that controversy,[267] Dzong-ka-ba (who mentions it frequently) refers to it only as concerning how emptiness is to be meditated on – by a mere stopping of conceptuality, which he rejects, or with analysis. However, Dzong-ka-ba is very much in the gradualist camp in as much as he sees the attainment of enlightenment as a gradual process that involves the sequential eradication of progressively more subtle levels of obstructions.

This is not to say that Dzong-ka-ba would describe a "partial" realization of emptiness. When emptiness is realized, it is realized fully, even by a conceptual consciousness; further, it is said that at the time of direct realization of emptiness, even though it is realized in terms of a specific phenomenon, that realization is a realization of the emptinesses of all phenomena. Nonetheless, there are differences in the potency of the wisdom consciousness realizing emptiness; with repeated familiarization, the wisdom consciousness becomes stronger and able to eradicate more subtle afflictions, the removal of which demarcate progress towards enlightenment. Thus, the ultimate truth, emptiness, is not the ultimate state but is the object which, through being taken to mind again and again in combination with the practices of method, makes possible the attainment of the ultimate state.

From Dzong-ka-ba's viewpoint, Nāgārjuna, too, propounded gradual progress towards enlightenment, as evidenced by his lengthy discussion in the *Precious Garland* of the ten Bodhisattva grounds (*sa*, *bhūmi*), which clearly indicate a progressive development culminating in the attainment of Buddhahood, and by his dedication in the *Sixty Stanzas of Reasoning* in which he speaks of beings accumulating the collections of merit and wisdom so that they might attain the Truth and Form Bodies of a Buddha.[268]

However, Nāgārjuna does not lay out the details, or the mechanics, of this process. These the Ge-luk-ba tradition finds elsewhere, the main sūtra source being the *Sūtra on the Ten Grounds* (*mdo sde sa bcu pa*, *daśabhūmikasūtra*) and the main śāstra, or treatise, sources being Chandrakīrti's *Supplement to (Nāgārjuna's) "Treatise on the Middle Way"* and autocommentary, Maitreya's *Ornament for Clear Realization* (*mngon rtogs rgyan*, *abhisamayālaṃkāra*) and Haribhadra's commentary on it, as well as Asaṅga's *Levels of Yogic Practice* (*rnal 'byor spyod pa'i sa*, *yogācāryabhūmi*) and *Compendium on the Mahāyāna* (*theg pa chen po bsdus pa*, *mahāyānasaṃgraha*). Dzong-ka-ba's writings on this topic are primarily found in his *Golden Rosary of Eloquence*, his first major work, and in his *Illumination of the Thought*, a commentary on Chandrakīrti's *Supplement to (Nāgārjuna's) "Treatise on the Middle Way"*. The Ge-luk-ba tradition has subsequently developed a genre of separate works on path structure which are used as adjuncts to the study of Maitreya's *Ornament for Clear Realization*.[269]

The understanding derived from later sources undoubtedly colors Dzong-ka-ba's understanding of Nāgārjuna. However, in the absence of strong evidence to the contrary of Dzong-ka-ba's understanding and given that Maitreya's *Ornament for Clear Realization* is based on the Perfection of Wisdom Sūtras just as is Nāgārjuna's *Treatise on the Middle Way*, it is not necessarily the case that it has caused Dzong-ka-ba to distort Nāgārjuna's meaning.

A basic assumption Dzong-ka-ba makes about Nāgārjuna's meaning that is at variance with the opinion of Mervyn Sprung is that enlightenment is achieved *by way of* the realization of emptiness. Sprung writes, "Nāgārjuna's truth – that the way of things is not given in terms of being or nonbeing – can be realized only by an enlightened person."[270] This is exactly opposite of Dzong-ka-ba's view and would from his viewpoint make religious effort pointless. If only an enlightened being could realize emptiness, there would be no reason to make effort at realizing emptiness and no way for the unenlightened to reach that state. Realization of emptiness eradicates ignorance and its latencies; initial direct cognition of emptiness is the boundary line between being an ordinary being and being a Superior (*'phags pa*, *ārya*) and subsequent enhancements of that realization with resultant eradication of more and more subtle levels of ignorance are the demarcations of progress on the Bodhisattva grounds. Liberation, enlightenment, is attained with the complete removal of ignorance.

Similarly, Sprung's description of a Bodhisattva as "an enlightened being, transcendent and immanent,"[271] confuses one who has achieved the result with one who is working to achieve it. Only a Buddha is fully enlightened (Foe Destroyers can be said to have achieved the enlightenment of their respective vehicles but are not *fully* enlightened). Bodhisattvas are those working to achieve enlightenment by way of the Mahāyāna Vehicle. Becoming a Bodhisattva is not determined by one's realization of emptiness, but rather by one's motivation, and one is said to become a Bodhisattva, and attain the level of the Mahāyāna path of accumulation, at the time that one initially develops non-artificial, or spontaneous, experience of a mind that seeks unsurpassed enlightenment for the sake of others.[272]

Finally, related with the mixing of ultimate truth with ultimate state, many authors equate the ultimate with the "silence of the Āryas" spoken of in the writings of Nāgārjuna and Chandrakīrti and then suggest that silence, a non-dual, non-conceptual state, is the final goal of the Mādhyamika. For example G.C. Nayak says, "Candrakīrti's answer is simply meant to point out that silence is the highest end for a philosophically enlightened person."[273] This suggests a quietism that Dzong-ka-ba would not accept. The goal of a Mahāyānist is Buddhahood, and such is said explicitly by both Nāgārjuna and Chandrakīrti. A Buddha has no conceptuality it is true, but the special feature of Buddhahood is the ability simultaneously to perceive both emptinesses and conventional phenomena.[274] Without ever rising from non-dualistic meditative equipoise, a Buddha is able to teach living beings in the manner most appropriate for each and thus is the supreme source of help and happiness for others. The goal is not mere silence, but rather a state of active participation in which others can truly and effectively be helped.

CONCLUSION

These three chapters have demonstrated at considerable length ways in which Dzong-ka-ba's Mādhyamika interpretation differs significantly from much that can be found in current literature on the topic: For Dzong-ka-ba, Mādhyamika is not a refutation of merely other systems, of language, or of reasoning, nor is it a refutation of all conventionalities or all conceptuality; it is not a "systemless system" with no views or theses of its own, but rather is a positive system directed towards realization of the Mādhyamika view by means of a refutation of inherent existence, inherent existence being defined as independence, or an existence of things in their own right or from their own side. The Mādhyamika view is sought as an antidote to ignorance, the innate misconception that is the root cause of all the sufferings of cyclic existence, for through the removal of ignorance, a state of liberation can be attained.

For the purposes of this discussion, attention has been focused primarily on those points where Dzong-ka-ba's interpretation differs significantly from current Mādhyamika interpretations, and it must be emphasized that there are also many significant points of agreement between his and those interpretations. However, the differences are substantial and should not be minimized.

In some cases Dzong-ka-ba's interpretation may differ because he brings to it perspectives gained from topics of Buddhist philosophy, such as epistemology and the structure of the path, articulated subsequent to the time of Nāgārjuna. However, Dzong-ka-ba was very aware of his sources; he understood the need, if he was to succeed in his claim to be giving an authentic Mādhyamika interpretation, to base it on authentic Mādhyamika texts. Thus, he was careful to support each specific point of his Mādhyamika interpretation with citation of passages from the writings of Indian Mādhyamikas widely accepted to be valid proponents of the Mādhyamika tradition.

Dzong-ka-ba did not base his interpretation only on the writings of Nāgārjuna, but relied heavily on his later followers, Āryadeva, Buddhapālita, and, most of all, Chandrakīrti. Thus, those who think that a correct understanding of Mādhyamika must be sought solely from the writings of Nāgārjuna may not accept Dzong-ka-ba's basic approach. However, such an attitude seems unnecessarily limited, first because, to borrow a point from Alex Wayman,[275] it must be pointed out that Western interpreters who, in seeking to understand Mādhyamika, would disallow interpretations of Nāgārjuna by later Mādhyamika authors as being too late, too far removed from the subject, too likely to introduce their own opinions, and so forth, might just as well rule out themselves as well, since they are even later. Of course, it is important to distinguish between what was actually said by Nāgārjuna and what is later commentary; nonetheless to refuse the assistance of trained scholars close to Nāgārjuna and steeped in the same intellectual and cultural milieu seems both arrogant and short-sighted, to say nothing of unlikely to succeed. Furthermore, Mādhyamika is not just Nāgārjuna, even though he was the founder of the system, but is the tradition that evolved and matured based on his writings, which includes the works of Āryadeva, Buddhapālita, Bhāvaviveka, Chandrakīrti, Kamalashīla, Shāntarakṣhita, and others.

In any case, the majority of current scholarly opinion on Mādhyamika seems theoretically willing (past descriptions of Mādhyamika based only on Nāgārjuna's *Treatise on the Middle Way* and *Refutation of Objections* notwithstanding) to include all the various writings of Nāgārjuna as well as the writings of later Mādhyamikas in efforts to understand that system.

Thus, on the whole, Dzong-ka-ba was relying on much the same sources as are modern scholars. That is to say, most of the sources accepted by modern scholars (with the exception of those texts that have survived only in Chinese) were known and used by Dzong-ka-ba. However, the body of texts relied on by Dzong-ka-ba goes far beyond that worked on by any single contemporary scholar that I know of, simply because there is so much ground that has not yet been covered in the field of Buddhist Studies.

Dzong-ka-ba used all the works widely accepted as authentically by Nāgārjuna. He used Āryadeva's *Four Hundred* and Buddhapālita's commentary on Nāgārjuna's *Treatise on the Middle Way* as well as Bhāvaviveka's *Lamp for (Nāgārjuna's) "Wisdom"* and his *Blaze of Reasoning*. He relied heavily on Chandrakīrti's *Clear Words*, his *Supplement to (Nāgārjuna's) "Treatise on the Middle Way"*, Chandrakīrti's own commentary to the *Supplement*, his *Commentary on (Āryadeva's) "Four Hundred"*, his *Commentary on (Nāgārjuna's) "Sixty Stanzas of Reasoning"*, and his *Commentary on (Nāgārjuna's) "Seventy Stanzas on Emptiness"*.

Of those texts, the writings of Nāgārjuna have received considerable attention from Western scholars, and a significant advance in availability is represented by Christian Lindtner's recently published *Nāgārjuniana*, which brings together in one volume all those texts he considers to be authentically composed by Nāgārjuna – except for Nāgārjuna's *Treatise* and his *Precious Garland* – with edited texts in Tibetan as well as Sanskrit where available and including English translations of those works previously not translated into a major European language. The *Precious Garland* is available in English translation by Jeffrey Hopkins and Lati Rinbochay. However, there is not yet a reliable English translation of Nāgārjuna's *Treatise on the Middle Way* in spite of several attempts.[276]

As far as the writings of Aryadeva, Buddhapālita, and Bhāvaviveka are concerned, an English translation of Āryadeva's *Four Hundred* by Karen Lang is just now becoming available.[277] As Christian Lindtner says of Buddhapālita's and Bhāvaviveka's commentaries on Nāgārjuna's *Treatise*, these works "have not yet received the general recognition to which their merits entitle them," and thus far, only two out of twenty-seven chapters of Buddhapālita's commentary have been published in English translation[278] and none of Bhāvaviveka's, although three chapters (18, 24, and 25) are available in David Eckel's as yet unpublished doctoral dissertation, "A Question of Nihilism: Bhāvaviveka's Response to the Fundamental Problems of Mādhyamika Philosophy". Of the portions that pertain to Mādhyamika, all that has been published in English of Bhāvaviveka's *Blaze of Reasoning* and the *Heart of the Middle Way*, on which it is a commentary, is a substantial portion of chapter three, translated by Shotaro Iida in his *Reason and Emptiness*.[279]

Concerning Chandrakīrti's writings, except for the *Clear Words*, none of these has received thorough attention in the West, although in the case of the *Supplement* and its auto-commentary, the work of young scholars such as Peter Fenner and C.W. Huntington, Jr. begins to remedy that situation. Even the *Clear Words*, which is one of the Mādhyamika texts most studied by modern scholars, is not available in a complete one volume translation, but rather one must seek chapters from here and there in various European languages, and the same is true for Chandrakīrti's *Supplement* and its auto-commentary.[280] Of the others, there are as yet no published European language translations.

Thus, Dzong-ka-ba was working from a wider body of texts than are modern interpreters, but most would consider them all valid sources. This is not to suggest that upon studying those sources everyone would – or should – draw the same conclusions as did Dzong-ka-ba. However, access to them would enrich our understanding as we saw the sources that Dzong-ka-ba has chosen to emphasize. Given that Dzong-ka-ba was a rigorously trained scholar who devoted his life to the study of these topics, it is evident that his interpretation must be considered as we seek to penetrate the meaning of the Mādhyamika teachings. Further, given the many differences even among Mādhyamika interpretations current in Buddhist scholarship as well as the differences from the interpretation of a great Tibetan Mādhyamika whose works cannot be discounted by responsible scholars, it is clear that the topic of Mādhyamika studies has not yet been closed. Our present understanding of that system is not definitive.

A basic need is more translations into Western languages of the Mādhyamika texts we are seeking to understand. For, the system will not be truly and widely understood until more reliable translations of the Mādhyamika texts are available. An ongoing debate between members of the scholarly community working in areas touched on by this discussion is whether the best mode of procedure is careful, philological translation, neutral in tone and aimed at presenting as clearly as possible the thought of the original author, or whether what is needed are interpretive and judgmental studies providing access to these ideas through vocabularies familiar to the West, often through comparisons with Western thinkers or through the application of methods such as linguistic analysis, and so forth. I would argue that the latter, though worthwhile, can only be successful when based upon a more extensive body of material than currently exists, made available by the former approach, for otherwise such attempts are much too likely to be compromised by inaccurate or incomplete understanding of the primary source materials.

7 *Summation: Emptiness and Ethics*

In summation, it is important, in considering Dzong-ka-ba and his work, to have in mind the broad perspective of who and what Dzong-ka-ba was and what he sought to do. He was a philosopher but in a culture in which religion and philosophy are intertwined, and his use of philosophy was within a religious system. Dzong-ka-ba was not setting forth an abstract theoretical system but was making use of rational philosophy in the service of a religious goal. Further, within his role as a religious figure, Dzong-ka-ba was not formulating a new and radically different system, but rather was forging a coherent system from an existent body of material.

One of Dzong-ka-ba's great contributions was that he integrated what might be seen as potentially conflicting strands of the Buddhist tradition into a consistent system, massive, tremendously complex, but rationally ordered and graspable. A hallmark of Dzong-ka-ba's style in this endeavor was his commitment to common sense. He insisted that the whole system should fit together, that it should make sense. For him, there are no paradoxes.

Although a brilliant and innovative thinker, he did not just make up a system of his own invention that worked logically. Rather, in a sense, Dzong-ka-ba was working from a revealed tradition, in that the basic orientation towards reality, the assessment of the way things are, of how an individual practitioner is to come to realize this, and to what such realization leads, all come from the teachings of Buddha – things taught, according to the tradition, by a fully realized being who then showed his path to others. Further, each of Dzong-ka-ba's major points of interpretation are supported from the basic texts of the Buddhist tradition, either of Buddha himself or the great Indian commentators.

However, the tradition also places strong emphasis on analysis and reasoning, and thus there is a great deal of leeway for individual interpretation, refinement, and so forth.

Further, that Dzong-ka-ba's system is rationally ordered does not mean that all aspects of it are readily graspable by ordinary analysis and conceptuality. The heart of the system lies in non-verbal, non-dualistic meditative experiences. The religious system is structured around these experiences, and is, in fact, justified and validated by them; although that structuring is rational and logical, the basic thrust of the system is that at some point ordinary conceptuality must be transcended and a new level of experience achieved. How this is to be achieved is a major theme in Dzong-ka-ba's writings, since it is his assertion that a careful and correct use of reasoning and conceptuality can lead directly to non-conceptual realization. Still, it must be kept in mind that Dzong-ka-ba's is a system based upon and only fully realized by non-conceptual experiences gained only through prolonged religious practice and meditation.

Thus, Dzong-ka-ba was not writing abstract philosophy, but rather was seeking to provide a correct verbal understanding that could serve as a basis for further thought and meditation, as a result of which its truth could and presumably would be ascertained in profound meditative experience. His text is often personal in tone with frequent bits of direct advice, and he emphasizes again and again how very difficult it is to gain a correct understanding of the middle way. In spite of a great deal of abstraction and technical detail, he was not writing out of mere love for scholarly quibble but was setting forth an interpretation he hoped would be taken to heart and put into practice.

An important aspect that must be considered is the figure of Dzong-ka-ba himself. As quickly becomes apparent from reading the biographies relied on by the Ge-luk-ba tradition,[281] Dzong-ka-ba was more than a scholar. Although he studied throughout his life, training under numerous great teachers from all the different Tibetan orders that flourished during his lifetime, he was, above all, a religious practitioner. He was initiated into tantric teachings from a very young age, and maintained their practice throughout his life; he spent years in meditative retreats and engaged as well in many other religious techniques directed towards purification and the accumulation of merit, such as prostrations, circumambulation of holy places and shrines, ritual offerings, and so forth.

Many of the fine distinctions that characterize Dzong-ka-ba's Mādhyamika interpretation have to do with differences between varying levels of experience: for instance, the fact that in our ordinary state we cannot distinguish between mere existence and inherent existence; the fact that at a time of direct realization of emptiness, all conventional phenomena vanish, such that one might erroneously come to think that they did not exist at all; the fact that subsequent to realization of emptiness, a difference between existence and inherent existence can be known and one realizes conventional phenomena as like illusions, appearing to inherently exist whereas they do not in fact; and so forth. Dzong-ka-ba describes these different levels, setting forth verbal distinctions such as between existence and inherent existence, between not being seen by a consciousness and being seen to be non-existent by a consciousness. These cannot now be verified in experience, in that they are things whose final verification comes only upon the attainment of advanced levels of realization. Never directly said, but implicit, is the suggestion that Dzong-ka-ba had verified them for himself.

There is a considerable supramundane aspect to the figure of Dzong-ka-ba. The traditional biographies report that an important aid to Dzong-ka-ba's development of the insights that led to his Mādhyamika interpretation were meetings with Mañjushrī, the incarnation of wisdom, that took place initially with a yogi, the Lama U-ma-ba, serving as an intermediary, and later in direct conversation.[282] It was Mañjushrī who originally told him that what Dzong-ka-ba thought was the Mādhyamika view was no view at all – that is, who told him that he was holding just that sort of misunderstanding that Dzong-ka-ba expended so much effort in the portion of the "Great Exposition" translated here to refute. It was also Mañjushrī who told him to value conventionalities, thus leading to Dzong-ka-ba's emphasis on valid establishment which relies so much on the epistemological system of Dignāga and Dharmakīrti.

Dzong-ka-ba was considered by his contemporaries to have attained very high levels of spiritual realization and his reputation has only increased with the passage of centuries. However, a point worth making is that even though Dzong-ka-ba is accorded tremendous personal reverence by the tradition he founded, and to a certain extent has been "deified", sometimes called "the second Buddha" and often described as an incarnation of Mañjushrī, the embodiment of wisdom, this does not mean that his writings are accepted completely uncritically, any more than he accepted uncritically the Indian sources from which he worked.

The educational system in the Ge-luk-ba monasteries is based on critical analysis as embodied in a structure of formal debate. Monks debate each other for hours every day, taking all sides of all issues, so that at times they are vigorously defending Dzong-ka-ba's positions but at others are just as vigorously attacking them. In no way is Dzong-ka-ba's interpretation unquestionable just because he said it. To be accepted, his points must be able to withstand probing and penetrating attack. As a result of such analysis, there has developed a large body of commentarial literature that criticizes, defends, explains, and elaborates on the interpretations set forth by Dzong-ka-ba, portions of which form the basic textbooks of the Ge-luk-ba monastic universities.

Dzong-ka-ba's interpretive grid, his hermeneutic of consistency and coherence, is not without its price. Much of the shock value of the original Mādhyamika writings is lost.

There is not the spontaneity found in other Mādhyamika interpretations that focus on the transcendent quality of realization of emptiness, the sense of simply shifting perspective and turning away from mundane descriptions.

Even more serious than mere loss of spontaneity is the danger that, because Dzong-ka-ba chose to emphasize a verbal distinction between existence and inherent existence which cannot be realized in ordinary experience, people will miss the Mādhyamika message altogether. They will not understand that Mādhyamika is attacking and refuting our very sense of existence and, misled by the verbal emphasis on inherent existence, will see Mādhyamika as refuting something merely intellectual, "out there", not immediate. In spite of cautions from within the Ge-luk-ba tradition that inherent existence should not be seen as like a hat to be put on the head and then taken off again, it is almost impossible to read Dzong-ka-ba without falling into such error, and Dzong-ka-ba has been criticized on this point even from within the Ge-luk-ba tradition.[283]

Also, there is a question of emphasis, of whether Dzong-ka-ba truly reflected the intentions of the Indian Mādhyamika authors. His gridwork of system and consistency assumes similar intentions for those authors, even if they did not make such clear in their writings. In the absence of detailed and clear expositions, Dzong-ka-ba felt justified in basing key points of his interpretation on small and often passing comments, and at times the evidence is slim.[284] Because the Indian Mādhyamikas did not write detailed systematic exegesis of the sort that Dzong-ka-ba's interpretation assumes they would have accepted, we have no way to know if he is right or wrong in his assumption, if he drew out what was in their minds or if he has simply added his own ideas. On the one hand, it is certainly true that most writing is not done in the encyclopaedic fashion of setting down on paper all that one knows, thinks, and assumes; people tend to write thematically, addressing a particular question or argument, and much about an author's basic assumptions must be inferred from passing comments, argumentative structure, what is not said, and so forth. On the other hand, the Indian Mādhyamikas were brief, often cryptic, and maybe chose to write that way in a conscious rejection of excess systematization. It can be argued either way.

What is gained through Dzong-ka-ba's approach is an ability to posit validly established conventional truths. This then allows for an integrated system in which the earlier teachings and practices are supported and validated by the higher and, above all, one in which ethical norms are justified and maintained. It is essential for the system to preserve ethics, a valuing of correct actions based upon the Buddhist doctrine of *karma*, that virtuous actions lead to good results and non-virtuous ones to bad results. Ethics are the basis of the religious system as a whole; even more are they the religious basis of an individual, for one's deeds determine one's future experiences, and it is taught that a loss of belief in *karma* will lead to unethical actions which will bring about great personal suffering in the future. All Buddhist practices can be included within the threefold trainings (*bslab pa gsum*, *triśikṣā*) – the training in higher ethics, higher meditative stabilization, and higher wisdom – and the latter two can only be developed upon a foundation of the former. Dzong-ka-ba says:[285]

> As causes for gaining the view, you should take as a basis the pure maintenance of the ethics you have promised [to maintain], and thereupon strive by way of many approaches to accumulate the collections and purify obstructions and, relying on the wise, make effort at hearing and thinking.

The emphasis within the training in wisdom is on philsophical understanding that not only leads to release from cyclic existence, but also sustains and validates the training in ethics. Expressing concern about the difficulty of this, Dzong-ka-ba says:[286]

> Thus, in the system of the masters Buddhapālita and Chandrakīrti, inherent existence, that is, establishment by way of the object's own entity, is refuted even conventionally. Hence it appears to be very difficult to posit conventional objects. If one does not know how to posit these well, without damage [by reasoning], one does not gain ascertainment well with respect to the class of deeds whereby it appears that most fall to a view of deprecation.

To avoid the nihilism to which emptiness misunderstood easily leads, Dzong-ka-ba is cautious in teaching emptiness and in his interpretation always emphasizes the valid establishment of conventionalities. The special insight section of Dzong-ka-ba's *Great Exposition* comes only after 364 folios describing essential Buddhist practices. Similarly, in the Geluk-ba monastic universities, Mādhyamika is begun only after years of study built on a foundation of what are called "The Collected Topics of Valid Cognition" (*bsdus grwa*), in which all the different types and categories of phenomena are analyzed and learned, and also only after study of path structure. This suggests the importance of being strongly based in what *does* exist before one commences the Mādhyamika negations that seek to eradicate adherence to a seeming concreteness of phenomena that does not exist, so that subsequent to what may in experience seem a total denial of everything, there is something to be left as an illusion-like but validly established appearance.

Dzong-ka-ba says again and again that a compatibility of emptiness and conventional presentations is the uncommon characteristic of Mādhyamika:[287]

> Hence, the allowability of asserting all the presentations of cyclic existence and nirvāṇa – objects produced, producers, refutation, proof, and so forth – within the non-existence of even a particle of inherent existence, that is to say, establishment by way of

> [object's] own entities, is a distinguishing feature of Mādhyamika.

He also says that as long as realization of emptiness and realization of the ineluctable relationship between actions and their effects are not realized in such a way that the realization of the one assists and enhances the realization of the other, one has not yet realized the thought of the Buddha:[288]

> As long as the two, realization of appearances – the inevitability of dependent-arising –
> And realization of emptiness – the non-assertion [of inherent existence] –
> Seem to be separate, there is still no realization
> Of the thought of Shākyamuni Buddha.

The two realizations must be seen not only to work together, but to facilitate and enhance each other, and it is said that if it is not possible to realize both, then it is better to give up emptiness than to give up belief in karma, the cause and effect of actions. The present Dalai Lama has said:[289]

> Knowledge of the final mode of subsistence of phenomena must be within the context of not losing the cause and effect of actions conventionally; if in an attempt to understand the final mode of subsistence one lost the presentation of conventionally existent cause and effect, the purpose would be defeated. . . . It is so important to be able to posit and have conviction in cause and effect that it is said that between giving up belief in the cause and effect of actions and giving up belief in emptiness, it is better to give up the doctrine of emptiness.

Dzong-ka-ba would certainly agree. However, the purpose of Dzong-ka-ba's lengthy identification of the object of negation in the "Great Exposition of Special Insight" is to show that if the Mādhyamika system is correctly understood, there is no need to make that choice.

Part Two
Translation of a Portion of Dzong-ka-ba's *Great Exposition of the Stages of the Path*

The translation that follows includes Dzong-ka-ba's introduction to the topic of special insight and his general consideration of over-negation.

Introduction

As was explained earlier,[290] you should not be satisfied with a mere calm abiding that possesses the features of (1) *non-conceptuality*, that is, the mind's staying in accordance with your wish on the single object of meditation on which it has been set, whereby it stays where it is placed, (2) *clarity* which is free from laxity, and (3) *benefit*, that is, joy and bliss. Rather, having generated the wisdom that ascertains non-erroneously the meaning of suchness, you should cultivate special insight.

Otherwise, since such mere meditative stabilization is shared even with Forders, no matter how much you cultivate that mere [meditative stabilization], you will not be released from mundane existence in just the same way as the seeds of the afflictions are not abandoned through the paths of [Forders].[291] The first of Kamalashīla's [three works on the] *Stages of Meditation* (*sgom rim, bhāvanākrama*) says:[292]

> Having thus made the mind steady with respect to an object of observation, one should analyze with wisdom. For, through the arising of the illumination of knowledge, the seeds of obscuration are thoroughly abandoned. [365b] If this is not done, then just like Forders, one cannot abandon the afflictions through mere meditative stabilization. [The *King of Meditative Stabilizations*] *Sūtra* (*ting nge 'dzin gyi rgyal po, samādhirāja*, IX.36) says:[293]

> Although worldly persons cultivate meditative stabilization,
> They do not destroy the discrimination of self.
> For them the afflictions return and disturb [the mind],
> Just as Udraka[294] cultivated meditative stabilization here.

[In the scripture cited above] the phrase, "although [worldly persons] cultivate meditative stabilization" means "although [persons] cultivate a meditative stabilization possessing the features of non-conceptuality, clarity, and so forth as explained before". The phrase, "They do not destroy the discrimination of self," means that although they cultivate such, they cannot abandon the conception of self. The fact that the afflictions will still be generated due to not having abandoned the conception of self is indicated by "the afflictions return and disturb [the mind]".

Through what sort of cultivation is liberation attained? Immediately following [the above passage], the scripture, as was cited earlier,[295] says:

> If selflessness is analyzed with respect to phenomena
> [And if one meditates in accordance with that individual analysis,
> This is the cause of the fruit, the attainment of nirvāṇa.
> There is no peace through any other cause]. (IX.37)

[The first line means], "If, having analyzed individually phenomena which are selfless, one generates the wisdom understanding the meaning of selflessness . . .". [The second line,] "If one meditates [in accordance with] that individual analysis," refers to sustaining and meditatively cultivating the view of selflessness that has been gained. [The third line,] "That is the cause of the fruit, the attainment of nirvāṇa" means that such is the cause of attaining the fruit which is nirvāṇa, or liberation.

Can liberation be attained through cultivating some other path without that [wisdom realizing selflessness][296] in the way in which it is attained through cultivating it? [The fourth line of the above scripture] says, "There is no peace through any other cause", meaning that although one cultivates a path which is other than that [of the wisdom of selflessness], [366a] without that [wisdom] there is no pacification of suffering and the afflictions. This scripture teaching very clearly that only the wisdom of selflessness severs the root of mundane existence was quoted in Kamalashīla's *Mādhyamika Stages of Meditation*[297] in order to damage [the assertions of the Chinese abbot] Hva-shang. Therefore, you need to gain ascertainment with respect to this, for although even the Forder sages have many good qualities such as meditative stabilization, the clairvoyances, and so forth, since they do not have the view of selflessness, they cannot cross beyond cyclic existence even a little. In this way, the *Scriptural Collection of Bodhisattvas* (*byang chub sems dpa'i sde snod, bodhisattvapiṭaka*), which was cited earlier, says that:[298]

> One who, without knowing the meaning of suchness explained in the scriptures, is satisfied with mere meditative stabilization might develop manifest pride[299] [mistaking] that for the path cultivating the profound meaning. Through that, such a person is not released from cyclic existence. I, thinking that, said that one who hears another will be released from aging and death.

The Teacher himself explains clearly [i.e., interprets] his own thought [when he earlier made the statement that one who hears another will be released from aging and death. Buddha explains that] "hear another" means to hear the explanation of selflessness from another. Therefore, it is unquestionable that Buddha said, "hears another," in order to stop the conception that [the profound view] is generated naturally without the hearing and thinking involved in listening to the meaning of selflessness from an external holy spiritual guide.

In general, of all the Conqueror's scriptures, some teach suchness directly and even those that do not directly teach it indirectly only flow to and descend to it. [366b] Since the darkness of obscuration is not overcome until the illumination of the knowledge of suchness arises, but is overcome when that arises, through mere calm abiding which is a one-pointedness of mind there is no pure exalted wisdom and the darkness of obscuration is also not overcome. Therefore, you should unquestionably seek wisdom, thinking, "I will seek the wisdom ascertaining the meaning of selflessness – suchness." Kamalashīla's middle *Stages of Meditation* says:[300]

> Then, having achieved calm abiding you should cultivate special insight, and should think, "All the sayings of the Supramundane Victor were spoken well; they all manifestly illuminate suchness directly or indirectly and flow to suchness. If one knows suchness, one will be separated from all nets of views, just as darkness is cleared away through the arising of illumination. Through mere calm abiding there is no pure exalted wisdom, and also the darkness of the obstructions is not cleared away. However, if, with wisdom, one meditates on suchness well, there will be very pure exalted wisdom and suchness will be realized. Only through wisdom are the obstructions thoroughly abandoned. Therefore, I, abiding in calm abiding, will, by means of wisdom, thoroughly seek suchness. I will not be satisfied with mere calm abiding." What is this suchness? Ultimately all things are just empty of the two selves – of persons and phenomena.

From among the perfections, suchness is realized by the perfection of wisdom. Since it cannot be generated by concentration and so forth [367a], you should, without mistaking mere concentration for the perfection of wisdom, generate wisdom. The *Sūtra Unravelling the Thought* (*mdo sde dgongs 'grel, saṃdhinirmocana*)[301] says:

> "Supramundane Victor, through what perfection should a Bodhisattva apprehend just the non-entityness of phenomena?"
>
> "Avalokiteshvara, it should be apprehended through the perfection of wisdom."

Thinking this, the *Sūtra of Cultivating Faith in the Mahāyāna* (*theg pa chen po la dad pa sgom pa'i mdo*, *mahāyānaprasādaprabhāvana*), quoted earlier, says that:[302]

> If they do not abide in wisdom, I do not say that those who have faith in the Bodhisattva Mahāyāna are delivered, no matter how much they engage in the Mahāyāna.

1 *The Interpretable and the Definitive*

Since this is so, [that is, since it is the case that mere calm abiding is not sufficient and special insight is needed], with respect to the second,[303] how to train in special insight, there are four parts: fulfilling the prerequisites for special insight, the divisions of special insight, how to cultivate special insight in meditation, and the measure of having achieved special insight through meditative cultivation.

FULFILLING THE PREREQUISITES FOR SPECIAL INSIGHT

Relying on scholars who know non-erroneously the essentials of the scriptures, you should hear the stainless textual systems. The generation of the view realizing suchness by means of the wisdoms of hearing and thinking is the indispensable prerequisite for special insight, for, if you do not have a view decisive with respect to the meaning of the mode of being [i.e., emptiness], you cannot generate the special insight realizing the mode [of being of phenomena, emptiness].

Also, such a view must be sought by one who, without relying on [scriptures] whose meaning requires interpretation, relies on those of definitive meaning.[304] Therefore, you must understand the meaning of scriptures of definitive meaning through having come to know the difference between that requiring interpretation and the definitive. [367b]

Furthermore, if you do not rely on treatises which are

commentaries on [Buḍdha's] thought by the great valid openers of the chariot-ways, you are like a blind person without a guide going in a direction of fright. Hence, you must rely on non-erroneous commentaries on [Buddha's] thought. On what sort of commentator on [Buddha's] thought should you depend? Since the Superior Nāgārjuna, renowned in the three levels [below, above, and on the earth], was very clearly prophesied by Buddha, the Supramundane Victor, himself in many sūtras and tantras as commenting on the profound meaning free from[305] all extremes of existence and non-existence, the essence of the teaching, you should seek the view realizing emptiness based on his texts.[306]

With respect to these [prerequisites for special insight], there are three parts: identifying scriptures requiring interpretation and scriptures of definitive meaning, the history of commentary on Nāgārjuna's thought, and how to settle the view of emptiness.

Identifying Scriptures Requiring Interpretation and Scriptures Of Definitive Meaning

Those who wish to realize suchness must rely on the Conqueror's scriptures. However, due to the various thoughts of trainees, the scriptures vary. Hence you might wonder in dependence on what sort [of scripture] you should seek the meaning of the profound. Suchness should be realized through reliance upon scriptures of definitive meaning.

Should you wonder, "What sort [of scripture] is of definitive meaning and what sort requires interpretation?", this is posited by way of the subjects discussed. Those teaching the ultimate are held to be scriptures of definitive meaning [368a] and those teaching conventionalities are held to be scriptures whose meaning requires interpretation. In that vein, the *Teachings of Akṣhayamati Sūtra* (*blo gros mi zad pas bstan pa*, *akṣayamatinirdeśa*) says:[307]

> What are sūtras of definitive meaning? What are sūtras whose meaning requires interpretation? Those which teach [within] establishing conventionalities are called sūtras of interpretable meaning.[308] Those which teach [within] establishing the ultimate are called sūtras of definitive meaning. Those teaching [about various objects by way of] various words and letters are called sūtras of interpretable meaning. Those teaching that which is profound, difficult to view, and difficult to realize are called sūtras of definitive meaning.

Question: What is the mode of teaching a conventionality, through the teaching of which [a sūtra] comes to be of interpretable meaning, and what is the mode of teaching the ultimate, through the teaching of which [a sūtra] comes to be of definitive meaning? This also is indicated very clearly in that sūtra. It says:[309]

> Those which teach things that must be expressed by way of various words [such as] self, sentient being, living being, the nourished, creature, person, born from Manu, child of Manu, agent, and feeler, in the manner of [there being an inherently existent] controller, for instance, when there is no [inherently existent] controller are called sūtras of interpretable meaning.
>
> Those which teach the doors of liberation – emptiness, signlessness, wishlessness, no [ultimate] composition, no [ultimate] production, not being [ultimately] produced, no [ultimate] existence of sentient beings, no [ultimate] existence of living beings, no [ultimate] existence of persons, and no [ultimate] existence of controllers – [368b] are called sūtras of definitive meaning.

Since it is said thus that those which teach selflessness, no [ultimate] production, and so forth in the manner of eliminating elaborations are of definitive meaning and those which teach self and so forth are of interpretable meaning, you should know that selflessness, no [ultimate] production, and so forth are the ultimate, and production and so forth are conventional. The *King of Meditative Stabilizations Sūtra* (VII.5) also says:[310]

> One knows as instances of sūtras of definitive meaning [those which teach]
> In accordance with the emptiness explained by the Sugata.
> One knows as of interpretable meaning all those [verbal] doctrines [i.e., sūtras]
> In which "sentient being", "person", and "creature" are taught.

Kamalashīla's *Illumination of the Middle Way* (*dbu ma snang ba*, *madhyamakāloka*) says:[311]

> Therefore, it should be understood that, "Only those which discuss the ultimate are of definitive meaning and the opposite are of interpretable meaning." Also, the *Ornament Illuminating the Exalted Wisdom Operating in the Sphere of All Buddhas* (*sangs rgyas thams cad kyi yul la 'jug pa ye shes snang ba'i rgyan*, *sarvabuddhaviṣayāvatārajñānālokālaṃkāra*) says, "That which is a definitive object is the ultimate," and also the *Teachings of Akṣhayamati Sūtra* teaches with respect to no [ultimate] production, and so forth, "[they] are definitive objects." Therefore, it is definite that only no [ultimate] production and so forth are called "ultimates".

Therefore, [Nāgārjuna's] Madhyamaka "Collections of Reasonings" as well as the commentaries on their thought are to be held as teaching the definitive meaning just as it is because they extensively settle the ultimate which is free from all the collections of elaborations such as [inherently existent] production, cessation, and so forth.

Why are those two that teach such [369a] called "[sūtras] of interpretable meaning" and "[sūtras] of definitive meaning"? Since [a sūtra's] meaning cannot be interpreted otherwise, it is called that of which the meaning is definite or of definitive meaning, for since that meaning is the meaning of suchness, it is the finality of that which is to be settled. It cannot be interpreted beyond that and cannot be interpreted as something other than that by some other person because it possesses valid proofs. Thus Kamalashīla's *Illumination of the Middle Way* says:[312]

> What is [a sūtra] of definitive meaning? That of which there is valid cognition and which makes an explanation in terms of the ultimate, for it cannot be interpreted by another [person] as something aside from that.

Through this statement one can implicitly understand [scriptures] of interpretable meaning. Those of which the meaning is to be interpreted, or which require interpretation, are those which, their meaning being unsuitable to hold just as it is, must be interpreted as some other meaning through explaining [their] thought. Or, they are those of which the meaning, although all right to hold as literal, is not the final suchness, and one must still seek that suchness as something other than that [mere appearance].

Qualm: Since sūtras of definitive meaning are literal, then if, "production does not exist," "persons do not exist," and so forth appear in those sūtras, one must hold that production and persons utterly do not exist; otherwise it would absurdly follow that since those [sūtras] would not be literal, they would require interpretation.

[*Answer*:] This does not appear to be correct, for when the teacher [Buddha] who is the speaker refutes production and so forth in that way, there are seen to be many sūtras of definitive meaning in which the qualification "ultimately" is affixed; [369b] and, if there occurs one affixing of the qualification, then since it is a common attribute it must be affixed even at points where it does not occur. Further, since [no production ultimately] is the suchness of those phenomena, how could that which teaches such not be of definitive meaning? Otherwise, through refuting the generality "production", instances [of production such as] words would also have to be refuted whereby there could also be no presentation even of sūtras of definitive meaning which teach such.

Therefore, you should know that the fact that it is not suitable to hold as literal what is taught in a few isolated words, out of context, not connecting it with what is said before or after in the general run of a sūtra or treatise, does not destroy [that text's] being a scripture of definitive meaning. You also should know that even though what is taught on the level of the words is suitable to be held as literal, it is not that it [necessarily] is not of interpretable meaning [that is, literal texts can still require interpretation].

2 *Reliable Sources*

THE HISTORY OF COMMENTARY ON NĀGĀRJUNA'S THOUGHT

What is the chronology of the stages of commenting on the thought of Nāgārjuna, who commented non-erroneously on the scriptures – the Perfection of Wisdom Sūtras and so forth – which teach in this way that all phenomena are without any inherently existent production, cessation, and so forth? Even the great Mādhyamikas such as the masters Buddhapālita, Bhāvaviveka, Chandrakīrti, and Shāntarakṣhita took Āryadeva to be valid like the master [Nāgārjuna]. Therefore, since both the father [Nāgārjuna] and his [spiritual] son [Āryadeva] are sources for the other Mādhyamikas, earlier [Tibetan scholars] used the verbal convention [370a] "Mādhyamikas of the model texts" (*gzhung phyi mo'i dbu ma pa*)[313] for those two and used the verbal convention "partisan Mādhyamikas" (*phyogs 'dzin pa'i dbu ma pa*) for the others.

Certain earlier spiritual guides said that when names are designated by way of how they posit conventionalities, Mādhyamikas are of two types: Sautrāntika-Mādhyamikas (*mdo sde spyod pa'i dbu ma pa*), who assert that external objects exist conventionally, and Yogāchāra-Mādhyamikas (*rnal 'byor spyod pa'i dbu ma pa*), who assert that external objects do not exist conventionally.[314] They are also of two types when names are designated by way of how they assert the ultimate: Reason-Established Illusionists (*sgyu ma rigs grub pa, māyopamādvayavādin*), who assert that a composite of the two, appearance and emptiness, is an ultimate truth, and Proponents of Thorough Non-Abiding (*rab tu mi gnas par smra ba, sarvadharmāpratiṣṭhānavādin*), who assert that the mere elimination of elaborations with respect to appearances is an ultimate truth.[315] They asserted that the former of these two are the masters Shāntarakṣhita, Kamalashīla, and so forth.

The verbal conventions "illusion-like" and "thoroughly non-abiding" are asserted also by some Indian masters.

Indeed, in general, some Indian and Tibetan masters who claimed to be Mādhyamikas did make such assertions, but what is to be settled here are just the systems of the great Mādhyamikas who are followers of the master Nāgārjuna. Who could explain [all] the subtle [distinctions]? Moreover, the statement by the great translator Lo-den-shay-rap (*blo ldan shes rab*, 1059–1109) that positing Mādhyamikas as twofold by way of their mode of asserting the ultimate is a presentation generating delight in the obscured is very good.[316]

For, their assertion appears to be an assertion that [for the Reason-Established Illusionists] the mere object that is comprehended by an inferential reasoning consciousness [370b] is an ultimate truth whereas it is said in both Shāntarakṣhita's *Ornament for the Middle Way* (*dbu ma rgyan, madhyamakālaṃkāra*) and Kamalashīla's *Illumination of the Middle Way* (*dbu ma snang ba, madhyamakāloka*) that the object comprehended by a reasoning consciousness is designated "ultimate" due to being concordant with an ultimate truth. Also, since the other great Mādhyamikas do not assert that the mere object which is an elimination through reasoning of elaborations is an ultimate truth, [these earlier scholars' explanation of Thoroughly Non-Abiding Mādhyamikas] is not good.

With respect to this [chronology of the commentaries on Nāgārjuna's thought], the master Ye-shay-day (*ye shes sde*) explains that the masters, the Superior [Nāgārjuna] and his [spiritual] son [Āryadeva], did not make clear in their Mādhyamika treatises whether external objects do or do not exist and that after them the master Bhāvaviveka, refuting the system of Consciousness-Only, presented a system in which external objects exist conventionally. Then the master Shāntarakṣhita set forth a different Mādhyamika system which teaches, in dependence on Yogāchāra texts, that external objects do not exist conventionally and also teaches that the mind is without inherent existence ultimately. Thereby, two forms of Mādhyamika arose, and the former is designated Sautrāntika-Mādhyamika and the latter Yogāchāra-Mādhyamika.[317]

The chronology is evident as [Ye-shay-day says]. However, although the master Chandrakīrti asserts that external objects exist conventionally, he does not do so in accordance with other proponents of tenets, and thus it is unsuitable to call him a "Sautrāntika[-Mādhyamika]". Similarly, the assertion that he accords with the Vaibhāṣhikas is also very unreasonable.[318]

The usage by scholars of the later dissemination [of the Buddhist doctrine] to the land of snowy mountains [Tibet] of the two verbal conventions, Prāsaṅgika and Svātantrika, [371a] for Mādhyamikas accords with Chandrakīrti's *Clear Words*. Hence, you should not think that it is their own fabrication.[319]

Therefore, [Mādhyamikas] are limited to the two, those who do and do not assert external objects conventionally, and also, if names are designated by way of how the view ascertaining emptiness, the ultimate, is generated in the continuum, they are limited to the two, Prāsaṅgikas and Svātantrikas.

Following which of those masters should one seek the thought of the Superior [Nāgārjuna] and his [spiritual] son [Āryadeva]? The great elder [Atisha] took the master Chandrakīrti's system as chief, and seeing this, the great earlier lamas of these precepts [of the stages of the path to enlightenment] who followed him also held that system to be chief.

The master Chandrakīrti [himself] saw the master Buddhapālita from among the commentators on Nāgārjuna's *Treatise on the Middle Way (dbu ma'i bstan bcos, madhyamaka-śāstra)*[320] as elucidating completely the thought of the Superior

[Nāgārjuna]. Thereupon, he took that system as his basis, and also taking many good explanations from the master Bhāvaviveka and refuting those that appeared to be a little incorrect, he commented on the thought of the Superior [Nāgārjuna]. Seeing the commentaries of those two masters [Buddhapālita and Chandrakīrti] to be most excellent with regard to explaining the texts of the Superior [Nāgārjuna] and his [spiritual] son [Āryadeva], here the thought of the Superior [Nāgārjuna] will be settled following the master Buddhapālita and the glorious Chandrakīrti.

3 *The Stages of Entry Into Suchness*

HOW TO SETTLE THE VIEW OF EMPTINESS [371b]

This has two parts: the stages of entry into suchness and the actual settling of suchness. With respect to the first, what is the nirvāṇa [i.e., the passing from sorrow], the suchness that is here the object of attainment, and by way of what sort of entry into suchness, that is, methods for attaining it, does one enter? The extinguishment in all forms of the conceptions of [inherently existent] I and mine, by means of pacifying all appearance of the varieties of internal and external phenomena as [their own] suchness whereas they are not [their own] suchness, along with their predispositions, is the suchness that is here the object of attainment, the Truth Body.

The stages of how you enter into that suchness are as follows: First, having contemplated the faults and disadvantages of cyclic existence and turned the mind [from it], you should generate a wish to cast that [cyclic existence] aside. Then, seeing that it will not be overcome if its cause is not overcome, you research its root, thinking about what the root of cyclic existence is. Thereby, upon inducing ascertainment from the depths with respect to the way in which the view of the transitory, or ignorance, serves as the root of cyclic existence, you need to generate a non-artificial wish to abandon it.[321]

Next, seeing that overcoming the view of the transitory depends upon generating the wisdom realizing the non-existence of the self conceived by that [view], you see that it is necessary to refute that self. Gaining ascertainment in dependence on scriptures and reasonings which damage the existence and prove the non-existence of that self is the indispensable method for one who is intent upon liberation. Having gained the view ascertaining in this way that the self and mine do not in the least have inherent existence, [372a] through familiarizing with that meaning the Truth Body will be attained.

Chandrakīrti's *Clear Words* says:[322]

> If all these afflictions, actions, bodies, agents, and effects are not [their own] suchness but nonetheless – like a city of scent-eaters (*dri za*, *gandharva*) and so forth – while not being [their own] suchness appear to childish [common persons] in the aspect of [being their own] suchness, then what is here suchness and how does one enter to that suchness?
>
> *Answer*: Here suchness is the extinguishment in all forms of the apprehension of [inherently existent] I and the apprehension of [inherently existent] mine with respect to the internal and external on account of the non-apprehension of internal and external things. With respect to entry into suchness, [my own] *Supplement to (Nāgārjuna's) "Treatise on the Middle Way"* (VI.120) says:
>
> > Yogis see with their minds that all afflictions
> > And faults arise from the view of the transitory
> > And having realized that the self is the object of
> > That [view], refute self. (VI.120)
>
> Thus, [a description of how to enter suchness] should be sought from such statements there.

[Chandrakīrti's *Clear Words*] also says:[323]

> Yogis who wish to enter into suchness and wish thoroughly to abandon all afflictions and faults investigate, "What does this cyclic existence have as its

> root?" When they thoroughly investigate in this manner, they see that cyclic existence has as its root the view of the transitory collection, and they see that the self is the object of observation of that view of the transitory collection. They see that the view of the transitory is abandoned through non-observation of self and that [372b] through abandoning that [view], all afflictions and faults are overcome. Hence, at the very beginning they investigate with respect to just the self – "What is this 'self', the object of the conception of self?"

Although many reasonings refuting inherent existence were set forth with respect to immeasurable individual subjects, when yogis [initially] engage [in practice], they meditate in an abridged way within settling the lack of inherent existence in terms of I and mine. The master Buddhapālita says that this is the meaning of the eighteenth chapter of Nāgārjuna's *Treatise on the Middle Way*, and in dependence on his statement, the master Chandrakīrti presents [the stages of entry into suchness thus in his *Supplement to (Nāgārjuna's) "Treatise on the Middle Way"*]; the teachings on the selflessness of the person in Chandrakīrti's *Supplement to (Nāgārjuna's) "Treatise on the Middle Way"* also are extensive explanations of just the eighteenth chapter [of Nāgārjuna's *Treatise*].

Qualm: Is this not [an occasion of] teaching the mode of entry into the suchness of the Mahāyāna? In that case, the mere extinguishment of the conception of [inherently existent] I and mine is unsuitable to be the suchness that is to be attained.[324] Also, since within the mere settling of the absence of inherent existence of I and mine, there is no settling of the selflessness of phenomena, it is not suitable to posit [just the former] as the path for entering into suchness.

Response: There is no fault. For, with respect to the extinguishment, in all ways, of the conception of I and mine, there are two types of which [the first,] the utter abandonment of the afflictions in the manner of their not being produced again, does indeed exist among Hīnayānists; however, [the second,] the abandonment by way of utter non-apprehension of all signs which are elaborations [even of the appearance of inherent existence] with respect to external and internal phenomena, is the Truth Body. Furthermore, when you realize that the self does not exist inherently, [373a] the conception also that the aggregates which are the branches of that [self] exist inherently is overcome. It is like the way in which when a chariot is burned, the wheels and so forth which are its parts are also burned.[325] Chandrakīrti's *Clear Words* says:[326]

> Those wishing liberation analyze whether [the self] which is imputed dependently, which serves as a basis for the strong adherence to self by those possessing the error of ignorance, and of which the five aggregates are seen to be the appropriated, has the character of the aggregates or does not have the character of the aggregates. When it is analyzed in all ways, those wishing liberation do not observe [a self having the character of the aggregates] and therefore, in those [aggregates, as Nāgārjuna's *Treatise* (XVIII.2ab) says:]
>
> > If the self itself does not exist
> > How could the mine exist?
>
> Because the self is not observed, also the mine,[327] the basis of designation as the self, will very much not be observed. When a chariot is burned, its parts also are burned and thus are not observed; similarly, when yogis realize the self as not [inherently] existent, they will realize the selflessness also of the mine, the things that are the aggregates.

Thus [Chandrakīrti] says that when you realize lack of inherent existence with respect to the self, you realize the lack of self, that is, inherent existence, also with respect to the mine, the aggregates.

Also, Chandrakīrti's *[Auto]commentary on the "Supplement to (Nāgārjuna's) 'Treatise on the Middle Way'"* says:[328]

> Because of error due to apprehending an intrinsic entity in forms and so forth, [Hearers and Solitary Realizers following Hīnayāna tenets] do not realize even the selflessness of persons. [373b] This is because they are apprehending [as inherently existent] the aggregates which are the basis of designation as self. [Nāgārjuna's *Precious Garland* (*rin chen phreng ba*, *ratnāvalī*, 35ab)] says:
>
> > As long as one conceives the aggregates [to be inherently existent]
> > So long does one conceive an [inherently existent] I with respect to them.

Thus it is said that if you do not realize the aggregates to be without inherent existence, you do not realize the selflessness of the person.

Qualm: If just that awareness realizing the absence of inherent existence with respect to the person realizes that the aggregates are without inherent existence, there would be the fault that the two awarenesses realizing the two selflessnesses would be one. [However] since the two, phenomena and persons, are separate, the two awarenesses realizing the lack of inherent existence of those two are also separate, like, for example, the awarenesses realizing the impermanence of a pot and of a pillar. [On the other hand] if just that awareness realizing the person to be without inherent existence does not realize the aggregates to be without inherent existence, then how can you posit [the meaning of Chandrakīrti's statement] that when one realizes the selflessness of the person, one realizes the lack of inherent existence of the aggregates?

[*Answer*:] Since we do not assert the first of those questions [that just that awareness realizing the lack of inherent existence with respect to the person realizes the aggregates as without inherent existence], I will explain the latter question. Although just that awareness realizing the person as without inherent existence does not engage in the thought, "The aggregates do not inherently exist," that awareness is able, without relying on another [reasoning or consciousness], to induce an ascertaining consciousness which ascertains that the aggregates lack inherent existence, whereby it is able to eliminate the superimpositions that superimpose inherent existence on the aggregates. Therefore, [Chandrakīrti] says that when the person is realized to lack inherent existence, the aggregates also are realized to lack inherent existence. This should be known in accordance with the statement in the *Buddhapālita Commentary on (Nāgārjuna's) "Treatise on the Middle Way" (dbu ma rtsa ba'i 'grel pa buddha pā li ta, buddhapālitamūlamadhyamakavṛtti)*:[329]

> Those which the so called "self" possesses are called the "mine". [374a] That self does not [inherently] exist, and if it does not [inherently] exist, how would these [mine which are the objects of use] of that [self] be correct?

For example, when you ascertain that a son of a barren woman does not occur, that awareness does not engage in the thought, "The ears of that [son of a barren woman] and so forth do not exist," but it is able to eliminate superimpositions conceiving the ears of that [son of a barren woman] to exist. Similarly, when you ascertain that the self does not exist as [its own] suchness, the conception that the eyes and so forth of that [self] exist as [their own] suchness is overcome.

Qualm: Even the Proponents of True Existence[330] of our own Buddhist schools who assert that the person is imputedly existent do not assert that the person is ultimately established. Therefore, even they would realize that eyes and so forth are without inherent existence.[331]

Response: In that case, since they assert gross objects such as eyes, sprouts, and so forth to be imputedly existent, they would realize them as without inherent existence.

[*Objector*:] That is so.

Response: If you accept such, it would contradict your own assertion [that Proponents of True Existence do not realize the lack of inherent existence of phenomena]. Also, it would not be necessary [for Mādhyamikas] to prove [to Proponents of True Existence] that sprouts and so forth do not truly exist. Further, complete paths of virtuous and non-virtuous actions are posited as continuums, and if [the Proponents of True Existence] asserted continuums to lack inherent existence, then there would be no purpose in [the Proponents of True Existence] disputing the Mādhyamikas' propounding that these, like dreams, lack true existence as is set forth in Haribhadra's *Clear Meaning Commentary* (*'grel pa don gsal*, *sphuṭārthā*):[332]

> [The Proponents of True Existence say to us Mādhyamikas:] If [all phenomena] are like dreams, then the ten non-virtues, giving, and so forth would not exist, whereby would not even the waking state become like the state of sleep?

Thus, there is a great disparity between ultimate and conventional establishment or non-establishment in the Proponents of True Existence's own system [374b] and conventional and ultimate establishment or non-establishment in the Mādhyamika system. Hence it is not at all contradictory that those things asserted by the [Proponents of True Existence] as conventionalities would, from the Mādhyamika perspective [have to be said to] be ultimately established and those things asserted by [the Proponents of True Existence] as ultimately established would, for the Mādhyamikas, come to be conventionally established. Therefore, these should be differentiated.

Furthermore, although the imputedly existent person of these [Proponents of True Existence] and the imputedly existent person of this master [Chandrakīrti] are similar in name,[333] the meaning is not the same. For, this master assserts that these [Proponents of True Existence] do not have the view realizing the selflessness of the person. This is because he asserts that if one has not realized the selflessness of phenomena, one has not realized the selflessness of the person. Therefore, since this master asserts that as long as one has not forsaken the tenet that the aggregates are substantially existent, one conceives the person also to be substantially existent, [he says that] these [Proponents of True Existence] do not realize that the person does not ultimately exist.

4 *Misidentifying the Object of Negation*

The actual settling of suchness has three parts: identifying the object of negation by reasoning, whether that negation is done by means of consequences or autonomous syllogisms, and how, in dependence on doing that, to generate the view in your continuum.

IDENTIFYING THE OBJECT OF NEGATION BY REASONING

This has three parts: the reason why it is necessary to identify well the object of negation, refuting other systems which [engage in] refutation without having identified the object of negation, and how the object of negation is identified in our own system.

THE REASON WHY IT IS NECESSARY TO IDENTIFY WELL THE OBJECT OF NEGATION

Just as, for example, in order to ascertain that a certain person is not here, you must know the person who is not here, [375a] so in order to ascertain the meaning of "selflessness", or "non-inherent existence", you also must identify well that self, or inherent existence, which does not exist. For, if the [meaning] generality of the object of negation does not appear well [to the mind], you will also not unerringly ascertain the negative of it. For, Shāntideva's *Engaging in the Bodhisattva Deeds* (*byang chub sems dpa'i spyod pa la 'jug pa, bodhisattvacaryāvatāra*, IX.140ab) says:[334]

> Without contacting the entity (*dngos po, bhāva*) which is imputed
> One will not apprehend the absence of that entity.

With respect to this, although the different features of the objects of negation are limitless, if they are negated from their root, which brings together [all of] the objects of negation, all the objects of negation will also be refuted. Moreover, if, not doing the refutation in terms of the final subtle essential of the object of negation, there is some remainder left over, you will fall to an extreme of existence and will generate a manifest conception of [the true existence of] things whereby you cannot be released from cyclic existence. If you engage in negation going much too far, without holding to the measure of the object of negation, you will lose belief[335] in the stages of the dependent-arising of cause and effect whereby you will fall to an extreme of annihilation and due to just that view will be led to a bad transmigration. Therefore, it is important to identify well the object of negation, for if it is not identified, you will unquestionably generate either a view of permanence or a view of annihilation.

SECOND, REFUTING OTHER SYSTEMS WHICH [ENGAGE IN] REFUTATION WITHOUT HAVING IDENTIFIED THE OBJECT OF NEGATION

This has two parts: refuting an overly broad identification of the object of negation and refuting a too limited identification of the object of negation.

FIRST, REFUTING AN OVERLY BROAD IDENTIFICATION OF THE OBJECT OF NEGATION

This has two parts: stating [others'] assertions and showing their incorrectness.

FIRST, STATING [OTHERS'] ASSERTIONS [375b]

Nowadays, most who claim to propound the meaning of the middle way[336] say that all phenomena ranging from forms through to exalted-knowers-of-all-aspects are refuted by the reasoning analyzing whether production and so forth are or are not established as [their own] suchness because when reasoning analyzes any [phenomenon] which is asserted, there does not exist even a particle that is able to bear analysis and also because all four alternatives – existence, non-existence, and so forth – are refuted and there does not exist any phenomenon not included in those.

Moreover, [they assert that] a Superior's exalted wisdom perceiving suchness perceives production, cessation, bondage, release, and so forth as not existing in the least, and since those must be just as they are comprehended by that [exalted wisdom], production and so forth do not exist.

[They say that] if one asserts production and so forth, are these or are these not able to bear analysis by a reasoning analyzing suchness with respect to them? If these are able to bear [analysis], then there would exist things able to bear analysis by reasoning, whereby there would be truly existent things. If they are unable to bear analysis, how is it feasible that objects which have been negated by reasoning exist?

Similarly, [these misinterpreters of Mādhyamika say that] if production and so forth are asserted to exist, are these or are these not established by valid cognition? In the former case, since an exalted wisdom perceiving suchness perceives production as non-existent, it is not feasible that [production] be established by it. Further, if one asserts that [production] is established by conventional eye consciousnesses and so forth, because it is refuted [in sūtra and by Chandrakīrti as cited below] that those *are* valid cognizers, it is not feasible that they be valid cognizers establishing [production and so forth]. The *King of Meditative Stabilizations Sūtra* (IX.23) says:[337]

> The eye, ear, and nose [consciousnesses] are not valid cognizers.

The tongue, body, and mental [consciousnesses] are
also not valid cognizers;
If these sense [consciousnesses] were valid cognizers,
[376a]
Of what use to anyone would the Superiors' path be?

Also, Chandrakīrti's *Supplement to (Nāgārjuna's) "Treatise on the Middle Way"* (VI.31a) says,[338] "In all respects worldly [consciousnesses] are not valid cognizers." An assertion that [production, and so forth] exist even though they are not established by valid cognition is not feasible, for one oneself does not assert such and it is also not reasonable.

[Those proponents also say] that if one were to assert production, since it is not asserted ultimately, it would have to be asserted conventionally, but that is unreasonable, for Chandrakīrti's *Supplement to (Nāgārjuna's) "Treatise on the Middle Way"* (VI.36) says:[339]

Through that reasoning through which [it is seen] on
the occasion of analyzing suchness
That production from self and other are not reasonable,
[It is seen] that [production] is not reasonable even
conventionally.
If so, through what [reasoning] would your production be [established]?

Thus, [they feel that Chandrakīrti] says that the reasoning refuting ultimate production also refutes conventional [production].

Furthermore, [they say that] if one asserts production even though there is no production from any of the four – self, other, and so forth – then, in the refutation of ultimate production, it would not be refuted through refutation upon investigating the four alternatives because there would exist a production which was not any of those [four].

[Also they say that] if production were from one from among the four alternatives, then it must be from other since one does not assert the other three [production from self, both self and other, or causelessly]. However, that is not reasonable,[340] for Chandrakīrti's *Supplement to (Nāgārjuna's) "Treatise on the Middle Way"* (VI.32d) says,[341] "Production from other does not exist even in the world." Because of that [they say that] one should not, in the refutation of production, affix even the qualification "ultimate", for Chandrakīrti's *Clear Words* refutes the affixing of the qualification "ultimate".

Among those [who assert such] some say that they do not assert production and so forth even conventionally whereas some do assert [those] as existing conventionally. However, all of them [376b] stretch out their necks and [boldly] explain: "A refutation by reasoning of an inherent existence, that is to say, an establishment by way of their own entities,[342] in phenomena is undeniably the system of this master [Chandrakīrti], for inherent establishment is refuted in terms of both truths; if there is thus no inherent existence, then what does exist? Therefore, affixing the qualification 'ultimate' to the object of negation is the system of only the Svātantrika-Mādhyamikas."

5 *The Uncommon Feature of Mādhyamika*

Second, showing that those [assertions] are incorrect, has two parts: showing that those systems refute the uncommon distinguishing feature of Mādhyamika and showing that the damages expressed do not overwhelm [our position].[343]

FIRST, SHOWING THAT THOSE SYSTEMS REFUTE THE UNCOMMON DISTINGUISHING FEATURE OF MĀDHYAMIKA

This has three parts: identifying the distinguishing feature of Mādhyamika, how those systems refute this [distinguishing feature], and how a Mādhyamika responds to them.[344]

FIRST, IDENTIFYING THE DISTINGUISHING FEATURE OF MĀDHYAMIKA

With respect to this, Nāgārjuna's *Sixty Stanzas of Reasoning* (*rigs pa drug cu pa*, *yuktiṣaṣṭikā*, stanza 60) says:[345]

> Through this virtue may all beings,
> Upon accumulating the collections of merit and exalted wisdom,
> Attain the two excellences
> That arise from merit and exalted wisdom.

In accordance with this statement, the attainment – by trainees who progress by way of the supreme vehicle [the Mahāyāna], on the occasion of the fruit – of the two, the excellent Truth Body and the excellent Form Body, depends upon accumulating on the occasion of the path, as explained earlier [in the discussion of Bodhisattvas' training, not included in this translation], the immeasurable collections of merit and exalted wisdom, that is, on inseparable method and wisdom. This, in turn, definitely relies upon attaining ascertainment with respect to the varieties, an ascertainment induced from the depths with respect to the relationship of cause and effect, [an understanding] that such and such beneficial and harmful effects arise from such and such causes, these being conventional causes and effects. [377a] It also definitely relies on attaining ascertainment with respect to the mode [of existence], an ascertainment gained from the depths that all phenomena are without even a particle of inherent existence, that is to say, establishment by way of their own entities. For, without both of these, a training from the depths of the heart in the complete factors of the path of both method and wisdom will not occur.

Not mistaking the essentials of the path causing attainment of the two bodies in that way at the time of the effect depends upon settling the view of the bases; the mode of settling the view upon which this depends is the gaining of ascertainment with respect to the two truths as has just been explained. With respect to this, except for Mādhyamikas, other persons do not know how to explain these [two truths as interpreted by Mādhyamikas] as non-contradictory, seeing them as only a collection of contradictions. However, those skillful persons possessing subtle, wise, and very vast intelligence, called "Mādhyamikas", through skill in the techniques for realizing the two truths, have settled [them] as without even a scent of contradiction, [thereby] finding the finality of the Conqueror's thought. In dependence on that, they generate wonderful and very great respect for our teacher and his teaching and with pure speech and words induced by that respect proclaim again and again with great voice, "Knowledgeable Ones, the meaning of emptiness, that is to say, the emptiness of inherent existence, is the meaning of dependent-arising; it does not mean the non-existence of things, that is to say, an emptiness of capacity to perform functions."[346]

Scholars of our own [i.e., Buddhist] schools, Proponents of True Existence, even though they have great training in many topics of learning, [377b] do not accept this Mādhyamika view, and their dispute with the Mādhyamikas is just this thought: "If all phenomena are empty, without any inherent existence, that is to say, establishment by way of their own entities, then there is no way to posit all the presentations of cyclic existence and nirvāṇa – bondage, release, and so forth." For, Nāgārjuna's *Treatise on the Middle Way* (XXIV.1), [citing an objection by the Proponents of True Existence], says:[347]

> If all these are empty,
> There would be no arising and no disintegration;
> It would follow that for you [Mādhyamikas]
> The four noble truths would not exist.

Thus they say that if [phenomena] are empty of inherent existence, then production, disintegration, and the four truths would not be feasible. Also Nāgārjuna's *Refutation of Objections* (*rtsod bzlog*, *vigrahavyāvartanī*, stanza 1) [sets forth an objection by the Proponents of True Existence]:[348]

> If an inherent existence of all things
> Does not exist in anything,
> Then your words also are without inherent existence
> And cannot refute inherent existence.

Saying that if words are without inherent existence, then they cannot refute inherent existence nor prove a lack of inherent existence, [the Proponents of True Existence] debate [with the Mādhyamikas] within the thought that if there is no inherent existence, then objects produced, producers, as well as activities of refutation and proof would not be feasible. With this [mode of debate], they debate within understanding that the reasonings refuting inherent existence refute all activities.

Therefore, when Proponents of True Existence and Mādhyamikas debate with respect to their uncommon tenets, they debate only about the suitability or unsuitability of positing all the presentations of cyclic existence and nirvāṇa within an emptiness of inherent existence. Hence, the allowability of asserting all the presentations of cyclic existence and nirvāṇa – objects produced, producers, refutation, proof, and so forth — within the non-existence of even a particle of inherent existence, that is to say, establishment by way of [objects'] own entities, is a distinguishing feature of Mādhyamika. The twenty-fourth chapter of Nāgārjuna's *Treatise on the Middle Way* (XXIV.13–14) says:[349] [378a]

> The consequence [expressing] the fallacy [that actions, agents, and so forth are unpositable]
> Is not correct with respect to [the Mādhyamika] emptiness;
> Thus, your abandonment of emptiness
> Is not correct with respect to me.
>
> In that [system] in which emptiness is
> Suitable, all is suitable;
> In that [system] in which emptiness is not
> Suitable, all is not suitable.

[Nāgārjuna] says that not only does the fallacy [expressed above by the Proponents of True Existence, XXIV.1], "If all these are empty, [there would be no arising and no disintegration] . . ." and so forth, not arise for those who propound an absence of inherent existence, but also production, disintegration, and so forth are suitable within a position of emptiness of inherent existence, whereas they are not suitable within a position of non-emptiness of inherent existence. Thus, Chandrakīrti's *Clear Words* [making the transition between XXIV.13 and 14] also says:[350]

> Not only does the consequence [expressing] fallacy set forth [by you Proponents of True Existence] just not apply to our position, but also [in our position]

> all presentations of the truths and so forth are very correct. In order to indicate this, [Nāgārjuna] said [in XXIV.14], "In that [system] in which emptiness is suitable . . .".

Thus [Chandrakīrti] makes an explanation citing that passage [from Nāgārjuna's *Treatise*].

The twenty-sixth chapter of Nāgārjuna's *Treatise on the Middle Way* teaches the stages of the production in the forward process of the twelve [links] of dependent-arising and the stages of their cessation in the reverse process.[351] Twenty-five chapters mainly refute inherent existence. The twenty-fourth chapter, that analyzing the noble truths, extensively settles how all presentations of cyclic existence and nirvāṇa, arising, disintegration, and so forth, are unsuitable within a non-emptiness of inherent existence and how all those are suitable within the emptiness of inherent existence. Hence, one needs to know to carry this [twenty-fourth] chapter over to the other chapters.

Therefore, the present-day proposition [378b] by those who claim to propound the meaning of the middle way that causes and effects – produced, producers, and so forth – are necessarily not suitable within an absence of inherent existence is the system of the Proponents of True Existence. Hence, it is the assertion of the protector Nāgārjuna that one must seek the emptiness of inherent existence and the middle path in dependence on just the presentation of cause and effect – the production and cessation of such and such effects in dependence on such and such causes and conditions. The twenty-fourth chapter [of Nāgārjuna's *Treatise on the Middle Way*, XXIV.18–19] says:[352]

> That which arises dependently
> We explain as emptiness.
> That [emptiness] is dependent designation;
> Just it is the middle path.
>
> Because there is no phenomenon
> That is not a dependent-arising,

There is no phenomenon
That is not empty.

Do not turn around this statement [of Nāgārjuna's] that dependent-arisings are necessarily empty of inherent existence and propound that those things produced in dependence on causes and conditions are necessarily inherently established. Nāgārjuna's *Refutation of Objections* similarly says (stanza 70 and concluding homage):[353]

For whom emptiness is possible
All objects are possible;
For whom emptiness is not possible
Nothing is possible.

I bow down to the Buddha,
Unequalled, supreme of speakers,
[Who taught] emptiness, dependent-arising,
And the middle path as of one meaning.

Also, Nāgārjuna's *Seventy Stanzas on Emptiness* (*stong nyid bdun cu pa*, *śūnyatāsaptati*, stanza 68) says:[354]

The unequalled Tathāgata thoroughly taught
That because all things
Are empty of inherent existence
Things are dependent-arisings.

Also, Nāgārjuna's *Sixty Stanzas of Reasoning* (stanzas 43–5) says:[355]

Those who adhere to the self
Or the world as not dependent
Are, alas, captivated by views [379a]
Of permanence and impermanence.

How could those faults of permanence
And so forth not accrue also
To those who assert dependently [arisen]
Things to be established as [their own] suchness?

Those who assert dependently
[Arisen] things as not real but
Not unreal, like a moon in water,
Are not captivated by [such wrong] views.

Also, Nāgārjuna's *Praise of the Supramundane [Buddha] ('jig rten las 'das par bstod pa, lokātītastava*, 21–2) says:[356]

Suffering is asserted
By [bad] logicians to be produced
From itself, other, both, or causelessly;
You [Buddha] said it arises dependently.

You asserted that whatever arises
Dependently is empty;
That there are no self-powered things
Is your unequalled lion's roar.

Thus [Nāgārjuna] says that by reason of being dependent-arisings [phenomena] are just empty of inherent existence. This dawning of the meaning of dependent-arising as the meaning of emptiness, that is to say, no inherent existence, is the uncommon system of the protector Nāgārjuna.

Therefore, taking this emptiness which is a lack of inherent existence from the Mādhyamika's own side, but, uncomfortable with making in one's own system a presentation of dependently arisen cause and effect, relying [for that] on others, and so forth, is not the meaning of dependent-arising. For [Nāgārjuna's statement in the *Treatise on the Middle Way* (XXIV.14, cited above)], "In that [system] in which emptiness is suitable ..." says that all the dependent-arisings of cyclic existence and nirvāṇa are feasible in the system which is a system of an absence of inherent existence.

6 *Dependent-Arising and Emptiness*

What is the system of the suitability of all of cyclic existence and nirvāṇa within a position asserting emptiness? Those who propound that all things are just empty of inherent existence propound such by reason of [things'] arising in dependence on causes and conditions. [379b] This will be explained [later].

This being the case, dependent-arising is feasible within that [emptiness of inherent existence], and when that [i.e., dependent-arising] is feasible, suffering is also feasible, for suffering must be posited to that which arises in dependence on causes and conditions, and suffering is not suitable in that which does not arise dependently. When true sufferings exist, then the sources from which those arise, the cessations that are the stopping of those sufferings, and the paths proceeding to those [cessations] are feasible; thereby, [all] four truths exist. When the four truths exist, then [respectively] knowledge of them, abandonment of them, actualization of them, and cultivation of the paths of them are suitable; when those exist, then all, the Three Jewels and so forth, are suitable. In that way, Chandrakīrti's *Clear Words* says:[357]

> For that [system] in which this emptiness of inherent existence of all things is suitable, all the [above]-mentioned are suitable. How? Because we call dependent-arising "emptiness"; [358] therefore, for that [system] in which this emptiness is suitable,[359] dependent-arising is suitable, and for that [system] in which dependent-arising is suitable, the four noble truths are reasonable.[360] How? Because just those

> which arise dependently are sufferings, not those which do not arise dependently. Since those [which arise dependently] are without inherent existence, they are empty.
>
> When suffering exists, the sources of suffering, the cessation of suffering, and the paths progressing to the cessation of suffering are suitable. Therefore, thorough knowledge of suffering, abandonment of sources, actualization of cessation, [380a] and cultivation of paths are also suitable. When thorough knowledge and so forth of the truths, suffering and so forth, exist, the fruits are suitable. When the fruits exist, abiders in those fruits are suitable; when abiders in the fruits exist, approachers to [those fruits] are suitable. When approachers to and abiders in the fruits exist, the spiritual community is suitable.
>
> When the noble truths exist, the excellent doctrine is also suitable, and when the excellent doctrine and spiritual community exist, then Buddhas are also suitable. Therefore, the Three Jewels are also suitable.
>
> All special realizations of all mundane and supramundane topics (*dngos po*, *padārtha*) are also suitable as well as the proper and improper, the effects of those,[361] and all worldly conventions. Therefore, in that way, [Nāgārjuna says, XXIV.14ab], "For that [system] in which emptiness is suitable, all is suitable."[362] For that [system] in which emptiness is not suitable, dependent-arising would not exist, whereby all is unsuitable.

Therefore, [here the meaning of] "suitable" and "unsuitable" is to be understood as those things' existing and not existing.

As cited earlier, (see p.183) an objection [by the Proponents of True Existence to the Mādhyamika position] was set forth in Nāgārjuna's *Refutation of Objections*:

[If an inherent existence of all things
Does not exist in anything,
Then your words also are without inherent existence
And cannot refute inherent existence. (stanza 1)]

In answer to that, the master [Nāgārjuna] clearly gives the answer that activities are feasible within an absence of inherent existence. The *Refutation of Objections* (stanza 22) says:[363]

We propound that which is the dependent-arising
Of things as "emptiness";
For, that which is a dependent-arising
Is just without inherent existence. [380b]

Also, his [Nāgārjuna's] own commentary on this [the *Commentary on the "Refutation of Objections"* (*rtsod pa bzlog pa'i 'grel pa, vigrahavyāvartanīvṛtti*)] says:[364]

You [Proponents of True Existence], not understanding the meaning of the emptiness of things and seeking a point of censure, propound, "Because your words [that is, the words of you Mādhyamikas] are without inherent existence, refutation of the inherent existence of things is not feasible." Here [in Mādhyamika] that which is the dependent-arising of things is emptiness. Why? Because of being just without inherent existence. Those things that arise dependently do not have inherent existence because of being without inherent existence. Why? Because of having reliance on causes and conditions. If things had inherent existence, they would exist even without causes and conditions; since such is not the case, they are without inherent existence. Therefore, we speak of them as "empty".

Similarly, my words also are dependent-arisings and therefore are without inherent existence. Because they are just without inherent existence, that they are said to be "empty" is correct. Because pots,

> woolen cloth, and so forth are dependent-arisings, they are empty of inherent existence but are able [respectively] to hold and receive honey, water, and milk soup and to thoroughly protect from cold, wind, and sun.[365] Just so, my words also, because of being dependent-arisings are without inherent existence but can thoroughly establish that things are without inherent existence. Therefore, that which is propounded [by you] with respect to this, saying, "Because your words are just without inherent existence, it is not feasible that they refute the inherent existence of all things," is unsuitable.[366] [381a]

Thus [Nāgārjuna] speaks very clearly about the counter-pervasion that whatever is inherently established does not rely on causes and conditions and the pervasion that whatever relies on causes and conditions is without inherent existence and says very clearly that non-inherently existent words can perform the activities of refutation and proof.

What need to speak of the two – dependent-arising, the production and cessation of thoroughly afflicted and very pure phenomena in dependence on causes and conditions, and non-inherent existence – coming together in a common locus. This [system] in which just such dependent-arising serves as the unsurpassed reason for realizing non-inherent existence should be known as the distinguishing feature of only the wise Mādhyamikas. And, if, holding that dependent production and dependent cessation are necessarily established by way of their own entities, you refute the dependent-arising of production and cessation with the reasoning refuting inherent existence, then [that reasoning], like a god who has turned into a demon, will become a great obstacle to finding the meaning of the middle way as it actually is.

Thus, if it is the case that 1) when you induce ascertainment that phenomena do not have even a particle of inherent existence, that is to say, establishment by way of their own entities, you have no way to induce ascertainment in your own system with respect to the relationship of cause and effect and must rely on others and so forth [as do the Tibetans who negate too much] or 2) when you induce ascertainment well in your own system with respect to cause and effect, you have no way to induce ascertainment through your own system with respect to non-inherent existence and claim that one must interpret [in another way] the thought [of Buddha] with respect to [his speaking of] the absence of inherent existence [as do the Proponents of True Existence], then know that you have not yet gained the Mādhyamika view.[367]

As causes for gaining the view, you should take as a basis the pure maintenance of the ethics you have promised [to maintain], [381b] and thereupon strive by way of many approaches to accumulate the collections and purify obstructions, and, relying on the wise, make effort at hearing and thinking.

Since this composite of the two, inducing ascertainment with respect to such appearance and emptiness, almost does not occur, the view of the middle way is very difficult to gain. Thinking of this, Nāgārjuna says in the twenty-fourth chapter of the *Treatise on the Middle Way* (XXIV.12):[368]

> Therefore, knowing that for those of weak mind
> The depths of this doctrine are difficult to realize,
> The mind of the Subduer turned away
> From teaching this doctrine.

Nāgārjuna's *Precious Garland* (116–18) says:[369]

> When the body, which is respectively unclean,
> Coarse, an object of direct perception,
> And always appearing,
> Does not remain[370] in the mind [as impure],
>
> Then how could the excellent doctrine,
> Baseless, subtle, not [an object
> Of ordinary beings'] direct perception,
> And profound, easily enter the mind?[371]

Therefore, the Subduer [Buddha], having become enlightened
And realizing that this doctrine, because of its profundity
Is difficult for beings to understand,
Turned away from teaching the doctrine.

Thus, it is said in treatises and scriptures that [the view of the middle way] is very difficult to realize.

Unlike that, some mistake the meaning of statements in certain valid texts that settle the lack of inherent existence through the reasoning analyzing whether pots and so forth are one with or different from their parts; when, upon analyzing whether pots and so forth are any of their parts – lip, neck, and so forth – they do not find them as any of those, they induce the ascertainment, "There are no pots." [382a] Then, analyzing similarly also the analyzer, they ascertain, "There is also no analyzer." At that time, thinking, "If an analyzer is not to be found, who is it that knows, 'Pots and so forth do not exist'?", they say, "[Things] do not exist and also do not not exist." Were one to posit the inducing of such erroneous ascertainment by way of certain counterfeit reasonings as having gained the [Mādhyamika] view, then this [gaining of the view] would appear to be the easiest of things.

Therefore, those with intelligence should induce ascertainment, undivertable by others, with respect to the statements in scriptures of definitive meaning and in pure Mādhyamika texts – treatises commenting on the thought of those [scriptures] – that the meaning of emptiness is the meaning of dependent-arising, this distinguishing feature of the wise Mādhyamikas, the subtle topic that is the thought of the Superior [Nāgārjuna] and his [spiritual] son [Āryadeva] and was commented on in complete form in particular by the master Buddhapālita and the glorious Chandrakīrti, this mode of bestowing ascertainment of the absence of inherent existence in dependence on dependent-arising, and this way in which things empty of inherent existence dawn as cause and effect.

SECOND, HOW THOSE SYSTEMS REFUTE THIS [DISTINGUISHING FEATURE OF MĀDHYAMIKA][372]

Thus, the system of the protector Nāgārjuna is that:

> Phenomena do not have even a particle of inherent existence, that is, establishment by way of their own entities. Also, if there were inherent establishment, one could not make all the presentations of cyclic existence and nirvāṇa, and it is not suitable not to make those presentations. Hence, all the presentations of bondage, release, and so forth are to be posited, whereby one must definitely assert no inherent existence.

However, [it seems that] you [misinterpreters of Mādhyamika] say:

> When things have no inherent existence, that is, establishment by way of their own entities, [382b] then what else is there? Therefore, without it being necessary to affix a qualification such as "ultimately" in the refutation of bondage, release, production, cessation, and so forth, [just those] are refuted by the reasoning refuting inherent existence.

If you say this, think about how you could not be refuting [Nāgārjuna's system in which] within no inherent existence it is allowable to posit bondage, release, arising, disintegration, and so forth.

You might think: "The assertion of the master [Chandrakīrti] is that the presentations of cyclic existence and nirvāṇa – bondage, release, and so forth – are [made] conventionally, and we also assert those conventionally. Hence, there is no fault." This is not reasonable, and the reason is as follows: Even you accept that the master Chandrakīrti's assertion is that phenomena do not have inherent existence, that is, establishment by way of their own entities, even conventionally. In that case, because the reasoning which refutes inherent existence must refute that inherent existence even conventionally and because you assert that the reasoning which refutes inherent existence refutes also bondage, release, and so forth, it is very clear that [in your system] bondage, release, and so forth are refuted even conventionally.

In brief, if you assert that an absence of inherent existence [on the one hand] and bondage, release, production, cessation, and so forth [on the other hand] are contradictory, then since the feasibility of all the presentations of cyclic existence and nirvāṇa within the emptiness which is an emptiness of inherent existence is unsuitable [to be posited] within either of the two truths, you have refuted the unique distinguishing feature of Mādhyamika.

If you do not assert those as contradictory, then you have no correct reason whatsoever for asserting that the reasoning refuting inherent existence refutes production, cessation, bondage, release, and so forth within [claiming] that it is not necessary to affix any qualification at all [such as "ultimately"] to the object of negation. Therefore, [383a] if the reasoning refuting inherent existence refutes cause and effect, then you are asserting that production, disintegration, and so forth are not suitable within an absence of inherent existence. In that case, it is very clear that [your position] does not differ in the slightest from the objection by a Proponent of True Existence set forth in the twenty-fourth chapter [of Nāgārjuna's *Treatise on the Middle Way*, (XXIV.1)]:[373]

> If all these are empty,
> There would be no arising and no disintegration;
> It would follow that for you [Mādhyamikas]
> The noble truths would not exist.

Or from the objection by a Proponent of True Existence set forth in Nāgārjuna's *Refutation of Objections* (stanza 1):[374]

> If an inherent existence of all things
> Does not exist in anything,
> Then your words also are without inherent existence
> And cannot refute inherent existence.

You might think: "Production, disintegration, and so forth are not suitable within either an emptiness of inherent existence or a non-emptiness of inherent existence; since we do not assert either emptiness of inherent existence or non-emptiness of inherent existence, we have no fault." This is not in the least suitable to be the meaning of the [Mādhyamika] texts. For, Chandrakīrti's *Clear Words* establishes:[375]

> Not only do we not have the fault that arising, disintegration, and so forth are not feasible, but also the four truths and so forth are feasible.

Also, Nāgārjuna's *Treatise on the Middle Way* speaks within differentiating well the suitability of those within a position of an emptiness of inherent existence and their unsuitability within a position of non-emptiness. Further, Chandrakīrti's *Supplement to (Nāgārjuna's) "Treatise on the Middle Way"* (VI.37–38ab) says:[376]

> It is not that empty things such as reflections that depend
> On a collection [of causes] are not renowned [to the world as falsities].
> Just as here, from those empty reflections and so forth,
> There are produced consciousnesses having their aspects [i.e., an eye consciousness seeing the reflection],
> Similarly, even though all things are empty, [383b]
> From those empty [things, effects] are thoroughly produced.

Moreover, if reasoning refutes bondage, release, and so forth, then, since [according to your assertion] it is not suitable to refute [those] ultimately [i.e., affixing the qualification "ultimately" to the refutation], they must be refuted conventionally, and at that time, all the presentations of cyclic existence and nirvāṇa would be refuted even conventionally. Such a Mādhyamika is unprecedented.

7 *Mādhyamika Response*

THIRD, HOW A MĀDHYAMIKA RESPONDS TO THOSE [WHO REFUTE THE DISTINGUISHING FEATURE OF MĀDHYAMIKA][377]

To the objection, "If things were empty of inherent existence, the causes and effects of cyclic existence and nirvāṇa would not be positable," the protector Nāgārjuna says that since the fault which was to be flung [to others] by the Mādhyamikas has been flung at them, he, turning it around, will fling [back at the opponent] that fault [of the unsuitability of positing the causes and effects of cyclic existence and nirvāṇa]. The twenty-fourth chapter of Nāgārjuna's *Treatise on the Middle Way* [XXIV.15–16] says:[378]

> You turn your own faults
> To us as faults[379]
> Like someone who, while riding on a horse,
> Forgets that very horse.
>
> If you view things
> As existing inherently,
> In that case you view
> All things as without causes and conditions.[380]

Also [XXIV.20]:[381]

> If all this is not empty,
> There would be no arising and no disintegration;
> It would follow that for you [Proponents of True Existence]
> The four noble truths would not exist.

Etc. Therefore, it is clear that you who propound, "If there is no inherent existence, that is to say, establishment by way of [objects'] own entities, then what else is there?" have unquestionably not differentiated the two, the absence of inherent existence of a sprout and the non-existence of a sprout. And, because of that, you have also not differentiated the two, the existence of a sprout and the establishment of a sprout by way of its own entity, [384a] whereby it is clear that you assert that whatever exists, exists by way of its own entity, and if something is not established by way of its own entity, it does not exist. Otherwise, why would you propound that the reasoning refuting establishment by way of [an object's] own entity refutes mere existence, mere production and cessation, and so forth?

When you propound in this way that as long as sprouts and so forth are asserted to exist, they exist in the sense of being established by way of their own entities and propound that if [sprouts] are utterly without establishment by way of their own entities, they are utterly non-existent, you unquestionably fall to the two extremes. Therefore, your mode of understanding is no different from that of the Proponents of True Existence. For, Chandrakīrti's *Commentary on (Āryadeva's) "Four Hundred"* says clearly:[382]

> According to the Proponents of True Existence, as long as there is an existence of things, there is[383] also an intrinsic entity [of those things]. When devoid of an intrinsic entity, then, for them, these things would be non-existent in all ways, like the horn of a donkey, whereby [these Proponents of True Existence] do not pass beyond propounding the two [extremes]. Therefore, all of their manifest [i.e., explicit] assertions are difficult to fit together.

As long as you do not realize this differentiation by the glorious Chandrakīrti between the four – inherent existence and existence [on the one hand] and absence of inherent existence and non-existence [on the other hand], you will unquestionably fall to the two extremes, whereby you will not realize the meaning of the middle free from the extremes. For, when a phenomenon comes to be utterly without establishment by way of its own entity, it will [for you] come to be utterly non-existent; in that case, since there is utterly no way to posit cause and effect within the empti[ness] which is an empti[ness] of inherent existence, you fall to an extreme of annihilation. Also, once a phenomenon is asserted as existing, [384b] it must [for you] be asserted as established by way of its own entity; in that case, since there comes to be no way to take cause and effect as illusion-like, appearing to exist inherently whereas they do not, you fall to an extreme of permanence.[384]

Therefore, through realizing that all phenomena are, from the beginning, without even a particle that is established by way of its own entity, you do not fall to an extreme of existence. And, when you induce an ascertaining consciousness which ascertains that even so [i.e., even though they lack inherent existence], things such as sprouts and so forth, without coming to be non-things[385] empty of the capacity to perform functions, have the power to perform their own functions, you abandon the extreme of non-existence.

A clear differentiation between the absence of inherent existence and non-existence also is set forth in Chandrakīrti's *Clear Words*:[386]

> [A Proponent of True Existence] says: "If you posit in this way that things do not exist inherently, then through this you eliminate all those things stated by the Supramundane Victor [Buddha, such as], 'The fruition of actions done by oneself are experienced by oneself,' and you deprecate actions and [their] effects. Therefore, you are the chief of Nihilists."
>
> *Answer*: "We are not Nihilists; having refuted the propounding of the two [extremes] of existence and non-existence, we illuminate the path free from those two that leads to the city of nirvāṇa. We also

> do not propound, 'Actions, agents, effects, and so forth do not exist.' What do we propound? We posit, 'These do not inherently exist.' If you think, 'There is fault because performance of activity is not feasible within an absence of inherent existence,' [385a] that [fault] also is not existent because activities are not seen among just those which have inherent existence and because activities are seen among just those without inherent existence.

The proposition by the Proponents of True Existence that if there is no inherent existence,[387] that refutation of inherent existence eliminates the arising of fruitions from actions does not differ in assertion from the assertion [by Tibetans claiming to be Mādhyamikas] that the reasoning refuting inherent existence refutes cause and effect.

Both the Mādhyamikas and the Proponents of True Existence are alike in asserting that if cause and effect are refuted, one becomes the chief of those having a view of annihilation. However, the Mādhyamikas do not assert that cause and effect are refuted. Nevertheless, the Proponents of True Existence, thinking that if one refutes inherent existence, one must also definitely refute cause and effect, call the Mādhyamikas "Nihilists", or "Annihilationists". Most of the Tibetans claiming to be Mādhyamikas appear to accord with the Proponents of True Existence in asserting that if one refutes inherent existence, that reasoning must also refute cause and effect; however, [those Tibetans,] taking this reasoned refutation of cause and effect to be the Mādhyamika system, appear to admire it.

In answer to the objection [raised by the Proponents of True Existence in the above passage, Chandrakīrti responds, in paraphrase]: "We [Mādhyamikas] are not Nihilists; avoiding propounding the two [extremes] of existence and non-existence, we illuminate the path to liberation." The remainder [of the passage] indicates how [Mādhyamikas] avoid propounding [the extremes of] existence and non-existence.

About that, through saying, "We do not propound that actions, effects, and so forth are non-existent," propounding [the extreme of] non-existence is avoided [385b] – whereas we would be Nihilists if we asserted cause, effect, and so forth to be non-existent, we do not assert such. To the question, "Well, what do you propound?", [Chandrakīrti] says, "We posit, or assert, that these – actions, effects, and so forth – are without inherent existence." Through this he avoids propounding [an extreme of] existence.

[The statement], "Since performance of activity is not feasible within an absence of inherent existence, the fault remains as before," indicates the objection by the Proponents of True Existence – "Even though you [Mādhyamikas] say, 'We do not propound non-existence; we propound an absence of inherent existence,' you still cannot abandon the fault stated earlier that if there is no inherent existence, cause and effect are not feasible." They object thus since in their system there is no difference between the two – an absence of inherent existence and non-existence. In answer to that, [Chandrakīrti] says that activities such as causes' producing effects and so forth are unsuitable within inherent existence and those are suitable within only an absence of inherent existence.

Also, Chandrakīrti's *Commentary on (Āryadeva's) "Four Hundred"* says:[388]

> We do not propound things as non-existent because we propound dependent-arising. If you ask, "Are you a Proponent of Things [that is, of truly existent things]?", we are not because of just being proponents of dependent-arising. If you ask, "What do you propound?", we propound dependent-arising. Furthermore, if you ask, "What is the meaning of dependent-arising?", it has the meaning of non-inherent existence, that is, it has the meaning of non-inherent production, it has the meaning of the arising of effects whose nature is similar to a magician's

> illusions, mirages, reflections, cities of scent-eaters, emanations, and dreams, and it has a meaning of emptiness and selflessness.

Thus [Chandrakīrti] indicates how, through asserting [things] as dependent-arisings, [386a] the propounding of the two extremes of the existence and non-existence of things is avoided. Moreover, through explaining that the meaning of dependent-arising is no inherently existent production he avoids propounding things as existent [i.e., as inherently existent], and through indicating the arising of effects that are like a magician's illusions and so forth as the meaning of dependent-arising, he avoids propounding things as non-existent [that is, as devoid of all capacity to perform functions].

Therefore, "thing" (*dngos po*, *bhāva*) can be taken as "inherent existence" (*rang bzhin*, *svabhāva*) or can be taken as "the capacity to perform a function" (*don byed nus pa*, *arthakriyā-śakti*). From among these two, "thing" in "propound things as existent" refers to only inherent establishment, and "thing" in "propound things as non-existent" refers to things which perform functions. For, when [Chandrakīrti] avoids those two [extremes, i.e., propounding things as existent or as non-existent] he refutes inherent existence and indicates that causes and effects which are like a magician's illusions exist.

Moreover, Chandrakīrti's *Commentary on (Āryadeva's) "Four Hundred"* says:[389]

> If someone asks, "Do you [Mādhyamikas propound] that a memory consciousness having a past thing as its object does not exist?", [we Mādhyamikas answer:] who would propound that such does not exist? We [Mādhyamikas] do not eliminate dependent-arising. The way in which it exists was posited by the master [Āryadeva] himself [XI.25bcd]:
>
> > Therefore, the "memory" which arises is only an unreal [subject]
> > Having an object which is unreal.

> Therefore, the object of observation of a remembering consciousness is a past thing. If [the past thing] did exist by way of its own entity, then because the memory of it would be observing an object that [inherently] exists, [that memory] would be established by way of its own entity. But, when that past thing [is shown to be] without inherent existence, then the remembering consciousness observing it also is without inherent existence. Therefore, [Āryadeva] has established that [the past object and the remembering consciousness] are unreal.
>
> "Unreal" does not mean something other than "without inherent existence" and "dependent-arising"; [386b] the non-existence of things [which perform functions] is not the meaning of "unreal".
>
> A past thing is not non-existent in all ways because of being an object of memory and because effects of it are seen. It also does not exist by way of its own entity because it would [absurdly] follow that it was permanent and because it would [absurdly] follow that it would be actually apprehended [i.e., the remembering consciousness would actually contact the past object].

Hence [Chandrakīrti] says that these past objects and so forth are not utterly non-existent and are also not established by way of their own entities and that the meaning of unreal or false is the meaning of dependent-arising and does not mean that things are non-existent.

Therefore, if you assert these phenomena to be established by way of their own entities, you are propounding things [i.e., inherent existence], or fall to an extreme of [inherent] existence; however, propounding these as merely existent is not a propounding of things [i.e., inherent existence], or a propounding of [inherent] existence. Similarly, if you assert that internal and external things are non-things, empty of the capacity to perform functions, you are propounding the non-existence of things, or fall to an extreme of [utter] non-existence; however, through propounding them as without inherent existence, you do not fall to an extreme of [utter] non-existence.

When, not differentiating in this way utter non-existence, no inherent existence, establishment by way of [an object's] own entity, and mere existence, you [try to] prevent falling to the extremes of existence or non-existence through putting hope in just propounding, "We do not propound [such and such] as non-existent (*med pa*); we say it is not existent (*yod pa ma yin pa*). We do not propound [such and such] as existent (*yod pa*); we say it is not non-existent (*med pa ma yin pa*)," you are propounding only a collection of contradictions and do not set forth even slightly the meaning of the middle way.[390]

For, when you [who claim to be Mādhyamikas] refute others, since you engage in refutation within having investigated the two [possibilities] of inherent existence, no inherent existence, and so forth, [387a] you yourself assert that the possibilities must be limited to two, and yet, you assert a meaning that is neither of those two. This is as follows: Since you are investigating with respect to some base [i.e., any phenomenon] whether it exists inherently or not, you must assert that the possibilities are limited to those two; if there were a third possibility not included in those [two], it would not be reasonable to investigate, "Which of these two, inherently existent or not inherently existent, is it?" For example, it would be like asking when something exists as a color, "Is it blue or is it yellow?"

Also, being limited in this way to the two, inherent existence and no inherent existence, depends upon in general being limited to the two, existence and non-existence, with regard to objects of knowledge. This is like the way in which, for example, being limited to truly existent one or truly existent many with respect to true existence depends upon being limited in general to the two, one or many. When there is such limitation, this must eliminate any third possibility; hence, asserting a phenomenon that is neither of those two is senseless babble. For, Nāgārjuna's *Refutation of Objections* (stanza 26cd) says:[391]

> If no inherent existence were overturned,
> Inherent existence would be thoroughly established.

Moreover, those who assert such, since they have no way to make a definite enumeration that eliminates any third possibility, can only be doubtful. For, eliminating one possibility such as "exists" or "does not exist" would not positively include [or affirm] the other possibility.[392]

If you assert that with respect to some things such as "is" (*yin*), "is not" (*min*), and so forth there is no third possibility, it is utterly the same also with respect to "exists" (*yod*) and "does not exist" (*med*).[393] Since it appears that such is asserted due to mistaking the mere words of Mādhyamika texts [387b] that say, "is not existent", "is not non-existent", then just as [according to you] it is unsuitable to propound "exists" or "does not exist", so also it would be unreasonable to propound, "is not existent", "is not non-existent" because such is said with respect to all four possibilities.[394]

Therefore, Nāgārjuna's *Treatise on the Middle Way* (XV.10) says:[395]

> Saying "exists" is a conception of permanence;
> Saying "does not exist" is a view of annihilation.
> Hence the wise should not dwell
> In either existence or non-existence.

Even this statement is not said with respect to mere existence and non-existence; rather, it is said clearly that asserting things as inherently established comes to be a view of permanence and annihilation. Chandrakīrti's *Clear Words*, after explaining that the conceptions of existence and non-existence [spoken of] in the earlier text [i.e., in the passage from Nāgārjuna's *Treatise on the Middle Way* just cited] refer to the views of inherent existence and inherent non-existence (*dngos po yod med*), says:[396]

> Why is it that when one has views of things and non-things [or inherent existence and inherent non-existence] it follows that one has views of permanence and of annihilation? As follows: [Nāgārjuna's *Treatise on the Middle Way*, XV.11 says:]
>
> > Whatever exists inherently is permanent
> > Since it does not become non-existent.
> > If one says that what arose formerly [as inherently existent] is now non-existent,
> > Through that [an extreme of] annihilation is entailed.
>
> Since the inherently existent is not overcome, something that is said to be inherently existent does not ever become non-existent; in that case it follows that through asserting [something] as just inherently existent, one has a view of permanence.
>
> Also, through asserting an inherent existence of things when formerly they were abiding and then asserting that now, later,[397] they are destroyed whereby they do not exist, it follows that one has a view of annihilation.

Thus [Chandrakīrti] calls the assertion of inherent existence a view of permanence and says that if one asserts the later destruction of what was formerly inherently existent, such is a view of nihilism. He does not call mere existence and mere disintegration [views of permanence and annihilation].

Also the *Buddhapālita Commentary on (Nāgārjuna's) "Treatise on the Middle Way"* [388a] clearly explains that [XV.11]:

> Whatever exists inherently [is permanent
> Since it does not become non-existent.
> If one says that what arose formerly (as inherently existent) is now non-existent,

> Through that (an extreme of) annihilation is entailed.]

indicates the type of permanence and annihilation [intended when XV.10, cited above] explains that saying "exists" and saying "non-exists" are views of permanence and annihilation.[398]

In brief, if you propound that the emptiness which is the absence of inherent existence is not the excellent emptiness and refute it, due to abandoning the doctrine, that is, abandoning the Perfection of Wisdom, you will go to a bad transmigration. Further, even if you have interest in the absence of inherent existence, but thinking, "If there is no inherent existence, what is there?", assert that all phenomena do not exist at all, you will still fall into the chasm of a view of annihilation.[399] In that way also [Nāgārjuna's *Treatise on the Middle Way*, XXIV.11ab] says:[400]

> If they wrongly view emptiness,
> Those of small wisdom will be ruined.

As commentary on this, Chandrakīrti's *Clear Words* says:[401]

> If, on the one hand, one were to think, "All [phenomena] are empty, that is, all do not exist," at that time one would be viewing [emptiness] wrongly. In this vein [Nāgārjuna's *Precious Garland*] (stanza 119) says:
>
> > This doctrine apprehended wrongly[402]
> > Ruins the unwise, for
> > They sink into the filth
> > Of nihilistic views.
>
> On the other hand, if you do not assert a deprecation of all [phenomena, but] at the same time say, "How could these things, having been observed, be just empty? Therefore, the meaning of an absence of inherent existence is not the meaning of emptiness," you have definitely abandoned emptiness.[403] Having

abandoned [emptiness] in this way, you will definitely go to a bad transmigration due to the action of having become bereft of dharma. As Nāgārjuna's *Precious Garland* (stanza 120) says:

> Further, if they hold this [doctrine] wrongly,[404]
> The stupid who fancy themselves wise [388b]
> Having a nature intractable due to abandoning [emptiness]
> Go headdown to the most tortuous hell.

Some persons might think: If we, having asserted things formerly, later viewed them as non-existent, we would have a view of annihilation. However, since we from the very beginning do not assert them as existing, what is annihilated [so that] there would come to be a view of annihilation? For, [Nāgārjuna's *Treatise on the Middle Way*, XV.11cd], says:

> If one says that what arose formerly [as inherently existent] is now non-existent,
> Through that [an extreme of] annihilation is entailed.

Thus [Nāgārjuna] says that such is a view of annihilation. Also, Chandrakīrti's *Clear Words* says:[405]

> Yogis, who, having realized conventional truths – which are produced only by ignorance – as without inherent existence, then realize that the emptiness of those has the character of the ultimate do not fall to the two extremes. Thinking, "When a certain thing [such as a seed] becomes non-existent [upon disintegrating] now [at the time of a sprout], then at the time [of the seed], what would have [inherently] existed?", since they do not observe an inherent existence of things formerly, they do not realize them later as non-existent.

[*Answer*:] This [argument] is not reasonable because if, in order to have a view of annihilation, it were necessary to have asserted formerly whatever thing was annihilated, then it would absurdly follow that even the worldly Materialists (*rgyang phan pa*, *āyata*) would not have a view of annihilation since they do not propound former and future lives, actions and their effects and so forth, as later non-existent having asserted them formerly, but rather do not assert them as existing from the very start.

Therefore, [Nāgārjuna's] statement, "If one says that what arose formerly [as inherently existent] is now non-existent, through that [an extreme of] annihilation is entailed," (XV.11cd) means that Proponents of True Existence who assert that things have inherent existence, that is, are established by way of their own entities, unquestionably come to have views of permanence or annihilation. [389a] For, if they assert that that [which has] inherent existence does not change at any time, they come to have a view of permanence, and if they assert that what existed [inherently] at a former time is later destroyed, they come to have a view of annihilation.

Therefore, when indicating that [the Mādhyamikas] do not have a view of annihilation in which an inherent existence that existed at a former time is held to be destroyed at a later time, their [the Mādhyamikas'] non-assertion of even a particle of inherent existence, that is, establishment by way of their own entities, in things serves as the reason [for this]. All views of annihilation are not abandoned through this [assertion].

Another mode of [Mādhyamikas'] difference from those having a view of annihilation, who assert that actions and their effects do not exist, is set forth extensively in Chandrakīrti's *Clear Words* as follows:[406] Those having a view of annihilation assert that actions and their effects as well as other lifetimes do not exist, whereas Mādhyamikas assert those as without inherent existence; hence there is a difference in their theses. Mādhyamikas propound that actions and their effects and so forth are without inherent existence by reason of their being dependent-arisings; Annihilationists, since they do not assert that actions and their effects and so forth are dependent-arisings, do not take this as their reason; rather, they propound [actions and their effects] as non-existent having taken as their reason the fact that a present sentient being is not seen to come to this life from a former one and to go from this to a future one. Hence there is a great difference [also] in their reasons. Chandrakīrti's *Clear Words* says:[407]

> Some say that Mādhyamikas do not differ from Nihilists. Why? Because [Mādhyamikas] propound that virtuous and non-virtuous actions, agents, effects, and all worlds [i.e., former and future lives] are empty of inherent existence and Nihilists [389b] also propound those as non-existent. Hence they argue that Mādhyamikas do not differ from Nihilists.
>
> Such is not the case, for Mādhyamikas propound dependent-arising and propound that everything – this world, other worlds, and so forth – because of being dependent-arisings[408] are without inherent existence. Nihilists do not realize other worlds [lifetimes] and so forth as non-things (*dngos med*, *abhāva*) [that is, as without inherent existence] by way of their emptiness of inherent existence due to being dependent-arisings. What do they [propound]? They, observing as inherently existent[409] the aspects of the things in this world and not seeing them come to this world from another world and go from this world to another, deprecate those other things [former and future lives] which [in fact] are like the things observed in this world.[410]

Someone [else] might think: Even though the reasons cited by the two, Mādhyamikas and Annihilationists, are not the same, nonetheless, because they are similar in realizing that actions and their effects and former and future worlds are without inherent existence, that is, establishment by way of their own entities, their views of an absence of inherent existence are the same.

Even with respect to this they differ. For, since [Nihilists] assert non-inherent existence to be utter non-existence, they do not assert [actions and their effects and former and future lifetimes] as either of the two truths; however, Mādhyamikas conventionally assert those – actions and their effects and so forth – as existing. Chandrakīrti's *Clear Words* says:[411]

> Should someone say: "Even so, they are similar in one way, in terms of the view, because [Nihilists] realize the non-existence of an intrinsic entity of things as non-existence." [390a] This is not so. Because Mādhyamikas assert [those] as existing conventionally and these [Nihilists] do not assert them at all, they are just not similar.

This indicates that those claiming to be Mādhyamikas who do not assert actions, effects, and so forth even conventionally are similar in view to the Worldly Materialists (*'jig rten rgyang phan pa, lokāyata*).

Here the master [Chandrakīrti], as the reason for [Mādhyamikas] being different from those having a view of annihilation, did not say [as you who negate too much would], "Because they have assertions, whereas we do not." He also did not say, "They assert those as non-existent whereas we do not propound such as non-existent (*med pa*) but rather assert them as not existent (*yod pa ma yin*)." Instead, he spoke of [Mādhyamikas'] propounding [actions, effects, and so forth] as without inherent existence, of their stating dependent-arising as the reason for that, and of their conventionally asserting those presentations as existent.

Someone might think: "That actions, their effects, and so forth are without inherent existence, that is, establishment by way of their own entities, is correct [from your viewpoint], and since when those having a view of annihilation also assert them as non-existent, they assert them as without inherent existence, therefore from the viewpoint of [asserting] an absence of inherent existence they are similar to Mādhyamikas."

[*Answer*:] With respect to this also there is a very great difference. For example, with respect to a person who stole some jewels, one person, whereas he does not [in fact] know that a certain [person] committed the robbery, says by way of speaking falsely, "That person committed the robbery." Another person, having seen that thief steal the jewels says, "That person committed the robbery." In this case, indeed, in just the way that both of them said, "That person committed the robbery," that thief did steal. [390b] However, since one person spoke falsely and the other spoke truly, they are not alike. In this vein Chandrakīrti's *Clear Words* says:[412]

> Someone might say that they [Mādhyamikas and Nihilists] are the same in fact.[413] [*Answer*:] Even if they are the same with respect to the fact of non-establishment [by way of objects' own entities], still, because the realizers [of that fact] are different, they are just not the same. For example, with respect to a person who has committed a robbery, one person, although not knowing correctly [who did it], motivated by lack of closeness with that [robber] proclaims falsely, "This person committed the robbery." Another person makes the accusation having actually seen that [robbery]. Even though there is no difference between those two with respect to the fact, still, since there is a difference in the two realizers, of the one it is said, "That one spoke falsely," and of the other, "That one spoke truly." When one investigates correctly with respect to the former, this leads to ill-renown and a sense of unseemliness, but such is not the case with the latter.
>
> Similarly, here also,[414] when the [mode of] understanding and speaking of Mādhyamikas who know just as it is the self-entity of things [that is to say, non-inherent existence] is put together with that of Nihilists, who do not know just as it is the self-entity of things, the [modes of] understanding and expression are not alike.

Some persons, when they understand the absence of inherent existence, understand that actions, their effects, and so forth have been refuted by reasoning and hence [assert] that cause and effect are unpositable in their own system. This [passage by Chandrakīrti] refutes well the proposition [by some Tibetans] that although such persons are wrongly perspected with respect to the class of appearances – conventionalities – they have gained an unerring view of the class of emptiness.

Therefore, without emptiness coming to be an emptiness of the capacity to perform functions, [391a] you must have a way of positing the dependent-arising of causes and effects even though there is no inherent existence. Chandrakīrti's *Commentary on (Āryadeva's) "Four Hundred"* says:[415]

> In that case, regarding any object, [it is said]:
>
> > With respect to production, it does not come [here from somewhere]
> > And, similarly, with respect to cessation, it does not go [from here to somewhere]. (XV.10ab)
>
> [Hence], it definitely does not inherently exist.
>
> Should someone ask, "If these do not inherently exist, then what is there?", the answer is as follows: Those [objects] that are dependent-arisings, entities produced from the thoroughly afflicted and the very pure acting as causes, exist.

This clearly answers the question, "If there is no inherent existence, then what does exist?"

The master Buddhapālita also gives an answer differentiating clearly between existence and establishment by way of [an object's] own entity; the *Buddhapālita Commentary on (Nāgārjuna's) "Treatise on the Middle Way"*, commenting on the twentieth chapter [of Nāgārjuna's *Treatise*] says:[416]

> Someone might say, "If [as you Mādhyamikas say] time does not exist, and also causes, effects, and collections [of causes and conditions] do not exist, then what other thing does exist? Therefore, this [proposition by you Mādhyamikas] is just a proposition of Nihilism."

> *Answer*: It is not so. Time and so forth are not feasible in the way in which you thoroughly imagine them to exist from [their own] entityness. However, those are established as dependent designations.

Thus [Buddhapālita] engages in refutation, saying, "Establishment [of phenomena] by way of their own entities as the Proponents of True Existence assert is not feasible." Also, saying, "They are established as dependent designations," he says that dependent-arisings exist.

Thus, if you differentiate between the four – inherent existence and existence and no inherent existence and non-existence, you will overcome measureless wrong ideas. Further, you will not generate the mistake that the reasonings refuting inherent existence refute mere existence. [391b] Hence, since the main of the answers given by Mādhyamikas to scholars who are Proponents of True Existence are given by way of [differentiating] these four, I have explained this a little.

Part Three
Translation of the Corresponding Portion of *The Four Interwoven Annotations on (Dzong-ka-ba's) "Great Exposition of the Stages of the Path"*

Translator's Introduction

This commentary on Dzong-ka-ba's *Great Exposition of the Stages of the Path* is known as the *Four Interwoven Annotations to (Dzong-ka-ba's) "Great Exposition of the Stages of the Path" (lam rim mchan bzhi sbrags ma)*,[417] and in the Delhi edition of the text the annotations are identified as having been written by:

1 Ba-so Chö-gyi-gyel-tsen (*ba so chos kyi rgyal mtshan*, 1402–1473)
2 De-druk-ken-chen Ka-rok Nga-wang-rap-den (*sde drug mkhan chen kha rog ngag dbang rab brtan*, seventeenth century)
3 Jam-yang-shay-ba Nga-wang-dzön-drü (*'jam dbyangs bzhad pa ngag dbang brtson 'grus*, 1648–1712)
4 Dra-di Ge-shay Rin-chen-dön-drub (*bra sti dge bshes rin chen don grub*, seventeenth century).

Biographical information on the four annotators is sketchy, and there is some disagreement in the source literature as to who actually wrote the two earliest sets of annotations. Both editions (i.e., Delhi and Berkeley) of the *Four Interwoven Annotations* identify the author of the oldest annotations as Ba-so Chö-gyi-gyel-tsen. Ba-so, who lived from 1402–1473, was the younger brother of one of Dzong-ka-ba's two chief disciples, Kay-drup (*mkhas grub*), and was the sixth "holder of the throne of Ganden", a title indicating the head of the Ge-luk order. However, His Holiness the Dalai Lama as well as a number of other scholars whom I consulted in India disagreed with this identification, indicating that the author was not that

Ba-so but one of his later incarnations. Written confirmation of their opinion is supplied by A-gya-yong-dzin (*dbyangs can dga' ba'i blo gros, a kya yongs 'dzin*, eighteenth century), who says that the author of the first set of annotations was the fifth incarnation of Ba-so Chö-gyi-gyel-tsen, named Ba-so Hla-wang-chö-gyi-gyel-tsen (*ba so lha dbang chos kyi rgyal mtshan*). Further support for this identification is found in a record of teachings received (*gsan yik*) by A-ku-ching Shay-rap-gya-tso (*a khu ching shes rab rgya mtsho*, 1803–1875) who refers in his description of the transmission of the lineage of the annotations to Ba-so Hla-wang-chö-gyi-gyel-tsen.

A final bit of circumstantial evidence suggesting that the former Ba-so was not the author is the fact that none of three lists of his works – one in the *Yellow Cat's Eye Gem* (*vaidūrya ser po*), a history of the Ge-luk-ba monasteries in Tibet by Sang-gyay-gya-tso (*sangs rgyas rgya mtsho*, 1653–1705), another in the *Biographies of Eminent Gurus in the Transmission Lineages of the Teachings of the Graduated Path* by Ye-shay-gyel-tsen (*ye shes rgyal mtshan*, 1713–93), and a third in Long-döl La-ma's (*klong rdol bla ma*, 1719–1794) *Catalogue of the Collected Works of Certain Principal Ga-dam-ba and Ge-luk-ba Lamas* – mentions a commentary on the *Great Exposition*. The Ba-so *Annotations* are a sufficiently well-known work that had he been the author, it would probably have been included in a list of his writings.[418]

However, taking the fifth incarnation of Ba-so Chö-gyi-gyel-tsen as the author is also problematic since Sang-gyay- gya-tso says in the *Yellow Cat's Eye Gem* that the fourth incarnation was reputed to be alive at the time of his writing the text – in 1693. This would place the fifth Ba-so in the eighteenth century, making this set of annotations later than the second set and probably even the third, those of Jam-yang-shay-ba; this seems unlikely since they are widely renowned as the first set of annotations and since, as described below, Ba-so's annotations are included in a lineage of oral transmission of teachings that commences in the sixteenth century. Thus, the authorship and dating of the first set of annotations remains an open question.

About Nga-wang-rap-den, identified in the Delhi edition as the second annotator, almost no information is available. The preface to the Delhi edition reports that he wrote down the explanation by his teacher, Jam-yang Gön-chok-chö-pel (*'jam dbyangs dkon mchog chos 'phel*), of an oral tradition descended from Dak-lung-drak-ba (*stag lung brag pa*). Jam-yang Gön-chok-chö-pel was the thirty-fifth holder of the throne of Gan-den; a very famous teacher of his time, he lived from 1573–1646 and transmitted the lineage of the *Great Exposition of the Stages of the Path* to the fifth Dalai Lama. Dak-lung-drak-ba himself was the thirtieth holder of the throne of Gan-den and lived from 1546–1618. Although known as Dak-lung-drak-ba, the name of a place in Western Tibet, his given name was Lo-drö-gya-tso (*blo gros rgya mtsho*). He was a monk of the Jang-dzay (*byang rtse*) College of Gan-den Monastery who did a great deal to further that College and one of the main details mentioned about him in the *Yellow Cat's Eye Gem* is that he was someone who held the lineages of Dzong-ka-ba's *Great and Small Expositions of the Stages of the Path.*

The Berkeley edition of the *Annotations* identifies Dak-lung-drak-ba Lo-drö-gya-tso as the second annotator; however, this is probably a loose identification, referring to the tradition of the annotations rather than the actual person who wrote them down since other sources support the Delhi text identification. A-ku-ching says that Nga-wang-rap-den wrote down explanations by Gön-chok-chö-pel of the oral lineages of Gung-ru-chö-jung (*gung ru chos 'byung*) and Dag-lung-drak-ba. A-gya-yong-dzin says that what is known as the annotations of Dak-lung-drak-ba is a lineage descended from his teaching, set down at a later time by either Yar-lung-chö-dzay Losang-den-dzin (*yar klung chos mdzad blo bzang bstan 'dzin*) or Ka-rok Nga-wang-rap-den (*kha rog nga dbang rab brtan*).[419]

Jam-yang-shay-ba Nga-wang-dzön-drü, the third annotator, lived from 1648–1721, and is the textbook author for the Gomang College of Dre-bung Monastic University. He was born in Am-do, in eastern Tibet, and studied at the Go-mang College of Dre-bung as well as the Tantric College of Lower Hla-sa. From age fifty-three to sixty-two he served as abbot of Go-mang, and then, returning to Am-do, founded a monastery at Dra-shi-kyil (*bkra shis 'khyil*), where several years later he also founded a tantric college. He wrote prolifically on the full range of topics of Ge-luk-ba studies. According to A-gya-yong-dzin, he also served for a time as abbot of Pabong-ka (*pha bong kha*) Monastery, and it was during that period that he wrote his annotations to Dzong-ka-ba's *Great Exposition of the Stages of the Path*, entitled *The Golden Wheel* (*gser gyi 'khor lo*).[420]

The dates of the fourth annotator, Dra-di Ge-shay, are unknown, but the English preface to the Delhi edition places him in the seventeenth century. The biography of Jang-gya Rol-bay-dor-jay (*lcang kya rol ba'i rdo rje*, 1717–1786) mentions a Dra-di Ge-shay who was involved in putting forward an alternate candidate for recognition as the eighth Dalai Lama. This occurred in the period from 1758–65, which would place him in the eighteenth rather than the seventeenth century if he is the same person as the author of these annotations. Also supporting an eighteenth century date is the fact that Dra-di Ge-shay is one of the latest authors catalogued by Long-döl La-ma, who himself lived from 1719–1794. Dra-di Ge-shay was from Am-do, and was associated with the Jay (*byes*) College of Se-ra Monastic University. His annotations, entitled *Annotations Completely Untying All the Difficult Points of (Dzong-ka-ba's) Text (gzhung gi dka' gnad thams cad lhug par bkrol ba'i mchan bu rnams)* deal only with the special insight portion of Dzong-ka-ba's text.[421]

The text developed into its present form over a period of centuries. A-ku-ching's record of teachings received, which was written in 1875, describes the lineage of the oral transmission of teaching of the *Four Interwoven Annotations* that he received: The lineage begins in the sixteenth century with the twenty-eighth holder of the throne of Gan-den, Gen-dun-gyeltsen (*dge 'dun rgyal mtshan*, 1532–1607) with just two sets of annotations – those of Ba-so and Nga-wang-rap-den. It then becomes a lineage of three, adding in those of Jam-yang-shayba, and finally, with the addition of Dra-di Ge-shay's annotations, becomes four. Ge-shay Tsul-trim-nam-gyal (*dge bshes tshul khrims rnam rgyal*), the person who corrected the Tsay-chok-ling blocks and prepared the blocks from which the Delhi edition was printed, mentions checking the text against versions of the *Annotations* having one annotation, three annotations, and four annotations.[422] However, it seems that none of the earlier versions have survived to the present. Also, none of the annotations seem to exist as independent works; for instance, Jam-yang-shay-ba's *Annotations* do not appear in the edition of his collected works printed in New Delhi by Ngawang Gelek and are not mentioned in catalogues of his writings found in Lokesh Chandra's *Materials for a History of Tibetan Literature* nor are Dra-di Ge-shay's mentioned in Long-döl's catalogue of his writings.

THE RESPECTIVE STYLES OF THE ANNOTATIONS

The *Four Interwoven Annotations* is a commentary in the interlinear style, meaning that the commentary is woven into Dzong-ka-ba's text, with Dzong-ka-ba's words printed in large type and the annotators' additions printed smaller. The four sets of annotations are interwoven in such a way as to preserve the individual integrity of each commentary and yet also make it possible, in most cases, to read the four commentaries and Dzong-ka-ba's text as a cohesive, albeit somewhat repetitive, whole. It is not feasible exactly to mirror in English the Tibetan of the *Four Interwoven Annotations* because, for one, the differences between English and Tibetan syntax mean that a format which is quite sensible in Tibetan would be incomprehensible in English. Also, the Tibetan texts use different sizes of print to distinguish Dzong-ka-ba's text from the annotators', with the different sets of annotations separated by a bit of space and marked, in the Delhi edition of the text, by small letters over phrases of commentary to identify the author and, in the Berkeley text, by various patterns of dots and circles. Although this is a stylistic convention quite acceptable to a Tibetan scholar, it has no equivalent in English. Thus, I have chosen in translating the text to treat it the way that it is read by most Tibetan scholars, as a coherent whole, making note of differences in commentary or pointing out who the author of a particular annotation is only when such information enhances understanding of the text.

Following is a sample passage to illustrate how the *Four Interwoven Commentaries* work. It has been chosen not so much because it demonstrates particularly interesting or helpful commentary, but because it includes in a brief passage annotations from three of the four annotators. First I will cite the passage as it appears in the translation below:[423]

> *First, A Question as to Whether the Selflessness of Phenomena Is or Is Not Included in the Suchness and Selflessness Which Are the Object of Attainment*
> Someone, generating the following qualm, might say that both the identification of suchness and the mode of entering into it are incorrect: Nāgārjuna's *Treatise on the Middle Way* is an occasion [of explaining] the meaning of the Perfection of Wisdom Sūtras, and since this is an occasion of teaching the stages of the Mahāyāna path, should one not teach the mode of entry into suchness in terms of the Mahāyāna?

Next I will distinguish Dzong-ka-ba's text from that of the annotators by citing it in all capital letters and indicate which portions of commentary are by which annotator by putting the annotators initials in parentheses following his commentary. (J) stands for Jam-yang-shay-ba; (B) for Ba-so Chö-gyi-gyel-tsen; and (D) for Dra-di Ge-shay Rin-chen-don-drup:

> *First, A Question as to Whether the Selflessness of Phenomena Is or Is Not Included in the Suchness and Selflessness Which Are the Object of Attainment* (J)
> Someone, generating the following qualm, (D) might say that both the identification of suchness and the mode of entering into it are incorrect (B): Nāgārjuna's *Treatise on the Middle Way* is (J) an occasion (D) [of explaining] the meaning of the Perfection of Wisdom Sūtras (J), and since THIS is an occasion of teaching the stages of the Mahāyāna path (D),

> SHOULD ONE NOT TEACH THE MODE OF ENTRY INTO SUCHNESS in terms (D) OF THE MAHĀYĀNA?

This comes as close to mirroring the Tibetan as English syntax allows, but is not precise because in the Tibetan it is possible, and sometimes necessary, to read Dzong-ka-ba alone and to read each annotator with Dzong-ka-ba's text separately and sequentially and have each be a complete sentence. Done this way, Dzong-ka-ba's line reads:

> Is this not [an occasion] of teaching the mode of entry into the suchness of the Mahāyāna?

With Jam-yang-shay-ba's annotation added, this reads:

> *First, A Question as to Whether the Selflessness of Phenomena Is or Is Not Included in the Suchness and Selflessness Which Are the Object of Attainment*
> IS NOT THIS *Treatise on the Middle Way* [which explains] the meaning of the Perfection of Wisdom Sūtras TEACHING THE MODE OF ENTRY INTO SUCHNESS OF THE MAHĀYĀNA?

Ba-so's annotation added to Dzong-ka-ba reads:

> Someone might say that both the identification of suchness and the mode of entering into it are incorrect for IS NOT THIS TEACHING THE MODE OF ENTRY INTO SUCHNESS OF THE MAHĀYĀNA?

And Dra-di Ge-shay plus Dzong-ka-ba reads:

> Another person generates the following qualm: Since THIS is an occasion of teaching the stages of the Mahāyāna path, SHOULD ONE NOT TEACH THE MODE OF ENTRY INTO SUCHNESS in terms OF THE MAHĀYĀNA?

In most places, and this is one, the annotations are only mutually supportive (sometimes redundant) and do not make points that require separate translation and identification of the particular annotator. Those occasions where such is not the case and there is significant variation in meaning between the different annotations have been noted. However, the main benefit of the annotations, which would be lost in the turgidness of marking individually each separate annotation and repeating redundant annotations, comes from the fleshing out and amplification of Dzong-ka-ba's text that is the combined effect of all of the annotations together. Thus I have chosen to translate them in such a way as to emphasize this aspect. In a sense I have created a new document since it would be impossible to reconstruct the Tibetan of the separate annotations from my English translation. However, the combined, edited translation captures the spirit of the Tibetan better than would any other form of translation in that a skilled reader of the Tibetan would create such a synthetic message, ignoring redundancies and using the four annotations to amplify Dzong-ka-ba's text in a coherent way. Because the four annotations are not read with a primary intention of identifing four scholars' separate annotations, an edited combined translation reflects what a competent Tibetan scholar gains from the text.

How well they blend together notwithstanding, the four commentaries are distinct in terms of what is done by each. Ba-so's *Annotations* are quite brief, an explanatory phrase added in here and there, and are particularly helpful in explicating passages from texts by Indian Mādhyamikas such as Nāgārjuna and Chandrakīrti, which Dzong-ka-ba often cites without giving detailed explanation of their meaning. Nga-wang-rap-den's *Annotations* are mostly summaries, a few lines to a few paragraphs at the beginning or end of a section, making explicit the steps in Dzong-ka-ba's argument and so forth. Because his annotations are quite different in character from those of the other commentators and, rather than blending into the flow of the text, mostly stop and restate points, in the translation I have almost always noted where his annotations begin and end since otherwise the text seems unduly repetitive.

Jam-yang-shay-ba's *Annotations* are true commentary; he explains points that Dzong-ka-ba is making, gives examples, and provides more detail – for instance, if Dzong-ka-ba says in passing that ignorance is the root of cyclic existence, Jam-yang-shay-ba will add an identification of what that ignorance is as well as providing supporting Indian source quotes. Jam-yang-shay-ba has also inserted into the text an elaborate structural outline that serves as a guide to and commentary on the points Dzong-ka-ba is making. (The compiler of the second edition of the *Four Interwoven Annotations* that I used through a Berkeley microfilm, has replaced Jam-yang-shay-ba's outline with his own. He says that he took Jam-yang-shay-ba's as a basis, and in fact he has used large parts of it verbatim, merely changing the wording of some entries and altering somewhat the breakdown of different subheadings.)

Dra-di Ge-shay's *Annotations*, quantitatively the most extensive, are word commentary, spelling out in detail the referents of indefinite particles, making clear the grammatical connections between parts of a sentence, identifying who a hypothical opponent is, and providing some elaboration as well. For instance, the sentence, "Those sūtras that teach the establishment of the ultimate are said to be of definitive meaning," expands, with Dra-di's additions to, "Those sūtras that *mainly and explicitly* teach *the positing and* establishment of ultimate *entities which are the mere elimination of the elaborations of true establishment* are said to be *sutras of* definitive meaning." His addition of every little referent and grammatical expansion can be somewhat tedious and repetitive (and, in fact, most Tibetan scholars find it excessive), but is helpful to a translator in that it becomes almost impossible to misconstrue a passage.

TECHNICAL NOTE

The chapter breaks are my own, added to facilitate understanding. Also I have occasionally inserted some explanation – both my own and that of contemporary scholars – into the body of the text. These additions are substantially indented and easily identifiable.

Page numbers to the Delhi edition of the Tibetan text have been inserted into the translation in square brackets. Only brief references to texts cited by Dzong-ka-ba are given here. For full references and discussion, including Sanskrit where available, see the citations of the passages in the translation of Dzong-ka-ba's *Great Exposition*.

Introduction

The explanation of special insight has two parts: the need to achieve special insight even though one has a meditative stabilization having the four qualifications, and how to achieve special insight.

THE NEED TO ACHIEVE SPECIAL INSIGHT EVEN THOUGH ONE HAS A MEDITATIVE STABILIZATION HAVING THE FOUR QUALIFICATIONS

This has two parts: (1) with an example, showing that one is not released merely through meditative stabilization, and (2) the path of release as well as how it is cultivated.

WITH AN EXAMPLE, SHOWING THAT ONE IS NOT RELEASED MERELY THROUGH MEDITATIVE STABILIZATION

This has five parts.

EVEN THOUGH ONE HAS A MEDITATIVE STABILIZATION HAVING THE FOUR FACTORS OF CLARITY, JOY, BLISS, AND NON-CONCEPTUALITY, IF ONE WANTS RELEASE, IT IS NECESSARY TO CULTIVATE THE SPECIAL INSIGHT REALIZING SUCHNESS

As was explained earlier, at the point of calm abiding, you should not be satisfied with just the achievement of a calm abiding that possesses the three features.

> In his section heading Jam-yang-shay-ba speaks of four factors that qualify meditative stabilization whereas Dzong-ka-ba mentions only three. The difference comes because the third of Dzong-ka-ba's qualifications, benefit, which he explains to mean joy and bliss, can be treated as two separate qualifications – joy and bliss.

[The first] feature is that of non-conceptuality, the imprint of being free from excitement. [It is a non-conceptualizing] of any other object on which to set the mind, which stays just where it was put, in the way that you want, for as long as you intend, on the single object of observation. [139] [The second] feature is that of clarity, the imprint of freedom from laxity, due to the great intensity of the mode of apprehension. [The third] feature is that of effect, or benefit, of those [first] two features when you have familiarized with them – the mental joy of physical and mental pliancy as well as the bliss of physical pliancy.

A person who has achieved calm abiding should, taking it as a basis, initially seek and generate the special wisdom that ascertains and realizes the meaning of suchness, that is, emptiness, non-erroneously in the sense of not mistaking something else for it.

> Ge-shay Wangdrak identifed this as meaning that one should ascertain emptiness as posited by the Prāsaṅgika system, not mistaking the emptinesses posited by the lower tenets systems to be the emptiness to be realized here.

Then you should cultivate the special insight which is a sustaining [of meditation] by means of that wisdom in just the way that [the meaning of emptiness] was sought.

In dependence upon having achieved a meditative stabilization of calm abiding, you should cultivate special insight. Otherwise, if you hold the mere attainment of calm abiding to be sufficient, since that mere meditative stabilization of calm abiding is also attained by Forders, it is shared with Forders. Therefore, no matter how much you familiarized with that mere meditative stabilization, just as through the paths of Forders, except for only temporarily abandoning most of the manifest afflictions of the levels below the peak of cyclic existence, it is not possible to abandon seeds of afflictions forever, so you [could] not abandon forever the seeds of the afflictions. Hence, you could not be released from mundane, that is, cyclic, existence.

> The Buddhist position is that through meditative stabilization – advanced levels of concentration – it is possible for someone, Buddhist or non-Buddhist, to abandon temporarily the manifest gross form of the afflictions associated with the first eight of the nine levels of cyclic existence: the desire realm, the four concentrations, limitless space, limitless consciousness, and nothingness. However, one cannot get rid of those associated with the ninth level, the peak of cyclic existence, at all, and even those temporarily abandoned with respect to the lower levels will eventually reoccur. Only through realization and subsequent meditation of emptiness can one utterly abandon the afflictions and gain release from cyclic existence.

SECOND, THE EXPLANATION IN KAMALASHĪLA'S "STAGES OF MEDITATION" THAT IF SUCHNESS IS NOT REALIZED, ONE CANNOT BE RELEASED AS IS THE CASE WITH THE MEDITATIVE STABILIZATIONS OF NON-BUDDHISTS

With respect to such non-release, the first of Kamalashīla's [three works on the] *Stages of Meditation* (*sgom rim*, *bhāvanā-krama*) says that:[424]

> Having attained, or established, a calm abiding that is a steadiness of mind with respect to an object of observation in accordance with the mode of training in calm abiding as explained earlier, one should then meditate within analyzing suchness with wisdom

realizing the meaning of selflessness. [140] One should know the way in which through doing this the fruit [of such practice] arises: Through repeated analysis and meditation by means of that wisdom, a special insight endowed with the illumination of clear knowledge of suchness arises; in dependence on its arising, that is, by means of cultivating special insight into selflessness, the seeds of thorough obscuration – the conception of self – will be abandoned thoroughly, from the root, in the manner of their never returning again.

If one does not cultivate such special insight, but instead is satisfied merely with calm abiding, since such calm abiding also exists among Forders, then, just as Forders cannot abandon afflictions from the root no matter how much they cultivate calm abiding, so one will not be able to abandon afflictions from the root merely through the meditative stabilization of calm abiding.

THIRD, CITATION OF A DEFINITIVE SŪTRA WHICH IS A SOURCE FOR THAT

That such could not be done was also set forth by the Supramundane Victor in a sūtra [the *King of Meditative Stabilizations Sūtra* (*ting nge 'dzin gyi rgyal po*, *samādhirāja*)] in which he said that:[425]

> Some worldly common beings cultivate the actual meditative stabilizations of calm abiding, or calm abiding and [mundane] special insight, of the peak of cyclic existence and below, without realizing suchness. However, without realizing suchness, those cultivators of a meditative stabilization which is a concentration or formless absorption utterly do not, no matter how much they meditate, destroy and abandon through that path the root of cyclic existence – the discrimination apprehending self – due

> to not possessing the quintessential instructions of the Buddha's teaching. Although temporarily they can suppress manifest afflictions,[426] due to not having abandoned the conception of self, the afflictions – with the conception of self as their basis – [141] return and, having increased, thoroughly disturb their minds again. Having been caused to lack independence, they accumulate actions whereby they circle in cyclic existence. For example, although the Forder Udraka cultivated here, in this world, a meditative stabilization having the aspect of [viewing a lower level as] gross and [a higher level as] peaceful, a calm abiding and [mundane] special insight that is an actual meditative absorption of the peak of cyclic existence, his meditative absorption deteriorated.

This sūtra is cited in Kamalashīla's *Stages of Meditation*.

FOURTH, A WORLDLY MEDITATIVE STABILIZATION THAT IS A CONCENTRATION OR FORMLESS ABSORPTION CANNOT DESTROY EVEN THE MANIFEST CONCEPTION OF SELF

In that scripture, the phrase, "although [worldly beings] cultivate meditative stabilization" means, "although [worldly beings] cultivate a meditative stabilization possessing the three features of non-conceptuality, clarity, and bliss as explained before". That the conception of self cannot be abandoned even though one cultivates just such a meditative stabilization is indicated by "they do not destroy the discrimination of self".

FIFTH, SINCE THE CONCEPTION OF SELF HAS NOT BEEN ABANDONED THROUGH THAT MEDITATIVE STABILIZATION, AFFLICTIONS ARE GENERATED FROM THE CONCEPTION OF SELF, DUE TO WHICH ONE IS NOT RELEASED

The fact that the afflictions will still again, at some future time, be generated and increase due to not having abandoned the conception of self is indicated by "the afflictions return and disturb [the mind]".

SECOND, THE PATH OF RELEASE AS WELL AS HOW IT IS CULTIVATED

This has three parts: identifying the path of release, how it is cultivated in meditation, and proving through scripture and reasoning that one cannot be released by anything other than realization of suchness.

FIRST, IDENTIFYING THE PATH OF RELEASE

If liberation cannot be attained merely through meditative stabilization, through cultivating what sort of path is it attained? [142]

Answer: Just after that passage [from the *King of Meditative Stabilizations Sūtra*], one stanza is set forth as was quoted earlier on the occasion of [explaining the need to cultivate both special insight and] calm abiding:

> If selflessness is analyzed with respect to phenomena
> [And if one meditates in accordance with that individual analysis,
> This is the cause of the fruit, the attainment of nirvāṇa.
> There is no peace through any other cause]. (IX.37)

The meaning of the first line is, "If one does not set in mere calm abiding after one has cultivated it, but in addition to that analyzes individually phenomena that are selfless and generates the wisdom understanding the meaning of selflessness . . .".

SECOND, [HOW IT IS CULTIVATED IN MEDITATION]: IF ONE MEDITATES BY WAY OF ANALYZING SUCHNESS, ONE WILL BE RELEASED

Not only that, but also the second line says, "If one meditatively cultivates and sustains that view again and again in accordance with how ascertainment was gained upon investigating individually the meaning of selflessness . . .". This refers to sustaining the view of selflessness that has been gained and meditatively cultivating special insight.

As the cause of what does the meditative cultivation of such special insight serve? The third line says that such special insight is the cause of the attainment of nirvāṇa, which is posited as [its] effect. This line means that the cause of attaining the fruit of nirvāṇa, or liberation, is just special insight into suchness.

Chandrakīrti's *Supplement to (Nāgārjuna's) "Treatise on the Middle Way"* (*dbu ma la 'jug pa*, *madhyamakāvatāra*) says, ". . . a yogi will be released."[427] Nāgārjuna's *Precious Garland* (*rin chen phreng ba*, *ratnāvalī*, stanza 365) says:[428]

> Knowing thus truly and correctly
> That all animate beings are not [their own] reality,
> Not being subject [to rebirth] and without grasping,
> One passes from suffering like a fire without its cause.

Dharmakīrti's *Commentary on (Dignāga's) "Compendium on Valid Cognition"* (*tshad ma rnam 'grel*, *pramāṇavārttika*) says:[429]

> Therefore, all you who wish for release
> Should remove from the root the view of the transitory collection
> Which arises from seeds of similar type,
> Having its cause from beginningless time.

Āryadeva's *Four Hundred* (*bzhi brgya pa*, *catuḥśataka*, VIII.21) [143] says:[430]

> When one sees correctly, one has the supreme of situations.
> When one sees a little, one [gains] a good transmigration.
> Therefore, contemplating the self within
> The wise always generate intelligence.

> Ge-shay Wangdrak identified the meaning of "contemplating the self within" as identifying selflessness in terms of oneself, looking within.

Chandrakīrti's commentary on this [in his *Commentary on (Āryadeva's) "Four Hundred"* (*bzhi brgya pa'i 'grel pa, catuḥśatakaṭīkā*)] says:[431]

> When one sees suchness through the knowledge of the ultimate, one attains the supreme of situations, nirvāṇa. When one sees it slightly, that is, a little, one has a good transmigration as a god or human.

THIRD, PROVING THROUGH SCRIPTURE AND REASONING THAT ONE IS NOT RELEASED BY ANY METHOD OTHER THAN REALIZATION OF SUCHNESS

> Gyu-may Ken-sur Jampel Shenphen was careful to explain that this heading means, as is spelled out by the next subheading, that one must have realization of suchness in order to be released from cyclic existence; it does not mean that cultivation of attitudes of renunciation, compassion, and so forth are not methods for release from cyclic existence – for in conjunction with wisdom they are – but that merely through cultivating them *alone* one could not be released.

This has six parts.

WITHOUT THE PROFOUND VIEW, ONE IS NOT RELEASED

Can liberation be attained through cultivating some other path without such special insight in the way in which it is attained through cultivation? In answer to this, the fourth line [of the above scripture] says that through cultivating something other than that special insight as a cause one will not attain peace. This means that no matter how much you cultivate a path other than that cause [i.e., other than special insight], if you do not cultivate such special insight, you will not attain the liberation that is a pacification of suffering and afflictions.

This scripture teaching very clearly that only the wisdom of selflessness severs the root of mundane, that is, cyclic, existence was cited in Kamalashīla's *Mādhyamika Stages of Meditation* in order to damage the assertion of the Chinese abbot Hva-shang that the supreme of meditations takes all conceptuality such as individual analysis and so forth as the object of abandonment, setting aside all mental application. Therefore, you need to gain ascertainment with respect to the fact that the view of selflessness is indispensible for severing the root of cyclic existence; you should know that you cannot be released without analytical meditation, in that if you analyze the reasons for [selflessness] again and again, your ascertainment becomes stronger and stronger, whereby the conception of self is badly damaged. Those who want liberation should hold this to be important like their own life. [144]

Although even the Forder [non-Buddhist] sages have many good qualities such as meditative stabilizations which are concentrations or formless absorptions, clairvoyances, the immeasurables, and so forth, since they do not have such a view of selflessness, they cannot damage at all the root of cyclic existence though they strive in hundreds of ways; hence they cannot cross beyond [cyclic existence] even a little.

The entire next section about the root of cyclic existence (up to the next subheading) is added by Jam-yang-shay-ba; Dzong-ka-ba does not discuss this question until much later in the text (not included in this translation) and then only relatively briefly. However, in his *Medium Exposition of Special Insight* it is the first major topic he addresses.

Jam-yang-shay-ba is presenting in brief the Indian source quotes for the Prāsaṅgika position that the root of cyclic existence – i.e., the most basic among what must be eradicated in order to get out of cyclic existence – is ignorance; that this ignorance is of two types, the misconception of the nature of the person and the misconception of the nature of other phenomena such as the aggregates; that these two misconceptions are in a causal relationship – the misconception of the nature of the aggregates leading to the misconception of the nature of the self; but that this nonetheless does not entail that there are two roots of cyclic existence because the mode of apprehension of both misconceptions is exactly the same – in both cases there is a conception of inherent existence whereas such does not exist.

Āryadeva's *Four Hundred* (XII.13ab) says:[432]

> . . . .
> The door of peace having no second,
> The destroyer of bad views.

Chandrakīrti's *Commentary on (Āryadeva's) "Four Hundred"*, commenting on that, says:[433]

> That which is the door of peace having no second is selflessness. That which destroys bad views is selflessness.

Hence, because there is no more than one root of cyclic existence, there is no more than one door of peace. Since the root of cyclic existence does not involve consciousnesses that have many discordant modes of apprehension, the root of cyclic existence is posited as one. However, the conception of the true existence of the aggregates – the conception of a self of phenomena – and the view of the transitory collection – the conception of a self of persons – are both roots of cyclic existence. For, with respect to the former, Nāgārjuna's *Precious Garland* (stanza 35) says:[434]

> As long as one conceives the aggregates [to be inherently existent]
> So long is there conception of the I [as inherently existent] with respect to them.
> When this conception of an [inherently existent] I exists, there is again action . . .

Nāgārjuna's *Seventy Stanzas on Emptiness* (*stong nyid bdun cu pa*, *śūnyatāsaptati*, stanza 64) says:[435]

That which conceives things produced
From causes and conditions to be real
Was said by the Teacher to be ignorance;
From it the twelve branches arise.

[With respect to the latter, the view of the transitory,] Chandrakīrti's *Supplement to (Nāgārjuna's) "Treatise on the Middle Way"* says that the innate view of the transitory collection is the root of cyclic existence.[436] Therefore, it is clear that one must make a distinction between [this system] and Svātantrika and so forth [that is, Svātantrika, Chittamātra, Sautrāntika, and Vaibhāṣhika].

> What the Prāsaṅgikas and the lower schools identify as the innate view of the transitory collection is not the same.[437] In Prāsaṅgika it is the innate conception of the person as inherently existent. In the lower schools it is the innate conception of the person as substantially established or self-sufficient. Thus, though all say that the innate view of the transitory collection is the root of cyclic existence, what they mean by it is quite different. Further, Prāsaṅgikas can say that there are not two roots of cyclic existence – even though both the conception of a self of persons and the conception of a self of phenomena are identified as the root of cyclic existence – because the modes of apprehension of the two are the same. In Svātantrika where the modes of apprehension are not the same, a distinction is made between the root of cyclic existence – the conception of a self of persons – and the *final* root of cyclic existence – the conception of a self of phenomena.

SECOND, WITHOUT HEARING MUCH ABOUT SELFLESSNESS, ONE IS NOT RELEASED THROUGH MEDITATIVE STABILIZATION AND ETHICS

Like the teachings in sūtra and so forth above, the *Scriptural Collection of Bodhisattvas* (*byang chub sems dpa'i sde snod, bodhisattvapiṭaka*) (which is said to be in the *Avataṃsaka Sūtra*) quoted earlier at the point of calm abiding says that: [145]

> Dra-di Ge-shay identifies this as the *Avataṃsaka Sūtra* (*phal po che'i mdo*);[438] however, in the Tibetan Tripitaka, it is found as a chapter of the *Heap of Jewels Sūtra* (*dkon mchog brtsegs pa, ratnakūṭa*).

One who, without knowing the meaning of suchness as it is explained in the Conqueror's scriptures, is satisfied with merely attaining a meditative stabilization might mistakenly think that the cultivation of only this is the final path for meditating on the profound meaning, suchness, and thus the means of release from cyclic existence. Developing the pride of conceiving himself or herself to be supreme, that person might make this known, or manifest, to others, saying, "I am cultivating the profound path." Through that, [however, this person] will not be released. Implicit in what [Buddha] said is that not only will one not be liberated from cyclic existence, but also due to the increase of afflictions such as pride, [such meditation] binds one in cyclic existence.

That sūtra also says that I, the Tathāgata, thinking that a person is not released from cyclic existence through mere meditative stabilization without knowing the meaning of suchness, propounded to my retinue that a person who hears the quintessential instructions taught by another, an excellent spiritual guide, will be released from the faults of cyclic existence, the frights of aging and death.

> Ge-shay Wangdrak explained that this does not indicate that hearing is unnecessary for meditative stabilization, but that there is a danger of someone's feeling, upon the attainment of meditative stabilization, that there is no need for further hearing.

The teacher Buddha himself clearly explained his own thought, which is that one who does not create pride upon having attained a few good qualities, but hears concordant instructions from another, an excellent spiritual guide, will be liberated from cyclic existence. One should hear from that excellent spiritual guide an unmistaken explanation of the quintessential instructions on the meaning of the suchness of selflessness. Therefore, it says in sūtra, "Deterioration of ethics is not so bad; deterioration of view is."

> Ge-shay Gönchok Tsering explained this as meaning that falling from ethics is, *comparatively*, a more minor infraction, for if one falls from the correct view, one falls from the middle way to one of the extremes. Particularly if one falls into the extreme of nihilism and loses belief in the laws of karma, one is liable to engage in serious infractions which will lead to bad rebirths in the future. Ken-sur Denba Dendzin added that a falling from ethics could be "fixed up" by practices such as confession, and so forth, whereas if one has fallen from the view, one is likely outside the sphere of such ethical activities and hence a falling from the view is a more difficult situation.[439]

THIRD, WITHOUT SEEKING HEARING ON THE TOPIC OF SELFLESSNESS THROUGH RELYING ON ANOTHER, A SKILLED SPIRITUAL GUIDE, EMPTINESS CANNOT BE REALIZED [146]

Therefore, if the meaning of the above is summarized, it is unquestionable – that is to say, it is decided and definite – that Buddha said, "Hear another," in order to stop the wrong idea conceiving that the realization of the profound is naturally generated from within, through staying with one's eyes closed with the mind aimed at certain slight quintessential instructions on meditative stabilization, without doing any hearing or thinking by way of hearing about the non-mistaken meaning of selflessness from an excellent skillful spiritual guide who has the compassionate wish to help, does not procrastinate, and is external, i.e., is not included in your own continuum.

FOURTH, THE NEED FOR LISTENING TO AND THINKING ON THE SCRIPTURES SINCE ALL OF THE SCRIPTURES DIRECTLY OR INDIRECTLY TEACH ABOUT EMPTINESS

In general, all the scriptures of the Conqueror mainly teach only methods for release from cyclic existence. Seeing that in order to be released from cyclic existence it is definitely necessary to realize suchness, [Buddha] taught suchness directly by means of some scriptures. Even those scriptures that do not directly teach [suchness], flow toward or are directed toward the teaching of suchness indirectly and only descend toward the teaching of suchness. For, such is explained in many sūtras and treatises. Āryadeva['s *Four Hundred*] (XII.23) says:[440]

> [The doctrines spoken by the Tathāgatas
> In brief are non-harmfulness]
> And emptiness, nirvāṇa.
> Here there are only these two.

In his commentary on that, Chandrakīrti says:[441]

> These two doctrines teaching about non-harm and emptiness are the means for attaining high status and pure release. Hence, here there are only these two.

The *King of Meditative Stabilizations Sūtra* says:[442]

> The many doctrines taught by the Buddhas [147]
> Are the selflessness of all phenomena.

Also, the foremost precious one [Dzong-ka-ba] says [in his *Praise of Dependent-Arising*]:[443]

> All of your teachings stem
> From just dependent-arising.
> They also are for the sake of passing beyond sorrow.

> You [Buddha] have nothing that is not for the sake of peace.

The reason for this [that is, why all the scriptures either directly or indirectly teach emptiness] derives from the fact that the root of wandering in cyclic existence is the obscuration, like darkness, [which descends] upon mistaking self [i.e., making the mistake of conceiving inherent existence]. Therefore, it is necessary to clear away the darkness of obscuration, and this darkness that is an obscuration with respect to self is not overcome until the illumination of the wisdom knowing suchness arises. When that illumination arises, [the darkness of obscuration] is definitely overcome. Hence, [release from cyclic existence] depends upon the wisdom knowing suchness.

Since mere calm abiding that is a one-pointedness of mind does not have any capacity to damage the clouded perception of obscuration with regard to self [i.e., inherent existence], you cannot attain the pure exalted wisdom free from that clouded perception [through mere calm abiding], and the darkness which is obscuration with respect to self cannot at all be overcome. Since, if it is not overcome, you must wander in cyclic existence, you must hold such wisdom to be very important and definitely seek it, thinking, "I will definitely seek the wisdom ascertaining and realizing the meaning of suchness – selflessness." That this is needed is stated in Kamalashīla's middle *Stages of Meditation* which says that:[444]

> When, having trained in calm abiding, it is achieved, you should – in dependence on that calm abiding – definitely cultivate the special insight realizing suchness. Such meditators who have achieved calm abiding should think at the beginning of their meditative cultivation [of special insight]:
>
> > Since all the sayings (*bka'*) [148] of the Supramundane Victor were set forth only as methods for the realization of suchness – the path for release from cyclic existence – they were

spoken well, that is to say, non-erroneously, and only to help. For, all of his sayings manifestly, that is to say, directly, or indirectly illuminate – that is, purposely set forth mainly – the suchness of selflessness or just flow toward the teaching of suchness.

The reason why they illuminate suchness and flow toward suchness is that if one knows suchness, through the force of that, one attains pure exalted wisdom and is liberated from cyclic existence, having become free from all bonds of wrong views, such as the view of self, which are connected one to the other like a net. This is like, for example, the clearing away of darkness through the arising of illumination. Through mere calm abiding, the pure exalted wisdom free from clouded perception with respect to self is not attained, and the obscuration, like darkness, obscuring the path to liberation will also not be cleared away. However, if one analytically meditates well – non-erroneously – again and again on suchness by means of the wisdom ascertaining suchness, the very pure exalted wisdom free from the clouded perception of obscuration will be attained; suchness will be realized directly. Only through the wisdom realizing suchness will the obstructions of obscuration be thoroughly, that is, definitely, abandoned. Therefore, I, the meditator, definitely dwelling also in calm abiding, will by means of wisdom thoroughly seek suchness by way of all techniques and in all forms of its meaning. In other words, I will meditatively cultivate the special insight realizing suchness; [149] I will not be satisfied with just mere calm abiding without that wisdom.

> What is the suchness to be sought? Ultimately, all things, in terms of their own final mode of subsistence, are not established as any of the selves of persons or phenomena which are the objects of negation and, therefore, are just established as empty of those two objects of negation.

FIFTH, SINCE THE FIRST FIVE PERFECTIONS ARE LIKE BLIND PERSONS, FROM AMONG [THE PERFECTIONS], ONLY THE PERFECTION OF WISDOM, OR WISDOM, REALIZES SUCHNESS

From among the six perfections, through what perfection is the suchness that is to be sought in this way realized? It is realized by the perfection of wisdom. Since it cannot be realized by the other five perfections – concentration, and so forth – you should not make the mistake of thinking that you have found a perfection of wisdom when you have found only a concentration such as that of calm abiding; you should mainly generate the wisdom ascertaining suchness. The reason for this is set forth in the *Sūtra Unravelling the Thought* (*mdo sde dgongs 'grel, saṃdhinirmocana*) which says that:[445]

> Avalokiteshvara asked, "Supramundane Victor, a Bodhisattva does indeed apprehend the mode of subsistence of phenomena through realizing just their non-entityness, but from among the six perfections, through which perfection does he or she apprehend and realize such?" In answer [Buddha] said, "Avalokiteshvara, [150] mainly it is apprehended and realized only through the perfection of wisdom."

SIXTH, IF WISDOM, LIKE AN EYE, IS NOT GENERATED THROUGH HEARING AND THINKING, ONE IS NOT RELEASED

Thinking of that fact, the *Sūtra of Cultivating Faith in the Mahāyāna* (*theg pa chen po la dad pa sgom pa'i mdo, mahāyānaprasādaprabhāvana*), which was quoted before, says that:[446]

If the wisdom realizing suchness does not abide, that is to say, if one is devoid of it, then not only with respect to those of low or middling faculties – Hearers, Solitary Realizers, and so forth – but also with respect to those who have faith in the Bodhisattva Mahāyāna, those of naturally sharp faculties, no matter how much they perform giving and so forth within the Mahāyāna, I, the Teacher, do not say that they are dwelling in release, deliverance.

1 *The Interpretable and the Definitive*

Second, how special insight is achieved.[447] Since it is the case that mere calm abiding is not sufficient and special insight is needed, with regard to the second heading from above,[448] how to train in special insight, there are four parts: fulfilling the prerequisites for special insight, the divisions of special insight, how to cultivate special insight in meditation, and the measure of having achieved special insight through meditative cultivation.

FULFILLING THE PREREQUISITES FOR SPECIAL INSIGHT

This has two parts: the need to hear and think about the stainless scriptures and the need not to mistake the interpretable and the definitive.

THE NEED TO HEAR AND THINK ABOUT THE STAINLESS SCRIPTURES

This has three parts, the first of which is the need to hear and think about the scriptures. With respect to fulfilling the causal prerequisites for special insight, you should without error rely on excellent scholars – who know non-erroneously the essentials of the Conqueror's scriptures teaching suchness – in a manner pleasing them. Then, you should hear the stainless, pure textual systems that teach suchness unerringly in accordance with the scriptures of the Conqueror. Furthermore, the generation of the view realizing the meaning of suchness decisively by means of the wisdom of definitively hearing quintessential instructions from those spiritual guides [151] and the wisdom of thinking until you gain ascertainment yourself with respect to the meaning of the quintessential instructions as they have been heard is the indispensible prerequisite for special insight. For, if you do not have such a view realizing decisively the meaning of suchness, the mode of being, you can never generate the special insight type of realization realizing the mode [of being of phenomena], that is to say, suchness.

(With respect to the meaning of [the term] "decisively" [*phu thag chod pa*, more literally "decisive with respect to the full extent", which was used above], if in a particular area one lost, for instance, a horse, when one searches through the full extent of that area and comes to a decision that the horse is not there, one can speak of the search as decisive with respect to the full extent of that area. Similarly, in searching out the meaning of suchness, one is "decisive" with respect to suchness when one decides that the self which is the object of negation does not exist upon searching [for it] with complete forms of reasonings that involve modes of seeking it in all ways.)

SECOND, THE NEED TO FOLLOW ONE OF THE GREAT OPENERS OF THE CHARIOT-WAYS

Such a decisive view must be sought by one who, without relying with conviction on just sūtras of interpretable meaning, relies with conviction on and follows sūtras of definitive meaning, this [precept] being one from among the four reliances. Therefore, in order to follow sūtras of definitive meaning, you must understand the meaning of the scriptures of definitive meaning through having come to know the difference between sūtras requiring interpretation and of definitive meaning. Also, this understanding definitely must rely upon treatises by the great openers of the chariot-ways, who are valid in the sense of being incontrovertible, such as Nāgārjuna and Asaṅga, [152] which comment in accordance with the thought of the sūtras. If you do not rely on such, you are like a blind person who, without a guide, is approaching an area that is frightful due to having the fright of being a path along an abyss. Since you will thereby be harmed, you most definitely must rely on such non-erroneous treatises commenting on [Buddha's] thought. Because this [passage] explains that it is unsuitable to follow the stupid and unskillful, take care.

THIRD, SINCE CHANDRAKĪRTI'S "SUPPLEMENT TO (NĀGĀRJUNA'S) 'TREATISE ON THE MIDDLE WAY'" EXPLAINS THAT ONE IS NOT RELEASED UNTIL UNDERSTANDING NĀGĀRJUNA'S SYSTEM FROM AMONG THOSE [MANY SYSTEMS], IT IS NECESSARY TO DEPEND ON THAT

On what sort of valid commentator on [Buddha's] thought should you depend? The special being, the Superior Nāgārjuna was prophesied very clearly by Buddha, the Supramundane Victor, himself without any obscurity in many sūtras – such as the *Descent into Laṅkā* (*lang kar gzhegs pa, laṅkāvatāra*) and so forth – and tantras – such as the *Mañjushrī Root Tantra* (*'jam dpal rtsa rgyud, mañjuśrīmūlatantra*) and so forth – as properly commenting on the meaning of the profound suchness free from all extremes of permanence and annihilation, that is to say, true existence and utter nonexistence – this profound suchness being the essence of the Conqueror's teaching. He is thoroughly renowned in that the fame of his name is spread throughout the three levels – below the earth, on the earth, and above the earth – and is valid with respect to this [profound suchness]. Hence, you should seek the view realizing emptiness based on his texts – the "Collections of Reasonings" and so forth. For, Chandrakīrti's *Supplement to (Nāgārjuna's) "Treatise on the Middle Way"* (VI.79ab) says:[449]

There is no method of pacification outside
The path of the honorable master Nāgārjuna.

Furthermore, [153] it is established by scriptures such as the *Mañjushrī Root Tantra*, the *Descent Into Laṅkā*, the *Great Drum Sūtra* (*rnga bo che, mahābherīhārakaparivārta*) and so forth as well as by reasoning that Nāgārjuna realized the profound [emptiness] directly. For, Chandrakīrti's *Supplement to (Nāgārjuna's) "Treatise on the Middle Way"* (VI.3) says:[450]

Since the way that he [Nāgārjuna] realized the very profound doctrine
Is [established] by scripture as well as reasoning . . .

The *Mañjushrī Root Tantra* says:[451]

Four Hundred years after I,
The Tathāgata, have passed away
A monk called Nāga will arise.
He will have faith in and help the teaching.
Attaining the very joyful ground
He will live for six hundred years . . .
He will know the meaning of no inherent existence
(*dngos po med*).

The *Descent Into Laṅkā* says:[452]

In the south, in the area of Bheda [Vidarbha],
There will be a widely renowned monk, Shrīmān;
He, called by the name Nāga,
Will destroy the positions of existence and non-existence.
. . . .
Having attained the very joyful ground,
[He will go to the Joyous Pure Land].

Thus, since he attained the very joyful ground, he directly realized emptiness.

This is the establishment by reasoning: since sūtra says that Nāgārjuna attained the first ground and since in order to do so, one must realize emptiness directly, one can infer that Nāgārjuna realized emptiness directly. The words of the sūtras themselves are the establishment by scripture.

The commentary [Avalokitavrata's *Commentary on (Bhāvaviveka's) "Lamp for (Nāgārjuna's) 'Wisdom'"* (*shes rab sgron ma'i rgya cher 'grel pa, prajñāpradīpaṭīkā*)] explains that [Nāgārjuna], initially a common being, attained the first ground, but it accords with sūtra [to hold] that he was initially a Mahāyāna Superior who attained the eighth ground in this life.

Even though the sūtra and tantra cited above, as well as Avalokitavrata, say that Nāgārjuna attained the first Bodhisattva ground, the Very Joyful, there is another sūtra source, the *Great Drum Sūtra* which says, "Having set him in the seventh ground, I will bless him as an ordinary being." Jam-yang-shay-ba resolves this apparent conflict by finding special significance in the words "as an ordinary being", this meaning that Nāgārjuna *seemed* to be an ordinary being who attained the first ground during that life, but in fact was a seventh grounder who attained the eighth.[453]

From among the three great proclamations of doctrine which [Nāgārjuna] proclaimed, [his] explaining the *Perfection of Wisdom Sūtras* and appearing in the south four hundred years after [Buddha] had passed are the second [proclamation], and [his] explaining the *Great Drum Sūtra* for a hundred years when the [average] lifespan was eighty years is the third proclamation of doctrine. The *Great Cloud Sūtra* (*sprin chen, mahāmegha*) says:[454]

> That monk will die after proclaiming three proclamations of doctrine.... He will appear a final time.

The *Great Drum Sūtra* says:[455]

> Such a monk is very difficult to find;
> Gradually the illumination deteriorated.

> Then, there was one final
> Appearance in the southern area.

Dzong-ka-ba's *Great Commentary on (Nāgārjuna's) "Treatise on the Middle Way"* (*rtsa shes ṭik chen*) says:[456]

> It is said that the prophecy of such in the *Great Drum Sūtra* is of the final appearance in the south ... [154]

Therefore, it is as is set forth by both the *Great Cloud* and the *Great Drum.*

Here Jam-yang-shay-ba is giving only the briefest indication of the controversy over the three proclamations of doctrine attributed to Nāgārjuna by a Tibetan tradition and its sources. He deals with this in great detail in his *Great Exposition of Tenets* (*grub mtha' chen mo*) and *Great Exposition of the Middle Way* (*dbu ma chen mo*); following are the conclusions he draws in the latter text:[457]

This master [Nāgārjuna] appeared three times in the southern part of the country of Superiors [India] during one lifetime and proclaimed three proclamations of doctrine. For, in accordance with the *Mañjushrī Root Tantra* and the *Great Cloud Sūtra*:

1 He was born when four hundred years had elapsed after the Teacher passed away.

2 Then he proclaimed the first proclamation of doctrine.

3 Then, having gained adepthood, somewhere between his fiftieth and hundredth years he went to the land of dragons and, bringing back the *Perfection of Wisdom [Sūtra]*, appeared in the south a second time.

4 Having composed the *Fundamental Text Called "Wisdom"* [the *Treatise on the Middle Way*], he proclaimed the second proclamation of the doctrine of emptiness of the Great Vehicle for up to a hundred years.

Then, he went to [the northern continent called]

Unpleasant Sound and again appeared in the south for a third time.

6 During this final period, having brought back the *Great Drum Sūtra*, the *Great Cloud Sūtra*, and so forth, he proclaimed the third proclamation of doctrine, discourse examining the basic constituent, for a hundred years.

In accordance with the *Mañjushrī Root Tantra* and the *Laṅkāvatāra Sūtra*, in terms of how things appeared he displayed the mode of an ordinary being's attaining the Very Joyful ground in that lifetime, but in terms of actual fact he was a seventh grounder because such is established by many scriptures and reasonings.

Therefore, one should definitely depend on his [Nāgārjuna's] texts.

THE NEED NOT TO MISTAKE THE INTERPRETABLE AND THE DEFINITIVE

This has three parts: identifying the mode of requiring interpretation and the mode of being definitive from the viewpoint of which something becomes a scripture of definitive or interpretable meaning; the history of commentary on Nāgārjuna's thought; and how to settle the view of emptiness.

IDENTIFYING SCRIPTURES REQUIRING INTERPRETATION AND SCRIPTURES OF DEFINITIVE MEANING

This has two parts: the need to rely on sūtras of definitive meaning [in order to realize] the profound meaning; and the meaning of requiring interpretation and being definitive.

THE NEED TO RELY ON SŪTRAS OF DEFINITIVE MEANING [IN ORDER TO REALIZE] THE PROFOUND MEANING

Those wishing liberation who want to realize suchness should hold as chief the Conqueror's scriptures and rely on them. However, due to the different thoughts of various trainees, the scriptures – that to be relied on – arose in various forms – requiring interpretation and definitive. Hence, you might wonder in dependence upon what sort of scripture you should seek the meaning of the profound. The answer is that without depending upon a scripture of definitive meaning, through depending on other scriptures you cannot realize the meaning of the profound. However, if you definitely depend on scriptures of definitive meaning, you should realize suchness.

THE MEANING OF REQUIRING INTERPRETATION AND BEING DEFINITIVE

This has four parts: positing the interpretable and definitive by way of the subjects discussed, how [the interpretable and the definitive] are explained in the *Teachings of Akṣhayamati Sūtra* (*blo gros mi zad pas bstan pa, akṣayamatinirdeśa*), how they are explained in other sūtras and treatises, and a refutation of others' mistakes with regard to the interpretable and the definitive.

Positing the interpretable and the definitive by way of the subject discussed

Question: What sort of scripture is of definitive meaning and what sort of scripture is of interpretable meaning? [155]

Answer: That scriptures require interpretation or are definitive is not posited from the viewpoint of the means of expression (*rjod byed*) [that is, the words] but must be posited from the viewpoint of the subject discussed (*brjod bya*). For, this is an occasion of investigating interpretable meaning and definitive meaning in terms of sūtras, and "meaning" refers to the meaning expressed.[458]

The system of positing them from this viewpoint is that a scripture which mainly teaches explicitly, as its subject of discussion, the suchness of selflessness – the ultimate – is identified as of definitive meaning and one which mainly teaches explicitly, as its subject of discussion, variously appearing conventionalities – natures which are falsities – is identified as a scripture whose meaning requires interpretation.

Second, how [the interpretable and the definitive] are explained in the "Teachings of Akṣhayamati Sūtra"

This has four parts.

First, a brief indication

That these are to be held in this way was set forth in the *Teachings of Akṣhayamati Sūtra* which says that:[459]

> *Question*: "What are sūtras of definitive meaning? What are sūtras whose meaning requires interpretation?"
>
> *Answer*: Those sūtras that mainly and explicitly teach conventional truths in that they posit and establish mere entities of false natures, conventionalities, are called sūtras of interpretable meaning. Those sūtras that mainly and explicitly teach ultimate truths in the sense that they posit and establish the ultimate entities, ultimate truths, which are mere eliminations of the elaborations of true establishment, are called sūtras of definitive meaning.

Second, the extensive explanation of the body [of this text, the "Teachings of Akṣhayamati Sūtra"]

> *Question*: What is the mode of teaching the establishment of conventional entities?
>
> *Answer*: Conventionalities, such as persons, Buddhas, and so forth, which are different even in fact [not just in words] are false natures that appear as various objects; therefore, they must be indicated by way of various words that are their means of expression as well as letters, "a", "b", etc., the bases of those words. [156] Since [what is taught in] sūtras that mainly and explicitly teach those is not suitable to be the mode of subsistence of those phenomena, [those sūtras] are called sūtras of interpretable meaning. This is like, for example, [using the words] self, sentient being, and so forth with respect to persons.

Ken-sur Denba Dendzin: Each of these terms used with respect to persons conveys a different meaning. They are not all getting at the same meaning in the way in which the synonyms of emptiness are.

Question: What is the mode of teaching the establishment and positing of ultimate entities?

Answer: The teaching of a mere elimination of the elaborations of the object of negation is the mode of teaching the positing or establishment of the ultimate entity. Hence, that which is taught by scriptures which mainly and explicitly teach such – i.e., teach what is profound because its depth cannot be realized in the sense that it is difficult to fathom, what is difficult to view by way of methods such as examples, reasons, and so forth since it is difficult to see, and what is difficult to realize because it must be comprehended by the mind alone, and because although by way of those [examples and reasons] one knows the mere measure of how [the profound] exists, it is difficult to understand in the sense of being able to think, "The entity itself of this meaning is just like this," – is the mode of being of those phenomena, whereby those sūtras teaching such are called sūtras of definitive meaning. This is because self, sentient being, and so forth are undifferentiable in the sphere of reality.

The final nature of all phenomena is equally their emptiness of inherent existence.

Third, the explanation of the branches [that is, in more detail]

Question: What is an illustration of the mode of teaching a conventionality through the teaching of which as its subject of discussion [a sūtra] comes to be of interpretable meaning and what is an illustration of the mode of teaching the ultimate through the teaching of which as its subject of discussion [a sūtra] comes to be of definitive meaning?

An answer to this is also indicated very clearly in that sūtra. It [the *Teachings of Akṣhayamati Sūtra*] says that: [157][460]

> Called sūtras of interpretable meaning are those sūtras that explicitly teach as their subject of discussion, through the fabrications of words, such things as an independent controller, for instance, which appears [to exist] whereas there is none in fact, as well as objects having a false mode of appearance which must be expressed by way of various words, such as:
>
> *self* (*bdag, ātman*) – [so-called] due to the sense of authority, or due to the mind's being held as owned with respect to just the person;
>
> *sentient being* (*sems can, sattva*) – [so-called] due to possessing the exertion of intention (*sems pa, cetanā*), or because of possessing the power of heart (*snying stobs, sattva*) [as in *sattva, rajas,* and *tamas*];
>
> *living being* (*srog, jīva*) – because [life] acts as a basis of liveliness (*'tsho ba, jīvikā*), or in the sense of living;
>
> *the nourished* (*gso ba, poṣa*) – [a person is called the nourished] because of being that which is nourished through many causes of liveliness, or because of increasing;
>
> *creature* (*skyes bu, puruṣa*) – because of possessing capacity in the sense of having power with respect to actions; in Sanskrit this is *puruṣa*, translated [into Tibetan] as *skyes bu*;
>
> *person* (*gang zag, pudgala*) – because our continuums are filled (*gang*) with the afflictions and we have fallen (*zag*) into cyclic existence (this etymology is renowned to many [scholars, i.e., it has no scriptural source]);
>
> *born from manu* (*shed las kyes pa, manuja*) – because *shed* (*manu*) means power, or force, and this is one who is established from that nature;

child of manu (*shed bu, mānava*) – because, like the preceding, of being a child who is established from a nature of power or potency;
agent (*byed pa po, kāraka*) – because of being the accomplisher of resources;
feeler (*tshor ba po, vedakā*) – because of being the experiencer of feelings with respect to those resources; in another way, these last two are explained as: *agent* because of being the agent of actions (*las, karma*) and *feeler* because of being the experiencer of the feelings which are fruitions [of those actions].

Realization of the entity which is a mere elimination of all the elaborations of the object of negation, inherent existence, is the door of liberation. Therefore, called sūtras of definitive meaning are those sūtras that do not teach about entities appearing as various elaborations but mainly and explicitly teach as their subject of discussion the doors of liberation, those being:
emptiness (*stong pa nyid, śūnyatā*) – [so called] because phenomena's own entities are empty of inherent existence, or because the entities of phenomena do not truly exist; [158]
signlessness (*mtshan ma med pa, animitta*) – the non-true existence of signs which manifest unmixed with other causes of that [phenomenon], or due to the non-true existence of causes, means (*byed pa*), and so forth;
wishlessness (*smon pa med pa, apraṇihita*) – the non-existence of an entity suitable to be an object of wishing by way of hoping to attain its fruits ultimately; this is due to the fact that fruits and actions (*bya ba*) do not truly exist;
non-composition (*mngon par 'du byed pa med pa, anabhisaṃskāra*) – something cannot be produced from the point of view of being able to be composed, or put together, ultimately by other causes and conditions;

non-production (*skye ba med pa*, *anutpāda*) – the non-existence of the occurrence of the ultimate production of an effect since ultimately causes do not have that capacity;
not being produced (*ma skyes pa*, *ajāta*) – the non-production of effects from their own side since such [the ultimate production of an effect] does not occur;
non-existence of sentient beings (*sems can med pa*, *niḥ sattva*) who are under their own power;
non-existence of living beings (*srog med pa*, *nirjīva*) who are under their own power;
non-existence of persons (*gang zag med pa*, *niḥpudgala*) who are under their own power;
non-existence of controllers (*bdag po med pa*, *asvāmika*) who are under their own power.

[In summary,] with respect to those two modes of teaching, those which teach in the manner of "does not exist, does not exist" are [instances of] the mode of teaching the ultimate. Those which teach in the manner of "exists, exists" are [instances of] the mode of teaching conventionalities. Furthermore, not existing in "does not exist" refers to [not existing] ultimately and existence in "exists" refers to conventional [existence].

Moreover, those [terms listed above] from "self" to "feeler" are synonyms of "sentient being".[461]

Fourth, the meaning established [by the above sūtra]

This says that those sūtras that mainly and explicitly teach selflessness, no [ultimate] production, and so forth in the manner of eliminating elaborations are sūtras of definitive meaning; those sūtras that mainly and explicitly teach conventionalities which appear as various elaborations, such as a self, are sūtras of interpretable meaning. Therefore, you should know that the non-existence of a self that is under its own power, no [ultimate] existence of production, and so forth, are ultimate objects, and production and so forth are conventional objects.

Third, how [the interpretable and the definitive] are explained in other sūtras and treatises [159]

This has seven parts.

First, the explanation in the "King of Meditative Stabilizations Sūtra" that the interpretable and the definitive are posited by way of the subjects discussed

Not only that, the *King of Meditative Stabilizations Sūtra* also says that:[462]

> Those [sūtras] that explicitly teach a subject of discussion in accordance with the ultimate – the emptiness that is an emptiness of true establishment – explained in sūtra by the Sūgata are sūtras of definitive meaning. Also, one knows those that teach signlessness, wishlessness, and so forth as particulars, or instances, of sūtras of definitive meaning. All the sūtras, or verbal doctrines, that mainly and explicitly teach as their subject of discussion conventional phenomena, that is to say, conventional truths such as sentient beings, persons, beings, and so forth, are to be known as particulars of sūtras whose meaning requires interpretation.

Since the sūtras teaching those subjects of discussion are explained as sūtras of interpretable and definitive meaning [respectively], those things taught are established also as being interpretable objects and definitive objects. Based on that, the teachings, "does not exist, does not exist," in most of the texts of the protector Nāgārjuna are definitive, and the teachings, "exists, exists," in most of the Superior Asaṅga's texts are established as texts of the transmission of vast deeds and as texts of interpretable meaning.

Second, the explanation in Kamalashīla's treatise, the "Illumination of the Middle Way"

Not only that, Kamalashīla's *Illumination of the Middle Way* (*dbu ma snang ba, madhyamakāloka*) says that:[463]

> Therefore, the intelligent should understand that only sūtras that mainly and explicitly discuss the ultimate are sūtras of definitive meaning, and the opposite of those, sūtras that mainly and explicitly discuss conventional truths, are sūtras of interpretable meaning.

Third, the explanation by another sūtra that no ultimate production and so forth are definitive objects [160]

> The sūtra on the *Ornament Illuminating the Exalted Wisdom Operating in the Sphere of All Buddhas* (*sangs rgyas thams cad kyi yul la 'jug pa'i ye shes snang ba'i rgyan, sarvabuddhaviṣayāvatārajñānālokālaṃkāra*) says,[464] "That which is a definitive object is the ultimate." Also, no ultimate production is a definitive object, the ultimate; for, the *Teachings of Akṣhayamati Sūtra* teaches with respect to no ultimate production, and so forth, "[They] are definitive objects." Therefore, it is definite from those passages that only eliminations of the elaborations of the object of negation – no ultimate production and so forth – are ultimates, and objects appearing as various elaborations are just not ultimates.

Fourth, therefore [Nāgārjuna's] "Collections of Reasonings", the root texts and commentaries, are definitive texts

Because the difference between the interpretable and the definitive is such, the Madhyamaka "Collections of Reasonings" composed by Nāgārjuna as well as the valid treatises that serve as commentaries on their thought are to be held as treatises teaching the definitive meaning just as it is. This is because they extensively settle the ultimate free from all the collections of elaborations such as inherently existent production, cessation, and so forth.

Fifth, the meaning established and an etymology

Question: Why are these two, sūtras teaching ultimate truths and sūtras teaching conventional truths, respectively, called sūtras of definitive meaning and sūtras of interpretable meaning?

Answer: In that the ultimate truth which is the subject discussed in a sūtra of definitive meaning [161] cannot be interpreted as other than that meaning [i.e., as other than what is said there], it is definite and final as just that meaning. Hence, it is called that of which the meaning is definite or a definitive meaning. The meaning which is the subject being discussed abides as just that and is a meaning which does not pass beyond that. Therefore, it is the ultimate of what is to be settled and when decided as that meaning, there is no place other than that to which it could go. That meaning cannot be interpreted as some other meaning beyond that and cannot be interpreted by another person as something else because it possesses valid proofs according with the nature of things which determine and decide that meaning as being just that.[465]

Sixth, this definitive meaning must be true, [though] not in the sense of "true" [when the term "true" refers to] the object of negation, and must be established by valid cognition

> Jam-yang-shay-ba is making a careful qualification that even though definitive meanings must be true, this does not mean that Prāsaṅgikas would say that they are truly existent, or truly established. To go that far would be an over-reification and would fall within the sphere of what Prāsaṅgikas refute.

Thus Kamalashīla's *Illumination of the Middle Way* says that:[466]

[*Question*:] What is a sūtra of definitive meaning? *Answer*: A sūtra of definitive meaning is one that has valid cognition in the sense that there are proofs that determine the meaning which is taught in the sūtra as just that and it will not turn into something else. Also, it not being sufficient just to have such proofs, [it must be a sūtra] that makes an explanation in terms of mainly and explicitly settling ultimate truths, meanings proved [by that valid cognition].

That a sūtra of definitive meaning must have validity means that it must be literal – one must be able to accept the words spoken. Kamalashīla's second qualification is that it also must teach emptiness.

For, the meaning taught by that sūtra is definite as just that, it not being interpretable as something aside from that by another person, and the mode of subsistence of the object is not interpretable in any other way.[467]

Seventh, therefore, not only the non-literal but also the literal [162] the [final] mode of subsistence of which must be interpreted otherwise are of interpretable meaning

From the description of sūtras of definitive meaning in Kamalashīla's *Illumination of the Middle Way*, one can implicitly understand what sūtras of interpretable meaning are. They are sūtras in which, seeing damage to the meaning as it is taught, it is unsuitable to believingly hold it just as it is, it needing to be changed and interpreted to another meaning, explaining, "The aim of [Buddha's] thought in the explanation by this sūtra is such and such other meaning."

This is referring to non-literal sūtras, such as Buddha's saying that one should kill one's father and mother – meaning that one should eradicate existence (*srid pa*, *bhava*) and attachment (*sred pa*, *tṛṣṇa*), the tenth and eighth links, respectively, in the twelve-fold cycle of dependent-arising. Buddha

> did not in the least mean that one should kill one's physical father and mother, and hence the sūtra is non-literal.

Or, in a case in which one can believe what is literally taught just as it is, such as the statement, "From giving, resources; from ethics, a happy [transmigration]," it is permissible to hold it as being literal, but because merely such is taught mainly in terms of conventional truths, it is not the final mode of subsistence, that is to say, suchness; one must still seek the suchness that is the final status of that object as something other than this falsity which is a mere appearance of an object. Therefore, [these two types of sūtras] are those the meaning of which is to be interpreted, or those which require interpretation.

Fourth, removing others' [false] superimpositions with respect to the interpretable and the definitive

This has four parts: refuting the assertion that it is not necessary to affix "ultimately" to the object of negation; that otherwise it would [absurdly] follow that even the sūtras that refute [the object of negation] would be refuted; though a portion of a text is interpretable, this does not stop the treatise from being definitive; and that it is not contradictory for [a text] to be both literal and require interpretation.

First, refuting the assertion that it is not necessary to affix "ultimately" to the object of negation

> This does not mean that if a passage says "does not inherently exist", then it is necessary to say "ultimately does not inherently exist". Such would be Bhāvaviveka's viewpoint but is not asserted by Dzong-ka-ba. What is meant here is that if a passage says "does not exist", this means, "does not inherently exist".

Someone might raise the following qualm: Since sūtras of definitive meaning are literal, one must assert just what is explained in those sūtras; therefore, no matter what appears – such as that production does not exist, persons do not exist, and so forth – one must hold in accordance with the literal meaning that production, persons, and so forth utterly and totally do not exist. [163] Otherwise – if it did not have to be held that way – since it would not be suitable to assert those topics as literally taught, those texts would become non-literal whereby it would [absurdly] follow that they would become sūtras of interpretable meaning.

This [qualm] does not appear to be correct. When the Buddha, the Teacher who in sūtras is the speaker of "production does not exist" and so forth, refutes production and so forth, there are seen to be many sūtras of definitive meaning in which the qualification "ultimately" is affixed, as in, "There is no production ultimately." If, in a sūtra, the affixing of the qualification "ultimately" appears once at the beginning, end, or anywhere, then even at the points in the sūtra where that qualification is not [physically] affixed, it must definitely be affixed [that is, understood,] since it is a common attribute of all refutations of production and so forth.

No production ultimately and so forth – the attribute ["ultimately"] being affixed – is the mode of subsistence that is the suchness of phenomena such as production. Hence, it [no production ultimately] is established as the ultimate, the definitive object. How could a sūtra that mainly and explicitly teaches such a definitive object not be a sūtra of definitive meaning? It is only a sūtra of definitive meaning.

> The following paragraphs, through to the next section heading, are a summary by Nga-wang-rap-den of this section as well as a brief introduction to the remaining three sections.

With respect to the statement that sūtras of definitive meaning are necessarily literal, someone might raise the qualm, "If the statements in sūtras that production, cessation, and so forth do not exist are literal, then those [production and cessation] must not exist."

[*Answer*:] There is no such fault. When the Teacher refuted production, cessation, and so forth, he set forth many sūtras in which the qualification "ultimately" is affixed, and since [this qualification] is common to all sūtras of similar type, the qualification "ultimately" must be affixed [or understood] even in those in which it is not explicitly [that is, physically] affixed.

Since the negative of inherent existence in a phenomenon is the suchness of that phenomenon, through teaching such [a negative of inherent existence] the definitive object is taught. [164] Otherwise, if you assert that an utter non-existence of production, cessation, and so forth is the meaning of those sūtras, then those sūtras themselves would also become non-existent. This is because if, in general, production, cessation, and so forth do not exist, instances [of production] such as words possessing production and cessation must also not exist.

> Sūtras themselves are made up of words and are produced; so, if there is no production, then there could not be any sūtras.

Therefore, in either sūtras or treatises, the affixing of the qualification "ultimately" at any place in it is to be carried over to the general part [where it is not affixed]; it is not the case that since isolated words to which the qualification ["ultimately"] has not been affixed are not suitable to be held as literal, [that sūtra] is not of definitive meaning. Nor is it the case [conversely] that due to [the words at a particular spot] being suitable to be held as literal, [a sūtra] is of definitive meaning. With respect to the latter, for example, although the words, "Forms are impermanent," appearing in a Mind-Only text are suitable to be held as literal with respect to just their teaching that forms are impermanent, if you fit that passage together with the general body of the text, since it is qualified by true establishment, those words are not suitable to be held as of definitive meaning.

Second, otherwise [that is, if it were not necessary to affix "ultimately" to the object of negation] it would [absurdly] follow that even the sūtras refuting the object of negation would be refuted

If, without such a mode of affixing the qualification ["ultimately"], mere production were refuted, then since the generality "production" (production taken as a generality since it is both production and is a generality)[468] would be refuted, instances of production such as words which are its particulars would also be refuted. This is because the generality "production" pervades words, which are instances of it. If words are refuted, then sūtras of definitive meaning teaching such topics of discussion would also come to be refuted, whereby one could not make a presentation of sūtras of definitive meaning either.

Third, though a portion of a text is interpretable, this does not stop the treatise from being definitive

Therefore, the mere fact that it is not suitable to hold as literal what is taught in a few isolated words taken out of context, not connecting it with a qualification that is mentioned before or afterwards in that sūtra or treatise and is to be affixed in the general run of the sūtra or treatise does not destroy that sūtra or treatise's being a scripture of definitive meaning – [165] that is, it does not become not a scripture of definitive meaning.

Fourth, it is not contradictory for something to be both literal and require interpretation

You also should know that merely the fact that what is taught on the level of the words is suitable to be taken literally does not make the [sūtra or treatise necessarily] not a scripture of interpretable meaning.

2 *Reliable Sources*

THE HISTORY OF COMMENTARY ON NĀGĀRJUNA'S THOUGHT

This has six parts: transition [between what has been said and what will follow]; identifying the model Mādhyamikas; analyzing the names designated by earlier scholars; analyzing the chronology [of the arising of the Mādhyamika schools]; the correctness of the verbal conventions [used] by scholars of the later dissemination; and which masters are to be followed.

TRANSITION

Thus, the scriptures that mainly teach the final view realizing that all phenomena are without any inherent establishment whatsoever, that is, are without inherently existent production, inherently existent cessation, and so forth, are the Mahāyāna scriptures of definitive meaning – the Perfection of Wisdom Sūtras and so forth. Since the supreme valid being prophesied and praised by the Conqueror himself as commenting non-erroneously on the thought of those scriptures is the master, the Superior Nāgārjuna, what is the chronology of the commentators who commented on that master's [i.e., Nāgārjuna's] thought?

IDENTIFYING THE MODEL MĀDHYAMIKAS

Answer: With respect to this chronology, the chief of the Superior Nāgārjuna's actual students was Āryadeva. He, held to be valid like the master, the Superior Nāgārjuna, was taken as a believable source even by innumerable thoroughly renowned great upholders of the Prāsaṅgika-Mādhyamika and Svātantrika-Mādhyamika systems such as the masters Buddhapālita, the great founder of Prāsaṅgika; Bhāvaviveka, the great founder of Svātantrika; [166] Chandrakīrti, the chief upholder of the Prāsaṅgika system; and Shāntarakṣhita, the great founder of the Yogāchāra-Svātantrika system, and so forth. Therefore, by reason of the fact that both the father, the Superior Nāgārjuna, and his [spiritual] son, Āryadeva, are sources for the other Mādhyamikas – Prāsaṅgikas, Svātantrikas, and non-partisans – earlier scholars of Tibet called these two, father and son, the Mādhyamikas of the "model", "root", or "basic" texts – the "straight" texts of the Mādhyamika system that do not lean to one side or the other – and they used the verbal convention "partisan Mādhyamikas" for the others – Buddhapālita, Bhāvaviveka, and so forth.

ANALYZING THE NAMES DESIGNATED BY EARLIER SCHOLARS

This has two parts: their assertions and an analysis [of the second of those assertions].

ASSERTIONS

This has three parts.

FIRST, A DESIGNATION OF NAMES [TO MĀDHYAMIKAS] BY WAY OF HOW THEY POSIT CONVENTIONALITIES

Certain earlier great spiritual guides in Tibet said that there are two [divisions of] Mādhyamikas when names are designated by way of their having different ways of positing the presentations of conventional objects. What are the two? Sautrāntika-Mādhyamikas, (*mdo sde spyod pa'i dbu ma pa*) [so-called] because of according with the Sautrāntikas from the viewpoint of asserting that external objects that are separate entities from the internal mind exist conventionally, and Yogāchāra-Mādhyamikas, (*rnal 'byor spyod pa'i dbu ma pa*) [so-called] since they accord with the Chittamātrins from the viewpoint of asserting that such external objects do not exist conventionally. [167]

SECOND, A DESIGNATION OF NAMES [TO MĀDHYAMIKAS] BY WAY OF HOW THEY ASSERT THE ULTIMATE

Also, [certain earlier scholars said that] there are also two [divisions of] Mādhyamikas when names are designated by way of different ways of asserting the ultimate object: Mādhyamikas who are Reason-Established Illusionists, who assert that the illusion-like object that is a composite of the two – appearance and emptiness – about which reasoning has refuted true establishment with respect to the appearance of a subject is an ultimate truth; and Thoroughly Non-Abiding Mādhyamikas who assert that not such a composite of two factors, but a non-affirming negative that is a mere elimination of the elaborations of true existence with respect to appearances is an ultimate truth.[469] [Those earlier scholars] asserted that illustrations of the former of these two Mādhyamikas [when divided] by way of how they assert the ultimate, that is, those who assert that a composite of appearance and emptiness is an ultimate truth, are the masters Shāntarakṣhita, Kamalashīla, and so forth.

The verbal conventions of Illusion-Like Mādhyamikas and Thoroughly Non-Abiding Mādhyamikas are asserted not only by Tibetan scholars, but also by some Indian masters – the master Shūra, the Kashmīri Lakṣhmi, and so forth.[470]

THIRD, THERE ARE ALSO INDIANS WHO ACCORD WITH THE SECOND [MODE OF] DESIGNATION

If this is left *in general* without taking it as appropriate in this context [of presenting the *important* divisions of Mādhyamika], indeed, some Indian and Tibetan masters who asserted, or claimed, that they upheld the Mādhyamika system did make assertions in accordance with the above modes of designation.

In other words, the terms "illusion-like" and "thoroughly non-abiding" do appear as names for divisions of Mādhyamika, but not in important works and not necessarily indicating different modes of asserting the ultimate.

SECOND, ANALYSIS OF [THE SECOND OF] THOSE [ASSERTIONS]

This has three parts.

FIRST, A LACK OF ENTHUSIASM DUE TO ITS BEING OF LITTLE IMPORT

To be settled here are just the systems of the great upholders of Mādhyamika, who are renowned and established as the supreme of scholars, those followers of the master Nāgārjuna who are important for the settling of the view. [168] Who could explain all of the subtle differences in the modes of positing tenets in India and Tibet, the subtle distinctions of the five Svātantrikas, and so forth?

SECOND, THE WAY IN WHICH THE NAMES AND MEANINGS OF THIS [DESIGNATION FROM THE POINT OF VIEW OF] THE MODE OF ASSERTING THE ULTIMATE ARE [PRODUCTS OF] OBSCURATION

The great translator Lo-den-shay-rap (*blo ldan shes rab*, 1059–1109) in his *Epistolary Essay, Drop of Ambrosia*, said that such an assertion by earlier Tibetans who posited Mādhyamikas as of two types – Reason-Established Illusionists and Thoroughly Non-Abiding – by way of how they assert the ultimate is not a presentation pleasing excellent scholars, but rather is just a presentation generating delight in the obscured. What the great translator Lo-den-shay-rap said is very good and correct, for this occasion is one of explaining the ultimate of the Mādhyamikas that has five attributes. A sūtra [the *Extensive Sport* (*rgya cher rol pa*, *lalitavistara*)] says, "Profound, peaceful, free from elaborations, luminous, and uncompounded."[471]

Ge-shay Wangdrak: Jam-yang-shay-ba introduces this topic of the five attributes of the ultimate in order to indicate that a composite of appearance and emptiness could not be an ultimate truth since a composite lacks these five qualities which an ultimate truth must have.

Also, Nāgārjuna's *Treatise on the Middle Way* (XVIII.9) says:[472]

Not known from others, peaceful,
Not elaborated by elaborations,
Without conceptuality, without plurality –
These are asserted as the characteristics of the ultimate.

Earlier Tibetan scholars asserted that for the Reason-Established Illusionists a composite of appearance and emptiness is the ultimate truth. This appears to be an assertion that for the Reason-Established Illusionists the mere illusion-like object that is a composite of the attribute, non-true existence, with a subject such as a pot, which is comprehended by an inferential reasoning consciousness is an ultimate truth. However, in both Shāntarakṣhita's *Ornament for the Middle Way* (*dbu ma rgyan*, *madhyamakālaṃkāra*) and Kamalashīla's *Illumination of the Middle Way* (*dbu ma snang ba*, *madhyamakāloka*), it is said that the illusion-like explicit object of comprehension of a reasoning consciousness is designated with the name "ultimate" due to being concordant with the actual ultimate truth and "non-metaphoric ultimate" from the point of view of [its involving] a negative of the object of negation, true existence. [170]

The following paragraph of commentary from Jam-yang-shay-ba has to be read as distinct from the above paragraphs. The above two paragraphs are annotations, mainly by Dra-di Ge-shay, on a line of Dzong-ka-ba's which, without interpolated commentary reads: "Their assertion appears to be an assertion that [for the Reason-Established Illusionists] the mere object which is comprehended by an inferential reasoning consciousness is an ultimate truth whereas it is said in both Shāntarakṣhita's *Ornament for the Middle Way* and Kamalashīla's *Illumination of the Middle Way* that the object comprehended by a reasoning consciousness is designated 'ultimate' due to being concordant with an ultimate truth." Jam-yang-shay-ba's explanation is based on a very different interpretation of that line. Whereas Dra-di took "the mere object of comprehension of an inferential reasoning consciousness" to refer to the illusion-like composite of appearance and emptiness, which is clearly not an ultimate truth since it is an affirming negative rather than a non-affirming negative, Jam-yang-shay-ba takes the passage as referring to the non-affirming negative comprehended by an inferential reasoning consciousness. This, as he explains, can be said to be concordant with an actual ultimate, in that it is not realized in the same way as emptiness is realized by a non-conceptual wisdom consciousness, but it still is an actual ultimate truth. Interpreted in this way the passage hardly supports the point that Dzongka-ba is making, in that he is refuting the Reason-Established Illusionists' *misidentification* as an ultimate truth of what they consider to be the object comprehended by an inferential reasoning consciousness. See appendix one, pp.429–38, for a full discussion of this point.

Because an inferential consciousness is a conceptual consciousness, it is not free from the elaborations of conceptuality or from the elaborations of dualism; therefore, the non-affirming negative that is the object of comprehension of an inferential reasoning consciousness is an ultimate truth and is concordant with the ultimate which is free from elaborations.

For, Dzong-ka-ba's *Medium Exposition of the Stages of the Path* says:[473]

> Because [the object emptiness] is free from just a portion of the elaborations for a conceptual reasoning consciousness, it is not the actual ultimate that is free from both elaborations. However, this is not to say that in general [the emptiness comprehended by an inferential reasoning consciousness] is not an actual ultimate truth.

THIRD, A SUMMARY

Not only that, but also for the appearance factor of both a non-conceptual reasoning consciousness and a conceptual reasoning consciousness, there is no true establishment. Hence, great Mādhyamikas other than Shāntarakṣhita also do not assert that for the appearance factor of either a conceptual or non-conceptual reasoning consciousness the mere composite of the two, appearance and emptiness, the object with respect to which the elaborations of the object of negation, that is to say, true establishment, are eliminated by reasoning with respect to an appearing subject – an affirming negative which is a positive inclusion from among the two, the [mere] elimination and the positive inclusion – is an ultimate truth.

For, Dzong-ka-ba's *Medium Exposition of the Stages of the Path* says:[474]

> Also there is no great Mādhyamika who asserts that the mere object comprehended by an inference – the latter from among the two, the [mere] elimination and the positive inclusion, with respect to the elimination of the elaborations of the object of negation with respect to appearances – is an ultimate truth.

This [positive inclusion], the illusion-like emptiness of true existence, is a conventional truth.[475]

Therefore, the propounding that there are Thoroughly

Non-Abiding Mādhyamikas who assert that a mere elimination of elaborations with respect to appearances is an ultimate truth is not good [and] such a positing by earlier [Tibetan scholars] of verbal conventions for Mādhyamikas by way of how they assert the ultimate is not good.

> All that follows until the next section heading is a summary by Nga-wang-rap-den of the above discussion that he has supplemented with background material identifying the major source for the prevalent commentarial tradition that justifies some use of the terms "Reason-Established Illusionists" and "Proponents of Thorough Non-Abiding". It concludes with his own opinion that the terms are not acceptable in any context.[476]

Da-nak-nor-sang (*rta nag nor bzang*) [wrote] an *Answer to the Questions of Lay-chen-gun-gyal-ba* (*las chen kun rgyal ba*). [Lay-chen-gun-gyal-wa] asked in his sixth question whether if, when sustaining the view, the aspect of a positive phenomenon other than the non-affirming negative which is a mere negative of establishment by way of [an object's] own entity appears, one would be engaging in signs [i.e., in the conception of true existence]. His seventh question was how, if the subject does not appear to an inferential cognizer realizing the aggregates to be without inherent existence, could one take the composite of the subject [the aggregates] and their quality [emptiness] as one's object; if [the subject] does appear, then how could [this inferential consciousness] be one which has a mode of apprehension of a non-affirming negative? The following explanation was made by Da-nak-nor-sang in the course of giving an extensive answer to those questions:

> The great translator [Lo-den-shay-rap] said with respect to certain earlier scholars' assertion that Mādhyamikas [are divided into] Reason-Established Illusionists who assert that a composite of the two – appearance and emptiness – is an ultimate truth, and [Proponents of] Thorough Non-Abiding who assert that a mere elimination of elaborations with

respect to appearances is an ultimate truth, that such presentations generate delight in the obscured. Furthermore, the foremost lama, [Dzong-ka-ba] said that the great translator's saying such was good.

However, in general Mādhyamikas are divided into the two – Reason-Established Illusionists and [Proponents of] Thorough Non-Abiding – and, since the master Shūra [Ashvaghoṣha] explained in his *Precious Lamp, Essay on the Ultimate Mind of Enlightenment* that the former is Svātantrika and the latter Prāsaṅgika, the division is correct [but with a different meaning].

The earlier [Tibetan scholars'] saying that the Reason-Established Illusionists, or Svātantrikas, assert a composite of appearance and emptiness as an ultimate truth is said within making the mistake that the Reason-Established Illusionists assert that a composite of appearance and emptiness is the object (*yul*) as well as the object of comprehension (*gzhal bya*) of an inferential reasoning consciousness. For all Mādhyamikas – Prāsaṅgikas and Svātantrikas – assert similarly that a composite of appearance and emptiness [169] is not an ultimate truth and that the non-affirming negative which is a mere negative of true establishment in terms of the appearance of a subject is an ultimate truth.

Concerning the reason for the total incorrectness of the verbal convention, "Reason-Established Illusionist" [those who assert an establishment of illusion by a reasoning consciousness], it is clear at length below whether or not the object of comprehension by an inferential reasoning consciousness realizing a sprout as without true existence [174] is an ultimate, and so forth. Concerning calling those who assert that the mere elimination of elaborations with respect to appearances is an ultimate truth "Proponents of Thorough Non-Abiding", there does exist, in general, the verbal convention, "Thoroughly Non-Abiding Mādhyamikas". However, to consider that the holding of a chariot, for instance, as non-existent at the end of analysis with reasoning is a mere elimination of elaborations is incorrect.[477]

The position of those who negate too much (to be discussed in chapter four) is that when a chariot is analyzed with reasoning, it is found to be non-existent, and they call this non-existence an elimination of elaborations. However, in this system, not finding a chariot under such analysis does not mean that it has been found to be non-existent and is not at all the meaning of the elimination of elaborations. Rather, one has found the absence of inherent existence of the chariot, and this is its freedom from elaborations.

FOURTH, ANALYSIS OF THE CHRONOLOGY [OF THE ARISING OF THE MĀDHYAMIKA SCHOOLS]

This has five parts.

The following subdivisions are a case of Jam-yang-shay-ba's adding in commentary mainly by way of topical headings, even introducing a topic that Dzong-ka-ba himself does not mention at all, namely the question of whether or not Nāgārjuna refuted Chittamātra. Here Dzong-ka-ba merely cites Ye-shay-day's opinion that Nāgārjuna and Āryadeva did not make a clear statement in their Mādhyamika treatises as to whether or not external objects exist, not indicating agreement of disagreement with that opinion. Although Dzong-ka-ba does not pursue the issue here in the *Great Exposition*, he mentions it briefly in his *Essence of the Good Explanations* and Jam-yang-shay-ba has taken that as the source for his interpretation.[478]

FIRST, THE INCORRECTNESS [OF THE ASSERTION] THAT THE SUPERIOR FATHER [NĀGĀRJUNA] AND HIS [SPIRITUAL] SON [ĀRYADEVA] DID NOT REFUTE CHITTAMĀTRA

With respect to the chronology of the commentaries on Nāgārjuna's thought, the master Ye-shay-day (*ye shes sde*) [171] said that the Superior father Nāgārjuna and his [spiritual] son Āryadeva did not, in the treatises settling the Mādhyamika system that they composed, such as the "Collections of Reasonings", the *Four Hundred*, and so forth, make clear whether external objects that are a different substantial entity from the internal mind exist or not.[479] His statement is incorrect because such was already refuted elsewhere[480] and because it contradicts Nāgārjuna's statement in the *Precious Garland*:[481]

> Just as a grammarian [first] makes
> [His students read the alphabet,
> So Buddha taught his trainees
> The Doctrines which they could bear.
>
> To some he taught doctrines
> To discourage sinning,
> To some, doctrines for achieving merit,]
> To others, doctrines based on duality.
>
> To some he taught doctrines based on non-duality,
> To some he taught what is profound and frightening
> to the fearful,
> Having an essence of emptiness and compassion,
> The means of achieving [the highest] enlightenment.
> (394–6)

SECOND, THE ASSERTION THAT THE INITIAL REFUTER OF CHITTAMĀTRA WAS ONLY BHĀVAVIVEKA IS INCORRECT

[Ye-shay-day further said that] after the composition of Mādhyamika treatises by the father [Nāgārjuna] and his [spiritual] son [Āryadeva], the master Bhāvaviveka refuted the system of Mind-Only, or Consciousness-Only, by way of eradicating it through reasoning. He established, newly opening the way, a Mādhyamika system in which external objects, that is, [objects] that are substantial entities other than the mind, exist conventionally.

THIRD, HOW SHĀNTARAKṢHITA OPENED THE WAY OF YOGĀCHĀRA-SVĀTANTRIKA

After Bhāvaviveka had made such a presentation, the master Shāntarakṣhita, in dependence on the textual system of Yogāchāra, or Mind-Only, newly set forth a different system establishing Mādhyamika texts that teach the non-existence of external objects conventionally and the non-inherent existence of the internal mind ultimately. Thereby, two forms of Mādhyamika arose, one earlier and one later. [Ye-shay-day explains that] the verbal convention "Sautrāntika-Mādhyamika" (*mdo sde spyod pa'i dbu ma pa*) was designated to the former, that is, to Bhāvaviveka and his followers, [172] and the verbal convention "Yogāchāra-Mādhyamika" (*rnal 'byor spyod pa'i dbu ma pa*) was designated to the latter, that is, to Shāntarakṣhita and his followers. This is the description of the chronology of the opening of the chariot ways of those two Mādhyamika [systems].

The chronology of the masters who are the authors of the treatises and the founders of the systems is evident to have occurred in accordance with the above explanation by Ye-shay-day. However, because Shūra, a Mādhyamika who asserted external objects, and Āryavimuktisena, who asserted that external objects did not exist, appeared before those two [before Bhāvaviveka and Shāntarakṣhita, respectively, Dzong-ka-ba] indicates [implicitly in the *Medium Exposition of Special Insight*] that this [presentation] is unsuitable as a mere chronology.[482]

FOURTH, THE NEED TO KNOW IN ACCORDANCE WITH KAY-DRUP'S "THOUSAND DOSAGES" THAT ALTHOUGH THESE NAMES ARE SUITABLE, THE [DIVISIONS OF MĀDHYAMIKA] ARE NOT THUS IN FACT[483]

Although the chronology is thus, with respect to the affixing of verbal conventions, Mādhyamikas are not limited to the two – Sautrāntika and Yogāchāra; for although the master Chandrakīrti does assert that external objects exist conventionally, since this is not done in accordance with another system of tenets, Vaibhāṣhika, Sautrāntika, Chittamātra, and so forth, it is not suitable to designate this master with the verbal convention "Sautrāntika".

FIFTH, A [FURTHER] UNSUITABILITY OF THOSE VERBAL CONVENTIONS FOR CHANDRAKĪRTI

Similarly, the assertion by some Tibetan scholars that since the master Chandrakīrti asserts external objects conventionally and does not assert self-knowers, he accords in tenet with the Vaibhāṣhikas is also very unreasonable. This is because the root of that master [Chandrakīrti's] asserting that external objects are not established substantially and his not asserting self-knowers derives from his non-assertion of the establishment [of phenomena] by way of their own character.

FIFTH, THE CORRECTNESS OF THE VERBAL CONVENTIONS "PRĀSAṄGIKA" AND "SVĀTANTRIKA" [USED BY SCHOLARS] OF THE LATER DISSEMINATION

This has three parts.

FIRST, AN INDICATION THAT THIS IS THE THOUGHT OF CHANDRAKĪRTI'S "CLEAR WORDS"

With respect to the position that is the correct way of designating Mādhyamikas, scholars at the time of the later dissemination of the doctrine to the land of snowy mountains, Tibet,

[173] used for Mādhyamikas the verbal conventions "Prāsaṅgika" – because [that group] asserts that an inferential cognizer realizing a probandum can directly be generated merely though a consequence (*prasaṅga*) – and "Svātantrika" – because [this group] asserts that such cannot be done merely through a consequence, but rather, autonomous (*svatantra*) reasons are definitely needed. This accords with the explanation in Chandrakīrti's commentary [on Nāgārjuna's *Treatise on the Middle Way*], the *Clear Words* (*tshig gsal*, *prasannapadā*). Thus, you should not think that [these verbal conventions] were fabricated by those Tibetan scholars themselves.

SECOND, THE DIVISION INTO THE TWO, THOSE WHO DO AND DO NOT ASSERT EXTERNAL OBJECTS

For that reason, our own factually based system is as follows: Although Mādhyamikas are not limited to the two above modes of designating verbal conventions in comparison with the tenets of Sautrāntikas and Chittamātrins, they are in general limited to the two, those who do and do not assert external objects. Therefore, by way of their mode of asserting conventionalities, they are limited to two – Mādhyamikas who do assert external objects conventionally and Mādhyamikas who do not assert external objects conventionally.

THIRD, THE DIVISION [OF MĀDHYAMIKAS] INTO TWO, PRĀSAṄGIKAS AND SVĀTANTRIKAS, BY WAY OF HOW THE VIEW IS GENERATED IN THE CONTINUUM

Also, if names are designated by way of how the view ascertaining the ultimate, emptiness, is generated in the continuum, [Mādhyamikas] are limited to the two, Prāsaṅgikas – due to asserting that the view can be directly generated through merely a consequence (*prasaṅga*) – and Svātantrikas – due to asserting that [the view] cannot [be generated] through merely that, but rather, in order to directly generate the [view], autonomous (*svatantra*) reasons are definitely necessary.

With regard to the chronology of the commentaries on Nāgārjuna's thought, the verbal conventions "Sautrāntika-Mādhyamika" and "Yogāchāra-Mādhyamika" are in general correct, but because the glorious Chandrakīrti is neither of those, in general Mādhyamikas are not limited to those two.

The assertion of external objects by the master Bhāvaviveka is essentially the same as Sautrāntika. However, the glorious Chandrakīrti's saying that there are external objects is not of the same meaning as any Sautrāntika or Vaibhāṣhika even though the mere words are similar.[484]

SIXTH, WHICH MASTERS ARE TO BE FOLLOWED

This has three parts.

FIRST, AN INDICATION THAT THE EARLIER GA-DAM-BAS' (BKA' GDAMS PA) SEEKING THE VIEW FOLLOWING CHANDRAKĪRTI IS THE THOUGHT OF ATISHA

One might think: Since, as explained above, there are many masters who commented on the thought of the Superior Nāgārjuna and his spiritual son, with respect to how to settle the view of the Superior Nāgārjuna and his spiritual son, following which among those masters should one non-erroneously seek [Nāgārjuna's] thought?

[*Answer*:] The great elder, the glorious Atisha, held the system of the master Chandrakīrti, that is to say, his quintessential instructions for settling the view, to be reliable and took them to be chief. For, Atisha's *[Introduction to the] Two Truths* (*bden gnyis la 'jug pa*, *satyadvayāvatāra*, 15d–16ab) says:[485]

> Through the quintessential instructions transmitted
> from Chandrakīrti, student of Nāgārjuna . . .
> Reality, the truth, will be realized.

Since this was seen to be correct, following the great elder [Atisha], earlier great lamas who transmitted these instructions on the stages of the path to enlightenment, Bo-do-wa

(*Po-to-ba*) and so forth, took the system of Chandrakīrti to be reliable and held it as chief. [175]

SECOND, DZONG-KA-BA'S OWN ASSERTION THAT THE TWO SYSTEMS OF BUDDHAPĀLITA AND CHANDRAKĪRTI ARE CHIEF AND THAT AFTER THEM BHĀVAVIVEKA IS NEXT IN IMPORTANCE

Among the commentators on Nāgārjuna's *Treatise on the Middle Way* (*dbu ma'i bstan bcos, madhyamakaśāstra*), whose did the master Chandrakīrti, who has been taken to be reliable and held as chief, see as elucidating completely and just as it is the thought of Nāgārjuna? He saw that the master Buddhapālita elucidated completely and without error the thought of the honorable Superior Nāgārjuna. Having seen that, the glorious Chandrakīrti took the system of the master Buddhapālita as his basis and held it to be chief. Not only that, but also the honorable Chandrakīrti took many portions of good explanation even from the commentaries of the master Bhāvaviveka, and having uprooted by way of refuting well with reasoning those things in Bhāvaviveka's commentaries that appeared to be a little incorrect, he commented on the thought of the Superior Nāgārjuna just as it is.

THIRD, THE IMPORTANCE OF THESE TWO MASTERS AT ALL TIMES WITH REGARD TO EXPLAINING THE PROFOUND MEANING [OF EMPTINESS]

Therefore, because the commentaries by these two masters, the honorable Buddhapālita and Chandrakīrti, are seen to be most excellent with regard to explaining the texts of the Superior father, Nāgārjuna, and his [spiritual] son [Āryadeva], such as the *Treatise on the Middle Way* and so forth, here on the occasion of settling the view, the thought of the honorable Superior Nāgārjuna will be non-erroneously settled following the master Buddhapālita and the glorious Chandrakīrti. [176]

3 *The Stages of Entry Into Suchness*

Now, the actual explanation of how to settle the view of emptiness, the third heading from above [see chapter one, p.253] and the topic of this discussion, is to be known by way of two topics: initially, the stages of entry into suchness and, after that, the actual settling of suchness. The first of these has two parts: (1) explanation of the suchness that is the object of attainment and the stages of entry [into it], and (2) explanation that although [even in this system, Prāsaṅgika, practitioners of] the two vehicles meditate on the two selflessnesses individually [first the selflessness of persons and then of phenomena], the mode of realization [in Mādhyamika] is different from that among the Proponents of True Existence.

FIRST, EXPLANATION OF THE SUCHNESS THAT IS THE OBJECT OF ATTAINMENT AND THE STAGES OF ENTRY [INTO IT]

This has two parts: the actual [explanation] and an elimination of qualms.

FIRST, THE ACTUAL [EXPLANATION]

This has two parts, a question and an answer.

QUESTION

With regard to this point of the stages of entry [into suchness], there are two factors, the object of attainment into which one is entering and the stages that are the means of entering into it. From among those two, what is the nirvāṇa, the passing very much beyond suffering as well as its root, that is the suchness that is the object of attainment? Also, by way of just what sort of stages of entry into realizing suchness, the methods of attaining that nirvāṇa, must one enter into it?

ANSWER

This has two parts: an explanation of the suchness that is the object of attainment and of the stages of entry into it.

FIRST, EXPLANATION OF THE SUCHNESS THAT IS THE OBJECT OF ATTAINMENT

Answer: The object of attainment is as follows: The suchness that is the fruit to be attained here, in the Mahāyāna, is the non-abiding nirvāṇa that is a state of the utter extinguishment, in all forms and in all places and times, of all the mistakes of the conception of I and mine as established right with their own bases. [This is achieved] through pacifying, by way of abandoning them, all factors of erroneous dualistic appearance, the manifest obstructions to omniscience, obscurers of the mind – that is to say, erroneous appearances that are the various appearances of those things of conventional natures, external phenomena such as forms, sounds and so forth, and internal phenomena, eyes, and so forth, as [their own] suchness whereas they are not the suchness that is the basic mode of subsistence of those bases – along with their predispositions, the obstructions to omniscience. [177] That suchness is a Buddha's Truth Body.

SECOND, EXPLANATION OF THE STAGES OF ENTERING INTO THAT SUCHNESS

This has seven parts.

First, the need to see the faults of cyclic existence

The second question [asked above] is, "What are the stages that are the means of entry to, that is, that are how one enters into realizing, suchness?"

Answer: Having first contemplated in detail the sufferings of cyclic existence, its faults – causes such as attachment and so forth – and its disadvantages – effects such as birth, aging, and so forth – your mind becomes averse to those faults and disadvantages due to discouragement with and fear of them. Then you should generate a strong mind wishing to cast aside, or abandon, that cyclic existence.

Second, the need to identify the root that is the source

When such [a mind wishing to abandon cyclic existence] arises, then you need to see that if you do not overcome the causes of cyclic existence through abandoning [contaminated] actions and afflictions, cyclic existence will not be overcome. Upon seeing such, you [come to] wonder what the root of cyclic existence is. You need to research what that root is and, through researching it, to induce ascertainment from the depths with respect to a decided analysis of how the view of the transitory, or ignorance, serves as the root of cyclic existence, being able to ascertain that you experience limitless suffering in cyclic existence due to error through just that view of the transitory, or ignorance. You must then generate a non-artificial wish to abandon that ignorance, or view of the transitory, the root of cyclic existence. [178]

Third, the need for those of sharp faculties to realize that one can abandon the view of the transitory, the root source

Then you must see that overcoming that view of the transitory, the cause of cyclic existence, definitely depends upon generating the wisdom realizing well the way in which self [i.e., inherent existence] as it is conceived by the view of the transitory is utterly non-existent. Further, having seen such, since that self cannot be known to be non-existent through just staying as you are, you should see that it must be refuted by means of correct reasoning. Further, it not being sufficient just to see that [reasoning is necessary], you need to gain definite ascertainment, deciding in dependence on stainless scriptures and reasonings that damage its existence and prove its non-existence that such a self does not exist. Such ascertainment is an indispensible method for one who is intent on liberation.

Fourth, the truth body is attained through cultivating the view realizing selflessness by means of the path

Having, in the manner explained above, gained the view ascertaining that the self and the mine do not in the least have inherent establishment, you should not just leave the view that has been found but should familiarize again and again with the meaning found. Thereby, finally as its imprint you will attain a Buddha's Truth Body, the effect.

> The following paragraph is a summary by Nga-wang-rap-den intended to show that Dzong-ka-ba's identification of the suchness that is the object of attainment and of the stages of entry to it is also the thought of Nāgārjuna and his spiritual sons.

Just as "the pacification of elaborations" [mentioned in the opening verse of] the *Treatise on the Middle Way*[486] is the final nirvāṇa without remainder and [Nāgārjuna] paid homage to the teacher who taught just that as the chief object of meditation by trainees, so the final suchness that is the abandonment of the elaborations of dualistic appearances as well as their predispositions is both the object of attainment and the object of meditation. With respect to how you engage in the methods for attaining it, [179] you initially generate a wish for liberation through contemplating the faults of cyclic existence, true sufferings. Then having contemplated true sources, the stages of entering into cyclic existence, you see through the example of a stake to which a calf is bound that the root of the suffering of cyclic existence meets back to the view of the transitory, whereupon you refute the self as it is conceived by that [view]. This has the same meaning as the statement in Maitreya's *Sublime Continuum of the Great Vehicle* (*rgyud bla ma*, *uttaratantra*) that the error is baseless and rootless. Such is also set forth in Chandrakīrti's *Clear Words* in the transition to the next chapter [that is, at the beginning of the eighteenth chapter, commenting on] the end [the last verse] of the [seventeenth] chapter in which [Nāgārjuna] had said:[487]

> Afflictions, actions, and the body,
> [Agents, and effects
> Are like a city of scent-eaters,
> Like mirages, and like dreams.

The passage from Chandrakīrti is cited by Dzong-ka-ba immediately below.]

Fifth, the explanation in Chandrakīrti's "Clear Words"

That it is attained in that way is set forth in Chandrakīrti's *Clear Words* which says that:[488]

> Certain people wonder the following: The afflictions that are the initial cause, the actions motivated by those [afflictions], the body that is the fruition impelled by those actions, the person who is the agent of those actions, and the sufferings that are the effects to be experienced by that person in dependence on the body depend one upon the other and appear variously. Are all these [their own] suchness in the sense that they are established as their own mode of subsistence?
>
> They are not; they are not established by way of their own entities. Rather, they are false, like the example of a city of scent-eaters (*dri za*, *gandharva*) which appears to be an actual city though it is not and to possess obstructiveness though it does not. Similarly, whereas the above-mentioned afflictions, actions, agents, and so forth are not [their own] suchness in the sense of being established by way of their own mode of subsistence, they appear in the aspect of being [their own] suchness to the childish,

that is, to common beings. [180] In this sense they are only deceptive falsities.

If, here on this occasion of researching the objective suchness of things, the above explained afflictions, actions, body, and so forth are not the suchness of objects, then what is the suchness of objects that is to be sought or attained here in the Mahāyāna? Also, what are the stages of entering into that suchness, that is, the methods for attaining that [suchness]?

Answer: The non-abiding nirvāṇa that is a pacification in the sense of utterly extinguishing in all forms – in all times and places – all error with respect to internal and external things of the manifest determination, or conception, of [inherently existent] I and mine together with its seeds by means of becoming accustomed to the unobservability of things internal and external as inherently existent, that is to say, by way of having utterly abandoned and pacified all mistaken appearances – the appearance of things internal, such as eyes, and external, such as forms, sounds and so forth, as if they were [their own] suchness in the sense of being their own mode of subsistence whereas they are not – is the suchness that is the final object of attainment and the object of meditation, that to be sought on this occasion of researching the suchness of objects. It is just the Truth Body of a Buddha.

Sixth, how the stages of entering [into suchness] are explained in Chandrakīrti's "Supplement to (Nāgārjuna's) 'Treatise on the Middle Way'"

Question: What are the stages, or mode, of entering into suchness, that is, what are the methods for achieving that? In answer to this, [Chandrakīrti] makes reference to his *Supplement to (Nāgārjuna's) "Treatise on the Middle Way"* (VI.120) which says that:

> Yogis see through having researched with their own minds that not just part, but all of the faults, the afflictions of desire and so forth, and the disadvantages, birth, aging, sickness, and death, and so forth, of cyclic existence [181] arise from a root that is the view of the transitory, that is to say, the conception of the inherent establishment of I and mine, in that through abandoning the view of the transitory, one removes all those faults like the branches of a tree whose root is cut.
>
> There is a way to abandon the view of the transitory, for [yogis] do not just leave it at only seeing that [all the afflictions arise in dependence on the view of the transitory]. Rather, since they need to know that object which is the basis from which error arises, they then realize that the self or I, erroneously adhered to by that [view] in the conception, "This is the self which exists by way of its own entity," is the object of observation mistaken by the view of the transitory. Then, through seeing that the self does not exist objectively as it is conceived to by the view of the transitory, [that view of the transitory] is abandoned.
>
> Thereby, after that, the yogi, that is, one who has the yoga of a union of calm abiding and special insight and is seeking liberation, refutes with correct reasoning by means of the five reasons and so forth, such inherent establishment, the self that is the object of negation, which is such that although the referent object [of the conception of inherent existence] lacks an objective mode of subsistence, it appears to have such. . . .

Since through such [statements], Chandrakīrti explained in detail the stages of entering into suchness in his *Supplement to (Nāgārjuna's) "Treatise on the Middle Way"*, he makes reference to it, saying that one should seek [this explanation] there.

[Chandrakīrti's *Clear Words*] also says that:[489]

> Yogis intent on liberation, who wish to enter into suchness by way of such stages as explained above and who wish by way of that thoroughly to abandon all of the true sufferings and true sources, the afflictions, such as attachment, and the faults of cyclic existence such as birth, aging, and so forth, [182] investigate and analyze the final basic root that serves as a cause of cycling in cyclic existence, initially researching, "What sort of root does this wandering in cyclic existence have as its cause? From what does it arise?"
>
> When yogis thoroughly investigate and analyze in this manner with such a reasoned mode of researching, they see through the power of this analysis that cyclic existence has as its root, that is to say, arises from, the view of the transitory collection – the conception of I and mine [as inherently existent]. When they analyze whether or not the view of the transitory can be abandoned and what sort of object that view of the transitory is observing, they see that the I or self which appears to be established as [its own] suchness is the object of observation of the view of the transitory collection. When they investigate with reasoning the appearance of that object of observation, the self, as if [its own] suchness, they see with wisdom that the self apprehended thus by that view of the transitory as established objectively – its referent object – is just not observed [by valid cognition] to be its own suchness as it appears, that

is, is non-existent. Then, they see that through meditation in accordance with this perception, the wrong consciousness that is the view of the transitory can be abandoned.

[Finally] they see that through abandoning the view of the transitory, all afflictions and faults also will definitely be overcome since the root of all the afflictions, attachment and so forth, and the faults of cyclic existence such as birth, aging, and so forth derives from just the view of the transitory. [183]

If one does not want all the faults and disadvantages as explained above, then since the root of all of them meets back to the view of the transitory collection, and since the generation of them by the view of the transitory meets back to conceiving self, yogis who are the analyzers see the great importance of analyzing just that self. They investigate and analyze in the following way: What is this self that is the object of the view of the transitory conceiving self like? Is it established by way of its own entity or not? From among all possible objects of analysis, at the very beginning they investigate and analyze by way of reasoned individual investigation just the self. [184]

Seventh, these stages of entry [into suchness] are the thought of both these masters [Chandrakīrti and Buddhapālita] and also of Nāgārjuna's "Treatise on the Middle Way"

Although in general, in Nāgārjuna's *Treatise on the Middle Way*, and so forth, many reasonings refuting inherent establishment with respect to an immeasurable number of individual subjects in terms of persons and phenomena are set forth, when yogis initially enter into practice, abridging all these limitless subjects, they settle the lack of inherent establishment in terms of only the two, I and mine, familiarizing with just this mode of meditation. Since all the essentials are complete there, the master Buddhapālita says that this mode of meditation is the meaning of the eighteenth chapter of Nāgārjuna's *Treatise on the Middle Way.*

In dependence on his having said that, the master Chandrakīrti here in this commentary presents the mode of settling [the view] in that way. Even the sections in his *Supplement to (Nāgārjuna's) "Treatise on the Middle Way"* that teach the selflessness of persons are just extensive explanations of just the eighteenth chapter of Nāgārjuna's *Treatise on the Middle Way.*

The following sentence is a summary commentary from Nga-wang-rap-den.[490]

Although in Nāgārjuna's *Treatise on the Middle Way* many reasonings refuting self in relation to individual subjects were set forth, when yogis initially engage [in refuting self], they meditate in an abridged way within settling the lack of inherent existence of the I and the mine.

SECOND, AN ELIMINATION OF QUALMS

This has three parts: a question as to whether the selflessness of phenomena is or is not included in the suchness and selflessness that are the object of attainment; in answer to that, an explanation individually of the objects of attainment; and that the mode of realizing the two selflessnesses differs from that of the Proponents of True Existence.

FIRST, A QUESTION AS TO WHETHER THE SELFLESSNESS OF PHENOMENA IS OR IS NOT INCLUDED IN THE SUCHNESS AND SELFLESSNESS THAT ARE THE OBJECT OF ATTAINMENT

Someone, generating the following qualm, might say that both the identification of suchness and the mode of entering into it are incorrect: [185] Nāgārjuna's *Treatise on the Middle Way* is an occasion [of explaining] the meaning of the Perfection of Wisdom Sūtras, and since this is an occasion of teaching the stages of the Mahāyāna path, should one not teach the mode of entry into suchness in terms of the Mahāyāna? Indeed one should, and therefore, the nirvāṇa that is a mere extinguishment of the view of the transitory conceiving [an inherently existent] I and mine as [explained] above is not suitable to be posited as the suchness that is the object of attainment by Mahāyānists, the Truth Body, [because this explanation] did not indicate the selflessness of phenomena. Since the meaning of settling the selflessness of phenomena does not exist within the mere settling of the absence of inherent establishment of the objects I and mine, it is not suitable to posit that for a Mahāyānist the mere realization that I and mine do not inherently exist is the path of entering into suchness.

That qualm will be cleared away with the following.

SECOND, INDIVIDUAL EXPLANATIONS OF THE TWO [TYPES OF] SUCHNESS, OR NIRVĀṆA, THAT ARE THE OBJECTS OF ATTAINMENT

There is no fault such as that put forth in the first qualm [namely, that the identification of suchness is incorrect]; the reason there is no fault is that with regard to the extinguishment by way of abandoning in all ways the conception of I and mine, there are two different modes of extinguishment. Although utter abandonment of the afflictions – the conception of I and mine – in the manner of their not being produced again does exist even among Hīnayānists, the nirvāṇa that is the abandonment exhaustively in the manner of unapprehendability in all ways by way of pacifying completely all predispositions of the afflictions as well as the signs, that is, the elaborations of mistaken dualistic appearance, with regard to all phenomena external and internal that are produced by those [afflictions] along with their predispositions is just the Truth Body. [186]

THIRD, THE MODE OF REALIZING THE TWO SELFLESSNESSES DIFFERS FROM THAT OF THE LOWER SYSTEMS [THE PROPONENTS OF TRULY EXISTENT THINGS]

This has two parts: the actual explanation and an elimination of qualms.

FIRST, THE ACTUAL EXPLANATION

This has four parts.

First, when the self is realized as not existing inherently, the aggregates that are the basis of designation of the self are realized as not existing inherently

There does not exist the second fallacy of incorrectness of the mode of entry [into suchness] because[491] when you realize that the self is not established inherently, through the force of that, the conception also of the aggregates, the mine, that are the branches, or basis of designation, of that self as inherently existent is overcome – that is, becomes non-existent. It is like the way in which, for example, when a chariot – that which has parts – is burned by fire, the parts of that chariot, the chariot wheels and so forth, are also definitely burned.

The following is a summary from Nga-wang-rap-den.[492]

Someone might say that both this mode of identifying suchness and the mode of entering into it are incorrect. For here one is setting forth the Mahāyāna mode of entering into suchness, whereby the mere extinguishing of the conception of I and mine is not suitable to be the suchness that is the object of attainment. Also, since the mere settling of the lack of inherent existence of I and mine does not involve settling the selflessness of phenomena, it is not feasible as a path for entering into suchness [i.e., that suchness which is the final object of attainment].

[*Response*:] There is no fault of incorrectness with respect to the first, [the identification of suchness], for, with regard to extinguishing all forms of the conception of I and mine, there are two varieties, and although [the first], the abandonment of the afflictions in the manner of their never being generated again exists even among Hīnayānists, here it is an exhaustive abandonment of all signs, that is to say, elaborations of dualistic appearance, as well as their predispositions with regard to all external and internal phenomena, and just that is the Truth Body.

There is no fault of incorrectness with regard to the mode of entering into suchness because the sign [the reason advanced above by the opponent to prove his assertion of fault] – that at the time of realizing the I and mine to be without inherent existence, the selflessness of phenomena has not been settled – is not established. [In other words, in the Prāsaṅgika system, you *have* settled the selflessness of phenomena when you realize the lack of inherent existence of I and mine.] For, when you realize that the self does not inherently exist, the conception that the five aggregates that are the basis of designation of the self inherently exist is overcome. It is like the way in which, for example, when a chariot is burned its parts are also burned.

Second, with regard to the mode of investigating the lack of inherent existence of the self, one needs to analyze, in accordance with how the innate view of the transitory conceives it, whether or not the self has all the characteristics of the aggregates

Moreover, Chandrakīrti's *Clear Words* says that:[493]

> [The self] is merely imputed in dependence upon its basis of designation, the five aggregates, and serves as a basis for the strong adherence to self by childish common beings who have come under the influence of error due to the force of their minds being affected by the dimness of ignorance. [187] The five aggregates are that which is appropriated by the self and the self is that which appropriates, and thus these five aggregates are seen to be that which is appropriated by [the self], the appropriator.
>
> Just what is this triply qualifed self like? [The three qualifications are that it is just imputed in dependence on the five aggregates, that it is the basis of the strong conception of self, and that the five aggregates appear to be and indeed are its appropriation.] Does [the self] have the character of the aggregates, i.e, is it of one nature with them? Or, is

it without the character, or other than the nature of, the aggregates?[494] Analytical persons who wish liberation initially engage in such analysis.

Third, when sought in this way, it is not found by a reasoning consciousness

When analyzed in all ways with this mode of analysis, those who want liberation do not find, or observe, such a so-called self having the nature of the aggregates that are its basis of designation, and therefore, due to the self's not being established by way of its own mode of subsistence, [Nāgārjuna's *Treatise* says that]:

> In that the self, the designated phenomenon which is designated [in dependence] upon the aggregates that are its basis of designation, does not exist by way of its own mode of subsistence, how could the mine, that is, the aggregates and so forth that are its basis of designation, exist from the viewpoint of being established by way of their own mode of subsistence? They cannot.

Therefore, because the self is not observed [as] inherently existent in them, [188] then also the aggregates which are the mine, the basis of designation of the self, would very much not be observed [as] inherently existent. This is because the two selves are not posited by way of [one being] coarse and [the other being more] subtle. For example, when a chariot, the parts-possessor [the whole], is burned by fire, the parts of the chariot, its wheels and so forth, are also burned and thus do not exist and are not observed. Similarly, when yogis realize that the self does not inherently exist, they will realize the selflessness, or lack of inherent existence, or lack of establishment by way of their own entity,

> also of the mine, the things that are the aggregates which are the bases of designation of the self.

Thus, that passage says that when through having analyzed whether the self is of one character with the aggregates or not one character with the aggregates, an inferential cognizer explicitly realizes the self as without inherent existence, that is, as not established from its own side, the mine – the aggregates – also are realized through its force as without inherent existence, that is, as not established from their own side.

Not only is there the above [statement in Chandrakīrti's *Clear Words*], but also Chandrakīrti's *[Auto] commentary on the "Supplement to (Nāgārjuna's) 'Treatise on the Middle Way'"* says that:[495]

> If, because of the great mistake of the mental error by way of apprehending that forms and so forth – the bases of designation of that [self] – entities which are not established as [their own] suchness are established as [their own] suchness, that is, as inherently existent, Hearers and Solitary Realizers did not realize the selflessness of phenomena, then it would follow that they would not realize the selflessness of the person, that is, the absence of inherent existence of the self that is designated with respect to the aggregates. Why? [189] Because they apprehend the aggregates that serve as the basis of designation of the self within the superimposition of inherent establishment.

Fourth, this is not only explained in Chandrakīrti's "Supplement to (Nāgārjuna's) 'Treatise on the Middle Way'", but is the thought of Nāgārjuna's "Precious Garland"

As a source for this [Chandrakīrti cites] Nāgārjuna's *Precious Garland* (35ab) which says that:

> As long as, without coming to disbelieve in the referent object of the conception of true existence,

> one has conception – through the force of tenets – of the aggregates as inherently established, or true, for so long does the one apprehending such have a conception of the I, which is designated [in dependence] upon the aggregates, as inherently established, not having come to disbelieve in the referent object of that conception. This must be so because the modes of apprehension of those two [the conceptions of a self of persons and of phenomena] are the same and because the basis of designation [the aggregates] is being conceived to truly be the phenomenon designated [the self].

Thus, it is said that if you do not realize the aggregates to be without inherent existence, that is, if you have not turned your mind to tenets that settle the absence of inherent establishment of the aggregates, then you do not at all realize the selflessness of the person.

SECOND, AN ELIMINATION OF QUALMS

This has three parts: a question, the actual answer, and dispelling an objection [with respect to that answer].

First, a question

There are two questions, the first of which is as follows: If just that awareness realizing the person as without inherent existence, that is, as not established by way of its own entity, realizes the aggregates also as without inherent existence, that is, as not established by way of their own entities, there would be the fault that the two awarenesses realizing the two selflessnesses would be one.

We do not assert such, and the damage [to that assertion] is that if the two [awarenesses] were one, then there would be the fault that the subjects – phenomena and persons – that are the bases of the two selflessnesses would also be one. [190] Therefore, the two, phenomena and persons, are separate, and since that is the case, the two awarenesses realizing those two as without inherent existence are also established as separate, just as, for example, an awareness realizing a pot as impermanent and an awareness realizing a pillar as impermanent are separate.

The second question is that if just that awareness realizing the person as without inherent existence does not realize the aggregates as without inherent existence, then how can one posit the meaning of Chandrakīrti's statement in the *Clear Words* that when one realizes the selflessness of the person, one realizes the absence of inherent existence of the aggregates? One cannot.

Second, the actual answer

This has two parts, a [brief] indication and an [extensive] explanation.

First, a [brief] indication

Since we do not assert the first of those two questions – that just that awareness realizing the person as without inherent existence realizes the aggregates as without inherent existence – I will explain the latter question, the meaning of asserting that just that awareness realizing the person as without inherent existence does not realize that the aggregates are without inherent existence.

Second, the extensive explanation

This has three parts.

First, although that awareness [realizing the selflessness of the person] does not realize the absence of inherent existence of the aggregates, [the absence of inherent existence of the aggregates] is realized through its force. Since just that awareness realizing the person as without inherent existence does not engage in the thought, "The aggregates do not inherently exist," just that awareness itself does not realize [the absence of inherent existence of the aggregates]; however, by way of that mind, without relying on some other mode of realization, another awareness that is an ascertaining consciousness ascertaining that the aggregates are without inherent existence can be induced. [191] Therefore, by way of just that awareness realizing the absence of inherent existence of the person, superimpositions that superimpose inherent existence on the aggregates also can be eliminated without depending on any other [mind]. Hence, [Chandrakīrti] speaks of realization through the force of that [mind] as realization by it. For, Dzong-ka-ba's *Ocean of Reasoning, Explanation of (Nāgārjuna's) "Treatise on the Middle Way"* says:[496]

> This is like the way in which when a valid cognizer ascertaining the three modes in the proof of sound as impermanent is generated, [in dependence on its force, without relying on a succession of other intervening valid cognizers, there is a capacity to generate an awareness that is explicitly contradictory with the superimposition and mode of apprehension of the conception of sound as permanent. However,] it is not that the former valid cognizer implicitly establishes sound as impermanent or that it eliminates the superimposition apprehending sound as permanent.

Second, it is asserted that the mind realizes it when it eliminates superimpositions. This does not mean that just that former functioning of the reasoning settling [the selflessness of the person] and just the former functioning of that awareness's mode of realization [of the selflessness of the person] can induce ascertainment [of the selflessness of phenomena] without depending on another [mind]. Rather, it means that, in general, in dependence upon the former reasoning and the mind's former mode of realization, ascertainment [of the selflessness of phenomena] can be induced without relying on another mode of reasoning or realization. If it were otherwise, then just that awareness realizing the absence of inherent existence of the person would realize the absence of inherent existence of the aggregates whereby it would not be necessary to settle again the absence of inherent existence in terms of the aggregates.

Therefore, because there is this capacity [for the selflessness of the aggregates to be realized through the force of the realization of the selflessness of the person without depending on another reasoning], thinking of that, [Chandrakīrti] said that when one realizes that the person does not inherently exist, due to the fact that one has eliminated the superimpositions of the conception of true existence with respect to the aggregates, one realizes that the aggregates also are without inherent existence. Dzong-ka-ba's *Ocean of Reasoning, Explanation of (Nāgārjuna's) "Treatise on the Middle Way"* says:[497]

> This is like the way in which in Dharmakīrti's *Commentary on (Dignāga's) "Compendium on Valid Cognition"*, [in the passage] "Through its import that becomes an awareness [realizing] disintegration," "through its import" (*don gyis*) is explained as "implicitly" (*shugs kyis*) but this is not implicit realization (*shugs rtogs*).

> > Dzong-ka-ba's interpretation of Chandrakīrti's statement that when one realizes the selflessness of the person, one realizes the selflessness of phenomena is that this means not that the awareness realizing the selflessness of the person *itself* either explicitly or implicitly realizes the selflessness of the aggregates, but that through it one has gained a *capacity* for realizing such, and thus it can be said that the selflessness of phenomena is realized *through its force*. In dependence on just the functioning of the awareness realizing the selflessness of the person, the selflessness of phenomena can be realized subsequently without having to rely on any other reasoning or consciousness. Dzong-ka-ba supports this interpretation of Chandrakīrti by citing a passage from Dharmakīrti where just the same sort of interpretation is required. Even though Dharmakīrti says "implicitly", this does not mean actual implicit

realization by that very consciousness but indicates that something *can* be realized through the force of that consciousness.

It is very clear in Dzong-ka-ba's writings and some of my own lamas explained with particular emphasis that although right after realizing the absence of inherent existence of the person, you do not realize the absence of inherent existence of the aggregates, you have attained a *capacity* to do so. [192]

Following is summary commentary from Nga-wang-rap-den.

Moreover, if you ascertain that the aggregates, the basis of designation, do not inherently exist, because you have refuted the object of negation in terms of [those] objects, good ascertainment also of the absence of inherent existence of the person who is designated to those [aggregates] will come. However, while conceiving the inherent establishment of the aggregates, the basis of designation, though you might claim that the person, the phenomenon designated to those, does not inherently exist, the object of negation would have become [something additional to the appearance of the object] like a hat peeled off.

Since the awareness realizing the absence of inherent existence of the person is able, without relying on any other [reasoning or mode of realization], to induce a consciousness ascertaining the absence of inherent existence of the aggregates, it is also able to eliminate through its own force the superimposition of an inherent establishment of the aggregates, whereby it is *said* that when the person is realized as without inherent existence, the aggregates also are realized as without inherent existence. This point is made in accordance with the statement, "One who sees the suchness of one phenomenon [sees the suchness of all phenomena]".

The earlier statement in Chandrakīrti's *Clear Words* that right from the beginning of seeking the view one should engage in analysis as to whether or not [the self] is imputed within the situation of the aggregates that are the basis of designation of the self being inherently existent[498] is also said to establish that when the person is realized as non-inherently existent, the aggregates also are realized as non-inherently existent.

Third, in this system, due to the absence of true existence of the substratum, the conception of the true existence of its attributes is refuted. Also, this should be known in accordance with Buddhapālita's statement in the *Buddhapālita Commentary on (Nāgārjuna's) "Treatise on the Middle Way"* (*dbu ma rtsa ba'i 'grel pa buddha pā li ta, buddhapālitamūlamadhyamakavṛtti*) that:[499]

> Just those that are the objects of use by the so-called "self" are called the "mine". Therefore, in that the self which is the basis in dependence upon which the mine are apprehended does not exist by way of its own entity, that is, inherently, if it does not exist [thus], how could it be correct that these mine which, depending upon that self, are its objects of use be inherently existent? That is, the mine would not be established by way of its own entity. [193]

For example, when you ascertain that a son of a barren woman, the substratum, does not occur, although that very awareness ascertaining such does not engage in the thought, "The ears and so forth which are attributes of that son of a barren woman do not exist," in dependence upon just that awareness, superimpositions conceiving the ears and so forth of that son of a barren woman to exist can be explicitly eliminated. Similarly, when you ascertain that the self, the substratum, does not exist as [its own] suchness, in dependence on just that mind of ascertainment, the conception that the eyes and so forth which are attributes of that self exist as [their own] suchness is overcome.

Third, dispelling an objection

This has four parts: the objection, an answer, an assertion, and a refutation of that [assertion].

First, the objection

Someone might say: Even the Proponents of True Existence who assert that the person is imputedly existent, that is, Buddhist schools with the exception of the Vatsīputrīyas and so forth, do not assert that the person is ultimately established. Therefore, even those Proponents of True Existence would realize that eyes and so forth are without inherent existence.

Second, the answer: it would [absurdly] follow that they would realize also the absence of true existence of gross objects

If it were as you have reasoned, then since those Proponents of True Existence assert that gross objects – eyes, sprouts, and so forth – which are aggregations and composites of minute [particles] are imputedly existent, then those Proponents of True Existence would realize eyes, sprouts, and so forth as without inherent existence.[500] [194]

Third, an assertion

That person might say that he accepts that the Proponents of True Existence realize the absence of inherent existence of eyes, and so forth.

Fourth, the refutation of that [assertion]

This has four parts.

First, not only would this contradict your own assertion [that Proponents of True Existence do not realize the absence of inherent existence of phenomena] but also as a reason [why such cannot be accepted], it would [absurdly] follow that Haribhadra's explanation in his "Small Commentary" [his "Clear Meaning Commentary on (Maitreya's) 'Ornament for Clear Realization'"] of the absence of true existence to Buddhist Proponents of True Existence would not be correct [because it would be absurd to prove the absence of true existence to them if they already realized it]. If you accept such, then it contradicts your own assertion; previously you flung to the opponent the unwanted consequence that [the Proponents of True Existence] would realize the absence of inherent existence of eyes and so forth; thus it is your own assertion that Proponents of True Existence do not realize that eyes and so forth do not inherently exist, and you are contradicting that.

Not only that, it would not be necessary for Mādhyamikas to prove to Proponents of True Existence that sprouts and so forth do not truly exist. Further, complete paths of virtuous or non-virtuous actions are posited as continuums of moments; since a continuum is similar to a gross object, which is a composite of minute particles, the Proponents of True Existence would have to assert virtues and so forth to be without inherent existence by reason of their being continuums. If the Proponents of True Existence did assert such, then there would be no purpose in the Proponents of True Existence objecting to and disputing the propounding by Svātantrika-Mādhyamikas such as Haribhadra and so forth that all phenomena, virtues, non-virtues, and so forth, are like dreams, without true existence, refuting that these are posited through the force of appearing to a non-defective awareness. [195] The objection by the Proponents of True Existence is set forth in Haribhadra's *Clear Meaning Commentary* (*'grel pa don gsal, sputārthā*) as follows:[501]

> If all such phenomena were like dreams, then just as when elephants and so forth appear in a dream, the elephants and so forth do not exist, so the ten non-virtues as well as giving and so forth would not exist even conventionally, whereby would not even the waking state become like the state of sleep with no difference of error or non-error?

> The following paragraphs are a summary commentary by Nga-wang-rap-den.[502]

Someone might say: It [absurdly] follows that since all Buddhist Proponents of True Existence assert that the person is imputedly existent, the Proponents of True Existence would realize that phenomena such as eyes and so forth do not inherently exist. [197] For, they do not assert that the person is ultimately established, or, [in other words] they realize that the person is not ultimately established. This is because they assert it [the person] to be imputedly existent.

Response: In that case, it [absurdly] follows that the Proponents of True Existence realize that gross phenomena such as eyes, sprouts, and so forth do not inherently exist because they assert those as imputedly existent. You have asserted the entailment [that if the Proponents of True Existence assert something as imputedly existent, they necessarily realize it as without inherent existence]. That the reason [that is, that they assert gross phenomena such as eyes, sprouts, and so forth as imputedly existent] is so follows because they assert that gross things are imputedly existent and that partless minute particles and so forth are substantially existent. If you accept the basic consequence [that the Proponents of True Existence do realize the absence of inherent existence of gross things such as eyes, sprouts, and so forth], then that would contradict your own flinging to me earlier [the *unwanted* consequence that the Proponents of True Existence would realize that phenomena such as eyes and so forth do not inherently exist] as a means of clearing away my conviction [that when the absence of inherent existence of the person is realized, one has the capacity to induce realization of the absence of inherent existence of the aggregates] and would contradict your own assertion [that they do not].

Not only that, but also it would not be necessary to prove to Proponents of True Existence that sprouts and so forth do not truly exist. Furthermore, it would [absurdly] follow that the [Proponents of True Existence] would realize that complete paths of virtuous and non-virtuous actions do not inherently exist because they assert that those imputedly exist. You have asserted the entailment [that if they assert those to be imputedly existent, then they necessarily realize them to be without inherent existence]. It follows that [the Proponents of True Existence do assert complete paths of virtuous and non-virtuous actions to be imputedly existent] because they posit that [a complete path of virtuous or non-virtuous actions] is a continuum and they assert that collections and continuums are imputedly existent. If you accept the basic consequence [that the Proponents of True Existence realize a complete path of virtuous or non-virtuous actions to be without inherent existence], then it would [absurdly] follow that the explanation in Haribhadra's *Clear Meaning Commentary* of how the Proponents of True Existence dispute the Madhyāmikas' assertion that virtuous and non-virtuous actions are without inherent existence, like dreams, would be incorrect.

Second, not only are the measures of being ultimately and conventionally established not the same in the higher and lower tenet systems, it is necessary to distinguish that there are many forms even within one system. Therefore, although establishment or non-establishment ultimately and conventionally in the systems of the Proponents of True Existence and establishment or non-establishment ultimately and conventionally in the Mādhyamika system are similar in name, there is a great difference of meaning in the mode of being or not being established conventionally and in the mode of being or not being established ultimately.

Hence, from the Mādhyamika perspective, those things, gross objects, continuums, and so forth, which are asserted by the Proponents of True Existence as conventionally existent,[503] come to be what in the Mādhyamika system would be ultimately established. For instance, although the Sautrāntikas assert generally characterized phenomena as conventionalities, since they assert them to be established from their own sides, from the Mādhyamika perspective these generally characterized phenomena would be truly established. Also, those things that the Proponents of True Existence assert to be ultimately established[504] are for the Mādhyamikas conventionally established. For instance, although the Sautrāntikas assert that specifically characterized phenomena are truly established, according to the Mādhyamikas, specifically characterized phenomena are not truly established. Therefore, there is no contradiction at all in the need for the Mādhyamikas to prove the absence of true existence of those things that are asserted by the Proponents of True Existence to be conventionalities. Hence, a detailed differentiation of those differences should be known from Kamalashīla's *Illumination of the Middle Way* and so forth. [196]

Third, the difference that for those [Proponents of True Existence] the person is not merely nominally imputed whereas for this master [Chandrakīrti] it is. Furthermore, although the imputedly existent person in the systems of the Proponents of True Existence and the imputedly existent person in the system of this master [Chandrakīrti] are similar in mere name, they are completely dissimilar in meaning. For, this master [Chandrakīrti] asserts that since the Proponents of True Existence assert that the person is truly established in the sense of being inherently established, they do not have the view realizing the selflessness of the person. That is so because this master asserts that if one has not realized the selflessness of phenomena either explicitily, implicitly, or through the force [of another realization], or, if one's mind is not directed toward tenets for realizing that selflessness [of phenomena], one has not at all realized the selflessness of the person.

Fourth, therefore, as long as one has not forsaken the tenet that the aggregates are substantially existent, that is, are not just nominally imputed, one has a conception of the person as substantially existent. Therefore, this master [Chandrakīrti] asserts that as long as one has not forsaken the tenets of a system asserting that the aggregates are substantially existent, one conceives the person also to be substantially existent in the sense of being established inherently.

SECOND, ALTHOUGH [EVEN IN THIS SYSTEM, PRĀSAṄGIKA, PRACTITIONERS OF] THE TWO VEHICLES MEDITATE ON THE TWO SELFLESSNESSES INDIVIDUALLY [FIRST THE SELFLESSNESS OF PERSONS AND THEN OF PHENOMENA], THE MODE OF REALIZATION [IN MĀDHYAMIKA] IS DIFFERENT FROM THAT AMONG THE PROPONENTS OF TRUE EXISTENCE

Therefore, until those [Proponents of True Existence] forsake tenets asserting true establishment, that is to say, the substantial existence, of the aggregates, there is no occurrence of their realizing that the person does not ultimately exist.

4 *Misidentifying the Object of Negation*

The actual settling of suchness has three parts: identifying the object of negation by reasoning, whether that negation is done by means of consequences or autonomous syllogisms, and how, in dependence on doing that, to generate the view in your continuum.

IDENTIFYING THE OBJECT OF NEGATION BY REASONING

This also has three parts: the reason why it is necessary to identify well the object of negation, [198] refuting other systems that [engage in] refutation without having identified the object of negation, and how the object of negation is identified in our own system.

THE REASON WHY IT IS NECESSARY TO IDENTIFY WELL THE OBJECT OF NEGATION

This has five parts.

FIRST, WITHOUT IDENTIFYING THE OBJECT OF NEGATION, THE NON-AFFIRMING NEGATIVE WHICH IS THE NEGATIVE OF THAT [OBJECT OF NEGATION] WILL NOT APPEAR

For example, in order to ascertain that a certain person is not here, you must first know the person who is not here. Just so, in order to ascertain the meaning of "selflessness" or "absence of inherent existence", you must identify well the self or inherent existence that does not exist – you need to think, "If it did exist, it would be like this." The reason for this is that if the meaning-generality, or aspect, of that object of negation does not appear as an object of the mind by way of having been identified well, then you will also not unerringly ascertain and realize selflessness and so forth, the non-affirming negative which is the negative of that object of negation. For, Shāntideva's *Engaging in the Bodhisattva Deeds* (*bodhisattvacaryāvatāra*, IX.140ab) says that:[505]

> Without contacting and ascertaining, by way of its aspect appearing to the mind, the entity (*dngos po, bhāva*) that is the object of negation, true establishment, which is erroneously superimposed by the conception of true existence, one cannot apprehend the absence of that entity, that is, the non-existence of that true establishment, by way of realizing the absence of true existence with the mind.

SECOND, IT IS EASIER TO REFUTE THE OBJECTS OF NEGATION IF THEY ARE CONDENSED INTO THE TWO, THE COARSE AND SUBTLE, OR INTO THE TWO, A SELF OF PERSONS AND A SELF OF PHENOMENA

With respect to this need to identify the object of negation, the different features – the divisions in terms of type – of the objects of negation are limitless. However, if they are negated from their root, which contains all of the objects of negation without being merely partial, all the objects of negation will also be well refuted. [199]

THIRD, ONE WILL NOT BE RELEASED IF ONE DOES NOT REFUTE THE SUBTLE OBJECT OF NEGATION

With regard to this which is to be refuted, if you do not do the refutation by way of the subtlest form that is the finality of all of the essentials of the object of negation and there is some remainder of an object of negation left over, you will fall to an extreme of existence, or permanence, that is to say, you will conceive of true existence. Due to that, a manifest conception of the true existence of things will be generated, whereby you cannot be released from cyclic existence.

FOURTH, IF ONE'S NEGATION GOES TOO FAR, ONE WILL FALL TO AN EXTREME OF ANNIHILATION

If you engage in negation without holding to the measure of the object of negation, going far beyond negating the object of negation, then due to losing belief in the stages of the dependent-arising of causes and effects you will not know how to posit those [dependent-arisings of causes and effects] even conventionally, whereby you will fall to an extreme of annihilation. Due to that view of annihilation, you will definitely be led, or impelled, into a bad transmigration.

FIFTH, THE MEANING THAT HAS BEEN ESTABLISHED IS THAT IF THE OBJECT OF NEGATION IS NOT IDENTIFIED, ONE WILL FALL TO [AN EXTREME OF] EITHER PERMANENCE OR ANNIHILATION

Therefore, it is important to identify well the object of negation, for if this object of negation is not identified, you will unquestionably generate either a view of permanence or a view of annihilation.

SECOND, REFUTING OTHER SYSTEMS THAT [ENGAGE IN] REFUTATION WITHOUT HAVING IDENTIFIED THE OBJECT OF NEGATION

This has two parts: refuting an overly broad identification of the object of negation and refuting a too limited identification of the object of negation.

FIRST, REFUTING AN OVERLY BROAD IDENTIFICATION OF THE OBJECT OF NEGATION

This has two parts: stating others' assertions [200] and showing that those assertions are incorrect.

FIRST, STATING OTHERS' ASSERTIONS

This has eleven attributes.

First, [others' assertion that] all phenomena are included in the four extremes

Nowadays most Tibetans who claim to propound the meaning of the middle way say that the existence of all phenomena ranging from forms through to exalted-knowers-of-all-aspects is refuted by the reasoning analyzing whether the bases of analysis, production and so forth, are or are not established as [their own] suchness. Their reason for this is that when reasoning analyzes any phenomenon which is asserted, there does not exist even a particle able to withstand, that is, bear the burden of, investigation. Also, [this reasoning refutes the existence of all phenomena, they say,] because in many sūtras and treatises all four alternatives, or extremes – existence, non-existence, both existence and non-existence, and neither existence nor non-existence – are refuted and there does not in the least exist any phenomenon not included in those four alternatives.

Second, [others'] assertion that the meditative equipoise of a Superior perceives production, cessation, bondage, release, and so forth, as non-existent

Not only that, they also have another reasoning: [They say that] a Superior's exalted wisdom of meditative equipoise directly perceiving suchness perceives the phenomena of production, cessation, bondage, release, and so forth as not existing in the least. [202] And, since the status of phenomena must be just as they are comprehended by the meditative equipoise of Superiors, production and so forth are just non-existent.

Third, [others'] assertion that an object found by [a consciousness] analyzing the ultimate and [an object] able to bear analysis [by that consciousness] are synonymous

They say: "If you assert that production and so forth exist, then are those or are those not able to bear analysis by the reasoning analyzing suchness with respect to them [that is, investigating whether or not production and so forth exist as their own suchness]? If they are able to bear analysis by that reasoning, then you have to assert that there exist things able to bear analysis by reasoning, whereby they would be established as truly existent things. If they are not able to bear analysis by that reasoning [analyzing suchness], then since, having been refuted by reasoning, they would be negated, how is it feasible that objects negated by reasoning exist? It is not."

Fourth, [others'] assertion that production, cessation, and so forth are not established by valid cognition

[They also say that] just as by way of analyzing whether they can or cannot bear analysis by reasoning, production and so forth are not feasible [to exist], so there is another reasoning: If production and so forth are asserted to exist, they do not pass beyond being either established or not established by valid cognition; thus, between these two, which are they? If it is the former [case, that is, that production and so forth] are established by valid cognition, then they must definitely be established by the supreme of valid cognizers, a Superior's exalted wisdom of meditative equipoise directly perceiving suchness. Since that exalted wisdom perceives production and so forth as non-existent, it is not feasible that it establish production and so forth.

Further, if you assert that forms and so forth are established by conventional eye consciousnesses, ear consciousnesses, and so forth, because it was refuted by the sūtras and so forth to be cited below that those eye consciousnesses and so forth are valid cognizers, it is not feasible to assert that those eye consciousnesses and so forth are valid cognizers establishing forms and so forth. [203] With regard to the reason for that, the *King of Meditative Stabilizations Sūtra* (IX.23) says that:[506]

> The eye consciousness, the ear consciousness, and also the nose consciousness are not valid cognizers; the tongue consciousness, the body consciousness, and mental consciousness are also not valid cognizers. If these sense consciousnesses were valid cognizers, of what use to any meditator would the effort of cultivating the Superior path be? There would be no purpose at all.

Not only that, Chandrakīrti's *Supplement to (Nāgārjuna's) "Treatise on the Middle Way"* (VI.31a) says that:[507]

> In all respects worldly conventional consciousnesses, such as eye consciousnesses, that do not realize emptiness are not valid cognizers.

Thus, [they say] a Superior's meditative equipoise perceives production and so forth as non-existent, and worldly conventional eye consciousnesses and so forth are in all respects not valid cognizers; since there is no other valid cognizer establishing production and so forth, it is not feasible that production and so forth are established by valid cognition.

[They say to us,] you yourself do not assert that production and so forth are not established by valid cognition and yet exist, and such is also not reasonable. Therefore, such is not at all feasible.

Fifth, [others'] assertion that production, and so forth, do not exist even conventionally

[They say that] if you assert that production and so forth exist, then since you do not assert that they exist ultimately, you must assert that they exist conventionally. [However], to assert such is also very unreasonable, for Chandrakīrti's *Supplement to (Nāgārjuna's) "Treatise on the Middle Way"* (VI.36) says that:[508]

> If one analyzes by means of the reasoning [used] on the occasion of analyzing suchness from what agent

> of production, self or other, things are produced, [204] one sees that production from either of those two is not reasonable. Through the reasoning analyzing suchness which sees thus, [one sees that] the production of things even conventionally is not reasonable. If that is not reasonable, by what reasoning would there be production in your system? That is to say, it is not feasible that production exists by way of any reasoning.

Thus, [Chandrakīrti] says that the reasoning refuting production from the four extremes that refutes ultimate production also refutes conventional production.

Sixth, [others'] assertion that if [production and so forth] are not included in the four alternatives, such analysis is not feasible

[They set forth] another reasoning: If you assert that things are produced even though they are not produced from any of the four – self, other, both self and other, or causelessly, then, on the occasion of refuting ultimate production, ultimate production would not be refuted by the refutation upon investigating the four alternatives – [production from] self, other, and so forth. For, there would exist a production that was not any of the four alternatives, or extremes, that is to say, [not from] self, other, [both, or causelessly].

Seventh, [others'] assertion that because, from among the four alternatives, production from other does not exist, production does not exist

Since production is limited to these four extremes, if it is said that production is one from among the four alternatives, then since you do not assert production from the other three causes of production – self, both [self and other], or causelessly – things must be produced from other. If [you say that] they are produced from other, this is not reasonable. For, Chandrakīrti's *Supplement to (Nāgārjuna's) "Treatise on the Middle*

Way" (VI.32d) says, "Production from other does not exist even in the world."[509]

Eighth, [others'] assertion that it is not necessary to affix the qualification "ultimate" in the refutation of production [205]

Because of those previous reasons, it is all right to refute mere production, and in the refutation of production one should not affix even the qualification "ultimate" as in the statement, "Production does not exist ultimately." For, Chandrakīrti's *Clear Words* refutes the affixing of the qualification "ultimate".

> The following paragraph is commentary from Nga-wang-rap-den that summarizes the three sections to follow.

Therefore, [these misinterpreters of Mādhyamika] say [correctly] that it is undeniably the system of the glorious Chandrakīrti that all phenomena are without inherent existence, that is, are not established by way of their own entities. [They then mistakenly conclude:] In that they are thus without inherent existence, what does exist? Therefore, nothing – production, cessation, and so forth – exists. Amongst those who assert such, some assert that production, cessation, and so forth do not exist even conventionally. Others assert that they exist conventionally, but this does not serve as existing. In either case, they say that the reasoning analyzing the ultimate refutes production, cessation, and so forth.

Ninth, among those, there are two types, those who do and do not assert production conventionally

Those who claimed to be Mādhyamikas at that time [i.e., Dzong-ka-ba's time] mostly propounded such [that production and so forth are refuted by the Mādhyamika reasoning and hence do not exist], and among those who did so, two different types are seen, some saying that they do not assert production and so forth even conventionally and some asserting that production and so forth exist conventionally.

Tenth, all accord in refuting inherent existence

Except for that [difference – some saying that production exists conventionally and some saying that it does not], all of those systems accord in propounding the following: It is undeniable by anyone that it is the system of this master [Chandrakīrti] that an inherent existence, that is, an establishment by way of their own entities, of phenomena such as production and so forth is refuted by reasoning engaged in ultimate analysis; for, the inherent establishment of phenomena is refuted in terms of both truths.

Eleventh, the assertion that whatever does not inherently exist necessarily does not exist [206]

[Then these misinterpreters of Mādhyamika say that] thus, if phenomena do not inherently exist, what else is there beyond this absence of inherent existence? Because phenomena do not exist, an affixing of the qualification "ultimate" in the refutation of the object of negation – production and so forth – is not the system of the Prāsaṅgika-Mādhyamikas but is the system of only the Svātantrika-Mādhyamikas. Stretching out their necks and raising themselves up high, they explain it thus.

> The remainder of the chapter is a summary explanation from Nga-wang-rap-den.[510]

Let us set forth in one place [all] the modes of refuting too broad an object of negation: Someone might say that all phenomena ranging from forms through to exalted-knowers-of-all-aspects are the object of negation of a reasoning consciousness analyzing the ultimate. For, none of those has even a particle that is established as able to bear analysis by that reasoning consciousness. Also, [all phenomena are the object of negation by a reasoning consciousness analyzing the ultimate] because if those [phenomena] were not refuted by that reasoning and did exist, then they would have to exist as one of the four alternatives, whereas in sūtra all four alternatives were refuted in the statement, "If one is engaged in 'existence', then one is engaged in signs," [i.e., misapprehension of reality] and so forth. Also, [all phenomena are the object of negation by reasoning] because a Superior's meditative equipoise perceiving suchness sees production, cessation, and so forth as not in the least existent.

Therefore, production, cessation, bondage, release, and so forth do not exist at all. Otherwise, if they do exist, can they or can they not bear analysis by reasoning? In the former case [if they were able to bear analysis by reasoning], then they would be truly existent things; in the latter case, if they cannot bear analysis by reasoning, then it must be that they are not found by that [reasoning consciousness]. In that case they must be refuted by that reasoning, whereby they must not exist.

Further, if those [phenomena] exist, are they or are they not established by valid cognition? The former is not feasible because a Superior's meditative equipoise does not establish them since it sees them as non-existent and it is refuted that conventional eye consciousnesses and so forth are valid cognizers.

Furthermore, if production did exist, it would have to exist conventionally, and that is not feasible because Chandrakīrti's *Supplement to (Nāgārjuna's) "Treatise on the Middle Way"* says that the reasoning that refutes production ultimately refutes production even conventionally.

Further, if production does exist, are [things] produced from one among the four alternatives [that is, from self, other, both self and other, or causelessly] or not? In the former case [that is, if they are produced from one of the four alternatives], they would have to be produced from other since the other three [alternatives] are not feasible, but that is refuted in Chandrakīrti's *Supplement to (Nāgārjuna's) "Treatise on the Middle Way"*. [201] In the latter case [that is, if they are not produced from any of the four alternatives, but are produced], then when ultimately existent production is refuted, it would not be refuted through a refutation within analyzing the four alternatives because there would exist a production that was not included in any of the four alternatives.

Moreover, if a reasoning analyzing the ultimate does not find the production of things and so forth, those are refuted; this is like the way in which, for example, if you fear that there might be a robber in one of the rooms [of a house] and search but do not find a robber, then the existence of a robber there is refuted.

I have put together in order the systems of those who assert too broad an object of negation; I offer them for you to consider.

5 *The Uncommon Feature of Mādhyamika*

The second division from above, showing the incorrectness of those systems' assertions, has two parts: initially showing that those systems [described] above refute the most important uncommon distinguishing feature of Mādhyamika; and then showing that the damages expressed above do not damage and overwhelm the party to whom they are expressed [i.e., do not damage the correct Mādhyamika interpretation].

> This is part two of a heading that occurred in the previous chapter and was entitled "refuting an overly broad identification of the object of negation". Part one was a statement of others' assertions, and part two, begun here, is the demonstration that those assertions are incorrect.

FIRST, SHOWING THAT THEY REFUTE THE DISTINGUISHING FEATURE OF MĀDHYAMIKA

This has three parts: identifying the distinguishing feature of Mādhyamika; how the above systems refute this distinguishing feature; and how a Mādhyamika responds to such a mode of refutation.

FIRST, IDENTIFYING THE DISTINGUISHING FEATURE OF MĀDHYAMIKA

This has four parts: the Mādhyamikas' mode of assertion; the mode of objection by the Proponents of True Existence; the feasibility of cyclic existence and nirvāṇa even though there is no inherent existence; and the way in which emptiness and dependent-arising are of one meaning.

FIRST, THE MĀDHYAMIKAS' MODE OF ASSERTION

This has three parts, the first of which is the need to assert that the fruits, the two bodies [a Buddha's Form Body and Truth Body], arise from the two collections [of merit and wisdom].

The following three paragraphs are a summary by Nga-wang-rap-den of the explanation that is to come.

Even though it is easy to understand how these [assertions of the misinterpreters of Mādhyamika] are to be refuted, let me state it briefly in one place in accordance with my lama's words: In order to achieve the fruit, the two bodies, you must [at the time of] the path, accumulate the two collections. For that, you must know the view of how to posit the bases, the two truths. And, for that, not only must two factors – 1) ascertainment induced from the depths with respect to the relationship of cause and effect in the sense of [knowing] that such and such an effect arises from such and such a cause, [207] and 2) [understanding] that all phenomena are without even a particle of inherent establishment – be non-contradictory for your mind, but also [understanding of] the one must serve to assist [understanding of] the other. Since this is a distinguishing feature of only the wise Mādhyamikas, it is difficult for others to realize it.

Furthermore, Mādhyamikas assert that emptiness is the meaning of dependent-arising: because of being dependent-arisings, [things] depend on causes, conditions, and so forth and thus, since they do not exist as self-powered entities, they are empty of existing from their own sides or of being established inherently.

Such an uncommon Mādhyamika system is refuted by the earlier faction [of misinterpreters] because they refute the system of the non-contradiction of the two factors: the non-existence of even a particle that inherently exists and the feasibility of production, cessation, and so forth. This is because they, saying, "If there is no inherent existence, what does exist?" propound that if there is no inherent existence, then production, cessation, and so forth must not exist. Furthermore, they propound in a manner opposite to the statement in Nāgārjuna's *Treatise on the Middle Way* that dependent-arisings are necessarily empty of inherent existence. For, their proposition that if there is no inherent existence, one must then assert that production, cessation, and so forth do not exist, amounts to propounding that if production and so forth exist, they must inherently exist.

Nāgārjuna's *Sixty Stanzas of Reasoning* (*rigs pa drug cu pa*, *yuktiṣaṣṭikā*, stanza 60) says that:[511]

> Through the power of this virtue, the cause of attainment, may all sentient beings without exception come to accumulate the two vast collections of merit and exalted wisdom and attain the fruit, the two supreme excellences – the Truth Body, which arises from exalted wisdom, and the Form Body, which arises from merit accumulated thus. [208]

As [Nāgārjuna] says, those fortunate trainees – who progress by way of the supreme vehicle, the vehicle to Buddhahood, and who engage [in practice] through the force of wanting and aspiring to only that vehicle – finally attain, on the occasion of the fruit, the two, the excellent Truth Body and the excellent Form Body. On what does the attainment of these depend? It depends on accumulating, on the occasion of the path, the immeasurable collections of merit and exalted wisdom in a non-partial manner, that is, through the non-separation of the two, method realizing the conventional varieties and wisdom realizing the ultimate mode, as explained earlier.

On what root does this accumulation of the two collections by way of method and wisdom rely? One [needs to] induce ascertainment from the depths of the heart, without its being merely verbal, with respect to the relationship of cause and effect – [an understanding that] such and such beneficial effects such as happy transmigrations, liberation, omniscience, and so forth arise from such and such virtuous causes, and such and such harmful effects such as bad transmigrations and so forth arise from such and such non-virtuous causes, these being conventional causes such as virtues and non-virtues and conventional effects such as happy transmigrations, bad transmigrations, liberation, and so forth. This attainment of ascertainment with respect to the conventional varieties is a factor of method and therefore is *method*.

One also [needs to] gain wisdom that is an ascertainment from the depths of the heart seeing that all phenomena, when analyzed well with reasoning, do not have even a particle of inherent existence, that is to say, establishment by way of their own entities. This attainment of ascertainment with respect to the ultimate mode is *wisdom*. [209] Therefore, [the attainment of the two bodies] definitely depends upon those roots – method and wisdom. The reason for this is that training involving generation of a wish to train from the depths of the heart in the complete factors containing the entire corpus of the path, a union of both method and wisdom, will utterly not occur if these two, method and wisdom, are incomplete and do not exist in union.

SECOND, HOW THE POSITING OF SUCH CAUSE AND EFFECT [I.E., THE ATTAINMENT OF THE TWO BODIES IN DEPENDENCE ON THE ACCUMULATION OF THE TWO COLLECTIONS] DEPENDS ON THE TWO TRUTHS

What is the root of not mistaking the essentials of the causal path, the union of method and wisdom, in reliance on which the two bodies are attained on the occasion of the effect? It depends on just the mode of settling the view realizing the bases, the two truths. What is the mode of settling the view on which such [non-mistaking of the essentials of the causal path] relies? It is this mode of gaining ascertainment with respect to the two truths that was just explained.

THIRD, HOW THE NON-CONTRADICTION OF ULTIMATE TRUTHS – ABSENCE OF INHERENT EXISTENCE – AND CONVENTIONAL TRUTHS – NOMINAL POSITING – IS ASSERTED ONLY BY MĀDHYAMIKAS

With respect to such a gaining of ascertainment concerning the two truths, the root of the essentials of the bases, paths, and fruits, no one else except for Mādhyamikas, persons of profound broad intelligence, knows how to explain the two truths [as interpreted by Mādhyamikas] as non-contradictory, seeing them as only a collection of contradictions in that when they make a presentation of conventional causes and effects, the ultimate – the class of emptiness – becomes unsuitable, and when they make a presentation of the ultimate – the class of emptiness – they become unable to posit cause and effect, and so forth. On the other hand, those skillful persons possessing subtle, wise, and very vast intelligence, those renowned as Mādhyamikas, knowing how to do such, [210] settle through their skill in the techniques for realizing the two truths such a presentation of the two truths without even a scent of contradiction, never mind actually having contradiction. They have found the finality, the root, of the Conqueror's thought, the meaning of the two truths exactly as it is. In dependence on that, they generate wonderful respect viewing the teacher who teaches such and that teaching as very amazing; with pure speech and words without flattery or falseness, powerlessly induced from having generated [that wonderful respect] they raise up their necks and proclaim again and again with great voice to other fortunate persons, "Listen, O Knowledgeable Ones, the meaning of emptiness, that is to say, of things' emptiness of inherent existence, is a meaning manifesting in the context of dependent-arising, the relationship of cause and effect. It does not mean that things do not exist at all in the sense of things being empty of, devoid of, all capacity to perform the functions of cause and effect."

SECOND, THE MODE OF OBJECTION BY PROPONENTS OF TRUE EXISTENCE

Although scholars of our own [i.e., Buddhist] schools, Proponents of True Existence, who are not such Mādhyamikas – that is, Vaibhāṣhikas, Sautrāntikas, and so forth who possess the discrimination of having great familiarity and training with many, limitless, topics of learning – have such discrimination, they do not assert this Mādhyamika view. Not only do they not assert it, [211] they also debate with the Mādhyamikas who assert such a special view.

The root reason for this is, in sum, as follows: In the estimation of these scholars who are Proponents of True Existence, since Mādhyamikas assert that all phenomena are utterly without inherent existence, that is, establishment by way of their own entities, and since [these scholars feel that] if [phenomena] were empty in the sense of being utterly without inherent existence, there would be no basis for positing all the presentations of cyclic existence and nirvāṇa, bondage, release, and so forth, they think that there is absolutely no way [for the Mādhyamikas] to posit such presentations. [Their objection] stems from just this thought. For, Nāgārjuna's *Treatise on the Middle Way* (XXIV.1), on the occasion of setting forth the way in which Proponents of True Existence debate with Mādhyamikas, says that:[512]

> [The Proponents of True Existence say that] if you Mādhyamikas assert that all these [phenomena] are empty of being established by way of their own entities, then in your system there would be no way at all to posit the activities of dependent-arising – arising, or production, and disintegration, or cessation. Also, it would absurdly follow that in the system of you Mādhyamikas there would be no way at all to posit the four noble truths – suffering, sources, cessations, and paths.

Thus [Nāgārjuna] states [the Proponents of True Existence's] mode of debate, which is to say that if all things are empty of inherent existence, then production, disintegration, and presentations of the four truths would be utterly unfeasible.

Also, the way in which Proponents of True Existence debate with Mādhyamikas is set forth in Nāgārjuna's *Refutation of Objections* (stanza 1). This says that:[513]

> If in your Mādhyamika system an inherent existence, that is to say, an establishment by way of their own entities, of all things is asserted not to exist in any thing, then since your words refuting inherent existence, that is to say, establishment by way of [an object's] own entity, are only without inherent existence, [212] such non-inherently existent words cannot at all overcome inherent establishment.

Thus, they say that if words do not have inherent existence, that is, an establishment by way of their own entities, then those words cannot perform activities of refutation and proof – refutation of inherent existence, i.e., of establishment by way of [an object's] own entity, or proof of such non-inherent existence. In this way, thinking that if there is no inherent existence, that is to say, establishment from [an object's] own side, then all objects produced and producers, as well as all activities of refutation and proof would not be feasible, Proponents of True Existence debate with Mādhyamikas. Through this mode of debate, it can be surmised that they dispute with Mādhyamikas within understanding that the reasonings refuting inherent existence totally refute all activity and functioning in all things.

THIRD, THE FEASIBILITY OF CYCLIC EXISTENCE AND NIRVĀṆA EVEN THOUGH THERE IS NO INHERENT EXISTENCE

This has seven parts.

FIRST, ALTHOUGH THERE IS NO INHERENT EXISTENCE, CYCLIC EXISTENCE AND NIRVĀṆA ARE SUITABLE

Therefore, when Proponents of True Existence and Mādhyamikas debate with respect to their respective uncommon tenets, they debate disagreeing only about the suitability or unsuitability of positing all the presentations of cyclic existence and nirvāṇa within a position of the emptiness of inherent existence. Hence, the allowability of asserting the feasibility of all the presentations of cyclic existence and nirvāṇa – objects produced, producers, refutation, proof, and so forth – within taking as one's basis the non-existence of even a particle of inherent existence, that is to say, establishment by way of their own entities, in all things is only a distinguishing feature of the wise Mādhyamikas.

Furthermore, the twenty-fourth chapter of Nāgārjuna's *Treatise on the Middle Way* (XXIV.13–14) sets forth an answer to the objection raised above by the Proponents of True Existence; Nāgārjuna says that:[514]

> The flinging of many consequences by you Proponents of True Existence with the fallacies of all activities not being feasible, there being no arising, disintegration, and so forth, is done within your not knowing the meaning and purpose of emptiness. The flinging of such a consequence – that activities cannot be posited in the system of us Mādhyamikas who propound an emptiness that is an emptiness of inherent existence – [213] is not correct. Not only that, but also, within the emptiness of inherent existence, all activities are very correct. Therefore, you Proponents of True Existence have a wrong perspective on the meaning of emptiness. This fault of abandoning emptiness by way of propounding these many fallacies is very incorrect in my Mādhyamika system.
>
> Not only does the fallacy of the incorrectness of activities not apply to us Mādhyamikas, but also, all activities are very correct, for in just that Mādhyamika system in which emptiness, that is to say, the emptiness of inherent existence, is positable, all the presentations of the truths, dependent-arising, and so forth are positable. However, in the system of the

Proponents of True Existence, in which such an emptiness is not positable, all the presentations of activities – the truths, and so forth – are not positable.

SECOND, NOT ONLY ARE CYCLIC EXISTENCE AND NIRVĀṆA SUITABLE WITHIN NON-INHERENT EXISTENCE, BUT ALSO, IF THERE WERE INHERENT EXISTENCE, CYCLIC EXISTENCE AND NIRVĀṆA WOULD NOT BE SUITABLE

[Nāgārjuna] says that not only do the fallacies expressed earlier when setting forth the objection by Proponents of True Existence to Mādhyamikas (XXIV.1), "If all of these were empty, [there would be no arising and no disintegration] ...." (see p.327) not occur in the Mādhyamika system, which propounds the absence of inherent existence, but also, in the system of Mādhyamikas, who assert a position of an emptiness of inherent existence, all activities such as production, disintegration, and so forth are positable, whereas in other systems, which assert a position of a non-emptiness of inherent existence, all activities are not positable.

Furthermore, the way such [activities] are suitable is stated in Chandrakīrti's *Clear Words* [making the transition between XXIV.13 and 14]:[515]

> The consequence [expressing] fallacy that you Proponents of True Existence set forth, saying that all activities are not positable, does not apply to our Mādhyamika position, or thesis, which is an assertion of the emptiness of inherent existence. [214] Not only does it just not apply, but also due to the very assertion of an emptiness of inherent existence, all the presentations of conventionalities, the [four noble] truths and so forth, are established as just very correct. In order to indicate that meaning, Nāgārjuna says in the *Treatise on the Middle Way*, "In that system in which the emptiness that is an emptiness of inherent existence is positable ...".

Thus Chandrakīrti makes an explanation within citing that passage [in Nāgārjuna's *Treatise*].

THIRD, THE SUITABILITY OF THE TWELVE LINKS OF DEPENDENT-ARISING AND SO FORTH WITHIN THAT [EMPTINESS OF INHERENT EXISTENCE]

Moreover, from among the twenty-seven chapters of Nāgārjuna's *Treatise on the Middle Way*, the twenty-sixth teaches the stages of production by way of the forward process of the twelve links of dependent-arising, ignorance, and so forth, and teaches the stages of the cessation [of those twelve links] through the reverse process.

> The forward process is that from ignorance comes actions and so forth; the reverse process is that through stopping ignorance, actions are stopped, and so forth.

The twenty-fifth chapter mainly refutes inherent establishment with respect to those dependent-arisings.[516]

FOURTH, THE SUITABILITY OF EVERYTHING, THE FOUR TRUTHS, AND SO FORTH

The twenty-fourth chapter [of Nāgārjuna's *Treatise on the Middle Way*], that analyzing the noble truths, extensively settles how all presentations of cyclic existence and nirvāṇa such as arising, disintegration, and so forth, are not positable within the system of those who assert a non-emptiness of inherent existence and how all those activities are positable within the system of those who assert things that are empty of inherent existence. Therefore, it is important to know to carry this twenty-fourth chapter over to all the others.

FIFTH, IN THE SUPERIOR [NĀGĀRJUNA'S] SYSTEM EVERYTHING IS SUITABLE WITHIN DEPENDENT-ARISING

For the above reasons, the present-day proposition by those here in Tibet who claim to propound the meaning of the middle way that presentations of cause and effect, produced, producer, and so forth are necessarily not suitable within an absence of inherent existence is not the Mādhyamika system, [215] but rather is the system of the Proponents of True Existence.

Hence, it is the assertion of the protector Nāgārjuna, great opener of the middle way, that one needs to seek the emptiness of inherent existence and the middle path in dependence on just the positing of the presentations of cause and effect – the production of such and such effects in dependence on such and such causes and conditions and the cessation [of those] due to the incompleteness of causes and conditions – that is to say, [one needs to seek the emptiness of inherent existence and the middle path] through just the force of the correctness of such presentations of cause and effect. This is the final essential that is the root of [his] tenet system.

From what sources is it known that this is so? One can know this from Nāgārjuna's *Treatise on the Middle Way*; the twenty-fourth chapter (XXIV.18–19) says that:[517]

> Because those things that arise only mutually dependent on causes and conditions coming together are not established by way of their own power or through their own force, the perfect Buddha explained that they are empty* of being established by way of their own entities. (One must understand this as meaning "empty" of inherent existence; how could you understand it as being "emptiness"!) That which is empty, as explained above, is posited as only dependently designated without the subject's being established by way of its own power. This dependent-designation with respect to things that are only mere aggregations and collections of other causes and conditions – appearing as the meaning of the emptiness of inherent existence – is the middle

* translated thus in accordance with following commentary. The text says "emptiness".

> way beyond the two extremes of permanence, or establishment by [an object's] own power, and annihilation, or the non-existence of dependent-arising. Because that meaning is the object for progress by Mādhyamikas, it is the path, and therefore, it is the middle path.
>
> This emptiness of inherent existence, the final meaning to be realized, is not trifling, but applies to all phenomena. For, because there does not exist any phenomenon that is not a dependent-arising, [216] there also does not exist any phenomenon that is not empty of inherent existence. This is because dependent-arising is established as just the meaning of emptiness of inherent existence.

Thus, with respect to this very clear statement [by Nāgārjuna] that whatever is a dependent-arising is necessarily empty of inherent existence, you who claim to be proponents of the meaning of the middle way should not propound something opposite from what the master Nāgārjuna said, saying that whatever is produced in dependence on causes and conditions is necessarily inherently established.

SIXTH, THE SUPERIOR MASTER [NĀGĀRJUNA] SPOKE AGAIN AND AGAIN ABOUT SUCH SUITABILITY

In accordance with that statement [cited] above that dependent-arising is the meaning of emptiness, Nāgārjuna's *Refutation of Objections* says that:[518]

> For a system in which the emptiness of inherent existence is possible, in the sense of being positable, all objects – the [four noble] truths, dependent-arising, and so forth – are possible and positable. For a system in which an emptiness of inherent existence is not positable and not possible, no presentations of objects are positable or possible.
>
> Homage to the Buddha, the unequalled teacher,

> renowned as the Supramundane Victor, for whom nothing else can serve as an equivalent example, supreme speaker who taught as of one meaning 1) the emptiness of inherent existence, 2) dependent-arising, and 3) the path – [so called] since that meaning of the middle way that has abandoned the two extremes is what is travelled by Mādhyamikas. These three – the meaning of emptiness of inherent existence, the meaning of dependent-arising, and the meaning of the middle way – except for being different names – have the same meaning as the path entered by Mādhyamikas.

Not only that, but also Nāgārjuna's *Seventy Stanzas on Emptiness* (*stong nyid bdun cu pa*, *śūnyatāsaptati*, verse 68), in accordance with the above statements, says that:[519]

> The Tathāgata, unequalled by any, thoroughly taught transmigrating beings by means of various marvellous doctrines for the sake of settling just this mode of the dependent-arising of things by the reason of their being posited as empty, that is, by reason of the fact that all things – all bases – are empty of inherent establishment. (It is said that a more felicitous translation of Nāgārjuna's middle two lines [from Sanskrit into Tibetan] would be, [217] "The unequalled Tathāgata [taught that] because things are empty, they are dependent-arisings.")

Also, Nāgārjuna's *Sixty Stanzas on Reasoning* (stanzas 43–5) says that:[520]

> Those outside of this doctrine, Outsiders, or Forders, having destroyed the mode of dependent-arising through the force of great obscuration with respect to the mode of dependent-arising – [the fact that] the entities of things have definite causes and conditions, which turn into them, and definitely arise from unconfused [i.e., specific sets of] causes and

conditions – adhere to things as not dependent, that is, as not dependent-arisings, and adhere to a self, that is, to a permanent self who is the creator of everything, or to the world as created by the prior motivation of that [permanent self] and likewise adhere to the self or the world as permanent or impermanent, or having an end or not having an end, and so forth. They, alas, due to being obscured, that is, pressed down by the weight of such great misconception, have had their independence stolen away by views – the sixty-four bad views and so forth, viewing [self and the world] as permanent, i.e., a thing without production or disintegration, or as impermanent, i.e., as something the continuation of which is completely severed upon its destruction, and so forth. [Captivated by such views], they wreck their own opportunity for liberation and are led into bad transmigrations. [218]

Not only that, but also how could those faults of falling to the extremes – the view of true establishment, i.e., permanence, or the view of the severing and utter non-existence of a continuum upon destruction, i.e., annihilation – not accrue to those Buddhist Proponents of True Existence who assert that things, due to being dependent-arisings that rely on definite, non-confused causes and conditions, are established inherently, that is, exist as [their own] suchness? They do accrue to them; once one asserts the above, then those faults only accrue.

Mādhyamikas of superior intelligence see and assert that just due to dependently arising from definite and unconfused causes and conditions, things are not real in the sense of being established as their own mode of subsistence as they appear to be, that is, are not inherently established, yet also are not non-existent conventionally, and despite being established as unreal falsities are not unreal (*log pa*)

> in the sense of being unable to perform functions. [They see and assert this] as like, for example, the reflection of a moon in the water which due to the aggregation of the three causes and conditions – water, the moon, and illumination – appears to be a moon but is not established as having the nature of the moon. [Hence] their independence is not ever stolen away by bad views, and they eliminate all bad views.

Also, Nāgārjuna's *Praise of the Supramundane [Buddha]* (*'jig rten las 'das par bstod pa*, *lokātītastava*, stanzas 21 and 22) says that:[521]

> Most of those whose disposition is to impute (*rtog*) and discriminate (*dpyod*) the extremes of things, those logicians ranging from non-Buddhists to our own Pro-ponents of True Existence, assert that suffering is produced either from its own essence – for instance, the Sāṃkhyas [who assert that suffering is produced from causes that are of the same nature as itself] – or that it is created by causes that are established as inherently other than itself – as is asserted by most Buddhist and non-Buddhist schools which propound that things are inherently established – or that [suffering] is created by both self and other [i.e., causes that are both the same entity as the effect and different entities from the effect] – like the Jainas – or that suffering is produced causelessly – as is asserted by the Materialists (*rgyang phen pa*, *āyata*). [219] You, the Supramundane Victor, unequalled teacher, said that [suffering] is a dependent-arising in the sense of depending on definite and unconfused causes and conditions, [this position] having passed beyond all those extremes.
>
> Also, you, the Supramundane Victor, unequalled teacher, asserted that those things that arise in de-

> pendence on, relative to, upon the meeting of, causes and conditions are empty of inherent existence. Since things are dependent-arisings, they depend on causes and conditions; hence, there are no self-powered things, whereby there is no establishment from [objects'] own side. This is the roar of the fearless lion, you, unequalled teacher, king of subduers, possessing the unendurable roar of the supreme profound causing the wild animal Forders to quiver.

Thus, [Nāgārjuna] says that by reason of being dependent-arisings, [phenomena] are only empty of inherent existence. Thereby, this system in which the meaning of dependent-arising dawns as the meaning of emptiness, that is to say, of no inherent existence, is the uncommon system of the protector Nāgārjuna.

SEVENTH, THE SUITABILITY OF ALL THE ACTIVITIES OF CYCLIC EXISTENCE AND NIRVĀṆA WITHIN A SYSTEM OF NO INHERENT EXISTENCE

Others, [who claim to be Mādhyamikas but] do not know this, take this emptiness which is an absence of inherent existence as a system posited from the Mādhyamikas' own side, [220] but they are uncomfortable with, that is to say, cannot posit, the presentations of dependently-arisen causes and effects in their own [so-called] Mādhyamika system through the force of not knowing the essential of the emptiness of inherent existence. These persons whose thesis is that the Mādhyamikas have no system of their own but rely merely on the assertions of other persons [for a presentation of the dependent-arising of cause and effect] have the error of propounding that dependent-arising and emptiness are contradictory; they have not arrived at even a mere portion of the meaning of dependent-arising. For, such is completely contradictory with [Nāgārjuna's] statement in the *Treatise on the*

Middle Way (XXIV.14, cited above), "In that [system] in which emptiness is suitable, . . ." in which he says that all the dependent-arisings of cyclic existence and nirvāṇa are feasible in whosoever's system propounds an absence of inherent existence.

6 *Dependent-Arising and Emptiness*

FOURTH, THE WAY IN WHICH EMPTINESS AND DEPENDENT-ARISING ARE OF ONE MEANING[522]

This has two parts: the dawning of the absence of inherent existence as dependent-arising and the dawning of dependent-arising as the absence of inherent existence.

FIRST, THE DAWNING OF THE ABSENCE OF INHERENT EXISTENCE AS DEPENDENT-ARISING

This has two parts: a brief indication by way of reasoning and individual explanations through scripture.

First, a brief indication by way of reasoning

Question: What is the system of the suitability of all [the phenomena] of cyclic existence and nirvāṇa within a position asserting the emptiness of inherent existence?

[*Answer*:] The Mādhyamikas, who propound that all things are just empty of inherent existence, propound such a suitability of all [the phenomena] of cyclic existence and nirvāṇa within a position of the emptiness of inherent existence by reason of [things'] arising in dependence on causes and conditions. This will be explained in detail below.

Because [things] do arise in dependence on causes and conditions in this manner, all the presentations of dependent-arising are feasible within the emptiness of inherent existence. [221] When the presentations of dependent-arising are feasible, suffering also is feasible. The reason for this is that suffering must be posited with respect to that which arises in dependence on causes and conditions; suffering is not suitable in that which does not arise in dependence on causes and conditions. This is because suffering does not arise without causes and conditions.

> Ge-shay Wangdrak: In other words, the arising of suffering involves change; thus it cannot occur in the permanent, but can only arise when there are causes and conditions.
>
> The following paragraph is a summary by Nga-wang-rap-den.

Suffering is under the other-influence of [contaminated] actions and afflictions. When dependent-arising is feasible, reliance on causes and conditions is feasible, whereby it [suffering] is feasible. If dependent-arising were not feasible, [suffering] would be under its own power, not relying on causes and conditions, in which case it would not be feasible for it to be under the other-influence of [contaminated] actions and afflictions. Therefore, when dependent-arising is feasible, the sources [of suffering] and so forth are feasible.

When the existence of such true sufferings that arise in dependence on causes and conditions is feasible, then the sources from which those sufferings arise, the cessations that are the stopping of those sufferings, and the paths proceeding to those cessations are feasible, whereby the presentations of the four truths definitely exist. When the four truths exist, then, respectively, the knowledge of suffering, the abandonment of its sources, the actualization of cessation, and the cultivation of the paths are suitable and feasible. When those – knowledge [of suffering], abandonment [of sources], and so forth – exist, then all, the Three Jewels and so forth, are very feasible and suitable.

Second, individual explanations through scripture

This has six parts.

First, indicating that all is suitable within an absence of inherent existence

Stating the way in which such is the case, Chandrakīrti's *Clear Words* says that:[523]

> For that system in which the emptiness of inherent existence of all things is suitable, all the above mentioned presentations are suitable. [222] How are they suitable? As follows: Because we Mādhyamikas propound the emptiness of inherent existence within just this meaning of dependent-arising – that is, propound that emptiness and dependent-arising are of one meaning – therefore, for that system in which the meaning of the emptiness of inherent existence is positable, all presentations of dependent-arising are positable. For that system in which the presentations of dependent-arisings are positable, the four noble truths are reasonable to be posited.

Second, the suitability of asserting the four truths within that [emptiness of inherent existence]

> How is such reasonable? As follows: There comes to be suffering in dependence upon just dependently-arisen causes and conditions. It does not arise without dependence; without dependently-arisen causes and conditions, the establishment of suffering does not at all occur. Since that which is established in dependence on causes and conditions does not have inherent existence, that is, is not established under its own power, it is empty of inherent existence. When such suffering exists, then the sources that are the causes from which that suffering arises, the cessations that are the stopping of that suffering, and the paths that are the methods for proceeding to the cessations that are the stopping of suffering are also positable. Because those are positable, the fruits –

thorough knowledge of suffering, abandonment of the sources that are the causes of suffering, actualization of the cessations that are the stopping of suffering, and [223] cultivation of the paths that are the methods for actualizing those cessations – are also feasible and suitable.

Third, the suitability of Approachers to [and Abiders in] the fruit within this [emptiness of inherent existence]

When thorough knowledge, abandonment, and so forth with respect to the truths – suffering, sources, and so forth – exist, the four fruits, such as entering the stream, returning once, and so forth are suitable. When those fruits, such as entering the stream and so forth exist, then the persons who abide in those fruits are also suitable. When the persons who abide in those fruits exist, then those approachers who are approaching for the sake of attaining those fruits also are suitable.

Fourth, the suitability of the Three Jewels

When abiders in and approachers to the fruits exist, then the spiritual community of Superiors is suitable. When the four noble truths exist, then the excellent doctrine of the methods for turning away from cyclic existence and entering into nirvāṇa is also suitable. When the excellent doctrine and spiritual community exist, then Buddhas who have brought such to completion are also suitable. Therefore – because such spiritual community, doctrine, and Buddhas are suitable – the Three Jewels are also suitable.

Fifth, within this [emptiness of inherent existence] everything, the proper and the improper is suitable

In brief, because dependent-arising is suitable, through training in all the categories of the thoroughly afflicted and the very pure that are the topics of mundane common beings and supramundane Superiors, these are specially realized, or understood, better and better. [224] [Hence] all the presentations of increase [of the very pure] and decrease [of the thoroughly afflicted] are also positable. Not only that, but also all, such as the proper, i.e., virtues, the improper, i.e., non-virtues, the effects of virtues and non-virtues, as well as all worldly conventions, that is, the happiness, unhappiness, and so forth that are renowned to conventional consciousnesses, are also suitable.

Because dependent-arising is suitable within an emptiness of inherent existence, for that system in which emptiness, that is to say, the emptiness of inherent existence, is positable, all the presentations of conventionalities are suitable. For a system in which the emptiness of inherent existence is not positable, the presentation of dependent-arising does not exist, whereby all the presentations of conventionalities are not suitable to be posited.

Sixth, the meaning of suitable and unsuitable on this occasion

Here "suitable" and "unsuitable" are to be understood as referring to those presentations' existing or not existing.

SECOND, THE DAWNING OF DEPENDENT-ARISING AS THE ABSENCE OF INHERENT EXISTENCE

This has eight parts.

First, the mode of objection by the Proponents of True Existence for whom the meaning of dependent-arising does not dawn as emptiness

As cited earlier, an objection [by Proponents of True Existence to the Mādhyamika position] was set forth in Nāgārjuna's *Refutation of Objections*:

> If an inherent existence of all things
> [Does not exist in anything,
> Then your words also are without inherent existence
> And cannot refute inherent existence. (stanza 1)]

Nāgārjuna's answer is clearly given by way of the reason that activities are feasible within an absence of inherent existence. The *Refutation of Objections* (stanza 22) says that:[524]

> We Mādhyamikas propound that that which is things' arising in dependence on causes and conditions is called the emptiness of inherent existence, or [own] entityness, due to their not being established under their own power. [225] And, those things that arise in dependence on causes and conditions are just without inherent establishment.

To clarify the meaning, his [Nāgārjuna's] own commentary on this [the *Commentary on the "Refutation of Objections"* (*rtsod pa bzlog pa'i 'grel pa, vigrahavyāvartanīvṛtti*)] says that:[525]

> You Proponents of True Existence, not understanding and not knowing the meaning of the mode of emptiness, which is the emptiness, the reality, the so-called "absence of inherent existence" of things – subjects – say the following to us: "If there is no inherent establishment, then the words of you Mādhyamikas also do not inherently exist; hence the refutation of the inherent existence of things – their establishment by way of their own entities – is not feasible since words that do not inherently exist cannot refute anything." You propound such, seeking a point of censure, to argue.

Second, how, due to being dependent-arisings, [phenomena] are empty of being able to set themselves up, or of substantial existence

> Here, within Mādhyamika, the meaning of the arising of things in dependence on causes and conditions is the meaning of the emptiness of inherent existence. For what reason is this said? Because things are just without inherent existence. Let me explain this clearly. Those things that arise in dependence on causes and conditions do not have inherent establishment. This is because of [their] being established as without inherent existence due to only arising from causes and conditions. Why is such propounded? [226] Because these things that are without inherent existence rely on causes and conditions and are not under their own power.

Third, proving the concomitance and non-concomitance of the incorrectness of substantial existence in that which arises dependently

> If, in accordance with the assertions of you Proponents of True Existence, things did inherently exist, then you would have to assert the existence of things established even without causes and conditions. However, such is not asserted, since the establishment of things needs causes and conditions, and therefore things are established as without inherent existence. Thus, we speak of them as "empty" – empty of inherent existence. In accordance with the above explanation of how things are empty of inherent existence, my words also, [that is, the words of] the master Nāgārjuna, are dependent-arisings that rely on causes and conditions, whereby, because of being such dependently established dependent-arisings, my words do not inherently exist. Because my words are just without such inherent existence, that they are said to be "empty" – empty of inherent existence – is very reasonable and correct.
>
> What is an example of this? Because pots, woolen

cloth, houses, and so forth are just dependent-arisings that rely on causes and conditions, those pots and so forth are just empty of inherent existence. However, pots can perform the function of holding honey, water, and milk soup that have been poured inside them and can perform the function of receiving those from something else. Also, by wearing woolen cloth, it can perform the function of thoroughly protecting the wearer from cold, wind, and sun.

Just so, my words, [that is, the words of] the master Nāgārjuna, also are without inherent existence because of being dependent-arisings that depend on causes and conditions. However the functioning of those words can thoroughly establish that things are without inherent existence. Therefore, the proposition by you Proponents of True Existence, "Because the words of you Mādhyamikas are just without inherent existence, it is not feasible that those non-inherently existent words are able to refute the inherent existence, that is to say, establishment by way of their own entities, of all things," does not accord with the fact. Hence it is not suitable to propound such.

Thus, [Nāgārjuna] speaks very clearly about the counter-pervasion that if [things] are inherently established, then they must not rely on causes and conditions and the pervasion that if [things] rely on causes and conditions, they are necessarily without inherent existence and says very clearly that non-inherently existent words can perform the activities of refutation and proof.

The following paragraph is a summary of the above points by Nga-wang-rap-den.[526]

Therefore, here in our system, [227] dependent-arising and emptiness are of the same meaning. For, if things inherently existed, they would have to exist without relying on causes, conditions, and so forth; however, since they do not exist without relying on causes, conditions, and so forth, therefore, by reason of their being dependent-arisings that rely on causes and conditions, they do not exist under their own power or able to set themselves up. Hence, they do not inherently exist, or exist from their own sides. Therefore, although my words also do not inherently exist, they can perform the activities of refutation and proof. For instance, although pots and woolen cloth are imputedly existent and not substantially established, they can hold water and protect from the sun, the wind, and so forth.

Fourth, therefore, holding that dependent-arising and emptiness are contradictory is like a god who has fallen to being a demon

> Ge-shay Palden Drakpa explained this as meaning that the supreme reasoning has become an obstacle. According to Ge-shay Wangdrak, the suggestion is that if a god who is supposed to help you harms you, then what recourse is left?

Therefore, [228] the meaning established by the above explanation is as follows: What need is there to speak of the definite need for the coming together in a common locus – a correctness within one base – of the two, that posited as dependent-arising, the production and cessation of thoroughly afflicted and very pure phenomena in dependence on causes and conditions, and an absence of inherent existence. This system in which just such dependent establishment serves as the unsurpassed and indispensible reason, or means, for realizing the absence of inherent existence should be known as the distinguishing feature of only the wise Mādhyamikas, those whose discrimination is excellent and broad.

But, you Tibetans who claim to propound the meaning of the middle way understand the opposite of this. If, holding that dependent production and dependent cessation are necessarily established by way of their own entities, you assert that the reasoning refuting inherent establishment refutes the dependent-arising of production and cessation, then, like the example of a god who has turned into a demon, although you are relying on a good system, it has turned into a great error that causes ruin in this and future [lives]. Hence, it has become a great obstacle to finding, as it actually is, the meaning of the middle way.

This is similar to the statement in Dzong-ka-ba's *Answers to the Questions of Jang-chup-la-ma* (*byang chub bla ma'i dris lan*):

> Many of this snowy land [i.e., Tibetans], without having come to decisions about the modes of refutation and proof with the subtle reasonings of the Mādhyamikas and Prāmāṇakas, make bold proclamations with respect to these subtle points: They agree that whatever is without inherent existence, that is, establishment by way of its own character, does not exist, and for that reason, whatever exists must truly exist.... They are outside of the system of Nāgārjuna in which emptiness dawns as dependent-arising. [229]

Fifth, as long as dependent-arising and emptiness appear to be separate [that is, contradictory], one has not realized the profound meaning

According to your assertions, when one induces the ascertainment that phenomena do not have even a particle of inherent existence, that is, establishment by way of their own entities, there is no way to induce ascertainment in one's own system with respect to the dependent relation of cause and effect, and it comes to be necessary to rely on others' perspective and so forth, saying, "The conventions of cause and effect are asserted from the perspective of others."

> Ge-shay Wangdrak: "And so forth" includes the position that things exist but this does not serve as existing.

Also, when ascertainment is induced well in one's own system with respect to the dependent relation of cause and effect – that from such and such causes, such and such effects arise – there is no way to induce ascertainment in one's own system with respect to the meaning of the absence of inherent existence, and once such is the case, not being comfortable with positing the absence of inherent existence in one's own system, one claims that the thought of that teaching must be interpreted otherwise. If [this is the situation], definitely know that the need to do such is a correct sign [that is, a reason proving] that you have not yet properly gained the Mādhyamika view.

[Dzong-ka-ba] advises, "As causes, or methods, for gaining the Mādhyamika view, you should take as a very important basis the pure maintenance of the ethics that you have promised [to maintain]. Also you should strive by way of not just one, but many, approaches to accumulate the collections and purify obstructions, and, relying properly on excellent scholars, you should make effort in all ways at pure hearing and thinking – at hearing the vast quintessential instructions and thinking on the meaning of the quintessential instructions that have been heard." [230]

Sixth, when dependent-arising and emptiness dawn with the one assisting the other, that is the measure of having realized the view, and such is difficult[527]

> The following paragraph is an aside from Jam-yang-shay-ba. Its relationship to the rest of the text is not obvious.[528]

Some of our own excellent lamas say that if a chariot is established from the chariot's own side, that is the meaning of its being established from its own side; they do not take the chariot's merely being established as able to set itself up as the meaning of being established from its own side. They say that it is necessary to examine whether a chariot's being established under its own power is the measure of its being established from its own side.

Such a composite of the two modes of inducing ascertainment with respect to appearance – dependent-arising – and with respect to the emptiness of inherent existence as noncontradictory in one base almost does not occur. Hence, it is very difficult to gain such a middle way view. Thinking of this, Nāgārjuna says in the twenty-fourth chapter of the *Treatise on the Middle Way* that:[529]

> If those of little intelligence misapprehend this doctrine which is profound and difficult to realize, they are brought to great injury and harm. Therefore, knowing that it is very difficult to realize since low persons who have low and weak strength of intelligence temporarily cannot realize the depths of such a profound doctrine, the meaning of suchness, the mind of the Subduer, Buddha, for a short period of time temporarily turned away from teaching this profound doctrine as if not enthusiastic to do so, saying, "[I have found that which is] profound, peaceful, free of the elaborations, . . ." [see below, p.351, for a full citation of this verse] and displayed a manner of not teaching the doctrine.

Nāgārjuna's *Precious Garland* (stanzas 116–18) says that:[530]

> Never mind realizing such a very subtle and profound doctrine, beings' own bodies are always with them and are filled and dripping with a collection of filth, [231] coarse in that they are physical, an object of direct perception viewable by an eye consciousness whereby it is easy to realize, and not hidden to oneself but always appearing to be filthy. When [even though the bodies of beings are like that], due to being obstructed by great obscuration, ascertainment of them as having a nature of filth does not remain in the sense that the impermanence, miserableness, and so forth [of the body] appear to the mind, and rather one conceives [the body] to be pure, blissful, and so forth, would not one find emptiness similarly difficult to understand? This is definitely a case of its being very difficult for those who are not vessels to realize it.
>
> If, for the time being, even the coarse cannot be

realized, what need is there to mention the difficulty of realizing the subtle [emptiness]. If one is unable to realize such a gross thing that is easy to realize and always accompanies oneself, how could the profound doctrine – which offers no support in the sense of not being a base that is the target of the conception of signs [inherent existence], that is, which lacks being a base for an apprehension thinking, "The mode of subsistence of dependent-arising is such and such a sign of appearance", that is subtle and profound in that it is difficult to realize, not suitable to appear directly to ordinary beings because ordinary beings must realize it in dependence on a sign, a profundity the depths of which are supremely difficult to realize – easily enter into the mind by way of ascertainment being generated easily, without difficulty? It does not. Ascertainment of the meaning of this does not easily appear to the mind. [232]

You the unequalled Subduer, having displayed the mode of becoming enlightened, by reason of seeing and realizing that, because of the profundity of this doctrine of emptiness that is free from all extremes of elaborations, it is difficult for beings who are trainees to understand since they cannot penetrate such profundity, said [in the *Extensive Sport Sūtra*, XXV.1]:[531]

> I have found a doctrine profound, peaceful, free from
> Elaborations, luminous, uncompounded, like ambrosia.
> No matter whom I taught it to, they would not understand;
> Hence I will stay without speaking in the forest.

Thus, to the sight of some trainees, for a not very long time – forty-nine days – [Buddha] was averse

> to, in the sense of not being enthusiastic for, teaching such a doctrine to trainees and displayed a manner of not teaching it.

Hence treatises, as exemplified by this [*Precious Garland*], and scriptures of the Conqueror say that [the view] is very difficult to realize.

Seventh, it is unsuitable to hold that things utterly do not exist due to not finding them upon analyzing with a facsimile of [the reasoning of] the lack of being one or many

Unlike the mode of inducing ascertainment explained above, in which there is a composite [of the ascertainments] of appearance and emptiness, some see the statements in certain valid texts such as Nāgārjuna's *Treatise on the Middle Way* that it is necessary to settle the meaning of the absence of inherent existence through the reasoning, or reason, analyzing whether phenomena such as pots and so forth are one with or different from their own branches, or parts; and, although thinking they have settled this in accordance with its meaning, they are obscured, or mistaken, with respect to that mode. They see that when one analyzes initially what those phenomena such as pots, woolen cloth, and so forth are from among their branches, or parts – the lip or the neck [with respect to a pot], the thread [with respect to woolen cloth] – [233] pots and so forth cannot be found as any of those branches. Not finding [what they seek] in this way, they think the following: "If pots and so forth did exist, they would definitely have to be findable through such searching. However, there is not at all anything to be found; therefore, they do not exist." Thus, they induce an ascertainment that pots and so forth do not exist. Then they analyze in that same way the analyzer him/herself, thinking, "What is [the analyzer] amongst its own parts, head, and so forth?" whereupon they induce ascertainment thinking that they themselves – the analyzer – also do not exist.

When such ascertainment of non-existence has been induced with respect to the analyzer as the object, then the person thinks, "If the analyzer is not to be found and does not exist, then what knower could know and think, 'Pots and so forth do not exist?' Therefore, without an analyzer, from whose point of view are pots and so forth posited as existing or not existing? Thus, pots and so forth cannot be posited as anything – existent or non-existent." Hence, these persons' mode of assertion is to say, "Pots and so forth are not existent and also are not non-existent."

If such an erroneous mode of inducing ascertainment by way of certain counterfeit reasonings in which the mode of analysis is not proper were to be posited as gaining the [Mādhyamika] view, then since this [erroneous] mode of gaining ascertainment is not difficult, [gaining the Mādhyamika view] would appear to be the very easiest thing.

Eighth, advice to value greatly the dawning of dependent-arising as the meaning of emptiness, the meaning established by those [former points]

Because through such one is not even in the direction of gaining the Mādhyamika view, those intelligent ones seeking the view who are capable of analyzing the meaning should abandon afar such counterfeit [reasonings]; they should strive at techniques for inducing firm ascertainment that cannot be diverted – that is to say, led somewhere else and changed – through some other means by another person with respect to the essential meaning. What is the essential meaning that is [a common locus of being] (1) the union of appearance and emptiness, which is that the meaning of the emptiness of inherent existence dwells as the meaning of dependent-arising, this being stated in the scriptures of definitive meaning spoken by the Conqueror and in the pure, that is, unpolluted, Mādhyamika texts, [234] such as the *Treatise on the Middle Way*, valid treatises commenting on the thought of those scriptures, (2) the final essential that is the uncommon distinguishing feature of the system of the wise Mādhyamikas, and (3) in particular, the final subtle topic that is the thought of the two, the Superior father, Nāgārjuna, and his [spiritual] son, the Superior Āryadeva, commented on in complete form in particular just as it is by the master Buddhapālita and the glorious Chandrakīrti, the marvelous commentators on the Superior Nāgārjuna? It is just this mode of bestowing ascertainment of the absence of inherent existence in dependence on dependent-arising and the way in which things empty of inherent existence dawn as cause and effect.[532]

SECOND, HOW THOSE SYSTEMS OF EARLIER TIBETANS [EXPLAINED] ABOVE REFUTE THIS DISTINGUISHING FEATURE OF MĀDHYAMIKA

This has seven parts.

HOW THEY REFUTE [THE MĀDHYAMIKAS'] EXPLANATION THAT BONDAGE AND RELEASE ARE FEASIBLE WITHIN AN ABSENCE OF INHERENT EXISTENCE

As explained above, it is the system of the protector Nāgārjuna that phenomena do not have even a particle of inherent existence, that is, establishment by way of their own entities; that if [phenomena] were established inherently, one could not make all the presentations of cyclic existence and nirvāṇa; and that it is unsuitable not to make the presentations of cyclic existence and nirvāṇa. Hence, since they should be made, [235] one must posit all the presentations of bondage, release, and so forth, in which case one must definitely assert that all things are only without inherent existence.

However, you Tibetans, understanding the opposite of this, say, "If things do not inherently exist, that is, are not established by way of their own entities, then what else is left – that is, as a remainder of this, there are no things left. Due to things not existing, no matter what is refuted – bondage, release, production, cessation, and so forth – in that refutation there is no need to affix a qualification such as 'ultimately'; that very reasoning refuting inherent establishment refutes everything."

When such is propounded, how could it be that you have not refuted this good system in which it is possible to posit with respect to non-inherently existent things all activities – bondage, release, arising, disintegration, and so forth. Having put the textual system of the Superior Nāgārjuna and his followers as the judge, think on this in detail!

> Ge-shay Wangdrak took "textual system" as meaning the great books of Nāgārjuna and his followers.

SECOND, THUS [IN THIS WRONG SYSTEM] BONDAGE, RELEASE, AND SO FORTH ARE REFUTED EVEN CONVENTIONALLY

You might think, "The master Chandrakīrti's assertion is that the presentations of cyclic existence and nirvāṇa – bondage, release, and so forth – are made conventionally, and we also assert the making of those presentations conventionally. Therefore, we do not have that previously adduced fault of refuting [Nāgārjuna's system]."

If you think this, the meaning of what you are thinking is not reasonable. In what way? As follows: The assertion of the master Chandrakīrti is that phenomena do not have inherent existence, that is, establishment by way of their own entities, even conventionally. [236] You yourself assert that this is so. Thus – since the master's assertion is thus and you also assert it – it is very clear, without needing to investigate with other reasons, that you have refuted all the presentations of bondage, release, and so forth even conventionally because (1) that very reasoning that refutes inherent existence, that is to say, establishment from [the object's] own side, must definitely refute such inherent existence, that is to say, establishment from [the object's] own side, even conventionally and (2) because you assert that due to the refutation of inherent existence by means of the reasoning refuting such, there is no way to posit anything, whereby that very reasoning refutes bondage, release, and so forth.[533]

THIRD, ONE WHO ASSERTS BONDAGE AND RELEASE TO BE CONTRADICTORY WITH AN ABSENCE OF INHERENT EXISTENCE HAS REFUTED THE UNIQUE DISTINGUISHING FEATURE OF MĀDHYAMIKA

To abbreviate the above modes of refutation, if you assert that the two presentations – (1) of the absence of inherent existence, that is, existence from [the object's] own side, and (2) of bondage, release, production, cessation, and so forth – are contradictory in that they cannot be posited with respect to one basis, then the feasibility of all the presentations of cyclic existence and nirvāṇa within the fact that all the phenomena that are being presented are entities empty of inherent existence is not positable within either of the two truths, conventional or ultimate. Hence you have only definitely refuted the unique marvellous distinguishing feature of Mādhyamika, praised in the scriptures and in the commentaries on [Buddha's] thought – the non-contradictory union of dependent-arising and emptiness.

FOURTH, IF ONE DOES NOT ASSERT SUCH, THERE IS NO REASON NOT TO AFFIX A QUALIFICATION TO THE OBJECT OF NEGATION

Should you say, [237] "I do not assert the emptiness of inherent existence and the presentations of bondage, release, and so forth to be contradictory," then you cannot demonstrate any correct reason that fits together with what you yourself propound for asserting that, without needing to affix any qualification such as "ultimately" to the object of negation – production, cessation, bondage, release, and so forth – the reasoning refuting inherent establishment refutes production, cessation, bondage, release, and so forth themselves. Thus you have said this without any thought.

FIFTH, YOUR MODE OF ASSERTION DOES NOT DIFFER FROM THE MODE OF OBJECTION BY THE PROPONENTS OF TRUE EXISTENCE

Therefore – because you do not have reasons for such an assertion – your assertion is only an assertion that the reasoning refuting inherent establishment refutes all phenomena, cause, effect, and so forth, and that when those are refuted,[534] arising, disintegration, and so forth are not positable within an absence of inherent existence. The twenty-fourth chapter of Nāgārjuna's *Treatise on the Middle Way* (XXIV.1), when setting forth an objection by Proponents of True Existence, says that:

> Proponents of True Existence say: If you Mādhyamikas assert that all these phenomena are empty of inherent existence, there is great fault: there would not be any arising – production – or disintegration – cessation – positable of any things. Without arising or disintegration, it would follow that in your Mādhyamika system, the presentations of the four noble truths – the effects, true suffering; the causes, true sources; the true cessations that are the stoppage of sufferings and sources; and the true paths that are the techniques for stopping those – could not be posited.

Etc. Also, Nāgārjuna's *Refutation of Objections* (stanza 1) says that:

> Proponents of True Existence say: If [238] you Mādhyamikas propound that an inherent existence of all things – that is to say, an establishment by way of their own entities – does not exist in anything, then the words of you Mādhyamikas would also not have such inherent existence, whereby words without inherent existence could not refute inherent existence by way of overcoming it.

It is very clear from just the words of these root texts that there is no difference at all between your assertions and the assertions set forth as objections by Proponents of True Existence; hence your assertions are just those of opponents who debate against Mādhyamikas.

> The following paragraph is a summary of the preceding points by Nga-wang-rap-den.

Someone who asserts that the existence of bondage, release, and so forth conventionally does not serve as existence and that the reasoning analyzing the ultimate refutes production, cessation, and so forth says, "Since I assert those conventionally, I do not have the fault of refuting the uncommon Mādhyamika system." That is incorrect. For, you assert that the reasoning analyzing the ultimate refutes production, cessation, and so forth, and, since it is not suitable that those be refuted ultimately by that [reasoning], you must assert that they are refuted conventionally. Therefore, between your system and that of a Proponent of True Existence who is flinging the consequence, "It [absurdly] follows that arising, disintegration, and so forth do not exist because those do not inherently exist," except that the latter [the Proponent of True Existence] is taking the predicate of that consequence [i.e., that arising and disintegration do not exist] to be eliminated by valid cognition whereas you are giving the answer, "I accept that," there is no other difference.

SIXTH, THE UNREASONABLENESS OF THE ASSERTION THAT ONE HAS NO SYSTEM DUE TO THERE BEING FAULTS WITH BOTH INHERENT EXISTENCE AND AN ABSENCE OF INHERENT EXISTENCE

You might think: "Since the reasoning refuting inherent establishment refutes all phenomena, it is not suitable to posit arising, disintegration, and so forth within either an emptiness of inherent existence or a non-emptiness of inherent existence; we, in accordance with that, [239] do not assert either an emptiness or a non-emptiness of inherent existence. Therefore, we do not have faults such as those [adduced] above in the objection raised by Proponents of True Existence to Mādhyamikas."

Such propounding is utterly unsuitable to be posited as the meaning of texts such as Nāgārjuna's *Treatise on the Middle Way*. The reason for that unsuitability is established in Chandrakīrti's *Clear Words*; setting forth an answer to that objection by the Proponents of True Existence, Chandrakīrti says that:

> Not only do we Mādhyamikas not have the fault that arising, disintegration, and so forth are not feasible within a position of asserting an emptiness of inherent existence, but also, by reason of their being empty of inherent existence, the four truths and so forth are very feasible.

Also, Nāgārjuna's *Treatise on the Middle Way* speaks within differentiating well the individual modes of the suitability of those presentations in a position asserting an emptiness of inherent existence and their unsuitability in a position asserting a non-emptiness of inherent existence.

Not only that, Chandrakīrti's *Supplement to (Nāgārjuna's) "Treatise on the Middle Way"* says that:

> Empty things, that is to say, false things, such as reflections and so forth (the term "and so forth" including echoes, mirages, and so forth) arise in dependence upon a collection of causes and conditions, for, a reflection is established from the collection of three factors – a mirror, a face, and illumination – echoes in dependence on a cave and sound, and so forth. Those false things that depend on such a collection are not not renowned in the world as falsities, that is, they are renowned in the world as false objects. [240]
>
> For instance, in terms of conventions renowned in the world, from causes that are false things such as

reflections that appear to be a face and so forth but are empty of such, eye consciousnesses and so forth are produced as their fruits, having the aspects of those falsities – the reflection, and so forth. Likewise, although all things are empty of inherent existence, from those causal things empty of inherent existence acting as causes, effects that are empty of inherent existence are thoroughly produced.

SEVENTH, THERE IS NO MĀDHYAMIKA WHO REFUTES ALL OF CYCLIC EXISTENCE AND NIRVĀṆA EVEN CONVENTIONALLY THROUGH ULTIMATE ANALYSIS

Moreover – another reason – if reasoning refuted bondage, release, and so forth, since object of negation, negator, and so forth are not feasible ultimately, it is unsuitable to engage in negation ultimately. Since such is not suitable, bondage, release, and so forth must be refuted by that reasoning conventionally. When they are refuted thus, then even conventionally all presentations of cyclic existence and nirvāṇa would not be positable in one's own system and must be refuted. Therefore, Mādhyamikas who assert such a negation as their own system are new Mādhyamikas who did not occur before.

7 *Mādhyamika Response*

THIRD, HOW AN ACTUAL MĀDHYAMIKA RESPONDS TO THE REASONINGS OF THOSE TIBETAN SYSTEMS THAT REFUTE THE DISTINGUISHING FEATURE OF MĀDHYAMIKA [241][535]

This has six parts: flinging back to them [the consequence] that cyclic existence and nirvāṇa would not be suitable; how they fall to extremes in that they do not differentiate the four – inherent existence and existence, no inherent existence and non-existence; the way in which realization of the meaning of the middle way depends upon refuting the two extremes; the unsuitability of refutation and proof without explicit contradictories that are contradictories in the sense of mutual exclusion; though those who do not know how to posit cause, effect, and so forth, hold, "There is no inherent existence," they have not found emptiness; and how to differentiate the four – inherent existence, no inherent existence, [existence, and non-existence].

FIRST, FLINGING BACK TO THEM [THE CONSEQUENCE] THAT CYCLIC EXISTENCE AND NIRVĀṆA WOULD NOT BE SUITABLE

This has three parts.

FIRST, STATING BACK TO THEM [THE CONSEQUENCE] THAT CYCLIC EXISTENCE AND NIRVĀṆA WOULD NOT BE SUITABLE

To the objection raised to the Mādhyamikas, "If all things were empty of inherent existence, then the causes and effects of cyclic existence and nirvāṇa would not be positable," the protector Nāgārjuna made the answer, "That very fault that the Mādhyamikas were to fling there [to you] has been flung at us Mādhyamikas by you objectors; therefore, turning that back to you, I fling the fault spoken by you – that if there is no inherent existence, all would be unsuitable – back to you. In this manner, the twenty-fourth chapter of Nāgārjuna's *Treatise on the Middle Way* [XXIV.15–16] says that:[536]

> You objectors, Proponents of True Existence, are speaking just erroneously; not seeing yourselves as having the fallacies that apply to your own system, you have turned them to my faultless Mādhyamika system as faults, for you, having asserted dependent-arising, are stating damage to it. This is like, for example, while being manifestly mounted on a horse, [242] having forgotten that horse on which one is mounted and searching where there is no horse.
>
>> In other words, someone is mounted on a horse, but forgetting that fact, goes looking elsewhere for that very horse – which cannot be found elsewhere since it is right with the seeker. Nāgārjuna is saying to the opponent, "Just so, you have fault yourself, but unaware of this, look to impute fault elsewhere where there is none."
>
> For, if you objectors, Proponents of True Existence, are viewing and conceiving things as existing from the point of view of their own inherent establishment – and indeed you are – then if things are established inherently as you conceive them, you [should] hold and view all things as produced without causes and conditions since they would not be dependent-arisings and since it would be contradictory for whatever was not dependent to rely on causes

> and conditions. It would be reasonable for you to view such.

Also, [Nāgārjuna's *Treatise on the Middle Way*, XXIV.20] says that:[537]

> I will speak turning back to you, the objector, your own statement [set forth in XXIV.1 as an objection by Proponents of True Existence] that if all things are empty [then the four truths and so forth would not be feasible]: If one asserts in accordance with the assertions of you objectors, Proponents of True Existence, that all these things are not empty of inherent existence, then by the very reason of their being established inherently, there would be no arising or disintegration; without those, it would [absurdly] follow that the four noble truths would not be positable in the system of you objectors.

Thus [Nāgārjuna] indicates how to turn this fault back to them.

SECOND, NOT AFFIXING A QUALIFICATION TO THE OBJECT OF NEGATION IS A CASE OF NOT DIFFERENTIATING AN ABSENCE OF INHERENT EXISTENCE AND NON-EXISTENCE

Therefore, your propounding, "If there is no inherent existence, that is, establishment by way of [objects'] own entities, then what else is there," clearly and unquestionably, that is, definitely, indicates that you have not at all differentiated the two, the absence of inherent existence of a sprout and the non-existence of a sprout. [243] Because of not making that differentiation, you have also utterly not differentiated the two, the mere existence of a sprout and the establishment by way of its own entity of a sprout, whereby it is clear that you must assert that whatever phenomenon exists, necessarily exists by way of its own entity, and if something is not established by way of its own entity, then it does not exist at all.

If you do not assert the above, then think on why you propound that the reasoning refuting establishment by way of [objects'] own entities refutes all presentations of mere existence, mere production, mere cessation, and so forth!

THIRD, SUCH DOES NOT PASS BEYOND PROPOUNDING THE TWO [EXTREMES]

If, in accordance with your assertions explained above, you propound that as long as it is asserted that things such as sprouts and so forth exist, then those things only exist in the sense of being established by way of their own entities and propound that if there is utterly no establishment by way of [objects'] own entities, then no things exist at all, then you unquestionably, that is, only definitely, fall to the two extremes – [falling to] the extreme of permanence through propounding existence by way of [objects'] own entities, and [falling to] the extreme of annihilation through propounding that things do not exist at all. Therefore, the mode of understanding of the Proponents of True Existence and your mode of understanding do not differ, whereby you are not suitable to be Mādhyamikas. For, Chandrakīrti's *Commentary on (Āryadeva's) "Four Hundred"* clearly says that:[538]

> According to the assertions, or the system, of Proponents of Things as inherently existent, [244] as long as there is an existence of things, establishment by way of their intrinsic entities also just exists. When [things] are devoid of establishment by way of their intrinsic entities, that is, when they are posited as not established by way of their intrinsic entities, those things that appear conventionally with respect to those bases are posited as not existing at all, as unobservable in all ways. Therefore, they would become utterly non-existent, like the horn of a donkey, and thus those who propound such do not pass beyond propounding the two extremes – permanence and annihilation. Therefore, all the manifest assertions of these Proponents of True Existence are

mutually contradictory, former and latter not according, whereby they are difficult to fit together.

The following paragraph is a summary from Nga-wang-rap-den.[539]

The meaning of Chandrakīrti's *Commentary on (Āryadeva's) "Four Hundred"* is as follows: Until a Proponent of True Existence gives up the tenets of a Proponent of True Existence, for the mind of that person, the two – the existence of a thing and its existing from its own side – are not differentiated as separate and appear as if mixed. Also, as long as that Proponent of True Existence does not give up his/her own tenets, when a thing appears in the aspect of not being established from its own side, it is as if mixed with appearance of an aspect of not existing at all. The meaning of this is similar to the thought [of the statement in Dzong-ka-ba's *Essence of the Good Explanations*], "The two Proponents of [Truly Existent External] Objects ... do not know how to posit [things] as existing if their being established by way of their own character ... is negated,"[540] in which [Dzong-ka-ba's] reference is to the two Proponents of [Truly Existent External] Objects as long as they do not give up their tenets.

SECOND, HOW YOU FALL TO EXTREMES IF YOU DO NOT DIFFERENTIATE THE FOUR – INHERENT EXISTENCE, EXISTENCE, NO INHERENT EXISTENCE, AND NON-EXISTENCE

This has three parts: an explanation by way of reasoning, an explanation by way of scripture, and the meaning established [by these explanations].[541]

FIRST, AN EXPLANATION BY WAY OF REASONING

This has two parts.

FIRST, HOW ONE FALLS TO EXTREMES

As long as you do not realize this differentiation by the glorious Chandrakīrti between the four – the two, inherent existence and existence in general, [245] and the two, no inherent existence and non-existence in general, you will unquestionably fall to the two extremes – of permanence and annihilation. Hence, through such you will never realize the meaning of the middle way free from such extremes. For, when any phenomenon comes to be [understood as] utterly without establishment by way of its own entity, then that phenomenon will [for you] come to be utterly non-existent; in that case, there is utterly no way to posit the phenomena of cause and effect within those that are posited as empty, that is, as empty of inherent existence. Hence you fall to an extreme of annihilation.

Also, once a phenomenon is asserted as existing, then you will definitely have to assert it to be established by way of its own entity; in that case, there comes to be utterly no way for cause and effect to be taken as illusion-like, a composite of the two, emptiness and appearance – that is to say, appearing to inherently exist whereas they do not. Hence, you definitely only fall to an extreme of permanence.

SECOND, HOW THE TWO EXTREMES ARE AVOIDED

Therefore, through realizing that all phenomena are from the beginning – from their very basis – without even a particle that is established by way of its own entity, one does not fall to an extreme of existence. Also, when an ascertaining consciousness is induced that is able to ascertain the great correctness that although things, such as sprouts, are from their very basis without establishment by way of their own entities, they nonetheless do not come to be non-things, nothings, empty of or lacking the capacity to perform functions such as producing effects and so forth, but have the power to perform their own functions – [246] producing effects, and so forth, one abandons and avoids falling to the extreme of non-existence.

SECOND, AN EXPLANATION BY WAY OF SCRIPTURE

This has two parts: stating a scripture and explaining its meaning.

FIRST, STATING A SCRIPTURE

This has two parts: an objection [raised] within the scripture and the answer.

First, an objection to this mode of falling to extremes

A clear statement of the difference between the absence of inherent existence and non-existence was made in Chandrakīrti's *Clear Words* which says that:[542]

> A Proponent of True Existence says, "If in that way explained earlier, you Mādhyamikas posit that things do not exist inherently, then you Mādhyamikas, through this mode of propounding that all do not inherently exist, refute and eliminate all the modes of actions and their definite effects, these being the meanings set forth by the Supramundane Victor when he said, 'The fruitions of actions done by oneself – the agent – are definitely experienced by oneself – the agent.' Through refuting that, you deprecate as just non-existent the definiteness of actions and their effects; therefore, you Mādhyamikas are the chief of Nihilists, Annihilationists."

Second, the [Mādhyamikas'] answer

This has two parts: a brief indication by way of the fact that [Mādhyamikas] avoid the two extremes and lead [trainees] to the non-abiding nirvāṇa; and an extensive explanation of how this is done.

First, a brief indication by way of the fact that [Mādhyamikas] avoid the two extremes and lead [trainees] to the non-abiding nirvāṇa

> *Answer*: We Mādhyamikas are not Nihilists, or Annihilationists. We refute the likes of you who propound the two extremes of inherent, or ultimate, existence and non-existence even conventionally

[247] and illuminate and show the path that definitely leads to the city of nirvāṇa, the supreme goodness, by going on the straight Mādhyamika path of non-dualism free from those extremes.

Second, the extensive explanation of how this is done

This has two parts.

First, although actions and so forth are not refuted, their inherent existence is.

Not only do we Mādhyamikas illuminate those [paths to nirvāṇa], we also do not at all propound the non-existence of the definiteness of actions that are causes [of effects], agents of those actions, the effects of those actions, and so forth. What do we propound? We propound and posit that these phenomena, actions and so forth, do not exist inherently.

Second, if there is inherent existence, activities are not suitable; without such, they are suitable.

You Proponents of True Existence think that because performance of activity, such as a cause's producing an effect, production, cessation, and so forth, are not feasible among phenomena that do not inherently exist, we cannot avoid that fault expressed earlier and thus it remains without any degeneration. However, there is no such fault that cannot be avoided, for activities such as cause and effect, production, cessation, and so forth are not feasible among things that have inherent existence, that is, things that are established by way of their own entities, and presentations of such are not seen. Activities such as cause and effect, production, cessation, and so forth are feasible only among things

> that do not exist inherently, that is, are not established by way of their own entities, [248] and such presentations are seen.

SECOND, EXPLAINING THE MEANING OF THAT [PASSAGE FROM THE "CLEAR WORDS"]

This has eight parts.

First, the thought of Proponents of True Existence

The meaning of the [above] passage is as follows: Proponents of True Existence propound: "If, as you Mādhyamikas assert, all things are without inherent existence, then the reasoning refuting inherent establishment refutes and eliminates the arising of fruitions, or effects, from actions that are causes." Such a statement by Proponents of True Existence does not differ from the mode of assertion by you Tibetans claiming to be Mādhyamikas that the reasoning refuting inherent establishment refutes all cause and effect.

Second, how [Mādhyamikas and Proponents of True Existence] agree that without cause and effect, one falls to an extreme

With respect to the statement, "If one refutes cause and effect, one becomes the chief of Annihilationists," in general both Mādhyamikas and Proponents of True Existence assert similarly that if cause and effect are refuted, one passes to a view of annihilation. However, the way they disagree in this context is as follows: Mādhyamikas do not refute cause and effect and assert them to be non-existent. Nonetheless, Proponents of True Existence say, "You Mādhyamikas refute the inherent establishment of all phenomena, in which case through just such refutation you must definitely also refute cause and effect. When they are refuted, you are asserting that cause and effect do not exist, and through deprecating them, you come to have a view of annihilation." Thinking this,

[249] they express fault, calling the Mādhyamikas "Nihilists", or "Annihilationists".

Third, although Tibetans admire Mādhyamika, their assertions are like those of Proponents of True Existence

Thus, most Tibetans who claim to be Mādhyamikas assert that when inherent establishment is refuted with reasoning, the reasoning refuting such must also utterly refute cause and effect. In asserting this, they appear to accord with the assertions of Proponents of True Existence. However, the difference between Proponents of True Existence and these Tibetans is that [the latter], having taken this reasoned refutation of cause and effect to be the actual Mādhyamika system, are seen to admire an emptiness negating cause and effect.

Fourth, Mādhyamikas answer that they avoid the two extremes and propound the middle way

The answer [Chandrakīrti] gives above to the objection raised to Mādhyamikas by Proponents of True Existence – that if inherent establishment is refuted, cause and effect are refuted whereby one becomes an Annihilationist – is: "We Mādhyamikas are not Nihilists; we refute and eliminate the propounding of the two extremes of existence and non-existence and illuminate the mode of progress on the straight path to liberation." Having said that, the remaining words [of the passage cited] indicate how [Mādhyamikas] avoid being a system propounding the extremes of existence and non-existence.

Fifth, if actions and so forth did not exist, there would be that fault, but we assert actions and effects

With respect to the indication, by the remaining words, of how [the extremes] are avoided, through [Chandrakīrti's] saying, "We Mādhyamikas do not propound that actions, their effects, and so forth do not exist," he indicates how propounding the extreme of non-existence is avoided:

Whereas we would, as you Proponents of True Existence say, become Nihilists having a view of an extreme of annihilation if we did assert actions, effects, and so forth as non-existent, [250] we Mādhyamikas do not assert that actions and so forth do not exist. That is his answer.

Sixth, how the extreme of permanence is avoided

This answer having been given, Proponents of True Existence then ask, "What do you propound?" A Mādhyamika responds, "We posit, or assert, that these things, actions, effects, and so forth, are not utterly non-existent but are without inherent existence." Through propounding such, [Mādhyamikas] avoid propounding an extreme of existence.

Seventh, the objection [by Proponents of True Existence] that cause and effect are not suitable within an absence of inherent existence

Proponents of True Existence answer back that since the performance of activities of production, cessation, and so forth are not feasible within an absence of inherent existence, the fault of refuting cause and effect has not deteriorated and remains as it was. They say: "Although you Mādhyamikas give the answer, 'We do not propound that those do not exist; we propound that they do not inherently exist,' you still cannot abandon the fault that we stated earlier – that if there is no inherent existence, cause and effect are not feasible. Hence the fault remains." Proponents of True Existence raise this objection to Mādhyamikas because in the systems of Proponents of True Existence there is no difference between the two – an absence of inherent existence and utter non-existence.

Eighth, the answer that if there is no inherent existence, then cause and effect are feasible, and if there is inherent existence, then they are not, as well as the meaning established [by all this] [543]

As an answer to [Proponents of True Existence's] saying that the fault remains as before, Mādhyamikas say that activities such as causes' producing effects are not at all positable within inherent existence whereas those activities are positable within only an absence of inherent existence. [251]

THIRD, THE WAY IN WHICH REALIZATION OF THE MEANING OF THE MIDDLE WAY DEPENDS UPON REFUTING THE TWO EXTREMES

This has two parts: realizing dependent-arising and how one comes to realize falsity.

FIRST, REALIZING DEPENDENT-ARISING

This has three parts.

FIRST, HOW THE TWO EXTREMES ARE AVOIDED BY WAY OF DEPENDENT-ARISING

In accord with this, Chandrakīrti's *Commentary on (Āryadeva's) "Four Hundred"* says that:[544]

> To Proponents of True Existence saying to Mādhyamikas, "Since you propound that things do not inherently exist, you propound that things do not exist at all," the Mādhyamikas answer as follows: "We Mādhyamikas do not propound that things utterly do not exist in the sense of an annihilatory view of an emptiness of capacity to perform functions. For, we propound – just as it is – the way in which things are dependent-arisings that depend and rely on causes and conditions."
>
> Proponents of True Existence then ask, "Are you Mādhyamikas proponents of the extreme of things, that is, true establishment?" Mādhyamikas answer, "We are not proponents of existence in the sense of true establishment; we do not propound the extreme of things [i.e., inherent existence]. Why? Because

we propound – just as it is – the way in which things are dependent-arisings that depend and rely on causes and conditions."

SECOND, NO INHERENT EXISTENCE, DEPENDENT-ARISING, FALSITY, AND SO FORTH HAVE THE SAME IMPORT

Proponents of True Existence ask, "If you Mādhyamikas do not propound that things do not exist and you also do not propound that things inherently exist, then what do you propound?" To that Mādhyamikas answer, "We propound – just as it is – the way in which things are dependent-arisings that depend and rely on causes and conditions."

Then Proponents of True Existence ask further, "What is the meaning of this 'dependent-arising'?" [252]

Answer: There are two meanings. With respect to avoiding the extreme of existence, "dependent-arising" has the meaning of an absence of inherent existence; it means no inherently existent production due to [things] depending and relying on causes and conditions. With regard to avoiding the extreme of annihilation, because [things] are not under their own power due to just that reason [i.e., because they are not produced inherently], it has the meaning of the arising of various false effects that appear, through the force of causes and conditions, to exist by way of their own entities although they do not, having natures similar to falsities that appear to be something whereas they are not such, examples being such things as illusory horses, elephants, and so forth, the water of a mirage, a reflected face, a city of scent-eaters, an emanated human, the elephants of dreams, and so forth; it has the meaning of an emptiness of inherent existence even though [things]

> produce such effects and the meaning of the non-existence of a self that is an independent agent.

Thus [Chandrakīrti] indicates how, through asserting dependent-arising, the propounding of the two extremes of the existence and the non-existence of things is avoided.

With respect to the meaning indicated thus, through explaining that the meaning of dependent-arising is no inherently existent production, [Chandrakīrti] avoids propounding the extreme of the existence of things. Through indicating the way in which the arising of effects that are not inherently produced but are like a magician's illusions and so forth is the meaning of dependent-arising, he avoids propounding the extreme of the non-existence of things [i.e., the non-existence of a capacity to perform functions].

THIRD, HAVING AVOIDED THE TWO EXTREMES, INDICATING THAT ILLUSORY-LIKE CAUSE AND EFFECT EXIST

Therefore, the Sanskrit for "thing" (*dngos po*) – *bhāva* – is used for many meanings. Hence, with respect to "thing" here in the context of the existence of things and the non-existence of things, [253] between taking it as inherent existence (*rang bzhin*) – *svabhāva* – and the capacity to perform functions (*don byed nus pa, arthakriyāśakti*), "thing" in the statement "propound things as existing" must be taken as only inherent establishment, and "thing" in the statement "propound things as non-existent" must be taken as the thing that means capacity to perform functions. For, when those two extremes of the existence of things [inherent establishment] and the non-existence of things [the capacity to perform a function] are avoided, at the point of avoiding the extreme of the existence of things, [Chandrakīrti] refutes inherent establishment and at the point of avoiding the extreme of the non-existence of things, he indicates the existence of illusion-like cause and effect.

SECOND, HOW ONE COMES TO REALIZE FALSITY

This has six parts.

FIRST, CLEARING AWAY THE EXTREME OF NON-EXISTENCE, HOW DEPENDENT-ARISINGS ARE ASSERTED AS ILLUSION-LIKE

Furthermore, Chandrakīrti's *Commentary on (Āryadeva's) "Four Hundred"* says that:[545]

> To the Mādhyamikas' refutation of a consciousness that has no external object and is inherently established, a Chittamātrin might say the following: "Even if it were the case that for a subject to exist an object must exist, do you Mādhyamikas assert that a remembering consciousness, a subject that takes as its object a past thing, does not exist?" In answer to that, [the Mādhyamika] says: "Who would propound that such a memory consciousness does not exist? Because we Mādhyamikas do not refute and eliminate dependent-arising, we do not propound such. If the entity of that remembering consciousness is definite as abiding in accordance with how it exists,[546] then this "memory" which is a subject possessing as its object a past thing is an unreal subject, that is to say, it is only without inherent existence. [254] This is because its object or meaning, a past thing, is unreal, that is to say, without inherent existence; and there arises only a subject that is unreal, that is, without inherent existence, and having a nature of falsity, in that it observes that unreal, that is to say, falsely established or non-inherently existent, object. The master [Āryadeva] himself posits it this way. Therefore, the object of observation of a remembering consciousness is a past thing with which one became familiar earlier.

SECOND, SINCE THE OBJECT IS NOT ESTABLISHED FROM ITS OWN SIDE, THE SUBJECT IS ESTABLISHED AS AN UNREALITY, OR FALSITY, THAT IS NOT ESTABLISHED FROM ITS OWN SIDE

> If the object, the past thing, did exist by way of its own entity, then because the remembering consciousness which remembers that thing would be

observing an object that inherently existed, the remembering consciousness observing such would have to be established by way of its own entity. However, when through reasoning that past thing is shown to be without inherent existence, then also the remembering consciousness observing that past thing is established as just not inherently existent. Therefore – because the two, the remembering consciousness and the object of observation are established as without inherent existence – [Āryadeva] has established that those two are unreal, that is, just have a nature of falsity.

THIRD, FALSE ESTABLISHMENT, NO INHERENT EXISTENCE, AND DEPENDENT-ARISING HAVE SIMILAR IMPORT AND DO NOT MEAN UTTER NON-EXISTENCE

The meaning of "unreal" is not some meaning other than the two – an absence of inherent existence and dependent-arising – that is, it is established as just meaning an absence of inherent existence and dependent-arising. [255] Moreover, that things which perform functions do not at all exist is not the meaning of "unreal" or "false".

FOURTH, HOW THE TWO EXTREMES ARE AVOIDED

Thus, a past thing is not utterly, in all ways, non-existent, this being an extreme of annihilation. Why? Because of being an object remembered by a present remembering consciousness and because effects of those [past] things such as the generation of a remembering consciousness, fall harvests, and so forth are seen. That past thing also does not exist by way of its own entity, this being an extreme of permanence. This is because if it did exist thus, then since it would have to exist at this time of a present memory [of it], it would [absurdly] follow that it

> would be permanent in the sense that it would not be affected by anything; also it would exist even in the present; and since it would not be feasible for an object that exists by way of its own entity not to exist at the time of a subject's remembering [it], it would [absurdly] follow that the remembering consciousness would be a consciousness able to apprehend that thing upon actually contacting it. Therefore, "unreal" in this context is to be taken as without inherent existence and not as the mere non-existence of a thing.

FIFTH, THEREFORE, THE ASSERTION OF FALSITY AVOIDS THE TWO EXTREMES

Hence [Chandrakīrti] says that these things, past objects and so forth, are not utterly non-existent and also are not established by way of their own entities, and that the meaning of unreal or false is the meaning of dependent-arising and does not mean that things are utterly non-existent.

SIXTH, THE PROPOUNDING OF THE TWO EXTREMES IS NOT THE SAME AS PROPOUNDING AN ABSENCE OF INHERENT EXISTENCE AND SO FORTH

Therefore, if you assert these phenomena to be established by way of their own entities, you are propounding an extreme of things, or have fallen to an extreme of existence; propounding these phenomena as merely existent is not a propounding of an extreme of things, or an extreme of existence [i.e., true establishment]. [256] Similarly, if you assert external and internal things to be non-things empty of all capacity to perform functions, you are propounding an extreme of the non-existence of things, or have fallen to an extreme of [utter] non-existence; however, through propounding that these things are not inherently existent, that is, are not established by way of their own entities, you do not fall to an extreme of non-existence.

FOURTH, THE UNSUITABILITY OF REFUTATION AND PROOF WITHOUT EXPLICIT CONTRADICTORIES THAT ARE CONTRADICTORIES IN THE SENSE OF MUTUAL EXCLUSION

This has twelve parts.

FIRST, THE ASSERTION THAT [THINGS] ARE NOT EXISTENT AND NOT NON-EXISTENT IS AN EXPLICIT CONTRADICTION

You [who negate too much], not differentiating in this way the two, utter non-existence and no inherent existence, and the two, existence by way of [an object's] own entity and mere existence, [try to] avoid and stop falling to the extremes of existence and non-existence, saying the following: "We do not say [such and such] does not exist (*med pa*); we say it is not existent (*yod pa ma yin*)." Also you say, deceptively, without other proof, "We do not say exists (*yod pa*); we say is not non-existent (*med pa ma yin*)." Those who take refuge in just such words and hope to overcome the words of their opponent do not know the two types of contradictories in the sense of mutual exclusion – implicit contradictories such as permanent phenomenon and [functioning] thing and explicit contradictories such as permanent phenomenon and impermanent phenomenon – and in their own former and later words are propounding only a mass of explicit contradictions. With such words one is not setting forth in the least the meaning of the middle way that is beyond the two extremes.

Furthermore, when you [who claim to be Mādhyamikas] refute other persons, you state limits such as the two, inherently existent or not inherently existent, and so forth, and analyzing those, refute other systems. Therefore, you yourself assert that the possibilities must be limited to those two, inherent existence and no inherent existence. [257] However, within asserting that, you then assert a third category, something that is neither of those two, i.e., the two to which you are limiting [your opponent].

SECOND, IF THERE ARE NO CONTRADICTORIES AND THE OPTIONS ARE NOT LIMITED, THEN REFUTATION AND PROOF ARE NOT SUITABLE

This is as follows: When analyzing any basis, since you are investigating whether it inherently exists or not, you must assert that the possibilities to be investigated are limited to those two. If there were a third possibility not included in the two to be investigated, there would be no purpose in having investigated with respect to that base, "Which of the two is it – inherently existent or not inherently existent?" Also, it would not be reasonable to analyze in that way. For instance, it would be like, when something is a color, asking the senseless question, "Is it blue or yellow?", senseless in that many colors other than blue and yellow are seen.

THIRD, IF IN GENERAL THE POSSIBILITIES ARE NOT LIMITED TO THE TWO, EXISTENT AND NON-EXISTENT, IT IS NOT SUITABLE [TO BE LIMITED TO] THE TWO, INHERENTLY EXISTENT AND NOT INHERENTLY EXISTENT

Therefore, as explained before, the possibilities must be limited. Being limited to the two, inherent existence and no inherent existence – particulars – depends upon in general being limited to the two, existence and non-existence, with regard to objects of knowledge. For example, it is like the way in which the limiting of the truly established to one of the two possibilities, being either a truly established one or a truly established many, definitely relies upon a limiting of the existent in general to being either one or many.

FOURTH, [THESE TIBETANS] DO NOT UNDERSTAND EVEN AN IMAGE OF THE FACT THAT SUCH LIMITING OF THE POSSIBILITIES IS CALLED EXPLICIT CONTRADICTION

When there is in this way a limiting to two of the possibilities to be investigated, [258] a third possibility that is not either of those two must definitely be eliminated – must not exist – whereby if you assert that a phenomenon that is neither of those two – inherently existent or not inherently existent – exists, you are propounding confused talk, senseless babble, with no thought at all.

The reason why it is unsuitable to propound such is stated in Nāgārjuna's *Refutation of Objections* (stanza 26cd) which says that:[547]

> If you do not stay with no inherent existence and discard it, then [the thing in question] abides as and is thoroughly established as inherently existent.

Hence, [Nāgārjuna] says that if an absence of inherent existence is refuted in terms of a specific phenomenon, then [that phenomenon] becomes inherently existent. Since it appears that there are many nowadays among our own and others' [schools] to whom an image of this does not dawn, identify this!

FIFTH, IF THERE WERE NO EXPLICIT CONTRADICTORIES [DICHOTOMIES] THAT ELIMINATE A THIRD CATEGORY, THEN DUE TO DOUBT [NOTHING] COULD BE ESTABLISHED

Moreover, those who assert phenomena that are not either of those two can only be doubtful and can only be in a situation in which ascertainment cannot be gained when they analyze anything, since they have no way of making a limited enumeration in which a third possibility with respect to a particular phenomenon such as being both or being neither is eliminated and they can say, "It does not pass beyond this enumeration." The reason for this is because when analyzing whether something is either of the two possibilities such as existing or not existing, the refutation of one possibility upon eliminating it would not positively include the other possibility by way of its being affirmed.

SIXTH, EXPLICIT CONTRADICTORIES [DICHOTOMIES] APPLY TO ALL

If you [the opponent] say, "We assert that some things such as 'is' (*yin*) and 'is not' (*min*) do not have third possibilities such as both and neither (*gnyis yin dang gnyis min*)," it is the same in all respects also for existence (*yod*) and non-existence (*med*), and hence there is no third possibility.

SEVENTH, SHOWING THAT THOSE ARE CASES OF BEING MISTAKEN WITH REGARD TO THE MERE WORDS, NOT KNOWING HOW TO DISCRIMINATE THE MEANING OF THE TEXTS WITH REASONING

Therefore, [259] it appears that such systems are propounding "is not existent, is also not non-existent" from having mistaken the mere words of Mādhyamika texts such as the *Treatise on the Middle Way* that say, "not existent and not non-existent". [However,] if such is asserted, then just as it is unsuitable to propound [that something is] existent or non-existent, so it would be unreasonable to propound [that it] "is not existent and is not non-existent" because such is said with respect to all four possibilities, that is, it is said, "is not existent, is not non-existent, is not both of those, is not not both of those."

EIGHTH, HOW OTHERS DO NOT IDENTIFY PERMANENCE AND ANNIHILATION [PROPERLY]

Therefore, Nāgārjuna's *Treatise on the Middle Way* (XV.10) says that:[548]

> If one conceives of inherent existence, then one is conceiving of permanence; if one conceives of non-existence even conventionally, one has a view of annihilation. Therefore, with respect to both extremes, of inherent existence and of utter non-existence, one should not be satisfied with just the words of the text without analyzing the meaning. Hence, the intelligent wise ones do not conceive and abide in such.

The existence and non-existence mentioned here do not refer to mere existence and non-existence in general; rather it is said clearly that those who assert that things are inherently established come to have views of permanence and annihilation. Chandrakīrti's *Clear Words* explains that the two conceptions

– of existence and non-existence – as set forth in the earlier passage [from Nāgārjuna's *Treatise on the Middle Way*] where it says "saying exists . . ." and "saying does not exist . . .", are the two views of things' inherent existence and inherent non-existence. Then, after those words [in Chandrakīrti's text] on the meaning of things' existing and not existing, [Chandrakīrti] asks:[549]

> Why does it follow that when one has a view of things as existing and of things as non-existent [that is, of inherent existence and inherent non-existence], one has [respectively] views of permanence and of annihilation?" The answer is as follows: [260] [Nāgārjuna's *Treatise on the Middle Way*, XV.11] says that:
>
> > Because a phenomenon that inherently exists does not depend on anything and is unstoppable, it does not ever become non-existent whereby there comes to be an extreme of permanence. When it is asserted that something formerly arose that was inherently existent and now having ceased is non-existent, since something that does not depend on anything has become non-existent, it follows that through this there is an extreme of annihilation.
>
> The explanation [by Chandrakīrti] of the meaning of this statement [by Nāgārjuna] is as follows: A thing that is expressed and asserted as inherently existent does not ever become non-existent since the inherently existent does not change and is not overcome. Since it is the case that it does not ever become non-existent, due to asserting it as inherently existent, that is, as established by way of its own entity, it follows that one has a view of permanence. Also, having asserted an inherent existence, that is to say, an establishment by way of its own entity, of a thing in a prior state, through asserting that now, later,

> that thing is destroyed whereby it does not exist, it follows that one has a view of annihilation.

Thus [Chandrakīrti] calls the assertion of inherent existence a view of permanence and calls the viewing and assertion of the later destruction of a thing that was formerly inherently existent, that is, established by way of its own entity, a view of nihilism. He does not call viewing mere existence and mere disintegration views of permanence and annihilation.

Through this [mode of] explanation, the thought also of Buddhapālita is explained. The *Buddhapālita Commentary on (Nāgārjuna's) "Treatise on the Middle Way"* clearly explains that the statement in Nāgārjuna's *Treatise on the Middle Way* [XV.11]:

> Whatever exists inherently [is permanent
> Since it does not become non-existent.
> If one says that what arose formerly (as inherently existent) is now non-existent,
> Through that, (an extreme of) annihilation is entailed].

indicates the way in which, as was explained in [the previous verse of] the *Treatise on the Middle Way* [XV.10], those saying "exists" and "does not exist" come to have views of permanence and annihilation.

NINTH, HOW, IF THE TWO EXTREMES ARE NOT REFUTED, ONE IS RUINED THROUGH WRONGLY VIEWING EMPTINESS [261]

In brief, if you propound that the emptiness, that is, the absence of inherent existence, spoken of in the Perfection of Wisdom Sūtras and the commentaries on their thought is not the excellent emptiness and you refute this emptiness, you will accumulate a powerful action of abandoning the doctrine, that is, of abandoning the Perfection of Wisdom. And, when that is accumulated, you will, through the force of that, go to a bad transmigration. Further, even if you have some interest in the meaning of the absence of inherent existence, if [without correctly understanding it] you understand, "If there is no inherent existence, then what else is there?", and assert that all phenomena do not exist at all, then you will still fall into the chasm of the frightful view of annihilation. In that way, Nāgārjuna's *Treatise on the Middle Way* (XXIV.11ab) also says that:[550]

> If, wrongly viewing the emptiness of inherent existence, one holds that all phenomona are empty in the sense of being utterly non-existent, persons of small intelligence who apprehend such are ruined through going to bad transmigrations and so forth.

As commentary on this Chandrakīrti's *Clear Words* says that:[551]

> On the one hand – that is, between the two extremes of ruin – first the extreme of deprecation is to be explained: When some, due to obscuration, think and hold, "All phenomena are empty, that is to say, all phenomena utterly do not exist," at the time of conceiving such, those who conceive it come to view emptiness wrongly.
>
> When emptiness is taught, some understand it as meaning that nothing exists. Nāgārjuna's *Precious Garland* (stanza 119) says that:
>
> > If they hold this doctrine of emptiness wrongly, understanding that nothing exists due to there being no inherent existence, such unskilled stupid persons are wrecked and ruined by way of falling from both high status [i.e., lives as humans and gods] and definite goodness [i.e., liberation and omniscience]. [262] The way in which they are wrecked is as follows: Through understanding such [i.e., that the meaning of emptiness is that nothing exists], they go to a bad transmigration, having entered and sunk deep into the filthy mud

> filled with various bad views that are bad and unpleasant from all points of view, through the force of this view of non-existence, or annihilation. (There is also an interpretation that one sinks into filth and bad transmigrations.)

Most of you do such deprecation.

However, on the other hand, if it is the case that you do not deprecate all [phenomena], not saying, "All phenomena do not exist," [still] at the time of asserting that you are not engaged in deprecation, you say, "How could these things, having already been observed, that is, while being observed and seen to exist, be empty of inherent existence?! Being seen, they would not be without inherent existence. Because they could not be such, the meaning of an absence of inherent existence is not the meaning of emptiness." Superimposing inherent existence on all phenomena, these proponents definitely abandon emptiness. Having abandoned emptiness in this way, they accumulate the action of being bereft of dharma, due to which they will definitely – undoubtedly – go to a bad transmigration. Nāgārjuna's *Precious Garland* (stanza 120) says that:

> Not only for the former reason, but also if one wrongly apprehends this profound doctrine, the meaning of emptiness, one who conceives such has a nature such that he/she has an intractable mind due to abandoning the profound emptiness, saying, "If there is no inherent existence, then what does exist? Therefore, the emptiness that is an emptiness of inherent existence is an extreme of annihilation." Having the pride of claiming to be wise – to know the mode of what is interpretable and definitive – although being a fool who does not know, [263] one goes headdown to the most tortuous hell.

TENTH, AN OBJECTION BY OTHERS DUE TO THEIR NOT UNDERSTANDING THE TWO EXTREMES

Someone might think the following: You say that we assert that things formerly exist and then assert that they later become non-existent; if we did view such, then we would come to have a view of non-existence. However, since we, from the very start, do not assert those things as existing, how do we come to have a view of annihilation in which anything is annihilated? The meaning of a view of annihilation is stated in Nāgārjuna's *Treatise on the Middle Way* (XV.11) which says:

> If one says that what arose formerly [as inherently existent] is now non-existent,
> Through that [an extreme of] annihilation is entailed.

Thus [Nāgārjuna] says that such an assertion – that a thing that earlier arose is now non-existent – is a view of annihilation. Also, Chandrakīrti's *Clear Words* says that:[552]

> Yogis, having realized the meaning of conventional truths, i.e., that false things that are produced into having an appearance of truth despite being untrue and that are deceptive in the sense of only existing for, or being true for, ignorance – a concealer, or non-knowledge[553] – are without inherent existence, realize that the emptiness of those conventional truths has the character of the ultimate. They do not fall to the extremes of permanence and annihilation. They think, "Some thing, having now been destroyed, has become non-existent; then at the [previous] time when it did exist, what would have existed [inherently]?" Thus, due to not observing an inherent existence of things formerly, they do not realize [i.e. view] them as later [becoming] non-existent.[554]

ELEVENTH, REFUTATION OF THAT

[*Answer*:] That [position stated above] is not reasonable, and the reason is as follows: If it were the case that, in order to posit [something] as a view of annihilation, one definitely had to assert that whatever thing was annihilated formerly existed, then even the worldly Materialists (*rgyang phan pa*, *lokāyata*), who have a view of annihilation, would have to propound former and future lives, the effects of actions, and so forth as later non-existent, having asserted them as existing formerly. Whereas they would have to do so, they do not. Rather, the Materialists, from the very beginning, do not assert former and future lives and so forth as existent, and since they do not assert such, it would absurdly follow that for you the Materialists would not have a view of annihilation.

TWELFTH, THAT [PASSAGE IN NĀGĀRJUNA'S "TREATISE ON THE MIDDLE WAY"] DOES NOT INDICATE WHAT THE VIEWS OF THE TWO EXTREMES ARE IN GENERAL, BUT HOW THEY ARE FOR PROPONENTS OF TRUE EXISTENCE

Therefore, [Nāgārjuna's] saying that due to propounding the present non-existence of some inherently existent thing that arose formerly, it follows that one has a view of annihilation means that Proponents of True Existence who assert that things are inherently existent, that is, established by way of their own entities, unquestionably come to have either a view of permanence or of annihilation. The reason for this is that if you Proponents of True Existence assert things having inherent existence, that is, establishment by way of their own entities, as not changing at any time, you come to have a view of permanence. If you assert things having such inherent existence as existing at a former time and, having been destroyed, becoming non-existent at a later time, then you come to have a view of annihilation.

Therefore, it is indicated to an opponent that Mādhyamikas themselves do not have such a view of annihilation in which inherently existent things, established by way of their own entities, that existed formerly are held to be destroyed at a later time. [265] When such is indicated, the non-assertion of even a particle of inherent existence, that is to say, establishment by way of their own entities, in things serves as the reason. However, that reason does not explicitly abandon all views of annihilation such as viewing former and future lifetimes as non-existent.[555]

> The following paragraph is a summary of the above point by Nga-wang-rap-den.[556]

The non-assertion in the least of inherent establishment is stated by these ‹[texts] as the reason [the Mādhyamikas] abandon the view of annihilation that is the destruction in the second moment of a thing that formerly was inherently existent. [264] It is not [the reason refuting] all views of annihilation.

FIFTH, THROUGH NOT KNOWING [THE EXISTENCE OF THE] CAUSE AND EFFECT [OF ACTIONS] AND SO FORTH, ONE DOES NOT REALIZE THE ABSENCE OF INHERENT EXISTENCE

This has two parts: [Nihilists'] non-realization [of the absence of inherent existence] due to the fact that the thesis and the sign differ; and, although the mere [words of the] theses are similar, they have not realized [the absence of inherent existence] and the great fault in this.

FIRST, [NIHILISTS'] NON-REALIZATION [OF THE ABSENCE OF INHERENT EXISTENCE] DUE TO THE FACT THAT THE THESIS AND THE SIGN DIFFER

This has ten parts.

FIRST, THE MEANING OF MĀDHYAMIKAS' AND MATERIALISTS' ASSERTION THAT FORMER LIVES DO NOT INHERENTLY EXIST IS NOT THE SAME [WITH RESPECT TO WHAT THEY MEAN BY] EXISTENCE AND NON-EXISTENCE

Some might propound, "We have no assertions at all," thinking, "According to you, because Materialists treat former and future lifetimes, the effects of actions, and so forth as non-existent, they come to have a view of annihilation. Also, if one takes what arose formerly as later non-existent, one similarly comes to have a view of annihilation, and one will fall to [extremes of] permanence and annihilation through merely propounding existence and nonexistence in general. Therefore, if one propounds that one has no assertions, it accords with those passages [from Nāgārjuna's and Chandrakīrti's texts]." However, this is very incorrect, and the reasons for this can be understood by the above [explanation of the need for explicit contradictories].

Furthermore, another way in which Mādhyamikas who assert that [actions and their effects] do not inherently exist differ from Annihilationists who assert that actions and their effects do not exist is set forth extensively in Chandrakīrti's *Clear Words*. The mode of statement is as follows: There is a great difference between the theses and reasons of these two, [Annihilationists and Mādhyamikas]: Annihilationists assert that actions and their effects as well as other lifetimes are utterly non-existent; Mādhyamikas assert those – actions and so forth – *not* as utterly non-existent, but as without inherent existence. Hence there is a very great difference between their theses.

SECOND, THEY DO NOT MEAN THE SAME THING SINCE THERE IS A GREAT DIFFERENCE ALSO WITH RESPECT TO THE REASON, OR SIGN, [SET FORTH] BY THOSE TWO

Also, Mādhyamikas propound that those – actions, effects, and so forth – do not inherently exist, that is, are not established by way of their own entities, by reason of being dependent-arisings. [266] However, since Nihilists, or Annihilationists, do not assert that actions and their effects and so forth are dependent-arisings; when they propound those as non-existent, they do not take their being dependent-arisings as the reason. What do they take as a reason? Since they do not assert any valid cognition other than direct perception, they propound that [actions and their effects] are non-existent through taking as a reason their not seeing that such and such a present sentient being came here to this life from a former life and goes from this life to a future life. Therefore, there is also a great difference with respect to the reasons [used by Mādhyamikas and Nihilists respectively].

THIRD, HOW PROPONENTS OF TRUE EXISTENCE OBJECT THAT [ANNIHILATIONISTS AND MĀDHYAMIKAS] ARE THE SAME

Chandrakīrti's *Clear Words* says that:[557]

> Here someone – a Proponent of True Existence – disputes and objects: "You Mādhyamikas are not different from Nihilists, those having a view of annihilation. Why? You Mādhyamikas propound everything – virtuous and non-virtuous actions, the agents of those actions, the fruitions that are the effects of those actions, former and future worlds [i.e., lives] and so forth – as just empty of inherent existence; Nihilists, those having a view of annihilation, also propound that those – virtues, non-virtues, and so forth – do not exist. Therefore, you Mādhyamikas do not differ from Nihilists, those having a view of annihilation."

FOURTH, CHANDRAKĪRTI'S EXPLANATION THAT THE TWO THESES ARE NOT THE SAME FROM THE VIEWPOINT OF THEIR REASONS

> The Mādhyamikas' answer to that – that it is not the case that they do not differ from Nihilists – is as follows: "We Mādhyamikas propound dependent-arising, and because of their being dependent-arisings, we do not propound all – this world, other worlds, and so forth – as utterly non-existent, but rather propound them as without inherent existence. Nihilists [267] do not know and realize other worlds [lifetimes] and so forth as non-things (*dngos med, abhāva*) [i.e., without inherent existence], that is, as not established by way of their own entities, due to the way in which they are established within an emptiness of inherent existence by reason of their being dependent-arisings in the way explained above.

> What do [the Nihilists] propound? Those having a view of annihilation, imagining that the aspects of things in this life that are presently being seen in direct perception are observed inherently without being caused, and not seeing that the aspect of a thing observed in that way comes here from another world [lifetime] and goes to another world [lifetime] from this one, deprecate the other things, the other worlds, which are like the things observed now in this world, saying that they do not exist.

With respect to the meaning of this, [their thought is as follows]: Former lifetimes and so forth are not seen at the time of one's own former and future lifetimes as the present life is seen. Although [this lifetime] is seen at its own time, Materialists, due to their not seeing former and future lifetimes as they see this lifetime, make a deprecation saying, "These do not exist."

FIFTH, THE OBJECTION THAT ALTHOUGH THE SIGNS [REASONS] ARE NOT THE SAME, THE THESES ARE THE SAME

Someone [else] might think: Although it is the case that the reasons cited by Mādhyamikas and Annihilationists are not the same, nonetheless, the two, Nihilists and Mādhyamikas, are the same with regard to this view realizing the absence of inherent existence because both Annihilationists and Mādhyamikas realize actions and their effects and former and future worlds as without inherent existence, that is, establishment by way of their own entities, whereby their realizations are similar. [268]

SIXTH, THE ANSWER THAT ALTHOUGH THE WORDS OF THEIR THESES ARE SIMILAR, THE MEANINGS ARE NOT THE SAME

Their views realizing the absence of inherent existence are very different. Since the absence of inherent existence of the Annihilationists is asserted as utter non-existence, they do not assert [former and future lifetimes as] either of the two truths.

However, Mādhyamikas conventionally assert those – actions, effects, and so forth – as existing. Hence they differ greatly.

SEVENTH, A SOURCE FOR THE OBJECTION [BY THE OPPONENT] THAT THE THESES ARE THE SAME

Chandrakīrti's *Clear Words* says that:[558]

> Someone says, "Even though there is such a difference with respect to the reasons, because the Annihilationists realize things' non-existence by way of their own entityness as non-existence, from among these [many] features, in one way, by way of this view, the two – Annihilationists and Mādhyamikas – are similar.

EIGHTH, A SOURCE THAT THE THESES ALSO ARE NOT THE SAME

> They are not similar by way of this view, for Mādhyamikas assert other lifetimes and so forth as existing conventionally whereas Annihilationists do not assert those at all. Hence they are not similar.

Following is Nga-wang-rap-den's summary of the above point.

If one says that the two, Mādhyamikas and Annihilationists, are similar because they are the same in asserting cause and effect as without inherent existence, there is no such fault. For, the former [Mādhyamikas] assert cause, effect, and so forth as existing conventionally due to not being inherently existent, whereas the latter [Annihilationists] assert cause, effect, and so forth as utterly non-existent.

NINTH, THEREFORE, IT IS ESTABLISHED BY THIS THAT CHANDRAKĪRTI IS INDICATING THAT IF [MĀDHYAMIKAS] DID NOT ASSERT CAUSE AND EFFECT, THEY WOULD BE SIMILAR TO MATERIALISTS

These words of [Chandrakīrti's] commentary indicate that those claiming to be Mādhyamikas who do not assert actions, their effects, and so forth, even conventionally [269] are similar in view to Worldly Materialists.

TENTH, THEREFORE, IT IS ESTABLISHED THAT CHANDRAKĪRTI ASSERTS THESE CONVENTIONALLY

Therefore, according to you, the master Chandrakīrti would have to have stated here, as a reason for Mādhyamikas being different from Annihilationists, "Because Annihilationists have assertions and we do not." However, he did not. Also, according to you, Chandrakīrti should have said, "Annihilationists assert actions, their effects, and so forth as non-existent; we do not propound them as non-existent (*med par*) but assert [them as] not existent (*yod pa ma yin par*)." However, instead of saying such, he spoke of [Mādhyamikas'] (1) propounding an absence of inherent existence as the reason for the difference between those two, (2) stating dependent-arising as the reason for non-inherent existence, and (3) conventionally asserting the presentations of actions, their effects, and so forth as existent. You should think about this in detail and analyze what is correct.

SECOND, IF ONE DOES NOT ACCEPT CAUSE, EFFECT, AND SO FORTH, ALTHOUGH THE THESIS THAT THESE DO NOT INHERENTLY EXIST WOULD BE SIMILAR [TO THE MĀDHYAMIKA'S THESIS], ONE DOES NOT REALIZE EMPTINESS AND THERE IS GREAT FAULT

This has seven parts.

FIRST, THE OBJECTION THAT THE VERBAL THESES ARE THE SAME

Someone thinks: "According to you, it is correct that actions, effects, and so forth do not have inherent existence, that is, are not established by way of their own entities, and also, when Annihilationists assert that those actions, effects, and so forth do not exist, they assert that those actions, effects, and so forth are without inherent existence, that is, are not established from their own sides. Therefore, by way of their asserting an absence of inherent existence, of establishment from their own sides, Mādhyamikas and Annihilationists are similar."

SECOND, IN ANSWER, AN EXPLANATION OF AN EXAMPLE AND THE MEANING EXEMPLIFIED, THIS BEING THE WAY IN WHICH THEY HAVE NOT REALIZED [EMPTINESS] DUE TO NOT HAVING IDENTIFIED THE OBJECT OF NEGATION

Even in terms of asserting an absence of inherent existence, they differ greatly. Should someone think that the two – Mādhyamikas and Annihilationists [270] – are similar in the mere assertion that cause and effect do not inherently exist, whereby in that respect those two are similar, it is not so. For, the former [the Mādhyamikas] propound such within understanding the meaning of an absence of inherent existence, whereas the latter [the Annihilationists] propound such within not understanding the meaning.

With respect to how they differ, for example, when it is said, "That person stole the jewels," with respect to a person who did [in fact] steal the jewels, one person, whereas he does not know himself that the thief stole the jewels, says by way of a lie, "This thief stole [the jewels]." Another person, having himself seen the thief steal the jewels says, "This thief stole [the jewels]."

Indeed, in just the way that those two said, "This person, the thief, stole the jewels," that thief did steal. However, the former person who called that one a thief, whereas he did not see it, spoke within changing his discrimination – though he did not know that the person stole it, he pretended as if he did know – and spoke a lie. The latter speaker, since he did see it, spoke truly in accordance with what he himself saw. Hence there is a great difference between those two.

THIRD, A SOURCE FOR THIS MODE OF OBJECTION [THAT THE THESES ARE THE SAME]

In this vein, Chandrakīrti's *Clear Words* says that:[559]

Someone might say that the meaning of what the two, Mādhyamikas and Annihilationists, say, this non-inherent existence, is the same in fact.

FOURTH, A SOURCE FOR THE FACT THAT ALTHOUGH WHAT WAS SAID IS THE SAME, THE REALIZERS ARE NOT AT ALL THE SAME

Unlike that former dissimilarity, even so there is a similarity – as you say – in terms of the thing being expressed – just the non-establishment [of objects] by way of their own entities. However, even if there is similarity with respect to the mere non-establishment by way of their own entities of things, due to a difference in the minds of the realizers of the meaning of "absence of inherent existence", [271] [Mādhyamikas and Nihilists] are just not the same.

FIFTH, A SOURCE FOR THE EXAMPLE

To indicate an example of this, when two people say with respect to one human who committed a robbery, "You stole the jewels," one of them, whereas he did not see and does not know correctly that that [person] committed the robbery, pretends to know and due to a mind that is not friendly with or close to that robber, he changes, or fixes up, his mind [i.e., adjusts his discrimination of the events] and speaks falsely about that robber saying, "He stole the jewels." Another person, having actually seen the theft of the jewels himself, makes the [same] accusation – that is, speaks accusing words. Even if there is no difference in the meaning spoken by those two due to the thing being expressed being the same – just the robbery – with regard to the ascertainment by the minds of the realizers, there is the difference of the one [pretending to] know without having seen the robbery himself and the other knowing it from having actually seen it himself. Thus, it is said with respect to the one speaker that he spoke falsely and with respect to the other that he spoke truly.

SIXTH, A SOURCE FOR THE EXAMPLE THAT NOT ONLY DOES THE MATERIALIST NOT REALIZE [EMPTINESS] BUT ALSO THIS IS VERY BAD

Since there is such a difference in the minds [of the two accusers], when other persons investigate properly the words of the first speaker, non-renown – ill-fame – and a sense of unseemliness, or fault, is generated. However, the other person does not have ill-fame and faultiness. Just so, here on the occasion of Nihilists' and Mādhyamikas' propounding no inherent existence, [272] although they are not different with regard to the absence of inherent existence, that is, the self-entity of things, when one puts the mode of understanding and speaking of Mādhyamikas – at a time when they, knowing just as it is the mode of the meaning of no inherent existence, the self-entity of things, propound their mode of understanding this meaning in words that accord with that understanding – together with that of the Nihilists, those having a view of annihilation, who do not know and understand as it is the meaning of no inherent existence, the self-entity of things, there is a very great difference between their modes of understanding and modes of speaking. Therefore, such modes of understanding and speaking are not the same.

SEVENTH, THEREFORE, THE ASSERTION BY SOME THAT ALTHOUGH THEY DO NOT ASSERT CAUSE AND EFFECT, THEY HAVE REALIZED EMPTINESS IS MISTAKEN

There are some people who, when they understand that things do not inherently exist, understand that actions, their effects, and so forth have been refuted by the reasoning analyzing the ultimate, whereby they assert that in their own system cause and effect are not positable. These words of [Chandrakīrti's] commentary refute well the proposition by some Tibetans that although such a system is a deprecation that is wrongly perspected with respect to the class of appearances – conventionalities – [its adherents] have gained unerringly the view of the empty class.

SIXTH, ADVICE TO VALUE DIFFERENTIATING EXISTENCE AND INHERENT EXISTENCE, NON-EXISTENCE AND NO INHERENT EXISTENCE

This has three parts: how Chandrakīrti differentiates between inherent existence and existence and between no inherent existence and non-existence; how Buddhapālita differentiates those; and advice therefore to work hard at differentiating the four – inherent existence and existence, no inherent existence and non-existence.

FIRST, HOW CHANDRAKĪRTI DIFFERENTIATES BETWEEN INHERENT EXISTENCE AND EXISTENCE AND BETWEEN NO INHERENT EXISTENCE AND NON-EXISTENCE

Therefore, not letting emptiness become an emptiness of the capacity to perform functions, in which case there would be a contradiction between appearances and emptiness, you must dependent-arising of causes and effects even though there is no inherent existence. [273] With respect to the reason for this, Chandrakīrti's *Commentary on (Āryadeva's) "Four Hundred"* says that:[560]

> Thus, regarding any object, the meaning of its [inherent] production is its coming, its transferring from another place. And likewise, the meaning of the [inherent] cessation of an object is its going, transferring to another place. [In both cases] there is no such thing. [Hence] that object definitely does not exist inherently, that is, it is not established from its own

side. That is, things do not inherently exist because if they did, when a thing was produced, it would have to be demonstrated that it came from such and such place, and similarly when it ceased one would have to demonstrate that it went to such and such place, but such is not the case.

If it is asked, "If objects do not exist inherently, that is, are not established from their own sides, then what is there?", the answer is as follows: Those objects that are dependently arisen entities, entities produced from the thoroughly afflicted and the very pure acting as causes, exist since they do not utterly not exist. (The term "entities" [in the phrase above, "entities produced from . . ."] is said to indicate the two conventional valid cognitions, [one] in the continuum of sentient beings and [the other] in the continuum of Buddha Superiors, with respect to which those two [the thoroughly afflicted and the very pure, respectively] act as causes.)

In answer to the question, "If there is no inherent existence, that is, establishment [of phenomena] from their own sides, then what is there?", these words of [Chandrakīrti's] commentary clearly speak of existent objects – "[These phenomena] exist as dependently-arisen entities."

SECOND, HOW BUDDHAPĀLITA DIFFERENTIATES BETWEEN THOSE

This has two parts: an objection and the answer.

FIRST, AN OBJECTION

Not only that, but also the master Buddhapālita gives an answer differentiating clearly between mere existence and establishment by way of [an object's] own entity. [274] The *Buddhapālita Commentary on (Nāgārjuna's) "Treatise on the Middle Way"*, commenting on the twentieth chapter says that:[561]

> Proponents of True Existence say to Mādhyamikas: According to you, time does not exist, causes, effects, the collections of causes and conditions also do not exist; if those do not exist, what other thing is there left over that does exist? Therefore, this proposition by Mādhyamikas is just a proposition of Nihilism.

SECOND, AN ANSWER DIFFERENTIATING THOSE TWO

> The Mādhyamika answers: It is not as you say. Those things – time and so forth – are not feasible to be established in the way in which you Proponents of True Existence mentally imagine and propound that those things, time and so forth, are established and exist from their own entityness. Rather, time and so forth are established as mere entities that are mutually dependent designations, conventions of this and that with respect to individual appearances of things.

Thus [Buddhapālita] says that Mādhyamikas engage in refutation saying, "Establishment by way of [an object's] own entity as Proponents of True Existence assert is not feasible." Also, saying, "They are established as dependent designations," [Buddhapālita] says that there exist only dependent-arisings that are dependent designations.

THIRD, ADVICE TO WORK HARD AT DIFFERENTIATING THESE FOUR

Thus, if you differentiate between these four, inherent existence and existence in general, and no inherent existence and non-existence in general, you will overcome measureless wrong ideas that are wrong perspectives on the limits of things. Also, you will not at all generate the mistake that the reasonings refuting inherent existence are reasonings refuting mere existence in general. [275] Therefore, when the unskilled

Proponents of True Existence who are mistaken with regard to these differences debate against [Mādhyamikas], the main context for Mādhyamikas giving their answer is just this individual differentiation of these four; therefore, this is very important. Hence, I have explained it here a little.

Appendices

1 *The Division of Mādhyamikas Into Reason-Established Illusionists and Proponents of Thorough Non-Abiding*

Dzong-ka-ba, in describing the development of the commentarial traditions following Nāgārjuna, identifies the subdivisions of the Mādhyamika school as those who do or do not assert external objects conventionally or, from another viewpoint, Svātantrika-Mādhyamika and Prāsaṅgika-Mādhyamika. As part of his discusssion he briefly sets forth some opinions by earlier scholars as to divisions of Mādhyamika and indicates them to be erroneous. One of those positions is that Mādhyamikas, when differentiated by way of how they assert the ultimate, are of two types: Reason-Established Illusionists (*sgyu ma rigs grub pa, māyopamādvayavādin*) and Proponents of Thorough Non-Abiding (*rab tu mi gnas par smra ba, sarvadharmāpratiṣṭhānavādin*).[562]

Dzong-ka-ba's brevity in rejecting this division leaves room for varying assessments of his meaning, and over the centuries conflicting interpretations have arisen. The basic controversy concerns whether Dzong-ka-ba is rejecting merely the misinterpretation of these two by earlier scholars and, when interpreted correctly, they are acceptable as alternate names for Svātantrika and Prāsaṅgika, or whether he is rejecting these two entirely, in both name and interpretation, saying that not only are the interpretations of earlier scholars incorrect but also the actual assertions of the Reason-Established Illusionists and the Proponents of Thorough Non-Abiding are unacceptable, so that there is no way they can be taken as synonyms for Svātantrika and Prāsaṅgika respectively. For the contemporary student, the problem is compounded by the fact that Dzong-ka-ba never identifies who held the positions he rejects, merely referring to them as "earlier ones", "earlier scholars", or "someone", and thus it is difficult to develop a context for the positions he is refuting.

Later commentators are basically divided into two camps: the first, represented by Jam-yang-shay-ba, Jang-gya, A-gya-yong-dzin, Pa-bong-ka, and Dra-di Ge-shay, holds that the problem is merely that earlier Tibetan scholars misunderstood and hence misrepresented the assertions of the Reason-Established Illusionists and Proponents of Thorough Non-Abiding; when understood correctly, the term "Reason-Established Illusionists" indicates Svātantrika and "Proponents of Thorough Non-Abiding" indicates Prāsaṅgika. The second group, represented by Nga-wang-bel-den, Sha-mar-den-dzin, and Nga-wang-rap-den, holds that Dzong-ka-ba found unacceptable not just earlier scholars' explanations of Reason-Established Illusionists and Proponents of Thorough Non-Abiding, but those very assertions themselves. Thus, the two cannot be equated with Svātantrika and Prāsaṅgika.

In the end, the answer is of little import, given that, whether accepted or not, the terms play no appreciable role in the history or philosophy of Mādhyamika. However, the issues around which the argument must be settled – what appears to an inferential consciousness realizing emptiness, what the boundaries of ultimate truths are, what certifies the illusion-like composite of appearance and emptiness that appears to someone who has realized emptiness, whether emptiness is in fact an object of the mind – are very important. Thus the controversy is of interest for what the arguments reveal about these issues, about the use of various terminology in Mādhyamika, and as a display of the penetrating analysis Dzong-ka-ba's followers brought to bear on his writings. One learns much about Mādhyamika assertions in general as the various commentators set forth their views as to whether any interpretation of the Reason-Established Illusionists and Proponents of Thorough Non-Abiding can fit within these complex assertions.[563]

STATEMENT OF SOURCES

Following is what Dzong-ka-ba says on this topic. In the *Great Exposition* he writes:[564]

> [Certain earlier spiritual guides said that Mādhyamikas] are also of two types when names are designated by way of how they assert the ultimate: (1) Reason-Established Illusionists, who assert that a composite of the two, appearance and emptiness, is an ultimate truth, and (2) Proponents of Thorough Non-Abiding, who assert that the mere elimination of elaborations with respect to appearances is an ultimate truth. They asserted that the former of these two are the masters Shāntarakṣhita, Kamalashīla, and so forth.
>
> The verbal conventions "illusion-like" and "thoroughly non-abiding" are also asserted by some Indian masters.
>
> Indeed, in general, some Indian and Tibetan masters who claimed to be Mādhyamikas did make such assertions, but what is to be settled here are just the systems of the great Mādhyamikas who are followers of the master Nāgārjuna. Who could explain [all] the subtle [distinctions]? Moreover, the statement by the great translator Lo-den-shay-rap (*blo ldan shes rab*, 1059–1109) that positing Mādhyamikas as twofold by way of their mode of asserting the ultimate is a presentation generating delight in the obscured is very good.
>
> For, their assertion appears to be an assertion that [for the Reason-Established Illusionists] the mere object that is comprehended by an inferential reasoning consciousness is an ultimate truth whereas it is said in both Shāntarakṣhita's *Ornament for the Middle Way* (*dbu ma rgyan, mādhyamakālaṃkāra*) and Kamalashīla's *Illumination of the Middle Way* (*dbu ma snang ba, madhyamakāloka*) that the object com-

> prehended by a reasoning consciousness is designated "ultimate" due to being concordant with an ultimate truth. Also, since the other great Mādhyamikas do not assert that the mere object which is an elimination through reasoning of elaborations is an ultimate truth, [these earlier scholars' explanation of Thoroughly Non-Abiding Mādhyamikas] is not good.

In his *Medium Exposition of Special Insight*, written several years after the *Great Exposition*, Dzong-ka-ba says:[565]

> [Earlier spiritual guides said that Mādhyamikas] are also of two types when names are designated by way of how they assert the ultimate: (1) Reason-Established Illusionists, who assert that a composite of the appearance of a subject, such as a sprout, and its absence of true existence is an ultimate truth, and (2) Proponents of Thorough Non-Abiding, who assert that the positive inclusion (*yongs gcod*) in terms of the elimination of elaborations with respect to appearances is an ultimate truth. They assert that the former of these two are the masters Shāntarakṣhita, Kamalashīla, and so forth.
>
> The verbal conventions "illusion-like" and "thoroughly non-abiding" are asserted also by some Indians.
>
> The great translator [Lo-den-shay-rap] said that positing [Mādhyamikas] as twofold by way of how they assert the ultimate is a presentation generating delight in the obscured.

Much later in the *Medium Exposition* Dzong-ka-ba says:[566]

> Therefore, the Reason-Established Illusionists assert that a composite of the two, the appearance of a base such as the aggregates and its emptiness of true existence – [this composite] being the mere object established by an inferential reasoning consciousness – is an ultimate truth. It is a concordant ultimate,

> not an ultimate truth.... Also there is no great Mādhyamika who asserts that the mere object comprehended by an inference – the latter from among the two, the [mere] exclusion and the positive inclusion with respect to the elimination of the elaborations of the object of negation with respect to appearances – is an ultimate truth. Through this mode you should understand in detail also my explanation of the presentation of these in the extensive *Stages of the Path*.

ONE INTERPRETATION

Most of the scholars of the Ge-luk-ba tradition who have written on this point – Jam-yang-shay-ba, Jang-gya, A-gya-yong-dzin, and Pa-bong-ka (as well as implicitly the *Annotation* author Dra-di Ge-shay since he did not disagree with Jam-yang-shay-ba's interpretation) – have come down on the side of the interpretation initially advanced by Kay-drup Nor-sang-gya-tso (*mkhas grub nor bzang rgya mtsho*): (1) that Dzong-ka-ba is refuting merely *misinterpretations* of the Reason-Established Illusionists and Proponents of Thorough Non-Abiding by earlier Tibetan scholars who posit that they represent a way of dividing Mādhyamikas into two groups differentiated by way of how they assert the ultimate; and (2) that Dzong-ka-ba is not objecting to a correct interpretation of these two in which the Reason-Established Illusionists are the Svātantrikas and the Proponents of Thorough Non-Abiding are the Prāsaṅgikas.[567] This position is summarized succinctly by A-gya-yong-dzin:[568]

> [Dzong-ka-ba's] statement that the great translator [Lo-den-shay-rap's] refutation of earlier spiritual guides' positing the designation of names to Mādhyamikas as twofold by way of their mode of positing conventionalities and twofold by way of their mode of asserting the ultimate was very good does not mean that he [Dzong-ka-ba] asserted that in general

such verbal conventions for Mādhyamikas are incorrect. For, ... with respect to the latter, the master Shūra, in his *Precious Lamp, Essay on [the Stages of] Cultivating the Ultimate Mind of Enlightenment* (*don dam pa byang chub kyi sems bsgom pa'i yi ge rin po che'i sgron ma*, *ratnapradīpa-paramārthabodhicittabhāvanā*), called the Svātantrikas "Reason-Established Illusionists" and the Prāsaṅgikas "Proponents of Thorough Non-Abiding". Hence, [Dzong-ka-ba] is not asserting that merely such verbal conventions are incorrect....

Nonetheless, the interpretation [by earlier scholars] of the mode of assertion of the Reason-Established Illusionists and the Proponents of Thorough Non-Abiding is very incorrect. For, [in fact] the Reason-Established Illusionists assert that the illusion-like object that is a composite of the two, appearance and emptiness – the appearance of the quality (*chos*), an absence of true existence, in terms of a subject (*chos can*) such as a sprout – is an object of comprehension of an inferential reasoning consciousness, whereby that composite of appearance and emptiness is asserted to be an actual conventional truth and an imputed ultimate truth. There is no Mādhyamika at all who asserts it to be an actual ultimate truth.

[Dzong-ka-ba] in his *Medium Exposition of Special Insight* speaks of the two, [mere] elimination and positive inclusion, with respect to the mere elimination of elaborations regarding appearances. Hence, since the Thoroughly Non-Abiding Mādhyamikas assert that the [mere] elimination, a non-affirming negative, is an ultimate truth but do not assert that the positive inclusion, the affirming negative which is the composite of the two, appearance and emptiness, is an ultimate truth, the [earlier scholars'] mode of positing the Proponents of Thorough Non-

Abiding is also incorrect.

> Therefore, in the system of the Svātantrikas, or Reason-Established Illusionists, since an inferential reasoning consciousness that realizes a sprout to be without true existence takes as its object (*yul*) an object (*don*) that is a composite of a sprout and non-true existence, it is asserted that the subject, the sprout, also appears [to it]. And, even though that is the case, this does not contradict that this inferential consciousness has a mode of apprehension of a non-affirming negative; for, it apprehends [its object] within the thought, "The sprout is without true existence" and the non-true existence of the sprout is a non-affirming negative.
>
> Since in the system of the Prāsaṅgikas, or Thoroughly Non-Abiding [Mādhyamikas], an inferential reasoning consciousness does not take such a composite object as its object, it has a mode of apprehension of only a non-affirming negative.
>
> The root of there arising such a difference between the two, Svātantrika and Prāsaṅgika, is said to meet back to whether they do or do not assert that phenomena are established from their own sides. Therefore, it appears to be subtle.

This presentation of the position of those who accept the terms "Reason-Established Illusionist" and "Proponent of Thorough Non-Abiding" as alternate names for Svātantrika and Prāsaṅgika can serve as a basis for analyzing the issues involved in the controversy and from which to explain the reasons advanced by other scholars for rejecting any correct usage of the terms, an interpretation favored by Jam-yang-shay-ba's annotator, Nga-wang-bel-den, and by Sha-mar-den-dzin as well as by the *Great Exposition* annotator Nga-wang-rap-den. The main advantage of the above position is that it is straightforward and relatively simple; the main disadvantage is that it does not hold up well when subjected to detailed scrutiny.

REASON-ESTABLISHED ILLUSIONISTS

Because most of the argument focuses on the Reason-Established Illusionists, we will begin there. Two main questions are involved: (1) Is this term used by any valid Mādhyamika, and, in particular, is it used as a mode of subdividing Mādhyamika followers? (2) What do the Reason-Established Illusionists assert? In seeking to answer these questions, one immediately encounters the major reason for the controversy: lack of sufficient information. A secondary reason is undoubtedly the fact that Dzong-ka-ba himself is not merely brief, he is also not particularly clear in setting forth his position, dismissing it as minor. As will be discussed below, some of his statements might even be considered misleading.

WHO USES THE TERM "REASON-ESTABLISHED ILLUSIONIST"?

References to Reason-Established Illusionists and Proponents of Thorough Non-Abiding are few in the Indian texts that were translated into Tibetan, and even where the terms are used, there is no clear explanation of their meaning. There does not seem to be an unequivocal statement by an Indian scholar that Mādhyamikas, when divided by way of their mode of asserting the ultimate, are twofold, Reason-Established Illusionists and Proponents of Thorough Non-Abiding. Dzong-ka-ba's statement in the *Great Exposition* with respect to this is:

> The verbal conventions "illusion-like" and "thoroughly non-abiding" are also asserted by some Indian masters.
>
> Indeed, in general, some Indian and Tibetan masters who asserted that they upheld the Mādhyamika system did make such assertions, but what is to be settled here are just the systems of the great Mādhyamikas who are followers of the master Nāgārjuna. Who could explain [all] the subtle [distinctions]?

The main Indian commentator known in the Tibetan tradition who makes use of these terms is the master Shūra, considered in some Tibetan traditions to be another name for Ashvaghoṣha, who was roughly contemporaneous with Nāgārjuna, his use of the terms occurring in his *Cultivation of the Ultimate Mind of Enlightenment*.[569]

This brings us to the first point of difficulty with what Dzong-ka-ba has said: No one in the Ge-luk-ba tradition questions that Shūra was a great Mādhyamika author; how is this to be be reconciled with Dzong-ka-ba's statement, "What is to be settled here are just the systems of the great Mādhyamikas who are followers of the master Nāgārjuna," which implies clearly that in his opinion those Indians who did use the terms in question were minor figures?

Nor-sang-gya-tso's answer to this is that Shūra's text, the *Cultivation of the Ultimate Mind of Enlightenment*, which he says can be found in Atisha's *Hundred Short Doctrines* (*jo bo'i chos chung brgya rtsa*)[570] was not seen by Dzong-ka-ba. The passage in question from Shūra's text reads:[571]

> Mere illusions are deceptive due to being imputations.
> The mind is an illusory aspect.
> Enlightenment also is like an illusion.
> They do not see that great gloriousness
> Free from elaborations, abandoning verbal expressions.
> Illusory [phenomena] are not mere illusions
> Because if they were, they would not be established [objectively].
> If they were established [objectively], then it would [absurdly] follow
> That even in the textual systems of others
> Illusion-like phenomena [would be taught]. . . .
> Through synonyms such as emptiness, and so forth,
> Limitless examples such as being like a magician's illusions, and so forth,

And the skillful means of a variety of vehicles,
[Buddha] made known the meaning of the middle
way not abiding [in any extremes].

Based on these passages, Nor-sang-gya-tso, Jam-yang-shay-ba, and Jang-gya all conclude that Mādhyamikas can be divided into the two, Reason-Established Illusionists and Proponents of Thorough Non-Abiding. Nor-sang-gya-tso explains that had Dzong-ka-ba seen this text, he would also have been willing to accept such a division since there is no way that he would not hold Shūra's text to be valid.[572]

Sha-mar-den-dzin attacks this position in a number of ways.[573] First he says, quite cogently, that except for mentions of "illusory" and so forth, what Shūra is setting forth is not particularly clear and that to take the passage, as do the above scholars, as (1) setting forth the Svātantrika position, (2) then refuting it through showing inner contradictions in the Svātantrika assertions, and (3) then setting forth the correct Prāsaṅgika position, requires so much interpolation that it is barely admissible as an interpretation and certainly cannot be posited as a clear statement of a twofold division of Mādhyamikas into Reason-Established Illusionists and Proponents of Thorough Non-Abiding.

Sha-mar-den-dzin also attacks the attribution of the *Cultivation of the Ultimate Mind of Enlightenment* to the great Mādhyamika Shūra who was roughly contemporaneous with Nāgārjuna and Āryadeva. For Sha-mar, it is fanciful to think that Dzong-ka-ba might not have seen Atisha's *Hundred Short Doctrines*, in which the text is found. Saying that if Shūra did compose the text and one even allowed that it uses the verbal conventions of the two Mādhyamikas, it is very difficult to explain the meaning of Dzong-ka-ba's statement, "What is to be settled here are the systems of the great Mādhyamikas," Sha-mar-den-dzin concludes that the text was composed by another Shūra who lived much later. He cites as his source the *Dak-den History of the Doctrine* (*rtag brtan chos 'byung*) which says that the author of the *Stages of Cultivating the Ultimate Mind of Enlightenment* lived at roughly the same time as the

Tibetan lord Tri-rel-wa-jen (*khri ral ba can*) and the master of yoga, Ānandagarbha – which would place him in the ninth century.[574]

Nga-wang-bel-den advances a similar view in his *Annotations* to Jam-yang-shay-ba's *Great Exposition of Tenets*, reporting that some scholars say that the author of the *Stages of Cultivating the Ultimate Mind of Enlightenment* was not the master Shūra who lived at the time of Nāgārjuna but just someone having the same name.[575]

(This is not the only context in which the *Stages of Cultivating the Ultimate Mind of Enlightenment* is problematic. In his *Essence of the Good Explanations* Dzong-ka-ba says that it does not appear that Mādhyamika treatises by the master Shūra were translated into Tibetan. In that case, what is one to do with the *Stages of Cultivating the Ultimate Mind of Enlightenment*? One solution is that suggested above – to deny that the text is by this master Shūra. Another, chosen by Jam-yang-shay-ba, is to say that even though it is a Mādhyamika treatise, from within the threefold division into view, meditation, and behavior, this is a text on meditation, not on the view, and what Dzong-ka-ba meant to say was that none of the master Shūra's treatises on the Mādhyamika *view* had been translated.)[576]

In this way, Sha-mar rejects the position that the *Stages of Cultivating the Ultimate Mind of Enlightenment* is by the great Mādhyamika Shūra and thus clears Dzong-ka-ba of any fault in his statement that what is to be settled are just the systems of the great Mādhyamikas. He then offers up other passages by figures not so well renowned that might have been Dzong-ka-ba's referent when he said that the terms were used, but not by great Mādhyamikas. Jñānavajra's *Two Staged Path* (*lam rim pa gnyis pa*) says:

> Mantra does not have a view beyond
> That of thorough non-abiding; if it did,
> The view would come to have elaborations; the master would be obscured.
> However, it is surpassing through method.

Also, the *Precious Garland* (*rin po che'i phreng ba, ratnamālā*) composed by Chandrahari says:[577]

> If illusory [phenomena] were established by reasoning,
> It would follow that they would not be illusory but would be correct,
> But they are not. If you say they are established as illusions
> The meaning of established by reasoning would not be correct.

Also:

> Entities which thoroughly do not abide
> Do not exist, do not not exist, are not both [existent and non-existent] . . .

To summarize, the main source used by those holding the position that the terms "Reason-Established Illusionist" and "Proponent of Thorough Non-Abiding" are valid when interpreted correctly and are to be taken as alternate names for Svātantrika and Prāsaṅgika is the passage from the *Stages of Cultivating the Ultimate Mind of Enlightenment* which they attribute to the great Mādhyamika master Shūra, or Ashvaghoṣha, the greatness of the author requiring that one accept his use of the terms. Sha-mar-den-dzin has rejected their position on two grounds: he denies that the great master Shūra is the author, and he says that even if he were, the terms are used only vaguely and not in the manner of a clear expression of the divisions of Mādhyamika. In fact, the term "Reason-Established Illusionist" never appears, only the words illusion (*sgyu ma*) and illusion-like (*sgyu ma lta bu*). Doing away with even the reference, Sha-mar-den-dzin does not address the major issue in the discussion of whether or not "Reason-Established Illusionist" can be interpreted in such a way that its meaning is correct.

WHAT ARE THE ASSERTIONS OF THE REASON-ESTABLISHED ILLUSIONISTS?

This brings us to the next question to be considered: Is there a meaning of the term "Reason-Established Illusionist" that would fit the Svātantrika system? Or, is it the case that any interpretation would be completely unacceptable in Dzong-ka-ba's interpretation of Svātantrika? Or, is what is unacceptable merely the misinterpretation of the Reason-Established Illusionists set forth by other earlier Tibetans?

The undisputed aspect of the question is that earlier Tibetan scholars said Reason-Established Illusionists (Svātantrikas) (1) assert that an illusion-like object that is a composite of two factors, the *appearance* of a subject, such as a sprout, and the *emptiness*, the absence of true existence, with which that sprout is qualified, appears to an inferential reasoning consciousness realizing emptiness and (2) further assert that the illusion-like object is an ultimate truth. Given as examples of those who make such assertions are Shāntarakṣhita and Kamalashīla.

The basic error of this interpretation by earlier Tibetan scholars, according to all these Ge-luk-ba scholars, is the claim that, for Svātantrika, such an illusion-like object, which is a composite of a conventional truth and an ultimate truth, is an ultimate truth. It is not. Being a mixture of a conventional phenomenon, such as a sprout, and an ultimate one, the emptiness of the sprout, it itself is a conventional truth. It is an affirming negative – a positive phenomenon qualified by an absence, or negative, of true existence – whereas in the Ge-luk-ba system an ultimate truth must be a non-affirming negative, a mere absence of true existence. Only emptiness is an ultimate truth, not the myriad phenomena qualified by emptiness. As Kay-drup and Pa-bong-ka point out,[578] whatever exists is necessarily an illusion-like composite of appearance and emptiness, and certainly Shāntarakṣhita and Kamalashīla do not assert that whatever exists is an ultimate truth.

The difficulty comes in deciding whether the above interpretation of the Reason-Established Illusionists is just a misunderstanding of earlier Tibetan scholars or is in fact the Reason-Established Illusionists' assertion. Lacking a clear statement by anyone who claims to be a Reason-Established Illusionist, the Ge-luk-bas are forced to search for the answer among Dzong-ka-ba's writings.

The majority of references are found in Dzong-ka-ba's first major work, his *Golden Rosary of Eloquence* (*legs bshad gser phreng*), which is a commentary on Maitreya's *Ornament for Clear Realization* (*mngon rtogs rgyan, abhisamayālaṃkāra*). In that text there is a discussion of whether a consciousness of meditative equipoise has appearance of an object (*snang bcas*) or does not (*snang med*), and, according to Nga-wang-bel-den, in that discussion the Reason-Established Illusionists are those propounding the former position – that an illusion-like object appears – and the Proponents of Thorough Non-Abiding the latter – that nothing at all appears. The *Golden Rosary* is not primarily concerned with Mādhyamika philosophy, and as Sha-mar-den-dzin puts it, was written "prior to [Dzong-ka-ba's] showing the mode of having completed the analysis of the view".[579] Thus, according to both Sha-mar-den-dzin and Nga-wang-bel-den, when Dzong-ka-ba wrote concerning the view in that text, he merely wrote in accordance with the system of earlier Tibetan scholars, and what he wrote there was not necessarily his own later final position.

Specifically, as Sha-mar-den-dzin explains, in the discussion of whether a consciousness of meditative equipoise has appearance or not, Dzong-ka-ba in the *Golden Rosary* presented the Svātantrika assertions in accordance with the interpretation of those who say that it does – the Reason-Established Illusionists – this being the less objectionable of the two positions, and concentrated on refuting the position that it has no appearance of anything at all. However, in later works he rejected both positions for both Svātantrika and Prāsaṅgika. This is to be understood through Gyel-tsap's *Ornament for the Essence, Explanation [of Maitreya's "Ornament for Clear Realization" and Its Commentaries]* (*rnam bshad snying po rgyan*), a commentary on the same topic as the *Golden Rosary* by one of

Dzong-ka-ba's two chief disciples; it is considered to incorporate Dzong-ka-ba's final teachings on the subject and, in points where it disagrees with the *Golden Rosary*, to supercede it.

The earlier scholars whose interpretations of the Reason-Established Illusionists and Proponents of Thorough Non-Abiding are being refuted in the *Great Exposition* said that Shāntarakṣhita and Kamalashīla are illustrations of Reason-Established Illusionists; Dzong-ka-ba himself says in the *Golden Rosary*:[580]

> Ārya Vimuktisena and the two masters [Shāntarakṣhita and Kamalashīla] . . . explain that the affirming negative, the illusion-like dependent arising that, without true existence, is the object of observation of [an exalted wisdom of] meditative equipoise. . . .

However in Gyel-tsap's *Ornament for the Essence, Explanation [of Maitreya's "Ornament for Clear Realization" and Its Commentaries]* it is explained that the above statement cannot be taken as Vimuktisena, Shāntarakṣhita, and Kamalashīla's own position, but rather should be considered as Dzong-ka-ba's reporting a misinterpretation of their position by earlier scholars. Gyel-tsap says:[581]

> Whoever asserts that it is the assertion of these masters that a Superior's meditative equipoise directly realizes an illusion-like falsity which is a dependent-arising has not trained well in the systems of either Mādhyamika – Prāsaṅgika or Svātantrika – and is describing erroneously the assertions of these masters.

Also:

> Since the assertion that an illusion-like dependent-arising appears to the appearance factor of a learner Superior's meditative equipoise directly comprehending an ultimate truth does not have even the scent of Mādhyamika, one should know that [one who

> says such] is propounding erroneously within not having realized the thought of those masters.

Thus Gyel-tsap makes it very clear that it is wrong to say that highly respected Svātantrika scholars like Vimuktisena, Shāntarakṣhita, and Kamalashīla propound that an illusion-like composite is the object of a Superior's meditative equipoise, a position unacceptable because it would entail that that illusion-like composite is an ultimate truth.

There is a further statement that provides a link for concluding that, from Gyel-tsap's viewpoint (and hence presumably also from Dzong-ka-ba's), it is in fact the position of the Reason-Established Illusionists that an illusion-like *composite* is the object of a Superior's meditative equipoise and hence these great Svātantrikas are not Reason-Established Illusionists: Gyel-tsap says, again in his *Ornament for the Essence, Explanation [of Maitreya's "Ornament for Clear Realization" and Its Commentaries]*, that it is a deprecation if one asserts that the master Haribhadra is a Reason-Established Illusionist.[582] Haribhadra, Vimuktisena, Shāntarakṣhita, and Kamalashīla are all proponents of the same basic tenets; thus if Haribhadra were a Reason-Established Illusionist, they all would be, and if it is a deprecation to call Haribhadra a Reason-Established Illusionist, then it would also be a deprecation of Shāntarakṣhita and Kamalashīla to call them such.

This final statement by Gyel-tsap is one of three reasons given by Nga-wang-bel-den for why the Svātantrikas cannot be considered Reason-Established Illusionists.[583] He gives as his second reason the fact that Dzong-ka-ba, in his *Medium Exposition of Special Insight* says that the Reason-Established Illusionists *themselves* assert that a composite of the two, appearance and emptiness, is an ultimate truth, and we know that the Svātantrikas do not assert this. The passage in the *Medium Exposition* reads:[584]

> Therefore, the Reason-Established Illusionists assert that a composite of the two, the appearance of a base such as the aggregates and its emptiness of true existence – [this composite] being the mere object

> established by an inferential reasoning consciousness – is an ultimate truth.

Nga-wang-bel-den's point is well taken in that in this context Dzong-ka-ba is clearly stating what the assertions of the Reason-Established Illusionists are and not a misinterpretation of their assertions by former Tibetans. In his earlier *Great Exposition* he had said:[585]

> [Earlier spiritual guides said that Mādhyamikas] are also of two types when names are designated by way of how they assert the ultimate: Reason-Established Illusionists, who assert that a composite of the two, appearance and emptiness, is an ultimate truth . . .

In that passage the Tibetan syntax makes it impossible to decide definitely whether the speaker saying "Reason-Established Illusionists who assert . . ." is the earlier spiritual guides who are being refuted or is Dzong-ka-ba himself, and thus one cannot be sure whether Dzong-ka-ba is setting forth their misinterpretation of the Reason-Established Illusionists or his own reporting of their assertions. However, in the passage from Dzong-ka-ba's later work, the *Medium Exposition*, cited above by Nga-wang-bel-den, it is quite clear that Dzong-ka-ba is stating his opinion as to what the Reason-Established Illusionists assert.

Nga-wang-bel-den's third reason is also cogent: the fact that in no valid Indian or Tibetan text – such as those by Nāgārjuna, Āryadeva, Dzong-ka-ba, Gyel-tsap, or Kay-drup – is it explicitly set forth that Svātantrikas are Reason-Established Illusionists.

WHAT COULD THE TERM REASON-ESTABLISHED ILLUSIONIST MEAN?

Most problematic is the term "Reason-Established Illusionist" (*sgyu ma rigs grub pa*) itself. The literal meaning of the Tibetan term is "one who propounds an establishment by reasoning of an illusion-like composite of appearance and emptiness" (*sgyu ma lta bu'i snang stong gnyis tshogs rigs pas grub par 'dod pa po*). (The Tibetan term, *sgyu ma gnyis med*, and corresponding Sanskrit term, *māyopamādvayavādin*, "proponent of illusion-like non-dualism," found in early references is a more general one and thus does not incur the same technical fault. It lends itself more readily to the loose interpretation of the term described below, see pp.422–4, whereby it might possibly be accepted as applying to Svātantrika.)

In Dzong-ka-ba's system, phenomena are established, or certified, by the consciousnesses apprehending them, that is, by the consciousnesses that realize them. Thus ultimate phenomena – emptinesses – are established by ultimate cognizers – inferential or directly perceiving "reasoning" consciousnesses of meditative equipoise, and conventional phenomena are established by conventional valid cognizers, direct or inferential. To say that an illusion-like composite of appearance and emptiness – a conventional truth – is certified by a reasoning consciousness – an ultimate cognizer – would contradict this basic system.

Further, for a consciousness to certify an object, it is not sufficient for that object merely to appear to it, but rather that object must be the object of its mode of apprehension, must be ascertained by it. Thus, were it the case that the illusion-like composite of appearance and emptiness was certified by the reasoning consciousness realizing emptiness, this would entail that the illusion-like composite was the object of the mode of apprehension of that consciousness. This, in turn, would entail that the consciousness did not have a mode of apprehension of merely a non-affirming negative, contradicting another fundamental Ge-luk-ba tenet.

Thus, from the viewpoint of Ge-luk-ba exegesis, there seems to be no way to justify the term "Reason-Established Illusionist" itself. There is a consciousness that certifies the illusion-like composite of appearance and emptiness, but it is not a reasoning consciousness but rather a conventional valid cognizer, most probably a Superior's exalted wisdom of subsequent attainment, which occurs *after* meditative equipoise on emptiness.

How could one interpret "Reason-Established Illusionist" in such a way that it might be considered a name for Svātantrika? A possible answer necessitates a brief discussion of the perceptual process involved in meditating on emptiness. The basic Ge-luk-ba position, that is, a position held not only by Dzong-ka-ba but by all the textbook authors of the major Ge-luk-ba monastic universities, is that when emptiness is realized by means of an inferential cognition generated as the result of a lengthy and very precise process of reasoning, just emptiness – a non-affirming negative that is the mere absence of true existence and is an ultimate truth – is realized. Emptiness is the object of the mode of apprehension of that consciousness, and many scholars take the position that only emptiness appears to that consciousness. Emptiness, however, is realized in relation to particular phenomena, and subsequent to that realization, phenomena are again taken to mind but now appear differently than they did prior to realization of emptiness, appearing as illusion-like in that they appear to exist truly whereas in fact they are qualified by their emptiness of true existence. Such an illusion-like appearance, a composite of an appearing subject and that subject's emptiness of true existence, is an affirming negative rather than a non-affirming negative as is emptiness alone.

According to Dzong-ka-ba's system, both Svātantrika and Prāsaṅgika accept that an inferential consciousness realizing emptiness *realizes* just emptiness and that the realization of the illusion-like subject qualified by emptiness is subsequent. The debate centers on whether or not the illusion-like composite of appearance and emptiness *appears* to the inference realizing emptiness.

Those among Dzong-ka-ba's followers who hold that the term "Reason-Established Illusionist" can be used as another name for Svātantrika make a distinction between the two systems – Svātantrika and Prāsaṅgika – on this basis. They say that for the Svātantrikas, an inferential reasoning consciousness realizing a sprout as without true existence takes as its object an illusion-like subject that is a composite of the subject and its attribute emptiness, and hence the subject, the sprout, *appears*, although that reasoning consciousness is nonetheless posited as having a mode of *apprehension* of a non-affirming negative. In contrast, they say that for the Prāsaṅgikas, such an inferential reasoning consciousness does not take as its object an object which is a composite of the subject and the emptiness that qualifies it, but rather takes as its object a mere non-affirming negative, emptiness.

There is some question whether making a distinction as to whether the subject does or does not appear to an inferential consciousness realizing emptiness on a strict Svātantrika/Prāsaṅgika basis can be supported. Again the Indian literature does not provide a definitive answer.

(In general, it is a much debated topic among Ge-luk-ba scholars as to whether in Prāsaṅgika the subject appears or not. The general sūtra system position as delineated in the major monastic colleges is to say that the subject does not appear – that only the non-affirming negative emptiness appears. However in the tantric system, it is posited that the subject – the appearance as a deity – appears to the appearance factor of the consciousness while the ascertainment factor of that same consciousness ascertains its emptiness. The consciousness is still considered to have a mode of apprehension of a non-affirming negative since it is *ascertaining* only emptiness even if a divine form, etc., is *appearing* to it. Such is said to occur in tantra due to the force of special training. However, some scholars, such as Nga-wang-bel-den,[586] have posited that even in the sūtra system the subject such as a sprout appears to an inferential consciousness realizing emptiness, even though the consciousness ascertains only emptiness. Dzong-ka-ba's position on this is not totally clear; it is generally held to be his view that the subject does not appear in the Prāsaṅgika system, but there are a few passages in his *Great Exposition* which seem to suggest that the subject does appear.)[587]

A further problem with taking the term "Reason-Established Illusionist" as a name for Svātantrika is that one has to gloss over the words of Dzong-ka-ba's statement that for the

Reason-Established Illusionists an illusion-like composite is the *object of comprehension* of an inferential reasoning consciousness. That something is the object of comprehension of a consciousness generally conveys that it is the object of the mode of apprehension of that consciousness, i.e., that it is what that consciousness *realizes*. In the case of a reasoning consciousness, this should be only emptiness. To equate Reason-Established Illusionists with Svātantrika, one weakly has to interpret the term "object of comprehension of a reasoning consciousness" vaguely, saying that it refers only to the illusion-like composite of appearance and emptiness *appearing* to the consciousness.

The contemporary scholar Ge-shay Palden Drakpa of Drebung Lo-sel-ling was willing to accept "Reason-Established Illusionists" and "Proponents of Thorough Non-Abiding" as alternate names for Svātantrika and Prāsaṅgika based, not on a strict delineation in terms of what appears to an inference realizing emptiness, but rather on just a difference of emphasis within the two systems. According to him, the technical descriptions of the perceptual processes involved in realization of emptiness are basically the same in the two systems. However, in Svātantrika, the topic of illusion is a major focus of discussion, in that in Svātantrika literature the example of a magician's illusion and how it appears differently (1) to ordinary persons, (2) to those who have realized emptiness, and (3) to Buddhas is most extensively developed; thus there is in Svātantrika literature a greater *focus* on the states subsequent to realization of emptiness when one is taking to mind the illusion-like composite of appearance and emptiness. In Prāsaṅgika, on the other hand, the emphasis tends to be upon just the emptiness that is the object ascertained in the cognition of emptiness, the non-affirming negative that thoroughly does not abide in either extreme – of permanence or annihilation.

Ge-shay Palden Drakpa's interpretation of the terms makes a somewhat defensible case for taking "Reason-Established Illusionists" as an alternate name for Svātantrika. However, such can be done only through using the term in a vague way, accepting neither its literal import as "one who propounds an establishment by reasoning of an illusion-like composite of appearance and emptiness" nor giving a technical explanation of its meaning. It has the fault of peripheral significance since none of the great formulators of the Mādhyamika systems discussed it or used it as another name for Svātantrika. His point perhaps is merely that "Reason-Established Illusionists" *can* be used as a name for Svātantrika.

PROPONENTS OF THOROUGH NON-ABIDING

The next topic to be considered is the meaning and usage of the term "Proponents of Thorough Non-Abiding". In this case the term itself is not controversial nor is it particularly evocative as a term only for Prāsaṅgika. It merely means those who propound that which thoroughly does not abide in the extremes of either permanence or annihilation. As Sha-mar-den-dzin points out, in that all Mādhyamikas (Proponents of the Middle Way) are said to abide in the middle way free from those two extremes, there is nothing in the term itself to limit it to Prāsaṅgika rather than Svātantrika. However, there is also no reason why it could not be another name for Prāsaṅgika, given that in the Ge-luk-ba interpretation, only the Prāsaṅgikas actually adhere to the middle way free from all extremes.

For the Ge-luk-ba commentarial tradition, the problem with this term comes in piecing together exactly what wrong interpretation of "Proponents of Thorough Non-Abiding" Dzong-ka-ba is refuting. In the *Great Exposition* Dzong-ka-ba says:[588]

> ... Proponents of Thorough Non-Abiding, who assert that the mere elimination of elaborations with respect to appearances is an ultimate truth.... Also, since the other great Mādhyamikas do not assert that the mere object which is an the elimination through reasoning of elaborations is an ultimate truth [these

> earlier scholars' explanation of Thoroughly Non-Abiding Mādhyamikas] is not good.

The simple statement that "the mere elimination of elaborations with respect to appearances is an ultimate truth" need not be unacceptable in the Ge-luk-ba interpretation of the Prāsaṅgika system if what one understands by it is that the non-affirming negative – emptiness – that is the mere elimination of the elaborations of inherent existence with respect to appearances is the ultimate truth.

What Sha-mar-den-dzin posits as the interpretation of earlier Tibetan scholars which Dzong-ka-ba found unacceptable is that propounded by those who from Dzong-ka-ba's viewpoint negate too much in their Mādhyamika interpretation. In such an interpretation, when phenomena are subjected to ultimate analysis, they are not found and hence do not exist. Rather than saying, as do the Ge-luk-bas, that the non-affirming negative emptiness is found, that is to say, realized, these scholars say that there is nothing established as an ultimate phenomenon nor apprehendable by the mind and that the non-finding of anything at all is merely designated for others as an ultimate truth. In their system, therefore, "elaborations", rather than referring to the object of negation, inherent existence, refers to the non-establishment of any phenomenon as any of the conceptual elaborations of things, non-things, neither, and so forth. They further say that the verbal convention of "realizing freedom from elaborations" is merely designated with respect to an awareness that is in fact not apprehending anything at all since reality is beyond being an object of an awareness, and thus they posit that even a Superior's meditative equipoise is without an object.

Nga-wang-bel-den gives a similar explanation, taking as his source Dzong-ka-ba's *Golden Rosary*. He says:[589]

> Dzong-ka-ba's statement in the *Great Exposition of the Stages of the Path*, "Since the other great Mādhyamikas do not assert that the mere object which is the elimination of elaborations through reasoning is

an ultimate truth, [those earlier scholars' explanation of the 'Proponents of Thorough Non-Abiding'] is not good," does not entail that the mere elimination of the object of negation, true existence, is not an ultimate truth. For, this [statement of disapproval] refers to "freedom from elaborations" in a system which [wrongly] asserts that [the term] "ultimate" is nominally imputed for others with respect to that freedom from all elaborations of all phenomena in terms of appearing or not appearing, being produced or not produced, having or not having self, and so forth, when one investigates and analyzes. [In their wrong system, the term "ultimate"] does not refer to emptiness, the mode of subsistence, free from all elaborations, or nets of conceptuality, for a non-conceptual exalted wisdom of meditative equipoise [as it does] in our own system.

For, in the system of these earlier scholars, many different characters such as production, cessation, thorough arising, refutation, and proof appear to a consciousness which is not investigating or analyzing, and all those factors of appearance which, in terms of that consciousness, are without damage by reasoning are conventional truths. They assert that the non-establishment of anything – production, cessation, and so forth – upon investigation and analysis is merely nominally designated for others as an ultimate truth; there is nothing established as an ultimate phenomenon or apprehendable by the mind....

For them, "freedom from elaborations" refers to not being apprehendable by the mind as, "This exists, this does not exist, this is, this is not." Thus it is completely dissimilar to the explanation [of "freedom from elaborations"] in our own system as freedom from all elaborations of dualistic appearance for a particular mind.

> That system [of the earlier scholars] asserts that even a Superior's non-conceptual exalted wisdom of meditative equipoise is without an object and without appearance. Also, they assert that just as when one analyzes, no object at all is established, so also an awareness does not apprehend as an ultimate any extreme at all – existence, non-existence, and so forth; and, when all apprehensions are pacified, there is the mere designation of the verbal convention "seeing freedom from elaborations, or the mode of subsistence", but there does not exist an object, "reality", that is to be realized upon being taken as the [object of] the mode of apprehension of a reasoning consciousness.

This explanation of what Proponents of Thorough Non-Abiding intend when they assert that the mere object which is the elimination of elaborations through reasoning is an ultimate truth makes excellent sense: they are describing merely a nominal imputation of the term "ultimate truth" to the non-finding of anything at all, a "freedom from elaborations" in terms of phenomena's appearing or not appearing, when one analyzes, such that there is nothing at all taken as the object of a reasoning consciousness. This provides an explanation of the Proponents of Thorough Non-Abiding that is clearly unacceptable in Dzong-ka-ba's system and also differs substantially from the assertions of the Reason-Established Illusionists.

The difficulty with this interpretation comes when one takes into account Dzong-ka-ba's own later rephrasing in his *Medium Exposition of Special Insight* of his comments with regard to the Proponents of Thorough Non-Abiding. There he says:[590]

> ... Proponents of Thorough Non-Abiding, who assert that the positive inclusion (*yongs gcod*) in terms of the elimination of elaborations with respect to appearances is an ultimate truth....

And, he says at a point much later in the *Medium Exposition*:

> Also there is no great Mādhyamika who asserts that the mere object comprehended by an inferential consciousness – the latter from among the two, the [mere] elimination and the positive inclusion with respect to the elimination of the elaborations of the object of negation regarding appearances – is an ultimate truth. Through this mode you should understand in detail also my explanation of the presentation of these in the extensive *Stages of the Path*.

The most common usage of the terms "[mere] elimination" (*rnam bcad*) and "positive inclusion" (*yongs gcod*) is in the context of dichotomies. For example, permanent phenomenon and impermanent phenomenon are a dichotomy – whatever exists is either one or the other. With respect to an impermanent phenomenon, such as a sprout, that it is permanent is merely eliminated; its being impermanent is positively included. However, Dzong-ka-ba uses the terms a bit differently here; Jam-yang-shay-ba's interpretation of his meaning is that when one considers whether a sprout is empty of inherent existence or not, the emptiness of the sprout is the mere elimination and the sprout qualified by that emptiness is the positive inclusion.

Thus, Jam-yang-shay-ba, and following him, A-gya-yong-dzin and Pa-bong-ka, have interpreted Dzong-ka-ba to be saying that earlier scholars said that the Proponents of Thorough Non-Abiding assert that the object qualified by emptiness – the illusion-like composite of appearance and emptiness – is an ultimate truth. This would clearly be unacceptable in Dzong-ka-ba's own system since such an object is an affirming negative rather than a non-affirming negative and, as such, could not be an ultimate truth. However, Nga-wang-bel-den and Sha-mar-den-dzin take exception to this interpretation, lucidly pointing out that in that case the assertions of the Proponents of Thorough Non-Abiding would be no different from those of the Reason-Established Illusionists – since asserting such is exactly their error – and could hardly constitute two different sets of Mādhyamika assertions.

Nga-wang-bel-den and Sha-mar-den-dzin offer alternate interpretations which avoid such a fault. According to Nga-wang-bel-den, Dzong-ka-ba set forth his passage in the context of the opponents' assertions: Even though for them, the ultimate is in fact not suitable to be an object of any mind, having *imputed* as an ultimate the aspect of freedom from elaborations which is the non-establishment of anything at all, they assert that it is the object of comprehension of an inferential consciousness. Sha-mar-den-dzin supplies the further explanation that this imputed, or superimpositional, aspect is also asserted as a positive inclusion. Thus, in this case, the mere elimination refers to not being established as anything, and the positive inclusion is the superimposition of that as something that can be taken as the object of an inferential consciousness. To say that such a positive inclusion is an ultimate truth would be erroneous, and this is the meaning of Dzong-ka-ba's statement. This explanation by Nga-wang-bel-den and Sha-mar-den-dzin creatively avoids the fault of redundancy they find in Jam-yang-shay-ba *et al.*

It is Dzong-ka-ba himself who made the meaning of the passage difficult to explain due to the tantalizingly brief bit of explanation he added in the *Medium Exposition of Special Insight*.

ACTUAL AND IMPUTED ULTIMATES

There is one final topic requiring discussion with regard to Dzong-ka-ba's statements about the Reason-Established Illusionists. Dzong-ka-ba's lack of clarity suggests a questionable interpretation put forth by Jam-yang-shay-ba. Whereas most of the later commentators have allowed Jam-yang-shay-ba's explanation to pass without comment, Sha-mar-den-dzin objects to it and gives in its stead a somewhat convoluted but in the end more satisfying explanation. Quite aside from the point under discussion, his analysis is fascinating for what it reveals about the various uses of the term "ultimate". Dzong-ka-ba says in the *Great Exposition*:[591]

> The assertion of these [earlier scholars] appears to be an assertion that [for the Reason-Established Illusionists] the mere object that is comprehended by an inferential reasoning consciousness is an ultimate truth whereas it is said in both Shāntarakṣhita's *Ornament for the Middle Way* (*dbu ma rgyan*, *madhyamakālaṃkāra*) and Kamalashīla's *Illumination of the Middle Way* (*dbu ma snang ba*, *madhyamakāloka*) that the object comprehended by a reasoning consciousness is designated "ultimate" due to being concordant with an ultimate truth.

In the *Medium Exposition of Special Insight* Dzong-ka-ba says:[592]

> Therefore, the Reason-Established Illusionists assert that a composite of the two, the appearance of a base such as the aggregates and its emptiness of true existence – [this composite] being the mere object established by an inferential reasoning consciousness – is an ultimate truth. It is a concordant ultimate, not an ultimate truth.

The above statement in the *Medium Exposition of Special Insight* was made immediately following citation and discussion of the meaning of the passages by Shāntarakṣhita and Kamalashīla to which Dzong-ka-ba only alluded in the *Great Exposition* as sources for its being the position of Shāntarakṣhita and Kamalashīla that the object comprehended by a reasoning consciousness is only a concordant and not an actual ultimate. Those passages are as follows. Shāntarakṣhita's *Ornament for the Middle Way* says:[593]

> Because of according with the ultimate,
> This is called an "ultimate".

> Actually [the ultimate] is free from all
> The collections of elaborations.

Kamalashīla's *Illumination of the Middle Way* says:

> Because this non-production accords with the ultimate, it is called an "ultimate" but it is not so in fact because actually the ultimate is beyond all elaborations.

To explain the meaning of these passages, Dzong-ka-ba gives in the *Medium Exposition* an extensive explanation of different ways the term ultimate is used, explaining that whereas in fact just the object emptiness – the nature of phenomena – is to be taken as the ultimate, there are many cases of using the term "ultimate" also to describe the subject, the consciousness realizing emptiness. He cites as a source for this Kamalashīla's *Illumination of the Middle Way* which says, "All consciousnesses arising from correct hearing, thinking, and meditating, because they are non-erroneous subjects, are called 'ultimates'; for, they are the ultimate among them [that is, among consciousnesses]."[594]

Once the term "ultimate" is being used for the consciousnesses realizing emptiness, one then needs to make a differentiation between different types of "ultimate" consciousnesses. There are two types of reasoning consciousnesses: (1) the non-conceptual exalted wisdom of meditative equipoise of Superiors directly perceiving reality and (2) conceptual reasoning consciousnesses realizing suchness in dependence upon a sign. In this context the former of these are called actual ultimates and the latter concordant ultimates. The reason justifying this differentiation is that although both consciousnesses realize emptiness and hence have removed the elaborations of the conception of true existence, the exalted wisdom of Superiors, in that it is a direct perception in which cognizing subject and cognized object are fused undifferentiably, has also removed the elaborations of dualistic appearance. Conceptual reasoning consciousnesses, realizing emptiness only by means of a conceptual image, have not removed the elaborations of dualistic appearance and hence are considered merely to be concordant with directly perceiving ultimate consciousnesses. Thus, here the terms "actual" and "concordant" ultimate are used for directly perceiving and inferential consciousnesses realizing emptiness, although in fact neither consciousness is an actual ultimate, that status being reserved for the object, emptiness.

To further complicate matters, based on the usage of the terms "actual" and "concordant ultimate" for the consciousnesses realizing emptiness, there is a parallel application of those terms to the object, emptiness, as realized by those two consciousnesses. For a Superior's non-conceptual exalted knower, emptiness is an actual ultimate free from both elaborations; for a conceptual reasoning consciousness, emptiness is not an actual ultimate free from both elaborations since it is only free from one class of elaborations – those of true existence. However, even though in this context the emptiness realized by a conceptual reasoning consciousness is called a "concordant ultimate" and said not to be an actual ultimate, this does not mean that in fact it is not an actual ultimate truth. Emptiness is an ultimate truth, and hence, no matter what type of mind takes it as an object, it is in fact free from all elaborations.

In the *Medium Exposition* Dzong-ka-ba uses this explanation of the usage of the terms "actual" and "concordant ultimate" for the object, emptiness, based on the type of subject that is realizing it to explain the meaning of the passages from Shāntarakṣhita and Kamalashīla cited above (pp.430–1), and Jam-yang-shay-ba then uses it to explain the meaning of this passage from the *Great Exposition*. Dzong-ka-ba had said:[595]

> The assertion of these [earlier scholars] appears to be an assertion that [for the Reason-Established Illusionists] the mere object which is comprehended by an inferential reasoning consciousness is an ultimate truth, whereas it is said in both Shāntarakṣhita's *Ornament for the Middle Way* (*madhyamakālaṃkāra*)

> and Kamalashīla's *Illumination of the Middle Way* (*madhyamakāloka*) that the object comprehended by a reasoning consciousness is designated "ultimate" due to being concordant with an ultimate truth.

Jam-yang-shay-ba gives the following commentary:[596]

> Because an inferential consciousness is a thought consciousness, it is not free from the elaborations of conceptuality or from the elaborations of dualism; therefore, the non-affirming negative that is the object of comprehension of an inferential reasoning consciousness is an ultimate truth and is concordant with the ultimate that is free from elaborations. For, Dzong-ka-ba's *Medium Exposition of the Stages of the Path* says, "Because [the object emptiness] is free from just a portion of elaborations for a conceptual reasoning consciousness, it is not the actual ultimate that is free from both elaborations. However, this is not to say that in general [the emptiness comprehended by an inferential reasoning consciousness] is not an actual ultimate truth."

There are two problems with Jam-yang-shay-ba's explanation. The first is that when one uses an interpretation that takes the referent of Shāntarakṣhita's and Kamalashīla's statements to be the object, emptiness, then it is no longer valid to posit Shāntarakṣhita and Kamalashīla's statements as in substantive disagreement with the assertion of the Reason-Established Illusionists that the object comprehended by an inferential reasoning consciousness is an ultimate truth. For, the only difference would be in the use of terminology, not a disagreement as to the ontological status of the object, since the mere emptiness that is the object of an inferential reasoning consciousness is in fact an actual ultimate truth, even for Shāntarakṣhita and Kamalashīla, even if the term "concordant ultimate" is used for it to take into account the type of consciousness by which it is being realized.

The second problem is that Jam-yang-shay-ba, in interpreting Dzong-ka-ba's mention of "the mere object that is comprehended by an inferential reasoning consciousness" as referring to "the non-affirming negative that is the object of comprehension of an inferential reasoning consciousness", is contradicting Dzong-ka-ba's own indication of his referent as found in the *Medium Exposition of Special Insight* just following his explanation of the above way to interpret the passages from Shāntarakṣhita and Kamalashīla. He said there:[597]

> Therefore, the Reason-Established Illusionists assert that a composite of the two, the appearance of a base such as the aggregates and its emptiness of true existence – [this composite] being the mere object established by an inferential reasoning consciousness – is an ultimate truth. It is a concordant ultimate, not an ultimate truth.

Thus, Dzong-ka-ba himself indicates that what the Reason-Established Illusionists posit as the object of comprehension of an inferential reasoning consciousness is not mere emptiness – a non-affirming negative and actual ultimate truth – but is the illusion-like composite of appearance and emptiness – an affirming negative which is merely concordant with an ultimate truth. If one puts this identification of what is meant by "mere object established by an inferential consciousness" from the *Medium Exposition* together with Dzong-ka-ba's statement in the *Great Exposition* that the passages from Shāntarakṣhita and Kamalashīla indicate clearly that for them such an object is only a concordant and not an actual ultimate, then it becomes evident that one cannot use the interpretation of the meaning of those passages by Shāntarakṣhita and Kamalashīla given by Dzong-ka-ba in the *Medium Exposition*. For, there those passages were taken as referring to the object, emptiness, called a concordant ultimate merely because it is being realized by a conceptual rather than a non-conceptual reasoning consciousness; as explained above, interpreted in that way they would not constitute a substantial disagreement with the assertions of the Reason-Established Illusionists since the object, emptiness, is in fact an actual ultimate even when it is designated a concordant ultimate due to the type of consciousness perceiving it. What is needed in this context is that the referent of those passages from Shāntarakṣhita and Kamalashīla be the illusion-like composite of appearance and emptiness.

Sha-mar-den-dzin's resolution of this dilemma is to make the case, which he says is corroborated in Kay-drup's *Thousand Dosages*, that Dzong-ka-ba gave in his writings two different interpretations of those passages – one in his *Ocean of Reasoning, Explanation of (Nāgārjuna's) "Treatise on the Middle Way"* and the other in the *Medium Exposition of Special Insight* – and that the one to be followed here is the former. Sha-mar-den-dzin cites the *Ocean of Reasoning* where Dzong-ka-ba, just after citation of the passage in question from Kamalashīla, says:[598]

> That emptiness which is an affirming negative, a negative of ultimate production and so forth in terms of the aggregates and persons ... appears dualistically to an awareness seeing it directly. Further, since it does not appear free from dualistic appearance, it is an imputed ultimate but a fully qualified conventionality.

Thus, Sha-mar-den-dzin concludes:[599]

> Therefore, with respect to the meaning of the passages from the *Ornament for the Middle Way* and the *Illumination of the Middle Way*, one needs to know that there are two modes of explanation:
>
> (1) the following, namely that the emptiness that is an illusion-like affirming negative – forms and so forth which are empty of true existence – is concordant with the ultimate in terms of the factor of being a negative of true establishment. However, it is not an actual ultimate because it appears to an awareness

> directly realizing it accompanied by dualistic appearance. An actual ultimate has passed beyond all elaborations; it is the object found by a non-contaminated exalted wisdom, which seeing it directly, has pacified all elaborations of dualistic appearance.
>
> (2) a mode of explanation as [is found] in the *Medium Exposition of the Stages of the Path.*

Thus, it is possible to interpret the passages from Shāntarakṣhita and Kamalashīla, when they say that the object comprehended by a reasoning consciousness is designated "ultimate" due to being concordant with an ultimate truth, as intending the illusion-like composite of appearance and emptiness, and such an interpretation is set forth by Dzong-ka-ba in his *Ocean of Reasoning*. If one uses this interpretation and disregards the interpretation given by Dzong-ka-ba in the *Medium Exposition* in which the referent was taken as just the object, emptiness, then it is possible to make sense of Dzong-ka-ba's statement in the *Great Exposition*:

> The assertion of these [earlier scholars] appears to be an assertion that [for the Reason-Established Illusionists] the mere object which is comprehended by an inferential reasoning consciousness is an ultimate truth whereas it is said in both Shāntarakṣhita's *Ornament for the Middle Way* (*dbu ma rgyan, madhyamakālaṃkāra*) and Kamalashīla's *Illumination of the Middle Way* (*dbu ma snang ba, madhyamakāloka*) that the object comprehended by a reasoning consciousness is designated "ultimate" due to being concordant with an ultimate truth.

Dzong-ka-ba is saying that the Reason-Established Illusionists assert that the illusion-like composite of appearance and emptiness is an ultimate truth whereas Shāntarakṣhita and Kamalashīla said that it was merely a concordant ultimate; thus, it would be incorrect to call Shāntarakṣhita and Kamalashīla Reason-Established Illusionists. A coherent interpretation of

Dzong-ka-ba's meaning can be pieced together, but one would have to conclude that Dzong-ka-ba did not make it easy.

Nga-wang-bel-den, in the Svātantrika chapter of his *Presentation of the Two Truths*, provides a very helpful key to unravelling the terminology of actual, imputed, concordant, metaphoric, non-metaphoric and so forth used with respect to the ultimate.[600] His explanation can be summarized by the charts on the following two pages.

SUMMARY

To summarize the main points of the above presentation, Dzong-ka-ba, in discussing the subdivisions of the Mādhyamika tenet system, briefly indicated and rejected an assertion by earlier Tibetan scholars that Mādhyamikas, when divided by way of their assertions about the ultimate, are of two types: Reason-Established Illusionists and Proponents of Thorough Non-Abiding. Among Dzong-ka-ba's Ge-luk-ba followers there is disagreement as to whether Dzong-ka-ba's intention was merely to reject those terms as misinterpreted by the earlier Tibetan scholars or whether he rejected them entirely on the grounds that the actual assertions of Reason-Established Illusionists and Proponents of Thorough Non-Abiding are such that they cannot be accepted as true Mādhyamikas.

Nga-wang-bel-den and Sha-mar-den-dzin present a very convincing case for the latter position. They say that Reason-Established Illusionists are those who assert (1) that an illusion-like composite of an appearing subject and its emptiness of true existence appears to an inferential consciousness realizing emptiness and (2) that such a composite is an ultimate truth. They say that Proponents of Thorough Non-Abiding are those who (1) assert that a consciousness realizing emptiness apprehends no object at all, since for them emptiness cannot be taken as an object of the mind, and (2) therefore assert that the term "realizing an ultimate truth" is merely designated for others with respect to a consciousness that in fact is apprehending nothing at all.

Chart 1.

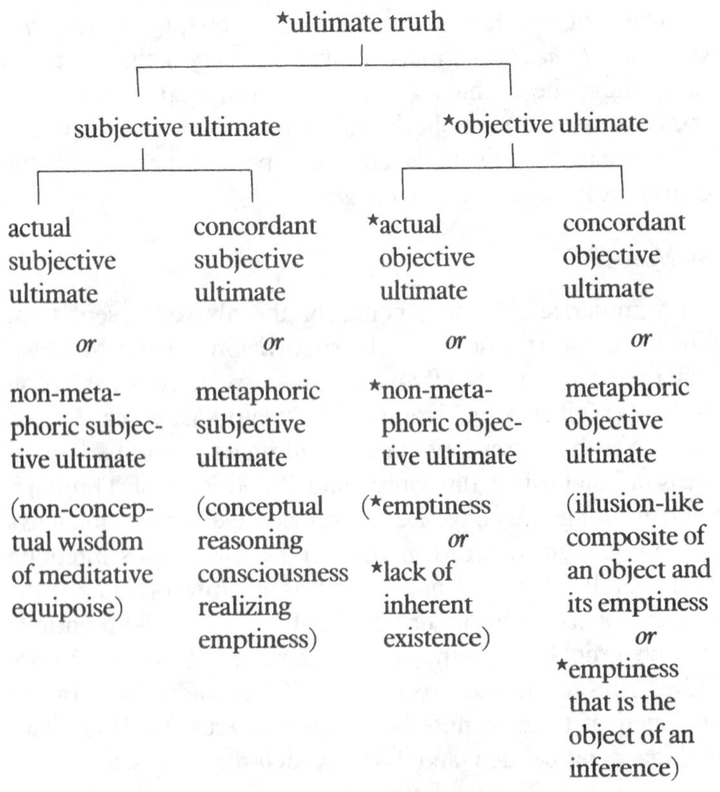

All items marked with an * are ultimate truths in fact.

Also, it is important to note that in actual usage the qualifiers "subjective" and "objective" are often omitted; thus, for example, the term "actual ultimate" could be referring either to the subjective ultimate – not an actual ultimate truth – or to an objective ultimate truth – an actual ultimate truth. The same is true for "metaphoric" and "non-metaphoric" ultimates. The referent must be determined from context.

An actual subjective ultimate, a concordant subjective ultimate, and a concordant objective ultimate can all be called "imputed ultimates".

Chart 2. The Tibetan terms of Chart 1.

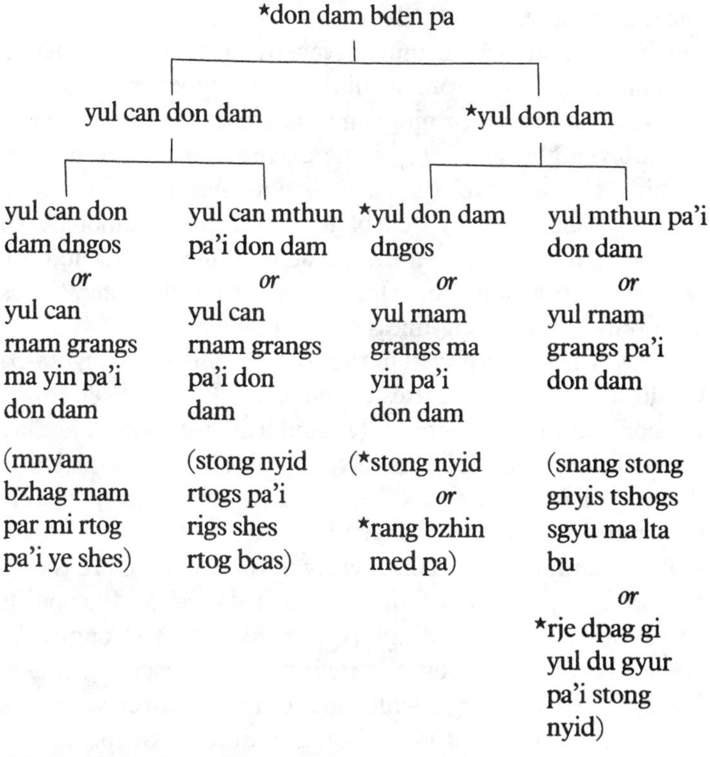

All items marked with an * are *don dam dngos*.

yul can don dam dngos, *yul can mthun pa'i don dam*, and *yul mthun pa'i don dam* can all be called *don dam btags pa ba*.

Neither of these positions is acceptable in Dzong-ka-ba's Mādhyamika interpretation. For him, an ultimate truth is necessarily an emptiness. It is an object, it is something that can be realized by the mind. Nevertheless, it is a negative phenomenon, and, from within the two types of negatives, affirming and non-affirming, an ultimate truth is necessarily a non-affirming negative – a mere elimination that implies nothing else in its place. An affirming negative, such as a sprout qualified by its lack of true existence, cannot be an ultimate truth. Also, even though an emptiness exists and is a phenomenon, when one realizes it, one is not thinking, "This *is* emptiness," or "Emptiness is this phenomenon."[601]

Thus, when interpreted in the above manner, Dzong-ka-ba would indeed reject all uses of the terms Reason-Established Illusionist and Proponent of Thorough Non-Abiding, finding them unacceptable not merely as a basis for an inclusive division of Mādhyamikas, but also fallacious as even merely descriptive of correct Mādhyamika tenets.

In the end, the basic controversy as to whether there is or is not an interpretation of the Reason-Established Illusionists and Proponents of Thorough Non-Abiding that Dzong-ka-ba would accept is of minor import. Further, the lack of detail in Dzong-ka-ba's writings, which led to the controversy, may in fact be seen, not as a fault, but as indicative of the way in which he concentrated on what was important rather than dwelling on minutia.

Nonetheless, there is a great deal of value in the care and attention given by Dzong-ka-ba's Ge-luk-ba followers to pursuing the secondary issues. The analysis used is of the same type as that brought to bear on the larger topics; it is based on the principles revealed by Dzong-ka-ba's presentation, using those principles to understand areas on which Dzong-ka-ba did not explicitly touch. This process serves to deepen understanding of the larger topics.

2 *Alex Wayman's Translation Considered*

The portion of Dzong-ka-ba's "Great Exposition of Special Insight" translated here has previously been translated by Alex Wayman in his *Calming the Mind and Discerning the Real* (New York: Columbia University Press, 1978, and reprint New Delhi: Motilal Banarsidass, 1979). Thus it is necessary here to explain why, in this writer's opinion, a new translation is warranted.

Professor Wayman, in an article, "Observations on Translation from the Classical Tibetan Language into European Languages", published in 1972 in the *Indo-Iranian Journal* sets forth his views on how translation from Tibetan should be done.[602] To summarize some of the main points that Professor Wayman makes in his article, the first is that mere knowledge of grammar, though essential, is insufficient for making competent translations from classical Tibetan. He also makes a strong case for literal translation, saying:

> In short, the attempt to render intelligible in another language what is difficult and obscure in the original can sometimes introduce elements quite at variance with the intentions of the original work. As Ruegg points out, clarifying remarks should be added (say in brackets) to, rather than replace the basic term. (p.166)

Wayman amplifies further:

> The translator who insists on making the entire sūtra

> intelligible even at the cost of departing from the words, introducing new material that does not correspond to the original text, and so on, is palming off his supposed "insight consisting of pondering" upon the unsuspecting reader. (p.168)

Also he emphasizes the importance of consistent translation of Tibetan technical terminology by non-interpretive translation equivalents that can be used in English in the same way as they are used in Tibetan. (For instance, in a well taken point, he criticizes Stcherbatsky's translation of *śūnyatā* (emptiness, or voidness) as "relativity" and *śūnya* (empty, or void) as "relative" since these translation equivalents are unworkable in a sentence such as "All dharmas are śūnya of svabhāva" (p.189). Finally, Wayman says that it is important not to skip over any part of the text, but to translate everything, even if the translation of some portions is tentative.

Wayman's translation of Dzong-ka-ba's *Great Exposition* is faithful to the principles he has articulated. It is very literal and reflects Dzong-ka-ba's text phrase by phrase, neither adding new material, except as indicated by parentheses, nor omitting difficult portions. The closeness with which it adheres to the Tibetan original, in fact, makes it particularly easy to check for accuracy, and such a check reveals that in terms of accuracy, Wayman's translation is severely flawed.

A number of problems with Wayman's translation have already been discussed by Geshe Sopa in a lengthy review.[603] However, a subsequent review by Robert Kritzer seems unaware of the seriousness of the problems with the translation, and, although the language is carefully couched, on the whole it is highly laudatory, calling Wayman's translation "a meticulous piece of scholarship".[604] Also Paul Williams remarks, in an article setting forth Dzong-ka-ba's views on conventional truths, on Wayman's "fine translation".[605] Thus, it seems appropriate to adduce further evidence of how flawed that translation is.

The major source of error in Wayman's translation is his misunderstandings of Tibetan grammar; other causes of difficulty are misconceptions about the meanings and uses of specific terms and a willingness to attempt translation that includes all the words of the Tibetan original but does not make sense of them in English. These will be discussed individually with representative samples of each.

GRAMMATICAL ERRORS

To show how quickly meaning can be distorted by a few simple errors in grammar and to give an idea of the sheer number of errors that can be found throughout Wayman's translation, let me cite the following passage. It is one that is fairly straightforward, difficult in neither syntax or meaning. Dzong-ka-ba is making the point that because both Nāgārjuna and Āryadeva were considered valid and used as sources by the Indian Mādhyamikas who came after them, earlier Tibetan scholars called those two "Mādhyamikas of the model texts" (*gzhung phyi mo'i dbu ma pa*) whereas they called the others "partisan Mādhyamikas" (*phyogs 'dzin pa'i dbu ma pa*). He says (see p.164):[606]

> Even the great Mādhyamikas such as the masters Buddhapālita, Bhāvaviveka, Chandrakīrti, and Shāntarakṣhita took Āryadeva to be valid like the master [Nāgārjuna]. Therefore, since both the father [Nāgārjuna] and [his spiritual] son [Āryadeva] are sources for the other Mādhyamikas, earlier [Tibetan scholars] used the verbal convention "Mādhyamikas of the model texts" for those two and used the verbal convention "partisan Mādhyamikas" for the others.

Wayman (p.181) translates this passage as follows:

> In this regard, the great Mādhyamikas Āryadeva,

> *ācārya* Buddhapālita, Bhāvaviveka, Candrakīrti, Sāntarakṣita, and others became authoritative like the *ācārya* (Nāgārjuna); but the Master and his disciples (Nāgārjuna and Āryadeva) are the source for the other Mādhyamikas, so the early teachers of Tibet called the texts of these two the "grandmother Mādhyamika" and applied the term "partisan Mādhyamika" to the others.

In this short passage Wayman has made five separate errors:

1) Not seeing that Dzong-ka-ba is saying that Buddhapālita, Bhāvaviveka, Chandrakīrti, Shāntarakṣhita, and so forth took *Āryadeva* to be just as authoritative as Nāgārjuna, Wayman has Dzong-ka-ba saying that Āryadeva, Buddhapālita, Bhāvaviveka, and so forth all became authoritative. He misidentifies "Buddhapālita, Bhāvaviveka, Candrakīrti, Sāntarakṣita, and others" as the object of the verb "to hold" or "to take" (*mdzad pa*, Wayman's "became") rather than as the agents. According to Wayman, these became authoritative for someone else, whereas Dzong-ka-ba is saying that they took Āryadeva to be authoritative.

Wayman makes this error first by ignoring a separative particle (*ni*) which sets Āryadeva off from the other names in the list as the object of the verb "hold" (the "logical" subject) and by then ignoring an instrumental (*kyis*) which establishes the others in the list as the agents who take Āryadeva to be authoritative. Thus, it is not that Āryadeva, Buddhapālita, Bhāvaviveka, Chandrakīrti, Shāntarakṣhita, and others became authoritative; rather, Buddhapālita, Bhāvaviveka, Chandrakīrti, Shāntarakṣhita, and so forth took Āryadeva to be authoritative.

2) Wayman does not take the term "*ācārya*" or "master" (*slob dpon*) as modifying "Buddhapālita, Bhāvaviveka, Chandrakīrti, Shāntarakṣhita, and so forth", but as referring only to Buddhapālita, whereas it is better understood as referring to all of them. Since the term appears only once at the head of

the list that begins with Buddhapālita, it is by context that one should understand that it applies to all members of the list. Additional support for applying it to all members of the list is the fact that Dzong-ka-ba uses the term in the pages immediately following the passage in question in reference to each of the individuals named in the list.

3) Because those masters took Āryadeva to be authoritative just as they took Nāgārjuna to be authoritative, earlier Tibetan scholars called Nāgārjuna and Āryadeva "Mādhyamikas of the model texts". Thus the first sentence or clause (whatever way one translates it) serves as the reason for the second one. Wayman, however, has not seen this, but has taken them to be in opposition, using the word "but". This reading is entirely unjustified because the Tibetan instrumental (*mdzad* PAS) is clearly an instrumental of reason.

4) Perhaps Wayman's phrase, "the Master and his disciples (Nāgārjuna and Āryadeva)," is a misprint for "the Master and his *disciple* (Nāgārjuna and Āryadeva)". If not, Wayman's parenthetical addition, "(Nāgārjuna and Āryadeva)", would be glossing "disciples", in which case Dzong-ka-ba would be referring, with the word "Master", to a third person who was a teacher of both Nāgārjuna and Āryadeva. It is clear, however, by its frequent use throughout the text, that *yab* ("father" or "Master") refers to Nāgārjuna and *sras* ("son" or "disciple") refers to Āryadeva. Any ambiguity might have been avoided had Wayman translated the term *gnyis ka* ("both") which modifies the term *yab sras* ("father and son", or "master and disciple"), making it unmistakably clear that only two individuals are the referents – "*both* the father [Nāgārjuna] and his [spiritual] son [Āryadeva] . . .".

5) In the last clause Dzong-ka-ba is saying that earlier Tibetans therefore called Nāgārjuna and Āryadeva "Mādhyamikas of the model texts" since they were accepted as valid by all the other Mādhyamikas – Buddhapālita, Bhāvaviveka, Chandrakīrti, Shāntarakṣhita, and so forth – whereas those scholars were called "partisan Mādhyamikas". Thus, *persons*

are the referents of the verb "called", being called "Mādhyamikas of the model texts" or "partisan Mādhyamikas".

Wayman, however, sees Dzong-ka-ba as saying that the term is applied to the *texts* of Nāgārjuna and Āryadeva rather than to the scholars themselves. He does this by mistranslating the grammatical particle *la*, which indicates those *for* whom the term was used ("earlier [Tibetan scholars] used the verbal convention 'Mādhyamikas of the model texts' *for* those two"). In his translation, Wayman inappropriately treats the particle *la* as if it were a genitive particle ("the early teachers of Tibet called the texts *of* these two the 'grandmother Mādhyamika'"). It should also be pointed out that here Wayman is inconsistent since in the final phrase of the passage ("and used the verbal convention 'partisan Mādhyamikas' *for* the others"), a parallel construction to the one under discussion here, he does translate the particle correctly ("and applied the term 'partisan Mādhyamika' *to* the others").

(I also disagree with Wayman's literalness in using the translation equivalent "grandmother" (in "grandmother Mādhyamika") for the term *phyi mo*. Although "grandmother" is found in the dictionary, the term is also used to translate the Sanskrit *mātṛkā*, as in Nāgārjuna's *Precious Garland*, verse 394, where it refers to a *model* of the alphabet which a grammarian uses in first teaching his students. Its usage thus as a basis, or model, or guide is more appropriate to the present context; these are "Mādhyamikas of the *model* texts" because they are taken to be valid, authoritative, by all the other Mādhyamikas. (See note 313.)

The net effect of all these errors is to obscure the basic point that all Mādhyamikas, whether Svātantrikas (Bhāvaviveka and Shāntarakṣhita) or Prāsaṅgikas (Buddhapālita and Chandrakīrti), accept Āryadeva to be as valid as Nāgārjuna and use both as sources. Almost all the later Mādhyamikas are differentiated into partisan camps as Svātantrika-Mādhyamikas or Prāsaṅgika-Mādhyamikas, and members of one camp would not necessarily accept the works of members of the other as reliable.

This passage is indicative of general types of errors found in Wayman's translation – misidentification of the subjects and objects and misuse or ignoring of the grammatical particles that determine the syntax of a sentence. I would like now to cite examples of classes of specific grammatical errors that Wayman makes on multiple occasions.

1. *Wayman frequently misses the non-case usage of the particle "la" and the genitive particles "kyi, gyi, gi, 'i, yi", where their meaning is "but", "and", or "whereas".*

Following is an example where Wayman mistranslates both. In a section where Dzong-ka-ba is showing how Mādhyamikas differ greatly from Nihilists, Dzong-ka-ba points out that when Chandrakīrti himself explicitly addresses this issue, he states as the reason why Mādhyamikas differ from Nihilists the fact that Mādhyamikas assert actions and so forth as existing conventionally. Dzong-ka-ba then uses Chandrakīrti as evidence for his position that Mādhyamika interpretations widespread in Tibet at his time were wrong, pointing out that Chandrakīrti did not say that Mādhyamikas differ from Nihilists because (1) Nihilists have assertions whereas Mādhyamikas do not or (2) because Nihilists say that actions and their effects do not exist (*med pa*) whereas Mādhyamikas merely say they are not existent (*yod pa ma yin*). In his translation of this passage, Wayman misses the non-case usage of the particle "*la*" twice and of the genitive particle "*yi*" once. Dzong-ka-ba says, (see p.212):[607]

> Here the master [Chandrakīrti], as the reason for [the Mādhyamikas] being different from those having a view of annihilation, did not say, "Because they have assertions, *whereas* we do not." He also did not say, "They assert those as non-existent *whereas* we do not propound such as non-existent (*med pa*) *but rather* assert them as not existent (*yod pa ma yin pa*)."

Wayman (p.212) translates this:

> Still, the *ācārya* (Candrakīrti), when differing from the nihilist in terms of the reason, does not say, "That's your thesis because it is not ours" [i.e., does not try to pin the Lokāyata doctrine on the opponent the way the latter tries to pin nihilism on the Mādhyamika]. He does not say, "We have nothing like your claim that those things do not exist" [since the *Prajñāpāramitā* scriptures have such teachings in the *paramārtha* sense]. Nor does he say, "We claim that an existent does not exist."

In the phrase, "Because they [the Nihilists] have assertions, *whereas* we [Mādhyamikas] do not," (Wayman's "That's your thesis because it is not ours"), Wayman ignores the disjunctive sense of the particle *la* ("whereas"), treating it merely as a phrase breaker and then applies the reason instrumental *pas* ("because") only to the second half of the phrase rather than the whole phrase. Wayman has not understood that Dzong-ka-ba is only giving a (hypothetical) reason clause showing how Chandrakīrti did *not* distinguish Mādhyamikas and Nihilists. In other words, Dzong-ka-ba is saying that Chandrakīrti did not say, "Mādhyamikas differ from Nihilists because the Nihilists have assertions whereas we Mādhyamikas do not." This basic error has then forced Wayman to misconstrue the demonstrative pronoun *de*, which means in this case "those [Nihilists]" or "they", as "your" and to misconstrue the first person plural particle *kho bo cag* "we", as "our", thereby adding an erroneous possessive sense.

The second part of the passage sets forth a second statement of what Chandrakīrti did not say when differentiating Mādhyamikas from Nihilists. He did *not* say that Mādhyamikas are different from Nihilists because the Nihilists assert actions and their effects as non-existent (*med pa*) whereas the Mādhyamikas assert them as not existent (*yod pa ma yin pa*). Dzong-ka-ba is refuting an interpretation of Mādhyamika in which negations of existence (*yod pa*) and non-existence (*med pa*) are taken without qualification and an unfounded difference is made between saying that something is non-existent (*med pa*) and that it is not existent (*yod pa ma yin pa*). Dzong-ka-ba's point is that although the Tibetan language allows one to differentiate these linguistically and some Mādhyamika interpretations are based on such a distinction, in terms of meaning there is no difference. Such a distinction is not a valid way of explaining Mādhyamika.

Wayman, based on not understanding the use of the non-case particles, fails to see that the remainder of the passage is one statement of what Chandrakīrti does not say, with its end indicated by the "quotation marker" *ces* – "He [Chandrakīrti] also did not say, 'They assert those as non-existent *whereas* we do not propound such as non-existent (*med pa*) *but rather* assert them as not existent (*yod pa ma yin pa*).'" (Wayman has handled the non-case particle *la* that separates the two statements of what Chandrakīrti did not say relatively correctly, treating it merely as a period. It would have been better to give an indication of its conjunctive sense, "and", indicated in my translation above by "also" – "He *also* did not say . . .") Wayman treats what is one statement of what Chandrakīrti did not say as two separate statements:

> He does not say, "We have nothing like your claim that those things do not exist" [since the *Prajñāpāramitā* scriptures have such teachings in the *paramārtha* sense]. Nor does he say, "We claim that an existent does not exist.

It is not two separate statements, but rather one phrase, composed of two equal clauses separated by the particle *la* ("whereas"), with the second clause itself being composed of two equal clauses separated by the particle *yi* ("but rather"). Wayman has run the first clause and the first part of the second together as one phrase ("We have nothing like your claim that those things do not exist"), ignoring the disjunctive *la* and adding in a "your" not in the Tibetan. Wayman then treats the third clause of the sentence (my "but rather assert them as not existent", Wayman's "Nor does he say, "We claim that an existent does not exist") as a separate independent clause, which it is not.

Wayman's inappropriate treatment of the clauses in this passage indicate another of his frequent tendencies – to take the *shad*, a textual mark used in Tibetan (which lacks punctuation such as commas, semicolons, periods, and so forth) to break up sections of text, as if it were the primary indicator of significant breaks in meaning. In fact, the *shad* often has less significance than Wayman assigns to it, and sometimes important meaning breaks are not marked by a *shad* at all.

Wayman's incorrect treatment of the clauses described above accords with how the sections of text are separated by the *shad*. The passage has two *shad* separating three sections of text, and Wayman took them as separating three equal clauses. This is not so, the grammatical units of the passage being determined by the grammatical particles of the sentence, not primarily by the *shad*. The first *shad* does indeed separate two equal clauses – the two statements of what Chandrakīrti did not say, but the second *shad* merely serves to separate the two clauses that make up the second part of the statement of what Chandrakīrti did not say. The break between the first and second clauses of the second statement of what Chandrakīrti did not say is marked only by the non-case particle *la*. Wayman, by mistranslating this particle and relying on the *shad* to indicate a break in meaning, has completely missed the point of the passage.

In mistranslating the passage, Wayman has obscured an important aspect of Dzong-ka-ba's Mādhyamika interpretation – namely, that Dzong-ka-ba does not feel that Mādhyamikas have no theses. Dzong-ka-ba suggests that if Chandrakīrti had held that Mādhyamikas have no theses, Chandrakīrti would have used this as a reason why Mādhyamikas differ from Nihilists. Also, Dzong-ka-ba does not believe that the Mādhyamika negations of both existence and non-existence can be taken without qualification since, as far as he is concerned, a denial of existence is the same as a statement of non-existence.

Further, Dzong-ka-ba does not believe that such was the intention of Nāgārjuna or Chandrakīrti, for again he feels Chandrakīrti would have used such as a reason if that were his opinion. These points could not possibly be understood from Wayman's translation.

Having missed Dzong-ka-ba's meaning, Wayman has sought to make his translation sensible by adding explanation in parentheses. The explanations, however, make the passage even more obscure.

In a second example where Wayman misunderstands the noncase usage of the particle *la*, Dzong-ka-ba is setting forth two different ways that Mādhyamikas can be divided: (1) into those who assert external objects and those who do not, or (2) into Svātantrikas and Prāsaṅgikas. He says (see p.166):[608]

> Therefore, [Mādhyamikas] are limited to the two, those who do and do not assert external objects conventionally, *and* also, if names are designated by way of how the view ascertaining emptiness, the ultimate, is generated in the continuum, they are limited to the two, Prāsaṅgikas and Svātantrikas.

Wayman (p.182) translates this as:

> There is certainty as to the Prāsaṅgika (*thal*) and the Svātantrika (*raṅ*) when one applies those names by way of the means of generating in the lineage of views certainty about whether they do or do not hold an external in conventional terms *and* [emphasis mine] certainty about *paramārtha*-voidness.

Wayman's basic error in this passage is that although he has treated the particle *la* as "and" (italicized above), he has not understood that it separates two independent clauses, each of which ends in "are limited to the two" (*gnyis su nges*). Dzong-ka-ba is setting forth two *different* ways in which a twofold division of Mādhyamika can be made. Wayman has run the two clauses together as one, and this leads him to make the incorrect statement that the division of Mādhyamikas into

Svātantrikas and Prāsaṅgikas has something to do with whether they do or do not assert external objects. This is not so because, as Dzong-ka-ba has just explained (see p.166), some Svātantrikas, those following Bhāvaviveka, do assert external objects and some, those following Kamalashīla and Shāntarakṣhita, do not. The division into Prāsaṅgika and Svātantrika is made purely on the basis of how the view is generated in the [mental] *continuum* (not "lineage" as Wayman translates it). Mādhyamikas who assert external objects include both Prāsaṅgika and Sautrāntika-Svātantrika; those who do not are the Yogāchāra-Svātantrikas.

Another problem with Wayman's translation that this passage reveals is his failure to differentiate between two distinct meanings of the Tibetan term *nges pa*. It can mean either "definite", or "limited", or it can mean "ascertain". Wayman makes the case that a Tibetan term should always be translated by the same English equivalent, and, in situations where the Tibetan original has only one meaning, I agree with him. However, in cases where a term has more than one distinct meaning, it is highly unlikely that one English equivalent can be found that will adequately serve those multiple meanings, and in those cases it seems, in the interest of a translation intelligible in English, more appropriate to employ different translation equivalents. Wayman's translation here of *nges pa* in all situations as "certainty" is a case in point, for it obscures the meaning of the passage cited above. Of the three times the term is used in this passage, in two cases it means "definite" or "limited" – "Mādhyamikas are *definite* as, or are *limited* to, the two . . ." – and in the third it means "ascertain" – "how the view *ascertaining* emptiness, the ultimate, is generated . . .".

2. *Wayman frequently misses the instrumental used to indicate the agent of an action, particularly when affixed to a term like wisdom (ye shes) or reasoning (rigs pa) which he tends to translate only in a passive sense.* Sometimes this is harmless as in the passage (see p.178):[609]

> ... a Superior's exalted wisdom perceiving suchness perceives production, cessation, bondage, release, and so forth as not existing in the least, ..."

Wayman translates this (pp.189–90):

> when with the noble knowledge that sees reality one sees that there is no (*dharma*) whatever of birth and decease, bondage and liberation, etc...

His adding in a "one" as a seer distinct from the "knowledge" that is the true agent of the passage, alters the meaning slightly but is not critical.

However, in other cases, such a practice leads to outright mistranslation. For instance, Dzong-ka-ba says (see p.196):[610]

> Moreover, if reasoning refutes bondage, release, and so forth ...

Wayman's translation (p.201) is:

> Furthermore, if one opposes with the principle of bondage and liberation, etc....

Having missed the fact that reasoning (Wayman's "principle") is the agent, and bondage and liberation are its object, he joins the two with an unjustified "of" and ends up with a "principle of bondage"! Wayman fabricates an unstated agent, "one", thereby causing him to ignore the true agent and introduce serious distortion of meaning.

To give a final example of misunderstanding of the agentive instrumental leading to serious error: Dzong-ka-ba makes the point that those who negate too much have not differentiated between inherent existence and existence and erroneously hold that a refutation of inherent existence is a refutation of existence. He says that such must be the case, for why else would they say that the reasoning refuting inherent existence refutes mere existence (see p.199):[611]

> Otherwise, why would you propound that the reasoning refuting establishment by way of [an object's]

> own entity refutes mere existence, mere production and cessation, and so forth?

Wayman translates this passage (p.202):

> (On the other hand), if this is not what (you believe), why do you interpose an objection saying there is only an existent thing and only arising and ceasing, etc. with your principle of cessation of accomplishment by own nature?

Wayman has taken *'gegs pa*, "refute", not as a verbal but as a noun, "objection" (even were it a noun, it would not mean "objection", but "refutation" or "negation"). Then, he has not seen that "mere existence" and "mere arising and cessation" are its object and that the agent of all this is the *reasoning* refuting establishment by way of [an object's] own entity (Wayman's "principle of cessation of accomplishment by own nature").

Wayman's translation results in Dzong-ka-ba's opponent saying that those things (my "mere existence, mere production and cessation"; Wayman's "only an existent thing and only arising and ceasing") exist, whereas Dzong-ka-ba's point is that they have erroneously been refuted by those who negate too much. Again, Wayman's mistranslation obscures one of the important points of Dzong-ka-ba's argument – that those who negate too much say that the reasoning refuting inherent existence also refutes arising, ceasing, bondage, liberation, and so forth, and that, from Dzong-ka-ba's viewpoint, such constitutes an extreme of Nihilism.

3. *Wayman seems not to understand either the participial or the agentive uses of the Tibetan genitive*. An example of the former can be found in the passage cited just above; in Wayman's "principle of cessation of accomplishment by own nature," (*rang gi ngo bos grub pa 'gog pa'i rigs pa*) "principle", or, if it were more accurately translated, "reasoning", is the agent of the participle, *'gog pa*, "refute", (Wayman's "cessation"), to which it is attached by the genitive particle *'i*. Hence it would

be better translated "reasoning refuting establishment by way of [an object's] own entity".

In an example of the latter, which leads to distortion of the meaning, Wayman speaks in his introductory chapters to the translation (p.61) of the "refutable of the path" (*lam gyi dgag bya*) and the "refutable of the principle" (*rigs pa'i dgag bya*). Here, his use of the non-committal "of" leaves open the possibility that the path and principle are in some fashion refuted. It is the opposite; the path and reasoning are the agents accomplishing the refutation – the afflictive obstructions and obstructions to omniscience are the objects to be refuted *by* the path, and inherent existence, or self, is the object to be refuted *by* reasoning.

4. *Wayman frequently ignores or mistakes the particle "ni", particularly when it is used to indicate the subject of a sentence.* For example, Dzong-ka-ba says (see p.210):[612]

> Another mode of [Mādhyamikas'] difference from those having a view of annihilation, who assert that actions and their effects do not exist, is set forth extensively in Chandrakīrti's *Clear Words* as follows:

Wayman (p.211) translates this as:

> The nihilistic view which holds that there is no *karma* and fruit as well as other different methods, are stated in the *Prasannapadā*, this way:

The particle *ni* is not usually translatable but does function within sentences. Wayman, by ignoring it, has in this case missed the subject of the sentence ("Another mode of the [Mādhyamikas'] difference from those having a view of annihilation who assert that actions and their effects do not exist"), which is set off by *ni*. Thus, he has completely missed the point of the sentence, which is to introduce a section setting forth yet another way that Chandrakīrti himself differentiates Mādhyamikas from Nihilists.

In taking as his subject "the nihilistic view . . . as well as other different methods", Wayman has misunderstood a common meaning of the particle *dang*. Although it often means "and" or "as well as", as Wayman has taken it here ("*as well as* other different methods), another very common meaning is as "from", which is what it means here, "difference *from* those having a view of annihilation". The *ni* indicating the subject is the real clue to which meaning is intended in this situation.

Finally, this passage reveals another error that Wayman makes on numerous occasions, a seeming lack of awareness of what is called in Tibetan the "term of ownership" (*bdag po'i sgra*), which adds a possessive sense to a term. What Wayman has translated as "the nihilistic view" in fact means "those having a nihilistic view", with the difference in Tibetan being between *chad lta* and *chad lta ba*. Wayman has ignored the *ba* particle.

5. *Wayman frequently misunderstands or does not make clear in his translation when passages are explanation of material cited previously rather than independent new material.* This mistake often distorts the meaning of what is being said, introducing new elements not intended by Dzong-ka-ba. For instance, Dzong-ka-ba, having just cited a passage from Chandrakīrti's *Clear Words* in which Chandrakīrti refers to Nāgārjuna's *Treatise on the Middle Way* (XXIV.ab), "For whom emptiness is suitable, all is suitable," and concludes "For whom emptiness is not suitable, dependent-arising would not *exist* [emphasis added], whereby all is unsuitable," (see p.189) says:[613]

> Therefore, "suitable" and "unsuitable" are to be understood as those things' existing and not existing.

Wayman (p.197) translates this as:

> One may understand from that passage when the valid and the invalid are present or absent.

Wayman has again misunderstood the usage of the particle *ni*, here also used to set off the subject of the sentence ("suitable" and "unsuitable"). He has taken it as "when", a meaning never justified by *ni* but an error which Wayman makes on more than one occasion.[614] Wayman's translation of *yod* and *med* ("existing and not existing") as "present" and "absent", although possible in some situations, is inappropriate here, where those terms mean simply "exists" and "does not exist".

Through mistranslating and misinterpreting the passage, Wayman has obscured another of Dzong-ka-ba's radical, but carefully made points – that emptiness can be said to exist, (not just be "suitable" as Nāgārjuna said literally), with the justification being Chandrakīrti's shift from "suitable" to "exists" in his concluding line of commentary.[615]

6. *Wayman frequently obscures the structure of Dzong-ka-ba's argument through mistaking when Dzong-ka-ba is setting forth his own opinion and when he is summarizing those of opponents.* It admittedly is not always easy to distinguish these, but usually there are clear grammatical clues, and these Wayman often ignores. For example, Wayman (p.210) translates a lengthy passage as follows:[616]

> (You say,) granted that we hold that prior entities did not exist later on, and in that sense do not exist; and we have not claimed that these (entities) exist primordially, so how does that amount to a nihilism view? (In reply) this is the way it has been said to be the nihilism view (*Mūlaprajñā*, XV, 11, c–d):
>
> > Saying that something does not exist now but existed formerly – reduces to nihilism.
>
> Your argument is discussed in the *Prasannapadā* (in XXIV, 11):
>
> > The yogin who is moved only by his deception about conventional truth (*saṃvṛti-satya*) and who has understood it to be without self-existence, when he discovers the voidness of it (= *saṃvṛti-satya*) to have the character of *paramārtha*, does not fall into the two extremes. (But:) when you think, "What is that thing which used to be and is

> not now?" you cannot thus perceptively reach the self-existence of the former entity, and so, also, you cannot discover its later non-existence.
>
> Since that was said, you think it over and say, "That is not right, . . ."

With this example I will, in the interests of space, ignore Wayman's errors of translation and concentrate only on his errors in identifying the flow of the argument. Wayman has the passage begin with an opponent's view – from "(You say)" through to "nihilism view?". Then, he returns to Dzong-ka-ba's viewpoint – beginning with "(In reply)" and continuing through the two quotations. Then he returns again to the opponent – "you think it over and say, "That is not right, . . .".

In fact, everything from the beginning of the passage through the end of the second quotation is the opponent's position. However, the line, "that is not right", which Wayman indicates as spoken by the opponent, is not the opponent's line at all, but is the beginning of Dzong-ka-ba's response refuting the opponent. That this is so is unmistakably clear from the Tibetan, in which the unit of the opponent's position is clearly demarcated at the beginning by the term *gal te*, "if", and at the end by *snyam na* "you were to think", from which Dzong-ka-ba's response follows naturally, "that is not reasonable" (*de ni rigs pa ma yin te*). Within the section that is the opponent's position, it is further made clear that the citation of the two quotes are by the opponent in support of his argument, for they are introduced by the particle *te* and are concluded by the indication that a reason has just been given, "because it is said" [i.e., in those passages cited] (*zhes gsungs pa'i phyir*), which, in logical discourse, are indicative of a reason clause.

Wayman's misinterpretation of who is speaking makes it impossible to follow the flow of Dzong-ka-ba's argument.

7. *Wayman frequently ignores the adverbial accusative (in Tibetan, "de nyid")*. Dzong-ka-ba says (see p.178):[617]

> ... since an exalted wisdom perceiving suchness perceives production as non-existent, it is not feasible that [production] be established by it.

Wayman (p.190) translates this as:

> ... since it is proved by that knowledge (= *ārya-samāpatti*) which sees reality (directly), it is not valid that it sees the non-existence of birth.

Wayman has made three major errors in this sentence:

1) He has ignored the adverbial accusative within the reason clause, "since an exalted wisdom perceiving suchness perceives production *as* non-existent." Instead he has translated that part of the phrase as "it sees the non-existence of birth," treating non-existence as the object of the verb and creating a genitive relationship between it and "birth", that is not found in the Tibetan.
2) He has ignored the basic rule that the entire clause governed by an instrumental of reason must precede that instrumental particle ("*since* an exalted wisdom perceiving suchness perceives production as non-existent") and has taken his verb "proved" ("since it is *proved* by that knowledge (= *ārya-samāpatti*) which sees reality (directly)"), from after it, again ignoring another adverbial accusative particle *ra* that is attached to the verb as he does so. He has also not included in the reason clause some material that should be there, ("perceives production as non-existent") which he puts in his main clause ("it sees the non-existence of birth"), again against the rules of Tibetan syntax.
3) By ignoring the second adverbial accusative particle *ra* just mentioned, he has failed to see that the verb to which it is attached, "proved", or "established", must be the referent of the term "valid", or "feasible" which follows it ("it is not feasible that [production] be established by it"). In fact, the two adverbial accusatives are in a parallel relationship and a

very literal translation of the passage would be, "Because production is perceived *as* (or *to be*) non-existent by an exalted wisdom perceiving suchness, [production] is not feasible *as* (or *to be*) established by that [exalted wisdom]." Wayman has taken "see" as what is not feasible ("it is not valid that it sees the non-existence of birth"), again jumping over the reason instrumental against the rules of Tibetan syntax.

Wayman's errors cause him to contradict directly the sense of Dzong-ka-ba sentence: whereas the point of the sentence is that, according to the opponent whose opinion is being cited, production and so forth are *not* "proved" or "established" by a Superior's exalted wisdom because it sees them to be non-existent, Wayman has that opponent saying that they are. Further, Wayman's mistranslation has obscured a passage that sets up another of Dzong-ka-ba's fine distinctions (which is drawn out in detail later, Wayman's translation, p.217) – the fact that a consciousness' not seeing something is not the same as its seeing that thing as non-existent, as is claimed by those who negate too much.

8. *Wayman consistently ignores basic rules of Tibetan syntax.* Errors two and three in the example just cited above are cases of this. To give another example, Dzong-ka-ba says in a section heading (see p.181):[618]

> Showing that those systems refute the uncommon distinguishing feature of Mādhyamika.

Wayman (p.191) translates this as:

> Showing that the special refutation of *dharma* by that school is not common to the Mādhyamika.

In this passage Wayman makes two major errors, both because of ignoring syntax. First he misunderstands what the adjective "uncommon" modifies, placing it with Mādhyamika rather than with "distinguishing feature". If it were as Wayman has interpreted it, there would not be a genitive particle between "Mādhyamika" and "uncommon", as there is (*dbu ma'i thun mong ma yin pa*), but instead there would be the particle *dang*, "with" (*dbu ma pa dang thun mong ma yin pa*).

Secondly, to arrive at the phrase "special refutation of dharma", Wayman has completely ignored word order and surrounding grammatical particles. The Tibetan word order here is *khyad chos bkag pa*, with *khyad chos* (feature) modified by the adjective "uncommon" (*thun mong ma yin pa*) that precedes it joined by a genitive particle *'i*. There is no way that Wayman's "special" (*khyad*) could be an adjective modifying "refutation" when it is separated from it by the term *chos*, especially not when it is bound to the term "uncommon" that precedes it by a genitive particle.

In addition, Wayman has further obscured the meaning by his choice not to translate the Tibetan *chos*, but instead to substitute its Sanskrit equivalent, *dharma*. *Dharma* and, correspondingly, *chos*, have at least ten different meanings.[619] No one English word can handle all those meanings, a fact which Wayman tacitly acknowledges by not attempting a translation but instead falling back to the Sanskrit. However, as a general practice this leads to potentially obscure translation, and in this case to outright error, since *chos* in connection with *khyad* is, in Tibetan, a technical term meaning "feature" or "attribute", being an abbreviation of *khyad par gyi chos*, and if one wants to be very literal, giving weight to both the syllables that make it up, it can be translated as "distinguishing feature" or "special attribute". Wayman, by trying to make the adjective "special" modify "refutation" has thus missed the technical term.

Wayman does on subsequent occasions translate the term *more* correctly as "special *dharma*" (pp.191 and 199), so he can be accused, not of not knowing at all that it is a technical term, but merely of error on this occasion and inconsistency in translation. I would still disagree with the translation "special *dharma*" as being unnecessarily obscure, particularly in a later situation where it is used in conjunction with another technical term, *khyad gzhi*. There *khyad gzhi* and *khyad chos* mean "substratum" and "attribute" and Wayman's translation of these (p.258) as "special basis" and "special *dharma*" make a passage that is already difficult unintelligible.

MISUNDERSTANDINGS OF TERMS

Often passages of Wayman's translation are obscured due to his not understanding the meaning of particular terms. Wayman mistranslates a number of such terms, frequently based on a very literal rendition of the parts of the term in situations where such literalness not only does not convey the sense of the term but introduces elements of error.

Wayman translates *srid mtha'* which means "almost not occuring" and might very literally be rendered as "an extreme of existence", as "The one who proceeded to the summit of the world" (p.198). Thus a sentence which should read, (see p.192) "Since this composite of the two, inducing ascertainment with respect to such appearance and emptiness, *almost does not occur*, the view of the middle way is very difficult to gain," comes out as, "The *one who proceeded to the summit of the world* with the double collection of certainty guidance in that sort of appearance and the void recalled the extraordinary difficulty of attaining the Mādhyamika view." Wayman perhaps is mixing the term *srid mtha'* with another, *srid rtse*, "the peak of cyclic existence" which refers to the highest realm within cyclic existence, the fourth of the four formless absorptions.

Wayman translates *gtan med*, "completely non-existent", as "not continuous" (p.203). Thus a passage which should read, (see p.199), "you ... propound that if [sprouts] are *utterly without* establishment by way of their own entities, they are *utterly non-existent*," is translated as, "... and you are asserting that if the accomplishment by own nature is *not continuous*, it is *not continuous*."

Wayman translates *med rgyu*, which is the Tibetan way of mirroring the Sanskrit gerundive and means "to be non-existent" or in English often simply "non-existent", as "with his cause for absence" (p.188) Thus a passage which should read (see p.176):

> Just as, for example, in order to ascertain that a certain person is not here, you must know the person who *is not* here, so in order to ascertain the meaning of "selflessness", or "non-inherent existence", you also must identify well that self, or inherent existence, which *does not exist.*

is translated by Wayman as:

> For example, to be certain about thinking that a (certain) person is not present, it is necessary to know this person *with his cause for absence*. In the same way, to be certain about the meaning of nonself and nonself-existence, it is also necessary to determine that "self" and "self-existence" with *cause for their absence*.

Wayman similarly translates *chad rgyu*, "annihilated" as "cause of annihilation" (p.210). Thus, the phrase, "if, in order to have a view of annihilation, it were necessary to have asserted formerly whatever thing was *annihilated*..." (see p.209) becomes, in Wayman's translation, "if it is necessary to accept a prior entity as a *cause of nihilism* for the nihilism view, ...".

Wayman translates the phrase "*med bzhin du*" which means "whereas [such and such] does not exist" or "while [such and such] does not exist" as "in that way it does not happen that". Thus the phrase, "in that case, since there comes to be no way to take cause and effect as illusion-like, appearing to exist inherently *whereas they do not*, you fall to an extreme of permanence," (see p.200) becomes, in Wayman's translation, (p.203), "in that way *it does not happen that* one regards as illusory-like the appearance there, which in fact is the cause and fruit without self-existence, and so one falls into the extreme of eternalism."

Also, Wayman seems not to understand that the term *rang gi sde pa*, or, in abbreviated form, *rang sde*, literally means "our schools" and hence "Buddhist schools". He sometimes ignores it altogether, as on p.187 where he translates the phrase "Even the Proponents of True Existence of *our own [Buddhist] schools*" (see p.173) as "the Sautrāntika realists"; (also, limiting the term *dngos smra ba*, Proponents of True Existence to just Sautrāntika does not accord with Dzong-ka-ba's intentions as discussed previously, pp.50–1). Another mistranslation of this term occurs on p.192 where he translates the phrase "Scholars of *our own [i.e. Buddhist] schools*, Proponents of True Existence," (see p.183) as "The learned realists *with their own position*."

Finally, as mentioned above, the term *nges pa* can mean "definite" or it can mean "to ascertain"; Wayman does not distinguish these two and thus mistranslates the phrase "gain *ascertainment* of the two truths" (see p.182) as "achieve the (two) *certainties*", (p.192).

NON-EVOCATIVE TRANSLATION

A final criticism of Wayman's translation is his willingness to translate the words of the Tibetan without making a decision as to their meaning, so that one is left with a string of phrases in English from which it is difficult to gain any understanding at all. To cite an example, in what is admittedly a very difficult passage, Dzong-ka-ba says:[620]

> Therefore, you should know that the fact that it is not suitable to hold as literal what is taught in a few isolated words, out of context, not connecting it with what is said before or after in the general run of a sūtra or treatise, does not destroy [that text's] being a scripture of definitive meaning. You also should know that even though what is taught on the level of the words is suitable to be held as literal, it is not that it [necessarily] is not [a passage of] interpretable meaning [that is, literal texts can still require interpretation].

Dzong-ka-ba's point is that the mere fact that a few words of a text out of context cannot be taken literally does mean that the text as whole is not of definitive meaning. Nor does mere literalness guarantee that a text is of definitive meaning; there are other criteria which must be met and some literal texts require interpretation.

Although Wayman's translation includes all of the words, I find it completely noncommunicative (p.180):

> Hence, one should know that for a preaching text of final meaning it is not proper to be "according to the words" with only the denotation at face value of each trivial word, not connecting what is said before and after of the general layout of the sutra or sastra – and there is no loss (of these final-meaning texts); and know that for a (preaching text of) provisional meaning, it is proper to be "according to the words" with denotation of the words – and there are still (these provisional meaning texts).

CONCEPTUAL ERRORS

Finally, in addition to errors of translation and understanding of particular terms, it appears, from his translation, that Wayman has not always grasped points that are central to Dzong-ka-ba's presentation and argument. Some have already been mentioned. Another, most basic, and one that has already been discussed by Geshe Sopa in his review of Wayman's translation (see pp.70–2), is Wayman's misidentification of who and what are intended by Dzong-ka-ba's refutation of those who negate too much or not enough. Given that Wayman, in his response to Geshe Sopa's review,[621] flatly denied that his identification of these was in error, it is appropriate to pursue the subject further.

Wayman says in the introduction to his translation of Dzong-ka-ba's text, (p.61) "He [Dzong-ka-ba] first treats the overpervasion in lengthy fashion (40 folios), then the non-pervasion rather briefly (4 folios), where the first of these fallacious positions, the overpervasion, affirms *svabhāva* (self-existence); and the second, the nonpervasion, denies *svabhāva*." As specific identifications of who is included within the scope of these refutations, Wayman says (p.61), "The opponents thus judged to be guilty of overpervasion are especially the realists, called the *vastu-satpadārthavādin* ... Other opponents are the mind-only (*cittamātra*) persons of the Yogācāra school of Buddhism as well as the Mādhyamika-Svātantrika of which Bhāvaviveka is the most famous exponent," and he says (p.63), "Under the nonpervasion, Tsoṅ-kha-pa places the insider of the Mādhyamika, Prāsaṅgika school who has quite properly denied *svabhāva* as a principle and then falsely denies *svabhāva* in the Buddhist path, i.e., takes it as the refutable of the path."

The starting point for Wayman's error in this section is the fact that he takes the terms "overpervasion" (*khyab ches pa*) and "under pervasion" (*khyab chung ba*) as technical logical terms. Geshe Sopa in his review (pp.70–1) correctly points out that while these terms do have technical meaning in Buddhist logic, they are also used in a non-technical way to mean "too broad" and "too narrow", and that this is how they are used by Dzong-ka-ba. Wayman, in his response to Geshe Sopa (pp.95–6), refuses to accept this, citing in his own support the fact that Dzong-ka-ba in the "Great Exposition of Special Insight" frequently uses other technical terms of logic in their technical sense. Except for pointing out that Wayman's argument is logically inconclusive since the mere fact that Dzong-ka-ba uses technical terms elsewhere in no way necessitates that that is his intention here, and that, furthermore, the whole weight of the Geluk-ba scholarly tradition is on the side of the more general usage, I will not pursue this line of discussion.

Rather, I will address the dispute from the viewpoint of the content of those sections of Dzong-ka-ba's discussion that proceed under the headings in question. For surely what Dzong-ka-ba talks about in those sections is the key to understanding what he means by his section headings.

Dzong-ka-ba divides his section refuting an overly broad identification of the object of negation – which Wayman calls "refutation of overpervasion in determining the refutable" – into two parts, (1) stating the assertions of such persons and then (2) indicating their incorrectness. His introductory sentence to the first part is, "Nowadays, most who claim to propound the meaning of the middle way say that all phenomena ranging from forms through to exalted-knowers-of-all-aspects [omniscient consciousnesses] are refuted by the reasoning analyzing whether production and so forth are or are not established as [their own] suchness . . ." (see p. 178). This certainly suggests that Dzong-ka-ba saw as those he was refuting his contemporaries, by implication, Tibetans, who considered themselves to be Mādhyamikas and not Proponents of True Existence, especially since, in this section setting forth the assertions of the opponents who are to be refuted, the term Proponents of True Existence (which Wayman translates as "realists" and whom he takes to be the opponents herein) is never once mentioned.

Dzong-ka-ba divides the second section, indicating the incorrectness [of those assertions], into two parts, (1) showing that those systems refute the uncommon distinguishing feature of Mādhyamika and (2) showing that the damages expressed do not overwhelm [our position]. He identifies the distinguishing feature of Mādhyamika as the ability both utterly to refute inherent existence and at the same time to make all the presentations of conventional phenomena and says that his contemporaries in Tibet who claim to be Mādhyamikas and yet find these two incompatible are no different from Proponents of True Existence.

In this portion of the "Great Exposition" Dzong-ka-ba makes far more mention of Proponents of True Existence than he does of Tibetan erstwhile Mādhyamikas, which perhaps explains Wayman's misconception that the Proponents of True Existence are the intended objects of Dzong-ka-ba's refutation. I think it could fairly be admitted that Dzong-ka-ba has a secondary purpose, in that having equated those

Tibetans who negate too much with the Proponents of True Existence, he is in fact negating both. Furthermore, since the ammunition for his argument is provided by the writings of Nāgārjuna, Āryadeva, and Chandrakīrti, who were negating Proponents of True Existence – who in fact negate too little – and were not negating those who negate too much, it could appear that the Proponents of True Existence were his primary referent and that Wayman's technical interpretation of the term *khyab ches pa* was justified.

However, to take it thus is to ignore the structure of Dzong-ka-ba's argument, which initially sets up as the assertions to be refuted those of Mādhyamikas in Tibet who claimed that all phenomena were refuted by the reasonings refuting inherent existence and then in the refutation of those assertions, proceeds one by one through a rebuttal of reasons advanced *by Mādhyamika interpreters*, not by Proponents of True Existence, to show why all phenomena are negated by the Mādhyamika reasonings. Dzong-ka-ba's primary purpose is to negate misinterpretations *of Mādhyamika by Mādhyamikas*, not the views of other schools of Buddhism.

Wayman has correctly translated numerous occasions where Dzong-ka-ba equates "erroneous" Mādhyamikas with Proponents of True Existence, so that a refutation of the one is a refutation of the other, and thus it seems that his error is basically in the identification of the primary referent of Dzong-ka-ba's refutation, perhaps because of his initial misconception that the term *khyab ches pa* is being used as a technical logical term. Wayman's statement, "the first of these fallacious positions, the overpervasion, affirms *svabhāva* (self-existence)" would be true were the primary and not the secondary object of Dzong-ka-ba's refutation the Proponents of True Existence. However, the true primary referent of Dzong-ka-ba's argument is those who claim not only to refute *svabhāva* but along with it would refute all conventional phenomena as well.

Wayman says of the second aspect of Dzong-ka-ba's refutation of those who misidentify the correct measure of the object of negation, "Under the nonpervasion, Tsoṅ-kha-pa places the insider of the Mādhyamika, Prāsaṅgika school who has quite properly denied *svabhāva* as a principle and then falsely denies *svabhāva* in the Buddhist path, i.e., takes it as the refutable of the path." (p.63) Again, Wayman seems to be confusing what Dzong-ka-ba discusses within the section refuting those who negate too little, (or as Wayman labels it, "nonpervasion"), with the basic structure of that argument. He also shifts Dzong-ka-ba's terminology with the result that he makes statements which, while understandable, do not, I believe, correctly reflect Dzong-ka-ba's intentions.

What Wayman sees as a two-staged progression in the opponent being refuted by Dzong-ka-ba, from proper denial of *svabhāva* as a principle and then false denial of *svabhāva* in the Buddhist path, describes the two major topics that Dzong-ka-ba addresses in this section. However it is clear that Wayman has not correctly understood Dzong-ka-ba's argument. First, what Wayman calls a "proper" denial of *svabhāva* is not so for Dzong-ka-ba. For, Dzong-ka-ba argues that these particular opponents have defined *svabhāva* in too narrow a fashion. They do deny the *svabhāva* they have so defined, but it is inconsequential. Not having gone far enough in their negation, they have not succeeded in refuting anything that would overcome innate afflictions. Hence their negation will not lead to release from cyclic existence and is hardly a "proper" denial. Wayman, in speaking of it as "proper", ignores Dzong-ka-ba's criticism of such a position.

Wayman is correct in pointing out that Dzong-ka-ba emphasizes the existence of a *svabhāva* that is realized on the Buddhist path, this *svabhāva* being reality, the final nature of each and every phenomenon. His mistake, as I see it, is to think that Dzong-ka-ba is refuting opponents who deny this *svabhāva*. This second aspect of Dzong-ka-ba's discussion, rather than being part of his argument against those guilty of under, or non, pervasion, is, I believe, in essence a digression, albeit one that flows naturally out of the material which preceded it. Let us look into this point in detail.

Those who negate too little take *svabhāva* as the object of negation, but they define it, based on two verses of Nāgārjuna's *Treatise on the Middle Way*, as that which has the threefold qualities of not being produced by causes and conditions, not changing into something else, and not depending on something else. Dzong-ka-ba refutes that *svabhāva* identified thus – rather than as inherent existence, or establishment by way of an object's own entity – is the Mādhyamika object of negation, on the grounds that it is inconsequential.

However, having concluded his refutation, further explanation of what those verses from Nāgārjuna's *Treatise* mean, as he understands them, is necessary, and this is the subject matter of the rest of the section. In explaining those verses, Dzong-ka-ba is able to elaborate his view that emptiness exists. He explains that the two verses do not concern merely the object of negation, but also indicate, with the last two lines of stanza two, the final nature, *svabhāva*, that does exist, realization of it being the purpose of the Mādhyamika path. This final nature is unchangeable, permanent, and not dependent on another consciousness as its positer.

This difference between the two parts of Dzong-ka-ba's explanation, the first, in which he is setting forth a wrong view and refuting it, and the second, in which he is raising hypothetical qualms and answering them, can be seen in the Tibetan, where the former is set forth by the standard "Someone says" (*kha cig na re*) construction[622] and the latter are phrased simply as questions, "Does such a nature exist?" (*'o na . . . she na*) and "Did you not earlier refute an inherent establishment with respect to all phenomena?" (*'o na . . . ma bkag gam snyam na*).[623] Wayman's error comes because he runs these two sections together.[624]

His description of this section as a whole as involving proper denial of *svabhāva* as a principle and then false denial of *svabhāva* in the Buddhist path additionally confuses things because he is mixing terminology. Dzong-ka-ba does speak of two types of *object of negation*, one by reasoning and one by the path. These Wayman translates (misleadingly, as discussed above) as "the refutable of the principle" and the "refutable of the path". Presumably because *svabhāva* when understood as inherent existence is the object of negation, or refutable, Wayman has supposed a parallel situation and, substituting *svabhāva* for "refutable", come up with "*svabhāva* as a principle" and "*svabhāva* in the Buddhist path". (These terms are entirely Wayman's; Dzong-ka-ba does not use them.) Wayman then sees the argument in Dzong-ka-ba's refutation of those who negate too little as concerning whether *svabhāva* is refuted as a principle or in the path. He has obscured the whole verbal point that, of the two meanings of *svabhāva* – inherent existence and the final nature of phenomena – only one, the former, is the object of negation. *Svabhāva* as meaning inherent existence is the object of negation by reasoning, and adherence to it is the object of negation by the path. *Svabhāva* in its second meaning, as the final nature of phenomena, is not an object of negation at all, but the reality that is to be realized.

The fact that only the first meaning of *svabhāva* can be called the object of negation is further evidence of why only the first part of Dzong-ka-ba's discussion in this section involves his basic argument, which is a refutation of those who assert too narrow an *object of negation*. Having dealt with that question, Dzong-ka-ba moves on to another important issue that evolves out of the same passages in the Indian texts as does the first question: whether *svabhāva*, when taken in its meaning of the final nature of phenomena, can be said to "exist" or not, given Mādhyamika refutations that seem on the surface to deny "existence" altogether. Proving that it does exist is the purpose of the second part of Dzong-ka-ba's exposition here and, although a very important argument, is in terms of the structural outline of the "Great Exposition of Special Insight" essentially a digression.

CONCLUSION

As should be evident from the preceding, lengthy discussion of errors to be found in Wayman's translation, I find it to be severely flawed and feel that one seeking to understand Dzong-ka-ba's "Great Exposition of Special Insight" could not rely on it with confidence. There are too many cases of key distinctions of Dzong-ka-ba's finely woven argument being distorted by mistranslation, as well too little clarity in revealing the structure of Dzong-ka-ba's argument due to misidentification of which passages set forth Dzong-ka-ba's own system and which indicate the opinions of others.

Among the introductory materials Wayman includes with his translation, the section entitled "Uses of Buddhist Logic", in which he discusses his ideas of who and what Dzong-ka-ba was refuting, is erroneous as was discussed above. However, other sections of the introduction are good and useful, such as Wayman's discussion of the *lam rim* lineage, his biography of Dzong-ka-ba, and his section, "Discursive Thought and the bSam-yas Debate".

One has to admire Wayman's courage and perseverance in tackling such a momentous task as the translation of the entire "calm abiding" and "special insight" sections of the *Great Exposition of the Stages of the Path*, for it is no small undertaking. Having myself begun with the intention of translating the whole "special insight" portion of the *Great Exposition* and having been forced to draw a line, for purposes of this volume, at something more like one-sixth of it, I am aware of the magnitude of Wayman's accomplishment. However, had Wayman attempted less, he might have been more successful in the final result.

I agree with much of Wayman's philosophy about translation. I, too, feel that translations should be quite literal, translating just what is in the Tibetan original with any clarifying material that is added clearly demarcated by parentheses or brackets. I also agree with Wayman that consistent translation of technical terminology is extremely important, although I take this point less literally than he does since I think it is important to translate the *meaning* of a term, and if a term has more than one meaning, then multiple translation equivalents will be required.

Professor Wayman is an important figure in the field of Buddhist Studies, particularly that of Tibetan Buddhism, where he has been a pioneer. He was one of the first to work with indigenous Tibetan texts, particularly those of the Ge-luk-ba school and has been an effective and articulate voice speaking for the inclusion of the viewpoint of the Tibetan tradition in contemporary efforts to understand Buddhism. As such, his contributions should not be minimized. He has done much to lay a foundation for later scholars to build on.

3 *Jam-yang-shay-ba's Topical Outline*

(The first set of page numbers refer to the location in the translation of the *Annotations*; the numbers in parentheses refer to the Delhi edition of the Tibetan.)

II The Explanation of Special Insight

A The need to achieve special insight even though one has a meditative stabilization having the four qualifications – p.229 (138.4)

1 With an example, showing that one is not released merely through meditative stabilization – p.229 (138.5)

a Even though one has a meditative stabilization having the four factors of clarity, joy, bliss, and non-conceptuality, if one wants release, it is necessary to cultivate the special insight realizing suchness – p.229 (138.5)

b The explanation in Kamalashīla's *Stages of Meditation* that if suchness is not realized, one cannot be released as is the case with the meditative stabilizations of non-Buddhists – p.231 (139.5)

c Citation of a definitive sūtra which is a source for that – p.232 (140.4)

d A worldly meditative stabilization that is a concentration or formless absorption cannot destroy even the manifest conception of self – p.233 (141.2)

e Since the conception of self has not been abandoned through that meditative stabilization, afflictions are generated from the conception of self, due to which one is not released – p.233 (141.4)

2 The path of release as well as how it is cultivated – p.234 (141.6)

a Identifying the path of release – p.234 (141.6)

b How it is cultivated in meditation – p.234 (142.2)

c Proving through scripture and reasoning that one is not released by any method other than realization of suchness – p.236 (143.2)

1 Without the profound view, one is not released – p.236 (143.2)

2 Without hearing much about selflessness, one is not released through meditative stabilization and ethics – p.239 (144.6)

3 Without seeking hearing on the topic of selflessness through relying on another, that is, a skilled spiritual guide, emptiness cannot be realized – p.241 (145.6)

4 The need for listening to and thinking on the scriptures since all of the scriptures directly or indirectly teach about emptiness – p.242 (146.3)

5 Since the first five perfections are like blind persons, from among [the perfections], only the perfection of wisdom, or wisdom, realizes suchness – p.245 (149.2)

6 If wisdom, like an eye, is not generated through hearing and thinking, one is not released – p.245 (150.1)

B How special insight is achieved/How to train in special insight – p.247 (150.3)

1 Fulfilling the prerequisites for special insight – p.247 (150.4)

a The need to hear and think about the stainless scriptures – p.247 (150.4)

1 The need to hear and think about the scriptures – p.247 (150.5)

2 The need to follow one of the great openers of the chariot-ways – p.248 (151.4)

3 Since Chandrakīrti's *Supplement to (Nāgārjuna's) "Treatise on the Middle Way"* explains that one is not released until understanding Nāgārjuna's system from among those [many systems], it is necessary to depend on that – p.249 (152.2)

b The need not to mistake the interpretable and the definitive – p.253 (154.1)

1 Identifying the mode of requiring interpretation and the mode of being definitive from the viewpoint of which something becomes a scripture of definitive or interpretable meaning/Identifying scriptures requiring interpretation and scriptures of definitive meaning – p.253 (154.2)

A′ The need to rely on sūtras of definitive meaning [in order to realize] the profound meaning – p.253 (154.3)

B′ The meaning of requiring interpretation and being definitive – p.254 (154.5)

1′ Positing the interpretable and definitive by way of the subjects discussed – p.254 (154.5)

2′ How [the interpretable and the definitive] are explained in the *Teachings of Akṣhayamati Sūtra* – p.255 (155.3)

a′ A brief indication – p.255 (155.3)

b′ The extensive explanation of the body [of this text, the *Teachings of Akṣhayamati Sūtra*] – p.255 (155.5)

c′ Explanation of the branches [that is, in more detail] – p.256 (156.4)

d′ The meaning established [by the above sūtra] – p.259 (158.4)

3′ How [the interpretable and the definitive] are explained in other sūtras and treatises – p.260 (158.6)

a′ The explanation in the *King of Meditative*

Stabilizations Sūtra that the interpretable and the definitive are posited by way of the subjects discussed – p.260 (158.6)

b′ The explanation in Kamalashīla's treatise, the *Illumination of the Middle Way* – p.260 (159.5)

c′ The explanation by another sūtra that no ultimate production and so forth are definitive objects – p.261 (159.6)

d′ Therefore [Nāgārjuna's] "Collections of Reasonings", the root texts and commentaries, are definitive texts – p.261 (160.3)

e′ The meaning established and an etymology – p.262 (160.5)

f′ This definitive meaning must be true, [though] not in the sense of "true" [when the term "true" refers to] the object of negation, and must be established by valid cognition – p.262 (161.3)

g′ Therefore, not only the non-literal but also the literal in which the [final] mode of subsistence must be interpreted otherwise are of interpretable meaning – p.263 (161.6)

4′ A refutation of others' mistakes with regard to the interpretable and the definitive/Removing others' [false] superimpositions with respect to the interpretable and the definitive – p.264 (162.4)

a′ Refuting the assertion that it is not necessary to affix "ultimately" to the object of negation – p.264 (162.5)

b′ Otherwise it would [absurdly] follow that even the sūtras that refute [the object of negation] would be refuted – p.266 (164.3)

c′ Though a portion of a text is interpretable, this does not stop the treatise from being definitive – p.267 (164.5) d′ It is not contradictory for [a text] to be both literal and require interpretation – p.267 (165.1)

2 The history of commentary on Nāgārjuna's thought – p.268 (165.2)

A′ Transition [between what has been said and what will follow] – p.268 (165.2)

B′ Identifying the model Mādhyamikas – p.268 (165.5)

C′ Analyzing the names designated by earlier scholars – p.269 (166.4)

1′ Their assertions – p.269 (166.4)

a′ A designation of names [to Mādhyamikas] by way of how they posit conventionalities – p.269 (166.4)

b′ A designation of names [to Mādhyamikas] by way of how they assert the ultimate – p.270 (167.1)

c′ There are also Indians who accord with the second [mode of] designation – p.270 (167.4)

2′ An analysis [of the second of those assertions] – p.271 (167.6)

a′ A lack of enthusiasm due to its being of little import – p.271 (167.6)

b′ The way in which the names and meanings of this [designation from the point of view of] the mode of asserting the ultimate are [products of] obscuration – p.271 (168.1)

c′ Summary – p.274 (170.2)

D′ Analyzing the chronology [of the arising of the Mādhyamika schools] – p.277 (170.6)

1′ The incorrectness [of the assertion] that the Superior father [Nāgārjuna] and his [spiritual] son [Āryadeva] did not refute Chittamātra – p.278 (170.6)

2′ The assertion that the initial refuter of Chittamātra was only Bhāvaviveka is incorrect – p.278 (171.3)

3′ How Shāntarakṣhita opened the way of Yogāchāra-Svātantrika – p.279 (171.5)

4′ The need to know in accordance with Kaydrup's *Thousand Dosages* that although these names are suitable, the [divisions of Mādhyamika] are not thus in fact – p.280 (172.3)

5′ A [further] unsuitability of those verbal conventions for Chandrakīrti – p.280 (172.4)

E′ The correctness of the verbal conventions "Prāsaṅgika" and "Svātantrika" [used] by scholars of the later dissemination – p.280 (172.6)

1′ An indication that this is the thought of Chandrakīrti's *Clear Words* – p.280 (172.6)

2′ The division into the two, those who do and do not assert external objects – p.281 (173.2)

3′ The division [of Mādhyamikas] into two, Prāsaṅgikas and Svātantrikas, by way of how the view is generated in the continuum – p.281 (173.4)

F′ Which masters are to be followed – p.282 (174.3)

1′ An indication that the earlier Ga-dam-bas' seeking the view following Chandrakīrti is the thought of Atisha – p.282 (174.3)

2′ Dzong-ka-ba's own assertion that the two systems of Buddhapālita and Chandrakīrti are chief and that after them Bhāvaviveka is next in importance – p.283 (175.1)

3′ The importance of these two masters at all times with regard to explaining the profound meaning [of emptiness] – p.283 (175.4)

3 How to settle the view of emptiness – p.284 (176.1)

A′ The stages of entry into suchness – p.284 (176.1)

1′ Explanation of the suchness that is the object of attainment and the stages of entry [into it] – p.284 (176.2)

a′ The actual [explanation] – p.284 (176.2)
1′ Question – p.284 (176.3)
2′ Answer – p.285 (176.5)
A″ An explanation of the suchness that is the object of attainment – p.285 (176.5)
B″ An explanation of the stages of entering into that suchness – p.285 (177.2)
1″ The need to see the faults of cyclic existence – p.285 (177.2)
2″ The need to identify the root that is the source – p.286 (177.4)
3″ The need for those of sharp faculties to realize that one can abandon the view of the transitory, the root source – p.286 (178.1)
4″ The Truth Body is attained through cultivating the view realizing selflessness by means of the path – p.287 (178.4)
5″ The explanation in Chandrakīrti's *Clear Words* – p.288 (179.3)
6″ How the stages of entering [into suchness] are explained in Chandrakīrti's *Supplement to (Nāgārjuna's) "Treatise on the Middle Way"* – p.289 (180.5)
7″ These stages of entry [into suchness] are the thought of both these masters [Chandrakīrti and Buddhapālita] and also of Nāgārjuna's *Treatise on the Middle Way* – p.292 (184.2)
b′ An elimination of qualms – p.293 (184.6)
1′ A question as to whether the selflessness of phenomena is or is not included in the suchness and selflessness that are the object of attainment – p.293 (184.6)
2′ In answer to that, an explanation individually of the objects of attainment/Individual explanations of the two [types of] suchness,

or nirvāṇa, that are the objects of attainment – p.294 (185.5)

3′ The mode of realizing the two selflessnesses differs from that of the Proponents of True Existence – p.294 (186.2)

A″ The actual explanation – p.295 (186.3)

1″ When the self is realized as not existing inherently, the aggregates that are the basis of designation of the self are realized as not existing inherently – p.295 (186.3)

2″ With regard to the mode of investigating the lack of inherent existence of the self, one needs to analyze, in accordance with how the innate view of the transitory conceives it, whether or not the self has all the characteristics of the aggregates – p.296 (186.5)

3″ When sought in this way, it is not found by a reasoning consciousness – p.297 (187.4)

4″ This is not only explained in Chandrakīrti's *Supplement to (Nāgārjuna's) "Treatise on the Middle Way"*, but is the thought of Nāgārjuna's *Precious Garland* – p.298 (189.1)

B″ An elimination of qualms – p.299 (189.4)

1″ A question – p.299 (189.5)

a″ Initial question – p.299 (189.5)

b″ Second question – p.300 (190.2)

2″ The actual answer – p.300 (190.3)

a″ A [brief] indication – p.300 (190.3)

b″ The extensive explanation – p.300 (190.4)

1″ Although that awareness [realizing the selflessness of the person] does not realize the absence of inherent existence of the aggregates, [the absence of inherent existence of the aggregates] is realized through its force – p.300 (190.5)

2" It is asserted that the mind realizes it when it eliminates superimpositions – p.301 (191.3)

3" In this system, due to the absence of true existence of the substratum, the conception of the true existence of its attributes is refuted – p.304 (192.5)

3" Dispelling an objection – p.304 (193.3)

a" The objection – p.305 (193.4)

b" The answer – p.305 (193.5)

c" An assertion – p.305 (194.1)

d" A refutation of that [assertion] – p.305 (194.1)

1" Not only would this contradict your own assertion [that Proponents of True Existence do not realize the absence of inherent existence of phenomena] but also as a reason [why such cannot be accepted], it would [absurdly] follow that Haribhadra's explanation in his *Small Commentary* [his *Clear Meaning Commentary on (Maitreya's) "Ornament for Clear Realization"*] of the absence of true existence to Buddhist Proponents of True Existence would not be correct [because it would be absurd to prove the absence of true existence to them if they already realized it] – p.305 (194.1)

2" Not only are the measures of being ultimately and conventionally established not the same in the higher and lower tenet systems, it is necessary to distinguish that there are many forms even within one system – p.308 (195.1)

3" The difference that for those [Proponents of True Existence] the person is not merely nominally imputed whereas for this master [Chandrakīrti] it is – p.309 (195.6)

4" Therefore, as long as one has not forsaken the tenet that the aggregates are substantially existent, that is, are not just nominally imputed, one has a conception of the person as substantially existent – p.309 (196.3)

2′ Explanation that although [practitioners of] the two vehicles meditate on the two selflessnesses individually [even in this system, Prāsaṅgika – first the selflessness of persons and then of phenomena], the mode of realization [in Mādhyamika] is different from that among the Proponents of True Existence – p.310 (196.5)

B′ The actual settling of suchness – p.311 (197.5)

1′ Identifying the object of negation by reasoning – p.311 (197.5)

a′ The reason why it is necessary to identify well the object of negation – p.311 (197.6)

1′ Without identifying the object of negation, the non-affirming negative which is the negative of that [object of negation] will not appear – p.311 (198.1)

2′ It is easier to refute the objects of negation if they are condensed into the two, the coarse and subtle, or into the two, a self of persons and a self of phenomena – p.312 (198.5)

3′ One will not be released if one does not refute the subtle object of negation – p.312 (199.1)

4' If one's negation goes too far, one will fall to an extreme of annihilation – p.313 (199.3)

5' The meaning that has been established is that if the object of negation is not identified, one will fall to [an extreme of] either permanence or annihilation – p.313 (199.4)

b' Refuting other systems that [engage in] refutation without having identified the object of negation – p.313 (199.5)

1' Refuting an overly broad identification of the object of negation – p.313 (199.6)

A" Stating others' assertions – p.314 (199.6)

1" [Others' assertion that] all phenomena are included in the four extremes – p.314 (200.1)

2" [Others'] assertion that the meditative equipoise of a Superior perceives production, cessation, bondage, release, and so forth, as non-existent – p.314 (201.5)

3" [Others'] assertion that an object found by [a consciousness] analyzing the ultimate and [an object] able to bear analysis [by that consciousness] are synonymous – p.314 (202.1)

4" [Others'] assertion that production, cessation, and so forth are not established by valid cognition – p.315 (202.3)

5" [Others'] assertion that production, and so forth, do not exist even conventionally – p.316 (203.5)

6" [Others'] assertion that if [production and so forth] are not included in the four alternatives, such analysis is not feasible – p.317 (204.3)

7" [Others'] assertion that because, from among the four alternatives, production from other does not exist, production does not exist – p.317 (204.5)

8″ [Others'] assertion that it is not necessary to affix the qualification "ultimate" in the refutation of production – p.318 (204.6)

9″ Among those, there are two types, those who do and do not assert production conventionally – p.318 (205.3)

10″ All accord in refuting inherent existence – p.319 (205.5)

11″ The assertion that whatever does not inherently exist necessarily does not exist – p.319 (205.6)

B″ Showing that those assertions are incorrect – p.322 (206.2)

1″ Showing that those systems [described] above refute the most important uncommon distinguishing feature of Mādhyamika – p.322 (206.2)

a″ Identifying the distinguishing feature of Mādhyamika – p.322 (206.4)

1″ The Mādhyamikas' mode of assertion – p.323 (206.5)

A★ The need to assert that the fruits, the two bodies [a Buddha's Form Body and Truth Body], arise from the two collections [of merit and wisdom] – p.323 (206.5)

B★ How the positing of such cause and effect [i.e., the attainment of the two bodies in dependence on the accumulation of the two collections] depends on the two truths – p.325 (209.2)

C★ How the non-contradiction of ultimate truths – absence of inherent existence – and conventional truths – nominal positing – is asserted only by Mādhyamikas – p.326 (209.4)

2″ The mode of objection by Proponents of True Existence – p.327 (210.5)

3″ The feasibility of cyclic existence and nirvāṇa even though there is no inherent existence – p.328 (212.3)

A* Although there is no inherent existence, cyclic existence and nirvāṇa are suitable – p.328 (212.3)

B* Not only are cyclic existence and nirvāṇa suitable within non-inherent existence, but also, if there were inherent existence, cyclic existence and nirvāṇa would not be suitable – p.330 (213.4)

C* The suitability of the twelve links of dependent-arising and so forth within that [emptiness of inherent existence] – p.331 (214.2)

D* The suitability of everything, the four truths, and so forth – p.331 (214.4)

E* In the Superior [Nāgārjuna's] system everything is suitable within dependent-arising – p.331 (214.5)

F* The Superior master [Nāgārjuna] spoke again and again about such suitability – p.333 (216.2)

G* The suitability of all the activities of cyclic existence and nirvāṇa within a system of no inherent existence – p.337 (219.6)

4″ The way in which emptiness and dependent-arising are of one meaning – p.339 (220.3)

A* The dawning of the absence of inherent existence as dependent-arising – p.339 (220.3)

1* A brief indication by way of reasoning – p.339 (220.4)

2* Individual explanations through scripture – p.340 (221.5)

a* Indicating that all is suitable within an absence of inherent existence – p.341 (221.5)

b* The suitability of asserting the four truths within that [emptiness of inherent existence] – p.341 (222.3)

c* The suitability of Approachers to [and Abiders in] the Fruit within this [emptiness of inherent existence] – p.342 (223.1)

d* The suitability of the Three Jewels – p.342 (223.3)

e* Within this [emptiness of inherent existence] everything, the proper and the improper, is suitable – p.342 (223.5)

f* The meaning of suitable and unsuitable on this occasion – p.343 (224.4)

B* The dawning of dependent-arising as the absence of inherent existence – p.343 (224.4)

1* The mode of objection by the Proponents of True Existence for whom the meaning of dependent-arising does not dawn as emptiness – p.343 (224.5)

2* How, due to being dependent-arisings, [phenomena] are empty of being able to set themselves up, or of substantial existence – p.344 (225.4)

3* Proving the concomitance and non-concomitance of the incorrectness of substantial existence in that which arises dependently – p.345 (226.1)

4* Therefore, holding that dependent-arising and emptiness are contradictory is like a god who has fallen to being a demon – p.347 (227.6)

5* As long as dependent-arising and emptiness appear to be separate [that is, contradictory], one has not realized the profound meaning – p.348 (229.1)

6* When dependent-arising and emptiness dawn with the one assisting the other, that is the measure of having realized the view, and such is difficult – p.349 (229.6)

7* It is unsuitable to hold that things utterly do not exist due to not finding them upon analyzing with a facsimile of [the reasoning of] the lack of being one or many – p.352 (232.4)

8* Advice to value greatly the dawning of dependent-arising as the meaning of emptiness, the meaning established by those [former points] – p.353 (233.5)

b″ How those systems of earlier Tibetans [explained] above refute this distinguishing feature of Mādhyamika – p.354 (234.4)

1″ How they refute [the Mādhyamikas']

explanation that bondage and release are feasible within an absence of inherent existence – p.354 (234.5)

2″ Thus [in this wrong system] bondage, release, and so forth are refuted even conventionally – p.355 (235.4)

3″ One who asserts bondage and release to be contradictory with an absence of inherent existence has refuted the unique distinguishing feature of Mādhyamika – p.356 (236.3)

4″ If one does not assert such, there is no reason not to affix a qualification to the object of negation – p.356 (236.6)

5″ Your mode of assertion does not differ from the mode of objection by the Proponents of True Existence – p.357 (237.3)

6″ The unreasonableness of the assertion that one has no system due to there being faults with both inherent existence and an absence of inherent existence – p.358 (238.5)

7″ There is no Mādhyamika who refutes all of cyclic existence and nirvāṇa even conventionally through ultimate analysis – p.360 (240.4)

c″ How a Mādhyamika responds to such a mode of refutation/How an actual Mādhyamika responds to the reasonings of those Tibetan systems that refute the distinguishing feature of Mādhyamika – p.361 (240.6)

1″ Flinging back to them [the consequence] that cyclic existence and nirvāṇa would not be suitable – p.361 (241.1)

A* Stating back to them [the consequence] that cyclic existence and nirvāṇa would not be suitable – p.362 (241.3)

B* Not affixing a qualification to the object of negation is a case of not differentiating an absence of inherent existence and non-existence – p.363 (242.5)

C* Such does not pass beyond propounding the two [extremes] – p.364 (243.3)

2'' How they fall to extremes in that they do not differentiate the four – inherent existence and existence, no inherent existence and non-existence – p.365 (244.6)

A* An explanation by way of reasoning – p.365 (244.6)

1* How one falls to extremes – p.365 (244.6)

2* How the two extremes are avoided – p.366 (245.5)

B* An explanation by way of scripture – p.366 (246.1)

1* Stating a scripture – p.367 (246.1)

a* An objection [raised] within the scripture/An objection to this mode of falling to extremes – p.367 (246.2)

b* The answer – p.367 (246.5)

*1** A brief indication by way of the fact that [Mādhyamikas] avoid the two extremes and lead [trainees] to the non-abiding nirvāṇa – p.367 (246.5)

*2** An extensive explanation of how this is done – p.368 (247.2)

A# Although actions and so forth are not refuted, their inherent existence is – p.368 (247.2)

B# If there is inherent existence, activities are not suitable; without such, they are suitable – p.368 (247.4)

2* Explaining the meaning of that [passage from the *Clear Words*] – p.369 (248.1)

a* The thought of Proponents of True Existence – p.369 (248.1)

b* How [Mādhyamikas and Proponents of True Existence] agree that without cause and effect, one falls to an extreme – p.369 (248.4)

c* Although Tibetans admire Mādhyamika, their assertions are like those of Proponents of True Existence – p.370 (249.1)

d* Mādhyamikas answer that they avoid the two extremes and propound the middle way – p.370 (249.3)

e* If actions and so forth did not exist, there would be that fault, but we assert actions and effects – p.370 (249.5)

f* How the extreme of permanence is avoided – p.371 (250.1)

g* The objection [by Proponents of True Existence] that cause and effect are not suitable within an absence of inherent existence – p.371 (250.2)

h* The answer that if there is no inherent existence, then cause and effect are feasible, and if there is inherent existence, then they are not – p.371 (250.5)

C* The meaning established [by these explanations] – p.371 (250.6)

3″ The way in which realization of the meaning of the middle way depends upon refuting the two extremes – p.372 (251.1)

A* Realizing dependent-arising – p.372 (251.1)

1* How the two extremes are avoided by way of dependent-arising – p.372 (251.1)

2* No inherent existence, dependent-arising, falsity, and so forth have the same import – p.373 (251.5)

3* Having avoided the two extremes, indicating that illusion-like cause and effect exist – p.374 (252.6)

B* How one comes to realize falsity – p.374 (253.3)

1* Clearing away the extreme of non-existence, how dependent-arisings are asserted as illusion-like – p.375 (253.3)

2* Since the object is not established from its own side, the subject is established as an unreality, or falsity, that is not established from its own side – p.375 (254.2)

3* False establishment, no inherent existence, and dependent-arising have similar import and do not mean utter non-existence – p.376 (254.5)

4* How the two extremes are avoided – p.376 (255.1)

5* Therefore, the assertion of falsity

avoids the two extremes – p.377 (255.4)

6* The propounding of the two extremes is not the same as propounding an absence of inherent existence and so forth – p.377 (255.5)

4" The unsuitability of refutation and proof without explicit contradictories that are contradictories in the sense of mutual exclusion – p.378 (256.2)

A* The assertion that [things] are not existent and not non-existent is an explicit contradiction – p.378 (256.2)

B* If there are no contradictories and the options are not limited, then refutation and proof are not suitable – p.379 (257.1)

C* If in general the possibilities are not limited to the two, existent and non-existent, it is not suitable [to be limited to] the two, inherently existent and not inherently existent – p.379 (257.4)

D* [These Tibetans] do not understand even an image of the fact that such limiting of the possibilities is called explicit contradiction – p.379 (257.6)

E* If there were no explicit contradictories [dichotomies] that eliminate a third category, then due to doubt [nothing] could be established – p.380 (258.3)

F* Explicit contradictories [dichotomies] apply to all – p.380 (258.5)

G* Showing that those are cases of being mistaken with regard to the mere words, not knowing how to discriminate the meaning of the texts with reasoning – p.381 (258.6)

H* How others do not identify permanence and annihilation [properly] – p.381 (259.3)

I* If the two extremes are not refuted, one is ruined through wrongly viewing emptiness – p.383 (260.6)

J* An objection by others due to their not understanding the two extremes – p.386 (263.1)

K* Refutation of that – p.386 (263.6)

L* That [passage in Nāgārjuna's *Treatise on the Middle Way*] does not indicate what the views of the two extremes are in general, but how they are for Proponents of True Existence – p.387 (264.3)

5″ Though those who do not know how to posit cause, effect, and so forth, hold, "There is no inherent existence," they have not found emptiness/Through not knowing [the existence of the] cause and effect [of actions] and so forth, one does not realize the absence of inherent existence – p.388 (265.1)

A* [Nihilists'] non-realization [of the absence of inherent existence] due to the fact that the thesis and the sign differ – p.388 (265.2)

1* The meaning of Mādhyamikas' and Materialists' assertion that former lives do not inherently exist is not the same [with respect to what they mean by] existence and non-existence – p.388 (265.2)

2★ They do not mean the same thing since there is a great difference also with respect to the reason, or sign, [set forth] by those two – p.389 (265.6)

3★ How Proponents of True Existence object that [Annihilationists and Mādhyamikas] are the same – p.390 (266.2)

4★ Chandrakīrti's explanation that the two theses are not the same from the viewpoint of their reasons – p.390 (266.5)

5★ The objection that although the signs [reasons] are not the same, the theses are the same – p.391 (267.5)

6★ The answer that although the words of their theses are similar, the meanings are not the same – p.391 (268.1)

7★ A source for the objection [by the opponent] that the theses are the same – p.392 (268.2)

8★ A source that the theses also are not the same – p.392 (268.4)

9★ Therefore, it is established by this that Chandrakīrti is indicating that if [Mādhyamikas] did not assert cause and effect, they would be similar to Materialists – p.392 (268.6)

10★ Therefore, it is established that Chandrakīrti asserts [these] conventionally – p.393 (269.1)

B★ Although the mere [words of the] theses are similar, they have not realized [no inherent existence] and the great fault in this/If one does not accept cause, effect, and so forth, although the thesis that these do not inherently exist would be similar [to the Mādhyamika's thesis], one does not realize emptiness and there is great fault – p.393 (269.4)

1* The objection that the verbal theses are the same – p.393 (269.4)

2* In answer, an explanation of an example and the meaning exemplified, this being the way in which they have not realized [emptiness] due to not having identified the object of negation – p.394 (269.6)

3* A source for this mode of objection [that the theses are the same] – p.394 (270.4)

4* A source for the fact that although what was said is the same, the realizers are not at all the same – p.395 (270.5)

5* A source for the example – p.395 (271.1)

6* A source for the example that not only does the Materialist not realize [emptiness] but also this is very bad – p.396 (271.5)

7* Therefore, the assertion by some that although they do not assert cause and effect, they have realized emptiness is mistaken – p.396 (272.3)

6″ How to differentiate the four – inherent existence, no inherent existence, [existence, and non-existence]/Advice to value differentiating existence and inherent existence, non-existence and no inherent existence – p.397 (272.5)

A* How Chandrakīrti differentiates between inherent existence and existence and between no inherent existence and non-existence – p.397 (272.5)

B* How Buddhapālita differentiates those – p.398 (273.6)

1* An objection – p.398 (273.6)

2* An answer differentiating those two – p.399 (274.2)

C* Advice therefore to work hard at differentiating the four – inherent existence and existence, no inherent existence and non-existence – p.399 (274.5)

2″ Showing that the damages expressed above do not damage and overwhelm the party to whom they are expressed [i.e., do not damage the correct Mādhyamika interpretation] – Vol II (275.2)

2′ Refuting a too limited identification of the object of negation – Vol II (386.6)

c′ How the object of negation is identified in our own system – Vol II (408.1)

2′ Whether that negation is done by means of consequences or autonomous syllogisms – Vol III (466.3)

3′ How, in dependence on doing that, to generate the view in your continuum – Vol IV (594.2)

2 The divisions of special insight – Vol IV (728.6)

3 How to cultivate special insight in meditation – Vol IV (742.3)

4 The measure of having achieved special insight through meditative cultivation – Vol IV (808.1)

4 *Emendations to the Delhi Edition of the "Four Interwoven Annotations"*

Two texts were used. The first is that published in New Delhi in 1972 by Chos-'phel-legs-ldan, which states in the prefatory matter that it was reproduced from a print of the corrected Tshe-mchog-gling blocks of 1842. It is referred to in abbreviated form as "Delhi".

The other is a text held at the University of California, Berkeley, of which I was able to obtain a microfilm. It has no publication data, but appears to have been printed for use in China as the pages are numbered on the right side in Chinese characters. It is referred to in abbreviated form as "Berkeley".

The following emendations are a list of all corrections made to the Delhi edition – the text from which the translation was made – plus indication of points where the Berkeley text differs in a significant way from the Delhi edition, but the Delhi edition was determined to be either the correct reading or an acceptable alternate reading. Numerous minor differences that have no effect on the meaning or translation are not noted.

Also, the outline headings in the Berkeley text are totally different from those in the Delhi edition in that the latter are by Jam-yang-shay-ba, whereas the compiler of the Berkeley edition says that he used Jam-yang-shay-ba's as a basis to write his own; accordingly no attempt has been made to note differences in the outlines.

In cases where the point of an emendation is to distinguish between Dzong-ka-ba's text and an added annotation, Dzong-ka-ba's text is transliterated in all capital letters and the annotation in small letters. In all other cases the transliteration is in small letters.

Introduction (Delhi, 138.4–150.3; Berkeley, 1–7a.2)

138.6 *bzhags* corrected to *bzhag pa* in accordance with Berkeley, 1a.5 (not actually translated here).

140.3 *mu stegs can rnams kyi* corrected to *mu stegs can rnams kyis* in accordance with Berkeley, 2b.6.

140.6 *mngon 'gyur ba mang* corrected to *mgnon 'gyur ba yang* in accordance with Berkeley, 3a.2.

140.6 *re zhig nyon mongs mngon gyur mgo non kyang*. Berkeley, 3a.4, reads *re zhig mngon gyur mgo gnon kyang*.

141.6 *tsam gyi* corrected to *tsam gyis* in accordance with Berkeley, 3b.2.

142.6 *'gro ba'i don byed* corrected to *'gro ba'i don med* in accordance with P5658, Vol.129, 180.4.4 (Peking *bstan 'gyur* edition of Nāgārjuna's *Precious Garland*).

142.6 *de bzhin du* corrected to *me bzhin du* in accordance with Berkeley, 3b.6, and P5658, Vol.129, 180.4.5.

142.6 *gnas med lan med* corrected to *gnas med len med* in accordance with Berkeley, 3b.6, and P5658, Vol.129, 180.4.5.

142.6 *thams cad pa'i* corrected to *thog med pa'i* in accordance with Berkeley, 3b.6, and the Pleasure of Elegant Sayings Printing Press, Sarnath, 1974 edition of Dharmakīrti's *Pramāṇavārttika*, 68.20–69.2.

143.1 *bsams pa la* corrected to *bsam pa la* in accordance with Berkeley, 4a.1, and Tokyo *sde dge* Vol.8, 142b.2 (Toh 3865, Chandrakīrti's *Commentary on (Aryadeva's) "Four Hundred"*).

143.2 *'das pa 'thob la* corrected to *'das pa thob la* in accordance with Berkeley, 4a.2, and Tokyo *sde dge* Vol.8, 142b.3.

143.5 *sgom rim du'ang*. Berkeley, 4a.5, reads *sgom rim du yang*. However, both the Dharmsala and Dra-shi-hlun-bo editions of Dzong-ka-ba's text read *'ang*.

144.1 *tshad med pa*. Berkeley, 4a.7, reads *tshad med bzhi*.

144.4 *phung por 'dzin*. Berkeley, 4b.3, reads *phung po 'dzin*. Reading in Delhi is supported by P5658, Vol.129, 174.3.6.

144.6 *zhes pa phal po che'i mdo yin gsungs*, identified in Delhi as by Dra-di Ge-shay, is identified as commentary by Ba-so in Berkeley, 4b.6. Delhi reading preferred.

145.5 *cung zad thob pa'i nga rgyal* corrected to *cung zas thob pas nga rgyal* in accordance with Berkeley, 5a.3.

145.6 *bsten* corrected to *brten*.

147.6 *gang zag de* corrected to *gang zag des* in accordance with Berkeley, 6a.2.

148.4 *'dra ba de 'ang*. Berkeley, 6a.5, reads *'dra ba de yang*, and *yang* occurs in Toh 3916, Tokyo *sde dge* Vol.15, 48a.6 (Kamalashīla's *Middle Stages of Meditation*). However, both editions of Dzong-ka-ba read *'ang* (366b.4 and 116.5, respectively).

148.6 *ste bdag med rtogs pa'i lhag mthong sgom par bya'o*. Berkeley, 6b.2, identifies this commentary as being by Ba-so.

149.1 *shes rab de med par*. Berkeley, 6b.1, identifies this commentary as by Dra-di Ge-shay.

149.2 Delhi reads *gnyis kyis stongs pa*. Berkeley, 6b.2, reads *nyid kyis stong pa*, as does Kamalashīla, Toh 3916, Vol.15, 48a.7. However, the Dharmsala edition of Dzong-ka-ba's text, 366b.6, reads *gnyis kyis stong pa*, and the Dra-shi-hlun-bo edition, 117.1, reads *gnyis kyis stongs pa*.

149.2–3 Berkeley, 6b.2–3, treats Jam-yang-shay-ba's outline heading as though it were commentary by Dra-di Ge-shay.

150.3 *ston pa ste gnas par*. In the Delhi text this appears to be all commentary by Ba-so. Berkeley, 7a.2 and 7a.3, identifies these as two different commentaries, *ston pa*, by Jam-yang-shay-ba, and *ste gnas par* by Ba-so. Read as two commentaries, the passage is far more sensible.

Chapter One (Delhi, 150.3–165.2; Berkeley, 7a.2–13b.2)

150.6 Delhi reads *mnyan*; Berkeley corrects this to *nyan*. However, both editions of Dzong-ka-ba read *mnyan*.

151.2 *thag chod pa'i phu thag chod par* corrected to *thag chod pa'i tshe phu thag chod par* in accordance with Berkeley, 7b.1. This accords with the explanation of the term given in A-gya Yong-dzin's *A Brief Explanation of Terminology Occurring in (Dzong-ka-ba's) "Great Exposition of the Stages of the Path"*, 163.3–4, *lung pa de'i phu'am phugs thams cad du btsal nas ma rnyed par thag chod pa'i tshe/phu thag chod par btsal ba zhes bya la/*.

151.4 Delhi reads *'ang*. Berkeley reads *yang*. *'ang* is supported by both editions of Dzong-ka-ba (Dharmsala, 367a.6, Dra-shi-hlun-bo, 117.6).

152.2 Delhi identifies the line *'dis ni blun po dang mi mkhas pa'i rjes su 'brang na mi rung bar bshad pas gces par gyis* as commentary by Dra-di. Berkeley, 7b.6, identifies it as by Jam-yang-shay-ba. This seems correct as it is more his sort of commentary than Dra-di's.

152.4 *lung bstan pa la* corrected to *lung bstan pa* in accordance with Berkeley, 8a.2.

153.2 *de 'das nas* corrected to *nga 'das nas* in accordance with Berkeley, 8a.5 and the Peking edition of the tantra, P162, Vol.6, 259.3.8.

153.3 *zhes sogs dang*. Berkeley, 8a.6, reads *sogs dang*. Delhi reading preferred.

153.3 *bhai ta* tentatively changed to *be da* in accordance with the sūtra, P775, Vol.29, 74.3.7.

153.3 *de'i ming klu zhes 'bod* corrected to *de ming klu zhes 'bod* in accordance with Berkeley, 8a.7 and the sūtra, P775, Vol.29, 74.3.8.

153.4 *so so skye bos*. Berkeley, 8a.7, reads *so so skye*. Delhi reading preferred.

153.4 *thegs chen pa tshe der* corrected to *theg chen 'phags pa tshe der* in accordance with Berkeley, 8b.1.

153.5 *rnga bo che'i mdor*. Alternate reading in Berkeley, 8b.1, *rnga bo che'i mdo*.

153.6 *rtsa she'i ṭīk chen nas* corrected to *rtsa shes ṭīk chen las* in accordance with Berkeley, 8b.3.

154.1 *gnyis ka nas gsungs/zhes pa ltar ro* corrected to *gnyis kas gsungs pa ltar ro* in accordance with Berkeley, 8b.3.

155.1 *mdo'i drang don nges don dpyad skabs spyi'i don la zhes pa'i rjod don byed pa'i phyir te* corrected to *mdo'i drang don nges don dpyad skabs yin cing don zhes pa brjod don la byed pa'i phyir te* accordance with Berkeley, 9a.2–3. Also, in accordance with Berkeley, that commentary is to be identified as by Jam-yang-shay-ba.

155.4 *brdzun pa'i rang bzhin* corrected to *rdzun pa'i rang bzhin* in accordance with Berkeley, 9a.5.

155.4 *ste grub byed* added in between *ste kun rdzob bden pa/* and *gtso bor dngos su* as commentary by Jam-yang-shay-ba in accordance with Berkeley, 9a.5–6.

156.1 *BA'I sgo nas* should be all small letters.

156.2 *yin zhe na*. Berkeley text, 9b.2, reads *yin ce na*.

156.2 *gtan tshig sogs thabs kyi SGO NAS* corrected to *gtan tshig sogs kyi thabs kyi sgo nas* in accordance with Berkeley, 9b.3.

156.4 *bdag dang sems can sogs chos kyi dbyings la dbyer med*. Berkeley, 9b.5, reads *bdag sems can sogs chos kyi dbyings su dbyer med*.

156.6 Commentary by Nga-wang-rap-den located in Delhi following *de nyid las* is located later in Berkeley (10a.5) which would correspond to Delhi, 157.6, following *zhes bya ba'o*.

157.1 *ston pa rnams*. Berkeley, 10a.5, reads *stong pa*; Delhi reading preferred.

157.1 *don dam dang*. Berkeley, 10a.5, reads *don dam pa dang*.

157.2 *sems pa'i rtsol ba dang ldan pa* to be identified as commentary by Dra-di rather than Jam-yang-shay-ba in accordance with Berkeley, 10a.1.

157.2 *'tsho bas na* to be identified as commentary by Jam-yang-shay-ba rather than Ba-so in accordance with Berkeley, 10a.1.

157.4 *sgrub pa po yin las* corrected to *sgrub pa po yin pas* in accordance with Berkeley, 10a.3 (Berkeley mistakenly reads *sgrub po yin pas*).

159.2 *par bya dgos so*, identified in Delhi as all commentary by Ba-so, is to be identified as two distinct commentaries *par bya* by Ba-so and *dgos so* by Dra-di in accordance with Berkeley, 10b.7.

159.4 Commentary beginning with *brjod bya de dag* to be identified as by Nga-wang-rap-den in accordance with Berkeley, 11a.2.

159.4 *de dag dang don* corrected to *de dag drang don* in accordance with Berkeley, 11a.2.

160.2 *don dam par nges pa'i don* corrected to *don dam pa nges pa'i don* in accordance with Berkeley, 11a.6.

160.4 *rnams na* corrected to *rnams ni* in accordance with Berkeley, 11b.1 and the Dharmsala edition of Dzong-ka-ba's text, 368b.6.

161.3 After *ldan pa'i phyir ro* Berkeley, 11b.6–7, adds in the following commentary: *'di'i don gzhan du drang dgos mi dgos kyi dbang du byas nas drang nges 'jog pa na gsung rab nyid drang nges kyi mtshan gzhir gzung la gzhan du drang dgos mi dgos kyi don la drang nges su 'jog pa na kun rdzob dang don dam la drang nges su bya ba'o.*

161.6 After *zhes gsungs so* Berkeley, 12a.3, adds in the following commentary: *ji ltar bstan pa ltar gyi don yod med la drang nges su byed na tshad ma dang bcas pas chog kyang des mi chog pas don dam pa'i dbang du mdzad ba zhes gsungs so.*

162.2 *dgongs pa'i gtang sa* corrected to *dgongs pa'i gtad sa* in accordance with Berkeley, 12a.5.

163.2 *mdor skye ba med sogs* corrected to *mdor skye ba med pa sogs* in accordance with Berkeley, 12b.3.

163.5 Commentary beginning *de ltar nges don* to be identified as by Nga-wang-rap-den in accordance with Berkeley, 12b.6.

163.6 *bkag pa ni chos de yi de kho na nyid yin pas de ltar bstan pas*; Berkeley, 13a.1, reads: *bkag pa ni de kho na yid yin pas de bstan pas*. Delhi reading preferred.

164.2 *don dam pa'i khyad par sbyar ba de ma sbyar ba spyi la 'khyer dgos pa la khyad chos de mi sbyor bar tshig re re'i ngo gdong sgra ji bzhin du bzung du mi rung bas nges don min pa dang bzung du rung bas kyang nges don yin par mi 'gyur ro*; Berkeley, 13a.2–3, reads: *don dam pa'i khyad bar sbyar ba'i spyi la 'khyer dgos pa'i khyad chos ma sbyor bar tshig re re'i ngo gdong sgra ji bzhin du bzung du mi rung bas nges don min pa dang/rung bas kyang drang don min par mi 'gyur ro*. Delhi reading preferred.

164.3 *grub pa'i khyad par* corrected to *grub pas khyad par* in accordance with Berkeley, 13a.4.

164.6 *khol 'don byas nas DE* corrected to *khol 'don byas nas de* in accordance with Berkeley, 13a.7, and the Dharmsala edition of Dzong-ka-ba's text, 369b.3.

165.1 *mi 'jog* corrected to *mi 'jig* in accordance with Berkeley, 13b.1, and the Dharmsala edition of Dzong-ka-ba's text, 369b.3.

Chapter Two (Delhi, 165.2–176.1; Berkeley, 13b.2–18a.5)

165.3 *mthar thug par gtso bor* corrected to *mthar thug pa gtso bor* in accordance with Berkeley, 13b.3.

165.4 *'GREL PAR rgyal ba nyid kyis lung bstan cing bsngags pa'i* corrected to *'GREL PAr rgyal ba nyid kyis lung bstan cing bsngags pa'I* in accordance with Dharmsala, 369b.5, and Berkeley, 13b.4.

167.4 Delhi omits commentary by Ba-so, *slob dpon dpa' po*, located in Berkeley on 14b.3 between *slob dpon kha cig* and *kyang 'dod do*.

168.1 *PHRA MO YOD PA RNAMS* corrected to *PHRA MO yod pa RNAMS* in accordance with Dharmsala, 370a.5, and Berkeley, 14b.5.

168.2 Berkeley, 14b.7, indicates the annotation *lo chen gyi springs yig bdud rtsi'i thigs pa las* to be by Ba-so and places it a bit later, following *bod snga rabs pa'i 'dod pa de 'dra ba ni* (end of 168.2 in Delhi text).

168.3 Berkeley, 15.3, indicates the annotation from 168.3–169.3 to be by Nga-wang-rap-den and places it later in the text – 170.4 in the Delhi edition, following *kun rdzob bden pa yin no*. Berkeley placement has been followed in the translation.

168.4 *'dod pa la lo chen*. Berkeley, 15b.3, reads *'dod pa lo chen*. Delhi reading preferred.

168.5 *rang rgyud pa dang gnyis pa*. Berkeley, 15b.4, reads *rang rgyud pa gnyis pa*. Delhi reading preferred.

168.6 *rjes dpag gis yul* corrected to *rjes dpag gi yul* in accordance with Berkeley, 15b.5.

168.6 *gzhal byar 'dod pa*. Berkeley, 15b.5, reads *gzhal bya 'dod pa*. Delhi reading preferred.

169.1 *bden grub bkag tsam*. Berkeley, 15b.6, reads *bden grub bkag pa tsam*. Delhi reading preferred.

169.2 *rnam par shar na* corrected to *rnam pa shar na* in accordance with Berkeley, 15b.7.

169.2 *mi snang na chos dang chos can* omitted from Berkeley, 15b.7. Delhi reading seems correct.

169.4 *de 'dir*. Berkeley, 15a.2, has same reading for this verse from Nāgārjuna's *Treatise on the Middle Way*; however, it should be corrected to *de ni* in accordance with the Pleasure of Elegant Sayings edition of Nāgārjuna's text, 47.6 and the Sanskrit, La Vallée Poussin's edition, 372.13.

169.5 Berkeley, 15a.3, adds in *sna rabs pa'i* at beginning of Baso commentary *sgyu ma rigs grub pa des*.

170.2 *gcig tsam dang bral dang* corrected to *gcig tsam dang bral bas* in accordance with Berkeley, 15a.5.

170.3 *rtog bral dang bcas*. Berkeley, 15a.6, reads *rtog bral dang rtog bcas*.

170.3–4 *la ni rnam* corrected to *la rnam* in accordance with Berkeley, 15a.7.

170.4 *yin de* corrected to *yin pas de* in accordance with Berkeley, 15a.7.

170.4 Commentary from *snang ba la* through to *dbu ma par smra ba* to be identified as commentary by Ba-so rather than Nga-wang-rap-den in accordance with Berkeley, 15b.2.

170.4 *snga rabs pas don dam*. Berkeley, 15b.1, mistakenly omits *pas*.

170.5 *rnam bcad yongs gcod*. Berkeley, 15b.1, reads *rnam bcad dang yongs gcod*.

170.5 *don tsam don dam*. Berkeley, 15b.2, reads *don de tsam ni don dam*.

171.2 *gnyis bstan pa* and *gnyis mi bstan* corrected to *gnyis brten pa* and *gnyis mi brten*, respectively, in accordance with Berkeley, 16a.5. This spelling also found in Hahn, ed. *Nāgārjuna's Ratnāvalī*, pp.129–31.

171.2 *'khu 'phrig*. Berkeley, 16a.5, reads *khu 'khrig*; Hahn, 131, shows readings of *khu 'phrigs* and *khu 'khrig*.

171.5 *legs ldan 'byed kyis de ltar rnam par bzhag pa'i rjes* omitted from Berkeley, 16b.1.

172.2 Commentary from *la phyi don 'dod pa'i dbu ma* through to *mi rung bar bstan* to be taken as commentary by Jam-yang-shay-ba rather than by Nga-wang-rap-den in accordance with Berkeley, 16b.4.

172.2 *grol sde gnyis* corrected to *grol sde de gnyis* in accordance with Berkeley, 16b.4.

172.6 Prior to the outline heading *snga pa*, Berkeley, 17a.1–2, adds the following commentary, identified as being by Nga-wang-rap-den: *slob dpon legs ldan 'byed phyi don bzhed pa mdo sde pa dang gnad gcig tu yod kyang dpal ldan zla ba ni phyi don yod ces pa'i tshig tsam 'dra yang mdo sde pa dang bye brag smra ba su dang yang don mi gcig go*.

173.5 Commentary from *dgongs 'grel* . . . through to *nges pa min no* to be identified as by Nga-wang-rap-den in accordance with Berkeley, 17b.1.

173.6 Commentary from *sgyu ma rigs* . . . to *mi 'thad do* on 174.2 to be placed, in accordance with Berkeley, 16a.1, at 169.3 and identified as by Nga-wang-rap-den.

174.1 *bcad tsam don dam bden par 'dod*. Berkeley, 16a.2, reads *bcad tsam du 'dod*. Delhi reading preferred.

174.1 *mi gnas par smra ba'o zhes*. Berkeley, 16a.2, reads *mi gnas pa zhes*. Delhi reading preferred.

174.2 *med par bzung ba spros pa*. Berkeley, 16a.2, reads *med par bzung bas spros pa*. Delhi reading preferred.

174.2 *byed la mi 'thad* corrected to *byed pa mi 'thad* in accordance with Berkeley, 16a.2.

Chapter Three (Delhi: *176.1–197.5*; Berkeley: *18a.5–28a.7*)

176.6 *shes sgrib yin pa* corrected to *shes sgrib yin pas* in accordance with Berkeley, 18b.4.

177.2 *theg chen skabs* to be identified as commentary by Jam-yang-shay-ba in accordance with Berkeley, 18b.5.

177.2 *'bras bu de kho na nyid* corrected to *'bras bu'i de kho na nyid* in accordance with Berkeley, 18b.6.

177.3 *rgyu chags sogs skyon* corrected to *rgyu chags sogs dang skyon* in accordance with Berkeley, 18b.7.

177.4 *nyes skyon de la yid* corrected to *nyes skyon de las yid* in accordance with Berkeley, 19a.1.

177.6 *'khor ba sdug bsngal* corrected to *'khor bar sdug bsngal* in accordance with Berkeley, 19a.3.

178.6 *yin pa de nyid* corrected to *yin la de nyid* in accordance with Berkeley, 19b.4.

179.1 *be'u 'dogs pa'i phur pa'i rtsa dpes*. Berkeley, 19b.5, reads *ba 'das phur pa'i rtsa'i dpes*.

179.4 *snang ba 'di dag* corrected to *'di dag* in accordance with Berkeley, 20a.1.

179.6 *la sogs dngos por*. Berkeley, 20a.2, reads *la sogs pa'i dngos por*.

180.2 *'i tshul de* to be identified as commentary by Ba-so in accordance with Berkeley, 20b.6.

180.5 *thob bya mthar thug dang bsgom bya'i*. Berkeley, 20b.1, identifies this as commentary by Jam-yang-shay-ba; Delhi identification as commentary by Ba-so is probably correct.

181.2 *des bdag* corrected to *des rang gi ngo bo nyid kyi bdag* in accordance with Berkeley, 20b.4.

181.3 *RTOGS pa BYAS* corrected to *RTOGS par BYAS*, commentary by both Ba-so and Nga-wang-rap-den, in accordance with Berkeley, 20b.5 and .6.

181.4 *zhi lhag zung 'brel gyi* to be identified as commentary by Jam-yang-shay-ba in accordance with Berkeley, 20b.5.

182.1 *'dra ba lta bu* to be identified as separate commentaries, *'dra ba* and *lta bu*, by Ba-so and Dra-di respectively in accordance with Berkeley, 21a.2.

182.2 *'khor ba de na* corrected to *'khor ba de ni* in accordance with Berkeley, 21a.4.

182.2 *las byung ba de* to be identified as commentary by Dra-di rather than by Ba-so in accordance with Berkeley, 21b.4.

182.3 *su la ji lta bu* corrected to *yul ji lta bu* in accordance with Berkeley, 21a.4.

183.2 *ngo bo nyid kyis grub ma grub ci 'dra ba* to be identified as commentary by Ba-so rather than by Jam-yang-shay-ba in accordance with Berkeley, 21b.4.

183.3 Commentary by Nga-wang-rap-den through 183.4 to be placed later, at 184.6, in accordance with Berkeley, 21b.7.

183.4 Commentary by Nga-wang-rap-den through 184.2 to be placed later, at 186.5, in accordance with Berkeley, 22b.6.

184.1 *phyir/bdag* corrected to *phyir te/bdag* in accordance with Berkeley, 23a.2.

184.2 *'gyur te/* corrected to *'gyur pa'i phyir* in accordance with Berkeley, 23a.3.

184.2 Commentary ending with *bzhin no* to be identified as by Nga-wang-rap-den rather than by Ba-so in accordance with Berkeley, 23a.3.

185.2 *theg chen las* corrected to *theg chen pas* in accordance with Berkeley, 22a.4.

185.4 *theg chen gyi gang zag ni bdag dang bdag gi ba rang bzhin gyis med par rtogs pa de tsam yang* to be identified as two separate commentaries – *theg chen gyi gang zag ni* by Jam-yang-shay-ba, and *bdag dang bdag gi ba rang bzhin gyis med par rtogs pa de tsam yang* by Dra-di, in accordance with Berkeley, 22a.5–6.

185.5 *dang po mi 'thad pa'i de 'dra'i dogs pa de'i* to be identified as two separate commentaries—*dang po mi 'thad pa'i* by Ba-so, and *de 'dra'i dogs pa de'i* by Dra-di, in accordance with Berkeley, 22a.7.

186.2 Commentary from *bdag dang bdag* through to *mi 'grub pa'i phyir* should be deleted. It is not found in Berkeley, 22b.2, and repeats commentary by Nga-wang-rap-den found on 184.1.

186.2 *gnyis pa 'jug tshul mi 'thad pa'i skyon med de* placed on 186.3, after the outline headings, in accordance with Berkeley, 22b.4.

186.3 *bdag gi ba'i gdags gzhi* corrected to *bdag gi bdag bzhi* in accordance with sense and the material in the section it heads.

187.1 *nye ba la blang bya* corrected to *nye bar blang bya* in accordance with Berkeley, 23a.7.

187.2 *nye bar byed pa* corrected to *nye bar bya ba* in accordance with Berkeley, 23a.7.

187.2 After *phung po'i mtshan nyid* and before *ste phung po*, the Berkeley compiler, 23a.7, adds the commentary *de rang bzhin gcig tu*.

187.3 After *mtshan nyid med* and before *pa zhig*, the Berkeley compiler, 23b.1, adds in the commentary *dam rang bzhin las gzhan pa*.

189.2 *bden par grub mtha'i dbang gi bden* which was identified as all commentary by Ba-so in Delhi corrected to three separate commentaries in accordance with Berkeley, 24 a.6–7: *bden par* by Ba-so, *grub mtha'i dbang gis* by Nga-wang-rap-den, and *bden par* by Jam-yang-shay-ba.

190.1 *skyon yod pa nges na* corrected to *skyon yod pa des na* in accordance with Berkeley, 24b.4.

190.6 *phung por rang bzhin* corrected to *phung po rang bzhin* in accordance with Berkeley, 25a.3, and the Dharmsala and Dra-shi-hlun-bo editions of Dzong-ka-ba, 373b.5 and 129.6 respectively.

191.2 *sgra mi rtag par bsgrub* changed to *sgra mi rtag pa sgrub* which accords with Berkeley, 25a.5, and follows the way Dzong-ka-ba himself wrote it in his *Ocean of Reasoning, Explanation of (Nāgārjuna's) "Treatise on the Middle Way"* (the *rje gsung dbu ma'i lta ba'i skor* edition, 504.1). However, it should be noted that the Delhi reading is preferable in terms of meaning.

191.2 *tshad ma snga mas shugs* changed to *tshad ma snga ma'i shugs* which accords with Berkeley, 25a.5, and follows the way Dzong-ka-ba himself wrote it in his *Ocean of Reasoning, Explanation of (Nāgārjuna's) "Treatise on the Middle Way"* (the *rje gsung dbu ma'i lta ba'i skor* edition, 504.4). However, it should be noted that the Delhi reading is preferable.

191.5 *sgro 'dog bcad* corrected to *sgro 'dogs bcad* in accordance with Berkeley, 25b.1.

191.6 *don gyi sde shugs kyi* corrected to *don gyis de shugs kyis* in accordance with Berkeley, 25b.2.

192.1 *rtsal du ston nas* to be corrected to *rtsal du bton nas* in accordance with Berkeley, 25b.3. In accordance with Berkeley, 25b.3–25b.7, the commentary only to this point is to be identified as by Jam-yang-shay-ba; the following commentary up to 192.5 to be identified as by Nga-wang-rap-den.

192.1 *des pa* to be corrected to *nges pa* in accordance with Berkeley, 25b.3.

192.3 *gang gi dngos* to be corrected to *gang gis dngos* in accordance with Berkeley, 25b.6.

192.5 *ngag rab kyi mchan las* to be deleted and entire passage taken as commentary by Nga-wang-rap-den rather than by Jam-yang-shay-ba in accordance with Berkeley, 25b.7.

193.5 Outline heading to be placed before *de la lan 'di skad brjod par bya sde* in accordance with Berkeley, 26a.7.

194.1 Between *'gyur ro* and *gsum pa ni* the Berkeley compiler adds his own commentary: *nyan thos sde pas rdul phra rab du ma bsags pa'i tshogs spyi yin pas rdzas su med par 'dod pa dang rten gcig la yod pa'am rigs gcig pa'i rdul rnams bsags pa'i bum pa lta bu rdzas yod dang rigs tha dad pa'am rten tha dad pa'i tshogs 'dus pa nags tshal lta bu btags yod du slob dpon legs ldan bzhed don gzhan la ma ltos par rang nyid bzung du yod pa tshugs thub pa kun gzhi sogs dang yul can sgra rtog la ma ltos par rang nyid mngon sum du rtogs byar yod pa'i tshugs thub bzugs sgra sogs don gzhan la ma ltos par rang gi ngo bo bzung du med pas tshugs mi thub pa gang zag lta bu dang yul can sgra rtog gang la ma brten par mngon sum du rtogs byar med pa'am mi thub pa gang rung gis bsdus pa'i chos de btags yod kyi mtshan nyid lta bu'o.*

194.5 *dngos smra ba* corrected to *dngos smra bas* in accordance with Berkeley, 27a.2.

195.1 *bzhag pa na yin pa bkag gi/* Berkeley, 27a.5, reads *bzhag pa ma yin pa bkag pa'i.* Delhi reading preferred.

195.1 Commentary by Nga-wang-rap-den from 196.6 to 197.5 – *kho na re* through to *mi 'thad par thal lo* – placed between *bden med do/* and *gnyis pa grub mtha'* in accordance with Berkeley, 27a.5.

195.4 *rigs pa dang rgyun* corrected to *rags pa dang rgyun* in accordance with Berkeley, 27b.5.

195.4 Between *de rnams* and *dbu ma pas gzhal na* the Berkeley compiler adds his own commentary, 27b.5: *yul steng nas 'jog pas de.*

195.5 Between *de dag gis* and *don dam par grub* the Berkeley compiler adds his own commentary, 27b.6: *gzhan dbang sogs.*

195.6 Instead of *pa la nges par dbu ma snang ba sogs las shes par bya'o* Berkeley, 28a.1, reads: *pa la der dbu ma snang ba dgos pas shes par bya'o.* Delhi reading preferred.

196.1 Between *slob dpon* and *'di'i* Berkeley, 28a.2, adds as commentary by Dra-di *sangs rgyas bskyangs.*

196.3 *dngos shugs dang stobs shugs gang rung la.* Berkeley, 28a.4, reads *dngos shugs gang rung la.* Delhi reading preferred.

196.4 *ma bor* corrected to *ma dor* in accordance with Berkeley, 28a.5.

196.4 *mdor ba'i bar* corrected to *ma dor ba'i bar* in accordance with Berkeley, 28a.5 and the Dharmsala edition of Dzong-ka-ba, 374b.4.

196.6 Text from *kho na re* through to *mi 'thad par thal lo*, 197.5, placed earlier, at 195.1, in accordance with Berkeley, 27a.5.

197.1 *grub par 'dod* corrected to *grub pa mi 'dod* in accordance with Berkeley, 27a.6.

197.1–2 *rang bzhin med pas rtogs* corrected to *rang bzhin med par rtogs* in accordance with Berkeley, 27a.7.

197.2 *des de dag btags yod* corrected to *des rags pa btags yod* in accordance with Berkeley, 27a.7.

197.4 *de'i tshogs pa dang* corrected to *des tshogs pa dang* in accordance with Berkeley, 27b.2.

Chapter Four (Delhi: 197.5–206.2; Berkeley: 28a.7–32a.5)

199.2 *nges dngos po* corrected to *des dngos po* in accordance with Berkeley, 29a.3. Also *des* is to be identified as commentary by Dra-di rather than Jam-yang-shay-ba.

200.1–201.2 moved to 206.2 after *byed do* and before *gong gi sa bcad* in accordance with Berkeley, 30a.1 and 31b.5. Also this is to be identified as commentary by Nga-wang-rap-den, not Jam-yang-shay-ba and Ba-so.

200.2 *rigs pa des* corrected to *rigs shes kyis* in accordance with Berkeley, 31b.6.

204.1 and twice on 204.2 *rang bzhin gyis skye ba* corrected to *skye ba* in accordance with Berkeley, 30b.5 and 30b.6; qualified by *rang bzhin gyis*, it would be stating the "correct" Prāsaṅgika position but at this juncture the assertions of the opponent are being set forth.

204.3 *'dus pa ni* corrected to *'dus pa na* in accordance with Berkeley, 30b.7.

205.2–3 To be identified as commentary by Nga-wang-rap-den rather than by Jam-yang-shay-ba and Ba-so.

206.2 *mgrin pa gsal* corrected to *mgrin pa bsal* in accordance with both editions of Dzong-ka-ba (Dharmsala, 376b.2; Dra-shi-hlun-bo, 135.1) and Berkeley, 31b.4.

Chapter Five (*Delhi:* 206.2–220.3; *Berkeley:* 32a.5–39a.1)

206.5–207.5 Commentary from *de 'gog pa'i* through to *yang song ba'i phyir* to be identified as all by Nga-wang-rap-den in accordance with Berkeley, 33b.7 and 45b.7. Also it should be noted that Berkeley places this commentary much later; the first portion, from *de 'gog pa'i* through to *dka' ba yin no*, 207.2, is placed in Berkeley at 33b.7; corresponding in Delhi to 210.5, just before the outline heading *gnyis pa*. The second portion, from 207.2 through to 207.5 is placed in the Berkeley text at 45b.7, corresponding in the Delhi text to 235.4, just before the outline heading *gnyis pa*.

207.3 *tha dad pa gnyis* corrected to *'thad pa gnyis* in accordance with Berkeley, 46a.2.

207.3 *lugs gnyis bkag* corrected to *lugs bkag* in accordance with Berkeley, 46a.2.

207.4 *med par 'dod dgos* corrected to *med dgos* in accordance with Berkeley, 46a.3.

207.4 *smras pa skye* corrected to *smras pas skye* in accordance with Berkeley, 46a.3.

208.1 *chos sku dam pa gzugs sku* corrected to *chos sku dam pa dang gzugs sku* in accordance with Berkeley, 32b.5, and the Dharmsala edition of Dzong-ka-ba's text, 376b.5.

208.5 *'dren thub pa'i 'drongs* corrected to *'dren thub pa'am 'drongs* in accordance with Berkeley, 33a.2.

211.1 *de rnams kyis bsams tshod* corrected to *de rnams kyi bsams tshod* in accordance with Berkeley, 34a.5.

211.4 *bzhags med* (end of line) corrected to *bhzag sa med* in accordance with Berkeley, 34b.2.

212.2 *go chod* corrected to *go tshod* based on sense.

212.6–213.1 *nyid smra ba'i lugs* to be identified as commentary by Ba-so in accordance with Berkeley, 35a.6.

214.6 *gzhin byas pa* corrected to *gzhir byas pa* in accordance with Berkeley, 36a.5.

215.4 *rang bzhin gyis stong pa go dgos kyi stong nyid yin par ga la go*. Berkeley, 36b.3, reads: *rang bzhin gyis stong pa go dgos kyi stong pa min par ga la go*. Delhi reading preferred.

215.4 *go la de ltar*. The break between commentary by Ba-so and by Dra-di Ge-shay comes after *go* rather than after *la* in accordance with Berkeley, 36b.2.

216.5 *gsum na* corrected to *gsum ni* in accordance with Berkeley, 37a.4.

217.5 *zhi gnas* corrected to *zhig nas* in accordance with Berkeley, 37b.4.

218.2 *zhi gnas* corrected to *zhig nas* in accordance with Berkeley, 37b.6.

218.2 *te 'gyur la/* to be identified as commentary by Ba-so in accordance with Berkeley 37b.7.

218.3 *ma tshol ba* corrected to *ma 'chol ba* in accordance with Berkeley, 38a.1.

218.4 *ste rang bzhin yod pa kyang*. Rather than all being commentary by Ba-so as identified in Berkeley, *ste rang bhzin yod pa* is to be identified as commentary by Ba-so and *kyang* as commentary by Dra-di in accordance with Berkeley, 38a.2.

218.6 Add in *gcer pa pas* before *de lta bu'i bdag gzhan* in accordance with Berkeley, 38a.5.

219.3 *dngos pos rgyu* corrected to *dngos po rgyu* in accordance with Berkeley, 38b.1.

219.4 *mi zad pa dang ldan pa'i* corrected to *mi bzod pa dang ldan pa'i* in accordance with Berkeley, 38b.1.

Chapter Six (Delhi: 220.3–240.6; Berkeley: 39a.1–48b.5)

220.6 *rgyu mtshan des* omitted by Berkeley, 39a.4; the Delhi reading is preferred.

221.3 *rten 'brel 'thad na kun 'byung sogs 'thad ces so* to be identified as commentary by Nga-wang-rap-den rather than by Ba-so in accordance with Berkeley, 39a.5.

221.3 *rgyu rkyen la brten nas 'byung ba* omitted by Berkeley, 39a.6; the Delhi reading is preferred.

221.4 *'gag* corrected to *'gog* in accordance with Berkeley, 39a.7.

225.4 *nged dbu ma pa'i skabs*; Berkeley, 41a.6, reads *nged dbu ma pas skabs*. The Delhi reading is preferred.

226.6 Commentary from *des na nged kyi* through to *pa bzhin no*, 227.3, to be placed on 227.6 just before *bzhi pa* in accordance with Berkeley, 42a.5.

227.1 *des rgyu* corrected to *des na rgyu* in accordance with Berkeley, 42a.5.

229.6 Berkeley, 43a.5, adds the following commentary, identified as by Jam-yang-shay-ba, after *brtson par bya'o* and before *zhes 'doms so: don 'di ni tsha kho dpon por gdams pa las/ snang ba rten 'brel bslu ba med pa dang/ stong pa khas len 'brel pa'i go ba gnyis/ ji srid so sor snang ba de srid du/ da dung thub pa'i dgongs pa rtogs pa med/ ces gsungs so/.*

229.6–230.1 Berkeley, 43a.6–7, places the commentary from *rang re'i bla ma* through to *dpyad gsung* before the outline heading *drug pa* and identifies the commentary as being by Nga-wang-rap-den rather than by Jam-yang-shay-ba. Stylistically it could be by either.

230.2 *ma 'gal bar* corrected to *mi 'gal bar* in accordance with Berkeley, 43a.7.

230.6–231.1 Commentary *kyis gang zhing mi gtsang ba rgyun du 'dzag pa gzugs can yin pas* to be identified as by Ba-so in accordance with Berkeley, 44a.2.

231.1 *rtogs sla ba*; Berkeley, 44a.2, reads *rtogs par sla ba*.

231.2 *shin tu rmongs pas bsgribs te mi gtsang ba'i rang bzhin du nges pa'i nges pa* to be identified as commentary by Dra-di Ge-shay and *mi rtag sdug bsngal sogs* as commentary by Ba-so in accordance with Berkeley, 43b.4–5 and 44a.2. Also, Berkeley adds the syllable *su* to the Ba-so commentary, so that the commentary reads: *mi rtag sdug bsngal sogs su*.

231.2–3 In Berkeley, 44a.3, the commentary *stong pa nyid de ltar go dka' 'am zhe na shes bya chos can/ snod min gyis ches rtogs par dga' ba nges par lags pa'i gnas* comes after the commentary *ste de'i phyir re zhig rags pa'ang rtogs par mi nus na phra ba rtogs par dka' ba lta ci smos zhes pa'o*. Either reading is acceptable; the translation follows Delhi.

231.6 *ste mi 'gyur la*. Berkeley, 44a.4, reads *ste mi 'gyur bar thal*. Either reading is acceptable.

232.3 *pha'i tshul* corrected to *pa'i tshul* in accordance with Berkeley, 44a.7.

233.4 *rigs pa s dpyod lugs*. Berkeley, 45a.1, reads *rigs pa 'i dpyod lugs*. The Delhi reading is preferred.

233.5 *de 'dra ba ni* corrected to *de 'dra bas ni* in accordance with Berkeley, 45a.2.

233.4 *rigs pas dpyod lugs*. Berkeley, 45a.1, reads *rigs pa'i* Berkeley, 45a.7–45b.2 adds the following commentary, identified as by Dra-di Ge-shay:

tsha kho dpon po ngag dbang grags pa la gdams pa las/ nam zhig res 'jog med par cig car du/ /rten 'brel mi blsur mthong ba tsam nyid nas/ /nges shes yul gyi 'dzin stangs kun 'jig na/ /de'i tshe lta ba'i dpyad pa rdzogs pa lags/ /zhes gsungs pa'i phyir dang/ tshig gsal dang bu ddha pā li ta bnyis las/ rgyang phan gyis skye ba snga phyi rang bzhin med par 'dzin pa stong nyid ma rtogs par bshad pa lta bu yin te/ tha snyad 'jog mi shes na chad mtha' las mi 'grol ba'i phyir dang/ mtha' gnyis ma khegs bar du dbu ma'i lta ba'i lam mi rnyed pa'i phyir dang/ lta ba de'i ngor tha snyad med kyang ming tsam la tha snyad 'thad tshul rtogs dgos par sngar yang bshad pa'i phyir/ byang chub bla ma'i dris lan las/ rten 'byung rgyu 'bras mi bslu ba la nges pa rnyed pas chad lta 'gog cing mtshan mar 'dzin pa'i dmigs gtad rdul tsam yang ma grub pa'i rang bzhin med pa'i stong nyid la nges pa rnyed pas rtag mtha' las grol ba'i phyir ro/ des na ngo bo nyid kyis stong bzhin du rgyu 'bras mi bslu ba'i nges pa rnyed pa'i lta ba ni rtag chad gnyis ka'i gol sa chod pa yin pas rmad du byung ba'i go ba yin no/ zhes gsungs so/

Based on stylistic considerations, this is probably commentary by Jam-yang-shay-ba.

235.4 The Berkeley text, 45b.7–46a.3, places here, before

the outline heading *gnyis pa*, material which the Delhi text placed much earlier, from 207.2–5 – from *de yang dbu ma pas ni* through to *yang song ba'i phyir*.

236.2 *gang yang bzhag pa med pas*. Berkeley, 46b.1, reads *gang yang bzhag sa med pas*. Either reading is acceptable although the latter mirrors such statements by Dzong-ka-ba.

236.3 Before the outline heading *gsum pa* the Berkeley compiler, 46b.2–3, adds the following commentary: *tha snyad du bcing grol sogs bkag pa yin te/ tha snyad du rang mtshan 'gag pa gang zhig rang mtshan 'gog pa'i rigs pas bcings grol sogs 'gog par 'dod pa'i phyir/*.

236.5 *'thad pa ni tha snyad*. Berkeley, 46b.5, reads *'thad pa'i tha snyad*. The Delhi reading is preferred.

237.3 After *de 'gog na* and before *ni rang* the Berkeley compiler, 47a.3–4, adds the following commentary: *rang bzhin dang rgyu 'bras bnyis med mnyam du 'dod pas*.

237.5 *'di ltar dngos sogs gang*. Berkeley, 47a.5, reads *'di ltar dngos po gang*. Either reading is acceptable.

237.6 *THAL BAR 'GYUR RO* corrected to *THAL BAR 'GYUR* in accordance with the Dharmsala edition of Dzong-ka-ba's text, 383a.2, and the Berkeley text, 47a.6.

239.1 *GANG YANG* corrected to *GANG DU YANG* in accordance with the Dharmsala edition of Dzong-ka-ba's text, 383a.4, and the Berkeley text, 47b.6.

239.4 *ste brdzun pa ni dngos po brdzun pa'o*. *ste brdzun pa* is to be identified as commentary by Ba-so, the remainder as by Dra-di in accordance with Berkeley, 48a.3.

239.5 *brag phug las sgra 'byung* corrected to *brag phug dang sgra 'byung* in accordance with Berkeley, 48a.5.

240.1 *yang nges stong* corrected to *yang des stong* in accordance with Berkeley, 48a.7.

240.2 *gzugs brnyan las brdzun*. Berkeley, 48b.2, reads: *gzugs brnyan la rdzun*. The Delhi reading is preferred.

Chapter Seven (Delhi: 240.6–275.2; Berkeley: 48b.5–64a.1)

241.1 *dbu ma pa don la gnas pas lan*. Berkeley, 48b.6, reads *dbu ma pas don la gnas pa'i lan*. Either reading acceptable.

241.6 *'i lugs dbu ma pa*. In accordance with Berkeley, 49a.3, to be read as two separate commentaries, *'i lugs*, by Dra-di Ge-shay, and *dbu ma ba* by Ba-so rather than as all one commentary by Ba-so.

241.6 *bsgyur* corrected to *sgyur* in accordance with La Vallée Poussin's citation of the Tibetan, 502, note 2, and the Berkeley text, 49a.3.

242.2 *RKYEN MED skyes pa nyid du rtsod PAR po* corrected to *RKYEN MED PAR skyes pa nyid du rtsod pa po* in accordance with Berkeley, 49a.6.

242.3 *rigs par 'gyur*. Berkeley text, 49a.7, reads: *rig par 'gyur*. Delhi reading preferred.

242.3 *dngos smra ba khyod*. Berkeley text, 49a.7, reads: *yang dngos smra ba khod kyis* and identifies the commentary as by Ba-so rather than by Jam-yang-shay-ba as identified in the Delhi text. Either reading acceptable.

242.3 *rtsod por khyod* corrected to *rtsod pa po khyod* in accordance with Berkeley, 49a.7.

243.1 *de ma byed pa* corrected to *de ma phyed pa* in accordance with Berkeley, 49b.4.

243.3 *'gogs* corrected to *'gegs* in accordance with Berkeley, 49b.6, and the Dharmsala edition of Dzong-ka-ba's text, 384a.2.

243.6 *des na dbu ma par mi rung ba'i phyir TE* corrected to *TE/ des na dbu ma par mi rung ba'i phyir* in accordance with Berkeley, 50a.2.

244.3–244.5 Commentary from *bzhi brgya pa'i 'grel pa'i don ni* through to *dgongs pa dang 'dra'o* identified by Berkeley, 50a.6, as commentary by Nga-wang-rap-den rather than by Ba-so as identified in the Delhi text. It could be by either but seems more in the style of Nga-wang-rap-den. Also Berkeley places the commentary after the phrase by Dzong-ka-ba *ZHES GSAL BAR*

GSUNGS PA'I PHYIR (Delhi, 244.4) rather than just before it as located in the Delhi text; the Berkeley placement is better.

244.6 *rigs pa'i bshad pa* corrected to *rigs pas bshad pa* based on sense.

245.4 *BYAS* corrected to *BYA SA* in accordance with Berkeley, 50b.5 and the Dra-shi-lhun-bo edition of Dzong-ka-ba's text, 151.1.

246.2 *rtsod pa na* corrected to *rtsod pa ni*.

246.6 *zhe na de yi lan* omitted from Berkeley, 51a.5. It seems completely redundant.

247.3 *zhes smra zhing ZHES* corrected to *ZHES smra zhing* in accordance with Berkeley, 51b.1.

247.4 Berkeley, 51b.1 and 51b.2, omits both bits of commentary by Ba-so: *kho na re* and *rgyus 'bras bu skyed pa sogs*. Delhi reading preferred.

247.4 *skye 'gag sogs kyis bya* corrected to *skye 'gag sogs kyi bya* in accordance with Berkeley, 51b.2.

247.5 *ma nus par* corrected to *mi nus par* in accordance with Berkeley, 51b.2.

248.1 *MTHOD PA'I PHYIR* corrected to *MTHONG PA'I PHYIR* in accordance with both editions of Dzong-ka-ba's text, the Berkeley *Annotations* and the Dharmsala edition of Chandrakīrti's text.

249.1 *bod kyi* corrected to *bod kyis* in accordance with sense.

252.1 The commentary by Jam-yang-shay-ba, *de'i don gnyis las yod mtha' sel ba*, is omitted in the Berkeley text, 53b.1, and occurs in somewhat altered form a bit below, Berkeley, 53b.2, which would still fall on 252.1 of the Delhi text, after *DON can DANG* and before *chad mtha' sel*. The Berkeley text reads: *zhes pas yod mtha' sel la*. Either reading acceptable.

252.1 *chad mtha' sel ba* to be identified as commentary by Jam-yang-shay-ba rather than by Dra-di Ge-shay in accordance with Berkeley, 53b.2. Also, Berkeley reads *chad mtha' sel ba ni*.

252.6 Berkeley, 53b.6–7, makes clear that the commentary *dngos po'i skad dod bhā va don du ma la 'jug pas 'di'i* is by Jam-yang-shay-ba and the commentary *'di dag gi skabs su dngos po yod pa dang dngos po med par bshad pa'i* is by Dra-di Ge-shay.

253.1 *BZHIN LA BYED DE* corrected to *BZHIN LA BYED PA* in accordance with Berkeley, 53b.7, and the Dharmsala edition of Dzong-ka-ba's text, 38b.2.

253.4 The Berkeley text, 54a.4, identifies the commentary from *dbu ma pas* through to *de yod dgos na* as by Ba-so rather than by Jam-yang-shay-ba as identified in the Delhi edition. Berkeley identification seems more plausible since most of the remaining commentary on the passage is by Ba-so and there is none by Jam-yang-shay-ba.

253.4 *rang bzhin gyis grub par bkag*. The Berkeley text, 54a.4, reads: *rang bzhin gyis grub pa bkag*. Delhi reading preferred.

254.1 *khyod kyis* corrected to *khyod kyi* in accordance with Berkeley, 54a.7.

254.1 *don dam* corrected to *don nam* in accordance with Berkeley, 54a.7.

254.1 *te yul*. Berkeley, 54a.7, places this commentary after *nyid LA* and before *yul can yang*. Delhi reading preferred.

255.2 *da lar gyi*. This commentary by Ba-so omitted in the Berkeley text, 54b.6. Delhi reading preferred.

255.2 *stan gyi lo thog* corrected to *ston gyi lo thog* in accordance with Berkeley, 54b.7.

255.2 *rtag mtha'*. Berkeley, 54b.7, identifies this as commentary by Ba-so rather than by Jam-yang-shay-ba as identified in the Delhi text. Delhi reading preferred given that earlier in the line there is the commentary *chad mtha'* attributed to Jam-yang-shay-ba.

255.3 *da ltar gyi dran pa'i dus su yod dgos pas*. In the Delhi text this is identified at the beginning of the passage as by Nga-wang-rap-den and at the end as by Jam-yang-shay-ba. Berkeley, 54b.7, identifies it as by Ba-so; Berkeley identification probably correct.

255.3 *da lta'ang de yod pa'i phyir*. The Berkeley text, 55a.2, reads: *de lta'ang de yod par*. Delhi reading preferred.

256.2 *gtan nas YE MED* corrected to *YE gtan nas MED* in accordance with Berkeley, 55a.6.

257.6 *don spyi mgo ba* corrected to *don spyi ma go ba* in accordance with Berkeley, 56a.4.

258.1 *gnyis pa gang yang* corrected to *gnyis po gang yang* in accordance with Berkeley, 56a.5.

258.1 *'dod pa na* corrected to *'dod pa ni* in accordance with Berkeley, 56a.5 and the Dharmsala edition of Dzong-ka-ba's text, 387a.4.

258.3 *da lta rang gzhan gnyis la don spyi ma shar ba mang du snang bas ngo shes bar gyis* to be identified as commentary by Jam-yang-shay-ba in accordance with Berkeley, 56a.7, rather than as by Nga-wang-rap-den and Dra-di Ge-shay as identified by the Delhi text.

258.4 *BZOS MED* corrected to *BZO SA MED* in accordance with Berkeley, 56b.1, and the Dra-shi-lhun-bo edition of Dzong-ka-ba's text, 156.4.

259.4 *mi bya ste dper na* corrected to *mi bya ste des na* in accordance with Berkeley, 57a.1.

259.4 *don la mi dpyod par gzhung gi tshig tsam gyis tshim par mi bya ste des na* to be identified as commentary by Dra-di Ge-shay in accordance with Berkeley, 57a.1, rather than Ba-so as identified in the Delhi text.

259.6 *dngos po yod med kyi don*. Berkeley text, 57a.3, reads: *dngos med kyi don*. Delhi reading preferred.

260.1 *dus nam gyi tshe yang*. Berkeley text, 57a.4, reads: *dus nam du yang*. Either reading acceptable.

260.2 *des ni rang bzhin* corrected to *de ni rang bzhin* in accordance with the Dharmsala edition of Dzong-ka-ba's text, 387b.4, and the Dharmsala edition of Chandrakīrti's *Clear Words*, 235.17.

260.2 *yod pa de LA 'gyur*. Berkeley text, 57a.6, reads: *yod pa de LAs 'gyur*. Delhi reading preferred.

261.5 *stong pa nyid bstan pa na ci yang med par bstan pa'i don*. Berkeley text, 58a.3, reads: *stong pa nyid bstan pa na ci yang med pa'i don*. Delhi reading preferred.

263.4 after *yod pa* and before *TSAM GYIS* the Berkeley compiler, 58b.7, adds the following commentary: *bden 'dzin gyi ngor bden pa.*

263.6 after *GSUNG PA'I* and before *PHYIR RO* the Berkeley compiler, 59a.2, adds the following commentary: *tshig gsal gyi chad lta'i don med pa'i phyir dang rang bzhin med par khas blangs pas chad lta sel ba'i.*

263.6–264.1 Commentary by Nga-wang-rap-den from *'di dag* through to *min no* is located later in the Berkeley text, 59b.4, which would be 265.1 in the Delhi text, just before the outline heading *lnga pa*. Berkeley placement preferred.

263.6 *'di dag gis ni.* Berkeley text, 59b.4, reads: *'di dag ni.* Delhi reading preferred.

263.6 *slar dngos po* corrected to *sngar dngos po* in accordance with Berkeley, 59b.4.

264.6 *rang bzhin can gyis dngos po* corrected to *rang bzhin can gyi dngos po* in accordance with Berkeley, 59b.2.

265.1 After *MIN NO* the Berkeley compiler, 59b.3, adds the following commentary: *des na rangs lugs rang bzhin pa'i sems sngar rang bzhin du yod pa chad pa'i chad lta 'gog nus kyang gcig shos 'gog mi nus pa bzhin gtan med du 'dzin pa la chad lta snga ma med kyang phyi ma 'byung ba'o/.* This added commentary immediately precedes the commentary by Nga-wang-rap-den which the Berkeley commentary locates here rather than at 263.6 as noted above.

265.3 *lugs de dag* corrected to *lung de dag* in accordance with Berkeley, 59b.6.

266.2 *kho rang gi* corrected to *kho rang gis* in accordance with Berkeley, 60a.4.

266.4 *'JIG RTEN sogs* corrected to *'JIG RTEN snga phyi sogs* in accordance with Berkeley, 60a.7.

266.4 *chad lta DAG KYANG* corrected to *chad lta ba DAG KYANG* in accordance with Berkeley, 60a.7.

267.4 Commentary by Nga-wang-rap-den from *zhes pa'i don* through to *zhes skur ba'o* placed after *ZHES*

GSUNGS SO, 267.5, rather than before it in accordance with Berkeley, 60b.5.

268.5 Commentary by Nga-wang-rap-den from *dbu ma pa* through to *zhes pa'o* should be placed after *ZHES GSUNGS SO*, 268.6, rather than before it in accordance with Berkeley, 61a.5.

268.6 *'brel ba'i tshig* corrected to *'grel ba'i tshig* in accordance with Berkeley, 61a.7.

269.1 *SLOB DPON ZLA GRAGS KYIS* corrected to *SLOB DPON zla grags KYIS* in accordance with Berkeley, 61b.1, and the Dharmsala edition of Dzong-ka-ba's text, 390a.2.

269.3 *MED PAS SMRAS* corrected to *MED PAR SMRAS* in accordance with Berkeley, 61b.3, and the Dharmsala edition of Dzong-ka-ba's text, 390a.3.

269.4 *bdun pas* corrected to *bdun las* in accordance with sense.

269.5 *NGANG GI NGO BO* corrected to *RANG GI NGO BO* in accordance with Berkeley, 61b.5.

270.3 *mi 'di la* corrected to *mi 'dis* in accordance with Berkeley, 62a.3.

270.4 *gsum pa rtsod tshul gyi shes byed ni* to be identified as by Jam-yang-shay-ba rather than by Nga-wang-rap-den in accordance with Berkeley, 62a.4.

270.5 *de nyid MTSHUNGS SO*. Berkeley text, 62a.4, reads: *de gnyis MTSHUNGS SO*. Delhi reading preferred.

270.6 *te ma grub pa*. Berkeley text, 62a.4, reads: *te grub pa*. Delhi reading preferred.

271.5 After *rang bzhin gyis* the Berkeley text, 62b.3, adds in the commentary *tshul bzhin gyis*. Either reading acceptable.

272.2 *MED PA PO* corrected to *MED PA BA* in accordance with Berkeley, 62b.6, and the Dharmsala edition of Chandrakīrti's text, 303.12.

274.1 *khyed de ltar na* corrected to *khyed ltar na* in accordance with Berkeley, 63b.2.

Glossary

Note

This glossary includes most of the technical terminology found in Dzong-ka-ba's *Great Exposition of the Stages of the Path to Enlightenment*, in the *Four Interwoven Annotations*, and in my discussion of those texts. Sanskrit terms that were not actually seen but are probable reconstructions are indicated with an asterisk.

I English-Tibetan-Sanskrit

abandonment	spong ba	prahāṇa
abider in the fruit	'bras bu la gnas pa	phalasthita
absence of inherent existence	rang bzhin gyis med pa	asvabhāva
accumulate the collections	tshogs bsags pa	sambhara/sañcaya
actions	las	karma
activities	bya ba/bya byed	vyāpāra/vyāpāra-karaṇa
actual	dngos	maula
actual objective ultimate	yul don dam dngos	
actual subjective ultimate	yul can don dam dngos	
actual ultimate	don dam dngos	
actualization	mngon du bya ba	sākṣātkaraṇa
affirming negative	ma yin dgag	paryudāsapratiṣedha
affix a qualification	khyad par sbyar ba	
affliction	nyon mongs	kleśa
afflictive ignorance	nyon mongs can gyi ma rig pa	*kliṣṭāvidyā
agent	byed pa po	kāraka/kartṛ
aggregates	phung po	skandha
aggregation	'dus pa	saṅghāta
aging and death	rga shi	jarāmaraṇa
allowability	chog pa	
almost does not occur	srid mtha'	bhavānta
alternative	mu/mtha'	koṭi/anta
altruistic intention to become a Buddha	byang chub kyi sems	bodhicitta

analysis	dpyod pa	vicāra
analytical meditation	dpyad sgom	
animal	dud 'gro	tiryak
annihilationist	chad lta ba	ucchedadārśika
annotations	mchan bu	
antidote	gnyen po	pratipakṣa
appearance/appearing	snang ba	pratibhāsa
apprehension of signs	mtshan mar 'dzin pa	nimittagrāha
approacher to the fruit	'bras bu la zhugs pa	phalapratipannaka
appropriated	nye bar len pa/nye bar blang bya	upādāna
appropriator	nye bar len pa po	upādātṛ
arbitrarily	'dod rgyal	yādṛcchika
argue	rgol par byed pa	codya
arising	'byung ba	udaya
artificial ignorance	kun btags pa'i ma rig pa	*parikalpitāvidyā
ascertain	nges pa	niś-ci/ni-yam
ascertaining consciousness	nges shes	*niścayajñāna
assert	'dod pa/khas blangs	iṣyate/abhyupagama
assertion	'dod pa	abhimata/abhilāṣa/icchā
attachment	chags pa/sred pa	sneha/tṛṣṇa
attribute	khyad chos	
autonomous syllogism	rang rgyud kyi sbyor ba	svatantraprayoga
awareness	blo	buddhi
bad transmigration	ngan 'gro	durgati
baseless	gnas med pa	anālaya
basis	gzhi/gzhi ma	adhikaraṇa/ādhāra
basis of designation	gdags gzhi	
bear analysis by reasoning	rigs pas dpyad bzod pa	
behavior	spyod pa	carita/caryā
being of great capacity	skyes bu chen po	mahāpuruṣa
being of middling capacity	skyes bu 'bring	madhyamapuruṣa

being of small capacity	skyes bu chung ngu	adhamapuruṣa
beings of the three capacities	skyes bu gsum	
benefit	phan yon	anuśaṃsa
birth	skye ba	jāti
bliss	bde ba	sukha
bodhisattva	byang chub sems dpa'	bodhisattva
body	lus	kāya
bondage	bcings pa	bandha
born from manu	shed las skyes pa	manuja
boundary	sa mtshams	
buddha	sangs rgyas	buddha
buddhahood	sangs rgyas kyi go 'phang	buddhapada
calm abiding	zhi gnas	śamatha
cannot withstand analysis	dpyad mi bzod pa	
capacity	nus pa	śakti
capacity to perform a function	don byed nus pa	arthakriyāśakti
cause	rgyu	hetu
causes and conditions	rgyu rkyen	hetupratyaya
cessation	'gag pa/'gog pa	nirodha
character of the aggregates	phung po'i mtshan nyid	skandhalakṣaṇa
characteristic	mtshan nyid	lakṣaṇa
child of a barren woman	mo gsham gyi bu	vandhyāputra
child of manu	shed bu	mānava
chronology	byung ba'i rim pa	
city of scent-eaters	dri za'i grong khyer	gandharvanagara
claim	khas 'che ba	pratijñā
clairvoyance	mngon par shes pa	abhijñā
clarity	gsal ba	saṃprakhyāna
class of deeds	spyod pa'i phyogs	*caryāpakṣa
clear	gsal ba	vyakta/sphuṭa
coarse	rags pa	sthūla/satataṃ
Collected Topics of Valid Cognition	bsdus grwa	

collected writings	gsung 'bum	
collection	tshogs pa	sāmagrī/saṃgati
collections of merit and wisdom	bsod nams dang ye shes kyi tshogs	puṇyajñānasambhāra
Collections of Reasoning	rigs tshogs	
common being	so so'i skye bo	pṛthagjana
common locus	gzhi mthun	samānādhikaraṇa
commonly appearing subject	chos can mthun snang	
compassion	snying rje	karuṇā
completely non-existent	gtan med	atyantābhāva
composite	tshogs pa/bsags pa	saṃgati/upacaya
composite of appearance and emptiness	snang sṭong gnyis tshogs	
compositional factor	'du byed	saṃskāra
concealer	kun rdzob	saṃvṛti
concentration	bsam gtan	dhyāna
conception of self	bdag 'dzin	ahaṃkāra
conception of mine	bdag gir 'dzin pa	mamakāra
conception of permanence	rtag par 'dzin pa	śāśvatagrāha
conceptual elaborations	rtog pa'i spros pa	*kalpanāprapañca
conceptual reasoning consciousness	rtog pa rigs shes	
conceptuality	rtog pa	vikalpa
concordant	mthun pa	anukūla
concordant objective ultimate	yul mthun pa'i don dam	
concordant subjective ultimate	yul can mthun pa'i don dam	
concordant ultimate	mthun pa'i don dam	
consciousness	shes pa/rnam par shes pa	jñāna/vijñāna
consequence/ contradictory consequence	thal ba/thal 'gyur/mi 'dod pa'i thal 'gyur	prasaṅga
contact	reg pa	sparśa
contaminated thing	zag bcas	sāsrava

continuum	rgyud/rgyun	santāna/prabandha
contradiction	'gal ba	virodha
contradictories in the sense of mutual exclusion	phan tshun spang 'gal/phan tshun 'gal ba	anyonyaparihara-virodha/paraspara-viruddha
contradictory	'gal ba	virodha
conventional consciousness	tha snyad pa'i shes pa	*vyavahāravijñāna
conventional phenomena	tha snyad pa'i chos	*vyavahāradharma
conventional truth	kun rdzob bden pa	saṃvṛtisatya
conventional valid cognition	tha snyad pa'i tshad ma	*vyavahārapramāṇa
conventionality	tha snyad/kun rdzob	vyavahāra/saṃvṛti
conventionally	tha snyad du/kun rdzob tu	vyavahāratas/saṃ-vṛtyā
correct	'thad pa	upapadyate
counter-pervasion	ldog khyab	vyatirekavyāpti
counterfeit reasoning	rigs pa ltar snang	*nyāyābhāsa
creature	skyes bu	puruṣa
cultivation	bsgom pa	bhāvanā
cyclic existence	'khor ba	saṃsāra
damaged	gnod pa	bādhana
damaged by reasoning	rigs pas gnod pa	
damages expressed	gnod byed brjod pa rnams	
debate	rtsod pa byed	vipravadati
definite	nges pa	niyama/niyata
definiteness of death	'chi ba nges pa	
definitive object/ definitive meaning	nges don	nītārtha
delusion	gti mug	moha
dependent-arising	rten 'byung/rten 'brel	pratītyasamutpāda
dependent designation	brten nas gdags pa/ brten nas gdags par bya ba	prajñaptir upādāya/ upādāya prajñap-yate
deprecation	skur pa 'debs pa	apavāda
designated phenomenon	gdags chos	

designation	gdags pa/btags pa	prajñapti
desire realm	'dod khams	kāmadhātu
destroy	'jig	vināśa
deterioration	nyams pa	upahata
dichotomy	dngos 'gal	
different/difference	tha dad	nānā/nānātva
different isolates	ldog pa tha dad	
different substantial entity	rdzas tha dad	
differentiate/ differentiation	phye ba/'byed pa	racayati/bhinna
Digambara	phyogs kyi gos can	digambara
direct antidote	dngos gnyen	
direct cause	dngos rgyu	sākṣātkāraṇa
direct perception/ direct perceiver	mngon sum	pratyakṣa
disadvantage	skyon	doṣa
disbelieve	sun 'byin pa	dūṣaṇa
discordant mode of apprehension	'dzin stangs mi mthun pa	
discrimination	'du shes	saṃjñā
disintegration	'jig pa	vyaya
dispute	rtsod pa	vivāda
distinguishing feature	khyad chos	
doctrine	chos	dharma
dream	rmi lam	svapna
ear	rna ba	śrotra
effect	'bras bu	phala
effort	brtson 'grus	vīrya
elaborations	spros pa	prapañca
elimination	rnam par bcad pa	apākṛta
emanation	sprul pa	nirmāṇa
emptiness	stong pa nyid	śūnyatā
emptiness of inherent existence	rang bzhin gyis stong pa nyid	svabhāvaśūnyatā
empty of capacity to perform functions	don byed pa'i nus pas stong pa	
enlightenment	byang chub	bodhi
entity	dngos po/ngo bo	bhāva/vastu
entityness of character	mtshan nyid ngo bo nyid	

entityness of [self-]production	skye ba ngo bo nyid	
entry into suchness	de kho na nyid la 'jug pa	tattvāvatāra
error/erroneous	phyin ci log	viparyāsa
establish	sgrub par byed pa	prasādhayati
established base	gzhi grub	*āśrayasiddhi
established by way of its own entity	rang gi ngo bos grub pa	svarūpasiddhi
establishment as [its own] reality	yang dag par grub pa	samyaksiddhi
establishment as its own suchness	de kho na nyid du grub pa	tattvasiddhi
establishment by way of own entity	rang gi ngo bo nyid kyis grub pa	svabhāvatā siddhi/ svarūpa siddhi/ svābhāvikī siddhi
establishment by way of [the object's] own character	rang gi mtshan nyid kyis grub pa	svalakṣaṇasiddhi
establishment from the object's] own side	rang ngos nas grub pa	svarūpasiddhi
ethics	tshul khrims	śīla
even a particle	rdul tsam yang	
exalted-knower-of-all-aspects	rnam mkhyen	sarvākārajñāna
exalted wisdom/ exalted wisdom consciousness	ye shes	jñāna
exalted wisdom of meditative equipoise	mnyam bzhag ye shes	samāhitajñāna
excellent doctrine	dam pa'i chos	saddharma
exist by way of its own character	rang gi mtshan nyid kyis yod pa	svalakṣaṇasat
existence	yod pa/srid pa	bhāva/sattva/bhava
existence by way of its own entity	rang gi ngo bos yod pa	svarūpeṇa vidyamāna
existence in its own right	rang ngos nas yod pa	svarūpasiddhi
existent	yod pa	bhāva
explicit contradictories	dngos 'gal	
explicit teaching	dngos bstan	
explicitly	dngos su	sākṣāt

explicitly affixed	dngos su sbyar ba	
explicitly teaches	dngos su bstan pa	
external object	phyi don	bahirdhārtha/ bāhyārtha
extreme of annihilation	chad pa'i mtha'	ucchedānta
extreme of existence	yod pa'i mtha'	
extreme of non-existence	med pa'i mtha'	
extreme of permanence/ extreme of reification	rtag pa'i mtha'	śāśvatānta
eye	mig	cakṣus
falsity	rdzun pa	mṛṣā
familiarization	goms pa	bhāvita/abhyāsa
fault	nyes pa	doṣa
feasible/feasibility	'thad pa	upapadyate
feature	khyad par/khyad chos	viśeṣa
feeler	tshor ba po	vedakā
feeling	tshor ba	vedanā
[final] nature	rang bzhin	svabhāva
final nature	rang bzhin mthar thug	*svabhāvaparyanta
final subtle essential	gnad mthar gtugs pa'i phra ba	
finality	mthar thug pa	paryanta
Foe Destroyer	dgra bcom pa	arhat
follow	rjes su 'brangs pa	anusaraṇa
Forder	mu stegs pa	tīrthika
form/visible form	gzugs	rūpa
Form Body	gzugs sku	rūpakāya
formless absorption	gzugs med kyi snyoms 'jug	ārūpyasamāpatti
forsaken the tenet	grub mtha' dor ba	
forward pervasion	rjes khyab	anvayavyāpti
forward process	lugs 'byung	anuloma
found to be non-existent by a reasoning consciousness	rigs shes kyis med par rnyed pa	

founder (lit. opener of the way)	srol 'byed	
four alternatives	mu bzhi	catuṣkoṭi
four concentrations	bsam gtan bzhi	catvāri dhyānāni
four noble truths	'phags pa'i bden pa bzhi	catvāri āryasatyāni
four possibilities	mu bzhi	catuṣkoṭi
four reliances	rton pa bzhi	catvāri pratisaraṇāni
four seals	phyag rgya bzhi	caturmudrā
free from dust	rdul bral	viraja
free from elaborations	spros bral	aprapañca
frighten	'jigs	bhayaṃkaraṃ
fruit	'bras bu	phala
fulfilling the prerequisites	tshogs bsten pa	
functioning thing/ thing	dngos po	bhāva
ge-luk-ba	dge lugs pa	
ge-shay	dge bshes	kalyānamitra
generality	spyi	sāmānya
generally characterized phenomenon	spyi mtshan	sāmānyalakṣaṇa
giving	sbyin pa	dāna
good quality	yon tan	guṇa
grasping	len pa	upādāna
Great Vehicle	theg pa chen po	mahāyāna
gross/gross objects	rags pa/rags pa rnams	audārika
ground	sa	bhūmi
grounds and paths	sa lam	
have conviction in	yid ches pa	
Hearer	nyan thos	śrāvaka
hearing	thos pa	śruta
hell-being	dmyal ba pa	nāraka
hidden/hidden phenomenon	lkog gyur	parokṣa
higher ethics	lhag pa'i tshul khrims	adhiśīla

higher meditative stabilization	lhag pa'i ting nge 'dzin	adhisamādhi
higher wisdom	lhag pa'i shes rab	adhiprajñā
Highest Yoga Tantra	rnal 'byor bla med kyi rgyud	anuttarayogatantra
Hīnayāna	theg dman	hīnayāna
holder of the throne of Gan-den	dga' ldan khri pa	
hungry ghost	yi dwags	preta
I	nga	ahaṃ
identifying	ngos 'dzin byed pa/ ngos bzung ba	
identifying the object of negation	dgag bya ngos bzung ba	
ignorance	ma rig pa	avidyā
illusion-like	sgyu ma lta bu	māyopama
immeasurable	dpag tu med pa/tshad med	aprameya/aparimāṇa
impermanence/ impermanent/ impermanent phenomenon	mi rtag pa	anitya/anityatā
implicit contradictories	brgyud 'gal	
implicit realization	shugs rtogs	
implicitly	don gyis/shugs kyis	arthāt/tarasā
imprint	lag rjes	
improper	chos ma yin pa	adharma
imputation	btags pa/kun brtags	parikalpita
impute	rtog	prekṣate
imputed	btags pa ba	
imputed dependently	brten nas brtags pa	upādāya prajñapyamāna
imputed existent	btags yod	prajñaptisat
imputed ultimate	don dam btags pa ba	
incontrovertible	mi slu ba	avisaṃvādin
incorrect	mi 'thad	anupapanna/ayukta
incorrectness	mi 'thad pa	anupapatti
indispensible	med du mi rung ba	
individual analysis	so sor rtog pa	pratisaṃkhyāna

inferential cognition	rjes dpag	anumāna
inferential reasoning consciousness	rigs shes rjes dpag	
inferential valid cognizer	rjes dpag tshad ma	anumānapramāṇa
inherent establishment	rang bzhin gyis grub pa	svabhāvasiddhi
inherent existence	rang bzhin	svabhāva/svarūpa
inherent existence of things	dngos po'i rang bzhin	bhāvasvarūpa
innate	lhan skyes	sahaja
instance	bye brag/khyad par	viśeṣa
Instructions on the view of the Middle Way	dbu ma'i lta khrid	
intention	sems pa	cetanā
interpretable object/ interpretable meaning	drang don	neyārtha
intrinsic entity	rang gi ngo bo	svarūpa
investigation	brtags pa/rtog pa	vitarka
isolate	ldog pa	vyatireka
joy	dga' ba	priya/prīti/rati
Kālachakra	dus 'khor	kālacakra
knowledge	chos mngon pa	abhidharma
knowledge, thorough	yongs su shes pa	parijñāna
lama	bla ma	guru
later dissemination	phyi dar	
laxity	bying ba	nimagna/laya
liberation	thar pa	vimokṣa
limited	nges pa/kha tshon chod pa	niyama/niyata
limitless	mtha' yas pa	ananta
limitless consciousness	rnam shes mtha' yas	vijñānānantya
limitless space	nam mkha' mtha' yas	ākāśānantya

literal	sgra ji bzhin pa	yathāruta
literal reading	sgras zin	
liveliness	'tsho ba	jīvikā
living being	srog	jīva
logician	rtog ge pa	tārkika
made up	bcos ma	kṛtrima
Mādhyamika	dbu ma pa	mādhyamika
magical power	rdzu 'phrul	ṛddhi
magician's illusion	sgyu ma	māyā
Mahāyāna/Great Vehicle	theg pa chen po	mahāyāna
Mañjughoṣha	'jam dbyangs	mañjughoṣa
Mañjushrī	'jam dpal	mañjuśrī
manifest/manifest phenomenon	mngon gyur	abhimukhī
manifest conception	mngon par zhen pa	abhiniveśa
manifest pride/pride of conceit	mngon pa'i nga rgyal	abhimāna
master	slob dpon	ācārya
Materialist	rgyang phan pa	āyata/carvāka
matter	bem po	kanthā
meaning	don	artha
means of expression	rjod byed	vācaka/abhidhāna
measure	tshad	pramāṇa
meditating/ meditation	sgom pa	bhāvanā
meditative equipoise	mnyam bzhag	samāhita
meditative stabilization	ting nge 'dzin	samādhi
memory consciousness	dran pa/dran shes	smṛti
[mere] elimination	rnam bcad	viccheda
mere elimination of elaborations	spros pa rnam par bcad tsam	
mere production	skye ba tsam	
merely nominal	ming tsam	nāmamātraka
merely posited by names and thought	ming dang rtog pas btags tsam	
metaphoric	rnam grangs pa'i	paryāya
metaphoric objective ultimate	yul rnam grangs pa'i don dam	

metaphoric subjective ultimate	yul can rnam grangs pa'i don dam	
method	thabs	upāya
middle path	dbu ma'i lam	madhyamapratipat
middle way	dbu ma	madhyama
mind	sems	citta
mind-basis-of-all	kun gzhi rnam shes	ālayavijñāna
mind of enlightenment	byang chub kyi sems	bodhicitta
mind-only	sems tsam	cittamātra
mind-training	blo sbyong	
mindfulness	dran pa	smṛti
mine	bdag gi/bdag gir/bdag gi ba/nga yi ba	ātmīya/mama
minute	phra rab	paramāṇu
mirage	smig rgyu	marīci
miserable	sdug bsngal ba	duḥkha
mode	tshul	naya
mode of abiding	gnas lugs	
mode of apprehension	'dzin stangs	muṣṭibandha
mode of being	yin lugs	
mode [of existence]	ji lta ba	yathā
mode of subsistence	gnas lugs/sdod lugs	
model	phyi mo	mātṛkā
model text	gzhung phyi mo	*granthamātṛkā
mundane	'jig rten pa	laukika
mundane existence	srid pa	bhava
mutually inclusive	don gcig	ekārtha
name and form	ming gzugs	nāmarūpa
negative of the object of negation	dgag bya bkag pa	
nihilism/nihilist	med par smra ba	nāstivāda/nāstivādin
Nihilist	med pa pa	nāstika
Nirgrantha	gcer bu pa	nirgrantha
nirvāṇa [i.e., passing from sorrow]	mya ngan las 'das pa	nirvāṇa
no composition	mngon par 'du byed pa med pa	anabhisaṃskāra
no inherent existence	rang bzhin med pa	niḥsvabhāva
no production	skye ba med pa	anutpāda

nominal positing	ming gis bzhag pa	
nominally imputed	ming gis btags pa	saṃjñākaraṇa
non-abiding nirvāna	mi gnas pa'i mya ngan las 'das pa	apratiṣṭhitanirvāṇa
non-affirming negative	med dgag	prasajyapratiṣedha
non-artificial experience	bcos ma ma yin pa'i myong ba	akṛtrimānubhava
non-conceptual exalted wisdom	rtog med ye shes	nirvikalpajñāna
non-conceptuality	mi rtog pa	avikalpa
non-contradictory	mi 'gal ba	aviruddha
non-defective awareness	blo gnod med	*nirvyathabuddhi
non-dualistic cognition	gnyis su med pa'i shes pa	*advayavijñāna
non-entityness	ngo bo nyid ma mchi pa nyid/ngo bo nyid med pa	asvabhāva/svabhāvato nāstikaṃ
non-entityness of character	mtshan nyid ngo bo nyid med pa	
non-entityness of [self-]production	skye ba ngo bo nyid med pa	utpattiniḥsvabhāvatā
non-erroneously	phyin ci ma log par	aviparyaya/aviparyāsa
non-existence/non-existent	med pa	abhāva/asat/nāsti
non-fabricated	bcos ma ma yin pa	akṛtrima
non-metaphoric	rnam grangs ma yin	aparyāya
non-metaphoric objective ultimate	yul rnam grangs ma yin pa'i don dam	
non-metaphoric subjective ultimate	yul can rnam grangs ma yin pa'i don dam	
non-mistaken	mi 'khrul ba	avyabhicārin
non-thing	dngos med	abhāva
non-virtuous	mi dge ba	akuśala
not able to bear analysis by reasoning	rigs pas dpyad mi bzod pa	
not being produced	ma skyes pa	ajāta
not existent	yod pa ma yin	
not found by a reasoning consciousness	rigs shes kyis ma rnyed pa	

not non-existent	med pa ma yin	
not unable	mi lcogs med	anāgamya
nothingness	ci yang med	ākiṃcanya
nourished	gso ba	poṣa
object	yul/don	viṣaya/artha
object of attainment	thob par bya ba	pratilambha
object of comprehension	gzhal bya	prameya
object of knowledge	shes bya	jñeya
object of negation	dgag bya	pratiṣedhya
object of negation by reasoning	rigs pa'i dgag bya	*nyāyapratiṣedhya
object of negation by the path	lam gyi dgag bya	*mārgapratiṣedhya
object of observation	dmigs pa/dmigs yul	ālambana
object of touch	reg bya	spraṣṭavya
objection	rtsod pa	vivāda
objective mode of subsistence	don gyi sdod lugs	
objective object of negation	yul gyi dgag bya	
objective ultimate	yul don dam	
objectively	yul steng nas	
obscuration, thorough	kun tu rmongs pa	saṁmūḍha
observed by valid cognition	tshad mas dmigs pa	*pramāṇālabdha
obstruction	sgrib pa	āvaraṇa
obstructions to liberation	nyon mongs pa'i sgrib pa/nyon sgrib	kleśāvaraṇa
obstructions to omniscience	shes bya'i sgrib pa/ shes sgrib	jñeyāvaraṇa
occurs	srid pa	prabhavati
odor	dri	gandha
omniscient consciousness	rnam mkhyen	sarvākārajñāna
one/oneness	gcig	eka/ekatva
one entity	ngo bo gcig	*ekarūpatā
one-pointed	rtse gcig pa	ekāgra
opener of the chariot-way	shing rta'i srol 'byed	

ordinary being	so sor skyes bu	pṛthagjana
[ordinary] consciousness	rnam shes	vijñāna
other-powered phenomenon	gzhan dbang	paratantra
our own system	rang lugs	svamata
overly broad	khyab ches pa	
overturned	bzlog pa	viparīta
own-character	rang mtshan	svalakṣaṇa
part	yan lag	aṅga/avayava
partisan Mādhyamika	phyogs 'dzin pa'i dbu ma pa	
parts-possessor [the whole]	yan lag can/cha can	avayavin/aṃśaka
passing from sorrow	mya ngan las 'das pa	nirvāṇa
path/path consciousness	lam	mārga
path of accumulation	tshogs lam	sambhāramārga
path of actions	las lam	
path of meditation	sgom lam	bhāvanāmārga
path of no more learning	mi slob lam	aśaikṣamārga
path of preparation	sbyor lam	prayogamārga
path of release	rnam grol lam	vimuktimārga
path of seeing	mthong lam	darśanamārga
patience	bzod pa	kṣānti
peaceful	zhi ba	śānta
peak of cyclic existence	srid rtse	bhavāgra
perfection of wisdom	shes rab kyi pha rol tu phyin pa	prajñāpāramitā
perfection	phar phyin	pāramitā
permanent/permanent phenomenon	rtag pa	nitya
person	gang zag	pudgala
pervasion	khyab pa	vyāpti
phenomenon	chos	dharma
pliancy	shin tu sbyangs pa	prasrabdhi/praśrabdhi

position	phyogs	pakṣa
positive inclusion	yongs gcod	pariccheda
positive phenomenon	sgrub pa	vidhi
possibility	phung gsum/mu	koṭi
pot	bum pa	ghaṭa
power of heart	snying stobs	sattva
Prāsaṅgika	thal 'gyur ba	prāsaṅgika
predispositions	bag chags	vāsanā
prerequisite	tshogs/rgyu'i tshogs	
presentation	rnam bzhag	vyavasthāpita
pride of conceit	mngon pa'i nga rgyal	abhimāna
pride of greatness	che ba'i nga rgyal	
principal	gtso bo	pradhāna
produced thing/ product	byas pa	kṛta
production	skye ba	utpatti
profound	zab pa	gambhīra
promised	khas blangs pa	abhyupagata
proof	sgrub pa	pratipad/sādhana
proper	chos yin pa	dharma
Proponent of Illusion-Like Non-Dualism	sgyu ma lta bu gnyis su med par smra ba	māyopamādvaya-vādin
Proponent of Thorough Non-Abiding	rab tu mi gnas par smra ba	sarvadharmāpratiṣṭhānavādin
Proponent of True Existence	dngos por smra ba/ dngos po yod par smra ba	vastusatpadārtha-vādin
propound	smra ba	varṇ
proven/thesis	bsgrub bya	sādhya
pure	rdul bral	viraja
purify	sbyang ba	viśodhana
purify obstructions	sgrib pa sbyang ba	
purpose	don	artha
qualification	khyad par	viśeṣa
quality	chos	dharma
quintessential instruction	man ngag	upadeśa

real	yang dag	samyak
reality	chos nyid	dharmatā
realize	rtogs pa	pratipad/adhigama
reason	gtan tshigs/rgyu mtshan	hetu
Reason-Established Illusionist	sgyu ma rigs grub pa	māyopamādvaya-vādin
reasoning	rigs pa	nyāya/yukti
reasoning consciousness	rigs shes	
reasoning of ultimate analysis	don dam dpyod byed kyi rigs pa	
reflection	gzugs brnyan	pratibimba
refuge	skyabs	śaraṇa
refutation	dgag pa	pratiṣedha
refuted	khegs pa	ityamya?
refuted by reasoning	rigs pas khegs	
reification	sgro 'dogs	samāropa
release	grol ba	vimukti
rely	rton	pratisaraṇa
remainder left over	lhag ma lus pa	śiṣyatā/avaśeṣa
renunciation	nges 'byung	niḥsaraṇa
research	rtsad bcad pa	
reverse process	lugs ldog	paryāya
root	rtsa ba	mūla
root of cyclic existence	'khor ba'i rtsa ba	
sage	drang srong	ṛṣi
same entity	ngo bo gcig pa	*ekarūpatā
satisfaction/be satisfied	chog shes pa	tṛptā/saṃtuṣṭa
Sautrāntika-Mādhyamika	mdo sde spyod pa'i dbu ma pa	sautrāntika-mādhya-mika
saying/word	bka'	vacana
scripture	gsung rab	pravacana
seed	sa bon	bīja
seeds of obscuration	kun tu rmongs pa'i sa bon	saṃmohabīja
seeing emptiness/ view of emptiness	stong nyid kyi lta ba	śūnyatādarśana

self	bdag	ātman
self-character	rang mtshan	svalakṣaṇa
self-instituting	tshugs thub	
self-powered things	dngos po rang dbang ba	bhāvāḥ svatantrāḥ
self-sufficient	rang rkya ba	
selflessness	bdag med	nairātmya
selflessness of persons	gang zag gi bdag med	pudgalanairātmya
selflessness of phenomena	chos kyi bdag med	dharmanairātmya
sense consciousness	dbang shes	indriyajñāna
sense power/sense faculty	dbang po	indriya
senseless babble	bab col	
sentient being	sems can	sattva
settle	gtan la 'babs pa	niścaya/viniścaya
settling of suchness	de kho na gtan la dbab pa	*tattvaviniścaya
shared	thun mong ba	sādhāraṇa
sign	mtshan ma	nimitta
sign/reason	rtags	liṅga
signlessness	mtshan ma med pa	animitta
Solitary Realizer	rang rgyal	pratyekabuddha
son of a barren woman	mo gsham gyi bu	vandhyāputra
sound	sgra	śabda
source	skye mched	āyatana
sources	kun 'byung	samudaya
space	nam mkha'	ākāśa
special insight	lhag mthong	vipaśyanā
special realization	khyad par du rtogs pa	viśeṣādhigama
specifically characterized phenomenon	rang mtshan	svalakṣaṇa
sphere of reality	chos kyi dbyings	dharmadhātu
spiritual community	dge 'dun	saṅgha
spiritual guide	dge ba'i bshes gnyen	kalyānamitra
stabilizing meditation	'jog sgom	
stages of entry	'jug pa'i rim pa	
stages of the path	lam rim	
state of sleep	gnyid log pa'i gnas skabs	*supta-adhikāra

stopping	'gags pa	niruddha
strong adherence	mngon par zhen pa	abhiniveśa
subject	chos can	dharmin
subject discussed/ subject matter	brjod bya	vācya/abhidheya
subjective/subject	yul can	
subjective ultimate	yul can don dam	
substantially existent	rdzas su yod pa	dravyasat
substratum	khyad gzhi	
subtle	phra rab	atisūkṣma
suchness	de nyid/de kho na nyid	tattva
suffering	sdug bsngal	duḥkha
suitability	rung ba	yuktatva
suitable	rung ba	yujyate
suitable for firmness of mind	yid brtan rung ba	
sung-bum	gsung 'bum	
superimposition	sgro 'dogs	samāropa
superior	'phags pa	ārya
supramundane	'jig rten las 'das pa	lokottara
Supramundane Victor	bcom ldan 'das	bhagavat
sūtra of definitive meaning	nges don gyi mdo	nītārthasūtra
sūtra of interpretable meaning	drang don gyi mdo	neyārthasūtra
Svātantrika	rang rgyud pa	svātantrika
syllogism	sbyor ba	prayoga
synonymous/ mutually inclusive	don gcig	ekārtha
system	lugs	naya/mata

tangible object	reg bya	spraṣṭavya
tantra	rgyud	tantra
tenet/tenet system	grub mtha'	siddhānta
tetralemma	mu bzhi	catuṣkoṭi
that which appropriates	nye bar len pa po	upādātṛ
that which is appropriated	nye bar blang bya	upādāna

that which is to be negated	dgag bya	pratiṣedhya
that which is to be proven	bsgrub bya	sādhya
thesis	dam bca'	pratijñā
thing	dngos po	vastu/bhāva
thinking	bsam pa	cintā
thoroughly afflicted	kun nas nyon mongs pa	saṃkleśa
thoroughly established	yongs grub	pariniṣpanna
thought	rtog pa	kalpanā
Three Jewels	dkon mchog gsum	triratna
threefold training	bslab pa gsum	triśikṣā
Tīrthika Nirgrantha	mu stegs gcer bu pa	tīrthika nirgrantha
too broad	khyab ches pa	
too limited/too narrow	khyab chung ba	
topic	dngos po	padārtha
trainee	gdul bya	vineya
training	bslab pa	śikṣā
transmigration	'gro ba	gati
treatise	bstan bcos	śāstra
trifling	nyi tshe ba	prādeśika
true cessation	'gog bden	nirodhasatya
true establishment	bden par grub pa	satyasiddha
true path	lam bden	mārgasatya
true source of suffering	kun 'byung bden pa	samudayasatya
true suffering	sdug bsngal bden pa	duḥkhasatya
truth	bden pa	satya
Truth Body	chos kyi sku	dharmakāya
Udraka	lhag dpyod	udraka
ultimate	don dam	paramārtha
ultimate establishment	don dam par grub pa	paramārthasiddhi
ultimate truth	don dam bden pa	paramārthasatya
ultimate valid cognition	don dam pa'i tshad ma	*paramārthapramāṇa
ultimately exist	don dam par yod pa	paramārthasat

uncertainty of the time of death	nam 'chi mi nges pa	
uncommon	thun mong ma yin pa	asādhāraṇa
uncommon distinguishing feature	thun mong ma yin pa'i khyad chos	
uncommon mode of subsistence	thun mong ma yin pa'i sdod lugs	
undeniably	bsnyon du med	
understand	khong du chud pa	avasāya/avagacchati /avabodha
unequalled	mnyam med/ mtshungs pa med pa	atula/apratima
unfeasible	mi 'thad	anupapanna/ayukta
union of calm abiding and special insight	zhi lhag zung 'brel	
unique distinguishing feature	khyad chos gcig bu	
unprecedented	sngon med pa	apūrva
unquestionably	gdon mi za bar	avaśya
unreal	log pa	nivṛtti/mithyā
unreasonable	mi rigs pa	ayukta/anupapatti
unsuitable	mi rung ba	na yujyate
unsurpassed	bla na med pa	anuttara
upholder of the system	srol 'dzin	
utter non-existence	ye med pa	
valid/valid cognition/ valid cognizer	tshad ma	pramāṇa
varieties	ji snyed pa	
Vātsīputrīya	gnas ma bu pa	vātsīputrīya
verbal convention	tha snyad	vyavahāra
very hidden phenomenon	shin tu lkog gyur	atyarthaparokṣa
very pure phenomena	rnam par byang ba'i chos	vaiyavadānika-dharma
view	lta ba	dṛṣṭi
view of annihilation/ deprecation	chad par lta ba	ucchedadarśana

view of nihilism	med par lta ba	nāstitvadarśana
view of permanence	rtag lta	śāśvatadarśana
view of selflessness	bdag med pa'i lta ba	nairātmyadarśana
view of the transitory	'jig tshogs la lta ba	satkāyadṛṣṭi
viewing emptiness/ view of emptiness	stong nyid lta ba	śūnyatādṛṣṭi
virtuous	dge ba	kuśala
waking state	gnyid ma log pa'i gnas skabs	
whole	yan lag can	avayavin
wisdom	shes rab	prajñā
wisdom realizing emptiness	stong nyid rtogs pa'i shes rab	
wise	mkhas pa	vicakṣaṇa
wishlessness	smon pa med pa	apraṇihita
without entityness	ngo bo nyid med pa	asvabhāva
without remainder	lhag ma ma lus pa	niravaśeṣa
withstand analysis by reasoning	rigs pas dpyad bzod pa	
woolen cloth	snam bu	paṭa
words	tshig 'bru	vyañjana
worldly conventions	'jig rten pa'i tha snyad	laukikasaṃvyavahāra
Worldly Materialists	'jig rten rgyang phan pa	lokāyata
wrong consciousness	log shes	mithyājñāna
wrong view	log lta	mithyādṛṣṭi
wrongful pride	log pa'i nga rgyal	mithyāmāna
Yogāchāra-Mādhyamika	rnal 'byor spyod pa'i dbu ma pa	yogācāra-mādhyamika
yogic direct perceiver/yogic direct perception	rnal 'byor mngon sum	yogipratyakṣa

2 *Tibetan-Sanskrit-English*

kun tu rmongs pa	saṃmūḍha	thorough obscuration
kun tu rmongs pa'i sa bon	saṃmohabīja	seeds of obscuration
kun btags pa'i ma rig pa	*parikalpitāvidyā	artificial ignorance
kun brtags	parikalpita	imputation
kun nas nyon mongs pa	saṃkleśa/sāṃkleśika	thoroughly afflicted
kun 'byung	samudaya	source
kun 'byung bden pa	samudayasatya	true source of suffering
kun rdzob	saṃvṛti	conventionality/ concealer
kun rdzob tu	saṃvṛtyā	conventionally
kun rdzob bden pa	saṃvṛtisatya	conventional truth
kun gzhi rnam shes	ālayavijñāna	mind-basis-of-all
dkon mchog gsum	triratna	Three Jewels
bka'	vacana	saying/word
rkyen	pratyaya	condition
lkog gyur	parokṣa	hidden/hidden phenomenon
skur pa 'debs pa	apavāda	deprecation
skyabs	śaraṇa	refuge
skye mched	āyatana	source
skye ba	jāti/utpatti	birth/production
skye ba ngo bo nyid		entityness of [self-]production
skye ba ngo bo nyid ma mchis pa nyid/ skye ba ngo bo nyid med pa	utpattiniḥsvabhāvatā	non-entityness of [self-]production

skye ba med pa	anutpāda	no production
skye ba tsam		mere production
skyes bu	puruṣa	creature
skyes bu chung ngu	adhamapuruṣa	being of small capacity
skyes bu chen po	mahāpuruṣa	being of great capacity
skyes bu 'bring	madhyamapuruṣa	being of middling capacity
skyes bu gsum		beings of the three capacities
skyon	doṣa	disadvantage/fault
kha tshon chod pa		limited
khas 'che ba	pratijñā	claim
khas blangs	iṣyate/abhyupagama	assert/promise
khegs pa	ityamya	refuted (?)
khong du chud pa	avasāya/avagacchati /avabodha	understand
khyad chos		attribute/feature/ distinguishing feature
khyad chos gcig bu		unique distinguishing feature
khyad par	viśeṣa	feature/instance/ qualification
khyad par du rtogs pa	viśeṣādhigama	special realization
khyad par sbyar ba		affix a qualification
khyad gzhi		substratum
khyab chung ba		too limited/too narrow
khyab ches pa		overly broad/too broad
khyab pa	vyāpti	pervasion
mkhas pa	vicakṣaṇa/paṇḍita	wise/skilled
'khor ba	saṃsāra	cyclic existence
'khor ba'i rtsa ba		root of cyclic existence
gang zag	pudgala	person
gang zag gi bdag med	pudgalanairātmya	selflessness of persons

goms pa	bhāvita/abhyāsa	familiarization
grangs can pa	sāṃkhya	Sāṃkhya
grub mtha'	siddhānta	tenet/tenet system
grub mtha' dor ba		forsaken the tenet
grub pa	siddha/āpatti	prove/establish
grol ba	vimukti	release
dgag pa	pratiṣedha	refutation
dgag bya	pratiṣedhya/niṣedhya	that which is to be negated/object of negation
dgag bya bkag pa		negative of the object of negation
dgag bya ngos bzung ba		identifying the object of negation
dga' ldan khri pa		holder of the throne of Gan-den
dga' ba	priya/prīti/rati	joy
dge 'dun	saṅgha	spiritual community
dge ba	kuśala	virtuous
dge ba'i bshes gnyen/ dge bshes	kalyānamitra	spiritual guide/ge-shay
dge lugs pa		ge-luk-ba
dgra bcom pa	arhat	Foe Destroyer
'gag pa/'gog pa/'gags pa	nirodha/niruddha	cessation/stopping
'gal ba	virodha	contradictory/ contradiction
'gog bden	nirodhasatya	true cessation
'gro ba	gati	transmigration
rga shi	jarāmaraṇa	aging and death
rgol par byed pa	codya	argue
rgyang phan pa	āyata/carvāka	Materialist
rgyu	hetu/kāraṇa	cause
rgyu dang rkyen	hetupratyaya	causes and conditions
rgyu mtshan	hetu/nimitta	reason
rgyu'i tshogs		prerequisite
rgyud	tantra	tantra
rgyun/rgyud	prabandha/santāna	continuum
sgom pa	bhāvanā	meditating/ meditation
sgom lam	bhāvanāmārga	path of meditation
sgyu ma	māyā	magician's illusion

sgyu ma lta bu	māyopama	illusion-like
sgyu ma lta bu gnyis su med par smra ba	māyopamādvaya-vādin	Proponent of Illusion-Like Non-Dualism
sgyu ma rigs grub pa		Reason-Established Illusionist
sgra	śabda	sound
sgra ji bzhin pa	yathāruta	literal
sgras zin		literal reading
sgrib pa	āvaraṇa	obstruction
sgrib pa sbyang ba		purify obstructions
sgrub pa	vidhi	positive phenomenon
sgrub pa	pratipad/sādhana	proof
sgrub par byed pa	prasādhayati	establish
sgro 'dogs	samāropa	reification/superimposition
brgyud 'gal		implicit contradictories
bsgom pa	bhāvanā	cultivation/meditation
bsgrub bya	sādhya	proven/that which is to be proven
nga	ahaṃ	I
nga yi ba	mama	mine
ngan 'gro	durgati	bad transmigration
nges don	nītārtha	definitive object/definitive meaning
nges don gyi mdo	nītārthasūtra	sūtra of definitive meaning
nges pa	niś-ci/niyata/niyama	ascertain/definite/limited
nges 'byung	niḥsaraṇa	renunciation
nges shes	*niścayajñāna	ascertaining consciousness
ngo bo gcig	*ekarūpatā	one entity/same entity
ngo bo nyid ma mchis pa nyid/ngo bo nyid med pa	asvabhāva/svabhāvato nāstikaṃ	non-entityness/without entityness
ngos 'dzin byed pa/ngos bzung ba		identify

dngos	maula	actual
dngos 'gal		dichotomy/explicit contradictories
dngos rgyu	sākṣātkāraṇa	direct cause
dngos gnyen		direct antidote
dngos bstan		explicit teaching
dngos po	bhāva/vastu/padārtha	entity/functioning thing/thing/topic
dngos po rang dbang ba	bhāvāḥ svatantrāḥ	self-powered things
dngos po'i rang bzhin	bhāvasvarūpa	inherent existence of things
dngos por smra ba/ dngos po yod par smra ba	vastusatpadārtha-vādin	Proponent of True Existence
dngos med	abhāva	non-thing
dngos su	vastutas/sākṣāt	explicitly
dngos su bstan pa		explicitly teaches
dngos su sbyar ba		explicitly affixed
mngon gyur	abhimukhī	manifest/manifest phenomenon
mngon du bya ba	sākṣātkaraṇa	actualization
mngon pa'i nga rgyal	abhimāna	manifest pride/pride of conceit
mngon par 'du byed pa med pa	anabhisaṃskāra	no composition
mngon par zhen pa	abhiniveśa	manifest conception/ strong adherence
mngon par shes pa	abhijñā	clairvoyance
mngon sum	pratyakṣa	direct perception
sngon med pa	apūrva	unprecedented

ci yang med	ākiṃcanya	nothingness
gcig	eka/ekatva	one/oneness
gcer bu pa	nirgrantha	Nirgrantha
bcings pa	bandha	bondage
bcom ldan 'das	bhagavat	Supramundane Victor
bcos ma	kṛtrima	made up
bcos ma ma yin pa	akṛtrima	non-fabricated

bcos ma ma yin pa'i myong ba	akṛtrimānubhava	non-artificial experience
cha can	aṃśaka	parts-possessor [the whole]
chags pa	sneha/tṛṣṇa	attachment
chad pa'i mtha'	ucchedānta	extreme of annihilation
chad par lta ba	ucchedadarśana	view of annihilation
che ba'i nga rgyal		pride of greatness
chog pa	paryāpti	allowability
chog shes pa	tṛptā/saṃtuṣṭa	satisfaction/be satisfied
chos	dharma	doctrine/ phenomenon/ quality
chos kyi sku	dharmakāya	Truth Body
chos kyi bdag med	dharmanairātmya	selflessness of phenomena
chos kyi dbyings	dharmadhātu	sphere of reality
chos mngon pa	abhidharma	knowledge
chos can	dharmin	subject
chos can mthun snang		commonly appearing subject
chos nyid	dharmatā	reality
chos ma yin pa	adharma	improper
chos yin pa	dharma	proper
mchan bu		annotations
'chi ba nges pa		definiteness of death
ji snyed pa		varieties
ji lta ba	yathā	mode [of existence]
'jam dpal	mañjuśrī	Mañjushrī
'jam dbyangs	mañjughoṣa	Mañjughoṣha
'jig	vināśa	destroy
'jig rten rgyang phan pa	lokāyata	Worldly Materialists
'jig rten pa	laukika	mundane
'jig rten pa'i tha snyad	laukikasaṃvyavahāra	worldly conventions
'jig rten las 'das pa	lokottara	supramundane

'jig pa	vyaya/vināśa	disintegration
'jig tshogs la lta ba	satkāyadṛṣṭi	view of the transitory
'jigs	bhayaṃkaraṃ	frighten
'jug pa'i rim pa		stages of entry
'jog sgom		stabilizing meditation
rjes khyab	anvayavyāpti	forward pervasion
rjes dpag	anumāna	inferential cognition
rjes dpag tshad ma	anumānapramāṇa	inferential valid cognizer
rjes su 'brangs pa	anusaraṇa	follow
rjod byed	vācaka/abhidhāna	means of expression
brjod bya	vācya/abhidheya	subject discussed/ subject matter
nyan thos	śrāvaka	Hearer
nyams pa	upahata	deterioration
nyi tshe ba	prādeśika	trifling
nye bar blang bya/ nye bar len pa	upādāna	that which is appropriated
nye bar len pa po	upādātṛ	that which appropriates
nyes pa	doṣa	fault
nyon sgrib	kleśāvaraṇa	obstruction to liberation
nyon mongs	kleśa	affliction
nyon mongs can gyi ma rig pa	*kliṣṭāvidyā	afflictive ignorance
nyon mongs pa'i sgrib pa	kleśāvaraṇa	obstruction to liberation
gnyid ma log pa'i gnas skabs		waking state
gnyid log pa'i gnas skabs	*supta-adhikāra	state of sleep
gnyis su med pa'i shes pa	*advayavijñāna	non-dualistic cognition
gnyen po	pratipakṣa	antidote
mnyam med	atula	unequalled
mnyam bzhag	samāhita	meditative equipoise
mnyam bzhag ye shes	samāhitajñāna	exalted wisdom of meditative equipoise
snying rje	karuṇā	compassion

snying stobs	sattva	power of heart
bsnyon du med		undeniably
ting nge 'dzin	samādhi	meditative stabilization
gtan med	atyantābhāva	completely non-existent
gtan tshigs	hetu	reason
gtan la 'babs pa	niścaya/viniścaya	settle
gti mug	moha	delusion/ bewilderment
btags chos		designated phenomenon
btags pa/kun brtags	prajñapti/parikalpita	designation/ imputation
btags pa ba		imputed
btags yod	prajñaptisat	imputed existent/ imputedly existent
rtag lta	śāśvatadarśana	view of permanence
rtag pa	nitya	permanent/ permanent phenomenon
rtag pa'i mtha'	śāśvatānta	extreme of permanence/ extreme of reification
rtag par 'dzin pa	śāśvatagrāha	conception of permanence
rtags	liṅga	sign/reason
rten	ādhāra	basis
rten 'brel/rten 'byung	pratītyasamutpāda	dependent-arising
rtog	prekṣate	impute
rtog ge pa	tārkika	logician
rtog pa	vikalpa/kalpanā/ vitarka	conceptuality/ thought/ investigation
rtog pa rigs shes		conceptual reasoning consciousness
rtog pa'i spros pa	*kalpanāprapañca	conceptual elaborations
rtog med ye shes	nirvikalpajñāna	non-conceptual exalted wisdom

rtogs pa	pratipad/adhigama	realize
rton	pratisaraṇa	rely
rton pa bzhi	catvāri pratisaraṇāni	four reliances
lta ba	dṛṣṭi/darśana	view
stong nyid rtogs pa'i lta ba		view realizing emptiness
stong nyid rtogs pa'i shes rab		wisdom realizing emptiness
stong pa nyid	śūnyatā	emptiness
brtags pa	vitarka	investigation
brten nas brtags pa/ brten nas gdags pa	upādāya prajñapti/ prajñaptir upādāya	imputed dependently/ dependent designation
bstan bcos	śāstra	treatise
tha snyad	vyavahāra	conventionality/ verbal convention
tha snyad du	saṃvṛtyā	conventionally
tha snyad pa'i chos	*vyavahāradharma	conventional phenomena
tha snyad pa'i tshad ma	*vyavahārapramāṇa	conventional valid cognition
tha snyad pa'i shes pa	*vyavahāravijñāna	conventional consciousness
tha dad	nānā/nānātva	different/difference
thabs	upāya	method
thams cad mkhyen pa	sarvajña	all-knowing/ omniscient
thar pa	vimokṣa	liberation
thal 'gyur/thal ba/mi 'dod pa'i thal 'gyur	prasaṅga	consequence/ contradictory consequence
thal 'gyur pa	prāsaṅgika	Prāsaṅgika
thun mong ba	sādhāraṇa	shared
thun mong ma yin pa	asādhāraṇa	uncommon
thun mong ma yin pa'i khyad chos		uncommon distinguishing feature
thun mong ma yin pa'i sdod lugs		uncommon mode of subsistence

theg pa chen po	mahāyāna	Mahāyāna/Great Vehicle
theg dman	hīnayāna	Hīnayāna/Lesser Vehicle
thob par bya ba	pratilambha/prāpaṇīya	object of attainment
thos pa	śruta	hearing
mtha'	koṭi/anta	alternative/extreme/possibility
mtha' yas pa	ananta	limitless
mthar thug pa	paryanta	finality
mthun pa	anukūla	concordant
mthun pa'i don dam		concordant ultimate
mthong lam	darśanamārga	path of seeing
'thad pa	upapadyate/upapatti	feasible/feasibility/correct
dam bca'	pratijñā	thesis
dam pa'i chos	saddharma	excellent doctrine
dud 'gro	tiryak	animal
dus 'khor	kālacakra	Kālachakra/wheel of time
de kho na nyid/de nyid	tattva/tathatā	suchness/reality
de kho na nyid du grub pa	tattvasiddhi	establishment as its own suchness
de kho na nyid la 'jug pa	tattvāvatāra	entry into suchness
de kho na gtan la dbab pa	*tattvaviniścaya	settling of suchness
don	artha	object/meaning/purpose
don gyi sdod lugs		objective mode of subsistence
don gyis	arthāt	implicitly
don gcig	ekārtha	synonymous/mutually inclusive
don dam	paramārtha	ultimate
don dam dngos		actual ultimate
don dam btags pa ba		imputed ultimate

don dam bden pa	paramārthasatya	ultimate truth
don dam pa'i tshad ma	*paramārthapramāṇa	ultimate valid cognition
don dam par grub pa	paramārthasiddhi	ultimate establishment
don dam par yod pa	paramārthasat	ultimately exist
don dam dpyod byed kyi rigs pa		reasoning of ultimate analysis
don byed nus pa	arthakriyāśakti	capacity to perform a function
don byed pa'i nus pas stong pa		empty of capacity to perform functions
drang don	neyārtha	interpretable object/ interpretable meaning
drang don gyi mdo	neyārthasūtra	sūtra of interpretable meaning
drang srong	ṛṣi	sage
dran pa/dran shes	smṛti	mindfulness/memory consciousness
dri	gandha	odor
dri za'i grong khyer	gandharvanagara	city of scent-eaters
gdags pa	prajñapti	designation
gdags gzhi		basis of designation
gdul bya	vineya	trainee
gdon mi za bar	avaśya	unquestionably/ undeniably
bdag	ātman	self
bdag gi/bdag gir/bdag gi ba	ātmīya	mine
bdag gir 'dzin pa	mamakāra	conception of mine
bdag med	nairātmya	selflessness
bdag med pa'i lta ba	nairātmyadarśana	view of selflessness
bdag 'dzin	ahaṃkāra/ātmagraha	conception of self
bde ba	sukha	bliss
bden pa	satya	truth
bden par grub pa	satyasiddhi	true establishment
mdo sde spyod pa'i dbu ma pa	sautrāntika-mādhya-mika	Sautrāntika-Mādhyamika
'du byed	saṃskāra	compositional factors
'du shes	saṃjñā	discrimination
'dus pa	saṅghāta	aggregation

'dod khams	kāmadhātu	desire realm
'dod rgyal	yādṛcchika	arbitrarily
'dod pa	iṣyate/abhyupagama/abhimata/abhilāṣa/icchā	assert/assertion
rdul bral	viraja	pure/free from dust
rdul tsam yang		even a particle
ldog khyab	vyatirekavyāpti	counter-pervasion
ldog pa	vyatireka/vyāvṛtti	isolate/reverse
ldog pa tha dad		different isolates
sdug bsngal	duḥkha	suffering
sdug bsngal bden pa	duḥkhasatya	true suffering
sdug bsngal ba	duḥkha/duḥkhita	miserable
sdod lugs		mode of subsistence
bsdus grwa		Collected Topics of Valid Cognition
nam mkha'	ākāśa	space
nam mkha' mtha' yas	ākāśānantya	limitless space
nam 'chi mi nges pa		uncertainty of the time of death
nus pa	śakti	capacity
gnad mthar gtugs pa'i phra ba		final subtle essential
gnas ma bu pa	vātsīputrīya	Vātsīputrīya
gnas med pa	anālaya	baseless
gnas lugs		mode of abiding/mode of subsistence
gnod pa	upakāra/bādhana/upaghāta	damage
gnod byed brjod pa rnams		damages expressed
rna ba	śrotra	ear
rnam mkhyen/rnam pa thams cad mkhyen pa	sarvākārajñāna	exalted-knower-of-all-aspects/omniscient consciousness
rnam grangs pa	paryāya	metaphoric
rnam grangs ma yin pa	aparyāya	non-metaphoric
rnam grol lam	vimuktimārga	path of release

rnam bcad/rnam par bcad pa	viccheda/apākṛta	[mere] elimination/ elimination
rnam par byang ba'i chos	vaiyavadānika-dharma	very pure phenomenon
rnam par shes pa	vijñāna	consciousness
rnam bzhag	vyavasthāpita	presentation
rnam shes	vijñāna	[ordinary] consciousness
rnam shes mtha' yas	vijñānānantya	limitless consciousness
rnal 'byor mngon sum	yogipratyakṣa	yogic direct perceiver/yogic direct perception
rnal 'byor spyod pa'i dbu ma pa	yogācāra-mādhya-mika	Yogāchāra-Mādhya-mika
rnal 'byor bla med kyi rgyud	anuttarayogatantra	Highest Yoga Tantra
snang stong gnyis tshogs		composite of appearance and emptiness
snang ba	pratibhāsa	appearance/appearing
snam bu	paṭa	woolen cloth
dpag tu med pa	aprameya/aparimāṇa	immeasurable
dpyad sgom		analytical meditation
dpyad mi bzod pa		cannot withstand analysis
dpyod pa	vicāra	analysis
spangs pa/spong ba	prahāṇa	abandonment
spyi	sāmānya	generality
spyi mtshan	sāmānyalakṣaṇa	generally characterized phenomenon
spyod pa	carita/caryā	behavior
spyod pa'i phyogs	*caryāpakṣa	class of deeds
sprul pa	nirmāṇa	emanation
spros pa	prapañca	elaborations
spros pa rnam par bcad tsam		mere elimination of elaborations
spros bral	aprapañca	free from elaboration

phan tshun spang gal/phan tshun 'gal ba	anyonyaparihara-virodha/paraspara-viruddha	contradictories in the sense of mutual exclusion
phan yon	anuśaṃsa	benefit
phar phyin	pāramitā	perfection
phung po	skandha	aggregate
phung po'i mtshan nyid	skandhalakṣaṇa	character of the aggregates
phung gsum		possibility
phyag rgya bzhi	caturmudrā	four seals
phyi dar		later dissemination
phyi don	bahirdhārtha/bā-hyārtha	external object
phyi mo	mātṛkā	model
phyin ci ma log par	aviparyaya/aviparyāsa	non-erroneously
phyin ci log	viparyāsa	error/erroneous
phye ba	bhinna/racayati	differentiation/differentiate
phyogs	pakṣa	position
phyogs kyi gos can	digambara	Digambara
phyogs 'dzin pa'i dbu ma pa		partisan Mādhya-mika
phra rab	paramāṇu/atisūkṣma	minute/subtle
'phags pa	ārya	Superior
'phags pa'i bden pa bzhi	catvāri āryasatyāni	four noble truths

bag chags	vāsanā	predispositions
bab col		senseless babble
bum pa	ghaṭa	pot
bem po	kanthā	matter
bya ba/bya byed	vyāpāra/vyāpāra-karaṇa	activities
byang chub	bodhi	enlightenment
byang chub kyi sems	bodhicitta	altruistic intention to become a Buddha/mind of enlightenment
byang chub sems dpa'	bodhisattva	bodhisattva
byas pa	kṛta	produced thing/product

bying ba	nimagna/laya	laxity
byung ba'i rim pa		chronology
bye brag	viśeṣa	instance
byed pa	kāraṇa	action
byed pa po	kāraka/kartṛ	agent
bla na med pa	anuttara	unsurpassed
bla ma	guru	lama
blo	buddhi	awareness
blo gnod med	*nirvyathabuddhi	non-defective awareness
blo sbyong		mind-training
dbang po	indriya	sense power/sense faculty
dbang shes	indriyajñāna	sense consciousness
dbu ma	madhyama	middle way
dbu ma pa	mādhyamika	Mādhyamika
dbu ma'i lta khrid		Instructions on the View of the Middle Way
dbu ma'i lam	madhyamapratipat	middle path
'byung ba	udaya	arising
'byed pa	racayati	differentiate
'bras bu	phala	fruit/effect
'bras bu la gnas pa	phalasthita	abider in the fruit
'bras bu la zhugs pa	phalapratipannaka	approacher to the fruit
sbyang ba	viśodhana	purify
sbyin pa	dāna	giving
sbyor ba	prayoga	syllogism
sbyor lam	prayogamārga	path of preparation
ma skyes pa	ajāta	not produced
ma yin dgag	paryudāsapratiṣedha	affirming negative
ma rig pa	avidyā	ignorance
man ngag	upadeśa	quintessential instructions
mi 'khrul ba	avyabhicārin	non-mistaken
mi dge ba	akuśala	non-virtuous
mi 'gal ba	aviruddha	non-contradictory
mi lcogs med	anāgamya	not unable
mi rtag pa	anityatā/anitya	impermanence/

		impermanent/ impermanent phenomenon
mi rtog pa	avikalpa	non-conceptual/ non-conceptuality
mi 'thad	anupapanna/ayukta	incorrect/unfeasible
mi 'thad pa	anupapatti	incorrectness
mi gnas pa'i mya ngan las 'das pa	apratiṣṭhitanirvāṇa	non-abiding nirvāṇa
mi rigs pa	ayukta/anupapatti	unreasonable
mi rung ba	na yujyate	unsuitable
mi slu ba	avisaṃvādin	incontrovertible/ ineluctable
mi slob lam	aśaikṣamārga	path of no more learning
mig	cakṣus	eye
ming gis btags pa	saṃjñākaraṇa	nominally imputed
ming gis bzhag pa		nominal positing
ming dang rtog pas btags tsam		merely posited by names and thought
ming tsam	nāmamātraka	merely nominal
ming gzugs	nāmarūpa	name and form
mu	koṭi/anta	alternative/possibility
mu stegs gcer bu pa	tīrthika nirgrantha	Tīrthika Nirgrantha
mu stegs pa	tīrthika	Forder
mu bzhi	catuṣkoṭi	four alternatives/four possibilities/ tetralemma
med dgag	prasajyapratiṣedha	non-affirming negative
med du mi rung ba		indispensible
med pa	abhāva/asat/nāsti	non-existence/ non-existent
med pa pa	nāstika	Nihilist
med pa ma yin		not non-existent
med pa'i mtha'		extreme of non-existence
med par lta ba	nāstitvadarśana	view of nihilism
med par smra ba	nāstivāda/nāstivādin	nihilism/nihilist
mo gsham gyi bu	vandhyāputra	child of a barren woman
mya ngan las 'das pa	nirvāṇa	nirvāṇa/passing from sorrow

dmigs pa/dmigs yul	upalabdhi/ālambana	observed/object of observation
dmyal ba pa	nāraka	hell-being
rmi lam	svapna	dream
rmugs pa	styāna	obscuration
smig rgyu	marīci	mirage
smon pa med pa	apraṇihita	wishlessness
smra ba	varṇ/vādin	propound/proponent
gtso bo	pradhāna	principal
rtsa ba	mūla	root
rtsad bcad pa		research
rtse gcig pa	ekāgra	one-pointed
rtsod pa	vivāda	dispute/objection
rtsod pa byed	vipravadati	debate/dispute
brtson 'grus	vīrya	effort
tshad	pramāṇa	measure
tshad ma	pramāṇa	valid/valid cognition/ valid cognizer
tshad ma ma yin pa	apramāṇa	not valid
tshad mas dmigs pa	*pramāṇālabdha	observed by valid cognition
tshad med	aprameya	immeasurable
tshig 'bru	vyañjana	words/syllables
tshugs thub		self-instituting
tshul	naya	mode
tshul khrims	śīla	ethics
tshogs bsten pa		fulfilling the prerequisites
tshogs pa	sāmagrī/saṃgati	collections/composite
tshogs lam	sambhāramārga	path of accumulation
tshogs bsags pa	sambhara/sañcaya	accumulate the collections
tshor ba	vedanā	feeling
tshor ba po	vedakā	feeler
mtshan nyid	lakṣaṇa	character/ characteristic
mtshan nyid ngo bo nyid med pa	lakṣaṇaniḥsvabhāvatā	non entityness of character

mtshan ma	nimitta	sign
mtshan ma med pa	animitta	signlessness
mtshan mar 'dzin pa	nimittodgrahaṇa	apprehension of signs
mtshung	tulya	similar/alike
mtshungs pa med pa	apratima	unequalled
'tsho ba	jīvikā	liveliness
'dzin stangs	muṣṭibandha	mode of apprehension
'dzin stangs mi mthun pa		discordant modes of apprehension
'dzin pa	grāha	grasp/apprehend
rdzas tha dad		different substantial entity
rdzas su yod pa	dravyasat	substantially existent
rdzu 'phrul	ṛddhi	magical power
rdzun pa	mṛṣā	falsity
zhi gnas	śamatha	calm abiding
zhi ba	śānta	peaceful
zhi lhag zung 'brel		union of calm abiding and special insight
gzhan dbang	paratantra	other-powered phenomena
gzhal bya	prameya	object of comprehension
gzhi	adhikaraṇa/ādhāra	basis
gzhi grub	*āśrayasiddhi	established base
gzhi mthun pa	samānādhikaraṇa	common locus
gzhi ma	adhikaraṇa/ādhāra	basis
gzhung phyi mo	*granthamātṛkā	model text
zag bcas	sāsrava	contaminated thing
zab pa	gambhīra	profound
gzugs	rūpa	form/visible form
gzugs sku	rūpakāya	Form Body
gzugs brnyan	pratibimba	reflection
gzugs med kyi snyoms 'jug	ārūpyasamāpatti	formless absorption

bzod pa	kṣānti	patience
bzlog pa	viparīta/nirvṛtta	overturned/reversed
yang dag	samyak	real/correct
yang dag par grub pa	samyaksiddhi	establishment as [its own] reality
yan lag	aṅga/avayava	part
yan lag can	avayavin	parts-possessor/whole
yi dwags	preta	hungry ghost
yid ches pa	adhimukti	have conviction in
yid brtan rung ba		suitable for firmness of mind
yin lugs		mode of being
yul	viṣaya	object
yul gyi dgag bya		objective object of negation
yul can		subjective
yul can mthun pa'i don dam		concordant subjective ultimate
yul can don dam		subjective ultimate
yul can don dam dngos		actual subjective ultimate
yul can rnam grangs pa'i don dam		metaphoric subjective ultimate
yul can rnam grangs ma yin pa'i don dam		non-metaphoric subjective ultimate
yul steng nas		objectively
yul mthun pa'i don dam		concordant objective ultimate
yul don dam		objective ultimate
yul don dam dngos		actual objective ultimate
yul rnam grangs pa'i don dam		metaphoric objective ultimate
yul rnam grangs ma yin pa'i don dam		non-metaphoric objective ultimate
ye med pa		utter non-existence
ye shes	jñāna	exalted wisdom/ exalted wisdom consciousness

yongs grub	pariniṣpanna	thoroughly established phenomenon
yongs gcod	pariccheda	positive inclusion
yongs su shes pa	parijñāna	knowledge/thorough knowledge
yod pa/srid pa	bhāva/sattva/bhava	existence/existent
yod pa ma yin	na asti/abhāva	not existent
yod pa'i mtha'		extreme of existence
yon tan	guṇa	good quality
rags pa/rags pa rnams	sthūla/satatam/audārika	coarse/gross/gross object
rang rkya ba		self-sufficient
rang gi ngo bo	svarūpa/svabhāva	intrinsic entity/own entity
rang gi ngo bo nyid kyis grub pa/rang gi ngo bos grub pa	svabhāvatā siddhi/svarūpasiddhi/svābhāvikī siddhi	establishment by way of its own entity
rang gi ngo bos yod pa	svarūpeṇa vidyamāna	existence by way of its own entity
rang gi mtshan nyid kyis grub pa	svalakṣaṇasiddhi	establishment by way of [the object's] own character
rang gi mtshan nyid kyis yod pa	svalakṣaṇasat	existence by way of its own character
rang rgyal	pratyekabuddha	Solitary Realizer
rang rgyud kyi sbyor ba	svatantraprayoga	autonomous syllogism
rang rgyud pa	svātantrika	Svātantrika
rang ngos nas grub pa	svarūpasiddhi	establishment from [the object's] own side
rang ngos nas yod pa	svarūpasat	existence in its own right
rang mtshan	svalakṣaṇa	own-character/self-character/specifically characterized phenomena

rang bzhin	svabhāva/svarūpa	[final] nature/ inherent existence
rang bzhin gyis grub pa	svabhāvasiddhi	inherent establishment
rang bzhin gyis stong pa nyid	svabhāvaśūnyatā	emptiness of inherent existence
rang bzhin gyis med pa	asvabhāva/niḥsva-bhāva	absence of inherent existence/no inherent existence
rang bzhin mthar thug	*svabhāvaparyanta	final nature
rang lugs	svamata	own system
rab tu mi gnas par smra ba	sarvadharmāpra-tiṣṭhānavādin	Proponent of Thorough Non-Abiding
rigs pa	nyāya/yukti	reasoning
rigs pa ltar snang	*nyāyābhāsa	counterfeit reasoning
rigs pa'i dgag bya	*nyāyapratiṣedhya	object of negation by reasoning
rigs pas khegs		refuted by reasoning
rigs pas gnod pa		damaged by reasoning
rigs pas dpyad mi bzod pa		unable to bear analysis by reasoning
rigs pas dpyad bzod pa		able to bear analysis by reasoning
rigs tshogs		Collections of Reasoning
rigs shes		reasoning consciousness
rigs shes kyis ma rnyed pa		not found by a reasoning consciousness
rigs shes kyis med par rnyed pa		found to be non-existent by a reasoning consciousness
rigs shes rjes dpag		inferential reasoning consciousness
rung ba	yuktatva/yujyate	suitability/suitable
reg pa	sparśa	contact

reg bya	spraṣṭavya	object of touch/ tangible object
lag rjes		imprint
lam	mārga	path/path consciousness
lam gyi dgag bya	*mārgapratiṣedhya	object of negation by the path
lam bden	mārgasatya	true path
lam rim		stages of the path
las	karma	action
las lam		path of actions
lugs	naya/mata	system
lugs ldog	paryāya	reverse process
lugs 'byung	anuloma	forward process
lus	kāya	body
len pa	upādāna	grasping
log lta	mithyādṛṣṭi	wrong view
log pa	nivṛtti/mithyā	unreal
log pa'i nga rgyal	mithyāmāna	wrongful pride
log shes	mithyājñāna	wrong consciousness
shing rta'i srol 'byed		opener of the chariot-way
shin tu lkog gyur	atyarthaparokṣa	very hidden phenomenon
shin tu sbyangs pa	prasrabdhi/praśrabdhi	pliancy
shugs kyis	tarasā	implicitly
shugs rtogs		implicit realization
shed bu	mānava	child of manu
shed las kyes pa	manuja	born from manu
shes sgrib/shes bya'i sgrib pa	jñeyāvaraṇa	obstruction to omniscience
shes pa	jñāna	consciousness
shes bya	jñeya	object of knowledge
shes rab	prajñā	wisdom
shes rab kyi pha rol tu phyin pa	prajñāpāramitā	perfection of wisdom

sa	bhūmi	ground
sa bon	bīja	seed
sa mtshams	sīma	boundary
sa lam		grounds and paths
sangs rgyas	buddha	Buddha
sangs rgyas kyi go 'phang	buddhapada	buddhahood
sun 'byin pa	dūṣaṇa	disbelieve/eradicate
sems	citta	mind
sems can	sattva	sentient being
sems pa	cetanā	intention
sems tsam	cittamātra	mind-only
so so'i skye bo/so sor skyes bu	pṛthagjana	common being/ ordinary being
so sor rtog pa	pratisaṃkhyāna	individual analysis
srid mtha'	bhavānta	almost does not occur
srid pa	bhāva/sattva/bhava/ prabhavati	existence/mundane existence/occurs
srid rtse/srid pa'i rtse mo	bhavāgra	peak of cyclic existence
sred pa	sneha/tṛṣṇa	attachment
srog	jīva	living being
srol 'byed		founder
srol 'dzin		upholder of the system
slob dpon	ācārya	master
gsal ba	saṃprakhyāna/ vyakta/sphuṭa	clarity/clear
gsung 'bum		sung-bum/collected works
gsung rab	pravacana	scripture
gso ba	poṣa	nourished
bsags pa	upacaya	composite
bsam gtan	dhyāna	concentration
bsam gtan bzhi	catvāri dhyānāni	four concentrations
bsam pa	cintā	thinking
bsod nams dang ye shes kyi tshogs	puṇyajñānasambhāra	collections of merit and wisdom
bslab pa gsum	triśikṣā	threefold training
lhag mthong	vipaśyanā	special insight

lhag pa'i tshul khrims	adhiśīla	higher ethics
lhag pa'i ting nge 'dzin	adhisamādhi	higher meditative stabilization
lhag pa'i shes rab	adhiprajñā	higher wisdom
lhag dpyod	udraka	Udraka
lhag ma ma lus pa	niravaśeṣa	without remainder/ completely
lhag ma lus pa	śiṣyatā/avaśeṣa	remainder left over
lhan skyes	sahaja	innate

3 *Sanskrit-Tibetan-English*

aṃśaka	cha can	parts-possessor/whole
akuśala	mi dge ba	non-virtuous
akṛtrima	bcos ma ma yin pa	non-fabricated
akṛtrimānubhava	bcos ma ma yin pa'i myong ba	non-artificial experience
aṅga	yan lag	part
ajāta	ma skyes pa	not produced
atisūkṣma	phra rab	subtle
atula	mnyam med	unequalled
atyantābhāva	gtan med	completely non-existent
atyarthaparokṣa	shin tu lkog gyur	very hidden phenomenon
advayajñāna	gnyis su med pa'i ye shes	non-dualistic exalted wisdom
*advayavijñāna	gnyis su med pa'i shes pa	non-dualistic cognition
adhamapuruṣa	skyes bu chung ngu	being of small capacity
adharma	chos ma yin pa	improper
adhikaraṇa	gzhi ma/gzhi	basis
adhigama	rtogs pa	realize
adhiprajñā	lhag pa'i shes rab	higher wisdom
adhimukti	yid ches pa	have conviction in
adhiśīla	lhag pa'i tshul khrims	higher ethics
adhisamādhi	lhag pa'i ting nge 'dzin	higher meditative stabilization
ananta	mtha' yas pa	limitless
anabhisaṃskāra	mngon par 'du byed pa med pa	no composition

anavaśeṣa	lhag med	without remainder
anāgamya	mi lcogs med	not unable
anālaya	gnas med pa	baseless
anitya/anityatā	mi rtag pa	impermanent/ impermanent phenomenon/ impermanence
animitta	mtshan ma med pa	signlessness
anukūla	mthun pa	concordant
anuttara	bla na med pa	unsurpassed
anuttarayogatantra	rnal 'byor bla med kyi rgyud	Highest Yoga Tantra
anutpāda	skye ba med pa	no production
anupapatti/ anupapanna	mi rigs pa/mi 'thad pa/mi 'thad	unreasonable/ incorrectness/ incorrect
anumāna	rjes dpag	inferential cognition
anumānapramāṇa	rjes dpag tshad ma	inferential valid cognizer
anuloma	lugs 'byung	forward process
anuśaṃsa	phan yon	benefit
anusaraṇa	rjes su 'brangs pa	follow
anta	mtha'	alternative/extreme
anyonyaparihara-virodha	phan tshun spang 'gal	contradictories in the sense of mutual exclusion
anvayavyāpti	rjes khyab	forward pervasion
aparimāṇa	dpag tu med pa	immeasurable
aparyāya	rnam grangs ma yin pa	non-metaphoric
apavāda	skur pa 'debs pa	deprecation
apākṛta	rnam par bcad pa	elimination
apūrva	sngon med pa	unprecedented
apraṇihita	smon pa med pa	wishlessness
apratima	mtshungs pa med pa	unequalled
apratiṣṭhitanirvāṇa	mi gnas pa'i mya ngan las 'das pa	non-abiding nirvāṇa
aprapañca	spros bral	free from elaborations
apramāṇa	tshad ma ma yin pa	not valid
aprameya	dpag tu med pa/tshad med	immeasurable

abhāva	med pa/mi srid pa/ dngos med	non-existence/ non-existent/ non-thing
abhijñā	mngon par shes pa	clairvoyance
abhidharma	chos mngon pa	knowledge
abhidhāna	rjod byed	means of expression
abhidheya	brjod bya	subject discussed/ subject matter
abhiniveśa	mngon par zhen pa	manifest conception/ strong adherence
abhimata	'dod pa	assert/assertion
abhimāna	mngon pa'i nga rgyal	manifest pride/pride of conceit
abhimukhī	mngon gyur	manifest/manifest phenomenon
abhilāṣa	'dod pa	assert/assertion
abhyāsa	goms pa	familiarization
abhyupagata/ abhyupagama	khas blangs ba/'dod pa	promise/assert/ assertion
ayukta	mi 'thad /mi rigs pa/ mi rung ba	unfeasible/ unreasonable/ incorrect/unsuitable
artha	don	object/meaning/ purpose
arthakriyāśakti	don byed nus pa	capacity to perform a function
arthāt	don gyis	implicitly
arhat	dgra bcom pa	Foe Destroyer
avagacchati	khong du chud pa/ rtogs pa	understand/realize
avabodha	khong du chud pa/ rtogs pa	understand/ realization
avayava	yan lag/cha shas	part
avayavin	yan lag can	parts-possessor/whole
avaśeṣa	lhag ma lus pa	remainder left over
avaśya	gdon mi za bar/nges par	unquestionably/ definitely
avasāya	khong du chud pa	understand
avikala	ma tshang ba med pa/tsang ba	complete
avikalpa	mi rtog pa	non-conceptuality
avidyā	ma rig pa	ignorance

aviparyaya/aviparyāsa	phyin ci ma log par	non-erroneously
aviruddha	mi 'gal ba	non-contradictory
avisaṃvādin	mi slu ba	incontrovertible
avyabhicārin	mi 'khrul ba	non-mistaken
aśaikṣamārga	mi slob lam	path of no more learning
asat	med pa/yod pa ma yin/bden pa ma yin	non-existence/non-existent/not true
asādhāraṇa	thun mong ma yin pa	uncommon
asvabhāva	rang bzhin gyis med pa/ngo bo nyid med pa/ngo bo nyid ma mchi pa nyid/	absence of inherent existence/non-entityness/without entityness
ahaṃ	nga	I
ahaṃkāra	ngar 'dzin/bdag 'dzin	conception of self
ākāśa	nam mkha'	space
ākāśānantya	nam mkha' mtha' yas	limitless space
ākiṃcanya	ci yang med	nothingness
ācārya	slob dpon	master
ātmagraha	bdag 'dzin	conception of self
ātman	bdag	self
ātmanīna	bdag gi	mine
ātmīya	bdag gi/bdag gir/bdag gi ba	mine
ādhāra	gzhi/rten	basis
āpatti	grub pa	establish
āyata	rgyang phan pa	Materialist
āyatana	skye mched	source
ārūpyasamāpatti	gzugs med kyi snyoms 'jug	formless absorption
ārya	'phags pa	Superior
ālambana	dmigs pa/dmigs yul	object of observation
ālayavijñāna	kun gzhi rnam shes	mind-basis-of-all
āvaraṇa	sgrib pa	obstruction
icchā	'dod pa	assert/assertion
indriya	dbang po	sense power/sense faculty

indriyavijñāna	dbang po'i rnam par shes pa	sense consciousness
iṣyate	'dod pa/khas blangs	assert
ucchedadarśana	chad par lta ba	view of annihilation/ view of deprecation
ucchedānta	chad pa'i mtha'	extreme of annihilation
utpatti	skye ba	production
udaya	'byung ba/skye ba	arising/production
udraka	lhag dpyod	Udraka
upaghāta	gnod pa byas pa/ gnod par gyur pa	to damage/is damaged
upacaya	bsags pa	composite
upadeśa	man ngag	quintessential instruction
upapadyate/upapatti	'thad pa	correct/feasible/ feasibility
upahata	nyams pa	deterioration
upādātṛ	nye bar len pa po	that which appropriates/ appropriator
upādāna	nye bar len pa/nye bar blang bya/len pa	appropriated/ grasping
upādāya prajñapyate/ upādāya prajñapyamāna	brten nas gdags par bya ba/brten nas brtags pa	dependent-designation/ imputed dependently
upāya	thabs	method
ṛddhi	rdzu 'phrul	magical power
ṛṣi	drang srong	sage
eka/ekatva	gcig	one/oneness
*ekarūpatā	ngo bo gcig pa	one entity/same entity
ekāgra	rtse gcig pa	one-pointed
ekārtha	don gcig	same meaning/ synonymous

audārika	rags pa/rags pa rnams	gross/gross objects
kanthā	bem po	matter
karuṇā	snying rje	compassion
kartṛ	byed pa po	agent
karma	las	action
kalpanā	rtog pa	thought/ conceptuality
*kalpanāprapañca	rtog pa'i spros pa	conceptual elaboration
kalyānamitra	dge ba'i bshes gnyen	spiritual guide
kāmadhātu	'dod khams	desire realm
kāya	lus	body
kāraka	byed pa po	agent
kālacakra	dus 'khor	Kālachakra/wheel of time
kuśala	dge ba	virtue/virtuous
kṛta/kṛtaka	byas pa	produced thing/ product
kṛtrima	bcos ma	made up/fabricated
koṭi	mu/mtha'	possibility/ alternative/extreme
*kliṣṭāvidyā	nyon mongs can gyi ma rig pa	afflictive ignorance
kleśa	nyon mongs	affliction
kleśāvaraṇa	nyon mongs pa'i sgrib pa	obstruction to liberation
kṣānti	bzod pa	patience
gati	'gro ba	transmigration
gandha	dri	odor
gandharvanagara	dri za'i grong khyer	city of scent-eaters
gambhīra	zab pa	profound
guṇa	yon tan	[good] quality
guru	bla ma	lama/teacher
*granthamātṛkā	gzhung phyi mo	model text
grāha	'dzin pa	apprehension
ghaṭa	bum pa	pot

cakṣus	mig	eye
caturmudrā	phyag rgya bzhi	four seals
catuṣkoṭi	mu bzhi/mtha' bzhi	four alternatives/four possibilities/ tetralemma
catvāri āryasatyāni	'phags pa'i bden pa bzhi	four noble truths
catvāri dhyānāni	bsam gtan bzhi	four concentrations
catvāri pratisaraṇāni	rton pa bzhi	four reliances
carita/caryā	spyod pa	behavior
*caryāpakṣa	spyod pa'i phyogs	class of deeds
carvāka	rgyang phan pa	Materialist
citta	sems	mind
cittamātra	sems tsam	mind-only
cintā	bsam pa	thinking
cetanā	sems pa	intention
codya	rgol par byed pa	argue/dispute
jarāmaraṇa	rga shi	aging and death
jāti	skye ba	birth
jīva	srog	living being
jīvikā	'tsho ba	liveliness
jñāna	shes pa/ye shes	consciousness/exalted wisdom/exalted wisdom consciousness
jñeya	shes bya	object of knowledge
jñeyāvaraṇa	shes bya'i sgrib pa/ shes sgrib	obstruction to omniscience
tattva	de nyid/de kho na nyid	suchness/reality
*tattvaviniścaya	de kho na gtan la dbab pa	settling of suchness
tattvasiddhi	de kho na nyid du grub pa	establishment as its own suchness
tattvāvatāra	de kho na nyid la 'jug pa	entry into suchness
tathatā	de bzhin nyid	suchness/reality
tantra	rgyud	tantra
tarasā	shugs kyis	implicitly

tārkika	rtog ge pa	logician
tiryak	dud 'gro	animal
tīrthika	mu stegs pa	Forder
tīrthika nirgrantha	mu stegs gcer bu pa	Tīrthika Nirgrantha
tulya	mtshungs	similar/same
tṛptā	chog shes pa	satisfaction/be satisfied
tṛṣṇa	sred pa	attachment
triratna	dkon mchog gsum	Three Jewels
triśikṣā	bslab pa gsum	threefold training
darśanamārga	mthong lam	path of seeing
dāna	sbyin pa	giving
digambara	phyogs kyi gos can	Digambara
duḥkha/duḥkhita	sdug bsngal/sdug bsngal ba	suffering/miserable
duḥkhasatya	sdug bsngal bden pa	true suffering
durgati	ngan 'gro	bad transmigration
dūṣaṇa	sun 'byin pa	disbelieve/eradicate
dṛṣṭi	lta ba	view
doṣa	skyon/nyes pa	disadvantage/fault
dravyasat	rdzas su yod pa	substantially existent
dharma	chos/chos yin pa	doctrine/ phenomenon quality/proper
dharmakāya	chos kyi sku	Truth Body
dharmatā	chos nyid	reality
dharmadhātu	chos kyi dbyings	sphere of reality
dharmanairātmya	chos kyi bdag med	selflessness of phenomena
dharmin	chos can	subject
dhyāna	bsam gtan	concentration
na yujyate	mi rung ba/mi rigs pa	unsuitable/ unreasonable
naya	lugs/tshul	system/mode
nānā/nānātva	tha dad	different/difference
nāmamātraka	ming tsam	merely nominal
nāmarūpa	ming dang gzugs	name and form

nāraka	dmyal ba/dmyal ba pa	hell/hell-being
nāsti	med pa	non-existence/non-existent
nāstika	med pa pa	nihilist
nāstitvadarśana	med par lta ba	view of nihilism
nāstivāda/nāstivādin	med par smra ba	nihilism/nihilist
niḥsaraṇa	nges 'byung	renunciation
niḥsvabhāva	rang bzhin gyis med pa	no inherent existence
nitya	rtag pa	permanent phenomenon
nimagna	bying ba	laxity
nimitta	mtshan ma	sign
nimittagrāha	mtshan mar 'dzin pa	apprehension of signs
niyata/niyama	nges pa/nges par	limited/definite/definitely
niravaśeṣa	lhag ma ma lus pa	without remainder/completely
niruddha	'gags pa	stopping/cessation
nirodha	'gag pa/'gog pa	cessation
nirodhasatya	'gog bden	true cessation
nirgrantha	gcer bu pa	Nirgrantha
nirmāṇa	sprul pa	emanation
nirvāṇa	mya ngan las 'das pa	nirvāṇa/passing from sorrow
nirvikalpajñāna	rtog med ye shes	non-conceptual exalted wisdom
nivṛtti	log pa	unreal/wrong/opposite
niś-ci	nges pa/gtan la 'babs pa	ascertain/settle
*niścayajñāna	nges shes	ascertaining consciousness
nītārtha	nges don	definitive object/definitive meaning
nītārthasūtra	nges don gyi mdo	sūtra of definitive meaning
neyārtha	drang don	interpretable object/interpretable meaning
neyārthasūtra	drang don gyi mdo	sūtra of interpretable meaning

nairātmya	bdag med	selflessness
nairātmyadarśana	bdag med pa'i lta ba	view of selflessness
nyāya	rigs pa	reasoning
*nyāyābhāsa	rigs pa ltar snang	counterfeit reasoning
*nyāyapratiṣedhya	rigs pa'i dgag bya	object of negation by reasoning
pakṣa	phyogs	position/direction
paṭa	snam bu	woolen cloth
padārtha	dngos po/don	topic/thing
paratantra	gzhan dbang	other-powered phenomenon
paramāṇu	phra rab/rdul phra rab	minute/minute particle
paramārtha	don dam	ultimate
*paramārthapramāṇa	don dam pa'i tshad ma	ultimate valid cognition
paramārthasat	don dam par yod pa	ultimately exist
paramārthasatya	don dam bden pa	ultimate truth
paramārthasiddhi	don dam par grub pa	ultimate establishment
parasparaviruddha	phan tshun 'gal ba/ phan tshun spang 'gal	contradictory in the sense of mutual exclusion
parikalpita	btags pa/kun brtags	imputation
*parikalpitāvidyā	kun btags pa'i ma rig pa	artificial ignorance
pariccheda	yongs gcod	positive inclusion
parijñāna	yongs su shes pa	knowledge/thorough knowledge
pariniṣpanna	yongs grub	thoroughly established phenomenon
parokṣa	lkog gyur	hidden/hidden phenomenon
paryanta	mthar thug pa	finality
paryāya	rnam grangs pa	metaphoric
paryudāsapratiṣedha	ma yin dgag	affirming negative
pāramitā	phar phyin	perfection
puṇyajñānasambhāra	bsod nams dang ye shes kyi tshogs	collections of merit and wisdom

pudgala	gang zag	person
pudgalanairātmya	gang zag gi bdag med	selflessness of persons
puruṣa	skyes bu	being/creature
pṛthagjana	so so'i skye bo/so sor skyes bu	common being/ ordinary being
poṣa	gso ba	nourished
prakṛti	rang bzhin	nature
prajñapti	btags pa/gdags pa	designation
prajñaptir upādāya	brten nas gdags pa	dependent designation
prajñaptisat	btags yod	imputed existent/ imputedly existent
prajñā	shes rab	wisdom
prajñāpāramitā	shes rab kyi pha rol tu phyin pa	perfection of wisdom
pratijñā	khas 'che ba/dam bca'	claim/thesis
pratipakṣa	gnyen po/mi mthun phyogs	antidote/discordant class
pratipad	rtogs pa/sgrub pa	realize/proof
pratibimba	gzugs brnyan	reflection
pratibhāsa	snang ba	appearance/ appearing
pratilambha	thob par bya ba	object of attainment
pratisaraṇa	rton	rely/reliance
pratiṣedha	dgag pa	refutation
pratiṣedhya	dgag bya	object of negation
pratisaṃkhyāna	so sor rtog pa	individual analysis
pratītyasamutpāda	rten 'brel/rten 'byung	dependent-arising
pratyakṣa	mngon sum	direct perception
pratyekabuddha	rang rgyal/rang sangs rgyas	Solitary Realizer
pradhāna	gtso bo	Principal
prapañca	spros pa	elaborations
prabandha	rgyun	continuum
prabhavati	srid pa	occurs
pramāṇa	tshad ma/tshad	valid/valid cognition/ valid cognizer/ measure
*pramāṇālabdha	tshad mas dmigs pa	observed by valid cognition
prameya	gzhal bya	object of comprehension

prayoga	sbyor ba	syllogism
prayogamārga	sbyor lam	path of preparation
pravacana	gsung rab	scripture
prasaṅga	thal ba/thal 'gyur/mi 'dod pa'i thal 'gyur	consequence/ contradictory consequence
prasajyapratiṣedha	med dgag	non-affirming negative
prasrabdhi/praśrab-dhi	shin tu sbyangs pa	pliancy
prasādhayati	sgrub par byed pa	establish/prove
prahāṇa	spong ba	abandon/ abandonment
prādeśika	nyi tshe ba	trifling
prāpaṇīya	thob par bya ba	object of attainment
prāsaṅgika	thal 'gyur ba	Prāsaṅgika
priya/prīti	dga' ba	joy
prekṣate	rtog	impute
preta	yi dwags	hungry ghost
phala	'bras bu	effect/fruit
phalapratipannaka	'bras bu la zhugs pa	approacher to the fruit
phalasthita	'bras bu la gnas pa	abider in the fruit
bandha/bandhana	bcings pa	bondage
bahirdhā-artha/ bāhya-artha	phyi don	external object
bādha/bādhana	gnod pa	damage
bīja	sa bon	seed
buddha	sangs rgyas	Buddha
buddhapada	sangs rgyas kyi go 'phang	buddhahood
buddhi	blo	awareness
bodhi	byang chub	enlightenment
bodhicitta	byang chub kyi sems	mind of enlightenment/ altruistic intention to become a Buddha
bodhisattva	byang chub sems dpa'	bodhisattva

bhagavat	bcom ldan 'das	Supramundane Victor
bhayaṃkaraṃ	'jigs	frighten
bhava	srid pa	mundane existence
bhavāgra	srid rtse	peak of cyclic existence
bhavānta	srid mtha'	almost does not occur
bhāva/sattva/bhava	yod pa/srid pa	existence/existent
bhāva/vastu	dngos po	entity/functioning thing/thing
bhāvanā	bsgom pa/sgom pa	cultivation/meditation
bhāvanāmārga	sgom lam	path of meditation
bhāvasvarūpa	dngos po'i rang bzhin	inherent existence of things
bhāvāḥ svatantrāḥ	dngos po rang dbang ba	self-powered thing
bhāvita	goms pa	familiarization
bhinna	phye ba/so so ba/tha dad pa	differentiate/individual/different
bhūmi	sa	ground
mañjughoṣa	'jam dbyangs	Mañjughoṣha
mañjuśrī	'jam dpal	Mañjushrī
mata	lugs	system
madhyama	dbu ma	middle way
madhyamapuruṣa	skyes bu 'bring	being of middling capacity
madhyamapratipad	dbu ma'i lam	middle path
manuja	shed las kyes pa	born from manu
mama	nga yi ba	mine
mamakāra	bdag gir 'dzin pa	conception of mine
marīci	smig rgyu	mirage
mahāyāna	theg pa chen po	Mahāyāna/Great Vehicle
mahāpuruṣa	skyes bu chen po	being of great capacity
mātṛkā	phyi mo	model
mādhyamika	dbu ma pa	Mādhyamika
mānava	shed bu	child of manu
māyā	sgyu ma	magician's illusion

māyopama	sgyu ma lta bu	illusion-like
māyopamādvaya-vādin	sgyu ma lta bu gnyis su med par smra ba	Proponent of Illusion-Like Non-Dualism
mārga	lam	path/path consciousness
*mārgapratiṣedhya	lam gyi dgag bya	object of negation by the path
mārgasatya	lam bden	true path
mithyā	log pa/phyin ci log	unreal/wrong/erroneous
mithyājñāna	log shes	wrong consciousness
mithyādṛṣṭi	log lta	wrong view
mithyāmāna	log pa'i nga rgyal	wrongful pride
muṣṭibandha	'dzin stangs	mode of apprehension
mūla	rtsa ba	root
mṛṣā	rdzun pa	false/falsity
moha	gti mug/rmongs pa	delusion/bewilderment/obscuration
maula	dngos	actual
yathā	ji lta ba	mode [of existence]
yathāruta	sgra ji bzhin pa	literal
yādṛcchika	'dod rgyal	arbitrarily
yukta/yuktatva	rung ba	suitable/suitability
yukti	rigs pa/'thad pa	reasoning
yujyate	rung ba	suitable
yogācāramādhyamika	rnal 'byor spyod pa'i dbu ma pa	Yogāchāra-Mādhyamika
yogipratyakṣa	rnal 'byor mngon sum	yogic direct perceiver/yogic direct perception
racayati	'byed pa	differentiate
rūpa	gzugs	form/visible form
rūpakāya	gzugs sku	Form Body

lakṣaṇa	mtshan nyid	characteristic
lakṣaṇaniḥsvabhāvatā	mtshan nyid ngo bo nyid med pa	non entityness of character
laya	bying ba	laxity
liṅga	rtags	sign/reason
lokāyata	'jig rten rgyang phan pa	Worldly Materialist
lokottara	'jig rten las 'das pa	supramundane
laukika	'jig rten pa	mundane
laukikavyavahāra	'jig rten pa'i tha snyad	worldly convention
vacana	bka'/gsung	saying/word/speech
vātsīputrīya	gnas ma bu pa	Vātsīputrīya
vandhyāputra	mo gsham gyi bu	child of a barren woman
varṇayati	smra ba/'chad pa/ brjod pa	propound/explain/ express
vastu/bhāva	dngos po/rdzas	thing/entity/ substantial entity
vastutas	dngos su	explicitly
vastusatpadārtha-vādin	dngos por smra ba/ dngos po yod par smra ba	Proponent of True Existence
vācaka	rjod byed	means of expression
vācya	brjod bya	subject discussed/ subject matter
vāsanā	bag chags	predisposition
vikalpa	rtog pa/rnam rtog	conceptuality
vicakṣaṇa	mkhas pa	wise
vicāra	dpyod pa/rnam par dpyod pa	analysis
viccheda	rnam bcad	[mere] elimination
vijñāna	rnam par shes pa	[ordinary] consciousness
vijñānānantya	rnam shes mtha' yas	limitless consciousness
vitarka	rtog pa/brtags pa	investigation
vidhi	sgrub pa	positive phenomenon
vināśa	'jig pa	destroy/destruction
viniścaya	gtan la 'babs pa	settle

vineya	gdul bya	trainee
viparīta	bzlog pa/phyin ci log	overturned/erroneous
viparyāsa	phyin ci log	error/erroneous
vipaśyanā	lhag mthong	special insight
vipravadati	rtsod pa byed	debate/argue
vimukti	grol ba	release
vimuktimārga	rnam grol lam	path of release
vimokṣa	thar pa	liberation
viraja	rdul bral	pure/free from dust
virodha	'gal ba	contradictory/contradiction
vivāda	rtsod pa	dispute/objection
viśeṣa	bye brag/khyad par/khyad chos	instance/feature/qualification
viśeṣādhigama	khyad par du rtogs pa	special realization
viśodhana	sbyang ba	purify
viṣaya	yul	object
vīrya	brtson 'grus	effort
vedakā	tshor ba po	feeler
vedanā	tshor ba	feeling
vaiyavadānikadharma	rnam par byang ba'i chos	very pure phenomenon
vyakta	gsal ba	clear
vyañjana	tshig 'bru	word/syllable
vyatireka	ldog pa	isolate
vyatirekavyāpti	ldog khyab	counter-pervasion
vyaya	'jig pa	disintegration
vyavasthāpita	rnam bzhag	presentation
vyavahāra	tha snyad	conventionality/verbal convention
*vyavahāravijñāna	tha snyad pa'i shes pa	conventional consciousness
*vyavahāradharma	tha snyad pa'i chos	conventional phenomena
*vyavahārapramāṇa	tha snyad pa'i tshad ma	conventional valid cognition
vyavahārasatya	tha snyad kyi bden pa	conventional truth
vyāpāra/vyāpārakaraṇa	bya ba/bya byed	activities
vyāpti	khyab pa	pervasion

śakti	nus pa	capacity/potency
śabda	sgra	sound
śamatha	zhi gnas	calm abiding
śaraṇa	skyabs	refuge
śānta	zhi ba	peaceful
śāśvatagrāha	rtag par 'dzin pa	conception of permanence
śāśvatadarśana	rtag lta	view of permanence
śāśvatānta	rtag pa'i mtha'	extreme of permanence/ extreme of reification
śāstra	bstan bcos	treatise
śiṣyatā	lhag ma lus pa	remainder left over
śīla	tshul khrims	ethics
śūnyatā	stong pa nyid	emptiness
śūnyatādarśana	stong nyid lta ba	seeing emptiness
śūnyatādṛṣṭi	stong nyid lta ba	viewing emptiness
śrāvaka	nyan thos	Hearer
śruta	thos pa	hearing
śrotra	rna ba	ear
saṃvṛti	kun rdzob/kun rdzob tu	concealer/ conventionality/ conventionally
saṃvṛtisatya	kun rdzob bden pa	conventional truth
saṃvṛtyā	tha snyad du/kun rdzob tu	conventionally
saṃsāra	'khor ba	cyclic existence
saṃskāra	'du byed	compositional factor
saṃkleśa/saṃkleśika	kun nas nyon mongs pa	thoroughly afflicted
saṅgati	tshogs pa	composite/collection
saṅgha	dge 'dun	spiritual community
saṅghāta	'dus pa	aggregation
saṃjñā	'du shes	discrimination
saṃjñākaraṇa	ming gis btags pa	nominally imputed
satataṃ	rags pa	coarse
satkāyadṛṣṭi	'jig tshogs la lta ba	view of the transitory collection
sattva	sems can/snying stobs	sentient being/power of heart

satya	bden pa	truth
satyasiddha	bden par grub pa	true establishment
saddharma	dam pa'i chos	excellent doctrine
santāna	rgyud/rgyun	continuum
saṃtuṣṭa	chog shes pa	satisfaction/be satisfied
samādhi	ting nge 'dzin	meditative stabilization
samānādhikaraṇa	gzhi mthun pa	common locus
samāropa	sgro 'dogs	superimposition/reification
samāhita	mnyam bzhag	meditative equipoise
samāhitajñāna	mnyam bzhag ye shes	exalted wisdom of meditative equipoise
samudaya	kun 'byung	source
samudayasatya	kun 'byung bden pa	true source of suffering
saṃprakhyāna	gsal ba	clarity
saṃbhāramārga	tshogs lam	path of accumulation
saṃmūḍha	kun tu rmongs pa	thorough obscuration
saṃmohabīja	kun tu rmongs pa'i sa bon	seed of obscuration
samyak	yang dag	real/correct
samyaksiddhi	yang dag par grub pa	establishment as [its own] reality
sarvadharmāpratiṣṭhānavādin	rab tu mi gnas par smra ba	Proponent of Thorough Non-Abiding
sarvākārajñāna	rnam mkhyen	omniscient consciousness/exalted-knower-of-all-aspects
sahaja	lhan skyes	innate
sākṣāt	dngos su	explicitly
sākṣātkaraṇa	mngon du bya ba/dngos rgyu	actualization/direct cause
sādhana	sgrub pa	proof
sādhāraṇa	thun mong ba	shared
sādhya	bsgrub bya	proven/to be proven
sāmagrī	tshogs pa	collection
sāmānya	spyi	generality
sāmānyalakṣaṇa	spyi mtshan	generally characterized phenomenon

sāsrava	zag bcas	contaminated
siddha	grub pa	proved/established
siddhānta	grub mtha'	tenets/tenet system
sīma	sa mtshams	boundary
sukha	bde ba	bliss
supta	gnyid log	sleep
*supta-adhikāra	gnyid log pa'i gnas skabs	state of sleep
sautrāntika-mādhyamika	mdo sde spyod pa'i dbu ma pa	Sautrāntika-Mādhyamika
skandha	phung po	aggregate
skandhalakṣaṇa	phung po'i mtshan nyid	character of the aggregates
styāna	rmugs pa	obscuration
sthūla	rags pa	coarse
sneha	sred pa/chags pa	attachment
sparśa	reg pa	contact
spraṣṭavya	reg bya	tangible object/object of touch
sphuṭa	gsal ba	clear
smṛti	dran pa/dran shes	mindfulness/memory/memory consciousness
svatantraprayoga	rang rgyud kyi sbyor ba	autonomous syllogism
svapna	rmi lam	dream
svabhāva	rang bzhin	[final] nature inherent existence
svabhāvatā siddhi/svarūpasiddhi/svābhāvikī siddhi	rang gi ngo bo nyid kyis grub pa	establishment by way of its own entity
*svabhāvaparyanta	rang bzhin mthar thug	final nature
svabhāvaśūnyatā	rang bzhin gyis stong pa nyid	emptiness of inherent existence
svabhāvasiddha	rang bzhin gyis grub pa/rang gi ngo bos grub pa	inherent establishment
svamata	rang lugs	own system
svarūpa	rang gi ngo bo	intrinsic entity/own-entity

svarūpasiddhi	rang gi ngo bos grub pa/rang ngos nas grub pa	established by way of its own entity/establishment from [the object's] own side/existence in its own right
svarūpeṇa vidyamāna	rang gi ngo bos yod pa	existence by way of its own entity
svalakṣaṇa	rang mtshan	own-character/self-character/specifically characterized phenomena
svalakṣaṇasat	rang gi mtshan nyid kyis yod pa	existence by way of its own character
svalakṣaṇasiddhi	rang gi mtshan nyid kyis grub pa	establishment by way of [the object's] own character
svātantrika	rang rgyud pa	Svātantrika
hīnayāna	theg dman	Hīnayāna/Lesser Vehicle
hetu	rgyu/rgyu mtshan/gtan tshigs	cause/reason
hetupratyaya	rgyu dang rkyen	causes and conditions

Bibliography of Works Cited

Note

Sūtras and tantras are listed alphabetically by English translation of the title in the first section. Indian and Tibetan treatises are listed alphabetically by author in the second. Works in Western languages are listed alphabetically by author in the third section.

"P", standing for "Peking edition", refers to the *Tibetan Tripiṭaka* (Tokyo-Kyoto: Tibetan Tripiṭaka research Foundation, 1956). "Toh" refers to the *Complete Catalogue of the Tibetan Buddhist Canons*, ed. by Prof. Hukuju Ui, and *A Catalogue of the Tohuku University Collection of Tibetan Works on Buddhism*, ed. by Prof. Yensho Kanakura (Sendai, Japan: 1934 and 1953). "Dharma" refers to the *sde dge* edition of the Tibetan canon published by Dharma Publishing – the *Nyingma Edition of the sDe-dge bKa'-'gyur and bsTan-'gyur* (Oakland, Ca.: Dharma Publishing, 1980). "Tokyo *sde dge*" refers to the *sDe dge Tibetan Tripiṭaka–bsTan ḥgyur preserved at the Faculty of Letters, University of Tokyo*, (Tokyo: 1977ff.).

References to the Peking edition of the Tibetan canon are given throughout. References to other editions are supplied only when those editions were actually consulted.

1 *Sūtras and Tantras*

Descent Into Laṅkā Sūtra
laṅkāvatārasūtra
lang kar gshegs pa'i mdo
P775, Vol.29
Sanskrit: *Saddharmalaṅkāvatārasūtram*, P.L. Vaidya, ed. Buddhist Sanskrit Texts No.3. (Darbhanga: Mithila Institute, 1963); also: Bunyiu Nanjio, ed. Bibl. Otaniensis, Vol.I. (Kyoto: Otani University Press, 1923)
English translation: D.T. Suzuki. *The Lankavatara Sutra*. (London: Routledge and Kegan Paul, 1932)

Extensive Sport Sūtra
lalitavistarasūtra
rgya cher rol pa'i mdo
P763, Vol.27
Sanskrit: *Lalitavistara*, P.L. Vaidya, ed. Buddhist Sanskrit Texts No.1. (Darbhanga: Mithila Institute, 1958)
English translation (from the French): Gwendolyn Bays. *The Lalitavistara Sūtra: The Voice of the Buddha, the Beauty of Compassion*. (Berkeley: Dharma Publishing, 1983)

Great Cloud Sūtra
mahāmeghasūtra
sprin chen po'i mdo
P898, Vol.35

Great Drum Sūtra
mahābherīhārakaparivartasūtra
rnga bo che chen po'i le'u'i mdo
P888, Vol.35

Heap of Jewels Sūtra
mahāratnakūṭadharmaparyāyaśatasāhasrikagranthasūtra
dkon mchog brtsegs pa chen po'i chos kyi rnam grangs le'u stong phrag brgya pa'i mdo
P760, Vol.22–24

Heart Sūtra/Heart of Wisdom Sūtra
prajñāhṛdaya/bhagavatīprajñāpāramitāhṛdayasūtra
shes rab snying po/bcom ldan 'das ma shes rab kyi pha rol tu phyin pa'i snying po'i mdo
P160, Vol.6
Sanskrit: in E. Conze. *Thirty Years of Buddhist Studies*. (Oxford: Cassirer, 1967), pp.148–53
English translation: E. Conze. *Buddhist Texts Through the Ages*. rpt. (New York: Harper, 1964), pp.152–3; also in Geshé Rabten's *Echoes of Voidness*. Stephen Batchelor, ed. and trans. (London: Wisdom, 1983), pp.18–19. Translation with explanation and Sanskrit text, E. Conze. *Buddhist Wisdom Books*. (London: George Allen & Unwin, 1958), pp.77–107.

Kālachakra Tantra/Condensed Kālachakra Tantra/Kālachakra, King of Tantras, Issued From the Supreme Original Buddha
paramādibuddhoddhṛtaśrīkālacakranāmatantrarāja
mchog gi dang po'i sangs rgyas las byung ba rgyud kyi rgyal po dpal dus kyi 'khor lo
P4, Vol.1
Sanskrit: *Kālacakra-Tantra And Other Texts*, Part 1. Prof. Dr. Raghu Vira and Prof. Dr. Lokesh Chandra, ed. (New Delhi: International Academy of Indian Culture, 1966)

Kāshyapa Chapter Sūtra
kāśyapaparivartasūtra
'od srung gi le'u'i mdo
P760.43, Vol.24

King of Meditative Stabilizations Sūtra
samādhirājasūtra/sarvadharmasvabhāvasamatāvipañcata-samādhirājasūtra
ting nge 'dzin rgyal po'i mdo/chos thams cad kyi rang bzhin

mnyam pa nyid rnam par spros pa ting nge 'dzin gyi rgyal po'i mdo
P795, Vol.31–2; Toh 127, Dharma Vol.20
Sanskrit: *Samādhirājasūtram*. P.L. Vaidya, ed. Buddhist Sanskrit Texts, No. 2. (Darbhanga: Mithila Institute, 1961)
Partial English translation (of chapters eight, nineteen, and twenty-two): K. Regamey. *Three Chapters from the Samādhirājasūtra*. (Warsaw: Publications of the Oriental Commission, 1938)

Mañjushrī Root Tantra
mañjuśrīmūlatantra
'jam dpal gyi rtsa ba'i rgyud
P162, Vol.6

Meeting of Father and Son Sūtra
pitāputrasamāgamasūtra
yab dang sras mjal ba'i mdo
P760.16, Vol.23

One Hundred and Fifty Means Perfection of Wisdom Sūtra
prajñāpāramitānayaśatapañcāśatikāsūtra
shes rab kyi pha rol tu phyin pa'i tshul brgya lnga bcu pa'i mdo
P121, Vol.5
English translation: E. Conze. in *The Short Prajñāpāramitā Texts*. (London: Luzac, 1973) pp.184–95

One Hundred Thousand Stanza Perfection of Wisdom
śatasāhasrikāprajñāpāramitā
shes rab kyi pha rol tu phyin pa stong phrag brgya pa
P730, Vol.12–18
See E. Conze. *The Large Sūtra on Perfect Wisdom*. (Berkeley: University of Calif. Press, 1975)

Ornament Illuminating the Exalted Wisdom Operating in the Sphere of All Buddhas Sūtra
sarvabuddhaviṣayāvatārajñānālokālaṃkārasūtra
sangs rgyas thams cad kyi yul la 'jug pa'i ye shes snang ba'i rgyan gyi mdo
P768, Vol.28

Questions of the King of Nāgas, Anavatapta, Sūtra
anavataptanāgarājaparipṛcchāsūtra
klu'i rgyal po ma dros pas zhus pa'i mdo
P823, Vol.33

Scriptural Collection of Bodhisattvas
bodhisattvapiṭaka
'phags pa byang chub sems dpa'i sde snod
P760.12, Vol.22–23; Toh 56, Dharma Vol.15–16

Sūtra of Cultivating Faith in the Mahāyāna
mahāyānaprasādaprabhāvanasūtra
theg pa chen po la dad pa rab tu sgom pa'i mdo
P812, Vol.32; Toh 144, Dharma Vol.21

Sūtra on the Four Reliances
catuḥpratisaraṇasūtra
rton ba bzhi'i mdo
[?]

Sūtra on the Ten Grounds
daśabhūmikasūtra
mdo sde sa bcu pa
P761.31, Vol.25
Sanskrit: *Daśabhūmikasūtram*. P.L. Vaidya, ed., Buddhist Sanskrit Texts No.7. (Darbhanga: Mithila Institute, 1967)
English translation: M. Honda. "An Annotated Translation of the 'Daśabhūmika'". In D. Sinor, ed., *Studies in Southeast and Central Asia*, Śatapiṭaka Series 74. (New Delhi: 1968), pp.115–276

Sūtra Unravelling the Thought
saṃdhinirmocanasūtra
dgongs pa nges par 'grel pa'i mdo
P774, Vol.29; Toh 106, Dharma Vol.18
Edited Tibetan text and French translation: Étienne Lamotte. *Saṃdhinirmocanasūtra: l'explication des mystères*. (Louvain: Université de Louvain, 1935)

Teachings of Akṣhayamati Sūtra
akṣayamatinirdeśasūtra
blo gros mi zad pas bstan pa'i mdo
P842, Vol.34

2 *Other Sanskrit and Tibetan Sources*

A-gya-yong-dzin (dbyangs can dga' ba'i blo gros, a kya yongs 'dzin, eighteenth century)
A Brief Explanation of Terminology Occurring in (Dzong-ka-ba's) "Great Exposition of the Stages of the Path"
byang chub lam gyi rim pa chen mo las byung ba'i brda bkrol nyer mkho bsdus pa
The Collected Works of A-kya Yoṅs-ḥdzin, Vol. 1
New Delhi: Lama Guru Deva, 1971

A-khu-ching (a khu ching shes rab rgya mtsho, 1803–1875)
Record of Teachings Received: A Drop of Water Taken Up with the Tip of a Hair From the Ocean of Ambrosia of Profound and Vast Sūtras and Tantras, Teachings Received of the Excellent Doctrine That is Virtuous in the Beginning, Middle, and End
thog mtha' bar du dge ba'i dam pa'i chos kyi thob yig mdo sngags zab rgyas bdud rtsi'i mtsho las skra rtses blangs pa'i chu thigs gsan yig
The Collected Works of A-khu-chiṅ Śes-rab-rgya-mtsho, Vol. 6
New Delhi: Ngawang Sopa, 1974

Advayavajra (gnyis su med pa'i rdo rje, eleventh century)
Precious Garland of Suchness
tattvaratnāvalī
de kho na nyid rin po che'i phreng ba
P3085, Vol.68

Āryadeva ('phags pa lha, second to third century, C.E.)
Four Hundred/Treatise of Four Hundred Stanzas

catuḥśatakaśāstrakārikā
bstan bcos bzhi brgya pa zhes bya ba'i tshig le'ur byas pa P5246, Vol.95
Edited Tibetan and Sanskrit fragments along with English translation: Karen Lang. *Āryadeva's Catuḥśataka: On the Bodhisattva's Cultivation of Merit and Knowledge*. (Copenhagen: Akademisk Forlag, 1986)
Italian translation from the Chinese of the last half: Giuseppe Tucci. "La versione cinese del Catuḥśataka di Āryadeva, confronta col testo sanscrito et la traduzione tibetana". *Rivista degli Studi Orientalia* 10 (1925), pp.521–567

Asaṅga (thogs med, fourth century)

Compendium on the Mahāyāna
mahāyānasaṃgraha
theg pa chen po bsdus pa
P5549, Vol.112
French translation and edited Chinese and Tibetan texts: Étienne Lamotte. *La somme du grand véhicule d'Asaṅga*, rpt. 2 vol. Publications de l'Institute Orientaliste de Louvain, Vol.8. (Louvain: Université de Louvain, 1973)

Levels of Yogic Practice/Actuality of the Levels
yogācāryābhūmi/bhūmivastu
rnal 'byor spyod pa'i sa/sa'i dngos gzhi
P5536–38, Vol.109–110

Ashvaghoṣha (rta dbyangs, third or fourth century [?])

Cultivation of the Ultimate Mind of Enlightenment/Essay on the Stages of Cultivating the Ultimate Mind of Enlightenment
paramārthabodhicittabhāvanākramavarṇasaṃgraha
don dam pa byang chub kyi sems bsgom pa'i rim pa yi ger bris pa
P5431, Vol.103

Atisha (982–1054)

Hundred Short Doctrines
jo bo je'i chos chung brgya rtsa
Paro, Bhutan: Lama Ngodrup and Sherab Drimey, 1979

Introduction to the Two Truths
satyadvayāvatāra
bden pa gnyis la 'jug pa
P5298, Vol.101; P5380, Vol.103
Edited Tibetan and English translation: Chr. Lindtner. "Atiśa's Introduction to the Two Truths, and Its Sources". *Journal of Indian Philosophy* 9 (1981), pp.161–214

Lamp for the Path to Enlightenment
bodhipathapradīpa
byang chub lam gyi sgron ma
P5343, Vol.103
English translation with Atisha's autocommentary: Richard Sherbourne, S.J. *A Lamp for the Path and Commentary*. (London: George Allen & Unwin, 1983)

Avadhūtipāda (avadhūtipa). See Advayavajra.

Avalokitavrata (spyan ras gzigs brtul zhugs, seventh or eighth century)

Explanatory Commentary on (Bhāvaviveka's) "Lamp for (Nāgārjuna's) 'Wisdom'"
prajñāpradīpaṭīkā
shes rab sgron ma'i rgya cher 'grel pa
P5259, Vol.96–7

Ba-so Chö-gyi-gyel-tsen (ba so chos kyi rgyal mtshan). See Jam-yang-shay-ba, et al.

Bhāvaviveka (legs ldan 'byed, c.500–570?)

Blaze of Reasoning, Commentary on the "Heart of the Middle Way"
madhyamakahṛdayavṛttitarkajvālā
dbu ma'i snying po'i 'grel pa rtog ge 'bar ba
P5256, Vol.96
Partial English translation (Ch.III. 1–136): S. Iida. *Reason and Emptiness*. (Tokyo: Hokuseido, 1980)

Heart of the Middle Way
madhyamakahṛdayakārikā
dbu ma'i snying po'i tshig le'ur byas pa

P5255, Vol.96
See directly above for partial translation
Lamp for (Nāgārjuna's) "Wisdom", Commentary on the "Treatise on the Middle Way"
prajñāpradīpamūlamadhyamakavṛtti
dbu ma rtsa ba'i 'grel pa shes rab sgron ma
P5253, Vol.95
Partial English translation (chapters 18, 24, and 25): David Eckel. "A Question of Nihilism: Bhāvaviveka's Response to the Fundamental Problems of Mādhyamika Philosophy", unpublished dissertation. (Harvard University, 1980)

Bu-dön (bu ston, 1290–1364)
History of the Doctrine
bde bar gshegs pa'i bstan pa'i gsal byed chos kyi 'byung gnas gsung rab rin po che'i mdzod
Lha-sa: zhol bka' 'gyur spar khang, n.d.
English translation by E. Obermiller. *History of Buddhism*. (Heidelberg: Harrasowitz, 1932). rpt. Suzuki Research Foundation

Buddhapālita (sangs rgyas bskyangs, c.470–540?)
Buddhapālita Commentary on (Nāgārjuna's) "Treatise on the Middle Way"
buddhapālitamūlamadhyamakavṛtti
dbu ma rtsa ba'i 'grel pa buddha pā li ta
P5254, Vol.95; Toh 3842, Tokyo *sde dge* Vol.1
Edited Tibetan edition: (Ch.1–12): Max Walleser. Bibliotheca Buddhica XVI. (Osnabrück: Biblio Verlag, 1970)
English translation of Ch.1: Judit Fehér. in Louis Ligeti, ed., *Tibetan and Buddhist Studies Commemorating the 200th Anniversary of the Birth of Alexander Csoma de Körös*, Vol.1. (Budapest: Akadémiai Kiado, 1984), pp.211–240
English translation of Ch.18: Chr. Lindtner. in *Indo-Iranian Journal* 23 (1981), pp.187–217.

Chandrahari
Precious Garland

ratnamālā
rin po che'i phreng ba
P5297, Vol.101

Chandrakīrti (zla ba grags pa, seventh century)

[Auto]commentary on the "Supplement to (Nāgārjuna's) 'Treatise on the Middle Way'"
madhaymakāvatārabhāṣya
dbu ma la 'jug pa'i bshad pa/dbu ma la 'jug pa'i rang 'grel
P5263, Vol.98
Also: Dharmsala: Council of Religious and Cultural Affairs, 1968
Edited Tibetan: Louis de la Vallée Poussin. *Madhyamakāvatāra par Candrakīrti*. Bibliotheca Buddhica IX. (Osnabrück: Biblio Verlag, 1970)
French translation (up to VI.165): Louis de la Vallée Poussin. *Muséon* 8 (1907), pp.249–317; *Muséon* 11 (1910), pp.271–358; and *Muséon* 12 (1911), pp.235–328.
German translation (VI.166–226): Helmut Tauscher. *Candrakīrti-Madhyamakāvatāraḥ und Madhyamakāvatārabhāṣyam*. (Wien: Wiener Studien zur Tibetologie und Buddhismuskunde, 1981)

Clear Words, Commentary on (Nāgārjuna's) "Treatise on the Middle Way"
mūlamadhyamakavṛttiprasannapadā
dbu ma rtsa ba'i 'grel pa tshig gsal ba
P5260, Vol.98
Also: Dharmsala: Tibetan Publishing House, 1968
Sanskrit: *Mūlamadhyamakakārikās de Nāgārjuna avec la Prasannapadā Commentaire de Candrakīrti*. Louis de la Vallée Poussin, ed. Bibliotheca Buddhica IV. (Osnabrück: Biblio Verlag, 1970)
English translation (Ch.I, XXV): T. Stcherbatsky. *Conception of Buddhist Nirvāṇa*. (Leningrad: Office of the Academy of Sciences of the USSR, 1927); revised rpt. (Delhi: Motilal Banarsidass, 1978), pp.77–222

English translation (Ch.II): Jeffrey Hopkins. "Analysis of Coming and Going". (Dharamsala: Library of Tibetan Works and Archives, 1974)

Partial English translation: Mervyn Sprung. *Lucid Exposition of the Middle Way, the Essential Chapters from the Prasannapadā of Candrakīrti translated from the Sanskrit*. (London: Routledge, 1979 and Boulder: Prajñā Press, 1979)

French translation (Ch.II–IV, VI–IX, XI, XXIII, XXIV, XXVI, XXVII): Jacques May. *Prasannapadā Madhyamakavṛtti, douze chapitres traduits du sanscrit et du tibétain*. (Paris: Adrien-Maisonneuve, 1959)

French translation (Ch.XVIII–XXII): J.W. de Jong. *Cinq chapitres de la Prasannapadā*. (Paris: Geuthner, 1949)

French translation (Ch.XVII): É. Lamotte. "Le Traité de l'acte de Vasubandhu, Karmasiddhiprakaraṇa". *MCB* 4 (1936), 265–288

German translation (Ch.V and XII–XVI): St. Schayer. *Ausgewählte Kapitel aus der Prasannapadā*. (Krakow: Naktadem Polskiej Akademji Umiejetnosci, 1931)

German translation (Ch.X): St. Schayer. "Feuer und Brennstoff". *Rocznik Orjentalistyczny* 7 (1931), pp.26– 52

Commentary on (Āryadeva's) "Four Hundred Stanzas on the Yogic Deeds of Bodhisattvas"

bodhisattvayogācāracatuḥśatakaṭīkā

byang chub sems dpa'i rnal 'byor spyod pa gzhi brgya pa'i rgya cher 'grel pa

P5266, Vol.98; Toh 3865, Tokyo *sde dge* Vol.8

Edited Sanskrit fragments: Haraprasād Shāstri, ed. "Catuḥśatika of Ārya Deva." Memoirs of the Asiatic Society of Bengal, III no. 8 (1914), pp.449–514

Also (Ch.8–16): Vidhusekhara Bhattacarya, ed. *The Catuḥśataka of Āryadeva: Sanskrit and Tibetan texts with copious extracts from the commentary of Candra-*

kīrti, Part II. (Calcutta: Visva-Bharati Bookshop, 1931)

Commentary on (Nāgārjuna's) "Seventy Stanzas on Emptiness"
śūnyatāsaptativṛtti
stong pa nyid bdun cu pa'i 'grel pa
P5268, Vol.99

Commentary on (Nāgārjuna's) "Sixty Stanzas of Reasoning"
yuktiṣaṣṭikāvṛtti
rigs pa drug cu pa'i 'grel pa
P5265, Vol.98, Toh 3864, Tokyo *sde dge* Vol.8

Supplement to (Nāgārjuna's) "Treatise on the Middle Way"
madhyamakāvatāra
dbu ma la 'jug pa
P5261, P5262, Vol.98
Edited Tibetan: Louis de la Vallée Poussin. *Madhyamakāvatāra par Candrakīrti*. Bibliotheca Buddhica IX. (Osnabrück: Biblio Verlag, 1970)
English translation (Ch.I–V): Jeffrey Hopkins. within *Compassion in Tibetan Buddhism*. (Valois, NY: Gabriel Snow Lion, 1980)
English translation (Ch.VI): Stephen Batchelor, trans. in Geshé Rabten's *Echoes of Voidness*. (London: Wisdom, 1983), pp.47–92
See also references under Chandrakīrti's *[Auto]-Commentary on the "Supplement"*

Den-dar-hla-ram-ba (bstan dar lha ram pa, 1759–?)

Presentation of Specifically and Generally Characterized Phenomena
rang mtshan spyi mtshan gyi rnam gzhag
Collected *gsung 'bum* of Bstan-dar Lha-ram of A-lag-sha, Vol.1
New Delhi: Lama Guru Deva, 1971

Dharmakīrti (chos kyi grags pa, seventh century)

Commentary on (Dignāga's) "Compendium on Prime Cognition"
pramāṇavārttikakārikā
tshad ma rnam 'grel gyi tshig le'ur byas pa
P5709, Vol.130

Also: Sarnath, India: Pleasure of Elegant Sayings Press, 1974

Sanskrit: *Pramāṇavārttika of Acharya Dharmakīrtti.* Swami Dwarikadas Shastri, ed. (Varanasi: Bauddha Bharati, 1968)

Dra-di Ge-shay Rin-chen-dön-drup (bra sti dge bshes rin chen don grub). See Jam-yang-shay-ba, et al.

Dzong-ka-ba (tsong kha pa blo bzang grags pa, 1357–1419)

Advice to the Lord of Tsa-ko, Nga-wang-drak-ba

tsha kho dpon po ngag dbang grags pa la gdams pa

See *The Three Principal Aspects of the Path*

Answers to the Questions of Jang-chup-la-ma

byang chub bla ma'i dri len

[?]

Concise Meaning of the Stages of the Path

lam rim bsdus don/byang chub lam gyi rim pa'i nyams len gyi rnam gzhag mdor bsdus

The Collected Works of Rje Tsoṅ-kha-pa Blo-bzaṅ-grags-pa, Vol.kha, *thor bu*, 65b.2–68b.1

New Delhi: Ngawang Gelek Demo, 1975ff

Essence of the Good Explanations, Treatise Discriminating the Interpretable and the Definitive

drang ba dang nges pa'i don rnam par phye ba'i bstan bcos legs bshad snying po

P6142, Vol.153

Also: Sarnath: Pleasure of Elegant Sayings Printing Press, 1973

English translation: Robert Thurman. *Tsong Khapa's Speech of Gold in the Essence of True Eloquence.* (Princeton: Princeton University Press, 1984)

Four Interwoven Annotations on (Dzong-ka-ba's) "Great Exposition of the Stages of the Path"

The Lam rim chen mo of the incomparable Tsong-kha-pa, with the interlineal notes of Ba-so Chos-kyi-rgyal-mtshan, Sde-drug Mkhan-chen Ngag-dbang-rab-brtan, 'Jam-dbyangs-bzhad-pa'i-rdo-rje, and Bra-sti Dge-bshes Rin-chen-don-grub

New Delhi: Chos-'phel-legs-ldan, 1972

Golden Rosary of Good Explanation/Extensive Explanation of (Maitreya's) "Ornament for Clear Realization, Treatise of Quintessential Instructions on the Perfection of Wisdom", As Well As Its Commentaries

legs bshad gser gyi phreng ba/shes rab kyi pha rol tu phyin pa'i man ngag gi bstan bcos mngon par rtogs pa'i rgyan 'grel pa dang bcas pa'i rgya cher bshad pa

P6150, Vol.154

Also: Sarnath: Pleasure of Elegant Sayings Press, 1970

Also: The Collected Works of Rje Tsoṅ-kha-pa Blo-bzaṅ-grags-pa, Vol.tsa. (New Delhi: Ngawang Gelek Demo, 1975ff)

Great Exposition of Secret Mantra/The Stages of the Path to a Conqueror and Pervasive Master, a Great Vajradhara: Revealing All Secret Topics

sngags rim chen mo/rgyal ba khyab bdag rdo rje 'chang chen po'i lam gyi rim pa gsang ba kun gyi gnad rnam par phye ba

P6210, Vol.161

English translation (Ch.1): by Jeffrey Hopkins. in *Tantra in Tibet*. (London: George Allen & Unwin, 1977)

English translation (Ch.2 & 3): by Jeffrey Hopkins. in *Yoga of Tibet*. (London: George Allen & Unwin, 1981)

"Great Exposition of Special Insight"

lhag mthong chen mo

In *rje tsong kha pa'i gsung dbu ma'i lta ba'i skor*, Vol.1

Sarnath, India: Pleasure of Elegant Sayings Press, 1975

English translation: Alex Wayman. *Calming the Mind and Discerning the Real*. (New York: Columbia University Press, 1978); reprint (New Delhi: Motilal Banarsidass, 1979)

Great Exposition of the Stages of the Path/Stages of the Path to Enlightenment Thoroughly Teaching All the Stages of Practice of the Three Types of Beings

lam rim chen mo/skyes bu gsum gyi rnyams su blang

ba'i rim pa thams cad tshang bar ston pa'i byang chub lam gyi rim pa
P6001, Vol.152
Also: Dharmsala: Shes rig par khang, no date
Also: The Collected Works of Rje Tsoṅ-kha-pa Blo-bzaṅ-grags-pa, Vol.pa. (New Delhi: Ngawang Gelek Demo, 1975ff.)

Illumination of the Thought, Extensive Explanation of (Chandrakīrti's) "Supplement to (Nāgārjuna's) 'Treatise on the Middle Way'"
dbu ma la 'jug pa'i rgya cher bshad pa dgongs pa rab gsal
P6143, Vol.154
Also: Sarnath, India: Pleasure of Elegant Sayings Press, 1973
English translation (first five chapters): Jeffrey Hopkins. in *Compassion in Tibetan Buddhism.* (Valois, New York: Gabriel Snow Lion, 1980)

"Medium Exposition of Special Insight"
lhag mthong 'bring
In *rje tsong kha pa'i gsung dbu ma'i lta ba'i skor*, Vol. 2
Sarnath, India: Pleasure of Elegant Sayings Press, 1975
English translation: Robert Thurman. "The Middle Transcendent Insight". in *The Life and Teachings of Tsong Khapa*, Robert A.F.Thurman, ed. (Dharamsala, Library of Tibetan Works and Archives, 1982), pp.108–85. Also: Jeffrey Hopkins, "Special Insight: From Dzong-ka-ba's *Middling Exposition of the Stages of the Path to Enlightenment Practiced by Persons of Three Capacities* with supplementary headings by Trijang Rinbochay", unpublished manuscript

Medium Exposition of the Stages of the Path
lam rim 'bring
P6002, Vol.152–3
Also: Dharmsala: Shes rig par khang, 1968
Also: Mundgod: Ganden Shardzay, n.d., (edition

including outline of topics by Trijang Rinbochay)

Ocean of Reasoning, Explanation of (Nāgārjuna's) "Fundamental Treatise on the Middle Way Called 'Wisdom'"
dbu ma rtsa ba'i tshig le'ur byas pa shes rab ces bya ba'i rnam bshad rigs pa'i rgya mtsho
P6153, Vol.156
Also: Sarnath: Pleasure of Elegant Sayings Press, no date
Also: in *rje tsong kha pa'i gsung dbu ma'i lta ba'i skor*, Vol.1 and 2 (Sarnath, India: Pleasure of Elegant Sayings Press, 1975)
English translation (of Chapter two): Jeffrey Hopkins. "Chapter Two of Ocean of Reasoning by Tsong-ka-pa". (Dharamsala: Library of Tibetan Works and Archives, 1974)

Praise of Dependent-Arising/Praise of the Supramundane Victor Buddha from the Approach of His Teaching the Profound Dependent-Arising, Essence of the Good Explanations
rten 'brel bstod pa/sangs rgyas bcom ldan 'das la zab mo rten cing 'brel bar 'byung ba gsung ba'i sgo nas bstod pa legs par bshad pa'i snying po
P6016, Vol.153
English tranlation: Geshe Wangyal. in *The Door of Liberation*. (New York: Lotsawa, 1978), pp.117–25. Also: Robert Thurman. in *The Life and Teachings of Tsong Khapa*. (Dharamsala, Library of Tibetan Works and Archives, 1982), pp.99–107

The Three Principal Aspects of the Path
lam gtso rnam gsum/tsha kho dpon po ngag dbang grags pa la gdams pa
P6087, Vol.153
English translation: Geshe Wangyal. in *The Door of Liberation*. (New York: Lotsawa, 1978), pp.126–60. Also: Jeffrey Hopkins and Geshe Sopa. in *Practice and Theory of Tibetan Buddhism*. (New York: Grove Press, 1976), pp.1–47. Also: Jeffrey Hopkins. Including commentary from the Dalai Lama, in Tenzin

Gyatso's *Kindness, Clarity, and Insight.* (Ithaca, N.Y.: Snow Lion, 1984) pp.118–56. Also: Robert Thurman. in *The Life and Teachings of Tsong Khapa.* (Dharamsala, Library of Tibetan Works and Archives, 1982), pp.57–8

Fifth Dalai Lama. See Nga-wang-lo-sang-gya-tso.

Gen-dun-chö-pel (dge 'dun chos 'phel, 1905?–1951?)

Ornament to Nāgārjuna's Thought, Eloquence Containing the Essence of the Profundities of the Middle Way

dbu ma'i zab gnad snying por dril ba'i legs bshad klu sgrub dgongs rgyan

Kalimpong: Mani Printing Works, no date

Gön-chok-jik-may-wang-bo (dkon mchog 'jigs med dbang po, 1728–91)

Precious Garland of Tenets/Presentation of Tenets, A Precious Garland

grub pa'i mtha'i rnam par bzhag pa rin po che'i phreng ba

Dharmsala: Shes rig par khang, 1969

English translation: Sopa and Hopkins. in *Practice and Theory of Tibetan Buddhism.* (New York: Grove, 1976), pp.48–145. Also: H.V. Guenther. in *Buddhist Philosophy in Theory and Practice.* (Baltimore: Penguin, 1972)

Presentation of the Grounds and Paths, Ornament Beautifying the Three Vehicles

sa lam gyi rnam bzhag theg gsum mdzes rgyan

The Collected Works of dkon-mchog-'jigs-med-dbang-po, Vol.7

New Delhi: Ngawang Gelek Demo, 1972

Gung-tang Gön-chok-den-bay-drön-me, (gung thang dkon mchog bstan pa'i sgron me, 1762–1823)

Beginnings of a Commentary on the Difficult Points of (Dzong-ka-ba's) "Differentiation of the Interpretable and the Definitive", the Quintessence of the "Essence of the Good Explanations"

drang nges rnam 'byed kyi dka' 'grel rtsom 'phro legs

bshad snying po'i yang snying
Sarnath: Guru Deva, 1965

Gyel-tsap, (rgyal tshab, 1364–1432)

Essence of Good Explanation, Explanation of (Āryadeva's) "Four Hundred"
bzhi brgya pa'i rnam bshad legs bshad snying po
Sarnath: Pleasure of Elegant Sayings Printing Press, 1971

Ornament for the Essence, Explanation [of Maitreya's "Ornament for Clear Realization" and its Commentaries]
rnam bshad snying po rgyan/shes rab kyi pha rol tu phyin pa'i man ngag gi bstan bcos mngon par rtogs pa'i rgyan gyi 'grel pa don gsal ba'i rnam bshad snying po'i rgyan
Sarnath: Gelugpa Student's Welfare Committee, 1980

Haribhadra (seng ge bzang po, late eighth century)

Clear Meaning Commentary/Commentary on (Maitreya's) "Ornament for Clear Realization, Treatise of Quintessential Instructions on the Perfection of Wisdom"
sphuṭārtha/abhisamayālaṃkāranāmaprajñāpāramitopadeśaśāstravṛtti
'grel pa don gsal/shes rab kyi pha rol tu phyin pa'i man ngag gi bstan bcos mngon par rtogs pa'i rgyan ces bya ba'i 'grel pa
P5191, Vol.90

Jam-yang-shay-ba ('jam dbyangs bzhad pa, 1648–1721)

Great Exposition of Tenets/Explanation of 'Tenets', Sun of the Land of Samantabhadra Brilliantly Illuminating All of Our Own and Others' Tenets and the Meaning of the Profound [Emptiness], Ocean of Scripture and Reasoning Fulfilling All Hopes of All Beings
grub mtha' chen mo/grub mtha'i rnam bshad rang gzhan grub mtha' kun dang zab don mchog tu gsal ba kun bzang zhing gi nyi ma lung rigs rgya mtsho skye dgu'i re ba kun skong
Musoorie: Dalama, 1962
English translation (beginning of the Prāsaṅgika

chapter): Jeffrey Hopkins. in *Meditation on Emptiness*. (London: Wisdom, 1983)

Great Exposition of the Middle Way/Analysis of (Chandrakīrti's) "Supplement to (Nāgārjuna's) 'Treatise on the Middle Way'", Treasury of Scripture and Reasoning, Thoroughly Illuminating the Profound Meaning [of Emptiness], Entrance for the Fortunate

dbu ma chen mo/dbu ma 'jug pa'i mtha' dpyod lung rigs gter mdzod zab don kun gsal skal bzang 'jug ngogs

Buxaduor: Gomang, 1967

Jam-yang-shay-ba et al. (Jam-yang-shay-ba, Ba-so Chö-gyi-gyel-tsen (ba so chos kyi rgyal mtshan), De-druk-ken-chen Nga-wang-rap-den (sde drug mkhan chen ngag dbang rab brtan), and Dra-di-ge-shay Rin-chen-dön-drub (bra sti dge bshes rin chen don grub)

Four Interwoven Annotations to (Dzong-ka-ba's) "Great Exposition of the Stages of the Path"/Clear Lamp of the Mahāyāna Path, Good Explanation by way of the Four Annotations on the Difficult Points of the "Great Exposition of the Stages of the Path to Enlightenment" Composed by the Unequalled Foremost Venerable Dzong-ka-ba

lam rim mchan bzhi sbrags ma/mnyam med rje btsun tsong kha pa chen pos mdzad pa'i byang chub lam rim chen mo'i dka' ba'i gnad rnams mchan bu bzhi'i sgo nas legs par bshad pa theg chen lam gyi gsal sgron)

Published as: *The Lam rim chen mo of the incomparable Tsong-kha-pa, with the interlineal notes of Ba-so Chos-kyi-rgyal-mtshan, Sde-drug Mkhan-chen Ngag-dbang-rab-brtan, 'Fam-dbyangs-bzhad-pa'i-rdo-rje, and Bra-sti Dge-bshes Rin-chen-don-grub*

New Delhi: Chos-'phel-legs-ldan, 1972

Different edition: *The Great Exposition of the Stages of the Path to Enlightenment Along With Annotations, Jewelled Source of Good Explanation*

byang chub lam gyi rim pa chen mo mchan 'grel dang bcas pa legs par bshad pa nor bu'i 'byung gnas

No publication data, printed in China

Jang-gya (lcang skya, 1717–86)

Presentation of Tenets/Clear Exposition of the Presentations of Tenets, Beautiful Ornament for the Meru of the Subduer's Teaching

grub mtha'i rnam bzhag/grub pa'i mtha'i rnam par bzhag pa gsal bar bshad pa thub bstan lhun po'i mdzes rgyan

Varanasi: Pleasure of Elegant Sayings Press, 1970

English translation (Sautrāntika chapter): Anne Klein. in "Mind and Liberation. The Sautrāntika Tenet System in Tibet: Perception, Naming, Positive and Negative Phenomena, Impermanence and the Two Truths in the Context of Buddhist Religious Insight as Presented in Ge-luk Literary and Oral Traditions". (Ann Arbor: University Microfilms, 1981)

English translation (Svātantrika chapter): Donald S. Lopez, Jr. in "The Svātantrika-Mādhyamika School of Mahāyāna Buddhism". (Ann Arbor: University Microfilms, 1982)

English translation (first half of the Prāsaṅgika chapter): Jeffrey Hopkins. *Emptiness Yoga*. (Ithaca, N.Y: Snow Lion, 1987)

Jñānavajra (ye shes rdo rje)

Two Staged Path

lam gyi rim pa gnyis pa

[?]

Kamalashīla (c.740–795)

Illumination of the Middle Way

madhyamakāloka

dbu ma snang ba

P5287, Vol.101

Stages of Meditation

bhāvanākrama

sgom pa'i rim pa

Sanskrit: *First Bhāvanākrama*. G. Tucci, ed. Minor Buddhist texts, II, Serie Orientale Roma IX, 2.

(Rome: IS.M.E.O., 1958), pp.185–229. *Third Bhāvanākrama*. G. Tucci, ed. Minor Buddhist texts, III, Serie Orientale Roma XLIII. (Rome: IS.M.E.O., 1971)

P5310–12, Vol. 102; Toh 3915–17, Dharma Vol.73, Tokyo *sde dge* Vol.15

Kay-drup Ge-lek-bel-sang-bo (mkhas sgrub dge legs dpal bzang po, 1385–1438)

Thousand Dosages/Opening the Eyes of the Fortunate, Treatise Brilliantly Clarifying the Profound Emptiness

stong thun chen mo/zab mo stong pa nyid rab tu gsal bar byed pa'i bstan bcos skal bzang mig 'byed

The Collected Works of the Lord Mkhas-grub rje dge-legs-dpal-bzaṅ-po, Vol.1, 179–702

New Delhi: Mongolian Lama Gurudeva, 1980

Wonderful, Amazing Biography of the Great Foremost Venerable Lama, Dzong-ka-ba, Entrance Way of the Faithful

rje btsun bla ma tsong kha pa chen po'i ngo mtshar rmad du byung ba'i rnam par thar pa dad pa'i 'jug ngogs

Varanasi: Lhundup and Samdup, 1966

Lo-den-shay-rap (blo ldan shes rab, 1059–1109)

Epistolary Essay, Drop of Ambrosia

spring yig bdud rtsi'i thigs pa

Incompletely cited in Ser-dok Paṇ-chen Shākya-chok-den's (*gser mdog paṇ chen shākya mchog ldan*, 1428–1507) *Explanation of the "Epistolary Essay, Drop of Ambrosia", Magical Rosary Fulfilling All Wishes* (spring yig bdud rtsi'i thigs pa'i rnam bshad dpag bsam yong 'du'i ljon phreng). The Collected works of Gser-mdog Paṇ-chen, Vol.24, 320.6–348.6. (Thimphu, Bhutan: Kunzang Topgey, 1978)

Lo-sang-da-yang (blo bzang rta dbyangs, also known as blo bzang rta mgrin, 1867–1937)

Brief Expression of the Presentation of the Grounds and Paths of the Three Vehicles According to the System of the Perfection Vehicle, Essence of the Ocean of Profound Meaning phar phyin theg pa'i lugs kyi theg pa gsum gyi sa dang lam gyi rnam bzhag pa mdo tsam du brjod pa zab don rgya mtsho'i snying po

The Collected Works of Rje-Btsun Blo-Bzaṅ-Rta-Mgrin, Vol.IV, pp.65–190

New Delhi: Guru Deva, 1975

Lo-sang-dor-jay (blo bzang rdo rje, twentieth century)

Ship for Entering Into the Ocean of Textual Systems, Decisive Analysis of (Dzong-ka-ba's) "[Great Exposition of] the Stages of the Path to Enlightenment", Special Insight Section

byang chub lam gyi rim pa'i mtha' dpyod gzhung lugs rgya mtshor 'jug pa'i gru gzings zhes bya ba las lhag mthong gi mtha' dpyod

New Delhi: Mongolian Lama Gurudeva, 1980

Lo-sang-gön-chok (blo bzang dkon mchog)

Word Commentary on the Root Text of (Jam-yang-shay-ba's) "Tenets", A Crystal Mirror

grub mtha' rtsa ba'i tshig ṭik shel dkar me long

In *Three Commentaries on the Grub mtha' rtsa ba gdoṅ lṅa'i sgra dbyaṅs of 'Jam-dbyaṅs-bźad-pa'i-rdo-rje ṅag-dbaṅ-brtson-'grus*

Delhi: Chophel Lekden, 1978

Long-döl La-ma Nga-wang-lo-sang (klong rdol bla ma ngag dbang blo bzang, 1719–94)

Catalogue of the Collected Works of Certain Principal Ga-dam-ba and Ge-luk-ba Lamas

bka' gdams pa dang dge lugs bla ma rag[s] rim gyi gsung 'bum mtshan tho

Lokesh Chandra, ed., *Materials for a History of Tibetan Literature*, Part Three, pp.607–696

New Delhi: International Academy of Indian Culture, 1963

Maitreya (byams pa)

Differentiation of the Middle Way and the Extremes

madhyāntavibhaṅga

dbus dang mtha' rnam par 'byed pa

P5522, Vol.108
Sanskrit: *Madhyānta-vibhāga-śāstra*. Ramchandra Pandeya ed. (Delhi: Motilal Banarsidass, 1971)
Partial English translation: T. Stcherbatsky. *Madhyānta-Vibhaṅga*. (Calcutta: Indian Studies Past and Present, 1971)

Ornament for Clear Realization
abhisamayālaṃkāra
mngon par rtogs pa'i rgyan
P5184, Vol.88
Sanskrit: *Abhisamayālaṃkāra-Prajñāpāramitā-Updeśa-Śāstra*. Th. Stcherbatsky and E. Obermiller, ed. Bibliotheca Buddhica XXIII. (Osnabrück: Biblio Verlag, 1970)
English translation: Edward Conze. *Abhisamayālaṅkāra*. Serie Orientale Roma VI (Rome: IS.M.E.O., 1954)

Sublime Continuum of the Great Vehicle
mahāyānottaratantraśāstra
theg pa chen po rgyud bla ma'i bstan bcos
Sanskrit: *The Ratnagotravibhāga Mahāyānottaratantra-śāstra*. E.H. Johnston (and T. Chowdhury) ed. (Patna: Bihar Research Society, 1950)
English translation: E. Obermiller. "Sublime Science of the Great Vehicle to Salvation". *Acta Orientalia*, 9 (1931), pp. 81–306. Also: J. Takasaki. *A Study on the Ratnagotravibhāga*. (Rome: IS.M.E.O., 1966)

Nāgārjuna (klu sgrub, first to second century, C.E.)

Commentary on the "Refutation of Objections"
vigrahavyavārtinīvṛtti
rtsod pa bzlog pa'i 'grel pa
P5232, Vol.95; Toh 3832, Tokyo *sde dge*, Vol.1
Sanskrit text edited by Johnston and Kunst, English translation by K. Bhattacharya. in *The Dialectical Method of Nāgārjuna*. (New Delhi: Motilal Banarsidass, 1978)

Commentary on the "Seventy Stanzas on Emptiness"

śunyatāsaptativṛtti
stong pa nyid bdun cu pa'i 'grel pa
P5231, Vol.95; Toh 3831, Tokyo *sde dge* Vol.1
Edited Tibetan: Chr. Lindtner. in *Nāgārjuna's Filosofiske Vaerker*. Indiske Studier 2, pp.219–44. (Copenhagen: Akademisk Forlag, 1982)

Essay on the Mind of Enlightenment
bodhicittavivaraṇa
byang chub sems kyi 'grel pa
P2665 and 2666, Vol.61
Edited Tibetan and Sanskrit fragments along with English translation: Chr. Lindtner. in *Nagarjuniana*. Indiske Studier 4, pp.180–218. (Copenhagen: Akademisk Forlag, 1982)

Praise of the Element of Qualities
dharmadhātustotra
chos kyi dbyings su bstod pa
P2010, Vol.46

Praise of the Supramundane [Buddha]
lokātītastava
'jig rten las 'das par bstod pa
P2012, Vol.46
Edited Tibetan and Sanskrit along with English translation: Chr. Lindtner. in *Nagarjuniana*. Indiske Studier 4, pp.121–38. (Copenhagen: Akademisk Forlag, 1982)

Precious Garland of Advice for the King
rājaparikathāratnāvalī
rgyal po la gtam bya ba rin po che'i phreng ba
P5658, Vol.129
Edited Sanskrit, Tibetan, and Chinese: *Nāgārjuna's Ratnāvalī, Vol.1, The Basic Texts (Sanskrit, Tibetan, and Chinese)*. Michael Hahn, ed. (Bonn: Indica et Tibetica Verlag, 1982)
English translation: Jeffrey Hopkins. in Nāgārjuna and the Seventh Dalai Lama's *The Precious Garland and the Song of the Four Mindfulnesses*. (New York: Harper and Row, 1975)

Refutation of Objections
vigrahavyāvartanīkārikā
rtsod pa bzlog pa'i tshig le'ur byas pa
P5228, Vol.95; Toh 3828, Tokyo *sde dge* Vol.1
Sanskrit text edited by Johnston and Kunst and English translation by K. Bhattacharya. in *The Dialectical Method of Nāgārjuna*. (New Delhi: Motilal Banarsidass, 1978)
Edited Tibetan and Sanskrit: in Chr. Lindtner. *Nagarjuniana*. Indiske Studier 4, pp.70–86. (Copenhagen: Akademisk Forlag, 1982)
Translation from the Chinese version of the text: G. Tucci. in *Pre-Diṅnāga Buddhist Texts on Logic from Chinese Sources*. Gaekwad's Oriental Series, 49. (Baroda: Oriental Institute, 1929)
French translation: S. Yamaguchi. "Traité de Nāgārjuna pour écarter les vaines discussion (Vigrahavyāvartanī) traduit et annoté." *Journal Asiatique* 215 (1929) pp.1– 86

Seventy Stanzas on Emptiness
śūnyatāsaptatikārikā
stong pa nyid bdun cu pa'i tshig le'ur byas pa
P5227, Vol.95; Toh 3827, Tokyo *sde dge* Vol.1
Edited Tibetan and English translation: Chr. Lindtner. in *Nagarjuniana*. Indiske Studier 4, pp.34–69. (Copenhagen: Akademisk Forlag, 1982)

Sixty Stanzas of Reasoning
yuktiṣaṣṭikākārikā
rigs pa drug cu pa'i tshig le'ur byas pa
P5225, Vol.95; Toh 3825, Tokyo *sde dge* Vol.1
Edited Tibetan with Sanskrit fragments and English translation: Chr. Lindtner. in *Nagarjuniana*. Indiske Studier 4, pp.100–119. (Copenhagen: Akademisk Forlag, 1982)

Treatise Called the Finely Woven
vaidalyasūtranāma
zhib mo rnam par 'thag pa zhes bya ba'i mdo
P5226, Vol.95

Treatise on the Middle Way/Fundamental Treatise on the Middle Way, Called "Wisdom"

madhyamakaśāstra/prajñānāmamūlamadhyamakakārikā

dbu ma'i bstan bcos/dbu ma rtsa ba'i tshig le'ur byas pa shes rab ces bya ba

P5224, Vol.95

Edited Sanskrit: *Nāgārjuna, Mūlamadhyamakakārikāḥ*. J.W. de Jong, ed. (Adyar: Adyar Library and Research Centre, 1977). Also: Chr. Lindtner. in *Nāgārjuna's Filosofiske Vaerker*. Indiske Studier 2, pp.177–215. (Copenhagen: Akademisk Forlag, 1982)

English translation: Frederick Streng. *Emptiness: A Study in Religious Meaning*. (Nashville, New York: Abingdon Press, 1967). Also: Kenneth Inada. *Nāgārjuna: A Translation of his Mūlamadhyamakakārikā*. (Tokyo, The Hokuseido Press, 1970). Also: David Kalupahana. *Nāgārjuna: The Philosophy of the Middle Way*. (Albany, N.Y.: State University of New York Press, 1986).

Italian translation: R. Gnoli. *Nāgārjuna: Madhyamaka Kārikā, Le stanze del cammino di mezzo*. Enciclopedia di autori classici 61. (Turin: P. Boringhieri, 1961)

Danish translation: Chr. Lindtner. in *Nāgārjuna's Filosofiske Vaerker*. Indiske Studier 2, pp.67–135. (Copenhagen: Akademisk Forlag, 1982)

For more detail on published editions and translations, see Ruegg's *Literature of the Madhyamaka School of Philosophy in India*, pp.126–7. For other translations included within commentary, see listings under Chandrakīrti's *Clear Words* and Buddhapālita.

Nga-wang-bel-den (ngag dbang dpal ldan, b.1797)

Annotations for (Jam-yang-shay-ba's) "Great Exposition of Tenets", Freeing the Knots of the Difficult Points, Precious Jewel of Clear Thought

grub mtha' chen mo'i mchan 'grel dka' gnad mdud grol blo gsal gces nor

Sarnath: Pleasure of Elegant Sayings Press, 1964

Explanation of the Conventional and the Ultimate in the Four Systems of Tenets/Presentation of the Two Truths

grub mtha' bzhi'i lugs kyi kun rdzob dang don dam pa'i don rnam par bshad pa legs bshad dpyid kyi dpal mo'i glu dbyangs/bden gnyis kyi rnam bzhag

New Delhi: Guru Deva, 1972

English translation (first chapter): John Buescher. in "The Buddhist Doctrine of Two Truths in the Vaibhāṣika and Theravāda Schools". (Ann Arbor: University Microfilms, 1982)

Presentation of the Grounds and Paths of Mantra/Illumination of the Texts of Tantra, Presentation of the Grounds and Paths of the Four Great Secret Tantra Sets

sngags kyi sa lam/gsang chen rgyud sde bzhi'i sa lam gyi rnam bzhag rgyud gzhung gsal byed

rgyud smad par khang edition, no other data

Nga-wang-lo-sang-gya-tso (*ngag dbang blo bzang rgya mtsho*, Fifth Dalai Lama, 1617–1682)

Sacred Word of Mañjushrī, Instructions on the Stages of Path to Enlightenment

byang chub lam gyi rim pa'i 'khrid yig 'jam pa'i dbyangs kyi zhal lung

Thimphu, Bhutan: kun bzang stobs rgyal, 1976

English translation ("Perfection of Wisdom Chapter"): Jeffrey Hopkins. in *Practice of Emptiness*. (Dharamsala: Library of Tibetan Works and Archives, 1974)

Nga-wang-rap-den (sde drub mkhan chen ngag dbang rab brtan). See Jam-yang-shay-ba, et al.

Pa-bong-ka-ba Jam-ba-den-dzin-trin-lay-gya-tso (pha bon kha pa byams pa bstan 'dzin 'phrin las rgya mtsho, 1878–1941)

About the Four Interwoven Annotations on (Dzong-ka-ba's) "Great Exposition of the Stages of the Path to Enlightenment", Set Forth In Very Brief Form to Purify Forgetfulness and Nourish the Memory

byang chub lam rim chen mo mchan bu bzhi sbrags kyi skor dran gso'i bsnyel byang mgo smos tsam du mdzad pa

The Collected Works of Pha-boṅ-kha-pa Byams-pa-bstan-'dzin-phrin-las-rgya-mtsho, Vol.5, 4–190
New Delhi: Chophel Legdan, 1973

Pur-bu-jok (phur bu lcog byams pa rgya mtsho, 1825–1901)
Explanation of the Lesser Path of Reasoning
rigs lam chung ngu'i rnam par bshad pa
in *Magical Key to the Path of Reasoning, Presentation of the Collected Topics Revealing the Meaning of the Treatises on Valid Cognition* (tshad ma'i gzhung don 'byed pa'i bsdus grwa'i rnam bzhag rigs lam 'phrul gyi sde mig)
Buxa, India: n.p., 1965
English translation (entire "Lesser Path of Reasoning"): Daniel Perdue. in "Practice and Theory of Philosophical Debate in Tibetan Buddhist Education" (Ann Arbor: University Microfilms, 1983)

Sang-gyay-gya-tso (sangs rgyas rgya mtsho, 1653–1705)
Vaiḍūrya-ser-po (A History of the Dge-lugs-pa Monasteries of Tibet)
vaiḍūrya ser po
New Delhi: International Academy of Indian Culture, 1960

Ser-dok Paṇ-chen Shākya-chok-den (gser mdog paṇ chen shākya mchog ldan, 1428–1507)
Explanation of the "Epistolary Essay, Drop of Ambrosia", Magical Rosary Fulfilling All Wishes
spring yig bdud rtsi'i thigs pa'i rnam bshad dpag bsam yong 'du'i ljon phreng
The Collected works of Gser-mdog Paṇ-chen, Vol.24, Thimphu, Bhutan: Kunzang Topgey, 1978

Sha-mar-den-dzin/Sha-mar Gen-dun-den-dzin-gya-tso (zhwa dmar dge bdun bstan 'dzin rgya mtsho, 1852–1910)
Lamp Illuminating the Profound Thought, Set Forth to Purify Forgetfulness of the Difficult Points of (Dzong-ka-ba's) "Great Exposition of Special Insight"
lhag mthong chen mo'i dka' gnad rnams brjed byang du bkod pa dgongs zab snang ba'i sgron me
Delhi: Mongolian Lama Guru Deva, 1972

Shāntarakṣhita (zhi ba 'tsho, eighth century)

Compendium of Principles

tattvasaṃgrahakārikā

de kho na nyid bsdus pa'i tshig le'ur byas pa

P5764, Vol.138

Sanskrit: *Tattvasaṁgraha*. D. Shastri, ed. (Varanasi: Bauddha Bharati, 1968)

English translation: Jha, G. *The Tattvasaṅgraha of Śāntirakṣita with the commentary of Kamalaśīla*. Gaekwad's Oriental Series, Vol.lxxx and lxxxiii. (Baroda: Oriental Institute, 1937–9)

Ornament for the Middle Way

madhyamakālaṃkāra

dbu ma'i rgyan gyi tshig le'ur byas pa

P5284, Vol.101

Shāntideva (zhi ba lha, eighth century)

Engaging in the Bodhisattva Deeds

bodhisattvacaryāvatāra

byang chub sems dpa'i spyod pa la 'jug pa

P5272, Vol.99

Sanskrit and Tibetan edition: *Bodhicaryāvatāra*. Vidhushekhara Bhattacharya, ed. (Calcutta: The Asiatic Society, 1960)

English translation: Stephen Batchelor. *A Guide to the Bodhisattva's Way of Life*. (Dharamsala: LTWA 1979). Also: Marion Matics. *Entering the Path of Enlightenment*. (New York: Macmillan Co, 1970)

Contemporary commentary: Geshe Kelsang Gyatso *Meaningful to Behold*. (London: Wisdom, 1980)

Shūra. See Ashvaghoṣha.

Tāranātha (b.1575)

History of Buddhism in India/Clear Teaching of How the Precious Holy Doctrine Spread in the Land of Superiors [India], Fulfilling All Needs and Wishes

rgya gar chos 'byung/dam pa'i chos rin po che 'phags pa'i yul du ji ltar dar ba'i tshul gsal bar ston pa dgos 'dod kun 'byung

Sarnath: Pleasure of Elegant Sayings Press, 1972

German translation: Anton Schieffer. *Geschichte des Buddhismus in Indien*. (St. Petersburg: 1869)

English translation: Chimpa and Chattopadhyaya. *Tāranātha's History of Buddhism in India*. (Calcutta: K.P. Bagchi & Company, rpt.1980)

Tu-gen (thu'u bkwan blo bzang chos kyi nyi ma, 1737–1802)

Mirror of the Good Explanations Showing the Sources and Assertions of All Systems of Tenets

grub mtha' thams cad kyi khungs dang 'dod tshul ston pa legs bshad shel gyi me long

Sarnath: Chhos Je Lama, 1963

Vasubandhu (dbyig gnyen, fl.360)

Treasury of Knowledge

abhidharmakośa

chos mngon pa mdzod

P5590, Vol.115

Sanskrit: *Abhidharmakośa & Bhāṣya of Ācārya Vasubandhu with Sphuṭārtha Commentary of Ācārya Yaśomitra*. Swami Dwarikadas Shastri, ed. Bauddha Bharati Series no.5. (Banaras: Bauddha Bharati, 1970)

French translation: Louis de La Vallée Poussin. *L'Abhidharmakośa de Vasubandhu*. (Paris: Geuthner, 1923–31)

Yaśomitra (rgyal po'i sras grags pa'i bshes gnyen, known as rgyal sras, fl.850)

Explanation of Vasubandhu's "Treasury of Knowledge"

abhidharmakośavyākhyā

chos mngon pa'i mdzod kyi 'grel bshad

P5593, Vol.116

Sanskrit: *Abhidharmakośavyākhyā (Spuṭārthā abhidharmakośavyākhyā, the work of Yaśomitra.* U. Wogihara, ed. (Tokyo: The Publishing Association of Abhidharmakośa-vyākhyā, 1932–36). Also *Abhidharmakośa & Bhāṣya of Ācārya Vasubandhu with Sphuṭārtha Commentary of Ācārya Yaśomitra*. Swami Dwarikadas Shastri, ed. Bauddha Bharati Series no.5.

(Banaras: Bauddha Bharati, 1970)
Ye-shay-gyel-tsen (tshe mchog gling ye shes rgyal mtshan, 1713– 1793)
Biographies of Eminent Gurus in the Transmission Lineages of the Teachings of the Graduated Path
byang chub lam gyi rim pa'i bla ma brgyud pa'i rnam par thar pa rgyal bstan mdzes pa'i rgyan mchog phul byung nor bu'i phreng ba
The Collected Works of Tshe-mchog-gliṅ Ye-śes-rgyal-mtshan, Vol.1
New Delhi: Ngawang Gelek Demo, 1970

3 *Works in Western Languages*

Ames, William. "The Notion of *Svabhāva* in the Thought of Candrakīrti". *Journal of Indian Philosophy* 10 (1982), pp.161–77.

Batchelor, Stephen, trans. *A Guide to the Bodhisattva's Way of Life*. Dharamsala: Library of Tibetan Works & Archives, 1979.

Bays, Gwendolyn. *The Lalitavistara Sūtra: The Voice of the Buddha, the Beauty of Compassion*. Oakland: Dharma, 1983.

Betty, L. Stafford. "Nāgārjuna's masterpiece – logical, mystical, both, or neither?" *Philosophy East and West* 33 (1983), pp.123–38.

Bhattacharya, Kamaleswar. *The Dialectical Method of Nāgārjuna*. Delhi: Motilal Banarsidas, 1978.

Buescher, John. "The Buddhist Doctrine of Two Truths in the Vaibhāṣika and Theravāda Schools". Ann Arbor: University Microfilms, 1982.

Bugault, Guy. "Logic and Dialectics in the *Madhyamakakārikās*". *Journal of Indian Philosophy* 11 (1983), pp.7–76.

Chandra, Lokesh, ed. *Materials for a History of Tibetan Literature*. Śata-piṭaka series, Vol.28–30. New Delhi: International Academy of Indian Culture, 1963.

———. *Vaidūrya-ser-po and the Annals of Kokonor*. New Delhi: International Academy of Indian Culture, 1960.

Chimpa, Lama and Chattopadhyaya, Alaka, trans. *Tāranātha's History of Buddhism in India*. Calcutta: K.P. Bagchi & Company, rpt.1980.

Conze, Edward. *Buddhist Thought in India*. Ann Arbor:

University of Michigan Press, 1967.

Daye, Douglas. "Japanese rationalism, Mādhyamika, and some uses of formalism". *Philosophy East and West* 24 (1974), pp.363–38.

———. "Major Schools of the Mahāyāna: Mādhyamika". in Charles Prebish, ed., *Buddhism: A Modern Perspective*, pp.76–96. University Park and London: Pennsylvania State University Press, 1975.

Demiéville, Paul. *Le concile de Lhasa: une controverse sur le quiétisme entre bouddhiste de l'Inde et de la Chine au VIIIe siècle de l'ère chrétienne*. Bibliothèque de l'Institut des Hautes Études Chinoises, VII. Paris: Imprimerie Nationale de France, 1952.

Eckel, Malcolm David. "Bhāvaviveka and the early Mādhyamika theories of language". *Philosophy East and West* 28 (1978), pp.323–37.

———. "A Question of Nihilism: Bhāvaviveka's Response to the Fundamental Problems of Mādhyamika Philosophy". Unpublished dissertation, Harvard, 1980.

Fehér, Judit. "Buddhapālita's *Mūlamadhyamakavṛtti*: Arrival and Spread of *Prāsaṅgika-Mādhyamika* Literature in Tibet". in Louis Ligeti, ed., *Tibetan and Buddhist Studies Commemorating the 200th Anniversary of the Birth of Alexander Csoma de Körös*, Vol.1, pp.211–40. Budapest: Akadémiai Kiado, 1984.

Fenner, Peter. "A Study of the Relationship Between Analysis (*vicāra*) and Insight (*prajñā*) Based on the *Madhyamakāvatāra*". *Journal of Indian Philosophy* 12 (1984), 139–97.

Fifth Dalai Lama. *Practice of Emptiness* (the "Perfection of Wisdom Chapter" of the *Sacred Word of Mañjushrī* [*'jam dpal zhal lung*]), Jeffrey Hopkins, translator. Dharamsala: Library of Tibetan Works and Archives, 1974.

Gomez, Luis O. "The Direct and the Gradual Approaches of Zen Master Mahāyāna: Fragments of the Teachings of Moho-yen". in Gimello and Gregory, ed., *Studies in Ch'an and Huayen*, pp.69–167. Honolulu: University of Hawaii Press, 1983.

———. "Indian Materials on the Doctrine of Sudden Enlightenment". in *Early Ch'an in China and Tibet*, Berkeley Buddhist Studies Series 5, pp.393–434. Berkeley: 1983.

Griffiths, Paul. "Buddhist Hybrid English: Some Notes on Philology and Hermeneutics for Buddhologists". *Journal of the International Association of Buddhist Studies* 4 (1981), pp.17–32.

Gudmunsen, Chris. *Wittgenstein and Buddhism*. London: The Macmillan Press, 1977.

Guenther, Herbert. *Buddhist Philosophy in Theory and Practice*. Baltimore: Penguin, 1971.

Gyatso, Kelsang. *Meaningful to Behold*. London: Wisdom, 1980.

Hopkins, Jeffrey. *Emptiness Yoga*. Ithaca, N.Y.: Snow Lion, 1987.

———. *Meditation on Emptiness*. London: Wisdom, 1983.

———, trans. Nāgārjuna and the Seventh Dalai Lama, *The Precious Garland and the Song of the Four Mindfulnesses*. New York: Harper and Row, 1975.

———, trans. Tsong-ka-pa's *Tantra in Tibet*. London: George Allen & Unwin, 1977.

———. *Yoga of Tibet*. London: George Allen & Unwin, 1981.

Houston, G.W. *Sources for a History of the bSam yas Debate*. Sankt Augustin: VGH Wissenschaftsverlag, 1980.

Huntington, C.W., Jr. "A 'nonreferential' view of language and conceptual thought in the work of Tsoṅ-kha-pa". *Philosophy East and West* 33 (1983), pp.326–39.

———. "The System of the Two Truths in the Prasannapadā and the Madhyamakāvatāra: A Study in Mādhyamika Soteriology". *Journal of Indian Philosophy* 11 (1983), pp.77–106.

Ichimura, Shohei. "A New Approach to the Intra-Mādhyamika Confrontation Over the Svātantrika and Prāsaṅgika Methods of Refutation". *Journal of the International Association of Buddhist Studies* 5 (1982), pp.41–52.

———. "A Study on the Mādhyamika Method of Refutation and its Influence on Buddhist Logic". *Journal of the International Association of Buddhist Studies* 4 (1981), pp.87–94.

Inada, Kenneth. *Nāgārjuna, A Translation of his Mūlamadhyamakakārikā with an Introductory Essay*. Tokyo: The Hokuseido Press, 1970.

Jayatilleke, K.N. "The Logic of Four Alternatives". *Philosophy East and West* 17 (1967), pp.69–84.

Jones, Richard Hubert. "The nature and function of Nāgārjuna's arguments". *Philosophy East and West* 28 (1978), pp.485–502.

Jong, Jan W. de. "A Brief History of Buddhist Studies in Europe and America". *The Eastern Buddhist*, NS 7, No. 1 (1974), pp.55–106; No.2 (1974), pp.49–82.

———. *Cinq chapitres de la Prasannapadā*. Paris: Geuthner, 1949.

———. "Emptiness". *Journal of Indian Philosophy* 2 (1972), pp.7–15.

———. "The Problem of the Absolute in the Madhyamaka School". *Journal of Indian Philosophy* 2 (1972), pp.1–6.

———. "Review of Guy Welbon's *The Buddhist Nirvāṇa and Its Western Interpreters*". *Journal of Indian Philosophy* 1 (1972), pp.396–403.

———. "Textcritical Notes on the Prasannapadā". *Indo-Iranian Journal* 20 (1978), pp.25–59 and 217–52.

Kachewsky, Rudolf. *Das Leben des Lamaistischen Heiligen Tsongkhapa Blo-Bzaṅ-Grags-Pa (1357–1419), dargestellt und erläutert anhand seiner Biographie "Quellenort allen Glücks"*. 2 vol. Asiatische Forschungen, Vol.32. Wiesbaden: Harrassowitz, 1971.

Kalupahana, David. *Nāgārjuna: The Philosophy of the Middle Way*. Albany, N.Y.: State University of New York Press, 1986.

Klein, Anne. "Mind and Liberation. The Sautrāntika Tenet System in Tibet: Perception, Naming, Positive and Negative Phenomena, Impermanence and the Two Truths in the Context of Buddhist Religious Insight as Presented in Geluk Literary and Oral Traditions". Ann Arbor: University Microfilms, 1981.

Kritzer, Robert. "Review of Alex Wayman, *Calming the Mind*

and Discerning the Real: Buddhist Meditation and the Middle View". *Philosophy East and West* 31 (1981), pp.380–2.

Kuijp, Leonard van der. *Contributions to the Development of Tibetan Buddhist Epistemology*. Wiesbaden: Franz Steiner Verlag, 1983.

———. "Phya-pa Chos-kyi Seng-ge's Impact on Tibetan Epistemological Theory". *Journal of Indian Philosophy* 5 (1977), pp.355–69.

Kunst, Arnold. "The Concept of the Principle of Excluded Middle in Buddhism". *Rocznik Orientalistyczny* 21 (1957), pp.141–7.

La Vallée Poussin, Louis de, trans. *L'Abhidharmakośa de Vasubandhu*. Paris: Geuthner, 1923–31.

———, trans. *Madhyamakāvatāra*. *Muséon* 8 (1907), pp.249–317; 11 (1910), pp.271–358; and 12 (1911), pp.235–328.

Lamotte, Étienne. "La critique d'interprétation dans le bouddhisme". *Annuaire de l'Institut de philologie et d'histoire orientales et slaves*, Vol. IX, pp.341–61. Brussels: Université Libre de Bruxelles, 1949.

———. *The Teaching of Vimalakīrti*. London: Pali Text Society, 1976.

———. "Le traité de l'acte de Vasubandhu, Karmasiddhiprakaraṇa". *MCB* 4, 1936, 265–88.

———. *Le traité de la grande vertu de la sagesse*, 5 vols. Louvain: Muséon, 1949–80.

———. *Saṃdhinirmocana-sūtra*. Louvain: Université de Louvain, 1935.

Lang, Karen. "Āryadeva on the Bodhisattva's Cultivation of Merit and Knowledge". Ann Arbor: University Microfilms, 1983.

———. "sPa tshab Nyi ma grags and the introduction of Prāsaṅgika Madhyamaka into Tibet", forthcoming in the Turrell Wylie memorial volume, 23pp.

Lati Rinbochay. *Mind in Tibetan Buddhism*. Elizabeth Napper, trans. and ed. Valois, New York: Snow Lion, 1980.

Lati and Lochö Rinbochays, Zahler, and Hopkins. *Meditative*

States in Tibetan Buddhism: The Concentrations and Formless Absorptions. London: Wisdom Publications, 1983.

Lindtner, Christian. "Atiśa's Introduction to the Two Truths, and Its Sources". *Journal of Indian Philosophy* 9 (1981), pp.161–214.

______. "Buddhapālita on Emptiness [*Buddhapālita-mūla-madhyamakavṛtti XVIII*]". *Indo-Iranian Journal* 23 (1981), pp.187–217.

______. *Nāgārjuna's Filosofiske Vaerker*. Indiske Studier 2. Copenhagen: Akademisk Forlag, 1982.

______. *Nagarjuniana*. Indiske Studier 4. Copenhagen: Akademisk Forlag, 1982.

Lochö Rinbochay. "Grounds and Paths". Unpublished transcript of lectures at the University of Virginia, 1978.

Lopez, Donald. "The Svātantrika-Mādhyamika School of Mahāyāna Buddhism". Ann Arbor: University Microfilms, 1982.

Loy, David. "How not to criticize Nāgārjuna: A Response to L. Stafford Betty". *Philosophy East and West* 34 (1984), pp. 437–45.

Matilal, Bimal Krishna. "A Critique of the Mādhyamika Position". in Mervyn Sprung, ed., *The Problem of Two Truths in Buddhism and Vedānta*. Dordrecht, Holland: D. Reidel, 1973.

______. *Epistemology, Logic, and Grammar in Indian Philosophical Analysis*. The Hague, Paris: Mouton, 1971.

May, Jacques. "On Mādhyamika Philosophy". *Journal of Indian Philosophy* 6 (1978), pp.233–41.

______. *Prasannapadā Madhyamakavṛtti, douze chapitres traduits du sanscrit et du tibétain*. Paris: Adrien-Maisonneuve, 1959.

McEvilley, Thomas. "Pyrrhonism and Mādhyamika". *Philosophy East and West* 32 (1982), pp.3–35.

Mehta, Mahesh. "Śūnyatā and Dharmatā: the Mādhyamika View of Inner Reality". in *Developments in Buddhist Thought: Canadian Contributions to Buddhist Studies*, pp.26–37. Waterloo, Ontario: Canadian Corporation for Studies in Religion, 1979.

Mimaki, Katsumi. *Blo Gsal Grub Mtha'*. Kyoto: Université de Kyoto, 1982.

———. "The *blo gsal grub mtha'*, and the Mādhyamika Classification in Tibetan *grub mtha'* literature". in E. Steinkellner and H. Tauscher, ed., *Contributions on Tibetan and Buddhist Religion and Philosophy*, pp.161–7. Wien: Universität Wien, 1983.

Murti, T.R.V. *The Central Philosophy of Buddhism*. London: George Allen & Unwin, rpt.1970.

———. "Saṁvṛti and Paramārtha in Mādhyamika and Advaita Vedānta. in M. Sprung, ed., *The Problem of Two Truths in Buddhism and Vedānta*, pp.9–26. Dordrecht, Holland: D. Reidel, 1973.

Nagatomi, Masatoshi. "*Mānasa-Pratyakṣa*: A Conundrum in the Buddhist *Pramāṇa* System". in *Sanskrit and Indian Studies*. Dordrecht, Boston, and London: D. Reidel, 1980.

Nayak, G.C. "The Mādhyamika attack on essentialism: A critical appraisal". *Philosophy East and West* 29 (1979), pp.477–90.

Obermiller, E. *History of Buddhism (Chos-hbyung) by Bu-ston*. Heidelberg: Otto Harrassowitz, 1931.

———. "Tson-kha-pa le Pandit". *MCB* 3 (1935), pp.319–38.

Perdue, Daniel. "Practice and Theory of Philosophical Debate in Tibetan Buddhist Education". Ann Arbor: University Microfilms, 1983.

Potter, Karl H. *Presuppositions of India's Philosophies*. Englewood Cliffs, N.J.: Prentice Hall, 1963.

Rabten, Geshé. *Echoes of Voidness*. Stephen Batchelor, trans. London: Wisdom, 1983.

Ramanan, K. Venkata. *Nāgārjuna's Philosophy as Presented in the Mahā-Prajñāpāramitā-Śāstra*. Varanasi: Bharatiya Vidya Prakashan, 1971.

Regamey, K. *Three Chapters from the Samādhirājasūtra*. Warsaw: Publications of the Oriental Commission, 1938.

Robinson, Richard. "Did Nāgārjuna Really Refute All Views?" *Philosophy East and West* 22 (1972), pp.325–31.

———. *Early Mādhyamika in India and China*. Madison,

Milwaukee, and London: University of Wisconsin Press, 1967.

———. Feature Book Review "K.N. Jayatilleke, Early Buddhist Theory of Knowledge". *Philosophy East and West* 19 (1969), pp.69–82.

———. "Some Logical Aspects of Nāgārjuna's System". *Philosophy East and West* 6 (1957), pp.291–308.

Roerich, George N. *The Blue Annals*. Delhi: Motilal Banarsidass, rpt.1979.

Ruegg, David Seyfort. "A propos of a Recent Contribution to Tibetan and Buddhist Studies". *Journal of the American Oriental Society* 82 (1962), pp.320–31.

———. "Does the Mādhyamika Have a Thesis and Philosophical Position?" in B.K. Matilal and R.D. Evans, ed., *Buddhist Logic and Epistemology*, pp.229–37. Dordrecht, Holland: D. Reidel, 1986.

———. "The Jo naṅ pas: A School of Buddhist Ontologists According to the *Grub mtha' šel gyi me loṅ*". *Journal of the American Oriental Society* 83 (1963), pp.73–91.

———. *The Literature of the Madhyamaka School of Philosophy in India*. Wiesbaden: Otto Harrassowitz, 1981.

———. "On the Knowability and Expressibility of Absolute Reality in Buddhism". *Journal of Indian and Buddhist Studies* 20 (1971), pp.495–89.

———. "On the Reception and Early History of the dbu-ma (Madhyamaka) in Tibet". in Michael Aris and Aung Suu Kyi, ed., *Tibetan Studies in Honour of Hugh Richardson*, pp.277–9. New Delhi: Vikas, 1980.

———. "On the Thesis and Assertion in the Madhyamaka/dBu ma". in E. Steinkellner and H. Tauscher, ed., *Contributions on Tibetan and Buddhist Religion and Philosophy*, pp.205–41. Wien: Universität Wien, 1983.

———. "Towards a chronology of the Madhyamaka School". in L.A. Hercus et al., ed., *Indological and Buddhist Studies*, pp.505–30. Canberra: Faculty of Asian Studies, 1982.

———. "The Uses of the Four Positions of the *Catuṣkoṭi* and the Problem of the Description of Reality in Mahāyāna

Buddhism". *Journal of Indian Philosophy* 5 (1977), pp.1–71.

Santina, Peter della. "The Madhyamaka and modern Western philosophy". *Philosophy East and West* 36 (1986), pp.41–54.

Scharfstein, Ben-Ami. *Mystical Experience.* Baltimore: Penguin, 1973.

Schmithausen, Lambert. "On the Problem of the Relation of Spiritual Practice and Philosophical Theory in Buddhism". in *German Scholars on India*, Vol.II. Bombay: Nachiketa Publications, 1976.

Schumann, Hans. *Buddhism. An Outline of its Teachings and Schools*. Wheaton, Illinois: Theosophical Publishing House, 1973.

Sherbourne, Richard, S.J. *A Lamp for the Path and Commentary*. London: George Allen & Unwin, 1983.

Siderits, Mark. "The Madhyamaka Critique of Epistemology. I and II". *Journal of Indian Philosophy* 8 (1980), pp.307–35 and 9 (1981), pp.121–160.

Smith, E. Gene. "Introduction". in the *Collected Works of Thu'u-bkwan Blo-bzang-chos-kyi-nyi-ma*, Vol.1. New Delhi: Ngawang Gelek Demo, 1969.

Sopa, Geshe. "Some Comments on Tsong kha pa's *Lam rim chen mo* and Professor Wayman's *Calming the Mind and Discerning the Real*" and "Geshe Sopa Replies to Alex Wayman". *Journal of the International Association of Buddhist Studies*, 3 (1980), pp.68–92 and 98–100.

Sopa and Hopkins. *Practice and Theory of Tibetan Buddhism*. New York: Grove, 1976.

Sprung, Mervyn. *Lucid Exposition of the Middle Way, the Essential Chapters from the Prasannapadā of Candrakīrti translated from the Sanskrit*. Boulder: Prajñā Press, 1979.

______. "The Mādhyamika Doctrine as Metaphysic". in *The Problem of Two Truths in Buddhism and Vedānta*, pp.40–53. Dordrecht, Holland: D. Reidel, 1973.

______. "Nietzsche and Nāgārjuna: The Origins and Issue of Scepticism". in Howard Coward and Krishna Sivaraman, ed., *Revelation in Indian Thought: A Festschrift in Honour of Professor T.R.V. Murti*, pp.159–70. Emeryville, Ca.: Dharma Publishing, 1977.

———. "Non-Cognitive Language in Mādhyamika Buddhism". in *Buddhist Thought and Asian Civilization*, pp.241–53. Emeryville, Ca.: Dharma, 1977.

Staal, Fritz. *Exploring Mysticism*. Berkeley: University of California Press, 1975.

Stcherbatsky, Theodore. *The Conception of Buddhist Nirvāṇa*. Delhi, Motilal Banarsidass, rpt. 1978.

Stoddard, Heather. *Le Mendiant de l'Amdo*. Paris: Societé d'Ethnographie, 1985.

Streng, Frederick J. *Emptiness: A Study in Religious Meaning*. Nashville, New York: Abingdon Press, 1967.

———. "The Significance of Pratītyasamutpāda for Understanding the Relationship Between Saṁvṛti and Paramārtha in Nāgārjuna". in M. Sprung, ed., *The Problem of Two Truths in Buddhism and Vedānta*, pp.27–39. Dordrecht, Holland: D. Reidel, 1973.

Suzuki, Daisetz T. *The Lankavatara Sutra*. London: Routledge and Kegan Paul, 1932.

Tachikawa, Musashi. "A Logical Analysis of the *Mūlamadhyamakakārikā*". in M. Nagatomi et al. ed., *Sanskrit and Indian Studies*, pp.159–81. Dordrecht, Boston, London: D. Reidel, 1980.

Tenzin Gyatso, Dalai Lama XIV. *The Buddhism of Tibet and the Key to the Middle Way*. Jeffrey Hopkins, trans. London: George Allen & Unwin, 1975.

——— and Jeffrey Hopkins. *The Kālachakra Tantra: Rite of Initiation*. London: Wisdom, 1985.

———. *Kindness, Clarity, and Insight*. Jeffrey Hopkins, trans. and ed.; Elizabeth Napper, co-editor. Ithaca, N.Y.: Snow Lion Publications, 1984.

———. *The Opening of the Wisdom Eye*. Wheaton, Illinois: Theosophical Publishing House, 1972.

———. *Opening the Eye of New Awareness*. Donald S. Lopez, Jr. with Jeffrey Hopkins, trans. London: Wisdom Publications, 1985.

Thurman, Robert. "Buddhist Hermeneutics". *Journal of the American Academy of Religion* XLVI (1978), pp.19–40.

______, ed. *The Life and Teachings of Tsong Khapa*. Dharamsala: Library of Tibetan Works and Archives, 1982.

______. "Philosophical nonegocentrism in Wittgenstein and Candrakīrti in their treatment of the private language problem". *Philosophy East and West* 30 (1980), pp.321–37.

______. *Tsong Khapa's Speech of Gold in the Essence of True Eloquence*. Princeton: Princeton University Press, 1984.

Tola, Fernando and Dragonetti, Carmen. "Nāgārjuna's Conception of 'Voidness' (Śūnyatā)". *Journal of Indian Philosophy* 9 (1981), pp.273–82.

Tsong-ka-pa. *Tantra in Tibet*. Translated and edited by Jeffrey Hopkins. London: George Allen & Unwin, 1977.

Tucci, Giuseppe. *First Bhāvanākrama of Kamalaśīla*. Minor Buddhist texts, II, Serie Orientale Roma IX, 2. Rome: IS.M.E.O., 1958.

______. *Pre-Diṅnāga Buddhist Texts on Logic from Chinese Sources*. Gaekwad's Oriental Series, 49. Baroda: Oriental Institute, 1929.

______, trans. "La versione cinese del Catuḥśataka di Āryadeva, confronta col testo sanscrito et la traduzione tibetana". *Rivista degli Studi Orientalia* 10 (1925), pp.521–67.

Ueda, Yoshifumi. "Two Main Streams of Thought in Yogācāra Philosophy". *Philosophy East and West* 17 (1967), pp.155–65.

Waldo, Ives. "Nāgārjuna and analytic philosophy, I and II". *Philosophy East and West* 25 (1975), pp.281–90, and 28 (1978), pp.287–98.

Wangyal, Geshe. *The Door of Liberation*. New York: Maurice Girodias, 1973; reprint, New York: Lotsawa, 1978.

Warder, A.K. "Is Nāgārjuna a Mahāyānist?". in Mervyn Sprung, ed., *The Problem of Two Truths in Buddhism and Vedānta*, pp.78–88. Dordrecht and Boston: D. Reidel, 1973.

Wayman, Alex. "Alex Wayman Replies to Geshe Sopa". *Journal of the International Association of Buddhist Studies* 3 (1980), pp.93–7.

———. *Calming the Mind and Discerning the Real*. New York: Columbia University Press, 1978; rpt. New Delhi: Motilal Banarsidass, 1979.

———. "Contributions to the Mādhyamika School of Buddhism". *Journal of the American Oriental Society* 89 (1969), pp.141–56.

———. "Introduction to Tsoṅ kha pa's Lam rim chen mo". *Phi Theta Annual*, Vol.3 (Berkeley, 1952), pp.51–82.

———. "Observations on Translation from the Classical Tibetan Language into European Languages". *Indo-Iranian Journal* 14 (1972), pp.161–92.

———. "Who understands the four alternatives of the Buddhist texts?". *Philosophy East and West* 27 (1977), pp.3–21.

———. "Yogācāra and the Buddhist Logicians". *Journal of the International Association of Buddhist Studies* 2 (1979), pp.65–78.

Welbon, Guy Richard. *The Buddhist Nirvāṇa and Its Western Interpreters*. Chicago: University of Chicago Press, 1968.

Williams, Paul. "A Note on Some Aspects of Mi Bskyod Rdo Rje's Critique of Dge Lugs Pa Madhyamaka". *Journal of Indian Philosophy* 11 (1983), pp.125–45.

———. "Review of Chr. Lindtner (1982) *Nagarjuniana: Studies in the Writings and Philosophy of Nāgārjuna*, Indiske Studier 4, Copenhagen: Akademisk Forlag". *Journal of Indian Philosophy*, 12 (1984) pp.73–104.

———. "rMa bya pa Byang chub brtson 'grus on Madhyamaka Method". *Journal of Indian Philosophy* 13 (1985), pp.205–25.

———. "Tsong-kha-pa on *kun-rdzob bden-pa*". in Aris and Aung, ed., *Tibetan Studies in Honour of Hugh Richardson*, pp.325–34. New Delhi: Vikas, 1980.

Willis, Janice. *On Knowing Reality*. New York: Columbia University Press, 1979.

Yamaguchi, Susumu. *Index to the Prasannapadā Madhyamakavṛtti*, Part Two Tibetan-Sanskrit. Kyoto: Heirakuji-Shoten, 1974.

———. "Traité de Nāgārjuna pour écarter les vaines discussion (Vigrahavyāvartanī) traduit et annoté". *Journal Asiatique* 215 (1929), pp.1–86.

Notes

Notes

The notes are numbered consecutively throughout the entire text. For easier reference, within the notes the part and chapter of the text to which they refer are identified.

Notes

PART ONE: ANALYSIS
INTRODUCTION

1 A standard medium-length Tibetan biography of Dzong-ka-ba is that written by his chief disciple Kay-drup (*mkhas grub*, 1385–1438), *Wonderful, Amazing Biography of the Great Foremost Venerable Lama, Dzong-ka-ba, Entrance Way of the Faithful* (*rje btsun bla ma tsong kha pa chen po'i ngo mtshar rmad du byung ba'i rnam par thar pa dad pa'i 'jug ngogs*, Varanasi: Lhundup and Samdup, 1966). A biography by the contemporary Ge-luk scholar, Geshe Ngawang Dhargey, that closely follows this one has been translated into English by Khamlung and Sherpa Tulkus in *The Life and Teachings of Tsong Khapa*, Robert Thurman, ed., Dharamsala: Library of Tibetan Works and Archives, 1982, pp.4–39. For a short and eloquent description of Dzong-ka-ba's life, see Robert A.F. Thurman's *Tsong Khapa's Speech of Gold in the Essence of True Eloquence* (Princeton: Princeton University Press, 1984), pp.65–89.

There is also a biography available in German that is based on a translation of a work by Char-har Ge-shay (*char har dge bshes*, 1740–1810): Rudolf Kachewsky, *Das Leben des Lamaistischen Heiligen Tsongkhapa Blo Bzaṅ Grags Pa (1357–1419), dargestellt und erläutert anhand seiner Biographie "Quellenort allen Glücks"* (Wiesbaden: Harrassowitz, 1971), as well as a brief biography in French by E. Obermiller: "Tson-kha-pa le Pandit", *Mélanges chinois et bouddhiques* 3 (1935), pp.319–38.

2 See Thurman's *Tsong Khapa's Speech of Gold in the Essence of True Eloquence*, pp.84–85, for a description of Dzong-ka-ba's visionary experience.

3 Leonard van der Kuijp in his *Contributions to the Development of Tibetan Buddhist Epistemology* (Wiesbaden: Franz Steiner Verlag, 1983), pp.24–5, questions whether, in the absence of "cogent and convincing analyses of pre-Tsong-kha-pa Buddhist thought", Dzong-ka-ba's Mādhyamika interpretation can be called a "reform". While there is undoubtedly a great need for such analyses, it is nonetheless clear from Dzong-ka-ba's tone in the *Great Exposition* (see particularly chapter four of the translation, pp.176–80) that he considered himself to be engaged in a "reform" of Mādhyamika interpretation. That he was also perceived as a reformer (to be disagreed with) by subsequent Tibetan scholars is shown by the criticisms of his writings by figures such as the Sa-gya scholar Dak-tsang (*stag tshang lo tsā ba shes rab rin chen*, b.1405) and the Ga-gyu hierarch Mi-gyö-dor-jay (*mi bskyod rdo rje*, 1507–54, the eighth Karmapa). See, for example, Paul Williams "A Note on Some Aspects of Mi Bskyod Rdo Rje's Critique of Dge Lugs Pa Madhyamaka", *Journal of Indian Philosophy* 11 (1983), pp.125–45. Thus, I find van der Kuijp's point unfounded.

4 The date and Dzong-ka-ba's age are taken from A-gya-yong-dzin's (*dbyangs can dga' ba'i blo gros, a kya yongs 'dzin*, eighteenth century) *A Brief Explanation of Terminology Occurring in (Dzong-ka-ba's) "Great Exposition of the Stages of the Path"* (*byang chub lam gyi rim pa chen mo las byung ba'i brda bkrol nyer mkho bsdus pa*, The Collected Works of A-kya Yoṅs-ḥdzin, Vol. 1, New Delhi: Lama Guru Deva, 1971), 82.3, and have been converted to the Western system. A-gya-yong-dzin actually says that Dzong-ka-ba was 46 years of age and

wrote *The Great Exposition of the Stages of the Path* in the water-male-horse year; however, the Tibetan way of determining age is that one is said to be the age of the number of years in which one has lived. Thus, children from the time of their birth until the new year are said to be one year; at the time of the new year, they are then said to be two.

The "water-male-horse year" refers to a 60 year cycle in which twelve animals, five elements, and the two polarities of male and female are combined such that they repeat themselves only every 60 years. This converts to the Western date 1402. Dzong-ka-ba's dates are 1357–1419; if one converts Dzong-ka-ba's age of 46 at the time of writing the text to the 45 it would be by our system of calculation and adds that to 1357 it yields 1402. Thus A-gya-yong-dzin's figure is both internally consistent and fits in with the generally accepted dates for Dzong-ka-ba's life.

5 It has been translated into English in Geshe Wangyal's *Door of Liberation* (New York: Girodias, 1973; rpt. New York: Lotsawa, 1978), reprint edition, pp.162–71. Another English translation can be found in Thurman, ed., *The Life and Teachings of Tsong Khapa*, pp.59–66.

6 The full title of this text is the *Stages of the Path to Enlightenment Practiced by Beings of the Three Capacities* (*skyes bu gsum gyi nyams su blang ba'i byang chub lam gyi rim pa*, P6002, Vol.152–3). The special insight portion of it has been translated into English by Robert Thurman in *The Life and Teachings of Tsong Khapa*, pp.108–85, and by Jeffrey Hopkins: "Special Insight: From Dzong-ka-ba's *Middling Exposition of the Stages of the Path to Enlightenment Practiced by Persons of Three Capacities* with supplementary headings by Trijang Rinbochay", unpublished manuscript.

The abbreviated names for this text can be somewhat confusing; it is often referred to as the "Small Exposition of the Stages of the Path" (*lam rim chung ba*), even though it is more formally known as the *Medium Exposition of the Stages of the Path* (*lam rim 'bring*) and as which it is also frequently cited. The special insight portion, however, when discussed apart from the rest of the text, is almost always called the "Medium Exposition of Special Insight" (*lhag mthong 'bring*). To avoid confusion, I refer to it in the translation as the *Medium Exposition* even when it is cited as the *Small Exposition.*

The date of the text's composition is from A-gya-yong-dzin, 82.3. He describes the *Medium Exposition* as differing from the *Great Exposition* in that Dzong-ka-ba has omitted extensive citation of sources and detailed refutation of others' positions and proof of his own, and instead gives a brief presentation of essential points (82.4).

7 *Essence of the Good Explanations, Treatise Discriminating the Interpretable and the Definitive* (*drang ba dang nges pa'i don rnam par phye ba'i bstan bcos legs bshad snying po*) P6142, Vol.153. Also: Sarnath: Pleasure of Elegant Sayings Printing Press, 1973 and in *rje tsong kha pa'i gsung dbu ma'i lta ba'i skor*, Vol.1, pp.262–458 (Sarnath, India: Pleasure of Elegant Sayings Press, 1975). There is available an English translation by Robert Thurman, *Tsong Khapa's Speech of Gold in the Essence of True Eloquence* (Princeton: Princeton University Press, 1984).

Thurman (p.88) identifies the text as having been written during the winter of 1407–8. K. Mimaki, in his "The *blo gsal grub mtha'*, and the Mādhyamika Classification in Tibetan *grub mtha'* literature," in *Contributions on Tibetan and Buddhist Religion and Philosophy*, Steinkellner and Tauscher, ed., (Wien: Universität Wien, 1983), p.164, identifies it as having been written in 1406.

8 *Ocean of Reasoning, Explanation of* (*Nāgārjuna's*) *"Fundamental Treatise on the Middle Way, Called 'Wisdom'"*, (*dbu ma rtsa ba'i tshig le'ur byas pa shes rab ces bya ba'i rnam bshad rigs pa'i rgya mtsho*) P6153, Vol.156. Also:

Sarnath, India: Pleasure of Elegant Sayings Printing Press, no date, and in *rje tsong kha pa'i gsung dbu ma'i lta ba'i skor*, Vol.1, pp.459–755, and Vol.2, pp.1–187 (Sarnath, India: Pleasure of Elegant Sayings Press, 1975). One chapter of this has been translated into English by Jeffrey Hopkins, "Chapter Two of *Ocean of Reasoning* by Tsong-ka-pa", Dharamsala, Library of Tibetan Works and Archives, 1974.

Concerning the order of composition of the above two texts, Kay-drup's biography, 96.12–14, says only that Dzong-ka-ba quickly composed the *Essence of the Good Explanations* and the *Ocean of Reasoning*; Kay-drup lists them in that order without explicitly saying that they were composed in this order. Geshe Ngawang Dhargey's biography (*The Life and Teachings of Tsong Khapa*, pp. 25–6) says that Dzong-ka-ba first wrote the *Ocean of Reasoning* and then wrote the *Essence of the Good Explanations*. However, in the *Essence of the Good Explanations* (*rje tsong kha pa'i gsung dbu ma'i lta ba'i skor*, Vol.1, 346.4–5), Dzong-ka-ba says, "... because I wish to compose a commentary on [Nāgārjuna's] *Treatise on the Middle Way*, here I will not write more than this," thus appearing to confirm that the *Essence of the Good Explanations* was written first. Robert Thurman in the introduction to his *Tsong Khapa's Speech of Gold in the Essence of True Eloquence*, p.11, resolves this seeming conflict with the information that the *Essence of the Good Explanations* was written in its entirety while Dzong-ka-ba was in the midst of writing the first chapter of his *Ocean of Reasoning*.

9 *Illumination of the Thought, Extensive Explanation of (Chandrakīrti's) "Supplement to (Nāgārjuna's) 'Treatise on the Middle Way'" (dbu ma la 'jug pa'i rgya cher bshad pa dgongs pa rab gsal*, P6143, Vol.154. Also: Sarnath, India: Pleasure of Elegant Sayings Press, 1973) and in *rje tsong kha pa'i gsung dbu ma'i lta ba'i skor*, Vol.2, pp.188–667 (Sarnath, India: Pleasure of Elegant Sayings Press, 1975). The first five chapters have been

translated into English by Jeffrey Hopkins in Tsong-ka-pa, Kensur Lekden, and Jeffrey Hopkins, *Compassion in Tibetan Buddhism* (Valois, New York: Gabriel Snow Lion, 1980). Translation of the sixth chapter by Jeffrey Hopkins and Anne Klein is in progress.

The date of composition comes from Kay-drup, 120.9–120.20. He says that Dzong-ka-ba completed the text in the year of the dog, which converts to 1418.

10 An example of the first type of situation can be found in the "Medium Exposition of Special Insight" (*rje tsong kha pa'i gsung dbu ma'i lta ba'i skor*, Vol.2, 733.1–2) where Dzong-ka-ba describes a questionable division of Mādhyamikas into Reason-Established Illusionists and Proponents of Thorough Non-Abiding and concludes, "Through this mode you should understand in detail also my explanation of the presentation of these in the extensive *Stages of the Path*". (See appendix one where this question is discussed extensively.) An example of the second type of situation is Dzong-ka-ba's treatment of the topic of commonly appearing subjects where the discussion in his *Essence of the Good Explanations* seems to supercede that in the *Great Exposition*. See Jeffrey Hopkins' *Meditation on Emptiness* (London: Wisdom, 1983) n.346, p.815 and n.424, p.830.

11 See Tsong-ka-pa, *Tantra in Tibet*, (London: Allen and Unwin, 1977) pp.110–16. See also the present Dalai Lama's discussion of this point in his *Kindness, Clarity, and Insight* (Ithaca, N.Y.: Snow Lion, 1984), pp.200–24.

12 For instance, Guy Welbon in his *The Buddhist Nirvana and Its Western Interpreters* (Chicago: University of Chicago Press, 1968), p.290, says, "From the time of Bournouf through the most famous writings of Louis de La Vallée Poussin, Europeans had been generally agreed that . . . there could be no doubt that the *śūnyatā* . . . theory of the Madhyamika stamped that school as completely nihilistic . . .". Richard Robinson advanced the

view that Mādhyamika was agnostic in his article, "Did Nagarjuna Really Refute All Philosophical Views?" in *Philosophy East and West* 22 (1971). Both Fritz Staal and Douglas Daye advance the position that the Mādhyamikas are merely seeking to demonstrate the inadequacy of language in, respectively, *Exploring Mysticism* (Berkeley: University of California Press, 1973), p.45 and "Major Schools of the Mahāyāna: Mādhyamika" in *Buddhism: A Modern Perspective*, Charles S. Prebish, ed. (University Park: Penn. State University Press, 1965), pp.94–5. T.R.V. Murti in his seminal work, *The Central Philosophy of Buddhism: A Study of the Mādhyamika System* (London: George Allen & Unwin, 1980), see pages 239 and 329, concludes that the Mādhyamikas were merely seeking to remove all conceptuality and that they have no position or view of their own at all. Such assessments of Mādhyamika are considered in detail in chapters four through six.

13 *Praise of Dependent-Arising/Praise of the Supramundane Victor Buddha from the Approach of His Teaching the Profound Dependent-Arising, Essence of the Good Explanations* (*rten 'brel bstod pa/sangs rgyas bcom ldan 'das la zab mo rten cing 'brel bar 'byung ba gsung ba'i sgo nas bstod pa legs par bshad pa'i snying po*) P6016, Vol.153. Translation by Geshe Wangyal in *The Door of Liberation* (New York: Lotsawa, 1978), pp.117–25, and by Robert Thurman in *The Life and Teachings of Tsong Khapa*, (Dharamsala, Library of Tibetan Works and Archives, 1982), pp.99–107. The following translation is taken from *The Door of Liberation*, p.123.

14 Dzong-ka-ba uses this same metaphor in the closing stanzas of his *Essence of the Good Explanations*. He says there:

> One respects from the heart all the good explanations
> Of those like adornments among the wise of the world.
> Still, the eye of intelligence, a garden of jasmine, is opened fully

By the white rays of good explanations come from the moon [Chandrakīrti] . . .

P6142, Vol.153, 208.5.5. Quoted in Jeffrey Hopkins' *Meditation on Emptiness*, p.583, from which the above translation is taken. See Thurman's, *Tsong Khapa's Speech of Gold in the Essence of True Eloquence*, pp.381–2.

15 The dates for Nāgārjuna are a subject of much scholarly controversy. According to the Tibetan tradition he lived for 600 years commencing 400 years after Buddha's death, which would place him from about 80 B.C.E. to 520 A.D., taking c.560 B.C.E. to c.480 B.C.E. as the dates for Shākyamuni Buddha. Western scholars place Nāgārjuna anywhere from the first to the third centuries A.D. See Ruegg's *The Literature of the Madhyamaka School of Philosophy in India*, Wiesbaden: Harrassowitz, 1981, pp.4–6, for a discussion of when Nāgārjuna lived as well as an extensive bibliography of Western scholarship on the issue.

16 These dates follow Ruegg, *The Literature of the Madhyamaka School of Philosophy in India*, who dates Buddhapālita c.470–540? and Bhāvaviveka c.500–570?, (p.58) and dates Chandrakīrti c.600–650? (p.71). See also Ruegg's "Towards a chronology of the Madhyamaka School" in L.A. Hercus et al., ed., *Indological and Buddhist Studies* (Canberra: Faculty of Asian Studies, 1982), pp.505–30. A Tibetan tradition, as reported by Hopkins in *Meditation on Emptiness*, p.364, places Nāgārjuna as living for six hundred years beginning from four hundred years after Buddha's death. This would mean from approximately 80 B.C.E. to 520 A.D. Chandrakīrti is said to have lived for three hundred years (i.e., from about 495 to 795 A.D.), overlapping Nāgārjuna for twenty five years, and is said to have been Nāgārjuna's direct disciple. Bhāvaviveka is placed a little before Chandrakīrti, and Buddhapālita a little before Bhāvaviveka.

17 Nāgārjuna's most famous work, the *Treatise on the Middle Way* (*rtsa ba shes rab*, *prajñā-mūla*, or *madhyamaka-śāstra*) was translated into Chinese (Taishō 1564); his other major Mādhyamika works were not. Also, the Chinese tradition attributes to Nāgārjuna works that are not found outside of China, a prime example being the *Ta chih tu lung* (*mahāprajñā-pāramitā-śāstra*, Taishō 1509). Western scholars disagree as to whether or not this work was actually by Nāgārjuna, the majority saying it was not. See É. Lamotte's *Le traité de la grande vertu de sagesse*, 5 vols. (Louvain: Muséon, 1949–80). There is also a commentary on the *Sūtra on the Ten Grounds* attributed to Nāgārjuna, the *Che tchou p'i p'o cha louen* (*daśabhūmikavibhāṣa*, Taishō 1521) that exists only in Chinese.

Āryadeva's most famous work, the *Four Hundred* (*bzhi brgya pa*, *catuḥśataka*), is not found *per se* in Chinese: it has rough analogues in a text translated by Kumarajīva, entitled the *Po louen* (*śata* or *śataka śāstra*, Taishō 1569); also, the last half of it was translated into Chinese by Hsüan tsang (Taishō 1570) and has been translated into Italian by Giuseppe Tucci, "La versione cinese del Catuḥśataka di Āryadeva, confronta col testo sanscrito et la traduzione tibetana," *Rivista degli Studi Orientalia* 10 (1925), pp.521–67.

Nothing by Buddhapālita or by Chandrakīrti was translated into Chinese, and of Bhāvaviveka's texts, only the *Lamp for Wisdom* (*shes rab sgron me*, *prajñāpradīpa*), Bhāvaviveka's commentary on Nāgārjuna's *Treatise on the Middle Way*, was translated into Chinese (Taishō 1566), and this not until the mid 7th century, by which time the Mādhyamika tradition in China was already fully formed. See Richard Robinson's *Early Mādhyamika in India and China* (Madison, Milwaukee, and London: University of Wisconsin Press, 1967), pp.26–39, for a discussion of Mādhyamika literature in Chinese.

18 See Ruegg's *Literature of the Madhyamaka School of Philosophy in India*, pp.124–8, for a listing of modern editions of Mādhyamika Sanskrit texts.

19 The edition I primarily used is that published by Chophel Lekden, New Delhi, 1972. The full title, as printed on the title page, is, translated, *Clear Lamp of the Mahāyāna Path, Good Explanation by Way of the Four Annotations on the Difficult Points of the "Great Exposition of the Stages of the Path to Enlightenment" Composed by the Unequalled Foremost Venerable Dzong-ka-ba* (*mnyam med rje btsun tsong kha pa chen pos mdzad pa'i byang chub lam rim chen mo'i dka' ba'i gnad rnams mchan bu bzhi'i sgo nas legs par bshad pa theg chen lam gyi gsal sgron*). This edition is a tracing of a copy made from the corrected blocks of Tsay-chok-ling (*tshe mchog gling*). The correcting of the blocks was completed in 1842; the original blocks were carved in 1802.

Through the assistance of E. Gene Smith of the Library of Congress in New Delhi I was able to procure a microfilm of another edition of the text held in the library of the University of California at Berkeley, entitled *The Great Exposition of the Stages of the Path to Enlightenment Along With Annotations, Jewelled Source of Good Explanation* (*byang chub lam gyi rim pa chen mo mchan 'grel dang bcas pa legs par bshad pa nor bu'i 'byung gnas*). The text includes no publication data; however, it does have Chinese page numbering on the right hand side of the pages, indicating that it was probably used in China. A brief description by the compiler of the text of how the different annotators are to be identified concludes with the statement "written by the monk Ye-dar, who is called *wang kya hu thog thu*", and the compiler also says that he has added to the four *Annotations* a bit more commentary from the oral lineages of Paṇ-chen Rin-bo-chay (*paṇ chen rin bo che*) and Jam-ba Rin-bo-chay (*byams pa rin bo che*) as well as explanations of his own.

It is clear that the two editions are printed from different sets of blocks, as even the style of identifying the annotators differs. They have been closely compared, and an extensive list of emendations to the Delhi edition is included as appendix four of this volume.

20 Sha-mar Gen-dun-den-dzin-gya-tso (*zhwa dmar dge bdun bstan 'dzin rgya mtsho*, 1852–1910) *Lamp Illuminating the Profound Thought, Set Forth to Purify Forgetfulness of the Difficult Points of (Dzong-ka-ba's) "Great Exposition of Special Insight"* (*lhag mthong chen mo'i dka' gnad rnams brjed byang du bkod pa dgongs zab snang ba'i sgron me*, Delhi: Mongolian Lama Guru Deva, 1972).

21 This is the special insight section, pp.551–713 of Lo-sang-dor-jay's (*blo bzang rdo rje*, twentieth century) *Ship for Entering Into the Ocean of Textual Systems, Decisive Analysis of (Dzong-ka-ba's) "[Great Exposition of] the Stages of the Path to Enlightenment"* (*byang chub lam gyi rim pa'i mtha' dpyod gzhung lugs rgya mtshor 'jug pa'i gru gzings zhes bya ba las lhag mthong gi mtha' dpyod*, New Delhi: Mongolian Lama Gurudeva, 1980).

22 A-gya-yong-dzin Yang-chen-ga-way-lo-drö (*dbyangs can dga' ba'i blo gros, a kya yongs 'dzin*, eighteenth century, *A Brief Explanation of Terminology Occurring in (Dzong-ka-ba's) "Great Exposition of the Stages of the Path"* (*byang chub lam gyi rim pa chen mo las byung ba'i brda bkrol nyer mkho bsdus pa*, The Collected Works of A-kya Yoṅs-ḥdzin, Vol.1, New Delhi: Lama Guru Deva, 1971).

23 Pa-bong-ka-ba Jam-ba-den-dzin-trin-lay-gya-tso (*pha bon kha pa byams pa bstan 'dzin 'phrin las rgya mtsho*, 1878–1941), *About the Four Interwoven Annotations on (Dzong-ka-ba's) "Great Exposition of the Stages of the Path to Enlightenment", Set Forth In Very Brief Form to Purify Forgetfulness and Nourish the Memory*, (*byang chub lam rim chen mo mchan bu bzhi sbrags kyi skor dran gso'i bsnyel byang mgo smos tsam du mdzad pa*, The Collected

Works of Pha-boṅ-kha-pa Byams-pa-bstan-'dzin-phrin-las-rgya-mtsho, Vol.5, 4–190, New Delhi: Chophel Legdan, 1973).

24 Limitations of space and the fact that this concluded a significant meaning unit of the text determined the stopping point for this volume. I am continuing to translate the entire *Great Exposition* and hope to have another volume ready for publication soon.

The edition I primarily worked from is one published in Dharmsala, India, by the Shes rig par khang, which is based on the Hla-sa (*lha sa*) blocks. I checked it closely against the Dra-shi-hlun-bo (*bkra shis lhun po*) edition published by Ngawang Gelek Demo and the versions contained within the two editions of the *Four Interwoven Annotations* (see above note 19). Any substantive variations or corrections (and there were relatively few) have been noted.

The whole of the special insight section of the *Great Exposition of the Stages of the Path* along with a fairly brief section on calm abiding (*zhi gnas*, *śamatha*) that precedes it has been translated into English by Professor Alex Wayman of Columbia University in his *Calming the Mind and Discerning the Real* (New York: Columbia University Press, 1978; rpt. New Delhi: Motilal Banarsidass, 1979). As is discussed in appendix two below, Wayman's translation is highly problematic both in terms of accuracy and of interpretation; also it is accompanied by only the briefest discussion of Dzong-ka-ba's treatment of issues in Mādhyamika philosophy. Thus it is appropriate to retranslate here a portion of the text. See the *Journal of the International Association of Buddhist Studies* 3 (1980), pp.68–92, for an extensive review of Wayman's work by Geshe Sopa of the University of Wisconsin that points out numerous problems in terms of accuracy of translation, clarity of presentation, and understanding of the philosophical issues.

CHAPTER ONE: AN OVERVIEW OF THE GREAT EXPOSITION

25 This work with its autocommentary has been translated into English by Richard Sherbourne, *A Lamp for the Path and Commentary* (London: George Allen & Unwin, 1983). An English translation of Atisha's *Lamp for the Path* alone can be found in Alex Wayman's *Calming the Mind and Discerning the Real*, pp.9–14.

26 *Great Exposition*, Dharmsala edition, p.304a.5.

27 *Great Exposition*, Dharmsala edition, p.307b.6–308a.1.

28 *Great Exposition*, Dharmsala edition, p.304b.5–6. See Hopkins, *Meditation on Emptiness*, pp.67–90, for a detailed discussion of calm abiding and the steps in its development. See also Lati Rinbochay, Lochö Rinbochay, Zahler, and Hopkins' *Meditative States in Tibetan Buddhism: The Concentrations and Formless Absorptions*, (London: Wisdom Publications, 1983), pp.52–91.

29 See *Meditative States*, pp.92–133, for a presentation of the concentrations and formless absorptions.

30 Hopkins, *Meditation on Emptiness*, p.87.

31 *Great Exposition*, Dharmsala edition, p.308a.1.

32 Hopkins, *Meditation on Emptiness*, p. 92. See pages 91–109 for a detailed presentation of special insight.

33 Gön-chok-jik-may-wang-bo (*dkon mchog 'jigs med dbang po*, 1728–91), *Presentation of the Grounds and Paths, Ornament Beautifying the Three Vehicles* (*sa lam gyi rnam bzhag theg gsum mdzes rgyan*), The Collected Works of dkon-mchog'jigs-med-dbang-po, (New Delhi: Ngawang Gelek Demo, 1972) Vol.7, 444.1. The rest of this paragraph is based on Gön-chok-jik-may-wang-bo's *Presentation of the Grounds and Paths*.

34 In Hopkins' *Yoga of Tibet* (London: George Allen & Unwin, 1981), pp.33–4, the Dalai Lama includes only the paths of accumulation and preparation in the first period of countless aeons. Denma Lochö Rinbochay in the "Grounds and Paths", an unpublished transcript of

his explanation of Gön-chok-jik-may-wang-bo's *Presentation of the Grounds and Paths* (cited in the previous note), includes the path of seeing, the first Bodhisattva ground, in the first period of countless aeons and then has the second period extend from the second through the seventh grounds (see p.144).

35 This is pp.304a.1–314a.4 in the Dharmsala edition of the *Great Exposition*.

36 This is a traditional Tibetan account of the outcome. The historical facts have been much argued by Western scholars. For a lengthy discussion of this debate, see Paul Demiéville, *Le concile de Lhasa: une controverse sur le quiétisme entre bouddhiste de l'Inde et de la Chine au VIIIe siècle de l'ère chrétienne*, Bibliothèque de l'Institut des Hautes Études Chinoises, VII (Paris: Imprimerie Nationale de France, 1952); Giuseppe Tucci, *First Bhāvanākrama of Kamalaśila*, Minor Buddhist texts, II, Serie Orientale Roma IX, 2 (Rome: IS.M.E.O., 1958; G.W. Huston, *Sources for a History of the bSam yas Debate* (Sankt Augustin: VGH Wissenschaftsverlag, 1980); Yanagida Seizan's "The *Li-tai fa-pao chi* and the Ch'an Doctrine of Sudden Awakening" in Lai and Lancaster, ed., *Early Ch'an in China and Tibet*, Berkeley Buddhist Studies Series 5 (Berkeley: 1983); and Luis Gomez' "Indian Materials on the Doctrine of Sudden Enlightenment" in *Early Ch'an in China and Tibet*, op. cit., as well as his "The Direct and the Gradual Approaches of Zen Master Mahāyāna: Fragments of the Teachings of Mo-ho-yen" in Gimello and Gregory, ed., *Studies in Ch'an and Hua-yen* (Honolulu: University of Hawaii Press, 1983). See also Wayman's chapter, "Discursive Thought and the bSam-yas Debate", pp.44–58, in his *Calming the Mind and Discerning the Real* for interesting disagreements with opinions set forth by Demiéville and Tucci. The Sam-yay debate is discussed further in chapter six, see p.135.

37 *Great Exposition*, Dharmsala edition, 306a.5.

38 Dzong-ka-ba does not at this juncture of his text directly address the qualms of those who feel that Mādhyamika is a systemless system without views, theses, and so forth. He goes into this at length later in the text, Dharmsala edition, pp.433a.6–447b.1, not included within the portion of the *Great Exposition* translated here. This is discussed further in chapter five, see pp.111–22.

39 This position also runs counter to the main thrust of Western opinion (as well as considerable opinion within the Buddhist tradition). See chapter six, pp.126–33, for further discussion.

40 Oral teachings of Ken-sur Yeshe Thupten.

41 Thurman, "Buddhist Hermeneutics", *Journal of the American Academy of Religion*, XLVI (1978), p.38, supplies Sanskrit for this verse as cited in Shāntarakṣhita's *Compendium of Principles (Tattvasaṃgraha*, D. Shastri, ed., Varanasi: Bauddha Bharati, 1968):

tāpācchedācca nikaśāt suvarṇam iva paṇḍitaiḥ
parīkṣya bhikṣavo grāhyaṃ madvaco na tu gauravāt//
v.3587.

The Sanskrit differs a little from the Tibetan and would best be translated as follows:

Monks, my words are to be accepted by scholars
Not [merely] out of respect,
But upon having analyzed them, like the way
Gold is accepted after scorching, cutting, and rubbing.

Gung-tang (*gung thang dkon mchog bstan pa'i sgron me*, 1762–1823), in his *Beginnings of a Commentary on the Difficult Points of (Dzong-ka-ba's) "Differentiation of the Interpretable and the Definitive", the Quintessence of the "Essence of the Good Explanations"* (*drang nges rnam 'byed kyi dka' 'grel rtsom 'phro legs bshad snying po'i yang snying*, Sarnath: Guru Deva, 1965), p.29, points out that there is more than one translation of this verse into Tibetan. That translated above, the most frequently cited in the Tibetan materials I have seen, is by Ra (*ra*).

Gung-tang cites another by Dro (*'bro*) which more closely parallels the Sanskrit:

sregs bcad brdar ba'i gser bzhin du/
mkhas pa rnams kyis yongs brtags nas/
bdag gsung blang bya dge slong dag/
gus pa'i phyir ni ma yin no/

42 *Great Exposition*, Dharmsala edition, 367a.1.

43 I follow Jeffrey Hopkins in translating the title of Chandrakīrti's *Madhyamakāvatara* (*dbu ma la 'jug pa*) thus, taking *avatāra* (*'jug*) as "supplement" rather than "introduction". For an explanation of the reasons behind this translation, see Hopkins' *Meditation on Emptiness*, n.545, pp.868–71. Translation of the following passage is taken from Hopkins' and Klein's unpublished manuscript, "Introduction to the Profound Emptiness", Part One, p.6. It is commentary leading into VI.4.

44 See pp.8b.3–14b.2 of the *Great Exposition*, Dharmsala edition.

45 *Great Exposition*, Dharmsala edition, 9b.5–6.

CHAPTER TWO: INTERPRETATION OF SCRIPTURE

46 See Étienne Lamotte, "La critique d'interprétation dans le bouddhisme," *Annuaire de l'Institut de philologie et d'histoire orientales et slaves*, Vol. IX (Brussels: Université Libre de Bruxelles, 1949), pp.341–61, for a discussion of this sūtra as well as other sūtra and śāstra references to the four reliances. Lamotte, p.342, provides a citation of this sūtra as found in Yashomitra's *Abhidharmakośa-vyākhyā (Sputārthā abhidharmakośavyākhyā, the work of Yaśomitra*, U. Wogihara, ed. (Tokyo: The Publishing Association of Abhidharma-kośa-vyākhyā, 1932–36), p.704:

catvārīmāni bhikṣavaḥ pratisaraṇāni. katamāni catvāri. dharmaḥ pratisaraṇaṃ na pudgalaḥ, arthaḥ pratisaraṇaṃ na vyañjanam, nītārthaṃ sūtraṃ pratisaraṇaṃ na neyārtham, jñānaṃ pratisaraṇaṃ na vijñānam.

For further discussion, see below, note 304.

47 See Robert A.F. Thurman's "Buddhist Hermeneutics" *Journal of the American Academy of Religion* XLVI (1978), pp.19–40, for a short description of Dzong-ka-ba's system of hermeneutics, or interpretation, as set forth in the *Essence of Good Explanations*. See also Thurman's translation of the *Essence of Good Explanations* in his *Tsong Khapa's Speech of Gold in the Essence of True Eloquence*.

48 This criterion is also used by some Hīnayāna systems, and Thurman's "Buddhist Hermeneutics", p.26, supplies a reference in La Vallée Poussin's translation of the *Abhidharmakośa*, Vol.V, p.246, n.2 for this in the Hīnayāna *abhidharma* tradition:

> "'definitive meaning' (*nītārtha*) is defined as 'meaning acceptable as literally expressed' (*yathārutavaśena jñatavyārtham*), and 'interpretable meaning' (*neyārtha*) as 'meaning acceptable after interpretation' (*niddharetva grahitavyārtham*)".

Although these are the meanings of "definitive" and "interpretable" most often reported in the Ge-luk-ba tradition as the assertions of the Hīnayānists, they are by no means a monolithic assertion of all Hīnayāna schools. See John Buescher's "The Buddhist Doctrine of Two Truths in the Vaibhāṣika and Theravāda Schools" (Ann Arbor: University Microfilms, 1982), pp.85–92, for a discussion of other meanings of those terms in Hīnayāna.

The Chittamātra system, based on the *Sūtra Unravelling the Thought (mdo sde dgongs 'grel, saṃdhinirmocanasūtra)*, relies on an extremely complex systematization to determine which scriptures are interpretable and which definitive; see Jeffrey Hopkins forthcoming book, *Reflections on Reality* for an in-depth discussion of this. However, the principle on which it is based is a determination of which scriptures can be accepted as literal.

49 The interpretation of this sūtra is supplied by Jang-gya Röl-bay-dor-jay (*lcang skya rol pa'i rdo rje*, 1717–86) in

his *Presentation of Tenets* (*grub mtha'i rnam bzhag*, Varanasi: Pleasure of Elegant Sayings Printing Press, 1970), p.317.4. English translation by Donald Lopez in "The Svātantrika-Mādhyamika School of Mahāyāna Buddhism" (Ann Arbor: University Microfilms, 1982), p.435.

50 A-gya-yong-dzin, 163.5–164.2.

51 See Thurman's *Tsong Khapa's Speech of Gold in the Essence of True Eloquence*, p.254.

52 P5287, Vol.101, 46.1.5–46.1.6.

53 This is the position set forth in Lo-sang-dor-jay's *Decisive Analysis of (Dzong-ka-ba's) "[Great Exposition of] the Stages of the Path to Enlightenment"*, p.577.3–6, and is supported by many Ge-luk-ba scholars including Sha-mar-den-dzin (see p.14.6). However, there are also scholars such as the former abbot of Namgyal Monastery, Losang Nyima, who say that, in Prāsaṅgika, for a scripture to be considered of definitive meaning, it need only be mainly and explicitly teaching emptiness and does not have to be literal. Losang Nyima's example of a non-literal definitive sūtra is the statement in the *Heart Sūtra* that forms do not exist. See immediately below for a discussion of another way to handle the passage from the *Heart Sūtra*.

54 *Heart of Wisdom Sūtra* (*prajñāhṛdaya*), P160, Vol.6, 166.2.4–166.3.1. The *Heart Sūtra* has been translated by E. Conze in *Buddhist Texts Through the Ages* rpt. (New York: Harper, 1964), pp.152–3; a translation is also found in Geshé Rabten's *Echoes of Voidness*, Stephen Batchelor, ed. and trans., (London: Wisdom, 1983), pp.18–19. Sanskrit text edited by E. Conze available in *Thirty Years of Buddhist Studies* (Oxford: Cassirer, 1967), pp.148–53. Sanskrit text with translation and Conze's explanation in E. Conze, *Buddhist Wisdom Books* (London: George Allen & Unwin, 1958), pp.77–107.

55 See Sha-mar-den-dzin, 15.1–2 and 15.4–5.

56 Sha-mar-den-dzin, 18.3–4.

57 See chapter five of the translation of Dzong-ka-ba's *Great Exposition*, particularly p.185.

58 Thurman, "Buddhist Hermeneutics", p.20.

CHAPTER THREE: DZONG-KA-BA'S ARGUMENT

59 See note 13 above.

60 The account of traditional Tibetan chronology interspersed throughout the next five pages is taken from Hopkins' *Meditation on Emptiness*, pp.356–64. For readers' convenience I have given approximate Western dates for the time periods described in the traditional chronology; however, it should be noted that these are highly tentative since the point from which the traditional history measures – Buddha's parinirvāṇa – is itself not really fixed within the system. I have used the widely accepted Western date of 483 B.C.E. (rounded to 480 B.C.E. because of the general nature of the traditional chronology). However, one widespread system of traditional astrological calculation places that date at 544 B.C.E. while another, a tradition of the *Kālachakra Tantra*, places it at approximately 880 B.C.E. (See Tenzin Gyatso and Jeffrey Hopkins, *The Kālachakra Tantra: Rite of Initiation* (London: Wisdom, 1985), pp.357 and 484.

61 The following account of the assertions of the various schools of Buddhist tenets is based on Tibetan sources such as Gön-chok-jik-may-wang-bo's (*dkon mchog 'jigs med dbang po*, 1728–91) *Precious Garland of Tenets* (*grub mtha' rin chen phreng ba*), English translation by Geshe Sopa and Jeffrey Hopkins in *Practice and Theory of Tibetan Buddhism* (New York: Grove, 1976), the theory portion; Lo-sang-dor-jay's *Decisive Analysis of Special Insight*; and Jang-gya's (*lcang skya*, 1717–86) *Presentation of Tenets* (*grub mtha'i rnam bzhag*).

62 The five Saṃmitīya schools, subschools of the Vaibhāṣhikas, are an exception to this since they hold that a

self-sufficient person exists. Thus, the only selflessness of the person they assert is the person's lack of being a permanent, unitary, and independent entity. See Sopa and Hopkins' *Practice and Theory of Tibetan Buddhism*, p.82. See also Lo-sang-dor-jay's *Decisive Analysis of Special Insight*, 620.5.

63 There is a considerable group of contemporary scholars who question whether Asaṅga himself asserted Mind-Only in an idealist sense of denying external objects; it includes such scholars as Lambert Schmithausen ("On the Problem of the Relation of Spiritual Practice and Philosophical Theory in Buddhism", in *German Scholars on India*, Vol.II, Bombay: Nachiketa Publications, 1976); Alex Wayman ("Yogācāra and the Buddhist Logicians", *Journal of the International Association of Buddhist Studies* 2 (1979), pp. 65–78); Yoshifumi Ueda ("Two Main Streams of Thought in Yogācāra Philosophy", *Philosophy East and West* 17 (1967), 155–65); and Janice Willis (*On Knowing Reality*, New York: Columbia University Press, 1979).

Such scholars would not be willing to apply many of the general statements about Chittamātra in the following paragraphs (which are based on the sources cited above in note 61) to Asaṅga. The question of the relationship between the view of reality put forward by Asaṅga in the "Chapter on Reality" in his *Bodhisattva Levels* (*byang sa*, *bodhisattvabhūmi*) and mind-only in the sense of no external objects is considered at length by Dzong-ka-ba in his *Essence of the Good Explanations* and amplified in later Ge-luk-ba commentarial literature, reaching the conclusion that the two are intertwined and Asaṅga does assert no external objects. See Jeffrey Hopkins' forthcoming *The Question of Mind-Only in the Early Yogic Practice School* for a detailed discussion of these issues.

64 This paragraph is based on Lo-sang-dor-jay's *Decisive Analysis of Special Insight*, 572.5–573.6.

65 Some examples of the way in which it is not strictly historical are that what the Ge-luk-bas include as Sautrāntika was primarily quite late in formulation, understood from the writings of Dharmakīrti, though Ge-luk-bas consider Dharmakīrti himself to have been a Chittamātrin. Also there is the fact that Prāsaṅgika is ranked at the top even though it was not the last school to develop, the Yogāchāra-Svātantrika school having come after it.

The disadvantage of the synchronic approach is that it encourages the idea of a monolithic system – for instance, Chittamātra – that does not take into account all the variations and intellectual developments of the individual people included within its sphere, leading to a sense of something more concrete and defined than can necessarily be found in the individual writings of its founding members. The advantage of such a system is that one has something compact, orderly, concrete, and graspable that facilitates the comparison of specific ideas across the different schools.

66 See Sopa and Hopkins' *Practice and Theory of Tibetan Buddhism*, p.117. For the following paragraph on Svātantrika assertions, see *Practice and Theory*, p.126, and Lo-sang-dor-jay's *Decisive Analysis of Special Insight*, 605.2– 606.5.

67 See Hopkins' *Meditation on Emptiness*, p.36, for a more extensive listing of synonyms of the object of negation. The list given here is intended for purposes of comparison with the other tenet systems. See also Lo-sang-dor-jay's *Decisive Analysis of Special Insight*, 610.4–5.

68 See Dzong-ka-ba's *Ocean of Reasoning, Explanation of (Nāgārjuna's) "Treatise on the Middle Way"* rje'i gsung dbu ma'i lta ba'i skor edition, Vol.1, 488.5–8 and Lo-sang-dor-jay's *Decisive Analysis of Special Insight*, 606.4–5. For what Svātantrika accepts, see Tu-gen's (*thu'u bkwan blo bzang chos kyi nyi ma*, 1737–1802) *Mirror of the Good Explanations Showing the Sources and*

Assertions of All Systems of Tenets (*grub mtha' thams cad kyi khungs dang 'dod tshul ston pa legs bshad shel gyi me long*, Sarnath: Chhos Je Lama, 1963), 24.13–15 and 20.10 as well as Sopa and Hopkins' *Practice and Theory of Tibetan Buddhism*, p.124.

69 The following three paragraphs are taken from Tu-gen, 20.3ff, with some refinement from Sopa and Hopkins' *Practice and Theory of Tibetan Buddhism*, *passim*.

70 The source for this Sanskrit term is Chandrakīrti's *Commentary on* (*Āryadeva's*) *"Four Hundred"*, edited Sanskrit fragments in: Haraprasād Shāstri, ed., "Catuḥ-śatikā of Ārya Deva," Memoirs of the Asiatic Society of Bengal, III no. 8 (1914), p.492.13.

71 This is the list of six most commonly found in Ge-luk-ba literature. See Paul Williams "Review of Chr. Lindtner (1982) *Nagarjuniana: Studies in the Writings and Philosophy of Nāgārjuna*, Indiske Studier 4, Copenhagen: Akademisk Forlag", *Journal of Indian Philosophy* 12 (1984), pp.76–83, for a discussion of other ways of adducing the six members of the list. Following are more complete references for the six I have listed:

Treatise on the Middle Way/Fundamental Treatise on the Middle Way, Called "Wisdom"

(*dbu ma rtsa ba'i tshig le'ur byas pa shes rab ces bya ba*, *madhyamakaśāstra/ prajñānāmamūlamadhyamakakārikā*) P5224, Vol.95. A Sanskrit edition of the text is available within the La Vallée Poussin edition of Chandrakīrti's *Clear Words*, a commentary on Nāgārjuna's text: *Mūlamadhyamakakārikās de Nāgārjuna avec la Prasannapadā Commentaire de Candrakīrti*, Bibliotheca Buddhica IV, (Osnabrück: Biblio Verlag, 1970). Also there is a more recent edition of the text without Chandrakīrti's commentary edited by J.W. de Jong: *Nāgārjuna, Mūlamadhyamakakārikāḥ*, (Adyar: Adyar Library and Research Center, 1977), as well as one by Chr. Lindtner: *Nāgārjuna's Filosofiske Vaerker* (Copenhagen: Akademisk Forlag, 1982), pp.177–215. Numerous scholars have translated various portions of it into a variety of European languages. There is not yet a definitive English translation. See the bibliography for a complete listing.

The text is commonly referred to in the Ge-luk-ba tradition by two abbreviated titles: *dbu ma'i bstan bcos* (*Treatise on the Middle Way*) and *rtsa ba shes rab* (*Fundamental Wisdom*). Although the later is probably numerically more prevalent, I have chosen always to refer to the text as the *Treatise on the Middle Way* since it is more evocative of the content of the text.

Treatise Called the Finely Woven

(*zhib mo rnam par 'thag pa zhes bya ba'i mdo, vaidalyasūtranāma*) P5226, Vol.95. The Sanskrit text has not survived. According to Chr. Lindtner (*Nagarjuniana*, Indiske Studier 4, Copenhagen: Akademisk Forlag, 1982, p.87) an English translation is forthcoming in the Indiske Studier series published in Copenhagen.

Seventy Stanzas on Emptiness

(*stong pa nyid bdun cu pa'i tshig le'ur byas pa, śūnyatāsaptatikārikā*) Toh 3827, Tokyo *sde dge* Vol.1; P5227, Vol. 95. The text does not survive in Sanskrit. An edited Tibetan edition and English translation by Chr. Lindtner is available in *Nagarjuniana*, pp.34–69.

Refutation of Objections

(*rtsod pa bzlog pa'i tshig le'ur byas pa, vigrahavyāvartanīkārikā*) P5228, Vol.95; Toh 3828, Tokyo *sde dge* Vol.1. A Sanskrit edition edited by Johnston and Kunst along with English translation by K. Bhattacharya is available in *The Dialectical Method of Nāgārjuna*, Bhattacharya, Johnston, and Kunst (New Delhi: Motilal Banarsidass, 1978). Edited Tibetan and Sanskrit is available in Chr. Lindtner, *Nagarjuniana*, pp.70–86. There is also a translation from the Chinese version of the text by G. Tucci in *Pre-Diṅnāga Buddhist Texts on Logic from Chinese Sources*, Gaekwad's Oriental Series, 49, (Baroda: Oriental Institute, 1929), as well as a French translation by S. Yamaguchi, "Traité de Nāgārjuna pour écarter les vaines discussion (Vigrahavyāvartanī) traduit et annoté," *Journal Asiatique* 215 (1929) pp.1–86.

Sixty Stanzas of Reasoning
(*rigs.pa drug cu pa'i tshig le'ur byas pa, yuktiṣaṣṭikākārikā*) P5225, Vol.95; Toh 3825, Tokyo *sde dge* Vol.1. An edited Tibetan edition with Sanskrit fragments and English translation is available in Chr. Lindtner, *Nagarjuniana*, pp.100–19.

Precious Garland of Advice for the King
(*rgyal po la gtam bya ba rin po che'i phreng ba, rājaparikathāratnavalī*) P5658, Vol.129. Sanskrit, Tibetan, and Chinese texts available in Michael Hahn's *Nāgārjuna's Ratnāvalī, Vol.1, The Basic Texts (Sanskrit, Tibetan, and Chinese)*, (Bonn: Indica et Tibetica Verlag, 1982). An English translation by Jeffrey Hopkins and Lati Rimpoche is available in Nāgārjuna and the Seventh Dalai Lama, *The Precious Garland and the Song of the Four Mindfulnesses*, (New York: Harper and Row, 1975).

72 For a description of the various purposes of Nāgārjuna's works, see Chandrakīrti's *Commentary on the "Sixty Stanzas of Reasoning"*, Toh 3864, Tokyo *sde dge* Vol.8, 2a.4–2b.2. See also Dzong-ka-ba's *Ocean of Reasoning, Explanation of (Nāgārjuna's) "Treatise on the Middle Way"*, rJe'i gsung dbu ma'i lta ba'i skor edition, Vol.1, 464.4–468.10 and Lo-sang-dor-jay's *Decisive Analysis of Special Insight*, 578.1– 580.2.

73 For example, Nga-wang-bel-den (*ngag dbang dpal ldan*, b.1797) in his *Explanation of the Conventional and the Ultimate in the Four Systems of Tenets* (*grub mtha' bzhi'i lugs kyi kun rdzob dang don dam pa'i don rnam par bshad pa legs bshad dpyid kyi dpal mo'i glu dbyangs*, New Delhi: Guru Deva, 1972), 46.6, says about the difference between Proponents of True Existence, or Truly Existent Things, and Proponents of No Entityness, i.e., Mādhyamikas:

Also, the Proponents of Truly Existing Things and the Proponents of No Entityness are divided by whether or not they assert functioning things to be truly established. As [Jam-yang-shay-ba's *Tenets*] says, "[By way of] asserting and refuting truly existent functioning things, there are Proponents of Truly Existing Things and [Proponents] of No Entityness." (Translation by Jeffrey Hopkins, unpublished manuscript, p.24.)

The term "Proponents of True Existence" often includes also non-Buddhist schools. Further, it must be noted that although its main usage is to distinguish Mādhyamikas and non-Mādhyamikas, in some contexts the Svātantrika-Mādhyamikas are included within its scope, and in others it is used to refer only to Hīnayānists, specifically Vaibhāṣhika and Sautrāntika. For this latter usage, see for example Dzong-ka-ba's *Essence of the Good Explanations*, Thurman's translation, p.238.

74 For full references on these texts including information on surviving Sanskrit texts and translations, see the bibliography.

75 Very little of the writings of any of the figures mentioned in this and the following paragraphs are extant, and, as a result, their views are known mainly from occasional references and citations in later sources. As more scholarly research on early Mādhyamika is done, it may be possible to identify with greater precision what their actual assertions were. Following are brief identifications of those mentioned.

Lo-den-shay-rap was one of the greatest translators of the second dissemination of Buddhism to Tibet and was one of the leading proponents of the Svātantrika branch of Mādhyamika philosophy during the introductory period of Mādhyamika to Tibet. See van der Kuijp's *Contributions to the Development of Tibetan Buddhist Epistemology*, Chapter 1, for a discussion of the life, writings, and views of Lo-den-shay-rap.

Tang-sak-ba was a student of the translator Ba-tsap Nyi-ma-drak (*spa tshab nyi ma grags*, 1055–114?), who was the translator responsible for bringing the Prāsaṅgika-Mādhyamika viewpoint to predominance in Tibet. Tang-sak-ba is known as one of Ba-tsap Nyi-ma-drak's "four sons", and thus would probably be placed in the early 12th century. He is known to have founded a school in Tang-sak (*thang sag*) and to have written and taught extensively on the Mādhyamika system. See Roerich's *Blue Annals*, rpt. (Delhi: Motilal Banarsidass, 1979), pp.343–4, and Karen Lang's "sPa tshab Nyi ma grags and the introduction of Prāsaṅgika Madhyamaka into Tibet", forthcoming in the Turrell Wylie memorial volume, pp.13–14. Ruegg describes Tang-sak-ba as being among those who accepted a Mādhyamika interpretation that said that "a theory of neither being nor non-being (*yod min med min gyi lta ba*) was the doctrine of Śrī-Candra" [that is, Chandrakīrti] ("The Jo naṅ pas: A School of Buddhist Ontologists According to the *Grub mtha' šel gyi me loṅ*", *Journal of the American Oriental Society* 83 (1963), p.89).

Cha-ba Chö-gyi-seng-ge was an indirect student of Lo-den-shay-rap, having studied with Lo-den-shay-rap's direct or indirect student, Gang-gya-mar-ba Jang-chup-drak (*gangs rgya dmar pa byang chub grags*, see below). Of great importance for his role in the development of epistemological studies in Tibet, Cha-ba also was a proponent of Svātantrika-Mādhyamika. See van der Kuijp's *Contributions to the Development of Tibetan Buddhist Epistemology*, Chapter 2, for a discussion of Cha-ba's life, writings, and views. See also his "Phya-pa Chos-kyi seng-ge's Impact on Tibetan Epistemological Theory", *Journal of Indian Philosophy* 5 (1977), pp.355–69.

Gun-kyen-rong-dön is known by the names Rong-dön-shākya-gyel-tsen (*rong ston shākya rgyal mtshan*) and Rong-dön-shay-ja-gun-sik (*rong ston shes bya kun gzigs*).

Ruegg identifies Rong-dön as a known opponent of Dzong-ka-ba ("On the Thesis and Assertion in the Madhyamaka/dBu ma" in *Contributions on Tibetan and Buddhist Religion and Philosophy*, Steinkellner and Tauscher, ed., Wien, 1983, p.216, n.30) and says also that he was a teacher of Shākya-chok-den (*shākya mchog ldan*, 1428–1507) and a follower of Svātantrika-Mādhyamika ("The Jo naṅ pas", p.89, n.75).

Concerning Bo-dong Chok-lay-nam-gyel, Ruegg says that Dzong-ka-ba is reported to have studied with a Bo-dong Chok-lay-nam-gyel, a follower of the Jo-nang-ba teachings, who lived from 1306–86, but that there is also a later Bo-dong Chok-lay-nam-gyel who lived from 1375–1450 ("The Jo naṅ pas", p.81, n.38). This latter figure extensively refuted Dzong-ka-ba, e.g., his demarcation of the difference between sūtra and tantra. Which Bo-dong is the intended referent here is not clear; it could easily have been the earlier, since Dzong-ka-ba is known to have refuted many Jo-nang-ba positions in his writings.

76 Lo-sang-gön-chok, *Word Commentary on the Root Text of (Jam-yang-shay-ba's) "Tenets", A Crystal Mirror* (*grub mtha' rtsa ba'i tshig ṭik shel dkar me long*) in *Three Commentaries on the Grub mtha' rtsa ba gdoṅ lṅa'i sgra dbyaṅs of 'Jam-dbyaṅs-bźad-pa'i-rdo-rje ṅag-dbaṅ-brtson-'grus*, Delhi: Chophel Lekden, 1978, 170.4–172.5.

Hva-shang Mahāyāna, as mentioned earlier, was a Chinese monk reputed to have debated Kamalashīla in the late eighth century. Although Dzong-ka-ba certainly disagreed with his views, he is an unlikely explicit referent of Dzong-ka-ba's refutation, since Dzong-ka-ba uses the time qualifier in his refutation, "*Nowadays*, most who claim to propound the meaning of the middle way . . ." (see p.270). However, it is possible that Dzong-ka-ba might have been referring to those whose view accorded with that of Hva-shang Mahāyāna, for it is reputed to have survived in Tibet long after Hva-shang's actual departure and Dzong-ka-ba does explicitly criticize Hva-shang's view at other points in the *Great Exposition*. See Karen Lang's "sPa tshab Nyi ma grags and the introduction of Prāsaṅgika Madhyamaka into Tibet", p.3, for a discussion of recent literature on the question of whether Hva-shang could be called a Mādhyamika.

Paṇ-chen Shākya-chok-den also could not have been one of Dzong-ka-ba's intended referents since he was not even born until nine years after Dzong-ka-ba's death. He undoubtedly ranks inclusion in the list of those having "unacceptable" views because of his own vigorous criticisms of Dzong-ka-ba's Mādhyamika interpretation. See van der Kuijp's *Contributions of the Development of Tibetan Buddhist Epistemology* (which is largely based on the writings of Shākya-chok-den), pp.10–22, for a biography of Shākya-chok-den and some description of his writings. See Ruegg's "The Jo naṅ pas", pp.89–90, for Tu-gen Lo-sang-chö-gyi-nyi-ma's (*thu'u bkvan blo bzang chos kyi nyi ma*, 1737–1802) brief – and highly critical – description of Shākya-chok-den from a Ge-luk-ba viewpoint.

Ma-ja Jang-chup-dzön-drü, d.1186[?], was initially a student of Cha-ba Chö-gyi-seng-ge and later of Ba-tsap Nyi-ma-drak (Lang, p.12). As such, he became a follower of Prāsaṅgika-Mādhyamika. Late in his life, he may have been a teacher of Sa-gya Paṇḍita (*sa skya paṇḍita*, 1182–1251) (see Paul Williams, "rMa bya pa Byang chub brtson 'grus on Madhyamaka Method", *Journal of Indian Philosophy* 13 (1985), p.216 and p.223, n.36) and was much admired by Shākya-chok-den. In a section of the *Great Exposition* not translated here, where Dzong-ka-ba explicitly addresses and refutes the position that Prāsaṅgikas have no theses or assertions of their own and merely refute others, the views of Ma-ja Jang-chup-dzön-drü are one of four positions addressed. See Ruegg's "On the Thesis and Assertion in the Madhyamaka/dbU ma", pp.229–30, for a discussion of this.

Ruegg brings up some problems regarding what the later commentarial tradition, specifically Jam-yang-shay-ba, has ascribed as positions of Ma-ja, and Williams picks up and elaborates on this point in great detail in his "rMa bya pa Byang chub brtson 'grus on Madhyamaka Method", concluding that the person actually holding that Mādhyamikas had no views or assertions and hence to be refuted was a different person with a very similar name, Ma-ja Jang-chup-ye-shay (*rma bya pa byang chub ye shes*). Williams offers a provocative political explanation, namely the high esteem in which Ma-ja Jang-chup-dzön-drü was held by a tradition that Jam-yang-shayba was seeking to refute, as one possible reason why his views might have been misrepresented.

Gang-gya-mar, full name Gang-gya-mar-ba Jang-chup-drak (*gangs rgya dmar pa byang chub grags*), was either a direct or indirect student of Lo-den-shay-rap and a teacher of Cha-ba Chö-gyi-seng-ge.

77 This summary of Dzong-ka-ba's argument relies heavily on Lo-sang-dor-jay's *Analysis of Special Insight*, 584.1–597.1.

78 The Tibetan of these terms is as follows:

rigs pas dpyad mi bzod pa – not able to bear analysis by reasoning

rigs pas gnod pa – damaged by reasoning, or *rigs pas khegs* – refuted by reasoning

rigs shes kyis ma rnyed pa – not found by a reasoning consciousness

rigs shes kyis med par rnyed pa – found as, or to be, non-existent by a reasoning consciousness.

79 The following definitions are taken from the chapter on "Established Bases" (*gzhi grub*) of Pur-bu-jok's (*phur bu lcog byams pa rgya mtsho*, 1825–1901) *Explanation of the Lesser Path of Reasoning* (*rigs lam chung ngu'i rnam par bshad pa*) in *Magical Key to the Path of Reasoning, Presentation of the Collected Topics Revealing the Meaning of the Treatises on Valid Cognition* (*tshad ma'i gzhung don*

'byed pa'i bsdus grwa'i rnam bzhag rigs lam 'phrul gyi sde mig), Buxa India: n.p., 1965. See Daniel Perdue's "Practice and Theory of Philosophical Debate in Tibetan Buddhist Education", a translation and explanation of the entire "Lesser Path of Reasoning", (Ann Arbor: University Microfilms, 1983), pp.364ff., for a discussion of these terms.

80 This passage is from the *King of Meditative Stabilizations Sūtra* (*ting nge 'dzin gyi rgyal po, samādhirāja*), IX.23ab. See chapter four of the translation of Dzong-ka-ba's "Great Exposition", pp.178–9, for citation of the entire verse as well as references to the Tibetan and Sanskrit.

81 P5265, Vol.98, Toh 3864, Tokyo *sde dge* Vol. 8, 5a.6. This is cited in the *Great Exposition*, Dharmsala edition, 396b.3.

82 Dharmsala edition, 386b.4–6. See chapter seven of the translation, pp.205ff.

83 T.R.V. Murti, *The Central Philosophy of Buddhism*, London: George Allen & Unwin, rpt.1970. Murti says, p.146:

> When one alternative is rejected or accepted the other is *eo ipso* accepted or rejected, else the Law of the Excluded Middle would be violated. The Mādhyamika flagrantly violates this law at every step; we find him cutting down all the alternatives that are, by the canons of formal logic, both exclusive and exhaustive.

He also says, p.131:

> How does the Mādhyamika reject any and all views? He uses only one weapon. By drawing out the implications of any view he shows its self-contradictory character. The dialectic is a series of *reductio ad absurdum* arguments .... The Mādhyamika *disproves* the opponents' thesis, and does *not* prove any thesis of his own.

The questions of whether Mādhyamikas do or do not accept the law of the excluded middle, the meaning and uses of the tetralemma, and the Mādhyamikas' use of logic in general have been widely addressed by numerous modern scholars, many but not all of whom disagree with Murti's conclusions. See, for example, Richard Robinson's *Early Mādhyamika in India and China*, pp.51–8; as well as his "Feature Book Review 'K.N. Jayatilleke, Early Buddhist Theory of Knowledge'", *Philosophy East and West*, 19 (1969), pp.69–82, especially pp.76–8; Seyfort Ruegg's, "The Uses of the Four Positions of the *Catuṣkoṭi* and the Problem of the Description of Reality in Mahāyāna Buddhism", *Journal of Indian Philosophy*, 5 (1977), pp.1–71, which includes a review of Western literature on the subject, pp.39–55; Alex Wayman's, "Who understands the four alternatives of the Buddhist texts?" *Philosophy East and West* 27 (1977), pp.3–21; K.N. Jayatilleke's, "The Logic of Four Alternatives," *Philosophy East and West* 17 (1967) pp.69–84; Fritz Staal's *Exploring Mysticism*, Berkeley: University of California Press, 1975; and Arnold Kunst, "The Concept of the Principle of Excluded Middle in Buddhism" *Rocznik Orientalistyczny*, 21 (1957), pp.141–7.

84 See also later in the *Great Exposition*, Dharmsala edition, 411a.1–412b.2, Wayman's translation, pp.246–9. This is not the only interpretation of the tetralemma set forth by Ge-luk-ba scholars or even by Dzong-ka-ba himself. For instance, at the point in the *Great Exposition* just noted, Dzong-ka-ba simply adds the qualification "established by way of their own entities" to all four possibilities. Thus, he says that what are being refuted are:

1) things (*dngos po, bhāva*) that are established by way of their own entities

2) non-things (*dngos med, abhāva*) that are established by way of their own entities

3) that which is both a thing and a non-thing that is established by way of its own entity

4) that which is not both which is established by way of its own entity.

See Hopkins' *Meditation on Emptiness*, note 500, pp.850–4, for a discussion of these different interpretations.

85 The Tibetan can be found in the Dharmsala edition of Chandrakīrti's *Clear Words*, 280.1–13. The Sanskrit is available in La Vallée Poussin's edition, 329.10–17. This passage is cited in its entirety in chapter seven of the translation, pp.200–1.

86 Toh 3865, Tokyo *sde dge* Vol.8, 201b.2–4. This is cited by Dzong-ka-ba in the *Great Exposition*, Dharmsala edition, 394b.6–395a.2.

87 VI.36. This is found in La Vallée Poussin's edition of the Tibetan, p.122.14–17. La Vallée Poussin's translation is in *Muséon*, 1910, p.315. See chapter four of the translation, p.179, for Dzong-ka-ba's citation of the passage. See the Dharmsala edition of the *Great Exposition*, 409a.6– 409b.5, for a second citation of the passage accompanied by explanation of how he understands it.

88 The *Questions of the King of Nāgas, Anavatapta, Sūtra* (*klu'i rgyal po ma dros pas zhus pa'i mdo, anavataptanāgarājaparipṛcchāsūtra*) P823, Vol.33. It is cited by Chandrakīrti in his *Clear Words*; the Sanskrit is available in La Vallée Poussin's edition of that text, 504.1. See the Dharmsala edition of the *Great Exposition*, 410a.5–410b.2, for citation of it by Dzong-ka-ba along with explanation of how he interprets it.

89 Jeffrey Hopkins has a lengthy article discussing this question of commonly appearing subjects and how it is used to differentiate Svātantrika and Mādhyamika, entitled "A Tibetan Delineation of Different Views of Emptiness in the Indian Middle Way School: Dzong-ka-ba's Two Interpretations of the *Locus Classicus* in Chandrakīrti's *Clear Words* Showing Bhāvaviveka's Assertion of Commonly Appearing Subjects and Inherent Existence", forthcoming in the *Journal of the Tibet Society*.

CHAPTER FOUR: DZONG-KA-BA AND MODERN INTERPRETERS I: NOT NEGATING ENOUGH

90 Ruegg, *The Literature of the Madhyamaka School*, p.2. Ruegg then goes on to say, "With the exception of the first five which are hardly appropriate in any context and become quite misleading when taken in their usual senses, such descriptions no doubt correspond to some aspect of Madhyamaka thought." Dzong-ka-ba would probably take exception with some others as well, as will become clear in the following discussion.

With regard to the question of labelling Mādhyamika, Douglas Daye makes the very apt comment ("Major Schools of the Mahāyāna: Mādhyamika" in Charles Prebish, ed., *Buddhism: A Modern Perspective*, (University Park and London: The Pennsylvania State University Press, 1975, p.77), "It seems fair to say that the different labels, approaches, and descriptions of Nāgārjuna's writings found in the history of modern scholarship reflect almost as much about the viewpoints of the scholars involved as do they reflect the content of Nāgārjuna's concepts."

91 For a detailed history of early Western scholarship on Mādhyamika, see J.W. de Jong, "Emptiness", *Journal of Indian Philosophy* 2 (1972), pp.7–15; his longer "A Brief History of Buddhist Studies in Europe and America", *The Eastern Buddhist*, NS 7, No. 1 (1974), pp.55–106; No.2 (1974), pp.49–82; Guy Richard Welbon, *The Buddhist Nirvāṇa and Its Western Interpreters* (Chicago: University of Chicago Press, 1968); and Malcolm David Eckel, "A Question of Nihilism: Bhāvaviveka's Response to the Fundamental Problems of Mādhyamika Philosophy", unpublished dissertation, Harvard, April, 1980, pp.12–50. Eckel's discussion is particularly relevant to the present context.

92 The most influential proponent of the absolutist inter-

pretation is T.R.V. Murti, whose *Central Philosophy of Buddhism*, published in 1955 (London: George Allen & Unwin) was the first book devoted totally to Mādhyamika philosophy. Although his strong absolutist interpretation is often disputed by modern scholars, Murti's work continues to exert a potent influence, and many still call Mādhyamika absolutism although usually in a more qualified way than does Murti. This topic will be discussed further (see pp.129–31) but, in brief, some of the current scholars who label Mādhyamika absolutism are B.K. Matilal, J.W. de Jong, G.C. Nayak, Mahesh Mehta, and Christian Lindtner.

93 "On the Reception and Early History of the dbu-ma (Madhyamaka) in Tibet", in Michael Aris and Aung Suu Kyi, ed., *Tibetan Studies in Honour of Hugh Richardson* (New Delhi: Vikas, 1980), pp.278–9.

94 Translation by Donald S. Lopez, Jr. with Jeffrey Hopkins, (London: Wisdom Publications, 1985), p.118. The text was previously translated by a team of Buddhist monks from Tibet, India, and Great Britain in a general paraphrase, entitled *The Opening of the Wisdom Eye* (Wheaton, Illinois: Theosophical Publishing House, 1972); the passage cited can be found on p.11 of that edition.

95 *Nagarjuniana*, Indiske Studier 4, Copenhagen: Akademisk Forlag, 1982, pp.249 and 258. Paul Williams, in a lengthy review of Lindtner's book (*Journal of Indian Philosophy* 12, 1984, pp.73–104) makes the very *a propos* comment, (p.97), "These references [supplied by Lindtner of Nāgārjuna's sūtra sources] enable us to see Nāgārjuna as a Buddhist monk on a direct continuum with the earlier traditions, to place him in his Indian religious context, to remove him from the position of an Indian proto-Wittgenstein, Nietzsche, Hegel, Kant or whoever is the currently fashionable Western philosopher – surely it must be Foucault and/or Derrida next!"

96 *Emptiness: A Study in Religious Meaning* (Nashville,

New York: Abingdon Press, 1967). See particularly chapter ten, "The Religious Meaning of 'Emptiness'", pp.155–69. In the same vein, David Eckel says, ("A Question of Nihilism: Bhāvaviveka's Response to the Fundamental Problems of Mādhyamika Philosophy", p.135):

> "To the Mādhyamikas philosophy was much more than a dialectical weapon to defeat the assertions of their opponents. It was a method for exploring the categories of the moral life, establishing those categories on a sound philosophical basis, and then using them to effect a radical change in the life of the practitioner. Mādhyamika therefore had the character of a Buddhist philosophy of religion, but a philosophy in which theory became the companion of practice."

Of course, there are still exceptions, such as those who believe that "religion" requires a Judeo-Christian type supreme deity, and thus Guy Bugault ("Logic and Dialectics in the *Madhyamakakārikās*", *Journal of Indian Philosophy*, 11, 1983, p.58) makes the qualified statement:

> "But for Nāgārjuna it is logic → dialectics → soteriology. His fundamental intention is – if not religious, for there is no God – at least one of therapy or liberation."

And Fernando Tola and Carmen Dragonetti, based, I believe, on a misconception of the scope of Nāgārjuna's refutation, understanding it to include even the Buddha and his teaching, make the stunning statement ("Nāgārjuna's Conception of 'Voidness' (Śūnyatā)", *Journal of Indian Philosophy*, 9, 1981, p.279):

> "The Buddhist theory of *śūnyatā* constitutes the most radical and rigorous conception, elaborated in India, of an Absolute in all the fullness of the work, without any concession to the religious feelings of man or to his religious needs."

Also, there is A.K. Warder, who stands nearly alone in raising the qualm as to whether, even though the Mahāyāna Buddhist tradition considers itself to stem from Nāgārjuna, Nāgārjuna himself was even a Mahāyānist. See his "Is Nāgārjuna a Mahāyānist?" in Mervyn Sprung, ed., *The Problem of Two Truths in Buddhism and Vedānta* (Dordrecht and Boston: D. Reidel, 1973), pp.78–88.

97 J.W. de Jong makes this point in his "Emptiness", pp.11– 12.

98 Lindtner's *Nagarjuniana* addresses just this question and arrives at a body of works that I think can be legitimately accepted as by Nāgārjuna, although Paul Williams in his feature review (*Journal of Indian Philosophy*, 12, 1984, pp.73–104) disagrees with one or two attributions. It is worth pointing out that those texts that Lindtner accepts as authentic parallel quite closely those relied on by the Ge-luk-ba tradition. Dzong-ka-ba, for example, does not cite in support of his Mādhyamika interpretation a single text which contemporary scholarship considers to be spuriously attributed to Nāgārjuna.

99 Richard Robinson says (*Early Mādhyamika in India and China*, Madison, Milwaukee, and London: University of Wisconsin Press, 1967, pp.57–8):

> "There do not seem to be any real paradoxes in the *Stanzas*. The seeming paradoxes are easily resolved once the definitions and the fundamental absurdity of the concept of own-being are taken into account."

Similarly, Seyfort Ruegg says ("The Uses of the Four Positions of the *Catuṣkoṭi* and the Problem of the Description of Reality in Mahāyāna Buddhism", *Journal of Indian Philosophy*, 5, 1977, p.5):

> "But at least in his theoretical scholastic treatises (*rigs ćhogs*), of which the *MMK* is most representative, he does not seem to have himself employed paradoxes as such in an attempt to speak of reality."

Imputation of paradox to Nāgārjuna by modern scholars will be dealt with as specific contexts arise in the following discussion.

100 One scholar vigorous in this opinion is Paul J. Griffiths,

who in an article noteworthy primarily for its heavy-handed and inflammatory tone ("Buddhist Hybrid English: Some Notes on Philology and Hermeneutics for Buddhologists", *Journal of the International Association of Buddhist Studies* 4, 1981, pp.17–32) claims (p.21) that a Buddhologist cannot be a Buddhist, since such apparently hopelessly cripples the powers of critical thought. One wonders if he would also say that Christianity can only be studied in a scholarly way by non-Christians, a requirement that would effectively end most scholarly study and negate most that has been done.

101 "Did Nāgārjuna really refute all philosophical views?", *Philosophy East and West* 22 (1972), p.331.

102 "Pyrrhonism and Mādhyamika", *Philosophy East and West* 32 (1982), p.3.

103 Douglas D. Daye, "Major Schools of the Mahāyāna: Mādhyamika", p.84.

104 *Buddhist Logic*, Vol.2 (New York: Dover, 1962) p.153, n.3. Stcherbatsky's comment is made in the context of differentiating between Prāsaṅgika-Mādhyamika which he says rejects logic altogether and Svātantrika-Mādhyamika which he sees as accepting logic. This view on the difference between the two Mādhyamika schools has had a great influence on subsequent scholars (see, for example, Streng's *Emptiness*, p.35). Given that Dzong-ka-ba does not accept that characterization of Prāsaṅgika, this is not how he makes the differentiation. Falling beyond the range of this discussion, that topic will be discussed in a subsequent study.

105 "Some Logical Aspects of Nāgārjuna's System", *Philosophy East and West* 6 (1957), p.307.

106 "Did Nāgārjuna really refute all philosophical views?", p.331.

107 *Exploring Mysticism*, (Berkeley: University of California Press, 1975) p.45.

108 *Buddhist Thought in India*, (Ann Arbor: University of Michigan Press, 1967) p.243.

109 "Nāgārjuna and analytic philosophy, II", *Philosophy East and West* 28 (1978), p.288. He is summarizing the conclusions of an earlier article, "Nāgārjuna and Analytic Philosophy", *Philosophy East and West* 25 (1975), pp.281–90.

110 "Major Schools of the Mahāyāna: Mādhyamika", p.83. A linguistic interpretation of Mādhyamika is a major stream of contemporary scholarship, most recently often based on comparison with Ludwig Wittgenstein, that begins with Richard Robinson and has been advanced by such subsequent scholars as Frederick Streng, Douglas Daye, and Chris Gudmunsen. It has been applied to the writings of Dzong-ka-ba by Robert Thurman ("Philosophical nonegocentrism in Wittgenstein and Candrakīrti in their treatment of the private language problem", *Philosophy East and West* 30, 1980, pp.321–37, and *Tsong Khapa's Speech of Gold in the Essence of True Eloquence*, Princeton: Princeton University Press, 1984, Introduction) and by C.W. Huntington, Jr. ("A 'nonreferential' view of language and conceptual thought in the work of Tsoṅ-kha-pa", *Philosophy East and West* 33, 1983, pp.326–39).

111 Ibid., p.94.

112 The first passage is from "The Madhyamaka Critique of Epistemology I", *Journal of Indian Philosophy* 8 (1980), p.320, and the second is from its continuation, "The Madhyamaka Critique of Epistemology II", *Journal of Indian Philosophy* 9 (1981), p.158.

113 "A Study on the Mādhyamika Method of Refutation and Its Influence on Buddhist Logic", *Journal of the International Association of Buddhist Studies* 4 (1981), p.88.

114 "Some logical aspects of Nāgārjuna's system", pp.307–8.

115 "The nature and function of Nāgārjuna's arguments", *Philosophy East and West* 28 (1978) p.499.

116 "Major Schools of the Mahāyāna: Mādhyamika". The first passage is from p.95; the second from p.96.

117 *Early Mādhyamika in India and China*, p.61.

118 He says this in his *Essence of the Good Explanations*. See Thurman's *Tsong Khapa's Speech of Gold in the Essence of True Eloquence*, p.364. See also Hopkins' *Meditation on Emptiness* (London: Wisdom Publications, 1983), p.558–9, where the purpose of Nāgārjuna's *Treatise* is discussed and this passage is cited.

119 Hopkins' *Meditation on Emptiness*, p.558, quoting Jang-gya's *Presentation of Tenets* (*grub mtha'i rnam bzhag*) 419.17–420.9. Dzong-ka-ba cites the passage from Buddhapālita in the *Great Exposition*, 423b.4–6, (Wayman's translation in *Calming the Mind and Discerning the Real*, p.267). It is commentary on Chapter 1 of Nāgārjuna's *Treatise*, located in Walleser's edition of the *Buddhapālita Commentary*, 3.6–3.11. Dzong-ka-ba cites the passage from Chandrakīrti in his *Essence of the Good Explanations* just prior to the passage from the *Essence* cited above. See Thurman's translation, p.364.

120 Douglas Daye, "Major Schools of the Mahāyāna: Mādhyamika" p.96.

121 *Central Philosophy of Buddhism*, p.146.

122 See the *Great Exposition*, Dharmsala edition, 422b.5–422b.6 (Wayman's translation, p.266). Murti's *Central Philosophy of Buddhism*, p.238, provides the *Śālistamba Sūtra* passage that is the source for this identification of ignorance as well as references to its citation in major Mādhyamika treatises.

123 *Nagarjuniana*, p.272.

124 *The Precious Garland and the Song of the Four Mindfulnesses*, Jeffrey Hopkins and Lati Rimpoche, trans., p.17.

125 This is found in the Dharmsala edition of the *Great Exposition*, 420.3–420.5, Wayman's translation, p.261 – mistranslated. (I will not make specific criticisms of Wayman's translation in this chapter except to indicate points where I feel his translation is erroneous or particularly unclear; Wayman's translation is considered in detail in appendix two.)

The formulation of this discussion in terms of the "object of negation" (*dgag bya, pratiṣedhya*) seems to be a late and perhaps Tibetan innovation. The term "object of negation" is used by Nāgārjuna in the *Refutation of Objections*, verses 14–16 (Lindtner's *Nagarjuniana*, p.78), but not in this context. Dzong-ka-ba (Dharmsala edition of the *Great Exposition*, 419b.4–420a.2, Wayman's translation, p.261) cites the *Refutation of Objections*, verse 27, and Nāgārjuna's commentary on it as indicating both objects of negation although the actual term is not used there.

The locus classicus for the non-existent object of negation, that refuted by reasoning, and the need to identify it well is the *Engaging in the Bodhisattva Deeds* (*spyod 'jug, bodhisattvacaryāvatāra*, IX.140ab) by the eighth century Mādhyamika, Shāntideva:

"Without contacting the entity which is imputed (*brtags pa'i dngos, kalpitaṃ bhāvaṃ*)
One will not apprehend the absence of that entity."

It is cited by Dzong-ka-ba at the opening of his section on the object of negation, see p.177.

The idea of contacting, or identifying, that which is to be negated is an important part of Ge-luk-ba meditation on emptiness where it is emphasized that prior to engaging in reasoned refutation of inherent existence, one must gain experientially a vivid sense of just what it is that one is refuting. See Sopa and Hopkins' *Practice and Theory of Tibetan Buddhism* (London: Rider & Co, 1976) pp.38–9 and the Fifth Dalai Lama's *Practice of Emptiness* [the "Perfection of Wisdom Chapter" of the Fifth Dalai Lama's *Sacred Word of Mañjushrī* (*'jam dpal zhal lung*)] (Jeffrey Hopkins, translator, Dharamsala: Library of Tibetan Works and Archives, 1974), pp.11–13.

126 The Dharmsala edition of the *Great Exposition*, pp.419b.1–427b.4 (Wayman's translation, 260–75). Dzong-ka-ba takes just the opposite approach in his

"Medium Exposition of Special Insight". He comes at the topic from the subjective rather than the objective side and, with no discussion of the object of negation by reasoning, gives an extensive discussion of afflictive ignorance. See Thurman's translation in *The Life and Teachings of Tsong Khapa*, pp.118–29.

127 Cited by Dzong-ka-ba in the Dharmsala edition of the *Great Exposition*, 423a.4–423a.6 (Wayman's translation, p.266). See Lindtner's *Nagarjuniana*, pp.62–5 (although Dzong-ka-ba is working from a different Tibetan translation than that cited by Lindtner).

128 Cited by Dzong-ka-ba in the Dharmsala edition of the *Great Exposition*, 422a.4–422a.5 (Wayman's translation, p.264). See Karen Lang's "Āryadeva on the Bodhisattva's Cultivation of Merit and Knowledge" (Ann Arbor: University Microfilms, 1983), pp.269–70 and 593.

129 This is commentary on VI.28, located in La Vallée Poussin's edition of the text, 107.6–8. It is cited by Dzong-ka-ba in the Dharmsala edition of the *Great Exposition*, 422b.2–422b.3 (Wayman's translation, p.265).

130 This is commentary on verse 65. It is cited by Dzong-ka-ba in the Dharmsala edition of the *Great Exposition*, 420b.4–420b.5 (Wayman's translation, p.262 – mistranslated). This passage is missing from the Sanskrit edition; see *The Dialectical Method of Nāgārjuna* (Delhi: Motilal Banarsidass, 1978), Bhattacharya, p.42 and Johnston and Kunst, pp.48–9.

131 Chandrakīrti's *Commentary on (Āryadeva's) "Four Hundred"*, commentary on XIII.11, Toh 3865, Tokyo *sde dge* Vol.8, 201b.2–4. Sanskrit does not survive. Cited by Dzong-ka-ba in the Dharmsala edition of the *Great Exposition*, 394b.6–395a.1 (Wayman's translation, p.219).

132 "The nature and function of Nāgārjuna's arguments", p.489.

133 *Lucid Exposition of the Middle Way, the Essential Chapters*

from the Prasannapadā of Candrakīrti translated from the Sanskrit, (Boulder: Prajñā Press, 1979), p.7.

134 "Non-Cognitive Language in Mādhyamika Buddhism" in Kawamura and Scott, ed., *Buddhist Thought and Asian Civilization*, (Emeryville, Ca: Dharma, 1977), p.247.

135 *Lucid Exposition of the Middle Way*, p.12.

136 "A Critique of the Mādhyamika Position", in Mervyn Sprung, ed., *The Problem of Two Truths in Buddhism and Vedānta* (Dordrecht, Holland: D. Reidel, 1973), p.61.

137 Dharmsala edition of the *Great Exposition*, 424b.6–425a.5 (Wayman's translation, pp.269–70 – mistranslated).

138 "Did Nāgārjuna Really Refute All Philosophical Views?", p.325.

139 Ibid., p.326.

140 See Thurman's *Tsong Khapa's Speech of Gold in the Essence of True Eloquence*, p.291. Dzong-ka-ba makes a similar statement in the *Great Exposition* that takes account also of non-Buddhist assertions:

> "When those things such as partless objects and subjects, self, the Principal (*gtso bo*, *pradhāna*), and Īshvara that are imputed by the uncommon assertions of the Proponents of True Existence among our own and others' schools are posited by them, they are posited upon analysis with reasoning as to whether such things are or are not established by way of their own entities and thereupon within the thought that those objects are found by reasoning analyzing in that way.... When analyzed in this way, these are unable to bear the burden of investigation by stainless reasoning, whereby upon not being found by that reasoning, they are refuted, for if they did exist, they would have to be found by those reasonings."

(The Dharmsala edition of the *Great Exposition*, 406a.3–406.6; Wayman's translation, pp.237–8.)

141 "Non-Cognitive Language in Mādhyamika Buddhism", pp.241 and 243.

142 Nga-wang-bel-den in the Sautrāntika chapter of his *Explanation of the Conventional and the Ultimate in the Four Systems of Tenets*, (*grub mtha' bzhi'i lugs kyi kun rdzob dang don dam pa'i don rnam par bshad pa legs bshad dpyid kyi dpal mo'i glu dbyangs*, New Delhi: Guru Deva, 1972, 39.5–39.6) says that some such as Prajñākaragupta, Suryagupta, Shāntarakṣhita, Kamalashīla, and Jetāri interpret Dharmakīrti's *Commentary on (Dignāga's) "Compendium of Valid Cognition"* (*tshad ma rnam 'grel, pramāṇavārttika*) as a Mādhyamika treatise. Taken as such, the points I am about to make would not apply. However, numerous Indian scholars such as Devendrabuddhi as well as the majority of Tibetan scholarship and the main body of Western scholarship would disagree, placing Dharmakīrti as a Chittamātrin or a Sautrāntika; in such a light my argument stands.

143 Nga-wang-bel-den's *Explanation of the Conventional and the Ultimate in the Four Systems of Tenets*, 34.4.

144 The Mongolian scholar Den-dar-hla-ram-ba (*bstan dar lha ram pa*, b.1759) says in his *Presentation of Specifically and Generally Characterized Phenomena* (*rang mtshan spyi mtshan gyi rnam gzhag*), a commentary on Sautrāntika tenets:

> "Thus, the term "pot" is known as a term of the prevailing wish. For, the initial affixer of the appellation affixed the appellation "pot" to the bulbous thing arbitrarily through the power of his wish, and, in dependence on that, "pot" prevails as the actual name of the bulbous thing. Later, although others designate names, these are unable to become renowned as its actual name.... However, the term "pot" is not unsuitable to be affixed to other than bulbous things because even if one affixes the name "pot" to woolen cloth, after some time, due to the power of conditioning, even the meaning-generality of pot could appear

for woolen cloth. Therefore, "pot" is not objectively established by the power of the fact with bulbous things."

Translation by Anne Klein in her doctoral dissertation, "Mind and Liberation. The Sautrāntika Tenet System in Tibet: Perception, Naming, Positive and Negative Phenomena, Impermanence and the Two Truths in the Context of Buddhist Religious Insight as Presented in Ge-luk Literary and Oral Traditions", (Ann Arbor: University Microfilms, 1981) pp.352–3.

145 See Hopkins' *Meditation on Emptiness*, p.369 and Sopa and Hopkins' *Practice and Theory of Tibetan Buddhism*, p.117. Dzong-ka-ba discusses this point in great detail and complexity in the Chittamātra portion of his *Essence of the Good Explanations*. See Thurman's *Tsong Khapa's Speech of Gold in the Essence of True Eloquence*, pp.209–53

146 See Sopa and Hopkins' *Practice and Theory of Tibetan Buddhism*, for descriptions of the path in each of the four tenet systems.

147 See the *Medium Exposition of Special Insight*, Thurman's translation in *The Life and Teachings of Tsong Khapa*, pp.162–3. See Anne Klein's discussion of the parallels between inexpressibility in Sautrāntika and Mādhyamika in her "Mind and Liberation. The Sautrāntika Tenet System in Tibet: . . .", pp.298–303.

148 "How not to criticize Nāgārjuna: A Response to L. Stafford Betty", *Philosophy East and West* 34 (1984), p.441. I would like to insert at this point the disclaimer that I am not trained in linguistic analysis nor competent to comment on Wittgenstein's writings *per se*. The purpose of the following pages is to address areas in which the ideas of Wittgenstein are said to overlap with those of Mādhyamika philosophy, and to comment on whether statements of comparison accord with Dzong-ka-ba's Mādhyamika interpretation. I have to trust that Wittgenstein has been represented accurately by those making the comparisons.

149 *Tsong Khapa's Speech of Gold in the Essence of True Eloquence*, p.98.

150 *Wittgenstein and Buddhism* (London: The Macmillan Press, 1977), p.39.

151 David Loy in the article just cited describes very perceptively some of the problems of a linguistic interpretation. In part, he says, (p.443):

> "... that the world is *śūnya* here amounts to a denial that words gain meaning by corresponding to something extralinguistic. This "neonominalism" emphasizes that language cannot describe the world. But by itself this approach also yields only half the truth about Mādhyamika.... To understand Mādhyamika only in a linguistic way is to ignore the religious context which Nāgārjuna as a Buddhist always took for granted and which provides the situation for his philosophical enterprise."

Concerning the problem of distortion through comparison, J.W. de Jong says, ("The Problem of the Absolute in the Madhyamaka School", p.1):

> "One must beware of drawing too hasty conclusions about analogies and proximities with western thought, because one runs the risk of distorting Indian thought and failing to recognize that each philosophy is an organic whole."

See also Peter della Santina's article, "The Madhyamaka and modern Western philosophy" *Philosophy East and West* 36 (1986), pp.41–54, where many of the problems of the comparative approach are addressed. See particularly pp.51–3 for specific problems of comparison with Wittgenstein.

Although comparisons can be helpful, particularly as a means of using something more familiar to get at something less familiar, there is a danger of distorting the overall picture of both systems being compared through focusing on aspects not necessarily central to either. Also, there is a tendency to over-extend the comparison, bringing, for example, to the understanding of Buddhism more of the elements of a particular western philosophy than are actually justified by the presence of some areas of similarity. This danger strikes me as particularly serious since it is so frequently unconscious. Finally, comparison *as a means of understanding Buddhism* is only truly helpful to those having some familiarity with the Western system being used to make the comparison; otherwise, there is merely the difficulty of understanding two new systems instead of one.

There is value in comparison, not primarily as an avenue of approach to an unfamiliar system, but as part of the study of ideas. However, it requires a high level of competency in both areas being compared, and such is not found in many comparative studies.

152 *Wittgenstein and Buddhism*, pp.51–2.

153 Dzong-ka-ba merely says in the *Great Exposition of Special Insight* (Dharmsala edition, 407a.3) that the sense consciousnesses are mistaken and does not elaborate. The major Indian source for this key Ge-luk-ba point of interpretation is a passage from Chandrakīrti's *Clear Words*:

> "Therefore, like the falling hairs [seen by] one with cataracts and so forth, when what does not exist [by way of its own character] is apprehended by [i.e., appears to] an erroneous [consciousness] as just existing [that way], how could even a portion of an object existent [by way of its own character] be observed."

Translation by Jeffrey Hopkins, *Meditation on Emptiness*, pp.509–510. It is found in La Vallée Poussin's Sanskrit edition, 30.3–30.4.

154 *Early Mādhyamika in India and China*, p.43. Cited by Gudmunsen in *Wittgenstein and Buddhism* on p.52.

155 See David Loy's "How not to criticize Nāgārjuna: A Response to L. Stafford Betty", pp.442–3, for his discussion of how Kantian and Wittgensteinian interpretations of emptiness both introduce distortion.

156 See pp.126–33 for a detailed discussion of the status of emptiness. Dzong-ka-ba has numerous citations from Chandrakīrti where such terminology is used to describe emptiness. See also William Ames, "The Notion of *Svabhāva* in the Thought of Candrakīrti", *Journal of Indian Philosophy* 10 (1982), pp.161–77.

157 In the technical vocabulary of the Ge-luk-ba tradition, an emptiness and the phenomenon it qualifies are different isolates (*ldog pa tha dad*), that is, they are nominally different, different for thought. A chair is not an emptiness and an emptiness is not a chair, and everything true of the one is not true of the other. However, they are one entity (*ngo bo gcig*); wherever there is a chair, there is also an emptiness of the chair and vice versa. This is considered essential if the realization of emptiness with respect to a particular phenomenon is to have any effect on one's misconceptions with regard to it. See Hopkins' *Meditation on Emptiness*, pp.413–15, for a discussion of these points.

158 "How not to criticize Nāgārjuna: A Response to L. Stafford Betty", p.438.

159 See also the Fifth Dalai Lama's *Practice of Emptiness*, pp.11–15.

Several modern commentators have, in their analysis of the Mādhyamika reasonings, worked out different levels of what the Mādhyamikas are analyzing. (See Douglas Daye, "Major Schools of the Mahāyāna: Mādhyamika", pp.82–4 and 91–3 and his "Japanese rationalism, Mādhyamika, and some uses of formalism", *Philosophy East and West* 24 (1974), pp.364–6. See also Richard Jones, "The nature and function of Nāgārjuna's arguments", pp.491–2.) Dzong-ka-ba's tradition applies the analyses across the board, to anything, substance or abstraction, which is susceptible to being reified into inherent existence. They are directed at the things around us, and thus Dzong-ka-ba would disagree with Douglas Daye's statement ("Japanese rationalism,

Mādhyamika, and some uses of formalism", p.365):

> "However, it is a mistake to assume that the Mādhyamika polemics concerning substance, causation (mutual and dependent coorigination, *paṭicca-samuppāda*) and emptiness refer directly to "things" of the conventionally described world. In fact the *MK* are really a third-order critique, in that they are criticizing their opponents' views and other Buddhist views, of the ontological and epistemic components of everyday 'things'."

According to Dzong-ka-ba, the things around us, forms, sounds, and so forth are not refuted by the Mādhyamika reasonings but those objects *as they are apprehended by our innate consciousness misconceiving inherent existence* are. He says:

> "Since the awarenesses which posit forms, sounds, and so forth are the six non-defective consciousnesses – eye and so forth – the objects established by them exist conventionally, whereby they are not refuted by reasoning. However, in the way that they are apprehended by ignorance they do not exist even conventionally because this is a superimposition of inherent existence, that is, establishment by way of their own entities, on things, and such inherent existence does not exist even conventionally. Therefore, [forms and so forth as they are apprehended by ignorance] are refuted even conventionally by reasoning; if they were not refuted, then conventionally things would not be established as like a magician's illusions."

(Dharmsala edition of the Tibetan, 407b.6–408a.3. For Wayman's translation of this passage, see *Calming the Mind and Discerning the Real*, pp.240–1.)

Since Dzong-ka-ba says that we cannot now distinguish between the existence and the inherent existence of the things around us, what he finds to be refuted by the Mādhyamika reasonings is very much of this world and very immediate.

160 *Wittgenstein and Buddhism* p.37. Although Gudmunsen is careful in his wording and does not make the statement that what linguistic and Mādhyamika analyses reveal is that words do not refer to anything, this is a claim often made. David Loy, although perhaps with some bias since he is not an enthusiast of the Wittgensteinian interpretation, says, ("How not to criticize Nāgārjuna: A Response to L. Stafford Betty", p.441) that Wittgensteinian interpretations see emptiness as indicating "the inability of language (systems of representation) to refer to anything." Mervyn Sprung's opinion, ("Non-Cognitive Language in Mādhyamika Buddhism", pp.247) is that Nāgārjuna is showing that "at no level and at no point does language in fact name anything. It does not 'refer' as we say," and Sprung further states (ibid., p.249) that "language cannot describe states of affairs." This is too complex an issue too far from the primary topic to be discussed here. However, the topic of naming, the fact that names do not describe objects as they are perceived in direct perception and yet can still refer to objects is a topic found in the Ge-luk-ba commentarial literature concerned with Sautrāntika tenets, and they consider it to be accepted by Mādhyamika as well. See Anne Klein's "Mind and Liberation. The Sautrāntika Tenet System in Tibet: ...", especially pp.200–204 and 281–86, for further discussion of these points.

161 *Wittgenstein and Buddhism*, p.37.

162 Both these passages are cited by Dzong-ka-ba in the "Medium Exposition of Special Insight" at the beginning of his section on conventional truths. Translation is from Hopkins, p.86. See Thurman's *Life and Teachings of Tsong Khapa*, p.153. Dzong-ka-ba cites three lines of the passage from Chandrakīrti's *Supplement* in the *Great Exposition*, Dharmsala edition, 407b.2–407b.4.

163 *Tsong Khapa's Speech of Gold in the Essence of True Eloquence*, p.99.

164 Ibid., p.102.

165 See Gudmunsen's *Wittgenstein and Buddhism*, chapter five, and Thurman's *Tsong Khapa's Speech of Gold in the Essence of True Eloquence*, pp.102–3.

166 Both passages from Wittgenstein cited by Gudmunsen on p.69 of *Wittgenstein and Buddhism.*

167 Both passages are found in *Wittgenstein and Buddhism*, p.71.

CHAPTER FIVE: DZONG-KA-BA AND MODERN INTERPRETERS II: NEGATING TOO MUCH

168 *Central Philosophy of Buddhism*, p.271. Murti also says ("Saṁvṛti and Paramārtha in Mādhyamika and Advaita Vedānta" in M. Sprung, ed., *The Problem of Two Truths in Buddhism and Vedānta*, Dordrecht, Holland: D. Reidel, 1973, p.9) that the Mādhyamika is negating "the conceptualist tendency (*vikalpa* or *dṛṣṭi*); for this is what falsifies reality which is Intuition (*prajñā*);" he spells this out (p.18):

> "In the Abhidharma, Vedānta and Vijñānavāda systems particular concepts or ways of viewing the real are *avidyā*. For the Mādhyamika, *avidyā* is much wider and more general in scope; conceptualization as such (not merely particular concepts), any view without exception, is *avidyā*. Reason or intellect (*buddhi*) as the faculty of conceptual construction is *avidyā* (*buddhiḥ saṃvṛtir ity ucyate*)."

Also (*Central Philosophy of Buddhism*, p.238):

> "The precise nature of avidyā in the Mādhyamika system consists in the inveterate tendency to indulge in conceptual construction (saṅkalpa). The Real is Indeterminate (śūnya); the viewing of it through thought forms is avidyā."

Christian Lindtner says (*Nagarjuniana*, p.257) that *avidyā* "is not merely lack or absence of knowledge but positively, *amitravat*, more or less a synonym of *abhiniveśa*, *dṛṣṭi*, *kalpanā*, or *grāha*, . . ."

Étienne Lamotte could perhaps also be included among those holding this view, in that he speaks, in the introduction to his translation, *The Teaching of Vimalakīrti* (London: Pali Text Society, 1976, English translation of Lamotte's French by Sara Boin, p.lxii), of "... Nāgārjuna, author of the famous Madhyamaka-kārikā which demonstrate the absurdity of all intellectual notions, the logical impossibility of any sensorial or mental experience."

169 "A Study of the Relationship Between Analysis (*vicāra*) and Insight (*prajñā*) Based on the *Madhyamakāvatāra*", *Journal of Indian Philosophy* 12 (1984), pp.139–97. He says (pp.152 and 154):

> "The contention of the Mādhyamika philosophers, and assumption on which the consequential (*prasaṅga*) analysis hinges is that predication is logically paradoxical in virtue of being embedded within a structure of logical opposites.... The aim of analysis is to clarify and expose the formally paradoxical structure of predication. ... Analysis is intended to demonstrate a paradox of predication that is opaque for a non-analytical intellect."

In other words, for Fenner, thought is inherently faulty because of its paradoxical nature, and thus the purpose of the Mādhyamika analyses is to reveal this paradox, leading finally to a stilling of thought. Nonetheless, for Fenner, thought – reasoning – does play a major role in actualizing its cessation.

170 Ben-Ami Scharfstein (*Mystical Experience*, Baltimore: Penguin, 1973), p.52.

171 Dzong-ka-ba's discussion is found in the Dharmsala edition of the *Great Exposition*, 495a.6–501b.1 (Wayman's translation, pp.390–9).

172 See the Dharmsala edition of the *Great Exposition*, 498a (Wayman's translation, p.394).

173 See Karen Lang's "Āryadeva on the Bodhisattva's Cultivation of Merit and Knowledge", pp.490 and 658.

This verse is cited in full by Dzong-ka-ba in the Dharmsala edition of the *Great Exposition*, 422a.2 (Wayman's translation, p.264) and the last two lines are cited on 498b.3–498b.4 (Wayman's translation, p.494), the latter citation in support of the point being made here.

174 For the passage from the *Four Hundred*, see Karen Lang's "Āryadeva on the Bodhisattva's Cultivation of Merit and Knowledge", pp.541–2 and 671. The passage from Chandrakīrti's *Commentary on (Āryadeva's) "Four Hundred"* is found in the Tokyo *sde dge* Vol.8, 238.2.1. It is cited by Dzong-ka-ba in the Dharmsala edition of the *Great Exposition*, 424b.1–424b.3 (Wayman's translation, p.268).

175 See for example the portions of Den-dar-hla-ram-ba's (*bstan dar lha ram pa*, b.1759) *Specifically and Generally Characterized Phenomena* (*rang mtshan spyi mtshan gyi rnam gzhag*) translated by Anne Klein in her "Mind and Liberation. The Sautrāntika Tenet System in Tibet: Perception, Naming, Positive and Negative Phenomena, Impermanence and the Two Truths in the Context of Buddhist Religious Insight as Presented in Ge-luk Literary and Oral Traditions", pp.324–97.

176 Cited by Dzong-ka-ba in the Dharmsala edition of the *Great Exposition*, 505a.3–505a.4 (Wayman's translation, p.405).

177 Not making a distinction such as Dzong-ka-ba does between psychological situation – the total disappearance of conventionalities for an ultimate consciousness realizing emptiness – and ontological fact – the conventional existence of those conventionalities – accounts, I believe, for C.W. Huntington Jr.'s statement ("The System of the Two Truths in the Prasannapadā and the Madhyamakāvatāra: A Study in Mādhyamika Soteriology", *Journal of Indian Philosophy* 11 (1983), p.95):

> ". . . on reading Candrakīrti one is after all still left with the lingering suspicion that the world is somehow absolutely rejected from the perspective of the ultimate truth."

One of Dzong-ka-ba's fine distinctions is the difference between something's not being seen by a consciousness and its being seen *as non-existent* by that consciousness. An ultimate consciousness does not see conventionalities, but it does not see them as non-existent, and thus does not negate them.

178 *The Precious Garland and the Song of the Four Mindfulnesses*, Jeffrey Hopkins and Lati Rimpoche, trans., p.24.

179 La Vallée Poussin edition of the Sanskrit, 368.14–15. Cited in chapter seven of the translation (see p.212). Since Dzong-ka-ba concludes, based on such passages, that it was not the intention of the Indian Mādhyamikas to deny unequivocally all conventional reality, from his viewpoint Tola and Dragonetti go too far when they say ("Nāgārjuna's Conception of 'Voidness'", p.276):

> "As a consequence of their argumentation and analysis, the *Mādhyamikas* deny the existence of the empirical reality, of all its manifestations, of all the elements that constitute it, of all the categories that manifest themselves in it, of all the characteristics which are proper to it, and they assign to everything that belongs to this empirical reality only an apparent, phantasmagoric, inconsistent existence."

(On p.273 they identify empirical reality as *saṃvṛtisatya*.)

The same is true for Mervyn Sprung, who even though denying that Mādhyamika is nihilism, says (*Lucid Exposition of the Middle Way*, p.3):

> "Mādhyamika does deny our most deeply rooted intellectual and vivial habits, holding that nothing, whether metaphysical or everyday, can be known in an unequivocal sense; holding that, hence, measured by knowledge, there is no difference between truth and falsehood, that no one, including all the Buddhas, has ever uttered one true word, that all conceptions, including that of an enlightened human being (*buddha*) fall short of the truth."

Sprung also says ("Nietzsche and Nāgārjuna: The Origins and Issue of Scepticism" in Coward and Sivaraman, ed., *Revelation in Indian Thought: A Festschrift in Honour of Professor T.R.V. Murti*, Emeryville, Ca.: Dharma Publishing, 1977, pp.165–6):

> "On this basis Mādhyamika sets out, as is well known, to undermine not only all philosophies and all ideologies but every last category and concept constituting the everyday world on which the philosophies and ideologies are founded. In this ruthless march through the everyday world all our familiar friends are slaughtered: people, things, cosmos, causality, time, knowledge, heaven and hell, and for the Buddhists ignorance and enlightenment, even Buddha himself. Events have no purpose; conventional existence is denied any meaning."

Dzong-ka-ba does not see empirical existence or ordinary categories as denied, but only any inherent existence of those. He is able – following Chandrakīrti (see pp.108–10) – to make a clear differentiation between the conventionally true and the utterly false. Buddhas, in his system, have no conceptuality, but their realizations, far from "falling short of the truth" are of the nature of things just as they are. A Buddha's teachings are considered true, and Dzong-ka-ba would never say that "events have no purpose" for in that case why would anyone seek or make effort at enlightenment?

180 See Christian Lindtner's "Buddhapālita on Emptiness *[Buddhapālita-mūla-madhyamakavṛtti XVIII]*", *Indo-Iranian Journal* 23 (1981), p.208, and La Vallée Poussin's Sanskrit edition of the *Clear Words*, 370.7–8.

181 I translate the term *pramāṇa* (Tib. *tshad ma*) both as "valid cognition" and "valid cognizer". "Valid cognition" is a more usual usage but "valid cognizer" conveys more accurately the sense of an agent of knowing rather than the action, as "cognition" conveys. The fault with "cognizer" is that it tends to suggest a person who cognizes rather than just the consciousness that cognizes.

Because of this problem, I use "valid cognition" in general situations but nonetheless switch to "valid cognizer" in cases where consciousness as an agent is being emphasized.

182 See for example Paul Williams article, "A Note on Some Aspects of Mi Bskyod Rdo Rje's Critique of Dge Lugs Pa Madhyamaka", *Journal of Indian Philosophy* 11 (1983), pp.125–45.

183 The following discussion is taken from the *Great Exposition*, Dharmsala edition, 405a.1–406b.4 (Wayman's translation, pp.236–8).

184 See the *Great Exposition*, Dharmsala edition, 396b.6–398b.5. The following discussion is taken from those pages. (Wayman's translation, pp.222–5 – translation garbled).

185 This ties in to what Dzong-ka-ba sees as a basic difference in tenet between the Dignāga-Dharmakīrti logicians and Chandrakīrti as to whether or not sense consciousnesses are mistaken. Both agree that phenomena appear to the sense consciousnesses to inherently exist, or, as the discussion is phrased in this context, as established by way of their own character. However, for Chandrakīrti this is a mistaken appearance caused by our predispositions for the conception of inherent existence whereas, for the Dignāga-Dharmakīrti logicians, this is the way phenomena exist. Again the argument centers over a differing identification of the object of negation.

186 The first passage is from Chandrakīrti's *Commentary on (Āryadeva's) "Four Hundred"*, Toh 3865, Tokyo *sde dge* Vol.8, 197b.5–197b.6, cited in the Dharmsala edition of the *Great Exposition*, 398b.2, in reference to a previous citation within a longer passage, 396b.6–397a.3 (Wayman's translation, p.225, misses this); the second is from Chandrakīrti's *Clear Words*, La Vallée Poussin edition of the Sanskrit, 75.9, cited in the Dharmsala edition of the *Great Exposition*, 398b.3 (Wayman's translation, p.225 – not clear).

187 La Vallée Poussin edition of the Sanskrit, 75.10–11, cited in the Dharmsala edition of the *Great Exposition*, 398b.4–398b.5 (Wayman's translation, p.225).

188 See Stephen Batchelor's translation in Geshé Rabten's *Echoes of Voidness* (London: Wisdom Publications, 1983), p.58. Cited by Dzong-ka-ba in the Dharmsala edition of the *Great Exposition*, 399a.1–399a.2 (Wayman's translation, p.226).

189 Toh 3865, Tokyo *sde dge* Vol.8, 225a.1–3. Commentary on XV.10. Cited by Dzong-ka-ba in the Dharmsala edition of the *Great Exposition*, 394a.6–394b.2 (Wayman's translation, p.219 – mistranslated).

190 See p.185.

191 *Wittgenstein and Buddhism*, p.44.

192 The first passage is found in La Vallée Poussin's Sanskrit edition, p.247; the second is found in La Vallée Poussin's Sanskrit edition, p.592. These passages are cited by numerous Western scholars as showing that Nāgārjuna rejects all views; see for example Robinson's *Early Mādhyamika in India and China*, p.43, and Frederick Streng's *Emptiness*, p.90.

193 "Major Schools of the Mahāyāna: Mādhyamika", p.77.

194 *Epistemology, Logic, and Grammar in Indian Philosophical Analysis* (The Hague, Paris: Mouton, 1971), p.147–8. Matilal cites in support of his position Murti's *Central Philosophy of Buddhism*, pp.145–6, "The Mādhyamika dialectic is not refutation; ... Refutation is the rejection of an opponent's view by an interested party having a view of his own to establish. A critique is the disinterested analysis of Reason by itself."

195 *Epistemology, Logic, and Grammar*, p.156. See Lamotte's introduction to his *Teaching of Vimalakīrti*, lxxi, where he cites the abovementioned verse from Nāgārjuna's *Treatise* (XXIII.8) "The Victorious Ones have proclaimed Emptiness to be the outlet of all the false views, but they have pronounced as incurable those who believe in Emptiness," and calls this an agnostic position.

196 "The nature and function of Nāgārjuna's arguments," p.485.

197 "Nāgārjuna's masterpiece – logical, mystical, both, or neither?" *Philosophy East and West* 33 (1983), p.129.

198 "Who understands the four alternatives of the Buddhist texts?" *Philosophy East and West* 27 (1977), p.14.

199 Dzong-ka-ba cites all three of these passages in his attempt to prove that Mādhyamikas have views; see the Dharmsala edition of the *Great Exposition*, 413b.5–414a.4 (Wayman's translation, 251–2). For the passage from Chandrakīrti's *Supplement to (Nāgārjuna's) "Treatise on the Middle Way"*, see La Vallée Poussin's edition of the text, 287.18–19 and Geshé Rabten and Stephen Batchelor's translation in *Echoes of Voidness*, p.82. For the passage from Chandrakīrti's *Commentary on (Āryadeva's) "Four Hundred"*, see Toh 3865, Tokyo *sde dge* Vol 8, 190b.7–191a.1. Sanskrit fragments exist for this portion of Chandrakīrti's text (see Haraprasād Shāstri's "Catuḥśatika of Ārya Deva," Memoirs of the Asiatic Society of Bengal, III no. 8, 1914, p.497) but do not include this passage.

200 The Dharmsala edition of the *Great Exposition*, 424b.5 (Wayman's translation, p.269).

201 *The Literature of the Madhyamaka School of Philosophy in India*, pp.2–3.

202 Cited by Dzong-ka-ba in the Dharmsala edition of the *Great Exposition*, 412b.6–413a.1 (Wayman's translation, pp.249–50). See pp.130–1, where Dzong-ka-ba's interpretation of this passage is discussed in more detail.

203 Cited by Dzong-ka-ba in the Dharmsala edition of the *Great Exposition*, 424b.6 (Wayman's translation, p.269). See Karen Lang's "Āryadeva on the Bodhisattva's Cultivation of Merit and Knowledge", pp.312–13 and 607.

204 La Vallée Poussin's edition, p.228; Geshé Rabten and Stephen Batchelor's translation in *Echoes of Voidness*, p.72. This is cited by Dzong-ka-ba in his *Essence of the Good Explanations*, see Thurman's *Tsong Khapa's Speech*

of Gold in the Essence of True Eloquence, p.365. It is also cited by Dzong-ka-ba in the *Great Exposition* in a different context; see the Dharmsala edition, 409a.2–409a.3 (Wayman's translation, p.242).

205 *Central Philosophy of Buddhism*, p.329.

206 See, for example, the Fifth Dalai Lama's *Practice of Emptiness*, passages from which are cited immediately below, and also the "Instructions on the Mādhyamika View" literature (*dbu ma'i lta khrid*), mentioned by Seyfort Ruegg in his assessment of Tibetan contributions to Mādhyamika studies (cited on p.69), the "view" being the view of emptiness.

207 *Practice of Emptiness*, p.17.

208 To cite some examples: B.K. Matilal says in *Epistemology, Logic, and Grammar in Indian Philosophical Analysis*, p.158, "But this theory of indeterminableness [i.e., emptiness] of the phenomenal world is not a theory itself . . ." and then, p.162, speaks of the "paradox of indeterminancy".

Karl Potter says of Nāgārjuna (*Presuppositions of India's Philosophies*, Englewood Cliffs, N.J.: Prentice-Hall, 1963, p.241), "he has no theories at all".

Jacques May says ("On Mādhyamika Philosophy", *Journal of Indian Philosophy* 6, 1978, p.238), "This Emptiness or universal unsubstantiality involves at the level of philosophical expression a particularly striking and singular consequence: namely, that the Mādhyamika has no thesis of his own, or, more generally speaking, no philosophical position." He also says, (p.234) "As for the Mādhyamika philosophical standpoint, there have been many attempts at defining it. It is actually a difficult thing to do, for the notion of 'Mādhyamika standpoint' is self-contradictory, . . ."

T.R.V. Murti says, (*Central Philosophy of Buddhism*, p.131) "*Prasanga* is disproof simply, without the least intention to prove any thesis," and (p.145) "He [the Mādhyamika] is a prāsangika – having no tenet of his own and not caring to frame a syllogism of his own."

Peter Fenner, as a continuation of his idea that thought per se is intrinsically faulty and is the object of negation says ("A Study of the Relationship Between Analysis (*vicāra*) and Insight (*prajñā*) Based on the *Madhyamakāvatāra*", pp.143–4), "Analysis employs the *prasaṅga*, tib. *thal 'gyur*, form of argumentation, a purportedly deductive form of argument that exposes absurd consequences by drawing out logical contradictions (*rigs-pai 'gal-pa*) that are thought to naturally and necessarily inhere in *all* theses."

G.C. Nayak says, ("The Mādhyamika attack on essentialism: A critical appraisal", *Philosophy East and West* 29 (1979), p.478), "This should make it clear that Mādhyamika, having no thesis of its own, cannot be regarded as a doctrine of the void either."

Shotaro Iida says ("An Introduction to Svātantrika Mādhyamika", Ann Arbor: University Microfilms, 1968, p.31), "The true Mādhyamika cannot uphold a position of his own . . . His sole endeavor is to reduce to absurdity the arguments of the opponents on principles acceptable to them."

Hans Schumann says (*Buddhism. An Outline of its Teachings and Schools*, Wheaton, Illinois: Theosophical Publishing House, 1973, p.143) "[Nāgārjuna] was concerned above all with demonstrating the untenability of any affirmative assertion and proving the inner inconsistency of all possible philosophical systems."

Herbert Guenther says (*Buddhist Philosophy in Theory and Practice*, Baltimore: Penguin, 1971, p.141), "Prāsaṅgikas. . . were pre-eminently concerned with pointing out the inherent shakiness of every postulate." He sees an end to the Prāsaṅgika's significance as a critical movement when they themselves "succumbed to the temptation of accepting certain premises."

209 See Thurman's *Tsong Khapa's Speech of Gold in the Essence of True Eloquence*, p.68 and pp.78–80.

210 See the Dharmsala edition of the *Great Exposition*, 433a.6–447b.6 (Wayman's translation, pp.284–309).

211 Both Jeffrey Hopkins and Robert Thurman, working with Ge-luk-ba materials, have addressed this topic and shown how such is not the case for Dzong-ka-ba. See Hopkins' *Meditation on Emptiness*, pp.471–5 and 549–51, and Thurman's *Tsong Khapa's Speech of Gold in the Essence of True Eloquence*, pp.155, 160, and 331–2.

Also, two recent articles by Seyfort Ruegg address this question using primarily Ge-luk-ba materials and arrive at a similar conclusion. See his "On the Thesis and Assertion in the Madhyamaka/dBu ma", in E. Steinkellner and H. Tauscher, ed., *Contributions on Tibetan and Buddhist Religion and Philosophy* (Wien: Universität Wien, 1983), pp.205–41, and "Does the Mādhyamika Have a Thesis and Philosophical Position?" in B.K. Matilal and R.D. Evans, ed., *Buddhist Logic and Epistemology* (Dordrecht, Holland: D. Reidel, 1986), pp.229–37.

212 The Dharmsala edition of the *Great Exposition*, 435b.5–436a.6 (Wayman's translation, pp.288–9).

213 See *The Dialectical Method of Nāgārjuna*, Bhattacharya, p.23 and Johnston and Kunst, p.29. Dzong-ka-ba cites this in the Dharmsala edition of the *Great Exposition*, 435b.4–435b.5 (Wayman's translation, p.288).

214 *Exploring Mysticism*, p.45.

215 "The Uses of the Four Positions of the *Catuṣkoṭi* and the Problem of the Description of Reality in Mahāyāna Buddhism", pp.49–50.

216 See *Meditation on Emptiness*, pp.550–1, where a lengthy passage from the *Great Exposition* is cited making just this point. See also the Dharmsala edition of the *Great Exposition*, 435b.3–435b.5 and 440a.3–440b.1 (Wayman's translation, pp.288 and 296 – mistranslated).

217 Dzong-ka-ba lists many of these. See the Dharmsala edition of the *Great Exposition*, 446a.5–447a.3 (Way-

man's translation, pp.306–8).

218 See p.187 for full references.

219 See p.212.

220 See the Dharmsala edition of the *Great Exposition*, 447a.1–447a.3 (Wayman's translation, p.308). Such a reference can be found in La Vallée Poussin's Sanskrit edition of Chandrakīrti's text, 81.17–18.

221 The following discussion is a paraphrase of Dzong-ka-ba's explanation as found in the Dharmsala edition of the *Great Exposition*, 442a.1–442a.6 (Wayman's translation, p.299). See also Hopkins' *Meditation on Emptiness*, p.473.

222 This sentence and the following discussion are taken from chapter seven of the translation, see pp.205–6.

223 Cited in the translation, p.206.

224 See Jeffrey Hopkins' *Meditation on Emptiness*, pp.442–530 for a detailed presentation of Bhāvaviveka's attack on Buddhapālita and Chandrakīrti's defense of Buddhapālita and criticism of Bhāvaviveka, in the course of which these fine distinctions are revealed.

225 *Central Philosophy of Buddhism*, p.145.

226 See his "A Study on the Mādhyamika Method of Refutation and Its Influence on Buddhist Logic", *Journal of the International Association of Buddhist Studies* 4 (1981), pp. 87–94 and "A New Approach to the Intra-Mādhyamika Confrontation Over the Svātantrika and Prāsaṅgika Methods of Refutation", *Journal of the International Association of Buddhist Studies* 5 (1982), pp.41–52, particularly the latter.

227 "Bhāvaviveka and the early Mādhyamika theories of language", *Philosophy East and West* 28 (1978), p.327.

228 Cited by Dzong-ka-ba in the "Medium Exposition of Special Insight", translation from Jeffrey Hopkins, p.142. See Thurman's *Life and Teachings of Tsong Khapa*, p.180.

CHAPTER SIX: DZONG-KA-BA AND MODERN INTERPRETERS III: OTHER ISSUES OF DIFFERENCE

229 *Journal of Indian Philosophy* 12 (1984) pp.139–197. p.139.

230 Let us cite a number of passages that comprise a more extensive survey of relevant comments than is cited by Fenner, in more or less chronological order. Theodor Stcherbatsky says (*Conception of Buddhist Nirvāṇa*, Delhi: Motilal Banarsidass, rpt. 1978, p.44, n.4), "The Mādhyamika denies the validity of logic, i.e., of discursive thought, to establish ultimate truth."

T.R.V. Murti says (*The Central Philosophy of Buddhism*, p.331), "thought is inherently incapable of revealing the real", and (p.304) "the absolute is beyond its [the intellect's] comprehension. The Absolute can be known only in intuition..." And, he speaks (p.229) of an Absolute characterized by "its utter indeterminateness and the consequent non-accessibility to Reason."

Edward Conze says (*Buddhist Thought in India*, Ann Arbor: University of Michigan Press, 1967, p.244):

> "It would be a mistake to treat the views of the Mādhyamikas as though they were the result of philosophical reasoning, when in fact they derive from age-old meditational processes by which the intuition of the Absolute is actually realized."

K.K. Inada says (*Nāgārjuna, A Translation of his Mūlamadhyamakakārikā with an Introductory Essay*, Tokyo, The Hokuseido Press, 1970, p.18), "the Buddhist truth, if forthcoming at all, is not the result of logic or dialectics". He also says (p.34, n.23), "whether *prasaṅga* is really a method for educing truth or only a method of criticism is a moot question".

J.W. de Jong says ("The Problem of the Absolute in the Madhyamaka School", p.5):

> "This knowledge, this 'state', is dependent on mystical intuition, which dispels ignorance and so leads to

deliverance. We are here beyond the realm of philosophical thought, where one proceeds with the aid of words and concepts, we are on the plane of individual experience, beyond all language and all thought. There is no doubt that *paramārtha*, being the 'supreme goal' of the believer, may be called 'the absolute'. But this absolute by its very nature is inaccessible to philosophical thought. One might try to approach it by indirect means, but all one could say or think about it would of necessity be false."

Frederick Streng is difficult to pin down on this issue because he seems to come down on both sides; some of this variation may reflect the chronology of his own thought. He says in his *Emptiness: A Study in Religious Meaning* (p.53), "Because of the danger in language to posit an essential reality within ideas, mental activity has been regarded with disfavor as a means for realizing Ultimate Truth." He also says (p.147–8), ". . . he who would perfect wisdom uses meditational exercises. Neither concepts nor logic, then, are used by Nāgārjuna in relation to an Absolute Reality which they might reflect." However, he also says (p.149), "Thus the dynamics of the dialectic is an effective force for realizing the emptiness of things. . . . In Nāgārjuna's negative dialectic the power of reason is an efficient force for realizing Ultimate Truth."

In an article written in 1973 ("The Significance of Pratītyasamutpāda for Understanding the Relationship Between Saṁvṛti and Paramārtha in Nāgārjuna", in M. Sprung, ed., *The Problem of Two Truths in Buddhism and Vedānta*, Dordrecht-Holland: D. Reidel, 1973, p.34) Streng says:

> "Likewise, Nāgārjuna's statements in the texts we are considering would affirm Jayatilleke's understanding of early Buddhist recogniton that the experiences in *jñāna* are not discontinuous with the processes of the mind in its everyday activity."

And, in that same article, (p.35):

"But when words are not regarded as representing some independent reality, they can function as practical forces in man's cessation of ignorance (attachment) to illusory objects. Even more, (empty) words used to express the *dharma* and the dialectic are not merely a destructive form which clears the ground for a constructive formulation of the truth, or simply a dissolution of all verbal formation that *then* allows a mystic intuition of an absolute unchanging reality to 'take over'. The dialectic itself can be a means of knowing. It provides the insight that there is no absolute or independent *saṁskṛta* or *dharma*."

Alex Wayman says, ("Who understands the four alternatives of the Buddhist texts?" *Philosophy East and West* 27 (1977), p.12):

"Hence the rejections, again, are aimed against all philosophical positions that resort to inference or to ordinary human reason in such matters, . . ."

Also, (pp.12–13):

"In the preceding illustrations, it is the Tathāgata or the Dharma or Nirvāṇa which is affirmed as the affirmation of absolute truth in the process of the denials, because these denials are a meditative act – and acts succeed where theories fail – which downgrades the role of inference and human reason generally, and upholds the role of vision, so – as Atīśa indicated – to promote insight."

However, Wayman also says (p.17):

"Even so, as was indicated previously, the Mādhyamika is not against reason as the faculty which denies a self, denies the alternatives, and so on, because this reason leads to the insight which realizes the absolute."

Mervyn Sprung says, ("Non-Cognitive Language in Mādhyamika Buddhism", p.243) "Language must be afflicted, as diseased as all other elements on the natural scene. It can hardly be used to uncover truth." And, (p.248), "all reasoning, based on the everyday understanding of language, must fail to be knowledge..."

One of the few scholars who clearly stands forth on the other side of the question is Karl Potter, who says (*Presuppositions of India's Philosophies*, p.238):

> "Nāgārjuna is not anti-rational; in fact, he elevates reason to the position of the prime means of attaining freedom. Unlike skepticism, his is a philosophy of hope: we *can* achieve freedom by our own efforts, through remorseless application of the dialectic. Yet freedom is release from the conceptual, for Nāgārjuna as for all Buddhists. This seems to be an insoluble paradox. How can we free ourselves from the conceptual by indulging in a dialectical play which is conceptual through-and-through? The answer is that through application of the dialectical method we convince ourselves that everything is inter-dependent, and we develop a special kind of insight (*prajñā*) into the void itself. This insight has no content – i.e., its content is the void. It is nonsensuous and nonconceptual, although it is rational in the sense that it is *developed* through a rational procedure."

Finally, Christian Lindtner says (*Nagarjuniana*, pp.269–70):

> "So to Nāgārjuna *prajñā* is at the outset a critical faculty constantly engaged in analysing the more or less common-sense notions presented to it by tradition or experience. The more it penetrates them and 'loosens them up' the more their apparent nature vanishes and in the final analysis their true nature turns out to be 'empty', i.e. devoid of substance, or simply illusory as it cannot really be determined as A or, for that matter, non-A. At this stage *prajñā* has also brought its own raison d'être to an end: by analysing its object away it has also deprived itself of an objective support (*ālambaṇa*) etc. At this moment the analytical understanding suddenly shifts into an

intuitive *jñāna* which has *śūnyatā* as its 'object', i.e., which has no object."

231 "A Study of the Relationship Between Analysis (*vicāra*) and Insight (*prajñā*) Based on the *Madhyamakāvatāra*", pp.139 and 143.

232 Fenner says, (p.152) "the contention of the Mādhyamika philosophers, and assumption on which the consequential (*prasaṅga*) analysis hinges is that predication is logically paradoxical in virtue of being embedded within a structure of logical opposites," and thus concludes, (p.154) "The aim of analysis is to clarify and expose the formally paradoxical structure of predication. . . . Analysis is intended to demonstrate a paradox of predication that is opaque for a non-analytical intellect." Dzong-ka-ba never frames his argument in anything like these terms and says repeatedly that not all thought, but merely the specific misconception of inherent existence is the object of negation.

233 See the *Great Exposition*, Dharmsala edition, 46b.2–50a.6, where Dzong-ka-ba lays out his views on this topic with clarity and precision.

234 Cited by Dzong-ka-ba in the "Medium Exposition of Special Insight", translation from Jeffrey Hopkins, p.138. See Thurman's *Life and Teachings of Tsong Khapa*, p.178. This is also cited by Dzong-ka-ba in the *Great Exposition*, Dharmsala edition, 505b.1–505b.3 (Wayman's translation, pp.405–6).

235 See the *Great Exposition*, Dharmsala edition, 431b.3–432a.3; Wayman's translation, pp.281–2. See also the *Medium Exposition*, Thurman's translation in the *Life and Teachings of Tsong Khapa*, pp.167–9.

236 Although Dzong-ka-ba in his *Great Exposition* often just speaks of "reasoning", the *Annotations* are very careful to spell this out as "reasoning consciousness". Further, as Dzong-ka-ba elaborates in the "Medium Exposition of Special Insight", (Hopkins' translation, p.116; Thurman's translation, p.168), "There are two types of

reasoning consciousnesses – (1) a Superior's non-conceptual exalted wisdom of non-conceptual meditative equipoise and (2) a conceptual reasoning consciousness comprehending suchness in dependence upon a sign, etc."

237 *Emptiness: A Study in Religious Meaning*, p.148. This may be unfair since Streng also says later, p.173, that the dialectical negation is an essential part of one's religious apprehension. But Streng does seem to make a split between formal logic, which is for others, and some almost indescribable way in which the dialectic functions religiously. See for instance p.33 where he says (emphasis mine) "Nāgārjuna affirms a limited use of conceptual forms and he appeals to phenomenal experience *when he refutes his opponents* who hold to assumptions of absolute distinctions and eternal essences . . ."

238 See Lati Rinbochay's *Mind in Tibetan Buddhism* (Valois, New York: Snow Lion, 1980) which I translated, edited, and introduced for a general presentation of a Ge-luk-ba view on consciousness. In particular, see pages 25–8 for a description of the progression from the ignorance misconceiving inherent existence through to a direct cognition realizing emptiness. The Ge-luk-ba texts on this topic take the works of Dignāga and Dharmakīrti as their primary sources, but have been systematized and standardized far beyond those sources.

239 See Masatoshi Nagatomi's "*Mānasa-Pratyakṣa*: A Conundrum in the Buddhist *Pramāṇa* System" in *Sanskrit and Indian Studies* (Dordrecht, Boston, and London: D. Reidel, 1980), pp.243–4.

240 Lamotte in the introduction to his *The Teaching of Vimalakīrti* (lxii–lxxi) sets forth a list of six "most important theses of the Madhyamaka" of which the sixth is "Emptiness is not an entity". Jacques May ("On Mādhyamika Philosophy", p.241) says that *śūnyatā* is a word and as such is on the side of conventional truth.

Edward Conze says, (*Buddhist Thought in India*, p.61), "it would be a mistake to regard it [emptiness] as a purely intellectual concept, or to make it into a thing, and give it an ontological meaning."

Frederick Streng (*Emptiness: A Study in Religious Meaning*, p.146) takes literally such statements about emptiness as that it neither exists nor does not exist (although just such statements are made about conventional phenomena as well). He also says (p.47) that "'emptiness' is simply a designation for conveying knowledge". This view that emptiness is merely a linguistic convention was set forth early on by Richard Robinson (*Early Mādhyamika in India and China*, p.43):

> "These stanzas [13:7–8; 20:17–18; 24:11] state that emptiness is not a term in the primary system referring to the world, but a term in the descriptive system (metasystem) referring to the primary system. Thus it has no status as an entity, nor as the property of an existent or an inexistent. If anyone considers it so, he turns the key term in the descriptive system into the root of all delusions."

This idea has been picked up by Douglas Daye, ("Major Schools of the Mahāyāna: Mādhyamika", pp.94–5) who says, "The word emptiness refers to the non-ontological, non-empirical referential status of certain pieces of the object languages...", by Guy Bugault, ("Logic and Dialectics in the *Madhyamakakārikās*", p.60), "Nowadays, we could say that voidness (*śūnyatā*) is not an existential category, and concerns statements rather than things – in brief, it belongs to metalanguage,"; and by Seyfort Ruegg, ("The Uses of the Four Positions of the *Catuṣkoṭi* and the Problem of the Description of Reality in Mahāyāna Buddhism", p.62, n.45):

> "The term *śūnyatā* could then be described as metalinguistic since it does not refer to any given (first-order) object or thing. Indeed, because it allows the

Mādhyamika philosopher to analyse the terms of the Ābhidharmika's philosophical parlance, which are second-order terms inasmuch as they do not refer directly to objects in the world but rather to analytical concepts such as the *dharma* lists, *śūnyatā* might even be called a third-order term."

In a related fashion G.C. Nayak sees emptiness as only having to do with concepts ("The Mādhyamika attack on essentialism: A critical appraisal", p.480): "But what is this ultimate truth or *paramārtha satya*? It is the exact significance of concepts as they are without any distortion which is nothing but *śūnyatā*, that is, *niḥsvabhāvatā* or essencelessness."

Mervyn Sprung says, ("The Mādhyamika Doctrine as Metaphysic", in *The Problem of Two Truths in Buddhism and Vedānta*, Dordrecht, Holland: D. Reidel, 1973, p.51), "This appears unequivocal and decisive: *śūnyatā* is not a term to which something real corresponds; it does not refer to anything of the nature of substance, to anything bhavic."

Finally, Tola and Dragonetti ("Nāgārjuna's Conception of 'Voidness' (Śūnyatā)", p.277) say, "We have said that is not possible to affirm with respect to *śūnyatā* that it exists or does not exist."

241 For instance, Sha-mar-den-dzin (*Difficult Points of (Dzong-ka-ba's) "Great Exposition of Special Insight"*, 76.1–76.4), listing some of those whose views Dzong-ka-ba was refuting gives the following examples:

> "Ngok-lo-tsā-wa (*rngog lo chen po*, i.e., Lo-den-shay-rap), thinking that since there was not in the least true establishment able to withstand analysis by reasoning, it was not feasible also that a reasoning consciousness establish reality (*chos nyid*), said that the ultimate truth was not an object of knowledge.... Dro-lung-ba-chen-bo (*gro lung pa chen po*), having divided that one awareness analyzing the ultimate by way of its isolate factors, explains that an object of a

reasoning consciousness [i.e., a non-conceptual awareness realizing the ultimate] does not exist, but an object of an inferential consciousness does exist."

(For more on Ngok Lo-den-shay-rap's views and the Geluk-ba response to them, see Hopkins' *Meditation on Emptiness*, pp.406–11, and Thurman's *Tsong Khapa's Speech of Gold in the Essence of True Eloquence*, pp.54–6.)

See Paul Williams article, "A Note on Some Aspects of Mi Bskyod Rdo Rje's Critique of Dge Lugs Pa Madhyamaka", pp.129ff; much of Mi-gyö-dor-je's criticism of Dzong-ka-ba stems from Dzong-ka-ba's assertion that emptiness exists. See also Seyfort Ruegg's "On the Knowability and Expressibility of Absolute Reality in Buddhism", *Journal of Indian and Buddhist Studies*, 20 (1971), pp.495–89, where he discusses this question in general, including mention of particular Tibetan interpretations.

242 "The Problem of the Absolute in the Madhyamaka School", p.4.

243 See the Dharmsala edition of Dzong-ka-ba's text, 416a.5–419b.1 (Wayman's translation, pp.255–60), where this topic is treated at length. It is included within Dzong-ka-ba's refutation of those who do not negate enough; however, after dispensing relatively quickly with that error, Dzong-ka-ba focuses most of his attention on the proof that emptiness exists, although it does not inherently exist.

In the *Medium Exposition of the Stages of the Path*, Dzong-ka-ba develops his argument that emptiness exists around showing that emptiness is an object of knowledge (Hopkins' translation, pp.104–14; see Thurman's *Life and Teachings of Tsong Khapa*, pp.162–4), addressing directly the many passages which seem to suggest that it is not, those that speak of seeing emptiness in the manner of non-perception, and so forth.

244 See William Ames' article "The Notion of *Svabhāva* in the Thought of Candrakīrti", *Journal of Indian Philosophy* 10 (1982), pp.161–77, which focuses on just these different meanings. It includes citation and discussion of the passages from Chandrakīrti cited in the following pages. Ames makes the point (pp.164–5) that although Chandrakīrti explicitly uses the term *svabhāva* in a positive way, there are no comparably clear and explicit uses of such by Nāgārjuna in the *Treatise on the Middle Way*; for instance, Nāgārjuna does not explicitly equate the terms *svabhāva* and *dharmatā* as does Chandrakīrti.

245 La Vallée Poussin edition of the Sanskrit, pp.259–62. Cited by Dzong-ka-ba, Dharmsala edition, 414b.5–415a.1 (Wayman's translation, p.253). See Sha-mar-den-dzin, 130.3 and 130.6, where this differentiation of two meanings, implicit in Dzong-ka-ba's treatment of the passage, is made explicit. See also Dzong-ka-ba's *Ocean of Reasoning, Explanation of (Nāgārjuna's) "Treatise on the Middle Way"*, *rje tsong kha pa'i gsung dbu ma'i lta ba'i skor* edition, Vol.1, 731.13–734.17, for Dzong-ka-ba's extended commentary on Nāgārjuna's verse and Chandrakīrti's commentary concerning this point.

Numerous scholars have taken the opening stanzas of chapter fifteen as referring only to the object of negation and not to the final nature of phenomena. Such an understanding leads Richard Robinson to say ("Some Logical Aspects of Nāgārjuna's System", p.299), "*Svabhāva* is by definition the subject of contradictory ascriptions. If it exists, it must belong to an existent entity, which means that it must be conditioned, dependent on other entities, and possessed of causes. But a *svabhāva* is by definition unconditioned, not dependent on other entities, and not caused. Thus the existence of a *svabhāva* is impossible."

And Frederick Streng, speaking from the same viewpoint, says (*Emptiness: A Study in Religious Meaning*, pp.44) that the first three verses of chapter fifteen are showing that "the notion of *svabhāva* is incompatible with the basic Buddhist position that all existence is produced dependent on other things."

Such views are essentially what Dzong-ka-ba argues against in the section of his presentation entitled "those who refute an overly narrow object of negation": If *svabhāva*, inherent existence, were merely not to be produced by causes and conditions, not to depend on something else, and not to change into something else, then even non-Mādhyamikas would realize the lack of inherent existence. For, all Buddhist schools realize that impermanent phenomena lack such *svabhāva*, that is, that they are produced by causes and conditions, do depend on other things, and do change into something else.

If things were inherently existent, there are many things that would be *entailed*, such as that they would possess the above three attributes, would be permanent, and so forth, but those attributes themselves are not the object of negation, for they are less subtle than the object of negation. They are used in the proofs that things lack inherent existence for just that reason; in that they are less subtle, they are easier to understand and hence serve as *means* to realize non-inherent existence: if some impermanent thing were inherently existent, it would have to be permanent since the inherently existent cannot change; it is clearly not permanent, hence it is not inherently existent.

Were one to think that the object of negation was a nature having the three attributes of (1) its entity not being produced by causes and conditions; (2) not depending on another positor; and (3) its state not changing to something else, and were one to refute merely this, it would not go far enough in that conceiving such to exist is not an innate misconception but rather is merely imputed by erroneous tenets. As such, it is not suitable to be that which binds all beings in cyclic existence, and refuting merely that will not be sufficient to lead to release from cyclic existence.

246 For instance, Mervyn Sprung says ("The Mādhyamika Doctrine as Metaphysic", p.47):

> "What is existence devoid of? What is it lacking? In a word, all things are lacking *svabhāva*: a simple, immutable own nature. What is real, by contrast, is precisely what the everyday world lacks. Only the real (*tattva*) which is *paramārthasatya* can be said to be *svabhāva*, i.e., real in its own right. And yet *paramārtha* has been expressly declared not to be real in the way in which named-things are wrongly taken to be real in the everyday, which is to say in the svabhavic way. This is a glimpse of the bedevilling paradox inherent in Mādhyamika...."

Not differentiating between the meaning intended when it is said that *svabhāva* exists – the final nature of phenomena – and that intended when it is said that *svabhāva* does not exist – existence from [an object's] own side – leads Sprung to say that the ultimate is exactly what is being refuted in terms of other phenomena: (pp.48–9)

> "*Saṁvṛti* is taking the everyday as if it were svabhavic – real in itself – but *paramārtha* is alone truly svabhavic. It *is* what the everyday is wrongly taken to be."

This amounts to saying that the ultimate inherently exists, a position Dzong-ka-ba refutes, see pp.129–31.

Seyfort Ruegg finds paradox in a similar dual usage of the term *svabhāva*: he says (*The Literature of the Madhyamaka School of Philosophy in India*, p.2):

> "Nāgārjuna has furthermore stated – paradoxically and perhaps by oxymoron – that whatever exists in dependence (*pratītya*) is still (*śānta*) 'by nature' (*svabhāvataḥ*, vii.16); it is clear from the doctrinal context that what is so must be precisely without the *svabhāva* postulated by his opponents."

Alex Wayman distinguishes the two meanings of *svabhāva* in a similar fashion to Dzong-ka-ba, but then he says (*Calming the Mind and Discerning the Real*, p.69):

> "Small wonder that this Mādhyamika school should be misunderstood, when it vigorously rejects the *svabhāva* that is something to establish by mundane reasoning, and then upholds the *svabhāva* that is something to realize in Yoga attainment."

Dzong-ka-ba would never call the first (non-existent) *svabhāva* something to be "established" by reasoning. Rather, it is to be refuted by reasoning, "refute" here meaning that one comes through a process of reasoning to understand that it does not and never did exist.

247 This is found in La Vallée Poussin's edition of Chandrakīrti's text, 305.19–306.12. It is cited by Dzong-ka-ba in the Dharmsala edition of the *Great Exposition*, 416a.6–416b.4 (Wayman's translation, pp.255–56).

248 This is found in La Vallée Poussin's Sanskrit edition, 263.5–264.4. It is cited by Dzong-ka-ba in the Dharmsala edition of the *Great Exposition*, 416b.6–417a.2 (Wayman's translation, pp.256).

249 The Dharmsala edition of the *Great Exposition*, 417a.2 (Wayman's translation, pp.256). Dzong-ka-ba considers at this juncture the qualm that since Chandrakīrti said that the "nature" is taught as existing upon imputation in order to dispell the fear of listeners, he does not actually assert it as existing. Dzong-ka-ba rejects this possibility on the grounds that such statements are made also with respect to other phenomena that clearly do exist, and thus if such qualification meant that emptiness did not exist, it would also mean that those phenomena would not exist. In addition, he points to the evidence of other statements such as that cited just above where Chandrakīrti is unequivocal in saying that such a nature exists and ties the purposefulness of religious practice to its existence.

250 *Central Philosophy of Buddhism*, p.139. Murti, in his "Saṁvṛti and Paramārtha in Mādhyamika and Advaita Vedānta", pp.22–3 says that he cannot agree with Frederick Streng that Mādhyamika is not absolutism, explaining, "Dr Streng accepts that *śūnyatā* serves a soteriological purpose and is religiously motivated. In that sense it differs from modern positivism or linguistic philosophy. But how can this purpose be secured if nothing is left over as Real, after the rejection of all things as relative? It is as if a man suffering from headache were told to cut off his head."

Sprung's statement is from his "The Mādhyamika Doctrine as Metaphysic", p.47; Matilal's is from his *Epistemology, Logic, and Grammar in Indian Philosophical Analysis*, p.147. Christian Lindtner also calls Mādhyamika a form of absolutism (see his "Atiśa's Introduction to the Two Truths, and Its Sources" (*Journal of Indian Philosophy* 9, 1981, pp.161–2) as does Mahesh Mehta (see his "Śūnyatā and Dharmatā: the Mādhyamika View of Inner Reality", in *Developments in Buddhist Thought: Canadian Contributions to Buddhist Studies*, Waterloo, Ontario: Canadian Corporation for Studies in Religion, 1979, p.36).

251 See the Dharmsala edition of the *Great Exposition*, 417b.3–417b.4 (Wayman's translation, p.257).

252 This is found in La Vallée Poussin's Sanskrit edition, 245.11–12. It is cited by Dzong-ka-ba in the *Great Exposition*, 411b.3. His discussion of it continues through 412b.6 (Wayman's translation, pp.247–9). See also the Fourteenth Dalai Lama, Tenzin Gyatso's *Buddhism of Tibet and the Key to the Middle Way* (London: George Allen & Unwin, 1975), pp.75–6, for citation of this passage and its meaning.

253 *Nāgārjuna's Philosophy as Presented in the Mahā-Prajñā-pāramitā-Śāstra*, (Varanasi: Bharatiya Vidya Prakashan, 1971), p.42. It is interesting to note that Venkata Ramanan's intepretations of many of these difficult points

in Mādhyamika philosophy, based on his work in Chinese on the *Mahā-prajñāpāramitā-śāstra*, or *ta chih tu lun*, accord more with Dzong-ka-ba's than those of most modern scholars with the exception of those working with indigenous Tibetan materials.

254 "Medium Exposition of Special Insight", Hopkins' translation, p.74; see Thurman's *Life and Teachings of Tsong Khapa*, p.148.

255 Toh 3842, Tokyo *sde dge* Vol.1, 220a.1–220a.4. It occurs near the end of chapter thirteen. It is cited by Dzong-ka-ba in the *Great Exposition*, Dharmsala edition, 413a.4–413a.5 (Wayman's translation, p.250 – mistranslated). Dzong-ka-ba explains that if this passage is not interpreted as referring to emptiness being conceived to exist inherently, the example would not be appropriate.

256 See pp.189 and 185; see note 349 for a full reference.

257 This is found in La Vallée Poussin's edition of Chandrakīrti's text, 307.4–307.7. It is cited by Dzong-ka-ba in the "Medium Exposition of Special Insight", Hopkins' translation, p.108; see Thurman's *Life and Teachings of Tsong Khapa*, p.164.

258 "Medium Exposition of Special Insight", Hopkins' translation, p.108; see Thurman's *Life and Teachings of Tsong Khapa*, p.164.

259 *Central Philosophy of Buddhism*, p.126. Others who echo this view include G.C. Nayak, who, equating wisdom and the ultimate, says ("The Mādhyamika attack on essentialism: A critical appraisal" p.485), "This *prajñā* (wisdom), in the sense of realization of *śūnyatā* (essencelessness), alone is considered to be the highest end or *paramārtha* according to the Mādhyamikas."

Also David Eckel ("A Question of Nihilism: Bhāvaviveka's Response to the Fundamental Problems of Mādhyamika Philosophy", pp.123–5 equates *paramārtha* with "experience" of the ultimate, and C.W. Huntington, Jr. equates both emptiness and nirvāṇa with realization: ("The System of the Two Truths in the Prasannapadā and the Madhyamakāvatāra: A Study in Mādhyamika Soteriology", p.91):

> "In fact, so far as I know, emptiness is nowhere defined as an object of knowledge (*jñeya*), but only as 'the direct seeing of phenomena as devoid of intrinsic being'."

Also (p.99):

> "*Nirvāṇa* is emptiness, [PP351] and emptiness is understood as the direct realization of the absence of intrinsic being within all phenomena [PP350]."

260 In the "Medium Exposition of Special Insight", Dzong-ka-ba cites a passage from Chandrakīrti's *Autocommentary on the "Supplement to (Nāgārjuna's) 'Treatise on the Middle Way'"* (Hopkins' translation, p.109; see Thurman's *Life and Teachings of Tsong Khapa*, pp.164–5):

> "Therefore, that suchness is realized is posited from imputation; actually there is no knowing of something by something because both knower and object known are non-produced."

He explains that passage as follows:

> "The meaning of the first part is that a positing of a realization of suchness with the two – the exalted wisdom and suchness – being taken as separate subject and object is a positing in terms only of a conventional consciousness, not for the exalted wisdom. That the knower is non-produced means that it has become like water put in water with respect to the meaning of non-inherent production."

261 The Dalai Lama takes just such a differentiation of whether one is describing the object, emptiness, or the subject, the wisdom realizing emptiness, as the basis for his explanation of the way in which all four schools of Tibetan Buddhism are getting at the same thing in spite of seemingly great differences in vocabulary and approach. See his *Kindness, Clarity, and Insight* (Ithaca, N.Y.: Snow Lion Publications, 1984), pp.206–20.

262 For instance, Karl Potter, *Presuppositions of India's Philosophies*, p.240 and David Eckel, "Bhāvaviveka and the early Mādhyamika theories of language", pp.331–2.

263 See Bhāvaviveka's *Blaze of Reasoning*, P5256, Vol.96, 27.3.1–27.3.4 and 27.5.7–28.1.1. Both of these passages are cited in the *Great Exposition* 431a.3–431b.3 (Wayman's translation, pp.280–1 – mistranslated). However, it must be emphasized that the only *actual* ultimates are emptinesses, objective ultimates. Subjective ultimates, consciousnesses realizing emptiness, are merely concordant ultimates. See appendix one, pp. 429–38, particularly the charts on pp.437–8, for a fuller discussion of this topic.

264 *Central Philosophy of Buddhism*, p.333. Similarly, Musashi Tachikawa ("A Logical Analysis of the *Mūlamadhyamakakārikā*", in Nagatomi et al. ed., *Sanskrit and Indian Studies*, Dordrecht, Boston, London: D. Reidel, 1980, p.159) says, "[Nāgārjuna] called the world of transmigration the profane world (*saṃvṛti*); enlightenment, ultimate truth (*paramārtha*)." See also J.W. de Jong, ("The Problem of the Absolute in the Madhyamaka School", p.5) "There is no doubt that *paramārtha*, being the 'supreme goal' of the believer, may be called 'the absolute' . . ." and G.C. Nayak ("The Mādhyamika attack on essentialism: A critical appraisal", p.489), "*Nirvāṇa* is thus nondifferent from critical insight par excellence which is free from all essentialist picture-thinking."

265 *Central Philosophy of Buddhism*, p.220.

266 *Presuppositions of India's Philosophies*, p.239.

267 See Paul Demiéville's *Le concile de Lhasa: une controverse sur le quiétisme entre bouddhiste de l'Inde et de la Chine au VIIIe siècle de l'ère chrétienne*, Bibliothéque de l'Institut des Hautes Etudes Chinoises, VII (Paris: Imprimerie Nationale de France, 1952); Yanagida Seizan's "The *Li-tai fa-pao chi* and the Ch'an Doctrine of Sudden Awakening" in Lai and Lancaster, ed., *Early Ch'an in China and Tibet*, Berkeley Buddhist Studies Series 5 (Berkeley:

1983); and Luis Gomez' "Indian Materials on the Doctrine of Sudden Enlightenment" in *Early Ch'an in China and Tibet*, op. cit., as well as his "The Direct and the Gradual Approaches of Zen Master Mahāyāna: Fragments of the Teachings of Mo-ho-yen" in Gimello and Gregory, ed., *Studies in Ch'an and Hua-yen* (Honolulu: University of Hawaii Press, 1983).

268 See the *Precious Garland and the Song of the Four Mindfulnesses*, verses 440–65, pp.84–7. The dedication to Nāgārjuna's *Sixty Stanzas of Reasoning* is cited by Dzong-ka-ba in the *Great Exposition* (see p.181).

269 During the approximately 20 year course of study in the Tibetan monastic universities that culminates in the attainment of the degree of "ge-shay" (*dge bshes*), the topic of "the Perfections" (*phar phyin*) is studied for about six years. This study is focused on Maitreya's *Ornament for Clear Realization* (*mngon rtogs rgyan, abhisamayālaṃkāra*) and Haribhadra's commentary on it, but many topics such as the grounds and paths (*sa lam*), the concentrations and formless absorptions (*bsam gzugs*), and so forth are extracted for special attention.

Each monastery has its own textbooks for these studies. For a presentation of the grounds and paths see, for example, Gön-chok-jik-may-wang-bo's (*dkon mchog 'jigs med dbang po*, 1728–91) *Presentation of the Grounds and Paths, Ornament Beautifying the Three Vehicles* (*sa lam gyi rnam bzhag theg gsum mdzes rgyan*, The Collected Works of dkon-mchog-'jigs-med-dbang-po, Vol. 7, New Delhi: Ngawang Gelek Demo, 1972) which is used by the Gomang College of Dre-bung Monastic University.

Most presentations of the grounds and paths are written from the viewpoint of the Svātantrika-Mādhyamika system since, although there are varying opinions as to whether the viewpoint of Maitreya's *Ornament for Clear Realization* is Yogāchāra, Svātantrika, or Prāsaṅgika, all the Ge-luk-ba colleges agree that Svātantrika-Mādhyamika is the viewpoint of Haribhadra's text.

(Both Edward Conze and Giuseppe Tucci felt that both Maitreya and Haribhadra wrote as Yogāchārins, and thus their interpretations of the meaning of those texts often differ widely from those of the Ge-luk-ba tradition.)

An interesting exception in the literature on path structure is the Mongolian scholar Lo-sang-da-yang's (*blo bzang rta dbyangs*, also known as *blo bzang rta mgrin*) *Brief Expression of the Presentation of the Grounds and Paths of the Three Vehicles According to the System of the Perfection Vehicle, Essence of the Ocean of Profound Meaning* (*phar phyin theg pa'i lugs kyi theg pa gsum gyi sa dang lam gyi rnam bzhag pa mdo tsam du brjod pa zab don rgya mtsho'i snying po*, the Collected Words (Gsung 'Bum) of Rje-Btsun Blo-Bzaṅ-Rta-Mgrin, Vol.IV, pp.65–190, New Delhi: Guru Deva, 1975), which is written from the viewpoint of Prāsaṅgika-Mādhyamika. It is the topic of a forthcoming Ph.D. dissertation by Jules Levinson of the University of Virginia.

270 "Nietzsche and Nāgārjuna: The Origins and Issue of Scepticism", p.168.

271 *Lucid Exposition of the Middle Way*, p.10.

272 Gön-chok-jik-may-wang-bo's *Presentation of the Grounds and Paths, Ornament Beautifying the Three Vehicles*, 444.1.

273 "The Mādhyamika attack on essentialism: A critical appraisal", p.487.

274 See the "Medium Exposition of Special Insight", Hopkins' translation, pp.110–12; Thurman's *Life and Teachings of Tsong Khapa*, pp.165–7.

275 See Wayman's "Contributions to the Mādhyamika School of Buddhism", *Journal of the American Oriental Society* Vol.8 (1969), p.151. Wayman says, justifying his use of an explanation by Abhayākara, an author from the last period of Indian Buddhism, of the meaning of a passage from Nāgārjuna, "It need not be thought that such an interpretation of Nāgārjuna is limited to a 'late'

Buddhist author (incidentally, modern scholars are still 'later')."

276 English translations of Nāgārjuna's verses without accompanying commentary have been made by Frederick Streng in his *Emptiness: A Study in Religious Meaning* and by Kenneth Inada, *Nāgārjuna: A Translation of his Mūlamadhyamakakārikā*. A translation of most of the verses with Chandrakīrti's commentary has been made by Mervyn Sprung, *Lucid Exposition of the Middle Way*. None is truly reliable. A recent translation by David Kalupahana, *Nāgārjuna: The Philosophy of the Middle Way*, (Albany, N.Y.: State University of New York Press, 1986), reached me too late to be included in this discussion; in a brief survey, I found many points of disagreement. More reliable translation into other European languages can be pieced together from various translations of Chandrakīrti's *Clear Words* as discussed below. Also R. Gnoli has translated all of the verses into Italian and Christian Lindtner has translated them into Danish, translations about which I have no means to comment. See the bibliography for full references.

277 Included within her doctoral dissertation, "Āryadeva on the Bodhisattva's Cultivation of Merit and Knowledge," it has appeared in revised form as volume 7 of the Indiste Studier series from Copenhagen, entitled *Āryadeva's Catuhśataka*.

278 Lindtner's comment is made in the introduction to his translation of chapter eighteen ("Buddhapālita on Emptiness [*Buddhapālita-mūla-madhyamakavṛtti XVIII*]", *Indo-Iranian Journal* 23 (1981), pp.187–217), p.188; a translation of chapter one by Judit Fehér is available in *Tibetan and Buddhist Studies Commemorating the 200th Anniversary of the Birth of Alexander Csoma de Körös*, Vol.1 (Budapest: Akadémiai Kiado, 1984), pp.211–40.

279 Tokyo: The Hokuseido Press, 1980.

280 See, for example, Fenner's "A Study of the Relationship Between Analysis (*vicāra*) and Insight (*prajñā*) Based on

the *Madhyamakāvatāra*", *Journal of Indian Philosophy* 12 (1984), pp.139–197, and Huntington's "The System of the Two Truths in the Prasannapadā and the Madhyamakāvatāra: A Study in Mādhyamika Soteriology", *Journal of Indian Philosophy* 11 (1983), pp.77–106. For a listing of where translations of the various parts of Chandrakīrti's *Clear Words*, *Supplement*, and its auto-commentary can be found, see the bibliography.

CHAPTER SEVEN: SUMMATION: ETHICS AND EMPTINESS

281 See Thurman's *Tsong Khapa's Speech of Gold in the essence of True Eloquence*, p.65–89 for a brief and eloquent biography of Dzong-ka-ba drawn from traditional sources.

282 See Thurman's *Tsong Khapa's Speech of Gold in the Essence of True Eloquence*, pp.77–82.

283 The twentieth century renegade Ge-luk-ba monk Gen-dun-chö-pel (*dge 'dun chos 'phel*, 1905?–1951?) wrote a work entitled *Ornament to Nāgārjuna's Thought, Eloquence Containing the Essence of the Profundities of the Middle Way* (*dbu ma'i zab gnad snying por dril ba'i legs bshad klu sgrub dgongs rgyan*, Kalimpong: Mani Printing Works, no date) leveling just such charges. For a discussion of Gen-dun-chö-pel and this issue, see Hopkins' *Meditation on Emptiness*, pp.544–7. There have been attempts within the tradition to rewrite history and deny Gen-dun-chö-pel's authorship of this text, probably in large part because of his attacks on Dzong-ka-ba, but they are not convincing. For more information on Gen-dun-chö-pel, see the study by Heather Stoddard, *Le Mendiant de l'Amdo* (Paris: Societé d'Ethnographie, 1985).

284 For instance, Dzong-ka-ba concludes that Bhāvaviveka asserted the mental consciousness to be the person and hence, since this would mean he asserted something

findable under analysis, that he asserts inherent existence. This is based on a brief passage in Bhāvaviveka's *Blaze of Reasoning* where Bhāvaviveka says that when another school tries to prove that the mental consciousness is the self, they are proving what is already established for him. See Hopkins' *Meditation on Emptiness*, pp.695–6, for a discussion of this point.

285 The Dharmsala edition of the *Great Exposition*, 381a.6–381b.1, see p.192.

286 The Dharmsala edition of the *Great Exposition*, 408b.1 (Wayman's translation, p.241).

287 The Dharmsala edition of the *Great Exposition*, 377b.5–377b.6, see p.184. See also p.191.

288 *The Three Principles of the Path* (*lam gtso rnam gsum*), translation by Geshe Sopa and Jeffrey Hopkins; see the Dalai Lama's *Kindness, Clarity, and Insight*, p.148.

289 *Kindness, Clarity, and Insight*, p.43.

PART TWO: TRANSLATION OF DZONG-KA-BA'S "GREAT EXPOSITION"

INTRODUCTION

290 The text translated here is the first sixth of the special insight portion of Dzong-ka-ba's *Great Exposition of the Stages of the Path*. The entire special insight section as well as a preceding one on calm abiding has been translated into English by Alex Wayman in his *Calming the Mind and Discerning the Real*, New York, Columbia University Press, 1978, reprint New Delhi, Motilal Banarsidass, 1979 (page numbers cited are to the reprint edition). See appendix two for a discussion of problems in Wayman's translation. Translations into other languages as identified by Wayman, p.497, are: Chinese translation by Fa-tsun, Peking, 1936; partial Russian translation by G.Z. Zubikov, *Bodhi mör*, Vostochnye Institut, Vladivostok, *Isviestiia*, 1914; translation into Japanese of the special insight section by Gadjin Nagao,

A Study of Tibetan Buddhism [in Japanese], Tokyo, 1954.

The edition used for this translation is that published in Dharmsala, India by the Shes rig bar khang, no date; the text is 523 folios in length and the portion translated here begins on page 365a.2 and goes through page 391b.1. Page numbers to this edition have been inserted into the translation in square brackets. The text has been checked against the Ngawang Gelek edition (New Delhi: 1976ff.) printed from the Dra-shi-hlun-bo blocks and against the versions of it found within the two editions of the *Four Interwoven Annotations* used.

Dzong-ka-ba's referent in the statement "as was explained earlier" is to the preceding chapter, that on the development of calm abiding (*zhi gnas*, *śamatha*). This introduction to his discussion of special insight is a restatement with somewhat different emphasis of a section at the beginning of his presentation of calm abiding entitled, "The reason why it is necessary to cultivate both [calm abiding and special insight]" (308b.5–312a.3).

291 Dzong-ka-ba refers here to the basic Buddhist position that advanced states of meditative concentration can be attained by Buddhists and non-Buddhists alike. However, no matter how subtle the concentrative level, one is still within cyclic existence and still subject to the process of repeated rebirth. According to Buddhism, what distinguishes it from the Hindu systems with which it was in competition is that Buddhism has techniques that enable one to succeed in removing oneself entirely from cyclic existence by eradicating, from its root, the ignorance that initiates the causal process of cyclic existence. This is done by means of special insight enhanced to the level of direct perception of truth.

"Forder" (*mu stegs pa*, *tīrthika*) is a term often used by Buddhists to refer to the Hindu systems in general. A-gya-yong-dzin (*dbyangs can dga' ba'i blo gros*, *a kya yongs 'dzin*, eighteenth century) in his *A Brief Explanation of Terminology Occurring in (Dzong-ka-ba's) "Great Exposition of the Stages of the Path"* (*byang chub lam gyi rim pa chen mo las byung ba'i brda bkrol nyer mkho bsdus pa* in The Collected Works of A-kya Yoṅs-ḥdzin, Vol.1, New Delhi, Lama Guru Deva, 1971), 162.4–5, gives an etymology of the Tibetan term *mu stegs pa* as follows: "*mu* is used to [denote] an 'end'; therefore, the end of cyclic existence is liberation. *stegs* is the method, or path, like a platform which reaches to that liberation. Hence, the path which, from their [the non-Buddhists'] own side, is discriminated as a path for attaining liberation and high status [within cyclic existence] is called a 'ford to the end' (*mu stegs*). Due to bearing and causing the increase of treatises teaching such, [the authors of those treatises] are called 'makers of the ford to the end' (*mu stegs byed, tīrthya-kara*) or 'those having a ford to the end' (*mu stegs can, tīrthika*)."

292 *First Bhāvanākrama*, edited in Sanskrit by G. Tucci, *Minor Buddhist Texts*, Part II, Serie Orientale Roma IX, 2, (Rome: IS.M.E.O., 1958), Sanskrit on pp.209–10, Tibetan on p.258. Tucci gives a summary of the text in English but does not actually translate it. Tibetan also in the *sDe dge Tibetan Tripiṭaka – bsTan ḥgyur preserved at the Faculty of Letters, University of Tokyo*, Tokyo, 1979, Vol.15, Toh 3915 (P5310) 32b.7–33a.2. (This edition of the *bstan 'gyur* portion of the Tibetan canon is hereafter referred to as the Tokyo *sde dge*.) The Sanskrit reads:

> tad evam ālambane cittaṃ sthirīkṛtya prajñayā vivecayet/yato jñānālokotpādāt sammohabījasyātyantaprahāṇaṃ bhavati/anyathā hi tīrthikānām iva samādhimātreṇa kleśaprahāṇaṃ na syāt/yathoktaṃ sūtre

293 *Samādhirājasūtra*: IX:36. Sanskrit available in P.L. Vaidya, ed., (Darbhanga: Mithila Institute, 1961), p.49; Tibetan in the *Nying-ma Edition of the sDe-dge bKa'-'gyur and bsTan'-gyur*, (Oakland, CA: Dharma Publish-

ing, 1980), Toh 127, Vol.20, 1318.7. (This edition of the Tibetan canon is hereafter referred to as the Dharma *sde dge*.) Partial translation by K. Regamey, (of chapters eight, nineteen, and twenty-two) *Three Chapters from the Samādhirājasūtra* (Warsaw: Publications of the Oriental Commission, 1938). This verse as cited in the sūtra itself differs slightly from that cited by Kamalashīla, and the form cited by Dzong-ka-ba is again slightly different. However, in terms of meaning, the differences are insignicant.

The Sanskrit in the P.L. Vaidya edition reads:

kim cāpi bhāveyya samādhi loke
na co vibhāveyya sa ātmasaṃjñām
punaḥ prakupyanti kileṣu tasya
yathodrakasyeha samādhibhāvanā

The Sanskrit cited within the *Bhāvanākrama* itself as found in Tucci's edition reads:

kiṃ cāpi bhāv[ay]et samādhim etam
na vāpi bhāvayet sā ātmasaṃjñā
punaḥ prakupyati kileṣu tasyā
yathodrakasyeha samādhibhāvanā

This difference is also reflected in the Tibetan editions. The Tibetan found in the Dharma *sde dge* edition of the sūtra reads:

'jig rten dag na ting 'dzin sgom byed kyang
de ni bdag tu 'du shes gzhig mi byed
de yi nyon mongs phyir yang rab tu ldang
lhag dpyod kyis ni ting 'dzin 'dir bsgom bzhin

The Tibetan for this verse as cited by Kamalashīla as found in the Tokyo *sde dge*, in the Peking edition (p.26.1.7), and in Tucci's edition reads:

ting nge 'dzin de sgom par byed mod kyi
de ni bdag tu 'du shes 'jig mi byed
de yi nyon mongs phyir zhing rab 'khrug ste
lhag dpyod 'di ni ting 'dzin bsgom pa bzhin

The version that occurs in Dzong-ka-ba's citation of Kamalashīla appears to be a combination of these two. It reads:

'jig rten dag ni ting 'dzin sgom byed kyang
de ni bdag tu 'du shes 'jig mi byed
de ni nyon mongs phyir zhing rab 'khrug ste
lhag spyod kyis ni ting 'dzin 'dir bsgoms bzhin

The difference in meaning between these different versions is insignificant.

294 *Udraka* (Tib., *lhag dpyod*) is identified by the *Mahāvyutpatti* (entry 3516) as "Udrako rāmaputraḥ, Rangs byed kyi bu lhag spyod". Sha-mar-den-dzin, (*zhwa dmar dge bdun bstan 'dzin rgya mtsho*, 1852–1910), in his *Lamp Illuminating the Profound Thought, Set Forth to Purify Forgetfulness of the Difficult Points of (Dzong-ka-ba's) "Great Exposition of Special Insight"* (*lhag mthong chen mo'i dka' gnad rnams brjed byang du bkod pa dgongs zab snang ba'i sgron me*, Delhi: Mongolian Lama Guru Deva, 1972), pp.4.6–5.4, says that according to an earlier oral tradition, Udraka was someone who cultivated meditative stabilization due to a sense of competitiveness with Buddha whereby, although he attained all eight concentrations and absorptions, upon seeing damage to his hair by a mouse he got angry and fell from his concentration. However, Sha-mar-den-dzin says that in the *Commentary on the King of Meditative Stabilizations Sūtra* (*ting nge 'dzin rgyal po'i mdo 'grel*), aside from saying that Udraka attained magical power (*rdzu 'phrul*), there is no clear statement about his attaining all eight meditative stabilizations.

His source of this appears to have been A-gya-yong-dzin's *A Brief Explanation of Terminology Occurring in (Dzong-ka-ba's) "Great Exposition of the Stages of the Path"*, pp.154.4–155.5. A-gya-yong-dzin gives these same two explanations but in somewhat more detail. He says that according to an oral tradition passed down through Yong-dzin Ye-shay-gyel-tsen Bel-sang-bo (*yongs 'dzin ye shes rgyal mtshan dpal bzang po*) and so forth, Udraka was a non-Buddhist Forder who, due to a sense of competitiveness with Buddha, let his hair grow long, held his breath, and through cultivating meditative stabilization for twelve years attained all eight concentrations (*bsam gtan, dhyāna*) and formless absorptions (*gzugs med kyi snyoms 'jug, ārūpya samāpatti*). When he rose from his equipoise, he saw that a mouse had eaten through the strands of his hair and made a nest of it, whereupon he generated strong anger. His attainment of the concentrations and absorptions immediately degenerated, and upon his death he was reborn in a hell.

The other explanation A-gya-yong-dzin identifies as coming from Achārya Jñānakīrti's *Commentary on the "King of Meditative Stabilizations Sūtra"*. It says that Udraka was a Digambara (*phyogs kyi gos can*), which A-gya-yong-dzin identifies as a name for the Tīrthika Nirgrantha (*mu stegs gcer bu pa*) school, who saw someone flying in the sky by means of magical powers, and wanting that feat entered into that person's teaching and achieved the ability to fly. He then returned to the Digambara teachings, still maintaining his ability to fly, but sometime later when another person questioned whether his teaching was an actual path, he fell from that magical power and crashed to earth. He subsequently took rebirth in a hell.

Ken-sur Yeshe Thupten, when explaining these passages, emphasized that the point being made was not that these non-Buddhists necessarily took rebirth in hells, nor that their rebirth there was a result of their meditations, but simply that even though one might cultivate these lofty meditative states and achieve considerable powers, since one had not interfered in the least with the root cause of cyclic existence, one would still take rebirth within it upon death, possibly even in its lowest state.

295 Dzong-ka-ba is referring to his previous citation of this scripture in the calm abiding section of the text, pp.311a.5–312a.3. He was citing Kamalashīla's middle *Stages of Meditation* (Toh 3916, Tokyo *sde dge* Vol.15 44b.1–45a.4) included within which Kamalashīla cited without explanation two verses of the *King of Meditative*

Stabilizations Sūtra. The first of those verses is that given just above (Kamalashīla cites only this one in his first *Stages of Meditation*); the second of those verses is what Dzong-ka-ba is about to explain here. He explains the entire verse, but cites only the first line and then says "and so forth"; I have supplied the remainder of the verse in brackets. The Tibetan as cited by Kamalashīla is:

gal te chos la bdag med so sor rtog
so sor de brtags gal te bsgom pa ni
de nyid mya ngan 'das thob 'bras bu'i rgyu
rgyu gzhan gang yin des ni zhi mi 'gyur

As cited in the Dharma *sde dge* edition of the sūtra itself, Vol.20, 1318.7–1319.1, the Tibetan reads:

gal te bdag med chos la rab rtog cing
de dag brtags nas gal te sgom byed na
'bras bu mya ngan 'das thob rgyu de yin
rgyu gzhan de dag zhi bar 'gyur mi srid.

The middle *Stages of Meditation* is not available in Sanskrit, so we have no Sanskrit for the verse as cited by Kamalashīla; as found in the Vaidya edition of the *Samādhirājasūtra* (p.49) the verse reads:

nairātmyadharmān yadi pratyavekṣate
tān pratyavekṣya yadi bhāvayeta
sa hetu nirvāṇaphalasya prāptaye
yo anyahetur na sa bhoti śāntaye.

296 The *Four Interwoven Annotations* identifies the referent of "that" as "special insight" but Dzong-ka-ba's concluding sentence seems to justify taking it as the "wisdom realizing selflessness", and this is how Ge-shay Palden Drakpa read it.

297 Toh 3916, Tokyo *sde dge* Vol.16, 44b.3–4.

298 The earlier citation was included within the citation from Kamalashīla just referred to (see note 295) and is found in Dzong-ka-ba on p.311b.3–5; it can be found in Kamalashīla's middle *Stages of Meditation* on p.44b.5–7, Tokyo *sde dge* Vol.16. Here Dzong-ka-ba is paraphrasing his earlier citation of the sutra. Dzong-ka-

ba's citation follows Kamalashīla; this differs somewhat from the sūtra itself (Toh 56, Dharma *sde dge* Vol.16, p.82.4.3–5) but the variations are not substantive. The *Scriptural Collection of Bodhisattvas* is included within the *Heap of Jewels Sūtra* (*dkon mchog brtsegs pa*, *ratnakūṭa*).

299 Although the *Four Interwoven Annotations* glosses this as developing pride and manifesting it to others, both Ge-shay Palden Drakpa and Go-mang Ken-sur Denba Dendzin took *mngon pa'i nga rgyal* as a technical term, meaning a type of pride in which one takes a small good quality and builds it up into something much bigger than it actually is. Ge-shay Palden Drakpa contrasted it to *log pa'i nga rgyal* in which one takes a fault and builds it up to be a good quality. These two types are included among a list of seven kinds of pride given in Nāgārjuna's *Precious Garland*, verses 406–12; they are mentioned in verse 411:

'bras ma thob par thob snyam pa
gang yin mngon pa'i nga rgyal te
sdig las byed la bstod pa ni
mkhas pas log pa'i nga rgyal stogs

Thinking one has won fruits not yet attained
Is pride of conceit.
Praising oneself for faulty deeds
Is known by the wise as wrongful pride.

(English translation by Jeffrey Hopkins, *The Precious Garland and the Song of the Four Mindfulnesses*, New York, Harper and Row, 1975.) In the Dharma *sde dge* edition of the sūtra itself, the term *mngon* is not used; it simply says *che ba'i nga rgyal*, pride of greatness (Toh 56, Dharma *sde dge* Vol.16, 82.3.3).

300 Toh 3916, Tokyo *sde dge* Vol.15, 48a.4–7.

301 Toh 106 (P774), Dharma *sde dge* Vol.18, 319.4.4–319.4.5. In Lamotte's translation of the sūtra (É. Lamotte, ed. and trans., *Samdhinirmocanasūtra: l'explication des mystères*, Louvain: Université de Louvain,

1935) this is IX.26, translation on p.253. This sūtra was also cited by Kamalashīla in his middle *Stages of Meditation* shortly after the passage just cited by Dzong-ka-ba – Tokyo *sde dge* Vol.15, 48b.1–2.

302 Here Dzong-ka-ba paraphrases a sūtra passage that he cited previously at the same point (312a.2–3) as the preceding quote from the *King of Meditative Stabilizations Sūtra*, both occurring within a citation from Kamalashīla, Tokyo *sde dge* Vol.15, 44b.1–45a.4. (This sūtra passage is found in Kamalashīla on 45a.2–3.) It is interesting to note that every sūtra reference given by Dzong-ka-ba in this section can be found in Kamalashīla; thus, it is probable that Kamalashīla was his source rather than the sūtras themselves.

CHAPTER ONE: THE INTERPRETABLE AND THE DEFINITIVE

303 This is the second of a three part heading, set forth on 314a.3 of the Dharmsala edition of Dzong-ka-ba's text and p.28.3 in Vol.II of the Annotations, where Dzong-ka-ba says that he will explain how to train in calm abiding and special insight individually in three parts: the first was "how to train in calm abiding", (pp.314a.3–365a.3, not included in this translation); the second (which begins here) is how to train in special insight; and the third (beginning on 514a.2, not translated here) is "how to conjoin those two".

304 "Rely" translates the Tibetan term *rton*; A-gya-yong-dzin, 163.4–5, identifies it as an archaic term meaning "to have conviction in" (*yid ches pa*), "suitable for firmness of mind" (*yid brtan rung ba*), "to assert" (*'dod pa*), or "to follow" (*rjes su 'brangs pa*). Dzong-ka-ba is alluding here to the four reliances (*rton pa bzhi*, *catvāri pratisaraṇāni*, see the *Mahāvyutpatti*, 1545):

> Rely not on the person (*gang zag*, *pudgala*), but on the doctrine (*chos*, *dharma*);

Rely not on the words (*tshig 'bru*, *vyañjana*), but on the meaning (*don*, *artha*);
Rely not on sūtras of interpretable meaning (*drang don gyi mdo*, *neyārthasūtra*), but on sūtras of definitive meaning (*nges don gyi mdo*, *nītārthasūtra*);
Rely not on [ordinary] consciousness (*rnam shes*, *vijñāna*), but on exalted wisdom (*ye shes*, *jñāna*).

These are set forth by Buddha in the *Sūtra on the Four Reliances* (*catuḥpratisaraṇasūtra*, see Étienne Lamotte, "La critique d'interprétation dans le bouddhisme," *Annuaire de l'Institut de philologie et d'histoire orientales et slaves*, Vol. IX (Brussels: Université Libre de Bruxelles, 1949) pp.341–61 for a discussion of this sūtra as well as other sūtra and shāstra references to the four reliances). According to Lamotte, p.342, the *Sūtra on the Four Reliances* is found in the sūtras of the Mādhyamika school as the *Teachings of Akṣhayamati Sūtra* (*blo gros mi zad pas bstan pa*, *akṣayamatinirdeśa*), P842, Vol.34, and certainly the four reliances are extensively discussed there, pp.63.5.1–64.5.8. The passage from the *Teachings of Akṣhayamati Sūtra* that Dzong-ka-ba cites just below (see pp.160–1) to explain what sūtras of definitive and interpretable meaning are is taken from that discussion.

305 367b.2, *de 'brel ba'i* corrected to *dang bral ba'i* in accordance with the Dra-shi-hlun-bo edition, 118.3, as well as both editions of the *Annotations* (Delhi, 152.4; Berkeley, 8a.2).

306 In this text, Dzong-ka-ba mentions only that the prophecies regarding Nāgārjuna exist. He goes into them in more detail in his *Great Commentary on (Nāgārjuna's) "Treatise on the Middle Way"* (*rtsa shes ṭik chen*; the full title of the text is *Ocean of Reasoning, Explanation of (Nāgārjuna's) "Treatise on the Middle Way"*, *dbu ma rtsa ba'i tshig le'ur byas pa shes rab ces bya ba'i rnam bshad rigs pa'i rgya mtsho*), Pleasure of Elegant Sayings Press edition, 3.14–5.11, and in his *Illumination of the*

Thought, Extensive Explanation of (Chandrakīrti's) "Supplement to (Nāgārjuna's) 'Treatise on the Middle Way'" (*dgongs pa rab gsal*), Pleasure of Elegant Sayings Press edition, 118.9–119.12, although he does not fully settle some of the questions raised by seeming contradictions between them.

Jam-yang-shay-ba gives very detailed attention to the topic in both his *Great Exposition of Tenets* (*grub mtha' chen mo*, Mussoorie: Dalama, 1962), ca 3b.3–6b.7, and his *Great Exposition of the Middle Way* (*dbu ma chen mo*, Buxaduor: Gomang, 1967), 194a.4–196b.1. Jeffrey Hopkins has translated these and discussed the issue extensively in "Wisdom in Tibetan Buddhism 1: the Opposite of Emptiness", Chapter Two: Prophecies, unpublished manuscript. See the *Annotations*, pp.252–3, for a brief summary of Jam-yang-shay-ba's conclusions.

307 P842, Vol.34, 64.3.6–64.4.1. This passage is translated in Hopkins' *Meditation on Emptiness*, pp.597–8, and also in Donald S. Lopez' translation of the Svātantrika chapter of Jang-gya's *Presentation of Tenets* ("The Svātantrika-Mādhyamika School of Mahāyāna Buddhism", Ann Arbor: University Microfilms, 1982), pp.428–34, where Jang-gya cites the passage and then gives considerable explanation of it. As Jang-gya explains, this is the major sūtra source cited by Indian Mādhyamikas in making their differentiation of scriptures of interpretable and definitive meaning – cited by Chandrakīrti in the first chapter of the *Clear Words* (*tshig gsal*, *prasannapadā*, P5260, Vol.98, 8.2.2; La Vallée Poussin Sanskrit edition, 43.4ff), by Avalokitavrata in his *Explanatory Commentary on (Bhāvaviveka's) "Lamp for (Nāgārjuna's) 'Wisdom'"* (*shes rab sgron ma'i rgya cher 'grel pa*, *prajñāpradīpaṭīkā*), and by Kamalashīla in his *Illumination of the Middle Way* (*dbu ma snang ba*, *madhyamakāloka*, P5287, Vol.101, 46.2.6–46.3.1).

Dzong-ka-ba's source for the passage was probably Kamalashīla's *Illumination of the Middle Way* rather than the sūtra itself (at least as found in the Peking edition of the canon) or Chandrakīrti. In the sūtra, the passage is not continuous; there are various additional lines intervening between those cited by Dzong-ka-ba (368a.1–3). Also there are numerous small differences: the sūtra reads *sgrub par bstan pa*, Dzong-ka-ba reads *sgrub pa bstan pa*; the sūtra reads *ces bya'o*, Dzong-ka-ba reads *zhes bya'o*; the sūtra reads *sna tshogs su bstan pa*, Dzong-ka-ba reads *sna tshogs bstan pa*; and, most differently, the sūtra reads *zab mo mthong bar dka' ba khong du chud par dka' ba* whereas Dzong-ka-ba reads *zab mo blta dka' ba rtogs par dka' ba*.

Also Dzong-ka-ba's citation differs substantially from Chandrakīrti's: Chandrakīrti cites a different middle two lines – found in the sūtra just before those cited by Dzong-ka-ba, "Those sūtras taught for the sake of causing one to enter to the path are said to be of interpretable meaning," (*mdo sde gang dag lam la 'jug pa'i phyir bstan pa de dag ni drang ba'i don zhes bya'o*/ *ye sūtrāntā mārgāvatārāya nirdiṣṭā ima ucyante neyārthāḥ*) and, "Those sūtras taught for the sake of causing one to enter to the fruit are said to be of definitive meaning," (*mdo sde gang dag 'bras bu la 'jug pa'i phyir bstan pa de dag ni drang ba'i don zhes bya'o, ye sūtrāntāḥ phalāvatāraya nirdiṣṭā ima ucyante nītārthāḥ*), and omits the next two lines cited by Dzong-ka-ba.

Dzong-ka-ba's citation of the passage is identical to that cited by Kamalashīla, differing only in one place, where Kamalashīla's reads *ces bya'o* and Dzong-ka-ba's *zhes bya'o*.

Dzong-ka-ba again cites this passage and accompanies it with considerable explanation in his *Essence of the Good Explanations*, Pleasure of Elegant Sayings edition, p.89– 91; see Thurman's *Tsong Khapa's Speech of Gold in the Essence of True Eloquence*, pp.253–6. The explanation given there clearly served as the basis for Jang-gya's explantion in the *Presentation of Tenets*.

308 Each annotator suggests a slightly different reading of the phrase *sgrub pa bstan pa*. As A-gya-yong-dzin says, 164.2–4, the difference in meaning is slight; I have chosen to translate the passage following Jam-yang-shay-ba, taking *sgrub pa* as *sgrub byed*, feeling that his interpretation intrudes the least on the actual words of the sūtra.

309 P842, Vol.34, 64.4.4–64.4.7; cited in Kamalashīla's *Illumination of the Middle Way*, P5287, Vol.101, 46.3.1–46.3.4; cited in Chandrakīrti's *Clear Words*, La Vallée Poussin edition, 43.6ff, Tibetan Publishing House edition, 30.8–17. Again Dzong-ka-ba's citation (368a.4–369b.1) accords almost exactly with Kamalashīla and differs in many small points from the Peking edition of the sūtra and from Chandrakīrti's citation of it. The sūtra reads *shed las skyes dang*, Dzong-ka-ba reads *shed las skyes pa dang*; the sūtra reads *sgra rnam par sna tshogs su bshad pa dang*, Dzong-ka-ba reads *skad sna tshogs kyis bshad par bya ba*; the sūtra reads *bdag po dang bcas par bstan pa*, Dzong-ka-ba reads *bdag po lta bur bstan pa*; the sūtra reads *ces bya'o*, Dzong-ka-ba reads *zhes bya'o*; the sūtra reads *mngon par 'du mi byed pa*, Dzong-ka-ba reads *mngon par 'du byed pa med pa*; the sūtra omits *skye ba med pa* but includes three others not present in Dzong-ka-ba, *ma byung ba dang/ dngos po med pa dang/ bdag med pa dang/*; and the sūtra reads *bdag po med pa dang rnam par thar pa'i sgo'i bar du bstan pa de dag ni nges pa'i don ces bya ste* whereas Dzong-ka-ba reads *bdag po med pa rnam par thar pa'i sgo ston pa de dag ni nges pa'i don zhes bya'o*.

In the Tibetan, Chandrakīrti's citation of the passage agrees with the Peking edition of the sūtra with two small exceptions: Chandrakīrti reads *shes bdag*, the sūtra *shed bu*; and Chandrakīrti reads *bdag po med pas na/ rnam par thar*, the sūtra *bdag po med pa dang/ rnam par thar*. The portion of the passage concerned with sūtras of interpretable meaning is missing from the Sanskrit of

Chandrakīrti's text. The Sanskrit of the remainder of the passage accords with the Tibetan. Mervyn Sprung's very loose translation of this passage is found on p.45 of his *Lucid Exposition of the Middle Way, the Essential Chapters from the Prasannapadā of Candrakīrti translated from the Sanskrit* (Boulder: Prajñā Press, 1979).

Dzong-ka-ba's citation of the passage differs from Kamalashīla's on only two small points: Kamalashīla reads *bdag po med pa las bdag po lta bur* whereas Dzong-ka-ba reads *bdag po med pa la bdag po lta bur*; and Kamalashīla reads *dngos po stong pa nyid* whereas Dzong-ka-ba reads just *stong pa nyid*.

310 P795, Vol.31, 281.1.5–281.1.6. The Sanskrit as found on 36.1–4 of Buddhist Sanskrit Texts 2 is:

nītārthasūtrāntaviśeṣa jānati
yathopadiṣṭā sugatena śūnyatā/
yāsmin punaḥ pudgala sattva pūruṣo
neyārthatāṃ jānati sarvadharmān//

This sūtra was also cited by Chandrakīrti in chapter one of the *Clear Words*, right after the above passage from the *Teachings of Akṣhayamati Sūtra*, La Vallée Poussin edition, 44.2–5, and also in chapter fifteen, La Vallée Poussin edition, 276.5–8. Sprung's translation of this passage – again very loose – is found on pp.45 and 163.

311 P5287, Vol.101, 46.3.5–46.3.8. This passage in Kamalashīla comes just after his citation of the *Teachings of Akṣhayamati Sūtra* – which, as discussed above, I believe was Dzong-ka-ba's source for the sūtra passage. The passage in the *Ornament Illuminating the Exalted Wisdom Operating in the Sphere of All Buddhas Sūtra* to which Kamalashīla refers is P768, Vol.28, 132.3.2. Kamalashīla seems to be stretching the meaning of the *Teachings of Akṣhayamati Sūtra* to find it saying that no [ultimate] existence of production and so forth are definitive *objects*, since the passage is clearly speaking of sūtras which teach such as being *sūtras* of definitive meaning.

312 P5287, Vol.101, 46.1.5–46.1.6. The wording of the reason clause of the passage as cited in the Peking edition of Kamalashīla's text differs slightly from that cited by Dzong-ka-ba. Dzong-ka-ba (369a.3) reads: *de ni de las logs shig* TU *gzhan* GYIS *gang du'ang drang bar mi nus pa'i phyir ro*. The Peking edition reads: *de ni de las logs shig gzhan gang du yang drang bar mi nus pa'i phyir ro*. Dzong-ka-ba's addition of *tu* and *gyis* make it more explicit that a passage of definitive meaning cannot be interpreted *as* anything else *by* anyone else.

CHAPTER TWO: RELIABLE SOURCES

313 The Tibetan *phyi mo* is sometimes used to translate the Sanskrit word *mātṛkā*, as in Nāgārjuna's *Precious Garland*, verse 394, where it refers to a *model* of the alphabet which a grammarian uses in first teaching his students. A-gya-yong-dzin (165.4) identifies it as an archaic term meaning "root" (*rtsa ba*) or "basis" (*gzhi ma*). See John Buescher's "The Buddhist Doctrine of Two Truths in the Vaibhaṣika and Theravada Schools", (Ann Arbor: University Microfilms, 1982), p.38–9, for a discussion of the usage of this term in early Buddhism. Buescher provides references to additional discussion of the term *mātṛkā* by Padmanabh Jaini in the introduction to his edition of the *Abhidharmadīpa* (Patna: Kashi Prasad Jayaswal Research Institute, 1977); by A.K. Warder in "The Mātikā", pp. xix ff. of A.K. Warder and A.P. Buddhadatta, eds., *Mohavicchedanī: Abhidhammamātikatthavaṇṇanā* (London: Pali Text Society, 1961), and by M. Hofinger, *Étude sur le concile de Vaiśālī* (Louvin: Bureau du Muséon, 1946), Bibliothèque du Muséon, Vol. 20, p.230.

314 These terms appear to have been widely used during the first dissemination of Buddhism to Tibet. David S. Ruegg in his *The Literature of the Madhyamaka School of Philosophy in India*, p.59, provides references to two late

eighth century works by renowned Tibetan scholars and translators in which such a division is set forth: the *Quintessential Instructions on the Stages of the View* (*lta ba'i rim pa'i man ngag*) by Ga-wa-bel-tsek (*ska ba dpal brtsegs*), fol. 140a–b, and the *Features of the View* (*lta ba'i khyad par*) by Ye-shay-day (*ye shes sde*), fol 252b, cf. Manuscrit Pelliot Tibétain 814, fol. 5a seq. and Manuscrit Pelliot Tibétain 116, p.112 seq. For a detailed discussion of the historical progression in the usage of such terminology in Tibet, see K. Mimaki's "The *blo gsal grub mtha'*, and the Mādhyamika Classification in Tibetan *grub mtha'* literature," and his *Blo Gsal Grub Mtha'* (Kyoto: Université de Kyoto, 1982).

Here Dzong-ka-ba only mentions that this way of dividing Mādhyamikas exists and moves immediately to a discussion and rejection of a second way of dividing Mādhyamikas – by way of how they assert the ultimate. (See appendix one for a detailed analysis of this question.) Dzong-ka-ba then returns to the first mode of division – by way of their assertions of conventionalities; he sets forth Ye-shay-day's view and accepts it as a rough chronology but not as an all-inclusive division since Chandrakīrti's Prāsaṅgika system could not be included within it.

315 Sanskrit for these two terms taken from Ruegg's *The Literature of the Madhyamaka School of Philosophy in India*, p.58, who provides a reference for their use by the eleventh century scholar Advayavajra in his *Tattvaratnāvali*, pp.14, 19 seq.

316 Lo-den-shay-rap made this statement in his *Epistolary Essay, Drop of Ambrosia* (*spring yig bdud rtsi'i thigs pa*). Lo-den-shay-rap's text does not appear to have survived, but it is incompletely cited in a commentary on it by the Sa-gya scholar Ser-dok Paṇ-chen (*gser mdog paṇ chen*, 1428–1507) written in 1488, the *Explanation of the "Epistolary Essay, Drop of Ambrosia", Magical Rosary Fulfilling All Wishes* (*spring yig bdud rtsi'i thigs pa'i rnam*

bshad dpag bsam yong 'du'i ljon phreng) available in the Collected works of Gser-mdog Paṇ-chen, (Thimphu, Bhutan: Kunzang Topgey, 1978) Vol.24, 320.6–348.6. The passage to which Dzong-ka-ba refers is at 334.1.2: sgyu ma gnyis med chos kun mi gnas dbu ma pa'i/ lugs gnyis rnam 'byed 'di yang rmongs pa mtshar skyed yin.

317 See three notes above for Ruegg's reference to this division in Ye-shay-day's *Features of the View*. Sha-mar-den-dzin, 31.4–5, adds the further information that in Ye-shay-day's text there is no clear mention of even the names of Buddhapālita and Chandrakīrti.

318 See later in the text, 401b.3–6, where Dzong-ka-ba cites a passage from Chandrakīrti's *Autocommentary on the "Supplement to (Nāgārjuna's) 'Treatise on the Middle Way'"*, in which Chandrakīrti explicitly states that it is unsuitable to compare Prāsaṅgika to any other proponents of tenets because the Prāsaṅgika system is unique. Pa-bong-ka, 105.1, identifies Ba-tsap Nyi-ma-drak as someone who erroneously compares Chandrakīrti to Vaibhāṣhika.

319 In other words, even though the actual terms Svātantrika and Prāsaṅgika as names of the two Mādhyamika schools are not found in Chandrakīrti's *Clear Words*, to separate these two terms out as names for the two schools is quite in accordance with the thought of the *Clear Words* in that a large portion of that text focuses on a defense of Buddhapālita's use of consequences (*prasaṅga*) and a rejection of Bhāvaviveka's use of autonomous (*svatantra*) syllogisms as means for generating in a person a correct understanding of emptiness, and these are concerned with a primary difference in tenet between the two systems.

320 The full title of this text is *Fundamental Stanzas on the Middle Way, Called "Wisdom"* (*dbu ma rtsa ba'i tshig le'ur byas pa shes rab ces bya ba*, *prajñānāmamūlamadhyamakakārikā*). When cited in Tibetan texts, it is usually referred to by one of two abbreviated titles: *Fundamental*

Wisdom (*rtsa ba shes rab*, *prajñamūla*) or *Treatise on the Middle Way* (*dbu ma'i bstan bcos*, *madhyamakaśāstra*). In order to avoid the confusion that would be engendered by referring to the same text with multiple titles, I have chosen to cite the text always as the *Treatise on the Middle Way* regardless of which occurs in the Tibetan. Also, although the former abbreviated title is numerically more prevalent, I have chosen to use the latter since it is more suggestive of the subject matter of the text while still not being overly long.

CHAPTER THREE: STAGES OF ENTRY INTO SUCHNESS

321 Here Dzong-ka-ba only mentions that the view of the transitory is the root of cyclic existence and, unlike his treatment in the *Medium Length Exposition of Special Insight*, does not discuss at all the many questions that this suggests. At this juncture in the *Medium Length Exposition of Special Insight*, he goes into the matter in depth. See Thurman's translation, pp.118–25, and Hopkins' translation, pp.8–50.

322 This passage is found in the Dharamsala edition at the beginning of chapter eighteen, 284.1–11. The Sanskrit for the passage (La Vallée Poussin edition, 340.3–12, including correction by de Jong in "Textcritical Notes on the Prasannapadā", [*Indo-Iranian Journal* 20 (1978), pp.25–59 and 217–52], p.224) is:

yadi kleśāḥ karmāṇi ca dehāś ca kartāraś ca phalāni ca sarvam etan na tattvaṃ kevalaṃ tu gandharvanagarād-ivad atatvam eva sattattvākāreṇa pratibhāsate bālā-nāṃ / kiṃ punar atra tattvaṃ kathaṃ vā tattvasyāvatāra iti // ucyate/ ādhyātmikabāhyāśeṣavastvanupalam-bhenādhyātmaṃ bahiś ca yaḥ sarvathāhaṃkārama-makāraparikṣaya idam atra tattvaṃ/ tattvāvatāraḥ punaḥ/satkāyadṛṣṭiprabhavān aśeṣān kleśāṃś ca doṣāṃś ca dhiyā vipaśyan/ātmānam asya viṣayaṃ ca buddhvā yogī karotyātmaniṣedham eva//ityādinā madhyamakāvatārādvistareṇāvaseyaḥ//

French translation by de Jong in *Cinq Chapitres*, p.1; English translation by Sprung on p.165. The Tibetan of the passage from Chandrakīrti's *Supplement to (Nāgārjuna's) "Treatise on the Middle Way"* can be found in La Vallée Poussin's edition of the Tibetan on p.233; La Vallée Poussin's translation of that into French is found in *Muséon* XII (1911), p.282.

This and the following two passages from the *Clear Words* as cited by Dzong-ka-ba differ in numerous small points from those passages in the Dharmsala edition of the *Clear Words* but none of the differences are substantive. The only difference which requires noting is that twice when citing Chandrakīrti – once in the *Clear Words* and once in the *[Auto]commentary* – Dzong-ka-ba quotes phrases referring to the aggregates as the *basis* (*gzhi*) of designation as the self whereas Chandrakīrti's texts themselves use the term *cause* (*gyu*).

The Dharmsala edition of Dzong-ka-ba's text, 373a.2, has been corrected from *snang ba yin no* to *snang ba yin na* in accordance with the Dra-shi-hlun-bo edition of Dzong-ka-ba, 126.3, and the Sanskrit of the *Clear Words*.

323 This follows almost immediately after the above passage, and is found in the Dharmsala edition, 284.12–285.2. The Sanskrit for the passage (La Vallée Poussin edition, 340.13–15, with corrections from de Jong, p.224) is:

iha yogī tattvam avatinīrṣu niravaśeṣakleśadoṣān parijihāsur eva upaparīkṣate kiṃmūlako 'yam samsāra iti/ sa caivam upaparīkṣamāṇaḥ satkāyadṛṣṭimūlakaṃ samsāram anupaśyaṃs tasyāś ca satkāyadṛṣṭer ālambanam ātmānam eva samanupaśyannātmānupalambhāc ca satkāyadṛṣṭiprahāṇaṃ tatprahāṇāc ca sarvakleśavyāvṛttiṃ samanupaśyan prathamataram ātmānam evopaparīkṣate ko 'yam ātmā nāmeti yo 'haṃkāraviṣayaḥ/

French translation by de Jong in *Cinq Chapitres*, pp.1–2; English translation by Sprung on p.165 –

Sprung has not caught the sense of the passage.

The Dharmsala edition of Dzong-ka-ba, 372a.6, has been corrected from *'jigs tshogs la lta ba spong* to *'jig tshogs la lta ba spong* in accordance with the Dharmsala edition of Chandrakīrti's *Clear Words* and the Dra-shi-hlun-bo edition of Dzong-ka-ba, 127.1.

324 The qualm is that all that has been described is a state of removing the obstructions to liberation – actions and afflictions – which is achieved even by Hīnayānists, and no mention has been made of removing the obstructions to omniscience, which must be eliminated if one is to achieve Buddhahood. The second part of the qualm concerns the fact that all that is explicitly mentioned is realization of the selflessness of the person, whereas Mahāyānists must realize the selflessness of both persons and all other phenomena.

The Dharmsala edition of Dzong-ka-ba, 372b.4, has been corrected from *thob pa'i de kho na nyid* to *thob bya'i de kho na nyid* in accordance with the Dra-shi-hlun-bo edition, 127.5, and the Delhi edition of the *Annotations*, 185.2.

325 373a.1, text corrected from *do'i yan lag* to *de'i yan lag* in accordance with the Dra-shi-hlun-bo edition, 128.2, and the Delhi edition of the *Annotations*, 186.5.

326 This passage is from chapter eighteen, Tibetan in Tibetan Government Printing Press edition, 288.10–20; Sanskrit for the passage (La Vallée Poussin edition, 345.13–346.3, with corrections by de Jong, p.225) is:

> upādāya prajñapyamāna eva tv avidyāviparyāsānugatānāmātmābhiniveśāspadabhūto mumukṣubhir vicāryate yasyedaṃ skandhapañcakam upādānatvena pratibhāsate kim asau skandhalakṣaṇa utāskandhalakṣaṇa iti/ sarvathā ca vicārayanto mumukṣavo naivam upalabhante bhāvasvabhāvataḥ/ tadaiṣāṃ
>
> ātmanyasati cātmīyaṃ kuta eva bhaviṣyati/ ātmānupalambhād ātmaprajñaptyupādānaṃ skandhapañcakam ātmīyam api sutarāṃ nopalabhante/ yathaiva

hi dagdhe rathe tadaṅgānyapi dagdhatvān nopalabhyante evaṃ yogino yadaivātmanairātmyaṃ pratipadyante tadaivātmī-yaskandhavastunairātmyam api niyataṃ pratipadyante//

French translation by de Jong in *Cinq Chapitres*, p.7; English translation by Sprung on pp.168–9.

The Dharmsala edition of Dzong-ka-ba, 373a.2, has been corrected from *ba rten* to *brten* in accordance with the Dra-shi-hlun-bo edition, 128.3, and the Dharmsala edition of the *Clear Words*, 288.10. Also, the Dharmsala edition of Dzong-ka-ba, 373a.3, has been corrected in two places from *dbyod* to *dpyod* in accordance with the Dra-shi-hlun-bo edition, 128.4, and the Dharmsala edition of the *Clear Words*, 288.13.

327 Dzong-ka-ba's citation of this passage omits here the phrase "five aggregates" as an appositive to "the mine" which is found in both the Sanskrit and the Dharmsala Tibetan edition of the *Clear Words*.

328 Chapter One, p.20.5–9 in the La Vallée Poussin edition of the Tibetan, pp. 17.20–18.3 in the Council of Cultural and Religious Affairs edition, commenting on I.8. La Vallée Poussin's translation is found in *Muséon* 8 (1907) p.269. The passage cited from Nāgārjuna's *Precious Garland* is verse I.35ab, for which the Sanskrit as cited in Hahn's Sanskrit-Tibetan-Chinese edition is:

skandhagrāho yāvad asti
tāvad evāham ity api/

Hopkins' translation of the *Precious Garland* verse is on p.22.

329 Toh 3842, Tokyo *sde dge* Vol.1, 240b.2, commenting on XVIII.2. An edited Tibetan text and English translation of chapter eighteen of Buddhapālita's text by Christian Lindtner is available in the *Indo-Iranian Journal* 23 (1981), pp.187–217. This passage is found on p.201.

330 See pp.50–1 for a discussion of this translation of the term *dngos por smra ba* (*vastusatpadārthavādin*).

331 The basic import of the qualm, according to Sha-mar-

den-dzin, 40.3–44.4, is the following: Dzong-ka-ba, based on Chandrakīrti, has just said that when one realizes the person as without inherent existence, one is at that point also able to realize phenomena as without inherent existence. In the Prāsaṅgika system, whatever is without inherent existence is necessarily an imputed existent, and if one had realized that something – for example, the person – was an imputed existent, one would have realized that it was without inherent existence. Therefore the qualm being raised is that since the non-Prāsaṅgika schools assert that the person is imputedly existent, this must mean that those schools realize the non-inherent existence of the person and from this it would follow that they would realize the non-inherent existence of the aggregates. This is unacceptable from the viewpoint of Prāsaṅgika which holds that selflessness is realized only by way of the Prāsaṅgika view. Furthermore, that Hīnayānists realize the selflessness of phenomena contradicts the tenets of the other Mahāyāna schools – Chittamātra and Svātantrika – which make the distinction that Hīnayānists realize only the selflessness of the person whereas Mahāyānists realize both the selflessness of persons and of phenomena.

The essence of Dzong-ka-ba's response to this qualm is to make the distinction that although the non-Prāsaṅgika schools may *assert* that the person is imputedly existent, this does not mean that they *realize* the person to be imputedly existent and hence also does not mean that they realize the person to be without inherent existence. He makes this distinction based on the fact that even though in all Buddhist schools (with the possible exception of the Vatsīputrīyas) the person is asserted as imputedly existent, there are many different meanings of "imputed existence" and not all are accepted by all tenet systems nor is the meaning intended in the assertion of the person as imputedly existent the same in all tenet systems.

In the systems of the Vaibhāṣhikas and the Sautrāntikas following scripture, imputed existent is coextensive with conventional truth, and its meaning can be understood from the definition of a conventional truth: that of which the mind apprehending it is suitable to be cancelled due to its being destroyed or broken down by the mind. The person is an imputed existent because the mind apprehending a person is cancelled when you remove all the parts of the person, as for instance, when you separate out the aggregates one by one.

In the system of the Sautrāntikas Following Reasoning, ultimate truths are those things which exist from their own side without being merely imputed by names and thoughts, and conventional truths are those phenomena which are merely imputed by terms and thoughts. All impermanent phenomena are ultimate truths, and all permanent ones are conventional truths, and there is one meaning of substantially and imputedly existent which parallels this division, substantial existence meaning the capacity to perform functions and imputed existence meaning an existent that lacks such capacity. In this sense the person is substantially existent since it is an impermanent phenomenon; however, there is another meaning for imputed existence based on whether or not a phenomenon can be identified without some other phenomenon having to appear to the mind, and in that sense the person is an imputed existent – the person can only be identified by way of the aggregates appearing to the mind and thus is an imputed existent.

The Chittamātrins and the Svātantrikas also rely mainly on that identification of the meaning of imputed existence when they posit the person as imputedly existent.

In Prāsaṅgika, however, the term takes on quite a different meaning. Substantial existence is equated with inherent existence or existence in its own right whereas imputed existence entails being merely nominally imputed. In the Prāsaṅgika system nothing is substantially existent, and all phenomena including the person are merely imputedly existent. Thus the Prāsaṅgika meaning of the term is considerably more far-reaching and subtle than what is posited by the other schools of tenets. If one had realized the person to be imputedly existent in the Prāsaṅgika sense, then one would indeed have realized the person's lack of inherent existence, but the Prāsaṅgikas say that the lower schools have not realized that imputed existence. The name is the same; they assert the person to be merely imputedly existent, but they have not realized this subtle meaning.

This same distinction holds true with respect to the response given in the next paragraph, that if one accepted the reasoning of the person raising the qualm, then one would be forced to assert that those Hīnayānists – the Vaibhāṣhikas and Sautrāntikas Following Scripture – who assert that gross objects such as eyes, sprouts, and so forth are imputedly existent would realize them to be without inherent existence. They do not realize such, and again the reason is that although they assert such gross objects to be imputedly existent, they do not realize this in the sense of its subtle meaning and hence do not realize non-inherent existence. That the non-Mādhyamika schools do not themselves assert that phenomena other than the person lack inherent existence is supported by the fact that Haribhadra – a Svātantrika-Mādhyamika – feels the need to bring up and refute an objection by Proponents of True Existence to the Mādhyamika assertion that such objects lack true existence.

Dzong-ka-ba's wording of the qualm is a bit difficult to follow, and Sha-mar-den-dzin offers the most promising line of explanation. In describing the objector's position, Dzong-ka-ba says: "Even the Proponents of True Existence of our own Buddhist sects who assert that the person is imputedly existent do not assert that the person is ultimately established." In fact, it is not the case that all of the Proponents of True Existence do not assert that the person is ultimately established. For Vaibhāṣhika and Sautrāntika Following Scripture, the person is asserted to be conventionally established, but for Sautrāntika Following Reasoning and Chittamātra the person is asserted to be ultimately established. Thus Sha-mar explains the line as indicating something that is forced on one by reasoning when one interprets the meaning of imputed existence in accordance with the Prāsaṅgika assertions. He interprets the passage as follows:

> Since the Proponents of True Existence assert that the person is imputedly existent, it is not suitable that they do anything else except not assert that [the person] is established ultimately. And, one must also assert that they realize that the person is not established ultimately. Therefore, in that case, they would realize that eyes and so forth are without inherent existence. (41.1–41.2)

332 *Clear Meaning Commentary* is the title used in Tibetan traditions to refer to Haribhadra's *Commentary on (Maitreya's) "Ornament for Clear Realization"* (*mngon par rtogs pa'i rgyan ces bya ba'i 'grel pa, abhisamayālaṃkāravṛtti*), P5191, Vol.90. This passage is from chapter four, 291.4.3–291.4.4, a point at which objections by the Proponents of True Existence are being discussed.

333 The Dharmsala edition of Dzong-ka-ba, 374b.3, has been corrected from *med* to *ming* in accordance with the Dra-shi-hlun-bo edition, 131.3, and the Delhi edition of the *Annotations*, 196.1.

CHAPTER FOUR: MISIDENTIFYING THE OBJECT OF NEGATION

334 *Bodhicaryāvatāra*, edited by Vidhushekhara Bhattacharya, (Calcutta: The Asiatic Society, 1960), p.221. The Sanskrit is:

kalpitaṃ bhāvam aspṛṣṭvā
tadabhāvo na gṛhyate/

English translation by Marion Matics in *Entering the Path of Enlightenment* (New York: Macmillan Co., 1970), p.224, (mistranslated) and by Stephen Batchelor in *A Guide to the Bodhisattva's Way of Life* (Dharmsala: Library of Tibetan Works & Archives, 1979), p.161. Commentary by the contemporary Ge-luk-ba scholar Kelsang Gyatso in *Meaningful to Behold* (London: Wisdom Publications, 1980), p.313.

335 "Lose belief" translates the Tibetan term *sun phyung ba*. This term usually means "to refute" or "to eradicate"; however it is often used in contexts in which it must refer to the agent of the verb rather than the object and in those situations it is better translated as "to lose belief". For instance, if it were taken in this context as referring to the object of verb and were translated as "refute", the passage would read, "you will refute the stages of the dependent-arising of cause and effect". This is something that cannot in fact be done, since the dependent-arising of cause and effect is a validly established existent. What can be done is that oneself will lose belief in those, and that such is the intention of the passage is supported by the remainder of the sentence, "whereby you will fall to an extreme of annihilation and due to just that view will be led to a bad transmigration." – The object of the action of the verb, the dependent-arising of cause and effect, has not been harmed due to being "refuted"; oneself, the agent of the verb, has been harmed due to a "loss of belief".

336 A-gya-yong-dzin, 167.6–168.2, identifies those holding this position as the followers of the great translator of Ngok, Lo-den-shay-rap, and his spiritual sons as well as the followers of Tang-sak-ba (*thang sag pa*) and so forth, and says that from among those, Lo-den-shay-rap, Cha-ba-chö-seng (*cha/phya pa chos seng*), Gun-kyen-rong-dön (*kun mkhyen rong ston*), and so forth upheld Svātantrika

tenets whereas Bo-dong Chok-lay-nam-gyel (*bo dong phyogs las rnam rgyal*) upheld the tenets of Chandrakīrti. See pp.85–7 and note 75 for further discussion.

337 P795, Vol.31, 283.5.1–283.5.2. The Sanskrit from the Vaidya edition, p.47, is:

na cakṣuḥ pramāṇaṃ na śrotra ghrāṇaṃ
na jihvā pramāṇaṃ na kāyacittam/
pramāṇa yady eta bhaveyur indriyā
kasyāryamārgeṇa bhaveta kāryam//

338 La Vallée Poussin's edition of the Tibetan, p.112.18. La Vallée Poussin's translation is found in *Muséon* 11 (1910), p.308.

339 La Vallée Poussin's edition of the Tibetan, p.122.14–17.
La Vallée Poussin's translation is found in *Muséon* 11 (1910), p.315.

340 376a.5, text corrected from *don mi rigs* to *de ni mi rigs* in accordance the Dra-shi-hlun-bo edition, 134.4, and the Delhi edition of the *Annotations*, 204.6.

341 La Vallée Poussin's edition of the Tibetan, p.114.4. La Vallée Poussin's translation is found in *Muséon* 11 (1910), p.309.

342 376b.1, text corrected from *rang gi ngo bos grub pas rang bzhin* to *rang gi ngo bos grub pa'i rang bzhin* in accordance with the Dra-shi-hlun-bo edition, 134.6, and the Delhi edition of the *Annotations*, 205.6.

CHAPTER FIVE: THE UNCOMMON FEATURE OF MĀDHYAMIKA

343 This is part two of a heading that occurred in the previous chapter and was entitled "refuting an overly broad identification of the object of negation". Part one was a statement of others' assertions, and part two, begun here, is the demonstration that those assertions are incorrect.

344 The Dra-shi-hlun-bo edition, 135.3, reads *dbu ma* PA'I *lan ji ltar btab pa* whereas the Dharmsala edition, 376b.4, reads *dbu ma* PAS *lan ji ltar btab pa*. The Dharmsala reading is preferred.

345 Toh 3825, Tokyo *sde dge* Vol.1, 22b.4–5; The Tibetan is also available in Lindtner's *Nagarjuniana*, p.160; his English translation is found on p.161.

346 Chandrakīrti makes a very clear statement to this effect in the *Clear Words* (Dharmsala edition of the Tibetan, 421.18– 422.1; Sanskrit in La Vallée Poussin's edition, 499.12– 13):

> You [Proponents of True Existence], superimposing a meaning of the non-existence of things as the meaning of emptiness, state [unwanted] consequences [to us]. We de not explain the meaning of emptiness as a meaning of the non-existence of things. Then what is it? It is a meaning of dependent-arising.

For a discussion of the way in which the meaning of emptiness serves as the meaning of dependent-arising, see Hopkins' *Meditation on Emptiness*, pp.170–71. Dzong-ka-ba gives a brief indication of this in his *Ocean of Reasoning, Explanation of* (*Nāgārjuna's*) *"Treatise on the Middle Way"*, *rje tsong kha pa'i gsung dbu ma'i lta ba'i skor* edition, 133.15–134.1 (commenting on Nāgārjuna's *Treatise on the Middle Way*, XXIV.18ab):

> With respect to the way in which the meaning of emptiness serves as the meaning of dependent-arising, this is for Mādhyamikas who have refuted inherent establishment with valid cognition, not for others. When such a Mādhyamika explicitly ascertains internal and external things as dependent-arisings which depend upon causes, in dependence upon the force of that very awareness, there is ascertainment of the meaning of the emptiness of inherent existence. For, [that Mādhyamika] realizes that what is inherently established does not depend on any other and realizes with valid cognition that that is contradictory with dependent-arising.

347 The Tibetan is found in the Dharmsala edition of the *Clear Words*, p.400.1–2. The Sanskrit from La Vallée Poussin's edition, p.475, is:

yadi śūnyam idaṃ sarvam udayo nāsti na vyayaḥ/
catūrṇām āryasatyānām abhāvas te prasajyate//

French translation by Jacques May can be found in *Candrakīrti Prasannapadā Madhyamakavṛtti*, p.206. English translation by Mervyn Sprung in the *Lucid Exposition of the Middle Way* is on p.223.

348 Toh 3828, Tokyo *sde dge* Vol.1, 28a.2. The Sanskrit as found in Lindtner's *Nagarjuniana*, p.76, is:

sarveṣām bhāvānāṃ sarvatra na vidyate svabhāvaś cet/
tvadvacanam asvabhāvaṃ na nivartayituṃ svabhāvam alam//

English translation by K. Bhattacharya can be found in *The Dialectical Method of Nāgārjuna*, (Delhi: Motilal Banarsidass, 1978), p.5.

349 The Tibetan is found in the Dharmsala edition of the *Clear Words*, pp.421.8–10 and 422.5–7. The Sanskrit from La Vallée Poussin's edition, pp.499 and 500, is:

śūnyatāyāmadhilayaṃ yaṃ punaḥ kurute bhavān/
doṣaprasaṅgo nāsmākam sa śūnye nopapadyate//

sarvaṃ ca yujyate tasya śūnyatā yasya yujyate/
sarvaṃ na yujyate tasya śūnyam yasya na yujyate//

The translation of XXIV.13 follows the Tibetan word order which differs a bit from that of the Sanskrit but accords with Chandrakīrti's commentary on the verse. In XXIV.14, the bracketing in of "system" as the referent of "that" is taken from Dzong-ka-ba's *Ocean of Reasoning, Explanation of (Nāgārjuna's) "Treatise on the Middle Way"*, *rje tsong kha pa'i gsung dbu ma'i lta ba'i skor* edition, 130.9.

A French translation of these verses by Jacques May can be found in *Candrakīrti Prasannapadā Madhyamakavṛtti*, pp.233 and 234. English translation by Mervyn Sprung in the *Lucid Exposition of the Middle Way* is found on pp.234 and 235.

Note that XXIV.14 offers support for the view that Indian authors sometimes used the terms *śūnya* – empty – and *śūnyatā* – emptiness – interchangeably; in this case Nāgārjuna's switch from one to the other is seemingly determined only by meter. Both were translated into Tibetan as *stong pa nyid* – emptiness.

The Dharmsala edition of Dzong-ka-ba's text, 378a.1, reads *gang de* NGA *la mi 'thad do*, whereas the Dra-shi-hlun-bo edition, 137.6, reads *gang de* DE *la mi 'thad do*. The Dharmsala reading is supported by the Sanskrit.

350 The Tibetan can be found in the Dharmsala edition of the *Clear Words*, 422.2–6. The Sanskrit from La Vallée Poussin's edition, 500.1–3, is:

> na ca kevalaṃ tathoktadoṣaprasaṅgo 'smatpakṣe nāvatarati api khalu sarvam eva satyādivyavasthānaṃ sutarām upapadyata iti pratipādayann āha/
> sarvaṃ ca yujyate tasya śūnyatā yasya yujyate/

French translation by Jacques May can be found in *Candrakīrti Prasannapadā Madhyamakavṛtti*, p.234. May's translation is a bit loose, missing the "not only this, but also that" sense of Chandrakīrti's commentary. English translation by Mervyn Sprung in the *Lucid Exposition of the Middle Way* is found on p.235.

351 The twelve links of dependent-arising are (1) ignorance, (2) action, (3) consciousness, (4) name and form, (5) sources, (6) contact, (7) feeling, (8) attachment, (9) grasping, (10) existence, (11) birth, and (12) aging and death. The stages of the generation of the forward process are that through ignorance, actions are generated; through actions, consciousness is generated, and so forth, and thus the process of cyclic existence continues. The stages of the cessation of the reverse process is that through stopping ignorance, actions are stopped; through stopping actions, consciousness is stopped, and thus the process of cyclic existence can be brought to a halt, with the key to stopping the process being the removal of ignorance.

352 The Tibetan is found in the Dharmsala edition of the *Clear Words*, pp.425.1–3 and 426.5–7. The Sanskrit from La Vallée Poussin's edition, pp.503.10–11 and 505.2–3, is:

yaḥ pratītyasamutpādaḥ śūnyatāṃ tāṃ pracakṣmahe
sā prajñaptir upādāya pratipat saiva madhyamā//

apratītya samutpanno dharmaḥ kaścin na yidyate/
yasmāt tasmād aśūnyo 'hi dharmaḥ kaścin na vidyate//

The translation of verse 18 does not follow the *Annotations*, but rather relies on the Sanskrit and Dzong-ka-ba's explanation of it in his *Ocean of Reasoning, Explanation of (Nāgārjuna's) "Treatise on the Middle Way"*. The bracketed material in the translation of verse 18 is taken from Dzong-ka-ba's *Ocean of Reasoning, Explanation of (Nāgārjuna's) "Treatise on the Middle Way"*, *rje tsong kha pa'i gsung dbu ma'i lta ba'i skor* edition, 132.8–11 and 134.7–8.

French translation by Jacques May can be found in *Candrakīrti Prasannapadā Madhyamakavṛtti*, pp.237 and 239. Mervyn Sprung's interpretive English translation can be found in the *Lucid Exposition of the Middle Way* on pp.238 and 239.

353 Toh 3828, Tokyo *sde dge* Vol.1, 29a.5–6. The Sanskrit as edited by Johnston and Kunst in *The Dialectical Method of Nāgārjuna*, p.52 and 53, is:

prabhavati ca śūnyateyaṃ yasya prabhavanti tasya sarvārthāḥ
prabhavati na tasya kiṃ cin na prabhavati śūnyatā yasya//

yaḥ śūnyatāṃ pratītyasamutpādaṃ madhyamāṃ pratipadaṃ ca
ekārthāṃ nijagāda praṇamāmi tam apratima-buddham//

The Tibetan of the concluding homage as found in the Tokyo *sde dge*, both in Nāgārjuna's *Refutation of Objections* (29a.6) and his *Commentary on the Refutation of*

Objections (Toh 3832, Vol.1, 137a.4) differs on one significant point from the way the verse is cited by Dzong-ka-ba. Dzong-ka-ba cites it as:

gang zhig stong dang rten 'byung *dang*
dbu ma'i lam du don gcig par

It is found in those texts as

gang zhig stong dang rten 'byung *dag*
dbu ma'i lam du don gcig par/

Whereas the latter versions would make the passage say that dependent-arising and emptiness are of one meaning as the Mādhyamika path, Dzong-ka-ba has taken it as saying that dependent-arising, emptiness, and the Mādhyamika path are of one meaning. His interpretation is supported by the Sanskrit and by Chandrakīrti's statement in the Chandrakīrti's *Clear Words* (Dharmsala edition of the Tibetan, 426.3–5; La Vallée Poussin edition of the Sanskrit, 504.15–16) that emptiness, dependent designation, and middle path are different names for dependentarising. (*de'i phyir de ltar na stong pa nyid dang/ brten nas gdags pa dang/ dbu ma'i lam zhes bya 'di dag ni rten cing 'brel par 'byung ba nyid kyi ming gi bye brag yin no*).

English translation of these two verses by K. Bhattacharya can be found in *The Dialectical Method of Nāgārjuna*, pp.47–8.

354 Toh 3827, Tokyo *sde dge* Vol.1, 26b.4–5. As found in the Tokyo *sde dge* edition, translation by Shu-nu-chok (*gzhon nu mchog*), Dar-ma-drak (*dar ma grags*), and Ku (*khu*), the verse differs significantly in wording (though not in meaning) from that same verse as found in Nāgārjuna's *Commentary on the "Seventy Stanzas on Emptiness"* (Toh 3831, Tokyo *sde dge* Vol.1, 120b.3), translation by Jinamitra and Ye-shay-day (*ye shes sde*). See Lindtner's *Nagarjuniana*, p.32, for a discussion of different versions of the text and p.65 for his English translation of this verse. Dzong-ka-ba's citation of the verse is basically that found in Nāgārjuna's *Commentary*.

There the verse reads:

dngos po thams cad rang bzhin gyis/
stong pa yin pas dngos rnams kyi*s*/
rten 'byung *de* ni de bzhin gshegs/
mtshungs pa med *par* nye bar bstan//

As cited by Dzong-ka-ba, the verse reads:

dngos po thams cad rang bzhin gyis/
stong pa yin pas dngos rnams kyi/
rten 'byung *phyir* ni de bzhin gshegs/
mtshungs pa med pa*s* nye bar bstan//

Dzong-ka-ba's use of the genitive rather than the instrumental in the second line and his use of the instrumental rather than the accusative in the fourth line accord with Nāgārjuna's commentary on the verse (120b.3–4): *dgnos po thams cad rang bzhin gyis stong pa yin pas/ dngos po rnams kyi brten nas 'byung ba 'di de bzhin gshegs pas nye bar bstan to/*. Also Lindtner has edited the verse thus in his *Nagarjuniana*, p.64. It is difficult to explain Dzong-ka-ba's use in the third line of *phyir* rather than *de*, and I have not followed his reading in translating the verse.

355 Toh 3825, Tokyo *sde dge* Vol.1, 22a.2–3. The Tibetan is also available in Lindtner's *Nagarjuniana*, p.114. The first line of stanza 43 reads *DE dag gis ni* in the Tokyo *sde dge* edition, whereas Dzong-ka-ba has cited it as *GANG dag gis ni*. Dzong-ka-ba's citation accords with Lindtner's edited edition and with sense.

356 The Tibetan can be found in Lindtner's *Nagarjuniana*, pp.134 and 136. The Sanskrit from Lindtner is:

svayaṃkṛtaṃ parakṛtaṃ dvābhyāṃ kṛtam ahetukam/
tārkikair iṣyate duḥkhaṃ tvayā tūktaṃ pratītyajam//

yaḥ pratītyasamutpādaḥ śūnyatā saiva te matā/
bhāvaḥ svatantro nāstīti siṃhanādas tavātulaḥ//

Dzong-ka-ba's citation of verse 21cd differs somewhat in wording from Lindtner's version, but the differences are not substantive. Dzong-ka-ba's says:

rgyu med *rtog ge pa yis* 'dod/
khyod kyis *rten cing 'brel par* gsungs//

Lindtner's version reads:

rgyu med *par ni rtog ge* 'dod/
khyod kyis *brten nas 'byung bar* gsungs//

It should be noted that the Tibetan translation of verse 22 says *stong pa* (empty) rather than the *stong pa nyid* (emptiness) which would be a literal translation of the Sanskrit; "empty" fits the passage better, and again this would seem to support the view that the two Sanskrit terms were used somewhat interchangeably. Following the Tibetan, I have translated the term as "empty". However, the Tibetan also differs from the Sanskrit in the placement of the adjective "unequalled" (*mnyam med*, *atulaḥ*); the Tibetan has it modify "you", whereas in the Sanskrit it agrees in gender and number with "lion's roar". In this, I have followed the Sanskrit.

Lindtner's English translation is found on pp. 135 and 137 of his *Nagarjuniana*.

CHAPTER SIX: DEPENDENT-ARISING AND EMPTINESS

357 The Tibetan is found in the Dharmsala edition of the Tibetan, 422.7–423.10. The Sanskrit as found in La Vallée Poussin's edition, 500.5–501.8, is cited below. The material in brackets is missing from the Tibetan; see the following five notes.

yasya hi sarvabhāvasvabhāvaśūnyateyaṃ yujyate tasya sarvametadyathopavarṇitaṃ yujyate/ kathaṃ kṛtvā/ yasmātpratītyasamutpādaṃ hi vayaṃ śūnyatetivyācakṣmahe/

[yaḥ pratyayairjāyati sa hyajāto
na tasya utpāda svabhāvato 'sti/
yaḥ pratyayādhonu sa śūnya ukto
yaḥ śūnyatāṃ jānati so 'pramattaḥ//

iti gāthāvacanāt// śūnyāḥ sarvadharmā niḥsvabhāvayogeneti prajñāpāramitābhidhānāt//] tasmādyasyeyaṃ śūnyatā yujyate [rocate kṣamate] tasya pratītyasamutpādo yujyate/ yasya pratītysamutpādo yujyate tasya catvāryāryasatyāni yujyante/ kathaṃ kṛtvā yasmātpratītyasamutpannameva hi duḥkhaṃ bhavati nāpratītyasamutpannaṃ/ tacca niḥsvabhāvatvācchūnyam/ sati ca duḥkhe duḥkhasamudayo duḥkhanirodho duḥkhanirodhagāminī ca pratipadyujyate tataśca duḥkhaparijñānaṃ samudayaprahāṇaṃ mirodhasaksātkaraṇaṃ mārgabhāvanā ca yujyate sati ca duḥkhādisatyaparijñānādike phalāni yujyante satsu ca phaleṣu phalasthā yujyante satsu ca phalastheṣu pratipannakā yujyante satsu ca pratipannakaphalastheṣu saṅgho yujyate āryasatyānāṃ ca sadbhāve sati saddharmo 'pi yujyate sati ca saddharme saṅghe ca buddho 'pi yujyate/ tataśca trīṇyapi ratnāni yujyante/ laukikalokottarāśca padārthāḥ sarve viśeṣādhigamā yujyante/ dharmādharmaṃ tatphalaṃ [sugatirdurgatir]laukikāśca sarvasaṃvyavahārā yujyante// tadevaṃ

sarvaṃ ca yujyate tasya śūnyatā yasya yujate/
[yasya sarvabhāvasvabhāvaśūnyatā yujyate tasya sarvametadyathoditaṃ yujyate saṃpadyata ityarthaḥ/]
yasya tu śūnyatā [yathoditā] na yujyate tasya pratītyasamutpādābhāvātsarvaṃ na yujyate/

French translation by Jacques May can be found in *Candrakīrti Prasannapadā Madhyamakavṛtti*, pp.234–6; English translation by Mervyn Sprung in the *Lucid Exposition of the Middle Way* is on pp.235–6.

358 The Sanskrit here includes some material missing from the Tibetan:

"For, a stanza [the *Questions of the King of Nāgas, Anavatapta, Sūtra* (*klu'i rgyal po ma dros pas zhus pa'i mdo, anavataptanāgarājaparipṛcchāsūtra*)] says:

Whatever is produced from conditions is not produced;
It does not have an inherent nature of production.
Whatever depends upon conditions is said to be empty;
One who knows emptiness is aware.

A Perfection of Wisdom Sūtra [the *One Hundred and Fifty Means Perfection of Wisdom Sūtra* (*shes rab kyi pha rol tu phyin pa'i tshul brgya lnga bcu pa'i mdo, prajñāpāramitānayaśatapañcāśatikāsūtra*)] explains, 'All phenomena are empty in the manner of being without inherent existence'." Both of these passages are cited again in the Sanskrit four pages later (La Vallée Poussin edition, 504.1–7) and they are found there in the Tibetan (Dharmsala edition, 425.6–13).

359 The Sanskrit adds here two more terms, "satisfactory" (*rocate*) and "permissible" (*kṣamate*).

360 The Tibetan use of the verb "reasonable" (*rigs pa*) is not mirrored by the Sanskrit which says *yujyate* – translated into Tibetan in all other occurrences in this passage as *rung ba*, "suitable".

361 The Sanskrit adds here as explanation of what those effects are, "good and bad transmigrations".

362 The Sanskrit adds a sentence: "This means that for that [system] in which an emptiness of inherent existence of all things is suitable, all these things mentioned above are suitable and agreeable."

363 Toh 3828, Tokyo *sde dge* Vol.1, 27b.5. There the Tibetan of the verse reads:

rten rnams 'byung ba'i dngos rnams gang/
de ni stong nyid ces brjod de/
gang zhig rten nas 'byung ba de/
rang bzhin med pa nyid yin no/

Dzong-ka-ba has cited the verse as it is found in Nāgārjuna's *Commentary on the "Refutation of Objections"*, Toh 3832, Tokyo *sde dge* Vol.1, 126b.2–3:

dngos rnams rten nas byung ba gang/
de ni stong nyid ces bya dang/
gang zhig rten nas 'byung ba de/
rang bzhin nyid med yin par smra/

(Dzong-ka-ba's citation of the last life differs in word order: he has cited it as *rang bzhin med nyid yin par smra*.) There is no significant difference in meaning between the two versions. The Sanskrit for the verse, as edited by Johnston and Kunst in *The Dialectical Method of Nāgārjuna*, p.23, mirrors the version found in the *Refutation of Objections* and is:

yaśca pratītyabhāvo bhāvānāṃ śūnyateti sā proktā/
yaśca pratītyabhāvo bhavati hi tasyāsvabhāvatvam//

The translation here accords with Dzong-ka-ba's citation of the verse except for following the Sanskrit and the *Refutation of Objections* version of the Tibetan in taking the connective between the second and third lines as "for" rather than "and" as cited by Dzong-ka-ba and found in the *Commentary on the "Refutation of Objections"* version.

An English translation by Bhattacharya can be found in *The Dialectical Method of Nāgārjuna*, p.17.

364 Toh 3832, Tokyo *sde dge* Vol.1, 126b.3–127a.1. Dzong-ka-ba's citation of the passage differs on numerous small points from the Tokyo *sde dge*; none are significant. The Sanskrit as edited by Johnston and Kunst can be found in *The Dialectical Method of Nāgārjuna*, p.24. (The bracketed material is not in the Tibetan; see the following two notes):

śūnyatārthaṃ ca bhavān bhāvānāmanavasāya pravṛtta upālambhaṃ vaktuṃ tvadvacanasya niḥsvabhāvatvād-bhāvānāṃ svabhāvapratiṣedho nopapadyata iti/ iha hi yaḥ pratītyabhāvo bhāvānāṃ sā śūnyatā/ kasmāt/ niḥsvabhāvatvāt/ ye hi pratītyasamutpannā bhāvās te na sasvabhāvā bhavanti svabhāvābhāvāt/ kasmāt/ hetupratyayasāpekṣatvāt/ yadi hi svabhāvato bhāvā bhaveyuḥ, pratyākhyāyāpi hetupratyayaṃ ca bhaveyuḥ/ na caivaṃ bhavanti/ tasmānniḥsvabhāvā niḥsvabhāvatvācchūnyā ityabhidhīyante/ evaṃ madīyam-api vacanaṃ pratītyasamutpannatvānniḥsvabhāvaṃ niḥsvabhāvatvācchūnyamityupapannam/ yathā ca pratītyasumutpannatvāt svabhāvaśūnyā api [ratha]paṭaghaṭādayaḥ sveṣu sveṣu kāryeṣu [kāṣṭhatṛṇamṛttā-haraṇe] madhūdakapayasāṃ dhāraṇe śītavātātapap-aritrāṇa[prabhṛtiṣu] vartante, evam[idaṃ] madīya-vacanaṃ pratītyasamutpannatvān niḥsvabhāvamapi niḥsvabhāvatvaprasādhane bhāvānāṃ vartate/ tatra yaduktaṃ niḥsvabhāvatvāt tvadīyavacanasya [śūnyatvaṃ śūnyatvāttasya ca tena] sarvabhāvasvabhāvapratiṣedho nopapanna iti tanna/

English translation by Bhattacharya is found in *The Dialectical Method of Nāgārjuna*, pp.17–18.

365 The Tibetan omits a third example found in the Sanskrit – that a cart is able to carry wood, straw, and earth. Also, whereas the Tibetan says that pots are able to receive and hold honey and so forth, the Sanskrit says only that they can "hold" (*dhārane*) those, and though the Tibetan speaks of "milk soup" (*'o thug*), the Sanskrit term seems just to mean "milk" (*payas*).

366 The Tibetan omits a phrase found in the Sanskrit. The final sentence reads in the Sanskrit, with the omitted portion underlined: "Therefore, that which [you] said, 'Your words, due to being without inherent existence *are empty; and due to being empty*, the refutation by them of the inherent existence of all things is not feasible,' is not so."

367 Sha-mar-den-dzin, 51.3–6, points out that one has to understand that the "ascertainment" Dzong-ka-ba speaks of in this paragraph is not actual ascertainment even though the usual usage of the term is to indicate correct and incontrovertible realization. Were one actually to have ascertained the non-inherent existence of phenomena, one would have realized that the meaning of the emptiness of inherent existence is the meaning of dependent-arising, and would not be left with an inability to posit cause and effect in one's own system. Thus, Dzong-ka-ba's referent here is to an erroneous ascertainment based on not having made the difference between non-existence and non-inherent existence. This is similar to the way in which Nihilists are sometimes said to have the view of non-inherent existence, even though they have not realized such, based on the fact that they propound cause and effect not to inherently exist – since they propound them not to exist at all.

The bracketed material in the passage is from Pabong-ka, 109.2–3.

In the Dharmsala text of Dzong-ka-ba, 381a.5, *drangs med* has been corrected to *drang sa med* in accordance with the Delhi and Berkeley editions of the *Annotations* (pp. 229.2 and 42b.7, respectively); 381a.6 *drangs med* has been corrected to *drang sa med* in accordance with the Dra-shi-hlun-bo edition of Dzong-ka-ba, 144.6, and both editions of the *Annotations* (pp.229.3 and 43a.2, respectively).

368 The Tibetan is found in the Dharmsala edition of Chandrakīrti's *Clear Words*, 420.11–13. The Sanskrit for this verse as found in La Vallée Poussin's edition, p.498, is:

ataśca pratyudāvṛttaṃ cittaṃ deśayituṃ muneḥ/
dharmaṃ matvāsya dharmasya mandairduravagāhatāṃ//

The Dharmsala edition of Dzong-ka-ba, 381b.2, has been corrected from *zhen* to *zhan*.

French translation by Jacques May can be found in *Candrakīrti Prasannapadā Madhyamakavṛtti*, p.233. English translation by Mervyn Sprung in the *Lucid Exposition of the Middle Way* is on p.234.

369 P5658, Vol.129, 176.1–3. The Sanskrit from Hahn, *Nāgārjuna's Ratnāvalī*, p.46, reads:

śarīrāśucitā tāvat
sthūlā pratyakṣagocarā/
satataṃ dṛśyamānāpi
yadā citte na tiṣṭhati//

tadātisūkṣmo gambhīraḥ
saddharmo 'yam anālayaḥ/
apratyakṣaḥ kathaṃ citte
sukhenāvatariṣyati//

sambudhyāsmān nivṛtto 'bhūd
dharmaṃ deśayituṃ muniḥ/
durjñānam atigāmbhīryāj
jñātvā dharmam imaṃ janaiḥ//

English translation by J. Hopkins in *The Precious Garland and the Song of the Four Mindfulnesses*, p.34.

370 The Peking edition of the Tibetan uses here the verb "appear" (*snang*) rather than "remain" (*gnas*) as cited by Dzong-ka-ba. Dzong-ka-ba's use of "remain" is supported by the Sanskrit (*tiṣṭhati*), and Michael Hahn has also given it as the primary reading in his edition of the text.

371 With respect to the term "subtle" in the second line of the verse, Dzong-ka-ba's citation of *phra zab* – "subtle and profound" – has been changed to *phra rab* – "subtle" – to avoid redundancy with the term "profound" in the fourth line. Sha-mar-den-dzin, 51.6–52.3, suggests this correction, citing Gyel-tsap's *Commentary on (Nāgārjuna's) "Precious Garland"* and many editions of Nāgārjuna's text in which *phra rab* appears; this also accords with the Sanskrit (*atisūkṣma*), with the Peking edition of the Tibetan, and with Michael Hahn's edition of the text. In line four Dzong-ka-ba has used the verb "enter" (*'jug*); whereas both the Peking edition of the Tibetan and Hahn's edition have the verb "appear" (*'char*), Dzong-ka-ba's use of "enter" is supported by the Sanskrit (*avatariṣyati*).

372 This is the second part of a topic that began on the first page of chapter five – "Showing that those systems [of those who negate too much] refute the uncommon distinguishing feature of Mādhyamika". The first part, which occupied all of chapter five and chapter six to this point, was "Identifying the distinguishing feature of Mādhyamika."

373 This was cited in the previous chapter; see p.183.

374 This was also cited in the previous chapter; see p.183.

375 This is a paraphrase of a passage from Chandrakīrti's *Clear Words* commenting on XXIV.13–14 that was cited in the previous chapter, see p.184.

376 This can be found in La Vallée Poussin's edition of the Tibetan, 123.11–16. La Vallée Poussin's translation into French is in *Muséon*, 1910, pp.315–16.

CHAPTER SEVEN: MĀDHYAMIKA RESPONSE

377 This is third of three subdivisions to the topic, "Showing that those systems [which negate too much] refute the uncommon distinguishing feature of Mādhyamika". The topic began on the first page of chapter five, and the first two subheadings, "Identifying the distinguishing feature of Mādhyamika" and "How those systems refute that distinguishing feature" formed the subject matter of chapters five and six.

378 Tibetan in the Dharmsala edition of Chandrakīrti's *Clear Words*, 423.15–17 and 424.3–4. Sanskrit in La Vallée Poussin's edition, 502.1–2 and 502.7–8:

sa tvam doṣānātmanīyānasmāsu paripātayan/
aśvamevābhirūḍhaḥ sannaśvamevāsi vismṛtaḥ//

svabhāvādyadi bhāvānāṃ sadbhāvamanupaśyasi/
ahetupratyayān bhāvāṃstvamevaṃ sati·paśyasi//

French translation by Jacques May in *Candrakīrti Prasannapadā Madhyamakavṛtti*, p.236.

379 Whereas the second line as found in La Vallée Poussin's edition and in the Dharmsala edition of Chandrakīrti's *Clear Words* reads *nga la yongs su sgyur byed pa*, as cited by Dzong-ka-ba it reads *nga la skyon du sgyur byed pa*. Although the basic meaning is the same in either case, the English translation reflects Dzong-ka-ba's repetition of the word "faults".

380 Whereas this line as found in La Vallée Poussin's edition and in the Dharmsala edition of Chandrakīrti's *Clear Words* reads *de lta yin na dngos po rnams*, as cited by Dzong-ka-ba it reads *de lta yin na dngos po kun* – "all things" rather than just "things" in the plural. The English translation reflects Dzong-ka-ba's citation.

381 Tibetan in the Dharmsala edition of Chandrakīrti's *Clear Words*, 426.20 and 427.1–2. Sanskrit in La Vallée Poussin's edition, 505.18 and 506.1:

yadyaśūnyamidaṃ sarvamudayo nāsti na vyayaḥ/
catūrṇāmāryasatyānāmabhāvaste prasajyate//

French translation by Jacques May in *Candrakīrti Prasannapadā Madhyamakavṛtti*, p.240.

Nāgārjuna has simply changed the word "empty" from stanza one of chapter twenty-four (cited in chapter five of the translation when setting forth an objection by the Proponents of True Existence) to "not empty" and thrown the very same consequence back to the Proponents of True Existence as he had them throw at the Mādhyamikas. Stanza one reads:

If all this were empty,
There would be no arising and no disintegration;
It would follow that for you [Mādhyamikas]
The four noble truths would not exist.

382 This is commentary on XI.10. Toh 3865, Tokyo *sde dge* Vol.8, 175b.2–3. Sanskrit in Haraprasād Shāstri, 492.13–15:

vastusatpadārthavādino hi yāvattasya vastuno 'stitvaṃ tāvattathāsvarūpasyaiva yadārthasvarūpa[na]dhigamastadāsya tadvastu sarvvathābhāvāt kharaviṣāṇaprakhyamiti dvayavādānatikramāt asya sarvvamevābhisamīhitaṃ durghaṭaṃ jāyate/

Note that this provides a Sanskrit source (*vastusatpadārthavādin*) for the Tibetan term *dngos po yod par smra ba* (Proponent of True Existence) which is usually abbreviated in Tibetan to *dngos smra ba*. See pp.50–1 for a discussion of this term and the reasons for translating it as "Proponent of True Existence".

383 Dzong-ka-ba's citation of this passage omits here the word *de ltar*, "accordingly" which is found in the Tokyo *sde dge* edition of the text, 175b.2, and in the Sanskrit, *tathā*.

384 384b.1 *lta bur byas* corrected to *lta bur bya sa* in accordance with the Dra-shi-hlun-bo edition of Dzong-ka-ba's text, 151.1, and the Berkeley edition of the *Annotations*, 50b.5.

385 384b.2, *dngos med mi 'gro* corrected to *dngos med du mi 'gro* in accordance with the Dra-shi-hlun-bo edition of

Dzong-ka-ba's text, 151.2, and both editions of the *Annotations*.

386 This is commentary following XVII.30. The Tibetan is found in the Dharmsala edition of Chandrakīrti's *Clear Words*, 280.1–13. Sanskrit from La Vallée Poussin's edition, 329.10–17, incorporating emendations suggested by De Jong in "Textcritical Notes", p.222:

> atrāha/ yadyevaṃ naiḥsvābhāvyaṃ bhāvānāṃ vyavasthāpitaṃ bhavati yattarhyetaduktaṃ bhagavatā svayaṃ kṛtasya karmaṇaḥ svayameva vipākaḥ pratyanubhavitavya iti tadetatsarvamamunā nyāyenāpākṛtaṃ bhavati/ karmaphalāpavādācca pradhānanāstiko bhavāniti// ucyate/ na vayaṃ nāstikāḥ/ nāstyastitvadvayavādanirāsena tu vayaṃ nirvāṇapuragāminamadvayapathaṃ abhidyotayāmaḥ/ na ca vayaṃ karmakartṛphalādikaṃ nāstīti brūmaḥ kiṃ tarhi niḥsvabhāvametaditi vyavasthāpayāmaḥ// atha manyase/ niḥsvabhāvānāṃ bhāvānāṃ vyāpārakaraṇānupapattestadavastha eva doṣa iti// etadapi nāsti sasvabhāvānāmeva vyāpārādarśanānniḥsvabhāvānāmeva ca vyāpāradarśanāt/

Dzong-ka-ba's citation of the passage differs on numerous small points from the Dharmsala edition of Chandrakīrti's text; none affect the meaning.

French translation by Lamotte in "Le Traité de l'acte de Vasubandhu, Karmasiddhiprakaraṇa", *MCB* 4, 1936, p.285.

387 385a.2 text corrected from *rar bzhin* to *rang bzhin* in accordance with the Dra-shi-hlun-bo edition of Dzong-ka-ba's text, 152.2, and both editions of the *Annotations*.

388 This is commentary leading into XIV.23. Toh 3865, Tokyo *sde dge* Vol.8, 220b.4–6. Sanskrit does not survive. Dzong-ka-ba's citation of the passage differs on four small points – none significant – from the passage as found in the Tokyo *sde dge* edition; on three of those points Dzong-ka-ba's reading is supported by the version of Chandrakīrti's text found in the Nar-tang edition of

the Tibetan canon as cited by Vidhushekhara Bhattacharya in his *The Catuḥśataka of Āryadeva* (Calcutta: Visva-bharati Bookshop, 1931), p.226.

389 This is commentary surrounding XI.25. Toh 3865, Tokyo *sde dge* Vol.8, 182b.6–183a.4. Sanskrit does not survive.

Ge-shay Palden Drakpa explained that this passage about memory consciousnesses being unreal – not truly existent yet also not totally non-existent – was cited as an easy example to show how falsities – all conventional phenomena – could still perform functions even though they lack inherent existence. Sha-mar-den-dzin, 54.5–57.2, offers explanation of the passage and its context within Āryadeva's *Four Hundred* which, in summary form is: Some non-Buddhists state as a proof that time is permanent and truly established the fact that one can remember past objects, specifically, former births, thinking, "In an earlier birth, I was such and such." As an answer to this, Āryadeva set forth XI.25:

> Things already seen do not appear.
> A [former] mind is not produced again [i.e., a past eye consciousness is not generated again today];
> Therefore, the "memory consciousness" which arises is only an unreal [subject]
> With respect to an object which is unreal.

This means that even though the object known in the past does not reoccur in the present, nor does the consciousness which knew that object in the past occur again, nonetheless one does generate a memory consciousness taking that past object to mind as if it were a present object. In that the object of that memory consciousness is unreal, i.e., not existing at present, the memory consciousnessness taking it to mind is also unreal in that the object appears to it to exist at present whereas it does not.

However, as Chandrakīrti goes on to make very explicit, that something is "unreal" does not mean that it is totally non-existent. For instance, the past object is something that could be remembered and which produced effects.

Karen Lang's translation of this verse is found on p.407 of her dissertation; I disagree with her treatment of lines c and d, having based my translation on the commentary cited above.

In both editions of Dzong-ka-ba's text (Dharmsala edition, 386a.4; Dra-shi-hlun-bo edition, 154.4) *nges na* should be corrected to *des na* in accordance with the Tokyo *sde dge* edition of Chandrakīrti's *Commentary on (Āryadeva's) "Four Hundred"*, 183a.1, further support on 182b.4. Dzong-ka-ba's citation of the passage differs on a number of small points from the version found in the Tokyo *sde dge* edition of Chandrakīrti's text; none are significant.

390 For Dzong-ka-ba, a negative is a negative, and two negatives make a positive. Thus, there is no difference between "non-existent" (*med pa*) and "is not existent" (*yod pa ma yin*); their meaning is identical – a negation of existence. Also, there is no difference between "not non-existent" (*med pa ma yin*) and "existent" (*yod pa*); in the former case, the two negatives cancel each other out, leaving the positive, "existence". Those who try to make such differences are seeking to take literally the famous Mādhyamika tetralemma, "not existent, not non-existent, not both, and not neither", and Dzong-ka-ba rejects the attempt as unacceptable, saying that instead one must understand what is intended by those negations – that "not existent" means "not inherently existent" and "not non-existent" means "not utterly non-existent".

391 Lindtner, *Nagarjuniana*, p.79. Sanskrit:

naiḥsvābhāvyanivṛttau svābhāvyaṃ hi prasiddhaṃ syāt//

English translation by Bhattacharya in *The Dialectical Method of Nāgārjuna*, p.20.

392 Dzong-ka-ba is making a very strong statement that Mādhyamikas do rely on dichotomies in their analyses; in some situations, the possibilities are limited to two, and by ruling out one, the other is established. In support of this, he cites a passage from Nāgārjuna's *Refutation of Objections*, that if non-inherent existence were to be ruled out, inherent existence would be established. The converse of this is also true – if inherent existence is ruled out, non-inherent existence is established. This is, for Dzong-ka-ba, a basic principle of Mādhyamika and is what makes it possible for them to assert a positive system of non-inherent existence; it is not that Mādhyamikas are merely negative, ruling out each possibility that comes along, but forever waiting for another that will have to be refuted in time. Rather, by limiting the possibilities to inherent existence and no inherent existence, they have ruled out inherent existence and established no inherent existence as the mode of being of all that exists.

The Dharmsala edition of Dzong-ka-ba's text, 387a.5, has been corrected from *bzos med* to *bzo sa med* in accordance with the Dra-shi-hlun-bo edition, 156.4.

393 The Tibetan verb of being takes two forms, one ontological – "exists" (*yod pa*) and "does not exist" (*med pa*) – and one linking – "is" (*yin*) and "is not" (*min*). Some might try to claim that the rule of two negatives making a positive and the equivalency of "not-is" (*ma yin*) and "is not" (*min*) is true of the linking form but not the ontological. Dzong-ka-ba rejects this, saying that the same rules apply to both.

394 Because in Mādhyamika texts, the possibilities of "exists" (*yod pa*) and "does not exist" (*med pa*) are both rejected, these misinterpreters try to propound, "is not existent and is not non-existent" (*yod min med min*). However, those same Mādhyamika texts reject four possibilities – exists, does not exist, both exists and does not exist, and neither exists nor does not exist. According to Dzong-ka-ba, by accepting "is not existent

and is not non-existent", these misinterpreters of Mādhyamika are in effect asserting that which is neither existent nor non-existent – the fourth of the four possibilities – and thus would themselves be contradicting the words of the Mādhyamika texts that they are trying so hard to take literally.

395 Tibetan in the Dharmsala edition of Chandrakīrti's *Clear Words*, 235.9–10. Sanskrit in La Vallée Poussin's edition, 272.14 and 273.3:

astīti śāśvatagrāho nāstītyucchedadarśanaṃ
tasmādastitvanāstitve nāśrīyeta vicakṣaṇaḥ

Dzong-ka-ba's citation of the third line differs a bit from the Tibetan cited in both of the above mentioned editions. There the line reads: *de phyir yod dang med pa la*. As cited by Dzong-ka-ba it reads: *de phyir yod med gnyis ka la*. I have reflected Dzong-ka-ba's use of *gnyis ka* by including the word "either" in the translation.

396 Chandrakīrti equates viewing existence and non-existence with views of inherent existence and inherent non-existence in his commentary leading into the verse just cited. This is based on the ambiguity of meaning of the term *bhāva* (Tib. *dngos po*); see above, p.203, where Dzong-ka-ba discusses the different meanings of this term. Chandrakīrti says (Tibetan in the Dharmsala edition of Chandrakīrti's text, 235.8–9; Sanskrit in La Vallée Poussin's edition, 272.11–12): "Nowadays some conceive things as existing and as not existing; with respect to such conception, [Nāgārjuna said that] it is definitely only the case that: 'Saying exists, . . .'" The passage about to be quoted comes immediately following Chandrakīrti's citation of the last two lines of XV.10 and is found in the Dharmsala edition of the Tibetan on 235.13–236.1; Sanskrit in La Vallée Poussin's edition, 273.4–9:

kasmātpunarbhāvābhāvadarśane sati śāśvatoccheda-darśanaprasaṅgo bhavatīti/ yasmāt/ asti yaddhisvabhāvena na tannāstīti śāśvataṃ nāstīdānīmabhūtpūrvamityucchedaḥ prasajyate//

yatsvabhāvenāstītyucyate svabhāvasyānapāyitvānna tatkadā cidapi nāstīti evam svabhāvasyāstitvābhyupagame sati śāśvatadarśanamāpadyate/ pūrvaṃ ca vartamānāvasthāyāṃ bhāvasvarūpamabhyupetyedānīṃ tadvinaṣṭatvānnāstīti paścādabhyupagacchata ucchedadarśanaṃ prasajyate//

397 The Tibetan clearly treats "later" as a gloss for the term "now", now being later than the earlier assertion of inherent existence. In the Sanskrit, it is placed as an adverb of time, modifying the verb "assert". Although the difference in meaning is not great, the Tibetan seems more clear.

398 See Buddhapālita's commentary leading into XV.11 (Toh 3842, Tokyo *sde dge* Vol.1, 226b.1): "To explain the way in which the fallacy of having views of permanence and annihilation is entailed if one views existence and nonexistence [Nāgārjuna says]:

Whatever exists inherently is permanent
Since it does not become non-existent.
If one says that what arose formerly [as inherently existent] is now non-existent,
Through that [an extreme of] annihilation is entailed."

399 There are two ways that one can misunderstand emptiness, and through either one one comes to have a view of annihilation. The first mentioned, "propounding that the emptiness which is the absence of inherent existence is not the excellent emptiness" is the position taken by, for example, the Buddhist Vaibhāṣhikas and Sautrāntikas, who say that the emptiness of inherent existence asserted by Mādhyamika goes too far and thus is not the true emptiness taught by Buddha. They fall to an extreme of annihilation as has been discussed in the preceding pages citing XV.11cd of Nāgārjuna's *Treatise on the Middle Way* through propounding the destruction of some inherently existent thing, this being an extreme of annihilation since whatever existed inherently could never be destroyed.

The other way one can misunderstand emptiness and fall into an extreme of annihilation is to assert that the absence of inherent existence means the non-existence of everything. Dzong-ka-ba would include in this group those Tibetan interpreters of Mādhyamika who from his viewpoint negate too much. The two modes of misconception are introduced in this order, but are then discussed by Chandrakīrti in the passage about to be cited in reverse order – first those who negate too much and then those who reject the Mādhyamika emptiness.

Distinguishing these two is important at this point in Dzong-ka-ba's argument because those who take the position that the Mādhyamika reasonings negate all phenomena try to protect themselves from the charge of having fallen to an extreme of annihilation by limiting what is meant by such an extreme to only the former meaning, and cite in their support XV.11 from Nāgārjuna's *Treatise*. Thus, Dzong-ka-ba spells out clearly that there are these two types of extreme of annihilation and suggests the absurd consequence that if there were only the former, then even the worldly Materialists – who are universally accepted as Nihilists having a view of annihilation – would have to be considered not to have such a view. They are considered Nihilists because they reject as non-existent former and future lives, the karmic doctrine of the effects of one's actions, and so forth, saying that these do not exist and never have; if in order to have a view of annihilation, one had to be propounding the later non-existence of something one asserted as having formerly existed, then these Materialists would not be Nihilists since they never propounded those things to exist.

400 Tibetan in the Dharmsala edition of Chandrakīrti's *Clear Words*, 417.20. Sanskrit in La Vallée Poussin's edition, 495.1:

vināśayati durdṛṣṭā śūnyatā mandamedhasaṃ/

French translation by Jacques May in *Candrakīrti Pra-*

sannapadā Madhyamakavṛtti, p.229.

401 Tibetan in the Dharmsala edition of Chandrakīrti's *Clear Words*, 418.19–419.10. Sanskrit in La Vallée Poussin's edition, 495.12–496.9:

yadi tāvatsarvamidaṃ śūnyaṃ sarvaṃ nāstīti parikalpayettadāsya mithyādṛṣṭirāpadyate/ yathoktaṃ

vināśayati durdṛṣṭo
dharmo 'yam avipaścitaṃ/
nāstitādṛṣṭisamale
yasmād asmin nimajjati//

atha sarvāpavādaṃ kartuṃ necchati tadā niyatamasya śūnyatāyāḥ pratikṣepa āpadyate/ kathaṃ hi nāmāmī bhāvāḥ sakalasurāsuranaralokairupalabhyamānā api śūnyā bhaviṣyanti/ tasmānna niḥsvabhāvārthaḥ śūnyatārtha ityevaṃ pratikṣipya saddharmavyasanasaṃvartanīyena pāpakena karmaṇā niyatamapāy-[ā]nyāyāt//

yathoktamāryaratnāvalyām/

aparo 'py asya durjñānān
mūrkhaḥ paṇḍitamānikaḥ/
pratikṣepavinaṣṭātmā
yāty avīcim adhomukhaḥ// iti/

French translation by Jacques May in *Candrakīrti Prasannapadā Madhyamakavṛtti*, p.231.

English translation by Jeffrey Hopkins of the two verses from the *Precious Garland* in *The Precious Garland and the Song of the Four Mindfulnesses*, pp.34–5.

402 As cited in editions of Nāgārjuna's *Precious Garland* (Hahn, pp.46–47, and P5658, Vol.129, 176.1.3), the line reads "*understood* wrongly" (*log par shes gyur na*, *durjñāto*).

403 The Sanskrit here differs from the Tibetan. Following the Sanskrit the above passage reads: "On the other hand, if you do not assert a deprecation of all [phenomena], then [still] an abandonment of emptiness occurs, saying, 'How could these so-called "things", being observed by the entire world of gods, demi-gods, and humans be empty? Therefore, the meaning of an absence

of inherent existence is not the meaning of emptiness.'"

404 As cited by Dzong-ka-ba, the first line ends in *na* – "if" or "when". However, as cited in the Peking edition of the *Precious Garland*, 176.1.3, and in the Dharmsala edition of Chandrakīrti's *Clear Words*, 419.8, it ends in *nas*, the ablative particle. This reading is supported by the Sanskrit *durjñānāt*. Translated in accordance with this reading, the first line would read, "Further, from holding this [doctrine] wrongly,".

405 Tibetan in the Dharmsala edition of Chandrakīrti's *Clear Words*, 418.2–6. Sanskrit in La Vallée Poussin's edition, 495.3–5:

> saṃvṛtisatyaṃ hyajñānamātrasamutthāpitaṃ niḥsvabhāvaṃ buddhvā tasya paramārthalakṣaṇāṃ śūnyatāṃ pratipadyamāno yogī nāntadvaye patati kim tadāsīdyadidānīṃ nāstītyevaṃ pūrvaṃ bhāvasvabhāvānupalambhātpaścādapi nāstitāṃ na pratipadyate

French translation by Jacques May in *Candrakīrti Prasannapadā Madhyamakavṛtti*, p.229.

Bracketed material in the translation of the passage taken from Sha-mar-den-dzin, 64.3–6. Sha-mar takes the final verb in the passage as "conceive" (*rtog*) rather than "realize" (*rtogs*) as cited by Dzong-ka-ba. Sha-mar's reading would be more comfortable, but Dzong-ka-ba's is supported by the Dharmsala edition of Chandrakīrti's text and by the Sanskrit.

406 The remainder of the chapter is no longer primarily concerned with rejecting the position of those Mādhyamika interpreters who negate too much, but instead lays out directly the way in which true Mādhyamikas – i.e., Chandrakīrti and Buddhapālita – defend themselves from the charges that Mādhyamikas are no different from Nihilists.

407 Chapter eighteen, commentary that comes between verses seven and eight. Tibetan in the Dharmsala edition of Chandrakīrti's *Clear Words*, 302.4–17. Sanskrit in La Vallée Poussin's edition, 368.4–12; bracketed material is missing from the Tibetan (see the following note):

nāstikāviśiṣṭā mādhyamikā yasmātkuśalākuśalaṃ karma kartāraṃ ca phalaṃ ca sarvaṃ ca lokaṃ bhāvasvabhāvaśūnyamiti bruvate/ nāstikā api hyetannāstīti bruvate/ tasmānnāstikāviśiṣṭā mādhyamikā iti//

naivaṃ/ kutaḥ/ pratītyasamutpādavādino hi mādhyamikā [hetupratyayān prāpya] pratītya samutpannatvātsarvamevehalokaparalokaṃ niḥsvabhāvaṃ varṇayanti/ [yathā svarūpavādino naiva] nāstikāḥ pratītyasamutpannatvād [bhāva]svabhāvaśūnyatvena na paralokādyabhāvam pratipannāḥ kim tarhi aihalaukikaṃ vastujātamupalabhya svabhāvatastasya paralokād ihāgamanamihalokācca paralokagamanamapaśyanta ihalokopalabdhapadārthasadṛśapadārthāntarāpavādaṃ kurvanti//

French translation by de Jong in *Cinq Chapitres de la Prasannapadā*, p.25.

408 The Sanskrit includes here a phrase not found in the Tibetan, "[arising upon] a meeting of causes and conditions" (*hetupratyayān prāpya*). Also, the above phrase "and so forth" is found only in the Tibetan. The next sentence includes in the Sanskrit a phrase missing from the Tibetan, *svarūpavādino naiva*. The negative, *na*, would seem to be a textual corruption, and de Jong, in his translation of this phrase (*Cinq Chapitres*, p.25) has avoided it entirely, translating the phrase as, "Quant aux nihilistes qui croient à l'existence de substances, . . ."

409 The phrase, "observing as inherently existent" (*rang bzhin gyis dmigs*, *upalabhya svabhāvatas*) is translated thus in accordance with Sha-mar-den-dzin, 65.3. Pa-bong-ka, 112.6, takes it as simply meaning that the Nihilists see the things of this life with direct perception. In accordance with his interpretation, the phrase would have to be translated, "observing naturally". One can make a case for either interpretation, but I find Sha-mar-den-dzin's the more plausible because it is found in the context of discussing propounding or not propounding inherent existence.

410 Dzong-ka-ba's citation of this passage differs on numerous small points from how the passage appears in the Dharmsala edition of Chandrakīrti's text. Most are insignificant. Two which bear noting are Dzong-ka-ba's use of the word "argue" (*rgol par byed do*) in the first paragraph whereas Chandrakīrti's text merely says "say" (*bya bar byed do*); also in the last sentence, in what is likely a copyist's omission, Dzong-ka-ba's text merely says "go from this world to another" (*'jig rten 'di nas pha rol tu 'gro ba*) whereas Chandrakīrti's text says "go from this world to another world" (*'jig rten 'di nas 'jig rten pha rol tu 'gro bar*). In both cases the Sanskrit accords with the version in the Dharmsala edition of Chandrakīrti's text.

411 This passage continues directly from that just cited. Tibetan in the Dharmsala edition of Chandrakīrti's *Clear Words*, 302.17–303.1. Sanskrit in La Vallée Poussin's edition, 368.13–15, incorporating emendations suggested by De Jong in "Textcritical Notes", p.228–9:

> tathāpi vastusvarūpeṇāvidyamānasyaiva te nāstitvaṃ pratipannā ityamunā tāvaddarśanena sāmyamastīti cet// na hi/ kutaḥ/ saṃvṛtyā mādhyamikairastitvenābhyupagamāt/ taiścānabhyupagamānna tulyatā//

French translation by de Jong in *Cinq Chapitres de la Prasannapadā*, p.25.

412 This passage continues directly from that just cited. Tibetan in the Dharmsala edition of Chandrakīrti's *Clear Words*, 303.1–14. Sanskrit in La Vallée Poussin's edition, 368.16–369.4:

> vastutastulyateti ced// yadyapi vastuto 'siddhistulyā tathāpi pratipattṛbhedādatulyatā/ yathā hi kṛtacauryaṃ puruṣamekaḥ samyagaparijñāyaiva tadamitrapreritastaṃ mithyā vyācaṣṭe cauryamanena kṛtamiti aparastu sākṣāddṛṣṭvā dūṣayati/ tatra yadyapi vastuto nāsti bhedastathāpi parijñātṛbhedādekastatra mṛṣāvādītyucyate aparastu satyavādīti/ ekaścāyaśasā cāpuṇyena ca samyak parīkṣyamāṇo yujyate nāparaḥ/ evamihāpi yathāvadviditavastusvarūpāṇāṃ mādh-

yamikānāṃ bruvatāmavagacchatāṃ ca vastusvarūpābhede 'pi yathāvadaviditavastusvarūpairnāstikaiḥ saha jñānābhidhānayornāsti sāmyaṃ//

French translation by de Jong in *Cinq Chapitres de la Prasannapadā*, p.25–6.

413 The Dharmsala edition of Chandrakīrti's text adds into this sentence the phrase *ma grub par*, which would result in the translation, "Someone might say that they are the same with respect to the fact of non-establishment [by way of objects' own entities]." (This phrase is repeated in the next sentence.) The phrase is not found in the Sanskrit.

Dzong-ka-ba's citation of this passage and the Dharmsala edition of Chandrakīrti's text differ on numerous other small points; none affect the translation except as described in the following note.

414 In what would appear to be a scribe's copying error (found in all editions of Dzong-ka-ba's text), Dzong-ka-ba's citation of this passage omits here a phrase found in the Dharmsala edition of Chandrakīrti's text, 303.11, "even though there is no difference in terms of the self-entity of things," (*dngos po'i rang gi ngo bo tha mi dad kyang/ dbu ma pa*); the phrase occurs in the Sanskrit.

415 This is commentary prior to, including, and subsequent to XV.10ab. Toh 3865, Tokyo *sde dge* Vol.8, 224b.2–3. Sanskrit does not survive.

The first phrase of the passage *de lta na yang* as cited by Dzong-ka-ba has been corrected to *de lta na* in accordance with the Tokyo *sde dge* edition and sense.

Lang's translation on p.507.

416 This is commentary at the very end of chapter twenty: Toh 3842, Tokyo *sde dge* Vol.1, 255b.3–4. Material in brackets is from Sha-mar-den-dzin, 67.3.

In the Dharmsala edition of Dzong-ka-ba's text, 391a.4, *med pa par smra ba* was corrected to *med par smra ba* in accordance with the Tokyo *sde dge* edition of Buddhapālita's text, 255b.4; also 391a.4, *rtogs par byed* was corrected to *rtog par byed* in accordance with the Dra-shi-hlun-bo edition of Dzong-ka-ba's text, 164.2, and the Tokyo *sde dge* edition of Buddhapālita's text, 255b.4.

PART THREE: TRANSLATION OF THE "FOUR INTERWOVEN ANNOTATIONS"

TRANSLATOR'S INTRODUCTION

417 See note 19 for full references to the two editions of the text used.

418 The identification as Ba-so Chö-gyi-gyel-tsen is found in the Delhi edition, Vol.1, 6.2–3, and in the Berkeley text is within a two page document entitled "Brief mode of identifying the enumeration of annotations with respect to the *Great Exposition of the Stages of the Path to Enlightenment Along With Annotations, Jewelled Source of Good Explanation*", 1.4. A-gya-yong-dzin's identification is found on 83.6–84.1 in his *A Brief Explanation of Terminology Occurring in (Dzong-ka-ba's) "Great Exposition of the Stages of the Path"*. A-ku-ching's reference is on 618.6 of his *Record of Teachings Received* (*thog mtha' bar du dge ba'i dam pa'i chos kyi thob yig mdo sngags zab rgyas bdud rtsi'i mtsho las skra rtses blangs pa'i chu thigs gsan yig*, in The Collected Works of A-khu-chiṅ Śes-rab-rgya-mtsho, Vol. 6, New Delhi: Ngawang Sopa, 1974), reference to the *Four Annotations* lineage, pp.618.6–620.3.

The list of Ba-so Chö-gyi-gyel-tsen's writings in the *Yellow Cat's Eye Gem* is found on 68.16 (Dr. Lokesh Chandra, ed., *Vaidūrya-ser-po and the Annals of Kokonor*, Delhi: International Academy of Indian Culture, 1960); it mentions three works: *The Stages of Generation and Completion of Kālachakra* (*dus 'khor bskyed rdzogs*), *Instructions on the View of the Middle Way* (*dbu ma'i lta khrid*), and *The Three Essential Meanings* (*snying po don gsum*).

Ba-so Chö-gyi-gyel-tsen's biography is found in Ye-shay-gyel-tsen's *Biographies of Eminent Gurus in the Transmission Lineages of the Teachings of the Graduated Path* (*byang chub lam gyi rim pa'i bla ma brgyud pa'i rnam par thar pa rgyal bstan mdzes pa'i rgyan mchog phul byung nor bu'i phreng ba*, New Delhi: Ngawang Gelek Demo, 1970) Vol.1, 923–30. In his list of what Ba-so wrote, 929.5, Ye-shay-gyel-tsen mentions the same three texts as listed above plus a fourth, *Instructions on the Stages of Generation and Completion of Vajrabhairava* (*rdo rje 'jigs byed kyi bskyed rdzogs kyi khrid*).

Long-döl's listing of Ba-so's collected works can be found in his *Catalogue of the Collected Works of Certain Principal Ga-dam-ba and Ge-luk-ba Lamas* (*bka' gdams pa dang dge lugs bla ma rag[s?] rim gyi gsung 'bum mtshan tho*, in Lokesh Chandra, ed., *Materials for a History of Tibetan Literature*, Part Three, pp.607–96, New Delhi: International Academy of Indian Culture, 1963). The listing of Ba-so's collected works is on p.611 and also does not mention annotations on Dzong-ka-ba's *Great Exposition*. (It lists four works by Ba-so Chö-gyi-gyel-tsen, but is a slightly different list than Ye-shay-gyel-tsen's. Long-döl treats *The Three Essential Meanings* not as a separate work but as a subtitle to Ba-so's *Condensed, Medium, and Extensive Instructions on the View of the Middle Way*; the other three works are the *Stage of Generation of Kālachakra*, the *Stage of Completion of Kālachakra*, and the *Stages of Generation and Completion of Bhairava*.)

419 In the Delhi edition, see the English preface and Vol.1, 6.3–4. Information on Gön-chok-chö-pel is from the English preface to the Delhi edition and the *Yellow Cat's Eye Gem*, 79.7–80.9. Information on Dak-lung-drak-ba is from the *Yellow Cat's Eye Gem*, 77.19–78.4. Identification of Dak-lung-drak-ba as the annotator in the Berkeley text is in the "Brief mode of identifying the

enumeration of annotations with respect to the *Great Exposition of the Stages of the Path to Enlightenment Along With Annotations, Jewelled Source of Good Explanation*", 2a.1–2. A-gya-yong-dzin's reference is on 84.1–2, and A-khu-ching's on 620.1–2.

420 Biographical information on Jam-yang-shay-ba is taken from Jeffrey Hopkins' *Meditation on Emptiness*, (London: Wisdom, 1983), p.567. Hopkins is following Lokesh Chandra's account in his *Materials for a History of Tibetan Literature* (New Delhi: International Academy of Indian Culture, 1963), Śata-piṭaka series, Vol.28, pp.45–6. A-gya-yong-dzin's reference is on 84.2. At that same point he also supplies the information that Baso's *Annotations* are known as the *Red Annotations*, Dak-lung-drak-ba's as the *Black Annotations*, and Jam-yang-shay-ba's as the *Yellow Annotations*.

421 For the connection with Jang-gya, see E. Gene Smith's synopsis of Jang-gya's biography in his introduction to the *Collected Works of Thu'u-bkwan Blo-bzang-chos-kyi-nyi-ma*, Vol.1 (New Delhi: Ngawang Gelek Demo, 1969), p.9. For Long-döl's listing of Dra-di Ge-shay's collected works, see Part 3 of Lokesh Chandra's *Materials for a History of Tibetan Literature*, pp.661–2.

422 For A-khu-ching, see his Collected Works, Vol.6, 618.6–619.6. Ge-shay Tsul-trim-nam-gyal's reference is in the *Four Interwoven Annotations*, Vol.1, 8.1.

423 For the context of the passage, see pp.293ff. The Tibetan, as it appears in the Delhi edition of the *Four Interwoven Annotations*, 184.6–185.2, is as follows. Dzong-ka-ba's words, which in the Tibetan appear in larger print, are transliterated all in capital letters. The letters "ja" over a phrase indicate commentary by Jam-yang-shay-ba; "ba" indicate commentary by Ba-so Chögyi-gyel-tsen, unmarked annotations are by Dra-di Ge-shay:

ja
dang po ni [thob bya'i de nyid dang bdag med la chos

ba
kyi bdag med yod med dri ba]/ GAL TE de la kho na re de kho na nyid kyi ngos 'dzin dang de la 'jug pa'i tshul
ba ja
de gnyis ka mi 'thad de/ rtsa shes 'dir sher mdo'i don

gzhan dag the tshom 'di ltar skyes te/ skabs 'DIR NI theg chen gyi lam gyi rim pa ston pa'i skabs yin pas THEG CHEN PA'I dbang du byas pa'i DE KHO NA NYID LA 'JUG PA'I TSHUL STON PA MA YIN NAM

INTRODUCTION

424 See note 292.
425 See note 293.
426 Ba-so's commentary on this point, if one follows the Berkeley text, is that, if one has not realized emptiness, one can suppress temporarily the manifest conception of self but cannot abandon the seeds of that conception. That the word "afflictions" is modified by "manifest" is not found in that edition (see 3a.2–4), and it is clear that Ba-so is saying that the seeds for the discrimination of self are not destroyed even though they might be temporarily suppressed. Jam-yang-shay-ba disagrees with this, saying that one cannot overcome even the manifest form of the conception of self, the root of cyclic existence, if one has not realized suchness. The controversy is avoided in the Delhi edition where the word "afflictions" is added in and becomes that which is modified by "manifest", for everyone agrees that manifest afflictions can be temporarily suppressed by concentrative states even though their seeds are not abandoned.
427 Jam-yang-shay-ba is citing the last line of VI.165, found in Louis de la Vallée Poussin's edition of the *Madhyamakāvatāra* (*Madhyamakāvatāra par Candrakīrti*, Bibliotheca Buddhica IX, Osnabrück: Biblio Verlag, 1970) on p.287. The line before that it is:

de phyir bdag dang bdag gi stong lta zhing.

Thus the entire passage reads," Therefore, viewing the emptiness of I and mine, a yogi will be released." La Vallée Poussin's translation is in *Muséon* 12 (1911), p.328. Dzong-ka-ba cites this line from Chandrakīrti in his *Illumination of the Thought*, Sarnath edition, p.62.

428 This translation is taken from J. Hopkins and Lati Rimpoche, trans., *The Precious Garland and the Song of the Four Mindfulnesses*, New York: Harper & Row, 1975) p.71. The Tibetan cited in the Delhi edition of the *Annotations* has been corrected in three places, as shown below, to accord with the version of the *Precious Garland* found in the Peking edition of the Tibetan Tripitaka (P5658, Vol.129, 180.4.4–5). The latter two of those changes are also supported by the Berkeley text of the *Annotations*. Version cited in the Delhi text (p.142.5–6):

de ltar yang dag ji bzhin du
'gro ba'i don *byed* shes nas ni
rgyu med pa yi *de* bzhin du
gnas med *lan* med mya ngan 'da'.

Corrected to:

de ltar yang dag ji bzhin du
'gro ba don *med* shes nas ni
rgyu med pa yi *me* bzhin du
gnas med *len* med mya ngan 'da'

The Sanskrit, as cited in Michael Hahn, *Nāgārjuna's Ratnāvalī, Vol.1, The Basic Texts (Sanskrit, Tibetan, and Chinese)*, Bonn, Indica et Tibetica Verlag, 1982, p.116 reads:

vyartham evam jagan matvā
yāthābhūtyān nirāspadaḥ/
nirvāti nirupādāno
nirupādānavahnivat//

Professor Ashok Aklujkar suggested the following reading as more closely mirroring the Sanskrit:

Having thus considered all the world substanceless,

He, being one without basis because of [the state of] being real [i.e., out of his knowledge of what reality is],
Passes beyond utterly [i.e., attains nirvāṇa]
Like a fire that has no material cause.

429 Occurring near the end of chapter two, this verse is found on 68.20–69.2 of the 1974 Pleasure of Elegant Sayings Printing Press edition of the Tibetan. The first line of the verse as cited in the Delhi edition of the *Annotations* has been corrected from *de phyir grol 'dod thams cad pa'i* to *de phyir grol 'dod thog med pa'i* in accordance with the Berkeley text and the Pleasure of Elegant Sayings edition. The Sanskirt for the verse is:

tasmād anādisantānatulyajātīyabījakām/
utkhātamūlāṃ kuruta sattvadṛṣṭiṃ mumukṣavaḥ/

Verse 258cd and 259ab, pp.87–8 of *Pramāṇavārttika of Acharya Dharmakīrtti*, Swami Dwarikadas Shastri, ed. (Varanasi: Bauddha Bharati, 1968). The Sanskrit *sattva-dṛṣṭi* – view of existence, or entity – has been translated into Tibetan as *'jig tshogs lta* (view of the transitory), usually used to translate *satkāyadṛṣṭi*.

430 The Sanskrit for this verse (as found on p.612 of Karen Lang, "Āryadeva on the Bodhisattva's Cultivation of Merit and Knowledge", Ann Arbor: University Microfilms, 1983) is:

samyag dṛṣṭe paraṃ sthānaṃ kiñcid dṛṣṭe śubhā gatiḥ/
tasmād adhyātmacintāyāṃ kāryā nityaṃ matir budhaiḥ//

Following the Sanskrit, the second part of the stanza says, more simply, "Therefore the wise engage the mind in thought relating to the self."

Lang's translation on p.322.

431 Toh 3865 (P5266), *bodhisattvayogācāra catuḥśatakaṭīkā*, *byang chub sems dpa'i rnal 'byor spyod pa bzhi brgya pa'i rgya cher 'grel pa*, Tokyo *sde dge* Vol.8, 142b.2–142b.4. The wording of the first phrase is slightly different

there, and serves as a better gloss of the verse. Rather than saying *don dam pa'i shes pas de kho na nyid mthong ba yod na*, as is found in both the Delhi and Berkeley editions of the *Annotations*, that text says *don dam pa'i shes pas de nyid yang dag par mthong ba yod na*, "When one sees suchness *correctly* through the knowledge of the ultimate . . .". The Sanskrit for this is found in Haraprasād Shāstri, ed., "Catuḥśatika of Ārya Deva," Memoirs of the Asiatic Society of Bengal, III no 8 (1914), p.478, and mirrors the wording found in the Tokyo *sde dge*:

paramārthajñānena khalu samyagdṛṣṭe paramārthe param sthānaṃ prāpyate nirvāṇam/ īṣat kiñcit dṛṣṭe śubhā devamanuṣyagatir bhavati

432 Sanskrit (Lang, p.638, English translation on pp.427–8):

advitīyaṃ śivadvāram kudṛṣṭīnāṃ bhayaṃkaram

The Sankrit term *bhayaṃkaram* means "to frighten" or "scare away" rather than "to destroy" as does the Tibetan *'jig byed*. Thus, following the Sanskrit, the second line would be translated, "That which scares away bad views," or "Frightening to holders of bad views". The Tibetan *'jig* (to destroy) is orthographically very close to the verb for frighten – *'jigs*. Thus, it is possible that the shift from *'jigs* to *'jig*, rather than being deliberate, was a spelling or scribe's error. However, more probably the translator was following a gloss given by Chandrakīrti in later commentary on the verse (Tibetan, 191a.4–5; Sanskrit, 498.3–5) in which Chandrakīrti says, "Because it is seen to utterly *destroy* (Sanskrit *vināśa*) all bad views that are based on thorough imputation of an own-entity of things . . .". In any case, as interpreted by Chandrakīrti and by Gyel-tsap (*rgyal tshab*), one of Dzong-ka-ba's two chief disciples, bad views and not the holders of those views are the object of the verb. Gyel-tsap's gloss of the line in his *Essence of Good Explanation, Explanation of (Āryadeva's) "Four*

Hundred" (*bzhi brgya pa'i rnam bshad legs bshad snying po*, Pleasure of Elegant Sayings Printing Press, Sarnath, 1971), chapter 12, p.9, is: "It is that which when realized destroys the bad views that are conceptions of extremes."

433 Tokyo *sde dge* Vol. 8, 190b.2. Commentary on XII.13 continueș until 191a.6. Sanskrit for the passage (Haraprasād Shāstri, p.497.22–23) is:

yat advitīyaṃ śivadvāram tan nairātmyaṃ yat kudṛṣṭīnāṃ bhayaṅkaram tan nairātmyaṃ

434 P5658, Vol.129, 174.3.6–7. The Sanskrit for this verse, as found on p.14 of Hahn is:

skandhagrāho yāvad asti
tāvad evāham ity api/
ahaṃkāre sati punaḥ
karma [janma tataḥ punaḥ//]

Translation by J. Hopkins in *The Precious Garland and the Song of the Four Mindfulnesses*, p.22.

435 There are two different translations of Nāgārjuna's *Seventy Stanzas on Emptiness* found in the Tokyo *sde dge*. Just the verses themselves were translated by Shön-nu-chok (*gshon nu mchog*), Dar-ma-drak (*dar ma grags*), and Ku (*khu*) – the *Seventy Stanzas on Emptiness* (*stong pa nyid bdun cu pa'i tshig le'ur byas pa*, *śūnyatāsaptatikārikā*) Toh 3827, Vol.1. A slightly different translation of the verses by Jinamitra and Ye-shay-day (*ye shes sde*) is found within their translation of Nāgārjuna's own *Commentary on the "Seventy Stanzas on Emptiness"* (*stong pa nyid bdun cu pa'i 'grel pa*, *śūnyatāsaptativṛtti*), Toh 3831, Vol.1.

The version of this verse cited here corresponds to that found in Jinamitra and Ye-shay-day's (*ye shes sde*) translation of Nāgārjuna's *Commentary on the "Seventy Stanzas on Emptiness"*, Vol.1 of the Tokyo *sde dge*, 120a.5. As cited in the Tokyo *sde dge* edition of the *Seventy Stanzas on Emptiness* (*stong pa nyid bdun cu pa'i tshig le'ur byas pa*), Vol.1, 26b.3, the verse differs slightly in wording, though not in meaning. It reads:

rgyu rkyen las skyes dngos po rnams
yang dag nyid du rtog pa gang
de ni ston pas ma rig gsungs
de las yan lag bcu gnyis 'byung

Chr. Lindtner has also noted this difference in his *Nagarjuniana*, Indiske Studier 4, Copenhagen: Akademisk Forlag, 1982, p.62. Lindtner's translation of this verse is on p.63.

436 He says this very clearly in VI.120, (p.233 of La Vallée Poussin's edition):

Yogis see with their minds that all afflictions
And faults arise from the view of the transitory
And having realized that the self is the object of
That [view] they refute self.

nyon mongs skyon rnams ma lus 'jig tshogs la
lta las byung bar blo yis mthong gyur zhing
bdag ni 'di yi yul du rtogs byas nas
rnal 'byor pa yis bdag ni 'gog par byed

(See chapter three of the translation, p.169.)

437 See Jeffrey Hopkins, *Meditation on Emptiness*, (London: Wisdom, 1983) pp.296–304.

438 In the Berkeley text, 4b.6, Ba-so is identified as the commentator making this identification. I have chosen to follow the Delhi edition based on the fact that this is the second time the *Scriptural Collection of Bodhisattvas* has been mentioned by Dzong-ka-ba; the first reference was in the introduction to the calm abiding section, which is where Ba-so would likely have made such an identification. Since Dra-di's commentary only begins with the special insight portion of the text, this is, for him, the first reference, and thus he seems the more likely author.

See note 298 for references for this sūtra passage and Dzong-ka-ba's earlier citation of it.

439 Āryadeva refers to this same sūtra statement in his *Four Hundred*, XII.11. (See Lang, p.425.) Chandrakīrti's

commentary on it is found in Toh 3865, Tokyo *sde dge* Vol.8, 189b.5–190a.5. His essential point is that the effects of even a minor falling from the view are far more severe than those of falling from ethics.

Gyel-tsap's *Essence of Good Explanation, Explanation of (Āryadeva's) "Four Hundred"* (Chapter 12, p.8) says that because deprecating emptiness brings great harm to oneself and others, the deterioration of ethics is not so bad, but one should not allow deterioration of the view of emptiness in the least. Through ethics, one attains the effect of proceeding to high states; through the view realizing reality, one proceeds to the supreme states of liberation and omniscience. (stong pa nyid la skur pa 'debs pa rang gzhan la gnod pa shin tu che bas tshul khrims las ni nyams pa sla yi stong pa nyid kyi lta ba las cis kyang nyams par bya ba ma yin te/ tshul khrims kyis ni 'bras bu mtho ris 'gro la de kho na nyid rtogs pa'i lta bas thar pa dang thams cad mkhyen pa'i go 'phang mchog tu 'gro bar 'gyur ro//)

440 Sanskrit: (Lang, p.641, English, p.433):

dharmaṃ samāsato 'hiṃsāṃ varṇayanti tathāgatāḥ/
śūnyatām eva nirvāṇaṃ kevalaṃ tad ihobhayam//

Chandrakīrti cites this verse in his *Clear Words*, La Vallée Poussin edition of the Sanskrit, 351.13–14.

441 Toh 3865, Tokyo *sde dge* Vol.8, 194b.3. His commentary on the entire verse goes from 194a.4 to 194b.4. Chandrakīrti explains that the doctrine of the Tathāgatas can be said, in brief, to be non-harmfulness because non-harmfulness means the opposite of any actions or thought of harm and hence includes the path of the ten virtues, as well as all help to others. Because the fruit of non-harmfulness is rebirth in high status and the fruit of realization of emptiness is the attainment of nirvāṇa, it is said that there are "only" these two doctrines, "only" meaning that these two are complete – no others are needed.

442 I have not been able to locate this passage in the sūtra.

443 P6016, Vol.153, 38.1.1–38.1.3. Translation by Geshe Wangyal in *The Door of Liberation* (New York: Lotsawa, 1978), p.122; by Robert A.F. Thurman in *The Life and Teachings of Tsong Khapa*, p.104.

444 Toh 3916, Tokyo *sde dge* Vol.15, 48a.4–7.

445 For the sūtra reference, see note 301.

446 For the sūtra reference, see note 302.

CHAPTER ONE: THE INTERPRETABLE AND THE DEFINITIVE

447 This is the second of the two parts of the "explanation of special insight". The first part, "the need to achieve special insight even though one possesses a meditative stabilization having the four qualifications" was the subject matter of the previous chapter.

448 The "above" referred to here is 314a.3 of the Dharmsala edition of Dzong-ka-ba's text, Vol.II, 28.3, of the Annotations, where Dzong-ka-ba says that he will explain how to train in [calm abiding and special insight] individually in three parts: how to train in calm abiding, how to train in special insight, and how to conjoin those two.

449 La Vallée Poussin edition, 174.16; French translation, *Muséon* 11 (1910) p.355. Pleasure of Elegant Sayings Printing Press edition, 87.9.

450 La Vallée Poussin edition, 75.17–21; French translation, *Muséon* 11 (1910), p.274 (De la manière dont cet [homme] a compris la nature profonde des choses (2) par l'Écriture et aussi par le raisonnement, de cette manière il faut exposer [cette nature des choses] d'après et en suivant le système (3) du noble Nāgārjuna). I have translated the passage in accordance with Jam-yang-shay-ba's obvious intention, and the Tibetan allows such a translation. However, such a translation does not accord with the explanation of the verse given in Dzong-ka-ba's *Illumination of the Thought* (in *rje tsong kha pa'i gsung dbu ma'i lta ba'i skor*, Vol.2, 304.1–8). Translated

in accordance with that commentary, the verse would read:

> Since with scripture as well as reasoning [Nāgārjuna
> Taught] how that [sixth ground Bodhisattva] realizes
> The very profound doctrine, I [Chandrakīrti] will speak
> In accordance with the system of the Superior Nāgārjuna.

(Translation by Jeffrey Hopkins and Anne Klein.) I feel that *Chandrakīrti's [Auto] commentary on the "Supplement to (Nāgārjuna's) 'Treatise on the Middle Way'"* (La Vallée Poussin, 76.1–9) is ambiguous and allows either reading.

451 P162, Vol.6, 259.3.8–259.4.2. Translation by E. Obermiller in the *History of Buddhism by Bu-ston* (Heidelberg: Harrasowitz, 1932), Part 2, p.111. He cites it as Kg. RGYUD. XI. 450a.5–6.

452 This translation follows Hopkins and Klein (unpublished manuscript, "Wisdom in Tibetan Buddhism 1: The Opposite of Emptiness", Part One: Chandrakīrti, p.5) who follow Nga-wang-bel-den's *Annotations for (Jam-yang-shay-ba's) "Great Exposition of Tenets", Freeing the Knots of the Difficult Points, Precious Jewel of Clear Thought* (*grub mtha' chen mo'i mchan 'grel dka' gnad mdud grol blo gsal gces nor*, Sarnath: Pleasure of Elegant Sayings Printing Press, 1964). See Hopkins' note 10 for an explanation of the translation. The passage is also translated by E. Obermiller in the *History of Buddhism by Bu-ston* (Heidelberg: Harrasowitz, 1932), Part 2, pp.110–11. The Sanskrit from the Buddhist Sanskrit Texts 3 edition (P.L. Vaidya, ed., *Saddharmalaṅkāvatārasūtram*, Darbhanga: Mithila Institute, 1963), chapter ten (*Sagāthakam*), verses 165 and 166cd, p.118.13–14 is:

> dakṣiṇā-patha-vedalyāṁ
> bhikṣuḥ śrīmān mahāyaśāḥ
> nāgāhvayaḥ sa nāmnā tu

sad-asat-pakṣa-dārakaḥ

. . . .

āsādya bhūmiṃ muditāṃ

yāsyate 'sau sukhāvatīm

Translation by D.T. Suzuki in the *Lankāvatāra Sūtra* (London: Routledge & Kegan Paul Ltd., 1973 rpt.), pp. 239–40.

453 See Jam-yang-shay-ba's *Great Exposition of the Middle Way*, 195b.4–196a.1. Translation by Jeffrey Hopkins in "Wisdom in Tibetan Buddhism 1: The Opposite of Emptiness", Part Three: Jam-yang-shay-ba, pp.15–16.

454 P898, Vol.35, 255.2.6–7.

455 P888, Vol.35, 99.4.5.

456 This is the abbreviated title most often used for Dzong-ka-ba's commentary on Nāgārjuna's *Treatise on the Middle Way*. Its full title is *Ocean of Reasoning, Explanation of (Nāgārjuna's) "Treatise on the Middle Way"* (*dbu ma rtsa ba'i tshig le'ur byas pa shes rab ces bya ba'i rnam bshad rigs pa'i rgya mtsho*) and it is also frequently referred to as simply the *Ocean of Reasoning* (*rigs pa'i rgya mtsho*). P6153, Vol. 156. Also: Sarnath, India: Pleasure of Elegant Sayings Printing Press, no date. The passage cited here is found in the Pleasure of Elegant Sayings Press edition, 4.17–4.18.

457 Jam-yang-shay-ba's *Great Exposition of the Middle Way*, 196a.2–196a.6. Translation by Hopkins in "Wisdom in Tibetan Buddhism 1: The Opposite of Emptiness", Part Three: Jam-yang-shay-ba, Chapter One, pp. 16–17.

458 This passage has been translated in accordance with the Berkeley text, 9a.2–3, which reads: *mdo'i drang don nges don dpyad skabs yin cing don zhes pa brjod don la byed pa'i phyir te*. The Delhi edition, 155.1, reads: *mdo'i drang don nges don dpyad skabs spyi'i don la zhes pa'i rjod don byed pa'i phyir te*. I find the latter impenetrable, and none of the Tibetan scholars consulted about it was able to shed light on its meaning.

459 P842, Vol.34, 64.3.6–64.4.1.

460 P842, Vol.34, 64.4.4–64.4.7. Sanskrit for the following terms is taken from Chandrakīrti's citation of the sūtra passage in the *Clear Words*, La Vallée Poussin's Sanskrit edition, p.43, and in cases where that passage differed from the version cited here, from Susumu Yamaguchi, *Index to the Prasannapadā Madhyamaka-vṛtti*, Part Two Tibetan-Sanskrit (Kyoto: Heirakuji-Shoten, 1974).

461 The above two paragraphs are summary from Nga-wang-rap-den. In the Delhi edition it was located before the sūtra citation (156.6); in the Berkeley text, it was placed in the middle of the sūtra passage, after sūtras of interpretable meaning and before those of definitive meaning (10a.5). I have moved it to the end of the sūtra passage so as to fit in better with the flow of the passage.

462 P795, Vol.31, 281.1.5–281.1.6.

463 P5287, Vol.101, 46.3.5–46.3.8.

464 P768, Vol.28, 132.3.2.

465 At this point, the compiler of the Berkeley text (11b.6–7) adds in the following commentary:

> When one posits the interpretable and the definitive in terms of whether the meaning of this [passage] (*'di'i don*) needs or does not need to be interpreted otherwise, then scriptures themselves are identified as the illustrations of the interpretable and the definitive; when one posits the objects (*don*), which need or do not need to be interpreted otherwise, as the interpretable and the definitive, then conventionalities and ultimates are taken as the definitive and the interpretable.

('di'i don gzhan du drang dgos mi dgos kyi dbang du byas nas drang nges 'jog pa na gsung rab nyid drang nges kyi mtshan gzhir gzung la gzhan du drang dgos mi dgos kyi don la drang nges su 'jog pa na kun rdzob dang don dam la drang nges su bya pa'o)

466 P5287, Vol.101, 46.1.5–46.1.6.

467 The Berkeley compiler, 12a.3, adds in the following commentary:

> If [the differentiation of] interpretability and definitiveness were made in terms of whether or not the object as it is taught exists or not, then merely to have valid cognition would be sufficient. However, since that is not sufficient, [Kamalashīla] says "[which makes an explanation] in terms of the ultimate".

(ji ltar bstan ba ltar gyi don yod med la drang nges su byed na tshad ma dang bcas pas chog kyang des mi chog pas don dam pa'i dbang du mdzad pa zhes gsungs so.)

468 This eliminates the idea that Dzong-ka-ba is speaking about a generality of production, such as existence, which is also *skye'i ba'i spyi* in Tibetan.

CHAPTER TWO: RELIABLE SOURCES

469 This is commentary which Dra-di Ge-shay has somewhat confusedly added here, making what is being said quite acceptable in the Prāsaṅgika system. According to Sha-mar-den-dzin and Nga-wang-bel-den, he is following Kaydrup's *Thousand Dosages* (*Thousand Dosages/ Opening the Eyes of the Fortunate*, *Treatise Brilliantly Clarifying the Profound Emptiness*, *stong thun chen mo/ zab mo stong pa nyid rab tu gsal bar byed pa'i bstan bcos skal bzang mig 'byed*, The Collected Works of the Lord Mkhas-grub rJe dGe-legs-dpal-bzaṅ-po, volume ka, New Delhi: Lama Gurudeva, 1980), 41a.6–41b.1 in doing so, but both commentators criticize him for contradicting the context of Dzong-ka-ba's statement. At this point Dzong-ka-ba is presenting this as an interpretation he rejects: all that he says in the *Great Exposition* is, "Proponents of Thorough Non-Abiding who assert that the mere elimination of elaborations with respect to appearances is the ultimate truth"; in the *Medium Exposition* he says, "Proponents of Thorough Non-Abiding who assert that *the positive inclusion* (*yongs gcod*) in

terms of the elimination of elaborations with respect to appearances is the ultimate truth".

In the commentarial literature there is a controversy over whether the designations Reason-Established Illusionist and Thoroughly Non-Abiding can be accepted in some form, and Dra-di is jumping ahead to this controversy by adding commentary to Dzong-ka-ba's words to show how he feels the term "Proponent of Thorough Non-Abiding" can be interpreted so that it becomes just another synonym for Prāsaṅgika-Mādhyamika. Since Dzong-ka-ba himself concludes this section of his text by saying that such an interpretation is not good, it is clear that he was not intending this passage to be interpreted in a fashion acceptable to his own system.

470 The Delhi text omits here the commentary of Ba-so, found in the Berkeley text on 14b.3, which adds in the name, "the master Shūra". A-gya-yong-dzin repeats this dual identification in his commentary, 167.3.

471 P763, Vol.27, 238.5.6, chapter 25; Sanskrit in Buddhist Sanskrit Texts No.1, 286.10.

gambhīra śānto virajaḥ prabhāsvaraḥ
prāptomi dharmo hyamṛto 'saṃskṛtaḥ

Translation follows the Tibetan. English translation (from the French) by Gwendolyn Bays (Berkeley: Dharma, 1983) Vol.II, p.594.

For a fuller discussion, see note 531, the reference for another citation of this passage that is found on p.351.

472 The Pleasure of Elegant Sayings edition of Nāgārjuna's *Treatise on the Middle Way*, 47.7. Sanskrit in La Vallée Poussin's edition, p.372.12–13:

aparapratyayaṃ śāntaṃ
prapañcair aprapañcitaṃ/
nirvikalpam anānārtham
etat tattvasya lakṣaṇaṃ//

The passage is found in the Tibetan of the *Clear Words*, Dharmsala edition, p.306 last line-310.6. French translation by J.W. de Jong, *Cinq Chapitres de la Prasannapadā* (Paris: Geuthner, 1949) p.29.

473 This passage is found in the *Medium Exposition*, edition

found in *rje tsong kha pa'i gsung dbu ma'i lta ba'i skor*, Vol.2, 732.3–5. Thurman's translation in *The Life and Teachings of Tsong Khapa*, pp.168–9. Hopkins' translation, p.117.

474 *Medium Exposition*, edition in *rje tsong kha pa'i gsung dbu ma'i lta ba'i skor*, Vol.2, 732.18–733.2. Thurman's translation, p.169. See Hopkins' translation, pp.118–19.

475 The above paragraph of commentary by Jam-yang-shay-ba was located in the *Annotations* after the next paragraph. I have moved it to this location to better maintain the flow of Jam-yang-shay-ba's argument.

476 Nga-wang-rap-den's commentary has been placed here in accordance with the Berkeley text, 15b.3. In the Delhi edition it is located near the beginning of the discussion, p.168.3 – between Dzong-ka-ba's statement that Lo-den-shay-rap's refutation of this mode of division of Mādhyamika was good and Jam-yang-shay-ba's commentary citing the *Extensive Sport Sūtra*; it seems to contribute more to the discussion and to be less disruptive to the flow of the argument as placed in the Berkeley edition. Also, in accordance with the Berkeley text, this commentary is identified as being by Nga-wang-rap-den, not by Ba-so and Dra-di Ge-shay as identified in the Delhi edition.

477 The preceding paragraph was moved to this location in accordance with the Berkeley text, 16a.1. In the Delhi edition this paragraph is located on 173.6, several pages below this point, and does not fit together with the rest of the text nearly as well as it does here.

478 See Dzong-ka-ba's *Essence of the Good Explanations*, Pleasure of Elegant Sayings Printing Press edition, 98.5–99.5. For English translation, see Thurman's *Tsong Khapa's Speech of Gold in the Essence of True Eloquence*, pp.258–9.

479 This is all that Dzong-ka-ba says; he cites Ye-shay-day's opinion without further comment. The following commentary from Jam-yang-shay-ba refutes Ye-shay-day's position on the grounds that Nāgārjuna did indeed

refute the Chittamātra position that there are no external objects. Dzong-ka-ba, judging from his *Essence of the Good Explanations* as cited above, would presumably agree that Nāgārjuna did refute Mind-only. However, whether such entails that he would consider Ye-shay-day's statement to be in error remains open to question given the exact phrasing of that statement. See the following two notes.

480 Jam-yang-shay-ba is probably referring to Nāgārjuna's *Essay on the Mind of Enlightenment* (*byang chub sems kyi 'grel pa, bodhicittavivaraṇa*), a text cited by Dzong-ka-ba in his *Essence of the Good Explanations* at the point of this discussion, which says:

The statement by the Subduer
That all these are mind-only
Is for the purpose of dispelling the fear of the childish
It is not so in reality.

This is indeed a refutation by Nāgārjuna of the Chittamātra teaching of mind-only. However, Sha-mar-den-dzin points out, 30.3–4, that this text is a spin-off from the *Guhyasamāja Tantra* and thus would be considered a tantric, not a Mādhyamika text. As such, it would not seem to contradict Ye-shay-day's statement that it is not made clear *in Mādhyamika treatises* by Nāgārjuna and Āryadeva whether external objects do or do not exist.

Although Christian Lindtner in his *Nagarjuniana* (p.11) has included the *Essay on the Mind of Enlightenment* within the works that he considers to be authentically by Nāgārjuna, Paul Williams in his review of Lindtner's book (*Journal of Indian Philosophy*, 12 (1984) pp.84–94) argues cogently and at length against attributing the work to Nāgārjuna and instead attributing it to a writer of the eighth or ninth century. One of his reasons against Nāgārjuna being the author of the text is its rejection of mind-only and use of Yogāchāra terminology that Williams finds no evidence in Nāgārjuna's other works to show he was familiar with.

481 Translation from Hopkins, trans. *The Precious Garland and the Song of the Four Mindfulnesses*, p.76. Sanskrit, as found in Hahn, pp.128–30, is:

yathaiva vaiyākaraṇo
mātṛkām api pāṭhayet/
buddho 'vadat tathā dharmaṃ
vineyānāṃ yathākṣamam//

keṣāṃ cid avadad dharmaṃ
pāpebhyo vinivṛttaye/
keṣāṃ cit puṇyasiddhyarthaṃ
keṣāṃ cid dvayaniśritam//

dvayāniśritam ekeṣāṃ
gambhīraṃ bhīrubhīṣaṇam
śūnyatākaruṇāgarbham
ekeṣāṃ bodhisādhanam//

As Sha-mar-den-zin, 31.2–3, points out, although these verses do seem to be indicating implicitly that the Chittamātra view is superceded by that of Mādhyamika, such is not clear in the literal words. Thus he feels that this passage also does not contradict Ye-shay-day's statement that it was not made *clear* in the Mādhyamika treatises of the Superior Nāgārjuna whether external objects exist or not.

482 A-gya-yong-dzin gives a somewhat fuller explanation, 167.3–5. Although Dzong-ka-ba says here in the *Great Exposition* that the chronology is evident to be thus, in the *Medium Exposition* (*rje tsong kha pa'i gsung dbu ma'i lta ba'i skor* edition, 670.9; Thurman's translation, p.117, Hopkins' p.6), he qualifies this statement, saying, "the chronology *of the clarification [of the texts by Nāgārjuna and Āryadeva] through great treatises* is evident to be thus". The reason for this qualification is that there were great Mādhyamikas of similar assertion who preceded both Bhāvaviveka and Shāntarakṣhita, and thus one can consider Ye-shay-day's account to be a chronology of the founding of those systems – i.e., setting

them forth in contradistinction to other systems – but not as a mere chronology of the persons who assert tenets in accordance with those systems.

483 See Kay-drup's *Thousand Dosages*, Gurudeva edition, 41b.5–43a.4, for his discussion of this topic. Quite aside from seconding the very specific objection brought up by Dzong-ka-ba concerning Chandrakīrti – saying that he cannot be considered to make assertions in accordance with any of the lower tenet systems – Kay-drup makes a broader objection (42a.2–3). He says that even Bhāvaviveka and Jñānagarbha – famed as Sautrāntika-Mādhyamikas – cannot be considered to accord with the Sautrāntikas in their presentations of conventionalities because they have many great dissimilarities from that system, such as not asserting self-knowers even conventionally. If something were posited as according with something else merely because of according in some partial way, then it would absurdly follow that all tenet systems accorded with each other.

484 In the Berkeley text, this paragraph was placed considerably earlier, at 17a.1–2; this would be p.401 of the English translation, coming just before the beginning of the heading, "Fifth, a further unsuitability ...".

485 P5380, Vol.103, 187.2.3. This is translated by Chr. Lindtner in "Atiśa's Introduction to the Two Truths, and Its Sources", *Journal of Indian Philosophy* 9, 1981, p.194. He has interpreted the Tibetan syntax a bit differently. The entire passage (15–16ab) reads:

stong nyid gang gis rtogs she na/
de bzhin gshegs pas lung bstan zhing/
chos nyid bden pa gzigs pa yi/
klu sgrub slob ma zla grags yin/
de las brgyud pa'i man ngag gis/
chos nyid bden pa rtogs par 'gyur/

My translation of it is:

Through what is emptiness realized?
Through the quintessential instructions transmitted from

Chandrakīrti, student of Nāgārjuna
Who was prophesied by the Tathāgata
And who perceived reality, the truth,
Reality, the truth, will be realized.

Lindtner's translation (p.194) is:

> But who has [actually] "understood" emptiness? – Nāgārjuna who was predicated (*vyākṛta*) by the Tathāgata, [and his] disciple (*śiya*) Chandrakīrti who [also] saw the absolute truth (*dharmatāsatya*). The absolute truth (*dharmatāsatya*) may be understood by means of the instructions (*upadeśa*) hailing from him.

Lindtner has interpreted the interrogative pronoun in the phrase *stong nyid* GANG *gis rtogs* as referring to a person, "Who has realized emptiness?" I feel that my interpretation of it as *what* – "Through what is emptiness realized?", is supported by the answer given in 16ab – "Through the quintessential instructions transmitted from him, reality, the truth, will be realized." Also, Lindtner has split the two lines, "Who was prophesied by the Tathāgata" (*de bzhin gshegs pas lung bstan zhing*), and "And who perceived reality, the truth" (*chos nyid bden pa gzigs pa yi*), so that the first applies to Nāgārjuna and the second to both Nāgārjuna and Chandrakīrti. Such a split is not justified by the Tibetan connective *zhing*, and given that only Nāgārjuna was prophesied by the Buddha, it is clear that both lines must refer to him.

CHAPTER THREE: STAGES OF ENTRY INTO SUCHNESS

486 The first verse of the *Treatise* says:

I bow down to the perfect Buddha,
The highest of speakers,
Who taught that dependent-arisings [in the face of uncontaminated meditative equipoise]

Are without cessation, without production,
Without annihilation, without permanence,
Without coming, without going,
Without difference, and without sameness –
Pacified of elaborations, peaceful.

See the La Vallée Poussin edition of Chandrakīrti's *Clear Words*, pp.11–12, for the Sanskrit and Tibetan. Dzong-ka-ba discusses this verse in his *Ocean of Reasoning, Explanation of (Nāgārjuna's) "Treatise on the Middle Way"*, *rje tsong kha pa'i gsung dbu ma'i lta ba'i skor* edition, Vol.1, 483.–8 through 484.–5, and the bracketed material in the translation above is drawn from 483.16.

487 Tibetan in the Dharmsala edition, 282.6–7; Sanskrit in the La Vallée Poussin edition, 334.5–6.

488 Tibetan in the Dharmsala edition, beginning of chapter eighteen, 284.1–11. Sanskrit in the La Vallée Poussin edition, 340.3–12.

489 Tibetan in the Dharmsala edition, 284.12–285.2. Sanskrit in the La Vallée Poussin edition, 340.13–15.

490 This commentary is placed here in accordance with the Berkeley text, 21b.7. In the Delhi text it was placed above, just before the section heading that begins, "Seventh ..."

491 This commentary by Ba-so is placed here in accordance with the Berkeley text, 22b.4. In the Delhi text it was placed just before the section headings.

492 This commentary is placed here in accordance with Berkeley, 22b.6. In the Delhi text it is found much earlier, 183.4–184.2, just before the section heading that begins, "Seventh ...".

493 Chapter eighteen, the Tibetan is found in the Dharmsala edition at 288.10–20; the Sanskrit is in the La Vallée Poussin edition, 345.13–346.3.

494 The translation of the previous two sentences follows the compiler of the Berkeley text. Ba-so gives a different interpretation of the passage, taking the investigation as

one analyzing whether or not the aggregates themselves are inherently existent, as follows:

> Is it something designated to a basis of designation having the character of the aggregates, that is, aggregates established from their own side, or inherently established? Or, is it designated to a basis of designation that is without the own-character of the aggregates?

495 Chapter One, p.20.5–9 in the La Vallée Poussin edition of the Tibetan, pp. 17.20–18.3 in the Council of Cultural and Religious Affairs edition.

496 Pleasure of Elegant Sayings edition, 45.20; *rje tsong kha pa'i gsung dbu ma'i lta ba'i skor* edition, Vol.1, 504.1. The bracketed middle portion of the passage, from "in dependence upon its force" through to "However," was indicated by ellipsis in the citation of this passage in the *Annotations*.

497 Pleasure of Elegant Sayings edition, 46.4; *rje tsong kha pa'i gsung dbu ma'i lta ba'i skor* edition, Vol.1, 504.5

498 Nga-wang-rap-den is referring to the passage from Chandrakīrti's *Clear Words* cited above (p.296) and is interpreting the passage as did Ba-so – see note 494 above. Another mode of interpretation, that set forth by the compiler of the Berkeley text, was followed in translating the above passage.

499 Chapter eighteen, Toh 3842, Tokyo *sde dge* Vol.1, 240b.2.

500 The compiler of the Berkeley text adds at this juncture, 26b.2–4, the following explanation of different meanings of "substantial" and "imputed" existence:

> The Hearer schools assert that since [a pot] is a collection generality which is a composite of many minute particles, it does not substantially exist. The master Bhāvaviveka asserts that a pot, for instance, which is a composite of particles existing in one base or of one type is substantially existent and that a forest, for instance, which is a collective aggregation

of different types or different bases is imputedly existent. Those which are self-instituting in the sense of their being apprehendable without depending upon other factualities are the basis-of-all and so forth. Those that are self-instituting in the sense of their being directly cognizable without depending upon object-possessors – terms or conceptual consciousnesses – are [for instance] forms, sounds, and so forth. Those that cannot be self-instituting since their entities are not apprehendable without depending upon other factualities are, for instance, persons. The definition of an imputed existent is: "a phenomenon that is included within those which are not or cannot be not directly cognizable without depending upon any object-possessor – a term or conceptual consciousness."

(nyan thos sde pas rdul phra rab du ma bsags pa'i tshogs spyi yin pas rdzas su med par 'dod pa dang rten gcig la yod pa'am rigs gcig pa'i rdul rnams bsags pa'i bum pa lta bu rdzas yod dang rigs tha dad pa'am rten tha dad pa'i tshogs 'dus pa nags tshal lta bu btags yod du slob dpon legs ldan bzhed don gzhan la ma ltos par rang nyid bzung du yod pa tshugs thub pa kun gzhi sogs dang yul can sgra rtog la ma ltos par rang nyid mngon sum du rtogs byar yod pa'i tshugs thub bzugs sgra sogs don gzhan la ma ltos par rang gi ngo bo bzung du med pas tshugs mi thub pa gang zag lta bu dang yul can sgra rtog gang la ma brten par mngon sum du rtogs byar med pa'am mi thub pa gang rung gis bsdus pa'i chos de btags yod kyi mtshan nyid lta bu'o)

501 P5191, Vol.90. This passage is from chapter four, 291.4.3–4.

502 This commentary has been placed here in accordance with the Berkeley text, 27a.5. In the Delhi text it is located two sides later – at 196.6 – which would have put it at the very end of this chapter.

503 The Berkeley compiler, 27b.5, adds here the phrase,

"since they are posited as existing objectively" (*yul steng nas 'jog pas de*).

504 The Berkeley compiler, 27b.6, adds here the phrase, "other powered phenomena and so forth" (*gzhan dbang sogs*).

CHAPTER FOUR: MISIDENTIFYING THE OBJECT OF NEGATION

505 *Bodhicaryāvatāra*, edited by Vidhushekhara Bhattacharya, (Calcutta: The Asiatic Society, 1960), p.221.

506 P795, Vol.31, 283.5.1–283.5.2.

507 La Vallée Poussin's edition of the Tibetan, p.112.18. La Vallée Poussin's translation in *Muséon* 11 (1910), p.308.

508 La Vallée Poussin's edition of the Tibetan, p.122.14–17. La Vallée Poussin's translation in *Muséon* 11 (1910), p.315.

509 La Vallée Poussin's edition of the Tibetan, p.114.4. La Vallée Poussin's translation in *Muséon* 11 (1910), p.309.

510 This commentary is placed here in accordance with the Berkeley text, 30a.1 and 31b.5. In the Delhi text it was placed at the beginning of the section; it seems more appropriate at the end. Also the commentary is identified as being by Nga-wang-rap-den in accordance with Berkeley; in the Delhi text, it was identified at the beginning as being by Jam-yang-shay-ba and at the end as by Ba-so. It accords with the style of neither of them but does with that of Nga-wang-rap-den.

CHAPTER FIVE: THE UNCOMMON FEATURE OF MĀDHYAMIKA

511 Toh 3825, Tokyo *sde dge* Vol.1, 22b.4–5; The Tibetan is also available in Lindtner's *Nagarjuniana*, p.160.

512 The Tibetan is found in the Dharmsala edition of the *Clear Words*, p.400.1–2. The Sanskrit is found in La

Vallée Poussin's edition of the *Prasannapadā*, p.475.

513 Toh 3828, Tokyo *sde dge* Vol.1, 28a.2. The Sanskrit is found in Lindtner's *Nagarjuniana*, p.76.

514 The Tibetan is found in the Dharmsala edition of the *Clear Words*, p.421.8–10 and 422.5–7. The Sanskrit is found in La Vallée Poussin's edition, pp.499 and 500.

515 The Tibetan is found in the Dharmsala edition of the *Clear Words*, 422.2–6. The Sanskrit is found in La Vallée Poussin's edition, 500.1–3.

516 Dra-di Ge-shay has changed Dzong-ka-ba's statement that twenty-five chapters of Nāgārjuna's *Treatise on the Middle Way* mainly refute inherent existence with respect to dependent-arisings to say that the twenty-fifth chapter mainly refutes dependent-arising. As Sha-mar-den-dzin points out, 45.3–6, this must be considered an error, since Dzong-ka-ba clearly means to say (see immediately below) that the twenty-sixth chapter teaches the mode of positing dependent-arisings, the twenty-fourth teaches the feasibility of the presentations of conventionalities within an emptiness of inherent existence, the other twenty-five mainly refute inherent existence, and one must know how to carry over the teaching of the feasibility of the presentation of conventionalities within an emptiness of inherent existence to those twenty-five chapters refuting inherent existence.

517 The Tibetan is found in the Dharmsala edition of the *Clear Words*, pp.425.1–3 and 426.5–7. The Sanskrit is found in La Vallée Poussin's edition, pp.503.10–11 and 505.2–3.

518 Toh 3828, Tokyo *sde dge* Vol.1, 29a.5–6. The Sanskrit as edited by Johnston and Kunst is found in *The Dialectical Method of Nāgārjuna*, p.52 and 53.

519 Toh 3827, Tokyo *sde dge* Vol.1, 26b.4–5.

520 Toh 3825, Tokyo *sde dge* Vol.1, 22a.2–3. The Tibetan can also be found in Lindtner's, *Nagarjuniana*, p.114.

521 In Lindtner's *Nagarjuniana*, pp.134 and 136.

CHAPTER SIX: DEPENDENT-ARISING AND EMPTINESS

522 This is the fourth of four subheadings to the topic, "Identifying the distinguishing feature of Mādhyamika". The first three formed the subject matter of the previous chapter.

523 The Tibetan can be found in the Dharmsala edition of the Tibetan, 422.7–423.10. The Sanskrit is found in La Vallée Poussin's edition, 500.5–501.8.

524 Toh 3828, Tokyo *sde dge* Vol.1, 27b.5. Dzong-ka-ba has cited the verse as it is found in Nāgārjuna's *Commentary on the "Refutation of Objections"*, Toh 3832, Tokyo *sde dge* Vol.1, 126b.2–3. The Sanskrit for the verse, as edited by Johnston and Kunst, is found in *The Dialectical Method of Nāgārjuna*, p.23.

525 Toh 3832, Tokyo *sde dge* Vol.1, 126b.3–127a.1. The Sanskrit from Johnston and Kunst is found in *The Dialectical Method of Nāgārjuna*, p.24.

526 This paragraph has been moved here in accordance with the Berkeley text, 42a.5. In the Delhi text it was located in the middle of the passage from Nāgārjuna's *Commentary on the "Refutation of Objections"* and seemed disruptive to the flow of the argument.

527 The Berkeley commentary, 43a.5, has at this juncture additional commentary, identified as by Jam-yang-shay-ba: "This meaning is set forth in the *Advice to the Lord of Tsako* (*tsa kho dpon por gdams pa*) [Dzong-ka-ba's *Three Principal Aspects of the Path*]:

As long as the two, realization of appearances, or
The inevitability of dependent-arising,
And realization of emptiness, or
The non-assertion [of inherent existence],
Appear to be separate,
There is still no realization
Of the thought of Shākyamuni Buddha."

The translation of the above verse is from Sopa and

Hopkins, *Practice and Theory of Tibetan Buddhism*, p.43. See the emendations to chapter six for the Tibetan of the passage.

528 The Berkeley text, 43a.6, identifies this paragraph as commentary by Nga-wang-rap-den rather than Jam-yang-shay-ba and places it before the outline heading rather than after. Stylistically it could be by either commentator and seems a superfluous commentary wherever it is placed.

529 The Tibetan is found in the Dharmsala edition of Chandrakīrti's *Clear Words*, 420.11–13. The Sanskrit for this verse is found in La Vallée Poussin's edition, p.498.

530 P5658, Vol.129, 176.1–3. The Sanskrit is found in Hahn, *Nāgārjuna's Ratnāvalī*, p.46.

531 P763, Vol.27, 238.5.6. The passage cited by Ba-so in the *Annotations* differs substantially in wording but not meaning from that found in the canon. As cited by Ba-so the verse reads:

zab zhi spros bral 'od gsal 'dus ma byas/
bdud rtsi lta bu'i chos ni kho bos rnyed/
su la bstan kyang go bar mi 'gyur bas/
des na mi smra nags su gnas par bya//

As found in the Peking edition of the sūtra it reads:

zab zhi rdul bral 'od gsal 'dus ma byas/
bdud rtsi chos ni bdag gis thob par gyur/
bdag gis bstan kyang gzhan gyis mi shes te/
mi smrar nags 'dab gnas par bya ba snyam//

The translation of this version differs slightly from that of the version cited by Ba-so:

I have attained a doctrine profound, peaceful,
Free from dust [i.e. pure], luminous, uncompounded, ambrosia.
Though I were to teach it, others would not understand;
Hence I should stay without speaking in the forest.

The Sanskrit, which supports the Peking edition citation, as found in Buddhist Sanskrit Texts, No.1, P.L. Vaidya ed., is:

gambhīra śānto virajaḥ prabhāsvaraḥ
  prāptomi dharmo hyamṛto 'saṃskṛtaḥ/
deśeya cāhaṃ na parasya jāne
  yannūna tūṣṇī pavane vaseyam//

It is interesting to note that one meaning of the Sanskrit term *virajaḥ*, usually translated as "pure", is "free from dust" which is how it is translated into Tibetan in the Peking edition (*rdul bral*). As cited by Ba-so, and as widely renowned in the Tibetan tradition, the term has become "free from elaborations" (*spros bral*) which usually translates the Sanskrit *aprapañca*.

English translation (from the French) by Gwendolyn Bays can be found in *The Lalitavistara Sūtra: The Voice of the Buddha, the Beauty of Compassion*, Vol.2, p.594.

532 The Berkeley text, 45a.6–45b.2, adds here the following commentary, not found in the Delhi text, identified as commentary by Dra-di Ge-shay:

For, it is said in the *Advice to the Lord of Tsa-ko, Nga-wang-drak-ba*, [Dzong-ka-ba's *Three Principal Aspects of the Path*]:

When [the two realizations exist]
Simultaneously without alternation
And when, from only seeing dependent-arising
As infallible, definite knowledge destroys
All the objects of the conception
[Of inherent existence], then the analysis
Of the view [of emptiness] is complete.

Also, it is as is explained in Chandrakīrti's *Clear Words* and in the *Buddhapālita Commentary on (Nāgārjuna's) "Treatise on the Middle Way"* that the Nihilists' conception that former and future lives do not inherently exist is not a realization of emptiness. For, if one does not know how to posit conventionalities, one is not released from the extreme of annihilation, and as long as one has not refuted the two extremes, one has not gained the path of the view of the middle way, and, as explained earlier, needs to realize the way in which conventionalities are feasible as mere nominalities even though conventionalities do not exist for the perspective of that view [that is, do not appear to an exalted wisdom consciousness realizing emptiness]. Dzong-ka-ba's *Answers to the Questions of Jang-chup-la-ma* says:

> Through gaining ascertainment of the inevitable causes and effects of dependent-arisings, the view of annihilation is stopped, and through gaining ascertainment of the emptiness that is the absence of inherent existence, the non-establishment of even a particle that is a focus for the conception of signs, one is released from the extreme of permanence. Therefore, since the view gaining ascertainment of infallible cause and effect within an emptiness of own entityness removes the possibility of the errors of both permanence and annihilation, it is the best of understandings.

Although the Berkeley text identifies the above as commentary by Dra-di Ge-shay, it is far more in Jam-yang-shay-ba's style, particularly since Jam-yang-shay-ba has cited previously within this chapter both Dzong-ka-ba's *Three Principal Aspects of the Path* (see note 527) and *Answers to the Questions of Jang-chup-la-ma* (p.348)

The translation of the above verse from Dzong-ka-ba's *Three Principal Aspects of the Path* is from Sopa and Hopkins, *Practice and Theory of Tibetan Buddhism*, p.43. See the emendations to chapter six for the Tibetan of the passage.

533 The Berkeley compiler, 46b.2–3, has added here the following commentary:

> Bondage, release, and so forth are refuted conventionally because (1) own-character is refuted conventionally and (2) you [misinterpreters of Mādhyamika] assert that the reasoning refuting own-character refutes bondage, release, and so forth.

(tha snyad du bcing grol sogs bkag pa yin te/ tha snyad du rang mtshan 'gag pa gang zhig rang mtshan 'gog pa'i rigs pas bcings grol sogs 'gog par 'dod pa'i phyir/)

534 The Berkeley compiler, 47b.2–3, adds here a phrase of commentary: "since you assert that the two – inherent

existence and cause and effect – are equally non-existent," (rang bzhin dang rgyu 'bras gnyis med mnyam du 'dod pas).

CHAPTER SEVEN: MĀDHYAMIKA RESPONSE

535 This is third of three subdivisions to the topic, "Showing that those systems [that negate too much] refute the uncommon distinguishing feature of Mādhyamika". The topic began on the first page of chapter five, and the first two subheadings, "Identifying the distinguishing feature of Mādhyamika" and "How those systems refute that distinguishing feature" formed the subject matter of chapters five and six.

The Berkeley text, 48b.6, places the adjective "actual" (*don la gnas pa*) somewhat differently from the Delhi text, and, as placed there, it would have to be translated as "factual". Following the Berkeley text, the heading would read: "How a Mādhyamika gives a factual answer to the reasonings of those Tibetan systems that refute the distinguishing feature of Mādhyamika." Either reading is acceptable.

536 Tibetan in the Dharmsala edition of Chandrakīrti's *Clear Words*, 423.15–17 and 424.3–4. Sanskrit in La Vallée Poussin's edition, 502.1–2 and 502.7–8.

537 Tibetan in the Dharmsala edition of Chandrakīrti's *Clear Words*, 426.20 and 427.1–2. Sanskrit in La Vallée Poussin's edition, 505.18 and 506.1.

538 This is commentary on XI.10. Toh 3865, Tokyo *sde dge* Vol.8, 175b.2–3. Sanskrit in Haraprasād Shāstri, 492.13–15.

539 The Delhi text identifies this as commentary by Ba-so whereas the Berkeley text identifies it as by Nga-wang-rap-den. Although it could be by either, it is more in the style of Nga-wang-rap-den, and thus the Berkeley identification has been accepted. Why Nga-wang-rap-den chose to make this point is not readily apparent.

540 Pleasure of Elegant Sayings edition of Dzong-ka-ba's *Essence of the Good Explanations*, 69.14–16. The entire passage reads: "The Two Proponents of [Truly Existent External] Objects do not know how to posit forms and so forth as existing if their being established by way of their own character as the basis of conception by thought and as the foundations of imputing terminology is negated." (Translation from Hopkins, unpublished manuscript). See Thurman's *Tsong Khapa's Speech of Gold in the Essence of True Eloquence*, p.238.

541 This third heading, "the meaning established [by these explanations]" is barely developed; it gets absorbed into a subheading that comes later – see p.371.

542 Tibetan in the Dharmsala edition of Chandrakīrti's *Clear Words*, 280.1–13. Sanskrit in La Vallée Poussin's edition, 329.10–17.

543 The phrase "as well as the meaning established by this" tacked on to the heading represents the third subdivision from a topic begun on p.365. Given the cursory treatment it receives, the heading appears to be superfluous.

544 This is commentary leading into XIV.23. Toh 3865, Tokyo *sde dge* Vol.8, 220b.4–6. Sanskrit does not survive.

545 This is commentary surrounding XI.25. Toh 3865, Tokyo *sde dge* Vol.8, 182b.6–183a.4. Sanskrit does not survive.

546 Dra-di Ge-shay has added in this rather obfuscating phrase of commentary based on a printing error that occurs in both editions of Dzong-ka-ba's text. Both texts (Dharmsala, 386a.4; Dra-shi-lhun-bo, 154.4) read *ji ltar yod pa de ltar ni* NGES *na*; however, as Sha-mar-den-dzin points out (54.5–57.1, *nb* 56.6), and as is supported by the *sde dge* edition of Chandrakīrti's text (182b.4 and 183a.1), the passage should read *de ji ltar yod pa de ltar ni* DES *na*, with the portion up to *ni* being commentary by Chandrakīrti and the *des na* being the last two syllables of Āryadeva's root text (XI.25b) which form a meaning unit with XI.25cd.

547 Lindtner, *Nagarjuniana*, p.79.

548 Tibetan in the Dharmsala edition of Chandrakīrti's *Clear Words*, 235.9–10. Sanskrit in La Vallée Poussin's edition, 272.14 and 273.3.

549 Tibetan in the Dharmsala edition on 235.13–236.1; Sanskrit in La Vallée Poussin's edition, 273.4–9.

550 Tibetan in the Dharmsala edition of Chandrakīrti's *Clear Words*, 417.20. Sanskrit in La Vallée Poussin's edition, 495.1. Dra-di Ge-shay, in interpreting "wrongly viewing emptiness" as referring only to understanding that all phenomena do not exist has, I believe, unnecessarily limited the import of Nāgārjuna's statement, which is worded broadly enough to allow multiple ways of "wrongly viewing emptiness". In his commentary on this verse, Chandrakīrti spells out two wrong views – one is that expressed in Dra-di Ge-shay's commentary, in which phenomena are understood not to exist at all because they are empty. The other mentioned by Chandrakīrti is the position of Hīnayāna schools, namely, to say that the emptiness taught by Mādhyamikas is not the emptiness taught by the Buddha because it goes too far.

551 Tibetan in the Dharmsala edition of Chandrakīrti's *Clear Words*, 418.19–419.10. Sanskrit in La Vallée Poussin's edition, 495.12–496.9.

552 Tibetan in the Dharmsala edition of Chandrakīrti's *Clear Words*, 418.2–6. Sanskrit in La Vallée Poussin's edition, 495.3–5.

553 The Berkeley compiler, 58b.7, adds around Dzong-ka-ba's words "due to mere", the phrase of commentary "DUE TO MERELY being true for a consciousness conceiving true existence" (bden 'dzin gyi ngor bden pa TSAM GYIS – Dzong-ka-ba's text in all capital letters).

554 The Berkeley compiler, 59a.2–3, adds in the following commentary at the end of the passage from Chandrakīrti's *Clear Words*:

> Therefore, we avoid the extreme of annihilation because we do not [assert] the meaning of a view of

annihilation [set forth] in the *Clear Words* and because we assert non-inherent existence.

(tshig gsal gyi chad lta'i don med pa'i phyir dang rang bzhin med par khas blangs pas chad lta sel ba'i PHYIR – Dzong-ka-ba's text in all capital letters.)

555 The Berkeley compiler, 59b.3–4, adds in here the following commentary:

Therefore, just as, in our own system, although [this reasoning] can refute the view of annihilation which is that a formerly inherently existent mind is annihilated, it cannot refute the other [that is to say, viewing former and future lifetimes as non-existent], so there would be [cases] of holding utter non-existence in which the former view of annihilation would not occur but the latter would.

(des na rang lugs rang bzhin pa'i sems sngar rang bzhin du yod pa chad pa'i chad lta 'gog nus kyang gcig shos 'gog mi nus pa bzhin gtan med du 'dzin pa la chad lta snga ma med kyang phyi ma 'byung ba'o)

556 This commentary is placed here in accordance with the Berkeley text, 59b.4. In the Delhi text it was placed earlier, on 263.6, just after the outline heading "eleventh, refuting those . . .", and seemed out of place.

557 Chapter eighteen, commentary that comes between verses seven and eight. Tibetan in the Dharmsala edition of Chandrakīrti's *Clear Words*, 302.4–17. Sanskrit in La Vallée Poussin's edition, 368.4–12.

558 This passage continues directly from that just cited. Tibetan in the Dharmsala edition of Chandrakīrti's *Clear Words*, 302.17–303.1. Sanskrit in La Vallée Poussin's edition, 368.13–15.

559 This passage continues directly from that just cited. Tibetan in the Dharmsala edition of Chandrakīrti's *Clear Words*, 303.1–14. Sanskrit in La Vallée Poussin's edition, 368.16–369.4.

560 This is commentary prior to, including, and subsequent to XV.10ab. Toh 3865, Tokyo *sde dge* Vol.8, 224b.2–3. Sanskrit does not survive.

561 This is commentary at the very end of chapter twenty: Toh 3842, Tokyo *sde dge* Vol.1, 255b.3–4.

APPENDICES

APPENDIX ONE: THE DIVISON OF MĀDHYAMIKAS INTO REASON-ESTABLISHED ILLUSIONISTS AND PROPONENTS OF THOROUGH NON-ABIDING

562 Sanskrit terms supplied by David Ruegg in his *Literature of the Madhyamaka School of Philosophy in India*, p.58–9, as corresponding to the Tibetan terms cited above. The Sanskrit term *māyopamādvayavādin* actually translates the Tibetan *sgyu ma lta bu gnyis su med par smra ba*: "proponent of illusion-like non-dualism", a Tibetan term used far less frequently in this context than is *sgyu ma rigs grub*. See below, note 577, for a reference on its use. The Tibetan *CHOS THAMS CAD rab tu mi gnas par smra ba*, which I have not actually seen used, would correspond more exactly to the Sanskrit *sarvadharmāpratiṣṭānavādin*.

563 The following discussion is primarily an interweaving of five sources:

1 Sha-mar-den-dzin, *Lamp Illuminating the Profound Thought, Set Forth to Purify Forgetfulness of the Difficult Points of (Dzong-ka-ba's) "Great Exposition of Special Insight"*, 19.4–30.2 (Sha-mar's discussion includes an extensive paraphrase of Kay-drup Nor-sang-gya-tso's (*mkhas grub nor bzang rgya mtsho*) assertions (19.4–21.6) which served as the source for that scholar's views);

2 Nga-wang-bel-den's *Explanation of the Conventional and the Ultimate in the Four Systems of Tenets* (usually referred to as the *Presentation of the Two Truths*, the full title is *grub mtha' bzhi'i lugs kyi kun rdzob dang don dam pa'i don rnam par bshad pa legs bshad dpyid kyi dpal mo'i glu dbyangs*, New Delhi: Guru Deva, 1972), 188.5–200.1;

3 Nga-wang-bel-den's *Annotations for (Jam-yang-shay-*

ba's) "Great Exposition of Tenets", Freeing the Knots of the Difficult Points, Precious Jewel of Clear Thought (*grub mtha' chen mo'i mchan 'grel dka' gnad mdud grol blo gsal gces nor*, Sarnath: Pleasure of Elegant Sayings Printing Press, 1964,) dbu 59b.7–62a.1 (note nya);

4 A-gya-yong-dzin's *A Brief Explanation of Terminology Occurring in (Dzong-ka-ba's) "Great Exposition of the Stages of the Path"*, 165.4–167.3;

5 Pa-bong-ka's *About the Four Interwoven Annotations on (Dzong-ka-ba's) "Great Exposition of the Stages of the Path to Enlightenment", Set Forth In Very Brief Form to Purify Forgetfulness and Nourish the Memory*, 103.1–104.3.

See also Kay-drup's *Thousand Dosages* (*Opening the Eyes of the Fortunate, Treatise Brilliantly Clarifying the Profound Emptiness, stong thun chen mo/ zab mo stong pa nyid rab tu gsal bar byed pa'i bstan bcos skal bzang mig 'byed*), 41a.6– 41b.5 in Vol.1 of The Collected Works of the Lord Mkhas-grub rje dge-legs-dpal-bzaṅ-po (New Delhi: Gurudeva, 1980) and see the *Four Interwoven Annotations*, Delhi edition, 166.4–170.6 and 173.6–174.2.

564 *Great Exposition*, Dharmsala edition, 370a.2–370b.2.

565 *Medium Exposition of Special Insight*, edition found in *rje tsong kha pa'i gsung dbu ma'i lta ba'i skor*, Vol.2, 669.13–20. English translation by Robert Thurman on p.117 of *The Life and Teachings of Tsong Khapa*, Robert A.F. Thurman, ed., Dharamsala, Library of Tibetan Works and Archives, 1982. English translation by Jeffrey Hopkins on p.5 of an unpublished manuscript, "Special Insight: From Dzong-ka-ba's *Middling Exposition of the Stages of the Path to Enlightenment Practiced by Persons of Three Capacities* with supplementary headings by Trijang Rinbochay".

566 *Medium Exposition of Special Insight*, edition found in *rje tsong kha pa'i gsung dbu ma'i lta ba'i skor*, Vol.2, 732.8–11 and 732.18–733.2. See p.169 of Thurman's transla-

tion, pp.117 and 118–19 of Hopkins' translation.

567 It is clear that Jam-yang-shay-ba accepts the term "Proponent of Thorough Non-Abiding" as another name for Prāsaṅgika-Mādhyamika. He says in the root text of his presentation of tenets: "They are known as Prāsaṅgikas, Only-Appearance Mādhyamikas, and Non-Abiding Mādhyamikas," and elaborates on this in his *Great Exposition of Tenets*, "Thus, because [Prāsaṅgikas] do not abide in even any of the extremes of permanence or annihilation, they are called Non-Abiding Mādhyamikas or Thoroughly Non-Abiding Mādhyamikas." (Translation from Hopkins' *Meditation on Emptiness*, pp.586 and 587.)

There is no similarly clear statement that he accepts the Reason-Established Illusionists as Svātantrika. Nga-wang-bel-den says in his *Presentation of the Two Truths*, 189.3–4, that since Jam-yang-shay-ba said in the *Great Exposition of Tenets* that the Prāsaṅgikas are Thoroughly Non-Abiding Mādhyamikas, one can implicitly understand that the Svātantrikas are Reason-Established Illusionists. Also, in his *Annotations to the "Great Exposition of Tenets"*, Nga-wang-bel-den says that it appears that Jam-yang-shay-ba accepts that the Reason-Established Illusionists are Svātantrikas since he says that those texts which refute the Reason-Established Illusionists are refuting Svātantrika.

Jang-gya's position can be found in his *Presentation of Tenets*, 289.18–290.13. English translation in Lopez, "The Svātantrika-Mādhyamika School of Mahāyāna Buddhism," (Ann Arbor: University Microfilms, 1982), pp. 388–9. A-gya-yong-dzin's interpretation is cited almost in its entirety below (see next note); Pa-bong-ka's position is found in the pages cited above.

568 A-gya-yong-dzin, 165.4–167.2. A few sentences – indicated by ellipses – that deal with the division of Mādhyamikas by way of how they assert conventionalities have been omitted in the interest of addressing the

issue at hand. A-gya-yong-dzin's including the twofold division of Mādhyamikas by way of how they posit conventionalities within the scope of that rejected by Lo-den-shay-rap seems to be unfounded. Dzong-ka-ba, in both the *Great* and *Medium Expositions*, mentions Lo-den-shay-rap only within his discussion of a twofold division by way of assertions regarding the ultimate, and the division of Mādhyamikas into Reason-Established Illusionists and Proponents of Thorough Non-Abiding is the only one discussed and rejected by Lo-den-shay-rap at the point in his *Epistolary Essay, Drop of Ambrosia* to which Dzong-ka-ba refers.

569 See Ruegg's *Literature of the Madhyamaka School*, p.119, for references in Tāranātha to the Tibetan view that Ashvaghoṣha, Shūra, Mātṛcheṭa, and Dharma/Dhārmika-Subhūti are all names referring to the same person as well as to Western scholars' views on the topic.

570 This text is not found in the Peking edition of the Tibetan canon among the works attributed to Atisha but is available as a separately published work from Bhutan (Paro: Lama Ngodrup and Sherab Drimey, 1979). It contains numerous short works by Atisha as well as works by other authors including Nāgārjuna, Vasubandhu, Shūra, and others. Included within it are works attributed to both Ashvaghoṣha and Shūra. The text in question, the *Cultivation of the Ultimate Mind of Enlightenment*, is found in the *Hundred Short Doctrines* from 418.6–422.6 and is attributed to Ashvaghoṣha.

571 P5431, Vol.103, 246.4.7–246.5.1 and 246.5.2–3. The passage is found in the *Hundred Short Doctrines*, 421.3–5 and 421.6. Translation is in accordance with commentary by Sha-mar-den-dzin, 20.1–21.3, who claims to be giving Nor-sang-gya-tso's interpretation. The last four lines are translated in Hopkins' *Meditation on Emptiness*, p.587.

572 Nor-sang-gya-tso's position and interpretation of the above passage are reported by Sha-mar-den-dzin, 19.5–21.6.

573 Sha-mar-den-dzin, 22.1–22.2 and 23.4–23.6.

574 *rtag brtan chos 'byung* seems to be another name for Tāranātha's *History of Buddhism in India* (*rgya gar chos 'byung*). Tāranātha was a member of the Jo-nang-ba school and its chief monastery was called Dak-den-pun-tsok-ling (*rtag brtan phun tshogs gling*). See p.284 of the translation of Tāranātha's text by Lama Chimpa and Alaka Chattopadhyaya (Calcutta: K.P. Bagchi & Company, rpt. 1980):

> Roughly speaking, the time of the death of this king was the same as that of the Tibetan king Khri-ral (Ral-pa-can). During the reign of this king lived *ācārya* Ānandagarbha, the Mādhyamika-prāsaṅgika Aśvaghoṣa, who wrote Saṃvṛti and Paramārtha *Bodhicitta-bhāvanā-krama* . . .

King Tri-rel-wa-jen (*khri gtsug lde bstan ral ba can*) reigned during the first half of the ninth century, which would indeed place the Ashvaghoṣha who wrote the *Stages of Cultivating the Ultimate Mind of Enlightenment* considerably later than Nāgārjuna.

575 *dbu* 62a.1–3, note *ta*. Ruegg in his *Literature of the Madhyamaka School*, p.120, says that the *Paramārtha-bodhicittabhāvanākrama* ascribed in Tibetan tenets literature to Ārya-Śūra is clearly a later composition, but offers no reasons.

576 See Hopkins' *Meditation on Emptiness*, p.588.

577 I was unable to locate the above text by Jñānavajra in either the Peking or *sde dge* editions of the Tibetan Tripiṭaka. It is cited by Sha-mar-den-dzin 22.5–6. Chandrahari's *Precious Garland* is P5297, Vol.101. The first passage cited by Sha-mar-den-dzin is 145.5.8; the second is 146.2.2. It should be noted that the first passage from Chandrahari is remarkably similar to the passage from Shūra cited above. Chandrahari's text also says, 144.5.5–6, "Buddhists are of seven types: Vaibhāṣhikas, Sautrāntikas, Solitary Realizers, Aspectarians, Non-Aspectarians, Illusionists, and Those Thoroughly Not Abiding."

Ruegg, in his *Literature of the Madhyamaka School*, p.58, gives another reference to the usage of the terms by an Indian scholar, the *Precious Garland of Suchness* (*de kho na nyid rin po che'i phreng ba*, *tattvaratnāvalī*, pp.14, 19 seq.) by the eleventh century scholar Advayavajra, in which he divides Mādhyamikas into those two groups. This is not cited by any of the Ge-luk-ba commentators writing on this controversy. In the Peking *bstan 'gyur* this text is P3085, Vol.68. The references Ruegg must be referring to are from 277.5.4–277.5.8. Again there is no clear statement that this is a way of dividing Mādhyamikas by way of their assertions regarding the ultimate nor is there use of the term "reason-established illusionist"; rather, the term used is "proponent of illusion-like non-dualism" (*sgyu ma lta bu gnyis su med par smra ba*). An interesting point for further study is the transformation of the Tibetan term *sgyu ma gnyis med* into *sgyu ma rigs grub*.

578 See Kay-drup's *Thousand Dosages*, Gurudeva edition, 41b.2–3, and Pa-bong-ka's *About the Four Interwoven Annotations on (Dzong-ka-ba's) "Great Exposition of the Stages of the Path to Enlightenment"*, 103.2–3.

579 Sha-mar-den-dzin, 25.5.

580 *Golden Rosary*, Ngawang Gelek edition, Vol.tsa, 548.4–5. Cited in Sha-mar-den-dzin, 25.1–2.

581 The first passage cited below is found in Gyel-tsap's *Ornament for the Essence*, Gelugpa Student's Welfare Committee edition, 231.12–15. The second is found on p.504.4–7. Both are cited in Sha-mar-den-dzin, 25.3–5.

582 *Ornament for the Essence*, Gelugpa Student's Welfare Committee edition, 504.7–8. Cited in Sha-mar-den-dzin, 26.2–3.

583 *Presentation of the Two Truths*, 189.5–7.

584 *Medium Exposition*, edition found in *rje tsong kha pa'i gsung dbu ma'i lta ba'i skor*, Vol.2, 732.8–10.

585 *Great Exposition*, Dharmsala edition, 370a.2–3.

586 See his *Presentation of the Grounds and Paths of Mantra* (*sngags kyi sa lam*, rgyud smad par khang edition, no other data), p.10.2, where he says, "... it must be asserted that the conceptual reasoning consciousness that realizes emptiness perceives the subject – the basis of emptiness ...." and cites as his reason the fact that such is stated in Dzong-ka-ba's *Ocean of Reasoning, Explanation of (Nāgārjuna's) "Treatise on the Middle Way"* and *Great Exposition of the Stages of the Path*. Nga-wang-bel-den cites those passages from Dzong-ka-ba in his *Presentation of the Two Truths*, 216.5–218.4; the first portion of the passage from the *Great Exposition* is given in the next note.

587 See for example 418a.4–5 where Dzong-ka-ba says:

> That emptiness – i.e., the emptiness of inherent existence with respect to which it is now being settled that a nature of phenomena established by way of its own entity is not established, not even a particle – exists as an attribute of those phenomena, forms and so forth, which serve as substrata. Thus, it is not contradictory that both those [that is, substrata and attribute] exist for one awareness.

In the last sentence, Dzong-ka-ba speaks of both the substrata and the attribute, that is, the phenomena qualified by emptiness and emptiness itself, existing for one awareness. This clearly suggests that both an object and its emptiness appear to that one awareness realizing emptiness.

588 *Great Exposition*, Dharmsala edition, 370a.3 and 370b.1–2.

589 *Presentation of the Two Truths*, 193.7–195.3.

590 The first passage in found on 669.16–17 of the *Medium Exposition*, edition found in *rje tsong kha pa'i gsung dbu ma'i lta ba'i skor*, Vol.2; the second passage is found on 732.18–733.2.

591 *Great Exposition*, Dharmsala edition, 370a.6–370b.1.

592 *Medium Exposition*, edition found in *rje tsong kha pa'i*

gsung dbu ma'i lta ba'i skor, Vol.2, 732.8–11.

593 These two passages are cited in the *Medium Exposition*, edition found in *rje tsong kha pa'i gsung dbu ma'i lta ba'i skor*, Vol.2, 730.13–15 and 730.11–13, respectively. See Thurman's translation, p.167 and Hopkins' translation, p.114.

594 Cited in the *Medium Exposition*, edition found in *rje tsong kha pa'i gsung dbu ma'i lta ba'i skor*, Vol.2, 731.6–8. See Thurman's translation, p.168 and Hopkins' translation, p.115.

595 *Great Exposition*, Dharmsala edition, 370a.6–370b.1.

596 *Four Interwoven Annotations*, 170.1–2.

597 *Medium Exposition*, edition found in *rje tsong kha pa'i gsung dbu ma'i lta ba'i skor*, Vol.2, 732.8–11.

598 Cited in Sha-mar-den-dzin, 28.4–5.

599 28.6–29.3. See Nga-wang-bel-den's *Presentation of the Two Truths*, 125.5–129 for a discussion of these two modes of interpretation and their implications as well as citation of the passage from Kay-drup's *Thousand Dosages* that Sha-mar-den-dzin referred to above.

600 Nga-wang-bel-den, *Presentation of the Two Truths*, 124.7–126.7. An Indian precedent for this sort of division of the ultimate can be found in Maitreya's *Differentiation of the Middle Way and the Extremes* (III.11ab), which says:

> The ultimate is asserted as of three aspects –
> Object, attainment, and practice.

In this context, "object ultimate" refers to emptiness, "attainment ultimate" to nirvāṇa, and "practice ultimate" to the path, specifically an exalted wisdom of meditative equipoise. (For the Sanskrit of the above passage, see the *Madhyānta-vibhāga-śāstra*, R. Pandeya, ed., Delhi: Motilal Banarsidass, 1971, p.95.)

601 See Tenzin Gyatso's *Buddhism of Tibet and the Key to the Middle Way* (New York: Harper & Row, 1975), p.77 for a description of emptiness and the qualities of the cognition realizing it.

APPENDIX TWO: WAYMAN'S TRANSLATION CONSIDERED

602 *Indo-Iranian Journal*, 14 (1972) pp.161–92.
603 *Journal of the International Association of Buddhist Studies*, 3 (1980), pp.68–92.
604 *Philosophy East and West*, 31 (1981), p.382.
605 "Tsong-kha-pa on *kun-rdzob bden-pa*", in Aris and Aung, ed., *Tibetan Studies in Honour of Hugh Richardson* (New Delhi: Vikas, 1980), pp.332.
606 The Dharmsala edition of the *Great Exposition*, 369b.4–370a.1 (portions under discussion emphasized):

'di la 'phags pa lha *ni slob dpon* sangs rgyas bskyangs dang legs ldan 'byed dang zla ba grags pa dang zhi ba 'tsho la sogs pa'i dbu ma pa chen po rnams *kyis* kyang slob dpon dang 'dra bar tshad mar mdzad *pas/ yab sras gnyis ka* dbu ma pa gzhan rnams kyi khungs yin pas snga rabs pa rnams de gnyis *la* gzhung phyi mo'i dbu ma pa zhes dang/ gzhan rnams la phyogs 'dzin pa'i dbu ma pa zhes tha snyad byed do/

607 The Dharmsala edition of the *Great Exposition*, 390a.2–3 (non-case particles emphasized):

'dir slob dpon gyis chad lta ba dang mi 'dra ba'i rgyu mtshan du de la khas len yod *la* kho bo la med pas zhes kyang ma gsungs *la/* de dag med par 'dod *la* kho bo cag de ltar med par mi smra *yi/* yod pa ma yin par 'dod ces mi gsung bar

608 The Dharmsala edition of the *Great Exposition*, 371a.1–2 (non-case particle emphasized):

des na tha snyad du phyi rol 'dod mi 'dod gnyis su nges *la* don dam pa stong pa nyid nges pa'i lta ba rgyud la bskyed tshul gyi sgo nas ming 'dogs na'ang thal rang gnyis su nges pa yin no/

609 The Dharmsala edition of the *Great Exposition*, 375b.2–375b.3 (agentive instrumental emphasized):

de kho na nyid gzigs pa'i 'phags pa'i ye shes *kyis* skye 'gog dang bcings grol sogs ci yang med par gzigs pas na

610 The Dharmsala edition of the *Great Exposition*, 383b.1 (agentive instrumental emphasized):

gzhan yang bcings grol sogs rigs *pas* 'gog na

611 The Dharmsala edition of the *Great Exposition*, 384a.1 (agentive instrumental emphasized):

de lta ma yin na rang gi ngo bos grub pa 'gog pa'i rigs *pas* yod tsam dang skye ba dang 'gag pa tsam la sogs pa ci'i phyir 'gegs par smra/

612 The Dharmsala edition of the *Great Exposition*, 389a.3 (portions under discussion emphasized):

las 'bras med par 'dod pa'i *chad lta ba dang* mi 'dra ba'i tshul gzhan *ni* tshig gsal las rgyas par gsungs te/

613 The Dharmsala edition of the *Great Exposition*, 380a.5:

zhes gsungs pas/ rung mi rung ni de dag yod pa dang med pa la go byar bya'o/

614 See also, for example, *Calming the Mind and Discerning the Real*, p.192, six lines from the bottom. The Tibetan for this is found in the Dharmsala edition of the *Great Exposition*, 377b.1. For my translation, see p.183, line three.

615 Other examples of Wayman's not correctly handling explanation of passages cited can be found on p.175 of his translation, first paragraph, (see my translation, pp.154–5); on p.214, first paragraph after the quote, (see my translation, p.215); and on pp.204–5 where all the material from 204 line 30 through 205, line 15 is explanation of a passage from Chandrakīrti cited previously, a fact that could never be gathered from Wayman's translation (see my translation, pp.201–2).

616 For my translation of this passage, see p.209. The Tibetan, as found in the Dharmsala edition of the *Great Exposition*, 388b.1–388b.4, is (portions under discussion emphasized):

gal te kho bo cag dngos po rnams sngar khas blangs nas phyis med par lta na med lta bar 'gyur yang kho bo cag ni gdod ma nas de dag yod par mi 'dod pas ci zhig chad pa'i chad lta bar 'gyur *te/* sngon byung da ltar med ces pa/ des na chad par thal bar 'gyur/ zhes de 'dra ba la chad lta bar gsungs shing/ tshig gsal las kyang/ rnal 'byor pa kun rdzob kyi bden pa mi shes pa tsam gyis bskyed pa rang bzhin med par rtogs nas de'i stong pa nyid don dam pa'i mtshan nyid can rtogs pa ni mtha' gnyis su ltung bar mi 'gyur te/ gang zhig de lta med par gyur ba de'i tshe na ni ci zhig yod par 'gyur zhes de ltar sngar dngos po'i rang bzhin ma dmigs pas phyis kyang med pa nyid du mi rtogs la/ *zhes gsungs pa'i phyir ro snyam na/* de ni rigs pa ma yin te/

617 The Dharmsala edition of the *Great Exposition*, 375b.5 (adverbial accusatives emphasized):

de kho na nyid gzigs pa'i ye shes kyis ni skye ba med par gzigs pas des grub par mi 'thad la/

618 The Dharmsala edition of the *Great Exposition*, 376b.2–376b.3:

lugs des dbu ma'i thun mong ma yin pa'i khyad chos bkag par bstan pa

619 See Bu-dön's *History of Buddhism*, E. Obermiller, trans., Vol.I, pp.18–23.

620 The Dharmsala edition of the *Great Exposition*, 369b.2–369b.3:

des na mdo'am bstan bcos de'i spyi'i lugs gong 'og tu smas pa mi sbyor bar tshig cung zad re'i ngo gdong gi bstan tshod sgra ji bzhin par gzung du mi rung bas nges don gyi gsung rab yin pa mi 'jig la/ tshig de'i bstan tshod sgra ji bzhin par bzung du rung bas kyang drang don ma yin par mi 'gyur shes par bya'o/

621 *Journal of the International Association of Buddhist Studies*, 3 (1980), pp.93–7, see particularly 95–7.

622 See the Dharmsala edition of the *Great Exposition*, 414b.5.

623 See the Dharmsala edition of the *Great Exposition*, 416a.5–6 and 416b.4.

624 The break between the two sections comes on p.255 of his translation, the new section beginning with "The question arises: . . .". Wayman has not even treated it as a new paragraph.

Index

Index

A-gya-yong-dzin 13, 52, 220, 221, 404, 407, 428, 726, 729–30, 733, 814
A-ku-ching Shay-rap-gya-tso 200–2
"A Question of Nihilism: Bhāvaviveka's Response to the Fundamental Problems of Mādhyamika Philosophy" 141
"A Study of the Relationship Between Analysis (vicāra) and Insight (prajñā) Based on the Madhyamakāvatāra" 123
Abhisamayālaṃkāra, see *Ornament for Clear Realization*
abiders in the fruits 189, 342
About the Four Interwoven Annotations on (Dzong-ka-ba's) "Great Exposition of the Stages of the Path to Enlightenment", Set Forth In Very Brief Form to Purify Forgetfulness and Nourish the Memory 13
actual ultimate 431–9, 720
Advayavajra 740, 818
Advice to the Lord of Tsa-ko 805, 807
affirming negative 408, 415, 417, 421, 428, 440
aggregates 296–8
Aklujkar, Ashok 783
Akṣayamatinirdeśa, see *Teachings of Akṣhayamati Sūtra*
alternatives, four 54, 60–1, 178, 179–80, 314, 317
Ames, William 713
analytical meditation 20, 124–5
Ānandagarbha 413
Annihilationists 388–96, see also Nihilists
Annotations Completely Untying All the Difficult Points of (Dzong-ka-ba's) Text 222
Annotations for (Jam-yang-shay-ba's) "Great Exposition of

Tenets" 413
Answers to the Questions of Lay-chen-gun-gyal-ba 275
Answers to the Questions of Jang-chup-la-ma 348, 808
appearance as a deity 422
appearance factor 422
approachers to the fruits 189, 342
Āryadeva 9–10, 82, 103, 139–40, 164–5, 268–9, 277–8, 375, 419, 445–6, 651
Āryavimuktisena 279, 417, 418
Asaṅga 26, 29, 42, 136, 260, 662
ascertainment factor 422
Ashvaghoṣha 276, 411, 816, 817, see also Shūra
Atisha 10, 17, 26, 166, 282, 411, 412
attachment 31
[Auto] commentary on the "Refutation of Objections" 83
[Auto] commentary on the "Supplement to (Nāgārjuna's) 'Treatise on the Middle Way'" 25, 51, 82, 96, 119, 127, 128, 131, 136, 140, 171, 298, 741
autonomous (*svatantra*) reasons 281
autonomous syllogisms 65, 121
Avalokitavrata 251, 735
Avataṃsaka Sūtra 240
Ba-so Chö-gyi-gyel-tsen 219–20, 226, 779–80, 782
Ba-so Hla-wang-chö-gyi-gyel-tsen 220
Ba-tsap Nyi-ma-drak 668, 670, 741
Beginnings of a Commentary on the Difficult Points of (Dzong-ka-ba's) "Differentiation of the Interpretable and the Definitive", the Quintessence of the "Essence of the Good Explanations" 657
beings of the three capacities 18
bhāva 203, 374
Bhāvanākrama, see *Stages of Meditation*
Bhāvaviveka 9–11, 29, 43–4, 121–2, 126, 132–3, 139–41, 164, 166, 264, 269, 279, 282, 283, 452, 650, 724–5, 797–8
Biographies of Eminent Gurus in the Transmission Lineages of the Teachings of the Graduated Path 220, 780
Black Annotations 781
Blaze of Reasoning 121, 132–3, 140, 141, 725
Bo-do-wa 282
Bo-dong Chok-lay-nam-gyel 52, 669, 751
Bodhisattva 18, 28, 137–8
Bodhisattva grounds 21, 135, 137, 656
Bodhisattvacaryāvatāra, see

Engaging in the Bodhisattva Deeds
Bodhisattvapiṭaka, see *Scriptural Collection of Bodhisattvas*
born from Manu 257
Brief Explanation of Terminology Occurring in (Dzong-ka-ba's) "Great Exposition of the Stages of the Path" 13, 644
bsdus grwa 149
Buddha 102, 137; dates for 661
Buddhahood, special feature of 137
Buddhapālita 9–11, 29, 44, 78, 130, 140, 164, 166–7, 170, 193, 215, 269, 283, 292–3, 396, 398–9, 650
Buddhapālita Commentary on (Nāgārjuna's) "Treatise on the Middle Way" 78, 106–7, 130–1, 140, 207, 214–5, 304, 383, 398–9, 807
Buddhapālitamūlamadhyamakavṛtti, see *Buddhapālita Commentary on (Nāgārjuna's) "Treatise on the Middle Way"*
Buddhism in Tibet 5
Buddhist Nirvana and Its Western Interpreters 648
Buddhists, seven types of 817
Buescher, John 659, 739
Bugault, Guy 116, 677, 710
Burnouf, Eugène 68
calm abiding 19–20, 29, 125, 153–6, 229–33
Calming the Mind and Discerning the Real 441, 654
capacity to perform functions 203, 374
Catalogue of the Collected Works of Certain Principal Ga-dam-ba and Ge-luk-ba Lamas 220, 780
Catuḥpratisaraṇasūtra, see *Sūtra on the Four Reliances*
Catuḥśataka, see *Four Hundred*
Catuḥśatakaṭīkā, see *Commentary on (Āryadeva's) "Four Hundred"*
cause and effect, illusion-like 374
Cha-ba Chö-gyi-seng-ge 52, 668, 670, 750
Chandrahari 414, 817
Chandrakīrti 9–11, 25, 29, 37, 44, 50–1, 59, 62, 63–4, 68, 78, 82, 83, 96, 104, 106, 108, 120, 127–9, 139–41, 164, 166–7, 170, 193, 199, 269, 280–3, 293, 302, 355, 365, 381, 396–8, 448, 651, 697, 713; dates for 650; presentation of valid cognizers 108–9
Char-har Ge-shay 643
Chittamātra/Chittamātrin 26, 28, 29, 30–3, 42–3, 44–5, 48, 50–1, 91,

277–9, 375, 659, 662, 663, 746, 747, 796–7; Chittamātrins Following Reasoning 48; Chittamātrins Following Scripture 48
city of scent-eaters 169, 203, 288, 373
Clear Meaning Commentary 174, 306, 308
Clear Words 51, 62, 106, 107, 109, 120, 129, 140, 141, 166, 169, 171, 184, 188, 196, 200, 206–7, 208–9, 210, 211, 212, 213, 280–1, 288–9, 291, 296, 300, 303, 318, 330, 341, 359, 367, 381–2, 384, 386, 389, 390, 392, 394, 807
Collections of Reasonings 161, 261
Commentary on (Āryadeva's) "Four Hundred" 51, 62, 83, 110, 113, 140, 199, 202, 203, 214, 236, 238, 242, 364–5, 372, 375, 397
Commentary on (Bhāvaviveka's) "Lamp for (Nāgārjuna's) 'Wisdom'" 251
Commentary on (Dignāga's) "Compendium of Valid Cognition" (tshad ma rnam 'grel, pramāṇavārttika) 91, 235, 302
Commentary on (Nāgārjuna's) "Seventy Stanzas on Emptiness" 140, 786–7
Commentary on (Nāgārjuna's) "Sixty Stanzas of Reasoning" 51, 59, 140
Commentary on the "King of Meditative Stabilizations Sūtra" 729
Commentary on the "Refutation of Objections" 190, 344
Compendium of Principles 657
Compendium on the Mahāyāna 136
composite of a conventional truth and an ultimate truth 415
conceptual reasoning consciousnesses 431–2
conceptuality 61, 103, 105; and ignorance 101–5; example of extinguishing 125; refuting all 22–3; view that it is refuted by the Mādhyamika reasonings 101–5
Concise Meaning of the Stages of the Path 6
concordant ultimate 406, 430–9, 720
Consciousness-Only, see Chittamātra and Mind-Only
consequences 65, 280–1
Contributions to the

Development of Tibetan Buddhist Epistemology 644
conventional establishment 174, 308–9
conventional existence, measure of 106–10
conventional phenomena 110
conventional truths 96–8, 415, 747
conventional valid cognizers 56–60, 106–9, 420
Conze, Edward 75, 98, 127, 704, 710, 722
Council of Lhasa, see Sam-yay debate
Cultivation of the Ultimate Mind of Enlightenment 411–14, 816
Cyclic existence, root of 168–70, 232, 238–9, 243, 286–92; sufferings of 286

Da-nak-nor-sang 275
Dak-den History of the Doctrine 412
Dak-lung-drak-ba 221
Dak-tsang 644
Dalai Lama 3, 12, 69, 95, 150, 219, 655, 719; Eighth 222; Fifth 116, 221
Daye, Douglas 74–6, 77–8, 112, 127, 649, 675, 689–90, 710
dbu ma chen mo, see *Great Exposition of the Middle Way*
De-druk-ken-chen Ka-rok Nga-wang-rap-den 219, see also Nga-wang-rap-den
de Jong, J.W., see Jong, J.W. de
Decisive Analysis of Special Insight 12–13
definitive meaning/definitive object 31–2, 659
Den-dar-hla-ram-ba 685–6, 694
Denba Dendzin, Ken-sur 12, 241, 256, 732
Denma Lochö Rinbochay 655
dependent-arising 3–4, 36, 40–1, 53–4, 149–50, 182–4, 211, 212, 333, 336–7, 373, 390; twelve links of 82, 185, 263, 331, 754; compatibility with emptiness 40–1, 53–4, 131, 149–50, 182–4, 188–93, 323–6, 339–54, 752
Descent Into Laṅkā Sūtra 41, 250
designation 96
dgongs pa rab gsal, see *Illumination of the Thought*
dharma 461–2
Dharmakīrti 90–1, 97, 125, 126, 235, 302, 663, 685, 697
dichotomies 120, 428, 770
differentiating inherent existence and existence 83–5, 199–207, 214–15 363, 365–6, 396–400

differentiating non-existence and no inherent existence 199–207, 214–15, 363, 365–71, 396–400
Difficult Points of (Dzong-ka-ba's) "Great Exposition of Special Insight" 12
Digambara 730
Dignāga 90, 97, 108, 125, 126, 697
Direct perception 91, 105, 126; of emptiness 91, 102, 105, 126, 132, 135, 137, 431–2, 719; yogic 126
doors of liberation 160, 258
Dra-di Ge-shay Rin-chen-dön-drub 219, 222, 227, 240, 272–3, 404, 407, 793
Dra-shi-kyil 222
Dragonetti, Carmen 127, 677, 695, 711
Dro-lung-ba 711
dualistic appearance 426, 432, 435
Dzong-ka-ba 5–11, 14, 27–9, 34–5, 36–7, 40–41, 51–4, 58–9, 60–1, 62–4, 78, 84–5, 107–8, 122, 135, 138–40, 143–50, 264, 276, 302–3, 403, 407–8, 411, 419, 420, 425, 429–30, 440, 449, 643, 644, 690; collected writings (*gsung 'bum*) 7; dates of 644–5; main sources for Dzong-ka-ba's views on Mādhyamika 7–11, 139–40, 166–7, 282–3; reliance on Chandrakīrti 9–10; visionary experience 6

Early Mādhyamika in India and China 68
Eckel, David 121, 141, 677, 718
Eighth Dalai Lama 222
elaborations 424–7, 431, 432–3
elimination of the elaborations of inherent existence with respect to appearances 425
emptiness 3–4, 23–4, 31, 40, 56, 104, 149–50, 188ff, 211, 258, 420–2, 425, 431–3; and dependent-arising as of one meaning 185–6, 191–2, 193, 323, 326, 339–54, 752; and reasoning 123–6; and the Kantian absolute 94; as an existent 94, 126–33, 440; as nihilism 4–6, 39–40, 67–8; compatibility of emptiness and dependent-arising 131–2, 149–50; danger of misunderstanding 25; direct realization of 91, 102, 105, 126, 132, 135, 137, 431–2, 719; non-finding analytically 3; not inherently existent 94,

130–1; ontological status of 94, 126–33, 709–11, 712; synonyms 127; two ways of misunderstanding 772–3; viewing wrongly 208–9, 383–5
Emptiness: A Study in Religious Meaning 71
Engaging in the Bodhisattva Deeds 176–7, 312, 682
entry into suchness 168ff
Epistolary Essay, Drop of Ambrosia 271, 740, 816
Essay on the Mind of Enlightenment 796
Essence of Good Explanation, Explanation of (Āryadeva's) "Four Hundred" 785–6
Essence of the Good Explanations, Praise of Munīndra 9
Essence of the Good Explanations, Treatise Discriminating the Interpretable and the Definitive 7, 30, 32, 122, 277, 365, 413, 646, 647, 662, 667, 810
ethics 4, 148, 192, 241, 788
exalted wisdom of meditative equipoise 417
examples: burning chariot 171, 295–7; cart 762; effects as like illusions 202–3, 373; falling hairs 688; forgetting a horse while riding on it 198, 362; god turned into a demon 191, 347; horn of a donkey 364; magician's illusions 110, 423, 690; moon in water 336; of no inherent existence 110; pots and woolen cloth 190–91, 345–6; reflections and echoes 359; robber in a house 321; robber truly and falsely accused 212–13, 395–6; son of a barren woman 173, 304
existence (*srid pa, bhava*) 31
existence by way of its own entity 83
existent, synonyms of 57
Explanation of the Conventional and the Ultimate in the Four Systems of Tenets 666
Explanation of the "Epistolary Essay, Drop of Ambrosia", Magical Rosary Fulfilling All Wishes 740
Extensive Sport Sūtra 271, 351
extremes, two 199–200, 205–10, 364–6, 374, 376–7, 381–8
extremes of permanence and annihilation 39–40, 376–7

feasibility of actions and so forth within emptiness 50, 100, 111, 149–50, 184–7,

188–94, 195–6, 201–3, 328–37, 339–49, 359
Features of the View 740
Fenner, Peter 101–2, 116, 123–4, 141, 693, 701, 708
Fifth Dalai Lama 116, 221
Finely Woven 49
Forders 153, 230, 232, 726
Form Body 181–2, 323–4
Four Hundred 82, 103, 104, 115, 140, 235, 238, 242, 651, 768
Four Interwoven Annotations to (Dzong-ka-ba's) "Great Exposition of the Stages of the Path" 11–12, 15, 219–27, 652
freedom from elaborations 424–7, 432–3
Fundamental Text Called "Wisdom" 252, see also *Treatise on the Middle Way*

Ga-dam-ba 17
Ga-wa-bel-tsek 740
Gang-gya-mar-ba Jang-chup-drak 53, 668, 671
Gangadean, Ashok 123
Ge-luk-ba 5, 14–15, 61, 95, 136, 146–7, 219, 415, 422, 424–5, 437, 691, 709; educational system 146, 721–2; view on consciousness 709
Ge-shay Tsul-trim-nam-gyal 222–3
Ge-shay Wangdrak 12, 230, 236, 240, 272, 340, 347, 348, 355
Gen-dun-chö-pel 724
Gen-dun-gyel-tsen 222
Golden Rosary of Eloquence 136, 416, 417, 425
Golden Wheel (gser gyi 'khor lo) 222
Gön-chok-chö-pel 221
Gönchok Tsering 12, 13, 241
Great Cloud Sūtra 252
Great Commentary on (Nāgārjuna's) "Treatise on the Middle Way" 252, 734, see also *Ocean of Reasoning*
Great Drum Sūtra 250, 251–3
"Great Exposition of Special Insight" 40, 103
Great Exposition of Tenets 252, 735, 815
Great Exposition of the Middle Way 252, 735
Great Exposition of the Stages of the Path 6, 8–9, 11, 15, 66, 82, 405, 410, 422, 424, 425, 430, 436; summary of, 17–19; translations of 725
greatnesses, four 26–7
Griffiths, Paul J. 678–9
grounds and paths 721
grub mtha' chen mo, see *Great Exposition of Tenets*
Gudmunsen, Chris 92–4, 96, 98–9, 111, 691

Guenther, Herbert 116, 701
Guhyasamāja Tantra 796
Gun-kyen-rong-dön 52, 668, 750
Gung-ru-chö-jung 221
Gung-tang 657
Gyel-tsap 417–18, 419, 785–6

Haribhadra 136, 174, 306, 418, 721–2, 748
Heap of Jewels Sūtra 240
Hearers 172
Heart of the Middle Way 141
Heart of Wisdom 33, see also *Heart Sūtra*
Heart Sūtra 33–5, 113, 660
Highest Yoga Tantra 8
Hīnayāna 41, 45–6, 49–50, 170, 294–5, 659, 667, 746–8
History of Buddhism in India 817
Holder of the throne of Ganden 219
Hopkins, Jeffrey 11, 140, 702
Hundred Short Doctrines 411, 412
Huntington, Jr., C.W. 141, 694, 718–19
Hva-shang Mahāyāna 22, 52, 102, 125, 155, 237, 669

Ichimura, Shohei 76, 121
ignorance 58, 78–80, 81, 103, 168–70, 237–9, 286–92, 681, 726; artificial and innate 85–7
Iida, Shotaro 116, 141, 701
Illumination of the Middle Way 32, 161, 261, 262–3, 309, 405, 431, 432, 433, 435, 735
Illumination of the Thought 27, 136, 734–5, 789
illusion-like affirming negative 435
illusion-like composite of appearance and emptiness 408–9, 415–24, 434, 436, 437
Illusion-Like Mādhyamikas 270, see also Reason-Established Illusionists
implicit realization 302
imputations 43, 48
imputed existence 174–5, 305–9, 746–9, 801–2
imputed ultimate truth 408, 429–39
Inada, Kenneth 123, 704
inference 126, 273–4
inferential consciousness realizing emptiness 404, 420–4, 432, 437; what appears to it 421–2, 819
inferential reasoning consciousness 409, 423, 432
inherent existence 23, 46–7, 50, 55–6, 79, 81–2,

85–9, 127–8, 203, 238, 374, 425
interpretable meaning 31–2, 659
interpretable object 31–2
interpretation of scripture, 24–6, 30–8, 42–3, 158–63, 247–67
Introduction to the Two Truths 282

Jainas 336
Jam-ba Rin-bo-chay 652
Jam-yang Gön-chok-chö-pel 221
Jam-yang-shay-ba 52, 219, 221–2, 237, 251–3, 262, 272, 273, 277, 349, 404, 407, 412, 413, 428, 429, 432–4, 782, 815; Jam-yang-shay-ba's *Annotations* 222, 227
Jampel Shenphen 11, 236
Jang-dzay College of Gan-den Monastery 221
Jang-gya Rol-bay-dor-jay 222, 404, 407, 412
Jay College of Se-ra Monastic University 222
Jayānanda 117
Jñanagarbha 798
Jñānakīrti 730
Jñānavajra 413
Jones, Richard 77, 84, 113
Jong, J.W. de 123, 127, 687, 704, 720
Ka-rok Nga-wang-rap-den 221, see also Nga-wang-rap-den
Kachewsky, Rudolf 643
Kālachakra Tantra 661
Kamalashīla 22–3, 29, 32, 102, 103, 125–6, 139, 153, 155, 161, 162, 165, 270, 405, 415, 417, 418, 431, 433–6.
karma 4, 148
Kashmiri Vaibhāṣhika 48
Kāshyapa Chapter Sūtra 105
Kay-drup 219, 280, 415, 419, 435, 643, 647, 798, 814
Kay-drup Nor-sang-gya-tso 407, 411–12, 813
King of Meditative Stabilizations Sūtra 31, 58, 102, 153–4, 161, 178–9, 232, 234, 242, 260, 315–16
Kritzer, Robert 442

La Vallée Poussin, Louis de 68
Lakṣhmi 270
Lalitavistara, see *Extensive Sport Sūtra*
lam rim chen mo, see *Great Exposition of the Stages of the Path*
lam rim mchan bzhi sbrags ma, see *Four Interwoven Annotations to (Dzong-ka-*

ba's) "Great Exposition of the Stages of the Path"
Lama U-ma-ba 145
Lamotte, Étienne 68, 112, 127, 693, 698, 709
Lamp for (Nāgārjuna's) "Wisdom" 140, 651
Lamp for the Path to Enlightenment 17, 26
Lang, Karen 140
language 89–100
Laṅkāvatāra Sūtra 253, see also *Descent into Laṅkā*
Lati Rinbochay 140
law of the excluded middle 61, 672
legs bshad snying po, see *Essence of the Good Explanations*
Levels of Yogic Practice 136
limiting possibilities 205–6, 378–81
Lindtner, Christian 70–1, 79, 101, 140–1, 692, 707, 717
literalness as a criterion of interpretability or definitiveness 30–3, 162–3, 263–7, 659
Lo-den-shay-rap 52, 165, 271, 275, 405, 667, 668, 671, 711, 750, 816
Lo-drö-gya-tso, see Dak-lung-drak-ba
Lo-sang-da-yang 722
Lo-sang-dor-jay 12
Lo-sang-gön-chok 52
Lokātītastava, see *Praise of the Supramundane [Buddha]*
Lokāyata, see Worldly Materialists
Long-döl La-ma 220, 222
Losang Nyima 13, 660
Loy, David 92, 95, 687, 691

Ma-ja Jang-chup-dzön-drü 53, 670–1
Madhyamakālaṃkāra, see *Ornament for the Middle Way*
Madhyamakāloka, see *Illumination of the Middle Way*
Madhyamakaśāstra, see *Treatise on the Middle Way*
Madhyamakāvatāra, see *Supplement to (Nāgārjuna's) "Treatise on the Middle Way"*
Mādhyamika/Mādhyamikas 4–6, 8–9, 10–11, 23, 26, 28, 31, 32–7, 40–4, 50, 61, 67–8, 71, 138–9, 182, 201, 210–14, 308–9, 339, 345, 370, 390, 417, 424–5; and absolutism 68, 198–203, 676, 717; and nihilism 4–6, 39–40, 67–8; and Wittgenstein, 92–9, 680; as a critique of language 75–6, 84–5,

67–8; as a positive system 115; as a refutation of conventionalities 105–11; as a refutation of other systems 74, 86–9; as an attack on conceptuality 101–5; as an attack on reasoning 74–5, 89; as having no view 111–16; as having no theses 111, 116–22; differentiated from Nihilists 210–15, 388–96, 447–51; divisions 164–7, 269–82, 403–29, 451–2; interpretations refuted by Dzong-ka-ba 8, 51–3, 177–80, 313–21; interpretations that negate too little 65, 73, 99, 177, 312–13, 468–71, 714–15; interpretations that negate too much 51–64, 73, 99–100, 101–22, 178–9, 191–2, 193, 195–7, 201–2, 314–20, 347–9, 352–3, 354–60, 425–7, 467–8, 772–3; Tibetan contributions to 68–9; transmission to Tibet 5; uncommon distinguishing feature of 100, 181–4, 187, 191, 193, 195, 322–37; view 115–16, 191–2, 349–54; views of western writers 8, 61, 67–9, 70–1 74–7, 101–2, 111–14, 116–18, 123–4, 126–8, 133–4, 136–7, 648–9, 677–8, 692–3, 695–6, 700–1, 704–8, 709–11, 718–19

Mādhyamika Stages of Meditation 155, 237, see also *Stages of Meditation*

Mādhyamikas of the model texts 164, 269, 443, 446

Mahābherīhārakaparivarta, see *Great Drum Sūtra*

Mahāmegha, see *Great Cloud Sūtra*

Mahāyāna 20–1, 29, 41, 45, 285, 293–5

Mahāyānaprasādaprabhāvana, see *Sūtra of Cultivating Faith in the Mahāyāna*

Mahāyānasaṃgraha, see *Compendium on the Mahāyāna*

Mañjushrī 117, 145–6

Mañjushrī Root Tantra 41, 249, 252, 253

Mañjuśrīmūlatantra, see *Mañjushrī Root Tantra*

Materialists 210, 336, 387, 388–96

Materials for a History of Tibetan Literature 223

Matilal, B.K. 85, 112, 116, 129, 700

mātṛka 446, 739

May, Jacques 116, 127, 700, 709

McEvilley, Thomas 74

meditation, analytical and stabilizing 124–5

Meditation on Emptiness 650
"Medium Exposition of Special Insight" 237, 279, 406, 408, 418, 427, 428, 430, 431, 432, 433, 434, 435, 646
Medium Exposition of the Stages of the Path 6, 274, 433, 436
Mehta, Mahesh 717
memory consciousness 203–4, 375–7, 768–9
mere elimination 408, 428–9
mere production 63
merit and wisdom, accumulation of 181–2, 323–5
metaphoric ultimate 437–9
method 324–5
Mi-gyö-dor-jay 644, 712
Middle Way School, see Mādhyamika
Mimaki, Katsumi 646, 740
mind-basis-of-all 48
Mind-Only 275, 662, see also Chittamātra
mind-trainings 18
mine 168–73, 296–8, 304
Murti, T.R.V. 61, 79, 101, 116, 121, 123, 129, 132, 134, 649, 672, 675–6, 692, 698, 700, 704, 717

Nāgārjuna 4, 9–10, 11, 26, 29, 41, 42, 49, 70–2, 80, 87, 98–9, 106, 130, 135, 164, 165, 183–7, 194, 249–50, 260, 268, 277, 278, 332, 337, 362, 411, 419, 446, 677, 796; and Wittgenstein 98–9; dates for 650; prophesies regarding and proclamations of doctrine 249–53, 734
Nagarjuniana: Studies in the Writings and Philosophy of Nāgārjuna 140
nature (*svabhāva*), three attributes of 65
Nayak, G.C. 127, 137, 701, 711, 718, 720
negating too little 65, 73, 99, 177, 312–13, 468–71, 714–15
negating too much 51–64, 73, 99–100, 101–22, 178–9, 191–2, 193, 195–7, 201–2, 314–20, 347–9, 352–3, 354–60, 425–7, 467–8, 772–3
neyārtha 32
Nga-wang-bel-den 91, 404, 409, 413, 416, 418–9, 422, 425, 428, 429, 437, 666, 685, 813
Nga-wang-rap-den 219, 221, 226, 265, 275, 287, 293, 295, 303, 306, 319, 323, 340, 346, 358, 365, 388, 392, 404, 409
Ngawang Dhargey, Geshe 643, 647
Ngok-lo-tsā-wa 711, see also Lo-den-shay-rap

Nihilism/Nihilists 106, 149, 200–1, 210–13, 367, 388–96, 448, 773, 807–8
nirvāṇa 154, 168, 234, 235, 236, 284–5, 294
non-affirming negative 23, 276, 409, 415, 421, 423, 425, 428, 433, 440
non-conceptual exalted wisdom of meditative equipoise 431
non-finding upon analysis 48–9
non-harmfulness 788
non-literal scriptures 33
non-metaphoric ultimate 437–9
Nor-sang-gya-tso 407, 411–12
not unable 19

object of comprehension of an inferential consciousness 165, 276, 429–37
object of negation 44–9, 50, 73, 176–80, 264–5, 311–13, 425, 682, 713–15; by reasoning and by the path 81; importance of identifying correctly 39–40, 313; objective and subjective 81
objective ultimate 438–9
"Observations on Translation from the Classical Tibetan Language into European Languages" 441
obstructions to liberation 744
obstructions to omniscience 744
Ocean of Reasoning, Explanation of (Nāgārjuna's) "Treatise on the Middle Way" 7, 301, 302, 435–6, 646–7
One Hundred Thousand Stanza Perfection of Wisdom 25, 36
Opening the Eye of New Awareness 69–70
Ornament for Clear Realization 136–7, 416, 721
Ornament for the Essence, Explanation [of Maitreya's "Ornament for Clear Realization" and Its Commentaries] 416–18
Ornament for the Middle Way 405, 430, 432, 435
Ornament Illuminating the Exalted Wisdom Operating in the Sphere of All Buddhas 161, 261
other-powered phenomena 43, 48

Pa-bong-ka 13, 404, 407, 415, 428, 741, 814
Pa-bong-ka Monastery 222
Palden Drakpa 12, 13, 347, 423, 732, 768

Paṇ-chen Rin-bo-chay 652
Paṇ-chen Shākya-chok-den 53, 670
paradox 34, 72, 102, 117–18, 128, 678, 693, 715
Partisan Mādhyamikas 164, 269, 443, 445–6
path of accumulation 30, 137
path in Mādhyamika 133–8
paths, five, 20–22
Perfection of Wisdom Sūtras 36, 42, 136, 164, 251, 252, 268, 293, 383
perfections, six 18–19, 156–7, 245
person (*gang zag*, *pudgala*), etymology 257
phenomena, manifest and hidden 104
positive inclusion (*yongs gcod*) 406, 408, 428–9
possibilities, four 63, see also alternative, four
Potter, Karl 116, 134, 700, 707
Praise of Dependent-Arising 9, 40, 242
Praise of the Element of Qualities 122
Praise of the Supramundane [Buddha] 118, 187, 336
Prajñāpradīpa, see *Lamp for (Nāgārjuna's) 'Wisdom'"*
Prajñāpradīpaṭkā, see *Commentary on (Bhāvaviveka's) "Lamp for (Nāgārjuna's) 'Wisdom'"*
prajñapti 96
Pramāṇavārttika, see *Commentary on (Dignāga's) "Compendium on Valid Cognition"*
Prāsaṅgika-Mādhyamika 7–8, 32–4, 36, 44–50, 60, 63, 65, 87, 166, 237, 239, 276, 281, 296, 403–4, 407–9, 421–5, 451–2, 668, 746–8
Prasannapadā, see *Clear Words*
Precious Garland 49, 71, 80, 99, 106, 107, 135, 140, 172, 192, 208, 209, 235, 238, 278, 298, 350, 384, 385, 414, 446, 732
Precious Garland of Suchness 818
Precious Lamp, Essay on the Ultimate Mind of Enlightenment 276
Presentation of the Grounds and Paths of Mantra 819
Presentation of the Two Truths 437
pride 732; of conceiving himself or herself to be supreme 240
production, see refutation of production
Proponents of No Entityness 666–7
Proponents of the Middle Way 424, see also Mādhyamika

Proponents of Things 202, see also Proponents of True Existence
Proponents of Thorough Non-Abiding 165, 270–1, 275–7, 403–9, 423–9, 437
Proponents of True Existence 49–51, 120, 174–5, 183–4, 199, 201–2, 215, 306–10, 327–9, 357–8, 362–5, 367, 369–74, 387, 399–400, 467, 666–7; explanation of term 50–1

Quintessential Instructions on the Stages of the View 740

Ramanan, Venkata 130, 717
Ratnakūṭa, see *Heap of Jewels Sūtra*
Ratnapradīpa, see *Precious Lamp, Essay on [the Stages of] Cultivating the Ultimate Mind of Enlightenment*
Ratnāvalī, see *Precious Garland*
Reason and Emptiness 141
Reason-Established Illusionists 164, 165, 270, 271–6, 403–24, 429–40
reasoning, role of 89, 99–100, 103–5, 123–6, 237; inclusion within analytical meditation 124–5
reasoning consciousness 126, 431–4, 708
Red Annotations 781
reflections as examples of empty things 359
Refutation of Objections 49, 50, 117, 119, 120, 183, 186, 189–90, 195–6, 206, 328, 333, 344, 357, 380, 770
refutation of production 63–4, 315–18; qualifying the refutation 179–80, 195–6, 265–7, 315–18
reliances, four 30, 658, 733–4
renunciation 18
robber, example of 213, 321
Robinson, Richard 68, 72, 74–5, 77, 78, 87–8, 94, 127, 648, 678, 710, 713
Rong-dön-shākya-gyel-tsen 668–9
Rong-dön-shay-ja-gun-sik 668–9
root of cyclic existence 168–70, 232, 237–9, 242, 286–92
rtsa shes ṭik chen, see *Great Commentary on (Nāgārjuna's) "Treatise on the Middle Way"*
Ruegg, D. Seyfort 67, 68–9, 72, 114, 117–18, 119–20,

441, 650, 668, 669, 675, 678, 710, 715, 739, 818

Śalistamba Sūtra 681
Sam-yay debate 22, 102, 135
Samādhirāja, see *King of Meditative Stabilizations Sūtra*
Saṃdhinirmocana, see *Sūtra Unravelling the Thought*
Saṃmitīya 48, 661
Sang-gyay-gya-tso 220
Sarvabuddhaviṣayāvatārajñā-nālokālaṃkāra, see *Ornament Illuminating the Exalted Wisdom Operating in the Sphere of All Buddhas*
Satyadvayāvatāra, see *Introduction to the Two Truths*
Sautrāntika 28, 44–5, 91, 105, 281, 308, 327, 663, 772, 798
Sautrāntika-Mādhyamika 164–6, 269, 277–82, 798
Sautrāntika-Svātantrika 452
Sautrāntikas Following Reasoning 48, 747, 749
Sautrāntikas Following Scripture 48, 747, 749
Scharfstein, Ben-Ami 102
Schayer, Stanislaw 68
Schmithausen, Lambert 662
Schumann, Hans 116, 701
Scriptural Collection of Bodhisattvas 102–3, 155, 239–40, 787
seals, four 41
self 39, 95, 176, 256, 257, 286, 290–1, 296–8, 303, 304; manifest conception of 782; triply qualified 296–7
selflessness 39, 41–3, 154, 234–5, 238; coarse 42, 45; in Hīnayāna 42; of persons 42, 45–6, 170–3, 174–5, 298–303, 309, 744, 746–9; of phenomena 45–8, 170–3, 174–5, 293–307, 309, 744, 746–9
sense consciousnesses as erroneous 46, 60, 108, 688, 697
sentient being, etymology 257
Ser-dok Paṇ-chen 740
Seventy Stanzas on Emptiness 49, 50, 82, 186, 238–9, 334
Sha-mar-den-dzin 12, 35, 404, 409, 412–14, 416, 424, 425, 428, 429, 435, 437, 711, 729, 768, 813
Shākya-chok-den 669, 670
Shāntarakṣhita 126, 139, 164, 165, 269, 270, 279, 405, 415, 417, 418, 433–6
Shāntideva 176, 312
Shūra 270, 276, 277, 408, 411–14
Siderits, Mark 76

silence of the Āryas 137
Six Collections of Reasoning 49–50, 664–6
Sixty Stanzas of Reasoning 49, 80, 118, 135, 181, 186, 324, 334
Smith, E. Gene 652, 781
Solitary Realizers 172
Sopa, Geshe 442, 466
special insight (*lhag mthong, vipaśyanā*) 6, 17, 19–22, 66, 125, 153, 158, 229–30, 243, 726; etymology 20
spheres of authority of different types of consciousnesses 55–8
Sphutārthā, see *Clear Meaning Commentary*
spiritual community 189
Sprung, Mervyn 84, 89, 116, 123, 127, 129, 136–7, 691, 695–6, 706, 711, 715
Staal, Fritz 75, 116, 117–18, 649
Stages of Cultivating the Ultimate Mind of Enlightenment 411–14
Stages of Meditation 22, 125, 153–6, 231, 243
stages of the path 14
Stcherbatsky, Theodor 68, 74, 442, 679, 704
Streng, Frederick 71, 116, 123, 126, 127, 705–6, 709, 710, 713–14
subjective ultimate 438–9, 720
Sublime Continuum of the Great Vehicle 287
substantial existence 708, 801–2
suchness 168–71, 284–92
sudden and gradual enlightenment 133–5
śunyatā, see emptiness
śunyatādarśana 114–15
śūnyatādṛṣṭi 114–15
Śūnyatāsaptati, see Seventy Stanzas on Emptiness
Superior 137
Superior's exalted wisdom of subsequent attainment 420
Supplement to (Nāgārjuna's) "Treatise on the Middle Way" 51, 63, 78, 96, 109, 113, 115, 136, 140–1, 169, 170, 179–80, 196, 235, 239, 249–50, 290–1, 293, 316–18, 359
sūtra, citation of 58, 64, 131–2
Sūtra of Cultivating Faith in the Mahāyāna 157, 245–6
Sūtra on the Four Reliances 30, 734
Sūtra on the Ten Grounds 136
Sūtra Unravelling the Thought 25, 42, 156–7, 245
sūtras of definitive meaning 159–63, 254–67, 660
sūtras of interpretable meaning 159–63, 254–67
svabhāva 65, 74, 80, 85, 88–9, 127–8, 203, 374,

469–71, 713–15; two meanings of 471, 713–15; see also inherent existence
Svātantrika-Mādhyamika 7, 33–4, 36, 43–6, 47, 48, 51, 65, 166, 180, 239, 276, 281, 319, 403–4, 407–9, 415, 416, 418, 421–4, 452

Tachikawa, Musashi 720
Tang-sak-ba 52, 668, 750
tantra 422
Tāranātha 817
Tattvasaṃgraha, see *Compendium of Principles*
Teachings of Akṣhayamati Sūtra 25, 31, 159–60, 254, 255–9, 261, 734
tenet systems, four 28, 44
Tenzin Gyatso, see Dalai Lama
tetralemma 34–5, 60–2, 673–4, 769
thoroughly established phenomena 43, 48
Thoroughly Non-Abiding Mādhyamikas 165, 270, 274–5, 277, see also Proponents of Thorough Non-Abiding
Thousand Dosages 280, 435, 798
Three Jewels 188, 340
three natures 42–3
Three Principal Aspects of the Path 150, 805, 807
three turnings of the wheel of doctrine 42–3
Thurman, Robert 92, 97, 643, 647, 702
Tola, Fernando 127, 677, 695, 711
"Towards a Chronology of the Madhyamaka School" 650
Treatise on the Middle Way 36, 49–50, 65, 112, 114, 127–8, 130, 131, 136, 139, 140, 170, 171, 183–6, 192, 195, 196, 206–9, 272, 287, 292–3, 297, 327, 329, 331, 332, 338, 350, 357, 359, 362, 381–4, 386, 456, 470, 651, 664–5, 713, 742, 804; purpose of 77–8
Tri-rel-wa-jen 413
Truth Body 168, 171, 181–2, 285, 287, 289, 294, 323
truths, four noble 18, 20, 188–9, 328, 339–42
truths, two 40, 96; compatability in Mādhyamika 182–7, 326
truths for a concealer, see conventional truths
Tucci, Giuseppe 722
Tuxen, Poul 68
Two Staged Path 403

Udraka 154, 233, 729–30
Ueda, Yoshifumi 662

ultimate 430, 820
ultimate analysis 55–6; non-refutation of conventional phenomena by 55–6
ultimate cognizers 420
ultimate establishment 173–4, 308–9
ultimate truth 126, 127–8, 262, 406, 408, 415, 424, 427, 429–39, 747; etymologies 132–3; five attributes 271–2; ontological status of 131–3; used for consciousnesses 431–440
ultimate valid cognizers 58, 107
Uttaratantra, see *Sublime Continuum of the Great Vehicle*

Vaibhāṣhika 28, 44, 48, 166, 282, 327, 661, 747, 748–9, 772
valid cognition/cognizer (*tshad ma, pramāṇa*) 107, 178–9, 263, 315–16, 696–7; four 108
van der Kuijp, Leonard 644, 670
Vātsīputrīyas 305
view, Mādhyamika 115–16, 191–2, 349–53; causes for gaining 192
view of emptiness 23, 115–16, 237
view of the transitory collection 168–70, 239, 286–92
views of permanence and annihilation 206–12, 381–8, 772–3
Vigrahavyāvartanī, see *Refutation of Objections*
Vigrahavyāvartanīvṛtti, see *Commentary on the "Refutation of Objections"*
Vimuktisena 417, 418

Waldo, Ives 75
Warder, A.K. 677–8
water in water, example of non-dualistic cognition 132
Wayman, Alex 113, 139, 441–73, 662, 706, 716, 722–3
Welbon, Guy 648
Williams, Paul 443, 644, 664, 671, 676, 796
Willis, Janice 662
Wittgenstein, 92–4, 97–9, 680
Wittgenstein and Buddhism 92
Word Commentary on the Root Text of (Jam-yang-shay-ba's) "Tenets" 52
Worldly Materialists 212, see also Materialists

Yar-lung-chö-dzay Lo-sang-den dzin 221

Ye-shay-day 165–6, 277–9, 740
Ye-shay gyel-tsen 220
Yellow Annotations 781
Yellow Cat's Eye Gem 220, 779, 780
Yeshe Thupten, Kensur 12, 13, 730
Yogācāryābhūmi, see *Levels of Yogic Practice*
Yogāchara 280, see also Chittamātra
Yogāchara-Mādhyamika 164–6, 270, 279–80
Yogāchara-Svātantrika 452, 663
Yong-dzin Ye-shay-gyel-tsen Bel-sang-bo 729
Yuktiṣaṣṭikā, see *Sixty Stanzas of Reasoning*

Wisdom Publications

Wisdom Publications, a not-for-profit publisher, is dedicated to making available authentic Buddhist works for the benefit of all. We publish translations of the sutras and tantras, commentaries and teachings of past and contemporary Buddhist masters, and original works by the world's leading Buddhist scholars. We publish our titles with the appreciation of Buddhism as a living philosophy and with the special commitment to preserve and transmit important works from all the major Buddhist traditions.

To learn more about Wisdom, or to browse books online, visit our website at wisdompubs.org. You may request a copy of our mail-order catalog online or by writing to:

WISDOM PUBLICATIONS
199 Elm Street
Somerville, Massachusetts 02144 USA
Telephone: (617) 776-7416
Fax: (617) 776-7841
Email: info@wisdompubs.org
www.wisdompubs.org

The Wisdom Trust

As a not-for-profit publisher, Wisdom is dedicated to the publication of fine Dharma books for the benefit of all sentient beings and dependent upon the kindness and generosity of sponsors in order to do so. If you would like to make a donation to Wisdom, please do so through our Somerville office. If you would like to sponsor the publication of a book, please write or email us at the address above.

Thank you.

Wisdom is a nonprofit, charitable 501(c)(3) organization affiliated with the Foundation for the Preservation of the Mahayana Tradition (FPMT).